ROUNDING THIRD

By

David Andrew Jacobsen

DALO PUBLISHING
Laramie, Wyoming

Dedicated to…

Edwin
EO, SeaBees
United States Navy
World War II: Served from 1941-1944
in the European Theater/DDay

William
Radio Operator
United States Merchant Marine
World War II: Served from 1941-1945
in the South Pacific

Zachary
Sergeant
United States Army
Operation Iraqi Freedom: Served from 2006-2007
in Baghdad, Iraq

And to Big Red…

Her Guardian Angel continues to bring everyone home

DALO
Publishing

ISBN 978-0-578-11803-1

There was nothing like minor league baseball. Sure, we got a few flubs, mental errors, but we also got desire in its purest form. We could smell the turkey in the oven and our mouths watered. We all knew what was at stake, that few were chosen. But we couldn't coast; we played our hearts out.

We loved the young kids who dreamed their world might be opening with their talent. We loved the guys who had been around the block who knew they would finish their careers in the bush but who gave it everything anyway, just for the love of the game.

We are all minor leaguers, when it comes down to it. Few of us ever get the call. We spend our lives on the assembly line or walking a beat. But we hold on to our dreams, no matter how tattered they become, and we play our hearts out, no matter how slim the glory.

Jack Kelly

BOOK I
THE PRESIDENTIAL

BOOK II
THE MIAMI METS

Do what you love to do and give it your very best. Whether it's business or baseball, or the theater, or any field. If you don't love what you're doing and you can't give it your best, get out of it. Life is too short. You'll be an old man before you know it.

Al Lopez

PROLOGUE

I'm sitting on a black metal bridge chair in front of my cubicle in the dingy locker room beneath the first base stands of Lawrence Stadium, home of the New York MetsTriple AAA team…the Norfolk, Virginia Tide. I've stripped down to a t-shirt and shorts and my sweaty, muddy, and somewhat bloody uniform is on the floor at my feet. The sweat came from a mixture of high humidity and exertion; the mud was the result of a light rain, some clay, and a slide into second base; and the blood was the outcome of an altercation prior to the game.

It's the blood that's got me nervous. Clyde McCullough, the manager, wants to see me. He probably wants to talk about what happened before the game but there's always the fear of being sent down. Since the season started last week out on the road, I only got three hits out of fifteen at bats in the first three games but in the last two games I lit up the pitchers from the Charlotte Knights and Richmond Braves. Then the Raleigh-Durham Phillies came in two days ago for our first home stand and I wasn't worth the price of a bus ticket back home. But I still don't think I'm about to be sent down to the Double AA Chicks in Memphis…because tonight I put it all together; it was the best game I've played this season.

My first opportunity to shine came in the bottom of the first inning. Our lead-off man doubled into left-center field and that rattled the Philly on the pitcher's mound, so he proceeded to walk our number two man on four straight pitches. McCullough has me batting third because, last year, I had the best on-base percentage and that gives our clean-up hitter, Jamie Bell, lots of opportunities to drive me in. In addition to being one hell of a nice guy Jamie is some kind of ballplayer. He was on the Ohio State national championship team in 1966 and up until this season, was playing great ball for the Toledo Mud Hens before being traded to us.

So up I came against this nervous Nellie left-handed pitcher. Like I said, the guy had two on and no outs and had already broken a big sweat. He knew he had to throw strikes and at the Triple AAA level, you can pretty much count on fastballs when a guy gets into trouble early in the game. I had mentally clocked the few heaters he'd thrown at our first two guys and figured the best he was doing was something in the high 80's with very little movement on the ball. So, I dug in and got the full barrel of the bat on his first pitch and everyone in the park knew it was gone from that sweet sound of the crack of an ash-wood Louisville Slugger meeting a full grained, alum tanned cowhide leather ball.

After that, it only got better! In the top of the fourth, their lead-off man hit one just inside the left field foul line into the corner. Luckily, I had been playing deep so I got to the ball in a heartbeat and threw a frozen rope to second base to get the guy sliding in trying for a double.

Then, in the bottom of the fourth inning, with one of our guys on first base, the pitcher threw me low and away and I leaned into it and pulled it down the right field line all the way to the fence. I gotta tell ya…I've got some speed…so I slid into third base for a triple.

When I came to bat in the bottom of the seventh, right after a roaring fan rendition of "*Take Me out to the Ballgame*," I lined one into the gap in left-center field and had an easy stand-up double.

So in the bottom on the ninth, sitting on the bench, I was feeling okay. I'd hit a dinger over the left field fence and showed power to both left-center and right. But I was still thinking about that altercation before the game and being told to see McCullough after I showered…and it didn't help that we were down by one run and maybe looking at a loss: the man hates it! I was scheduled to bat fourth in the inning with Jamie coming up after me if we got that far. He was sitting next to me and suddenly he grinned.

"What?" I asked

"You know, you could have just taken one for the team in the first inning so I could have come up and hit a grand slam."

"You gotta be kidding! Why should I get hit by a pitch so you can get all the glory?"

He gave me a shot in the arm and just kept grinning. "Well, you better do something up there because we're down by one and I want another shot at these guys."

"But I don't have to take one for the team, right?" I asked with my own shit-eaten smile.

He gave me another poke just as a roar went up from the crowd. Our lead-off hitter had hit one into right-center field and slid into second for a double. So, I knew I was going to get some licks and got up and grabbed a bat. Our next guy topped a slow roller back to the mound and their pitcher had no choice but to throw him out at first…while our guy made it to third. I headed for the on-deck circle and, as our next hitter dug in at the plate, I took some practice swings and started to time their pitcher. His motion was really slow to the plate, but his first three pitches were sliders with some heat…and all three were strikes!

So, I went to the plate in a do-or-die situation. Some guys don't like that kind of pressure but I've always thrived on it. I love being in a situation where you get a chance to win the game. And some pitchers like it too so this big hunker was staring me down and I was returning his glare. I figured he was coming with his a-one slider so I didn't take that fraction of a second guys take to figure out the pitch. And…

Thunk!

Damn!!

Jamie got his wish. I took a fastball in the left thigh just above my knee. Bones bruise and might even break but muscle just flat fucken hurts! So I limped alittle toward first and was surprised to see McCullough come out of the dugout and jog toward me.

"You okay?" he asked

"I'm fine."

"You think you can run at full speed?"

"Yes sir."

"Good. I'll give Jamie the take sign on the first pitch and you go for second. The pitcher has a slow delivery to the plate and the catcher has a good arm but won't expect you to steal. Knowing you've been dinged, I figure he'll try to throw you out to end the game and Cookie will break for home as soon as he tries to nail you. Sure you can do it?"

"Yes sir."

He gave me a pat on the ass and headed back for the dugout. Jamie dug in at the plate and I quickly noticed the first baseman was not trying to hold me close to the bag so the plan was looking good right from the git-go. The pitcher only checked me once and then started his slow, high-kick delivery to plate…and I let fly! McCullough was right. The catcher figured he could get me and was probably caught off guard because his throw wasn't anyway near as good as it had been all night. So in I went with a pop-up slide and the crowd roared as Cookie touched home plate and tied up the game.

McCullough gave me a thumbs-up and Jamie just grinned at me. And then Jamie got his second wish of the night: a game winning, walk-off homer to dead center field. What a night!

But now I've showered, tossed on some jeans and a t-shirt, and am heading for McCullough's office. His door is open so I go on in. He's sitting behind his desk, motions me to sit, and gets right to it.

"This isn't why I called you in but you got dinged at the plate for the fourth time and we're not much more than two weeks into the season. I think you're guessing too much and that isn't good. I want you to focus more on what's being thrown after it leaves the pitcher's hand, okay?"

"Okay, Mr. McCullough."

I've already learned that he comes right to the point, is short on words, and it's best to agree with him; in other words, he's a no-nonsense guy.

"Now," he continues, "tell me about the dust-up before the game. What was that all about? You say something to get Christensen riled up?"

"No sir. I was just sitting in front of my locker suiting up and without saying a word he slugged me in the jaw. Then he told me that the he'd just been sent down for a fifteen day rehab and that I was never going to take his place on the Mets roster."

"What did you do?"

"Other than bleed and have Klep sew me up, I didn't do anything."

"Why not?"

"In high school I retaliated once and it wasn't worth it."

"What happened?"

"A teammate thought I was making a move on his girlfriend so he biffed me. I told him I didn't even know who his girlfriend was and he biffed me again so I laid him out."

"And then?"

"The coach only saw me hit him and I got a one game suspension."

"That's not so bad."

"It was football and it was the last game of my senior year."

"Tough. Were you any good?"

"I had scholarship bites but my dad wanted me to be a big league ballplayer."

"Well, he's getting his wish, D Jack," McCullough says with a half smile. "Christensen was wrong. Pack your bags. You're going up.Tomorrow night you'll be playing left field in Shea Stadium. I'll bet your dad is going to be really proud of you."

My grimace says it all. "He died last December."

'I'm sorry to hear that. I really am," McCullough says sincerely. He gets up, comes around his desk and offers his hand as I stand up. "You're about the best I've seen, D Jack. When you get to New York, show them what you've got. Now get out of here!"

Like I said, he's all business. "Thanks Mr. McCullough."

He turns back towards his desk and I head out the door. I'm not a very religious guy but I stop, look up, and close my eyes.

We're going to the Show, Dad.

BOOK I

THE PRESIDENTIAL

To be good you've gotta have a lot of little boy in you. When you see Willie Mays and Ted Williams jumping and hopping around the bases after hitting a home run, and the kissing and hugging that goes on at home plate, you realize they have to be little boys.

Roy Campanella

I

THE PRESIDENTIAL AND THE PROS

Driving along, billboards on the fly
heading for home, another day gone by.....

Actually, I'm not heading for home and sadly, not heading for Shea Stadium either. But the billboards are on the fly and in eighteen hours, I will be heading back to the efficiency where I eat a little, drink a lot, and sleep on occasion…so call it home if you like. I don't, but people are supposed to have one and it ain't worth arguing with you. Anyway, it's 5:45 a.m. and I'm heading south towards Miami on I-95 and it's black as the ass end of Plato's cave with the weatherman on WTVJ predicting a 6:17 a.m. sunrise, clear, and the usual high humidity. His track record? Last week he predicted perfect weather for the Dolphins' game and just about the time the thunderheads moved in during the second quarter, Marcus the Clock, the guy who got us tickets in the Orange Bowl's ancient end zone, spotted him in the vicinity of the forty yard line around Row 12 standing and adjusting his rain gear. Unfortunately for him, the "Fish" were not ahead at the time and his t-shirted neighbors directed their hostility in his direction…along with some ice, cups, a brewsky or two, and a scoop of vanilla which did a number on his Coral Gables Stagg Shop London Fog. It's really amazing this guy survives, but people seem to thoroughly enjoy his ineptitude. Fact of the matter is, he's on the Turk's daily betting odds board in the locker room at the Presidential Golf Course and Country Club and that's exactly where I'm headed.

Immediately you envision a fancy sport shirt and designer slacks, a fifty-pound leather golf bag for some ex-pug barfly to drag around on his back, four matched woods for another pug to wash and rewrap if need be, and an arrogant sneer painted on a somewhat blotchy and spider-webbed martini face which can still make hungry young women wet. Sorry, ya gotta paint another picture. Sure, I'm headed toward the Club but I'm kicking down into third gear on my jet-black Yamaha 500cc, 4-stroke TX 500 with a breakfast cheek of H. B. Scott leaf tobacco. There's no fancy linen under my Arizona State sweatshirt, my jeans are as far away from designer as Eddie Fisher is from Liz Taylor, and my black work boots substitute for Bally loafers.

Having set the record straight, it should be obvious the Club is, for me, financial as opposed to recreational. Fact is I'm the guy who gets the bags to the carts or the caddies' backs, washes em, wraps 'em, and stores em for some $600 per night hotel guest. This should clearly convey to you that the joint is pure class with the Presidential Golf Course and Country Club being the best of the three golf venues that cater to the patrons of the multi-million dollar complex of the Diplomat Hotel, the pride of Hallandale Beach, Florida. Truth be known, this place has everything you can think of and at least a dozen things you couldn't even conjure up. Well, actually, you could dream up some dillies, but then after I told you they have it, you would say, "Naw, they don't really have that!" But honestly, friend, they really do have it…and if they don't, it's up to guys like me to procure it for a price. But as the cliché goes, if you can afford to stay here, don't ask how much. Strike that; I doubt you've got the stock portfolio and don't take it personal, okay?

This being the year of the bicentennial, lots of lists got announced and some fancy schmancy group named the Diplomat Hotel the number one resort in the history of our nationhood which, needless to say, gave management license to double the cost of everything, with a few triples thrown in to boot. My wages, along with everyone else on staff, remained the same and that's the primary reason I really scrounge, although that hasn't always been my line. But let's talk later; a bike ain't a good place for a conversation.

I kick her down into second, lay into a right turn off I-95, roar up the exit ramp to an overpass, and then throw a lazy left onto Miami Gardens Drive which leads me to NE 18th Avenue. After about another half mile or so, another left puts me on the Presidential's private entrance that points toward the top of a small hill upon which sits an architectural marvel of glass and wood. As I slow her down, I glide past lush trees and beautiful flower beds that line the cinnamon bricked road as it winds its way up to the elegant main entrance. The splash of red, yellow and blue petals greets you no matter what time of year. I think these flowerbeds are part of the "ain't this the greatest vacation ever" syndrome. A guest once told me it was the closest thing to the world famous Butchart Gardens she had ever seen, but I've never been to Victoria B.C. so I'll have to take her word for it. At the top of the hill, I ease the lean machine to the right off the main entrance and head for the lower parking area. You don't need a sign to figure out it's for the grunts; there isn't anything newer than a 1970 model vehicle in the whole lot and there's no brick in the tar. Some contrast. Give it a couple more hours and the players' parking lot will have wheels in it that make a BMW look sleazy. Well, maybe that's overdoing it a bit.

I ease out of the black saddle and push the relatively lightweight bike up on the double kickstand. Off comes the black astronaut style helmet that I lock to the metal bar just below and behind the 1.5-gallon tank. I stretch, yawn, and take in the aroma of acres of fresh grass…the green kind you mow! Funny thing…when I leave the efficiency in the morning, it's dark, and when I get back it's pitch black so I never get to see the little bit of grass that separates the place from the asphalt boardwalk that runs parallel to the shoreline of the Atlantic Ocean. Ever! Ya think this is a glimpse into my punitive and occasionally repulsive lifestyle? You got it; a seven-day-a-week gig starting with a 6:00 a.m. kick off and ending when the fat lady sings (actually Charlie T Moon's last song) sometime after midnight when the House closes down the Bengal Lounge. Only good thing I guess is the job is seasonal. I started a few weeks ago in mid-November and will hit the pavement on the 15th of April…unless…as the Brits like to say…I get cashiered. "Is that possible?" you ask. Let me put it to you this way. For those of us who toil for the rich and famous in the Presidential's parking lots, lounges, dining rooms, locker rooms, bag rooms, exercise rooms, and tee to green, the plush Presidential Golf Course and Country Club pays thirty-three cents an hour. Sure, we get tipped, but it becomes necessary to engage in extra-curricular activities if one is to finance any semblance of a quality of life. And you better not make waves; management frowns on such things. When we get to know each other a little better, I'll clue you in on how I manage to indulge myself with the reconditioning of my 1954 XK-120 Jaguar. I suspect you can imagine this kind of place is just full of unique and lucrative opportunities, and I'll tell you up front that smarts frequently ain't part of the rich and famous peoples' package.

I'm beginning to see rust and colors on the dented heaps in the parking lot, and two-to-one on the predicted 6:17 a.m. sunrise looks like a pretty solid bet. I already told you about the daily board which is actually in the men's locker room. The Turk makes a good pretense of being concerned about shoes, shirts, towels, cologne and who the hell knows what while he condescendingly attends to the patrons, but it's just his day job cover. He delegates most of the manual stuff to the caddy corps of walking wounded which allows him to spend the majority of the day in the back room attending to the board and engaging in his chosen profession: bookmaker! Right now, the focus is on the thoroughbreds with their silks flying and hooves pounding the turf at Tropical Park in Miami. College and pro football are big, while basketball and hockey pop up with a little bit of golf, but then, anything goes, like weather predictions! I place a few bets with the Turk every morning, because it helps make the long days go by a little more quickly. Losses are considered to be an investment in mental health around this place, while cashing in provides the pleasant surprise of new-found folding green in the jeans.

I walk up the hill to the circular driveway that leads from the entrance approach and upper parking area to the huge sculpted, double-paneled oak front doors. The first shuttle bus of the day has already arrived, loaded down with the golf bags of guests who will be playing the Presidential today. As mentioned, we are not only the most scenic of the three golf courses offered by the Complex but also the most demanding. Jerry Pate, who just got on the tour last year, supposedly remarked that he wouldn't have won the U. S. Open this year if it had been played out here. The less serious guests tee off at either the Diplomat or the Executive, both of which are located just across the Intracoastal Canal about a half-mile west of the high rise hotel on the Atlantic, often referred to in these parts as Sargasso Sea West. If I could harvest all that seaweed, I'd be hitting you up to back some exercise in entrepreneurship rather than taking up your time with idle chat.

Anyway, there are guests who play all three courses, so their bags have to be sent back and forth constantly. The two blue and white Mercedes shuttle buses have their engines running from before dawn 'til after dusk. The whole operation is like a huge Disneyworld with state-of-the-art transportation connecting the hotel to the three golf courses, a nasty par three, an amusement park for the kids, and two ballroom-sized night spots under one roof. Sure, there's dancing and big time entertainment in the Diplomat, but the big boys wanted the raucous stuff away from the hotel proper. Exclusive? Well, the whole operation is somewhat akin to public beaches in Connecticut: open to the public, if you can afford the parking. And while we're on the subject of affording things, the transportation arrangement is about the only similarity with Disneyworld; I mean, you can get a room in the Polynesian on the beach of the man-made lake across from the Magic Kingdom for about forty-nine bucks, but that won't even buy you a decent lunch around this place.

Regardless, the engine of one of the two Mercedes is purring somewhat like Morris the TV Cat after his morning bowl of whatevers. Unlike my ongoing XK-120 project, the shuttle actually idles in a motionless position. In fact, these vehicles are symbolic of the whole operation: tuned to perfection and designed to provide the utmost service, creature comforts, and unadulterated luxury. The sliding panel door is open, and G.D. is wrestling a huge, black-hooded bag out of the bus and adding it to a pile of four others, all of which appear to be soft, polished, and ostentatiously resplendent.

"Hey, G.D., how's it goin?" I inquire enthusiastically. He looks up slowly from the bags. I can never tell if he has a shaved skull or is just flat bald. His face is a layer of tan folds, his nose is mashed across his cheeks and, what's left of his eyebrows, appear to just kind of melt into his forehead. You remember I was telling you about pugs? Well, G.D. was what you call a journeyman which means he fought mostly prelims and under card stuff but he did get a few main events when he got in with guys who were on the verge of becoming contenders, ya know, like Marlon Brando's Terry Malloy in *On the Waterfront*. G.D. had been a fairly decent welterweight on the high end of a hundred and forty seven pounds who had a good left jab and nice right cross, but it left him wide open to the thunderous blows of Kid Gavilan. The story goes that Gavilan swung a machete in his homeland's sugar cane fields as a kid, and the motion lent itself to something like a half hook and a half uppercut that became his famous bolo punch. In just four rounds, the flashy Cuban in his white high tops put G.D. in Palookaville where he toiled for another five years as a punching bag for the up-and-comers. You got it right…that was about 15-16 fights a year; you don't see much of that anymore, but then, that's probably a damn good thing to put in the past along with six-ounce gloves. G.D. used to caddy until his legs went, and now he spends his days and nights standing in front of those big beautiful wooden doors waiting for the next shuttle and the bags he can barely tote.

"God dammit," he mumbles to himself. "Dis gotta be da lass season."

"Mine too!" I say with gusto as I give him a light, encouraging smack across his stooped shoulders. Again, he mutters softly, his words barely audible…"God damn lass season." Now you know why we call him G.D. Most of the guys working the place are ex-jocks with varied degrees of broken-down bodies and nicknames. Nope, I know what you might be thinking, but it hurts to tell you that I'm not the exception.

Like I said, I'm not playing baseball for the Mets and you might be wondering how I got here so I'll try to be as humble as possible; after all, I'm no Bo Belinsky who allegedly once said that his only regret in life was that he couldn't sit in the stands and watch himself pitch. But, truth be known, just like that last game I told you about in Norfolk, I was a fucken baseball phe-nom! And the stories you hear about pampered athletes are true. I pitched and played left field for the Hollywood Optimists at age ten and was being mollycoddled by age eleven. Age twelve I was throwing heat as an all-state Little League pitcher. At seventeen I threw a two-hit shutout against a Miami powerhouse and notched the first state championship for the Hollywood squad, while the teachers could have cared less what I was doing in class. A year later, a no-hitter against the glamour boys of The Bolles Academy in Jacksonville made it two in a row. Fortunately for me, a number of scouts had been following some pretty quality guys at that prestigious Jax prep school, and two months later at the tender age of 18, I found myself suiting up for the Met's Triple AAA affiliate, the Jacksonville Suns, in Wolfson Park down by the Gator Bowl on the St. Johns River. The classic minor league park had a twenty-five foot outfield brick wall with lots of billboard advertising, but the foul lines were only 320 feet and dead center was 390, so it was really a hitter's yard. Oh yeah, I forgot to mention that those last two years on the high school diamond I hit the long ball and batted .437 and .462 respectively. That kind of power, coupled with a right-armed gun capable of throwing frozen ropes, found the Sun's manager drooling to have me in the lineup on a daily basis so he ended my pitching career and I started patrolling left field. The ole Babe Ruth syndrome if you recall his shift from a Red Sox lefty on the mound to the Yankee Sultan of Swat out in right field. Sure, I know what you're thinking. High school ballplayers, even phe-noms, don't go straight to Triple AAA but the Mets had more or less been a disaster since their inception in '62 and the time was ripe. Maybe they were hoping for the next Al Kaline who, in '55, at the youthful age of 20, hit .340 for the Tigers to snag the American League batting title. And, of course, let's not forget that Casey saw something in Mickey Mantle and took him straight from Class C Joplin to right field in Yankee Stadium. Actually, it should have been the Mick in center, but DiMaggio just wasn't ready to let go.

Year one was a beaut. Played good glove which you had to do because, as Yogi put it, "If you don't catch the ball, you catch the bus home." Hit a solid .308 with 35 homers and 105 runs batted in. Was only one of two guys in the International League that year to bat over .300 with more than 30 dingers, and I think the only guy ever to nail the MVP *and* Rookie of the Year. The fact that we won the International League Championship was obviously a huge plus in adding to a potential super-star kind of status. The sportswriters for the *Florida Times Union* and the TV guys, like Dick Stratton on Channel 4, covered me daily, and the cops could care less about fans buying "D Jack" beers at Brinkman's Pub on Beach Blvd. Some guy even made a beer can with my picture on it, and that one twelve-ouncer became a unique addition to Brinkman's collection, hundreds of which are displayed in mahogany cases surrounding the bar and the many tables in the joint. Now, that doesn't exactly put me up there with Brooks Robinson. Some sportswriter said Robinson never asked anyone to name a candy bar after him or a beer for that matter; however, in Baltimore, people name their children after him. Hell, the guy has been playing for more than twenty years and is a lock for the Hall of Fame, so obviously a can of suds isn't much of a testament. Anyway, the groupies were frequently at Brinkman's usually nibbling on the specialty of the house, the "Big B," and I rarely spent a lonely night. But that only lasted for about a month until the blonde, busty captain of the cheerleaders of the Jacksonville Firebirds semi-pro football team staked her claim and ran off the competition. Other than long overnights in the broken-down team bus which stopped exclusively at fleabag motels and greasy spoons (with the good ole Waffle House being an exception, and my fav) life was about as good as it could get. All the signs pointed toward going to the show in New York the following spring…or maybe a month or so back in Jax at the start of the season and then the bigs. Hey, it was a given; this is the way it had been for almost ten years and there was no reason to believe it would change. But it did…in a tenth of second…but let me finish the glory part before we get to that.

The following April the 1969 season opened with two series on the road. The Mets had moved their Triple AAA team from Jax to Norfolk, and I killed the starting pitchers for the Charlotte Knights and then did the same against the Richmond Braves…but I think you already know that. The manager of the Norfolk Tide, Clyde McCullough, had been a solid and tough catcher for the Cubs and Pirates but didn't get a lot of press thanks to the Berra-Roy Campanella era. In short, he was a smart and savvy baseball man, and he kept my spikes nailed to the floor while the press started to pick up the chant, and the fans got ready to rattle the rafters in Lawrence Stadium. He did a good job because my ballcap was still fitting my head, and, in our first home stand against the Raleigh-Durham Phillies, if you recall, I played errorless ball in left and took their pitching apart.

So, as you know, I was called up to the Show. The Mets' left fielder, Christiansen, had gotten his spikes tangled up with the bag stealing second base and had twisted his ankle which put him on the fifteen-day disabled list. That's the way it breaks sometimes, no pun intended. Somebody gets lucky and somebody else's ox gets gored. Who knows, maybe I would be like Gehrig who stepped in as a pinch hitter, when the regular Yankee first baseman got a headache, and didn't come out for 2,130 games. But that would be asking for way too much and, anyway, no one is ever gonna come close to the record of the 'Iron Horse.'

So, on a Friday I had suited up for Norfold/Portsmouth in a ghost of a park, and on a Saturday I was lacing up my cleats in the dressing room of the magnificence of Shea Stadium, nestled in the New York borough of Queens. After batting practice, the manager, Gil Hodges, had attempted to shield me from the New York Press. That, of course, was impossible because the ballyhoo had already begun. You have to understand that the New York Metropolitan Baseball Club had basically been dead to the neck until the "Franchise", Tom Seaver, arrived in 1966 out of the University of Southern California. The fans were starting to hope for a competitive team what with guys like Bud Harrelson, Cleon Jones, and Tommy Agee really starting to cook, and Tug McGraw and Nolan Ryan in the bullpen waiting to bail out Seaver if need be, so the timing was perfect for the "Second Franchise" player. It didn't hurt that Mantle had retired just the previous year and that Broadway Joe Namath had pulled off his self-predicted Super Bowl upset against the mighty Baltimore Colts in January. You've got it! The stars were perfectly aligned, the table was set, and the sportswriters were all over me like stink on a skunk.

"What's the biggest difference between the pitching in the minors and the pitching up here?" the first one asked while I was sliding on my right sock that *always* came after the left one. I should have answered 'The questions here are more stupid,' but that wouldn't have been too smart a move.

"I'll tell you around 11:30 tonight," I responded with my best boyish smile. That got a good laugh out of the writers and a kind of half-smile out of Hodges, who was leaning against my locker in a somewhat protective stance. His look also had seemed to convey that I needed to say something a little more serious.

"I'm sure I'm gonna see more heat on their fast balls and more likely a curve on a 3-2 pitch which didn't happen all that much in Jacksonville or Norfolk."

A sly-looking sonuvabitch had kind of measured me up and I knew something nasty was coming, and he didn't disappoint. "I'm sure you know Mantle had big shoes to fill what with the legacies of Ruth and DiMaggio but that isn't the case here except for a few writers and fans who think you might be the second coming of Christ. How do you feel about that?" The locker room went to dead silence in less than a second while the wise guy with a shit-eaten grin under his battered fedora chomped on his half-smoked ten-cent cigar.

"Well, sure," I began, "this franchise doesn't have forty or fifty years of tradition, but over the past six or so seasons there have been…and are," I hastily added, "some great ballplayers, and I just hope I can contribute to bringing the first championship to the franchise and the fans. And, if I recall, the Mick was sent down to Kansas City in a matter of weeks, so I sure hope I still get a chance to talk with you guys next month." I wanted to finish up and, hearing some chuckles, I figured it was going okay, but they kept at me.

"Is this your first time in Shea Stadium?" Wow…another brilliant inquiry, but at least it had broken the ice.

"Yup…first time in any major league park."

"Big, isn't it?" said another guy wearing an equally battered fedora and a big dopey smile.

"Awesome," I responded, "and the really neato thing is that I've never played with the fans at my back. When I was shagging fly balls during warm ups a few minutes ago," I continued, "that bleacher area in left center was starting to fill up around the left field foul pole, and golly gee, there's three tiers up there. I played in front of about 8,000 when we won the International League World Series last year in Wolfson Park, but, hell, all the parks that I've played in, left field was so quiet you could hear the grass grow." That got another good laugh, but Hodges had had enough and told the guys to clear out while he promised some post game interviews.

So there I was, looking at the bigs, suiting up to play in front of fifty thousand fans against the St. Louis Cardinals and getting ready to stare down a big right-hander who threw a 97 m.p.h. heater…but good luck had kicked in before the game even started. Bob Gibson had been scheduled to go to the mound that Saturday night, and he was just coming off the '68 season with a 1.12 earned run average that was the lowest in more than fifty years. For reasons I didn't know about, or care about for that matter, Gibson was scratched at the last minute, and the next guy in the rotation had gotten the start. I remember there were some young Turks challenging his ass so I figured their starter was going to try to blow fast balls by me and secure the spotlight by welcoming the new kid on the block to the real world of big league baseball. I had figured right and jacked his first pitch more than 400 feet off the big black scoreboard in dead center. It was fucken mythological; I mean, I'm touching all the bags on my first at bat in the Show and the Big Apple is popping up out of the black top hat in right center, which happens every time a Met nails one in Shea. Then it just got better, because his testosterone must have gotten the best of him and he kept the heat coming, and I dinged him for a triple and a double even though it was a tough yard that night with lots of humidity. I mean, just think of it, the first pitch in my career had gone downtown, and if I could have gotten a single for my last at bat, I would have hit for the circuit in my first appearance in the majors. Hell, there are guys in Cooperstown who didn't get a single, double, triple, and homer in the same game during their entire careers.

In left field, the night was just as magical. I reeled in a few easy shots, one toughy off my shoe tops, and another one that had backed me up to the wall. Then, in the top of the eighth with guys on first and second and two down, Hodges waved me into shallow left and the light-hitting Cardinal at the plate put a one hopper between 3rd and short. I got on it in a heartbeat and threw the ole frozen rope straight to the plate where our catcher, Jerry Grote, made an easy tag.

Right after that, I led off the bottom of the eighth going for the circuit and figured he was finally gonna throw me a curve, so I dug in with my cleats kissen the dish. If you recall, that was exactly what McCullough told me not to do. Again, when I think about it, I guess he figured I was cocky and getting in his face so maybe it was chin music he was throwing. After all, he was young and undoubtedly getting some pointers from Gibson, who didn't take any shit off anybody: if you smiled at him, he'd put one in your ear! Regardless, I took that 'tenth of a second' I told you about expecting the breaking ball…and his heater came at me and slammed my left cheek, orbital, and nose. I guess it was one of those 'out of body' experience things 'cause I knew something bad had happened and thought I heard somebody shout, "For God's sake, don't move him!" Someone else was moaning and, after seeing the photos of all the blood a few weeks later, I figure the players must have been a lot more scared than me, 'cause truth is, I was in a daze sprawled across the plate and didn't know or feel a damn thing. The next thing I knew I was stretched out in a hospital bed barely comprehending the pronouncement every pro fears the most: the unequivocal utterance of a permanent, career-ending injury.

In my case, it wasn't clinical or anything like that the first day or so, but I do remember a serious-sounding guy talking to somebody else saying something like…'Poor sonofabitch will be trading in his Louisville Slugger for a red and white cane.' The actual doctors' prognosis came three days later with the announcement, from both an ophthalmologist and a neurosurgeon, of a blowout fracture of the orbit bone surrounding my left eye. If you want the anatomical dope, the *World Book Medical Encyclopedia* says, "A blow out fracture occurs when the eye or eye region is struck with enough force to cause pressure within the orbit (eye socket) to suddenly increase resulting in a break in one of the orbit bones." The worstcase scenario involves damage to the nerves and eye muscles in the orbit if they get pushed through the broken bone, and, unfortunately, that is precisely what happened to me. So, it was time to say goodbye to watching the ball leave the pitcher's hand and 'reading' those red seams on that pure white sphere which was the key to greatness...if, like Ted Williams, you could really do it.

The one thing that sticks in my mind, to this day, is how quick it all went from euphoria to dysphoria...that inexplicable feeling that everything had gone from unbelievably great to horribly wrong. I mean, I'm going to the plate for my first at bat in a Major League baseball game; hitting it out of the park; rounding third, heading for home; and soaking up the adulation of the fans. Three hours later, I'm unconscious in a hospital emergency room, unaware of the fact that it's all over. In the blink of an eye, literally, it was all gone. Damn!

After ten days in the hospital, the organization sadly, but fairly, settled my contract which wasn't much of a deal because I was making a hell of a less than the $38,000 they were paying Seaver. So, once again, I was rounding third, but this time I wasn't heading for home plate; this time, I had a one-way ticket to Ft. Lauderdale International Airport...and was heading abso-fucken-lutely nowhere.

That's when I decided to study philosophy. I really think, had I stayed healthy, I could have stayed at the Show for a long time, but then, I never got cut and I never got sent down. Or, to put it in another way, I didn't have to hear a manager like Casey Stengel say, "Son, we'd like to keep you around this season, but we're going to try to win a pennant." See what I mean: positive deep thinking...not that philosophy is always positive. And, of course, as you might know, the Miracle Mets not only won the pennant in the first ever National League Championship series by beating Atlanta but went on to take out Brooks and the Orioles and won the World Series for the city of Flushing, Queens, New York without D Jack, or the next coming of Christ for that matter. So, how's that for even more philosophizing?

Anyway, with some severance money in my pockets I figured I might as well try college life. Fortunately I graduated from high school with some decent standardized scores and a respectable GPA. The problem now was my eyesight...or lack thereof. I guess I mentioned this college thing to one of the doctors in New York who must have passed it on to someone in the Mets front office, because the day before I left the hospital, I got a letter from the registrar's office at Arizona State University. It informed me that if I applied for admission and was accepted, I would have all tuition fees waived, would serve as an assistant baseball coach, and would be assigned "student readers who will provide assistance due to your visual impairments."

Why not! Hell of a place, Reggie Jackson and Sal Bando had been there and the Sun Devils had a number of NCAA baseball championships tucked away. It wouldn't take Jackson long to be a unanimous MVP in 1973, but in '70 it was the year of the Orioles, who had bounced back from their defeat at the hands of the Miracle Mets to take out the Reds, and Boog Powell had been the best of the best. I had often played in Key West where Boog was nothing short of a living legend, but now that all seems like nothing more than a dusty memory.

Bittersweet; some guys are just made to play, and I spent too many hours in May instructing big-eyed kids while, in my heart, I was swinging the lumber at heaters and sliders. I hung in anyway, because it not only paid a modest stipend of twenty-six hundred dollars but also continued to waive all the academic fees. The first thing I did when I started my coursework in the fall was to enroll in an intro course in philosophy and it just seemed like neat stuff, so I majored in useless PH 101 right up through a Master of Arts. I'm not going to suggest to you that I started looking at the miles of Japanese flower gardens on Phoenix's Baseline Road with deep contemplation or that I began to wander up into the Superstition Mountains above Apache Junction looking for knowledge and wisdom from the lost Dutchman. The crimson and orange Arizona sunsets continued to look about the same when sipping a VO and sitting on a lawn chair in the dry bed of the Salt River which runs through Tempe, but all and all, life did kind of slow down which was a good thing during those five plus years.

Among other mind expanding activities, I learned to appreciate good jazz when the Newport Jazz Festival Road Show included Phoenix on its annual trek. I mean in a period of four hours on a Saturday night, I was exposed to Cannonball Adderly on alto with brother Nat blowing the horn; Jimmy Smith whose R&B, jazz, bebop style popularized the Hammond organ; Herbie Mann on flute with his trio; Thelonious Monk growling at everyone all by himself; and sixty glorious minutes of Dionne Warwick doing Burt Bacharach's stuff.

Even better than concerts, a grounds keeper named Ramon Gonzalez introduced me to everything from gaspacho to flan although he was unable to lure me from my VO to his blue something or other tequila. He got most of his recipes from his cousin who was the head waiter at the Cave in Nogales. We would go down there once a month and the restaurant actually was in an honest-to-God cave. It was kind of a hangout for the movie crowd who would often drive down the sixty-seven miles after a long day on the dusty sets in Old Tuscon, and I actually saw the cousin doctor up some turtle soup with his homemade tobasco sauce for John Wayne. Tell you what, pilgrim, the Duke looked like he was enjoying it, big time.

Relaxation was found in fingering my Yamaha G-51 classical guitar and writing story songs. I also did a little horseback riding up in South Mountain Park, engaged in brief and shallow relationships with co-eds mostly from California, and became an ardent hockey fan of the Phoenix Roadrunners which helped to heal the baseball scars…but not by much.

I spent most of my time on the Arizona State campus which was literally strewn with Frank Lloyd Wright architecture. The jewel was the Grady Gammage Auditorium which allegedly was designed for a shah who got deposed or something like that. I heard a speech in there by a guy named Rudolph Dreikurs who talked about the "Courage to Be Imperfect." Hell, that was easy in baseball; I mean if you're out 60 percent of the time, you're still batting .400 which puts you right up there with Ted Williams who actually was quoted as saying, "Baseball is the only field of endeavor in which a man can succeed three times out of ten and be considered a good performer." I doubt seriously the Splendid Splinter thought much about being imperfect.

Anyway, this edifice had great big arches studded with globes that blazed a path to the sand-colored circular palace…and across the street was the music building that looked like a birthday cake or maybe a top hat for a royal head of state. If you wanted tranquility, you could get a special dose of Frank Lloyd by driving up past Camelback Mountain in Scottsdale to his home away from home, Taliesan West. What was neat was that no matter how hot it would get, you were always cool in one of the many breezeways of the structure. The place looked more like God put it there as opposed to mere mortals erecting a studio home that kinda got absorbed by the desert. I think Wright's students actually built it and I'm pretty sure he died there in 1959.

I went to Taliesan pretty regularly and hit Bill Johnson's Big Apple on Van Buren in Phoenix on the way back to Tempe. The joint had the best ribs and slow cooked cowboy chili topped with cheddar cheese and crackers, and the deep dish apple pie was to kill for, but the main course was the waitresses, complete with gun belts slung around their tight blue-jeaned hips which provided a tantalizing sight as the girls' black boots kicked up sawdust from the wood-planked floors.

But none of it worked. A day didn't go by that I didn't think about that fateful day in Shea Stadium. In fact, it even found its way into my Master's Thesis. I don't want to take up your time with a bunch of academic mumbo-jumbo, so let me just try to give you the short version of the abstract; you know, the piece that introduces, and sums up, the whole scholarly work…so professors don't have to read the whole fucken thing!

Okay then, what I was trying to do was to establish a philosophically significant similarity between baseball and life. In baseball, although there are lots of scenarios, generally when you're rounding third and heading for home, you're doing it one of two ways: first, if you're a power hitter, like the 3 M boys…Mantle, Maris, and Mays…you're notching up another home run and jogging to the plate.

But, secondly, if you're like most players, you're touching the third base bag and running like hell, hoping to score. That's because you've seen the third-base coach's arms circling frantically…and you know there's going to be a play at the plate. So, you put your head down, and run ninety feet, for all you're worth. You don't think about it, and you don't know if you'll be safe or out; win or lose; succeed or fail.

Now, the connection I was aiming for is that in baseball, you run a path. In life, you travel a path; many paths, whether by choice, circumstance, fate…call it what you want. But just a handful of thoses paths will significantly impact your future. And, in life, just like in baseball, when you're rounding third, unlike the 3 M boys, something, or someone, is waiting for you at the plate.

It all gets somewhat speculative in the body of the thesis, but I won't push my luck. Thanks for hanging in!

Anyway, like Campanella said, "You have to have a lot of little boy in you to play this game," and this little boy had trouble putting things away, so upon graduation in the summer of 1975, I headed back south to Miami to be the 'has-been' who could attract the locals to move through the turnstiles to watch a semi-pro team play ball. Bad move…couldn't see out of that left eye and was doing little more than guessing and swinging. I would have been totally embarrassed if these guys were able to throw something other than fast balls which weren't all that fast. Hell, they only threw curves in 0-2 situations, so I just waited for the lukewarm heat. Truth is, having stepped in against some real flamethrowers, this stuff looked like slow motion and sure as hell could never split a lip.

What did come as a pleasant surprise, however, was that the fans in south Florida remembered me. Actually, I had become a trivia item with the question being, "Who was the only guy to ever play in the majors and have a lifetime batting average of .1000?" Also, there had been a lot of concern with the picture of me laid out at home plate on the front pages of all the sports sections, so the Commissioner of Baseball, Bowie Kuhn, had provided a photo op to assure the fans I was alive and well. I had actually gotten to throw out the first pitch at the '69 all-star game at R. F. K. Memorial Stadium in D. C. and, wow, it was a genuine rush!

My fifteen minutes of fame continued when I was flown up to New York City for a "hi-how-are-ya" on the Johnny Carson Show, and that had really gone well. Carson's opening inquiries, I guess, were designed to provide a bit of a sympathetic pity session, which I deflected with what was referred to in the morning papers as a terrific sense of humor. He had opened by asking me if I missed the game, and my response had been, "No, because in the off season you had to play a lot of celebrity golf tournaments, and on the links I was a total clod with a lousy wardrobe." Well, Carson just threw his head back the way he does, with that genuinely full blown laugh and it was nothing but fun and games from that point on. They told me after the show that Johnny had kept me on an extra seven minutes. Well, if that wasn't enough, in the next few shows he was still using my "golly gees" and "neato kazeatos", and, for me, that was really the whipped topping on the cake. On the very next morning, I was just as light-hearted while mixing in a respectable dose of baseball savvy, with my already apparent sense of humor, with ex-catcher Joe Garagiola in his role as anchor of the Today Show. The producer got ahold of me backstage after my appearance and told me I was a natural and might want to consider doing sports on TV. "Sure," I had laughed, "what with my 'pretty' face."

Anyway, I guess I had become a widespread, barroom "what if" kind of conversation. Seems as if I had died young but wasn't dead yet. Fortunately, I only played a few weeks in the old Miami Stadium downtown, or else I truly would have been in the grave or totally embarrassed at the very least. I used to love that place. Most of the fans seemed to be transplanted New Yorkers and you know what that means: rugged individuals who belly up a few bucks for a ducket which gives them license to say or do just about anything. Usually, half of 'em would boo at the seventh inning stretch because how can you take me out to where I already am? Like Bill Veeck used to say, "Baseball is the working man's game. A baseball crowd is a beer-drinking crowd, not a mixed-drink crowd."

That went double for the players on the way down from the bigs or Triple AAA, or the invalids who didn't play drunk, but sure as hell had hangovers, which didn't do much to up the ability level of this ragtag semi-pro team. There were a few kids who had some skill but probably didn't have much of a chance because of the growth of colleges as the top breeding grounds for future big leaguers, so most were guys in their middle to late 20's who were just trying to hang around the 'pop' of a glove and the 'crack' of a bat. God, we were lousy but for some of those guys, they hoped there was always a chance.

And, speaking of chances, unlike football and basketball, in the National Pastime, you can't take a knee, and there's no clock you can run out. There's always the bottom of the ninth, the pitcher has to bring it, and the visiting team still needs those final three outs to get to Miller time. As for those blue collar transplanted Yanks, Bums, Giants, and Mets' fans, we were so bad, there was always a bottom of the ninth so they got their bang for their buck.

One big plus remained. I was the big fish in the little pond when it came to the groupies. There were still a few Miami Swamp Angels who wanted to etch my initials on their headboards and it wasn't like I had a significant relationship going which might produce some kind of guilt complex. Truth is I really didn't have anything going at all so casual sex was a pleasant distraction, with one huge exception. Identical blonde strippers who worked in a pretty nice establishment in the Gables had let it be known that if any guy could hit two dingers in one game, they'd both swing for him. So, one night I was blindly flailing away at anything and everything and put two out of the park and, lo and behold, they met me at the players gate and escorted me to their apartment where I was treated to my first and, to date, only ménage a trois. I really have to be honest. It was mostly a lot of laughs and the sensory overload was too much to handle, so I wasn't very good, but that was okay because they really didn't seem to care. Eventually, they satisfied themselves, much to my visual delight. I've got to tell you, there really is something erotic about watching two broads working each other over, or maybe you already know that, whether watching or participating. Whatever.

I'm sure I would have been stupid enough to play and just hang in with the sweat and leather but the next night a guy named Harlan tracked me down in a sports bar. Turns out he was the head pro at the Presidential and felt I would be a nice addition to his retired sports staff stable as he so graciously put it. Like he said, people still remembered D Jack, the brightest one-year comet ever to flash across the International League sky and the one day wonder in the Show. I viewed it differently, I guess. I was more like G.D. who never saw the big money and who got knocked out in the first minute of the first round in the main event. Like I said a few minutes ago, I'm not the exception. Enough.

I'm still listening to G.D.'s grunts as I push open the ten-foot high double doors and am greeted by your standard magnificent wood-paneled Clubhouse foyer which funnels guests straight away to a huge lounge or sitting room or whatever the well-heeled call it. The place has deep soft leather couches, loveseats, and chairs with small cherrywood tables placed strategically for drinks and finger food. It's one of those rooms where there can be lots of people, but you just don't know they're there. The thick, rich, brown shag carpets are wall-to-wall and extend into an intimate bar and lounge to the left and a posh formal dining room to the right. The far end of the so-called sitting room is all glass which allows the lush grass and foliage of the 1st tee and the 18th green to pour into the room.

I hang a left for the Bengal Lounge which is decorated entirely with hardwoods and red leather-backed booths and barstools. I've never really been in a "gentleman's club", but I think this is what it's supposed to look like. The lighting is so soft you can hardly see the few deep-cushioned love seats and sofas behind a few tables at the far end of the room which also houses a small stage in the back right corner. Charlie T Moon plays from nine 'til one most nights, and I back him, on guitar, along with two brothers; one plays bass and the other is on drums and vocals. We do Chapin-Croce kinds of stuff, and the mellow sounds enhance the romantic ambiance of the room. We also play our own stuff. Charlie writes most of the music and I write most of the lyrics. Doing so makes it possible for guests to go back home and tell their equally pretentious friends about these guys who did originals and that they discovered them while enjoying their multiple hundred-a-day getaway. You know the shit; it's the "I did something or got something you didn't" deal or, in this case, the "I did something you didn't" vacation.

I had gotten sidetracked Saturday night and wasn't sure if the late custodial shift had put the Yamaha G behind the bar, but, sure enough, there she was. Not that anyone would bother to heist the beat-up old axe. I mean, come on, the clientele in the room on any given night is totally focused on a drink or two and an arrangement or two. A lot of wheeling and dealing, business and otherwise, transpires in this bar; in fact, this spot has to be the one place in the Club where the action is financial winning and losing, ulcer-incubating, and love-fire burning.

I head out of the bar and cross over to the formal dining room which encompasses a lot of space without sacrificing its intimacy. As with the lounge, the architect did his best to bring the outside in and, between you and me, he did a damn fine job of it. No matter where guests sit, they experience the vast panorama of manicured lawns, flowers, trees, bunkers, water hazards, and little hills through the large, irregularly-shaped panes of glass, all of which make their Crab Louis, Tournadoes Hongroise, or whatever, taste a little bit better. A couple of girls are already putting together the breakfast set-ups for the early birds who have 7:15 a.m. tee-off times. I head straight for the kitchen for a croissant and a half cup of black steaming coffee; I drink 'em by the halves so they stay good and hot. On the way out, one of the waitresses, a pert, short-haired ash blonde waves, smiles, and throws in a playful wiggle of her tight, curvaceous ass. You ask me, "Okay wise guy, how do you know her ass is tight?" Well, as they say in philosophical circles, I have empirical data through a primary source: me. I had caught her on a rebound and had filled a ten-day void until her boyfriend realized what he was missing. There were the obligatory tears, we kissed gently one night, and parted friends; nay, siblings would be more like it, although I'm really kind of lousy at the big brother thing.

Don't get me wrong. This isn't machismo bullshit; in fact, I've had very little success with the ladies, whether it's been an attempt at the serious or simply mattress recreational. Truth is I see myself as a 50's romantic. I like to get involved, you know, the whole idea of a meaningful relationship, but the few times I thought I was on track, things went south. You remember the cheerleader, Miss Firebird, right? Well, she isn't the focus of this brief discussion, but sure, if I was still in left field in New York, she would probably be purring in my penthouse, and I would be thinking it was the real deal because I was too green to realize the ladies seem to like to hang with the guys who are running the streak…and will do just about anything to keep the job.

This, of course, ain't true for the keepers, the ones who will hold your hand and go the distance, but guys like me have this remarkable inability to perceive all that, and then fuck up the real thing when it actually comes along. I think maybe the deeper problem for me is that unless I focus on an inanimate object, like whisky, I have this uncanny ability to say or do something so off the wall that I can't even fathom it myself. What I'm trying to say is that VO, which is best consumed when mixed with a splash of water and two or three ice cubes, depending upon the size of the glass, is an inanimate object and therefore very forgiving by nature. I can spill it, mix it with the wrong stuff, or even throw it against the wall, all stupid things, but that ole brown bottle will still be around tomorrow. That's pretty much the way I approach things, and so the only time I'm really in control is when I'm not shopping around or, put another way, could care less.

Example? During one monthly soiree in Nogales with Ramon, a fourteen- year-old black-haired youth tried to sell me a seascape. I think it was something like twenty bucks and it was just flat hideous. I wouldn't have bought it for three and I know what I am talking about because that was her final offer. I had 'no way' written all over me so she went back to the twenty spot, but that was for herself and fifteen minutes in the back seat of the nearby broken-down '52 Ford. After politely declining her offer, I kept motoring and two blocks closer to the aforementioned Cave I spied a white leopard in a large-hand carved wood frame. We started at a ten-spot and were working our way down to a five. The kid could smell it all over me, and he begrudgingly agreed to six bucks. My grin quickly ran off my face as he started to tear the felt artwork out of the frame. I had a hemorrhage. The frame had to be part of the deal, yes? The hell it was. We started all over again, and I finally walked away with the painting, in the frame, and a conspicuously absent ten-dollar bill. And so it is with the ladies and damn near everything else: it seems that when I really want something, I screw the pooch.

I head through the exterior glass doors of the dining room, hang a left, and head for the pro shop. This part of the Club is in the form of a "U", with the pro shop jutting out across the base, the ladies' lockers traveling up the left arm, the men's up the right arm, and the bag room and cart room occupying all the space in between the arms. The pen for the caddies is located at the open end of the "U" from which a flower-lined path curves around the building to the 1st and 10th tees. Obviously, this is the working part of the Club, but it, too, exhibits about a hundred-and-fifty-dollar square-foot construction. Actually, the pro shop is about as magnificent as the bar and comes complete with a big name from yesteryear: Hammering Harlan Bottomly. You remember Harlan; he's the head pro who brought me to this oasis in North Miami Beach about a year ago.

Harlan still plays a few rounds with guests, but only if they are celebrities or movers and shakers. He's more like the Joe Louis of the place. Shakes a lot of hands, smiles, lends himself to personalized photographs, and generally gives the paying public the thrill of being in his presence and exchanging a story or two. Bobby "Sticks" Wilson actually runs the pro shop and oversees most of the lessons. I'm not sure whether his nickname comes from his unusually long and skinny legs or the fact that a driver looks like a matchstick in his mammoth hands. The bottom line, however, is that Bobby Sticks never won a tournament, rarely finished in the big money or even made the cut, and forever doomed himself to the role of assistant pro. Hey, no tears here! A lot of guys hit the circuit for a few years and never come close to ending up with something as sweet as the Presidential. Yeah, no hearts and flowers for ole Bobby Sticks.

Sticks is doing something with shirts, and he shoots me a smile which I return along with a high-five sign as I head to the back of the pro shop and go through the middle of three sets of doors into the bag room. About ten feet in, a long Spanish-tiled counter runs parallel to the door with absolutely nothing on it except a copy of today's starting times sheet. I quickly look it over and note a foursome is inked into every slot between 7:15 a.m. and 1:30 p.m. Now that's about six hours or three hundred and sixty minutes divided by nine, as in minutes, which is the stagger time between tee offs. That gives us forty tee offs which means…holy shit! A hundred and sixty bags and that won't include stragglers and some of the fucken cheapskate doctors who start to play as late at 4:30 p.m. Whoa Nellie! Today is going to be an ass- buster because, like the Turk who gets others to do his grunt work, I've got to get the walking wounded caddies organized to undertake the bagroom chores while I try to average a couple of bucks per player with some special services. That, plus some private club rentals and hustling some convention booze might provide sufficient funds for a potentially beneficial investment with the Turk. Who knows what resources might pop up and supply today's income. Yes, sir! The Presidential Golf Course and Country Club is about to greet me with another sunrise.

II

BRUNETTE PIGTAILS AND A STRAWBERRY BLONDE

The sun comes up and I can see
the harsh light of reality…..

Those are some lyrics from one of our story songs. It makes me feel pretty good that Charlie likes to mix our work in with stuff that's on the charts, but it makes him feel even better that people staying at the Presidential think of him as kind of an American Gordon Lightfoot. He sings good and finger picks maybe two or three shades under Leo Kottke. Charlie sings songs like the billboards thing you caught earlier this morning which is part of the stuff we write about people at different stages of life. Our dusk songs focus on the twilight years, but, being in our late twenties, the lyrics obviously have nothing to do with us unless we forsee a dreaded future. They go on:

familiar faces melt away
I've got to start another day
sitting alone, reading the news
drinking a cup, feeling unused.

It's all part of future shock. I'm figuring if you live long enough, you're going to be alone and I guess it's gonna to be tough:

It's dinner time a place for one
the fading day is almost done
yet I am warmed throughout these eves
by the ones I loved and my memories
I turn down the bed
my tired eyes gleam
my mind is at peace
I welcome my dreams.

Charlie always checks the room before he does that one; if he sees a person, who appears to be over sixty at a table alone, he throws it out. Anyway, the sun has officially come up three minutes past the 6:17 a.m. which was well within the window posted on the odds board. It's now about 7:40 a.m., and the harsh light of reality is that I've had a pretty dull hour. On a long wall next to the caddy's pen, I had the guys stack a row of about a hundred or so golf bags which will take care of the players up through something like 11:00 a.m. By that time, I'll have made sure the other sixty plus have been lined up so I can have a couple of hours to provide random services. Then the bags start coming in as the golfers head for the mandatory nineteenth hole where a few toast the occasional birdie while the majority anesthetize their double and triple bogies. For most of the afternoon I'm supposed to make sure their clubs get cleaned but again, I pay a caddy out of my own pocket to labor over the sinks with the soap and towels. This, of course, gives me even more time for my randoms. Example? Patience, guys. I'm sure we'll come across something worthwhile before the day is out.

I walk into the starter's office which is a three-paneled smoked, cut glass cubicle with little more than standing room behind a counter that allows for monitoring the first tee which is dead away. Number ten is just down an asphalt golf cart trail to the left, the ninth green is nestled between the tenth and first tees, and the eighteenth green is off to the right. This compact setting allows the starter, Marcus the Clock, to efficiently oversee the daily ebb and flow of the guests at the points on the course that frequently offer up logjams. At this particular moment, he's sitting behind the counter patiently scrutinizing the starting sheet and undoubtedly anticipating the less than happy remarks, offered commonly in the form of raised and ominous voices, from the portfolioed clientele.

"Top o' the morning to you, D Jack," Marcus says without looking up from the sheets. His brogue is still quite pronounced in that he's a first-generation American from the Callahan clan, his vaudevillian daddy, Jerry, having set sail from Dublin with little more than a tam on his head, a battered pipe in his mouth, tap shoes in his back pocket, and a glint in his corn-blue eyes. I would say Marcus is somewhere in his late sixties, and he's kind of a frail looking sort with small, wire-rimmed spectacles perched on a rail-thin nose that separates sharp cheekbones beneath a thinning head of wavy brown hair with more than a touch of gray. Sometimes I really think a strong breeze could blow him on his bony ass but that's something even the mightiest guest has yet to accomplish. If you recall, he's the guy that gets us tickets to things…like Dolphin's games. Problem is we rarely can get away from this place so we generally scalp 'em through the Turk.

"Yo, Marcus. Looken busy, huh? Good?"

"Not good, D Jack. Got a full sheet and I heard from the Big House fifteen minutes ago that I've got to wedge in Michael Dawson."

"Terrific," I grunt with a smirk. "I thought golden-throat wasn't singing in the main room til next week."

"He isn't but Bottomly was told he's coming in early to show off his nineteen-year-old bride," Marcus answers in what I perceive to be a disapproving tone. "You're going have to keep an eye on her, Pirate. The way that schmuck behaves, she won't be more than window dressing when he hits the links and the word is that she doesn't know diddly squat about the game, or anything else for that matter."

"Doesn't stop Dawson much," I respond. "He don't know shit from shinola about golf but he manages to dig up the whole fucken course twice a year without dropping a dime on the help at the Big House, here, nowhere, nada, zilch! Like Paul Gallico said, 'if there's any larceny in a man, golf will bring it out.'"

"Who was he and where did you get that morsel from?"

"He was some writer who died this year and I saw the quote in his obit," I answer. "But who the fuck cares," I conclude, still miffed about the thought of dealing with Dawson.

Marcus the Clock is unmoved by my feeble attempt at a tirade. "That's what I like about you, Pirate. You're always looking to the bright side." He finally brings his eyes off the starting sheets and slowly works his way up all six feet of me. Well, five-eleven when the toes are in the sand but let's not make a federal case out of it. He finally makes eye contact, which usually happens when he wants to make a point. Ya know…the ole look em deep in the retina game which obviously doesn't work very well on me.

"Regardless, one small problem we've got is the man's bag hasn't arrived yet so you're going to have to set him up with some quality clubs."

"How about I give him Bottomly's bag? The ole man will be on the coast until Thursday and no one will know the difference." Now I'm getting the pointed forefinger but he's painted a half smile on his gaunt face.

"Okay, but I don't know about it, right? And be ready! I don't have the vaguest idea when the sonovabitch is coming and I want him out of here as quickly as possible. Got it?"

I shrug and nod in the affirmative. What are the options? After all, like you just heard, I'm also known around here, on rare occasions, as the Pirate, not the Captain. And while we're on that subject, only a handful of my "colleagues" refer to me as the Pirate and only when players are not within earshot. I've got to tell you, I'm not a hundred percent sure where it comes from, but it could be that I'm considered to be rather proficient at digging various treasures out of guests; or it might be that I commandeered a few things during the last season; or maybe it's simply the full dark reddish-brown beard that hides the New York City beanball scars that adorn my tanned face, what little of it you can see. Whatever, it's just another part of being on the team and, like it or not, you get tagged sooner or later…with Ralph being the lone exception. He takes care of the electric golf carts and I have it on good authority that his name actually is Ralph, but he looks so much like a Ralph, we just flat out have to call him Ralph. Just think of Gleason doing the Honeymooners. Now I ask you, ain't that a Ralph? You got it and maybe it's only my opinion, but I think Ralph's brain is somewhat on the Ralph side too.

Marcus returns his gaze to the sheets so I exit his domain and head for the expansive area where the carts are stored and electrically charged overnight. As expected, Ralph is popping pairs of golf bags on the backs of the sleek, spotless four-wheeled vehicles. One thing I'll say for him, he's strong as a bull and proud of it. I used to make a point of telling him so, but then he always tried to prove it by loading all the carts every morning. See what I mean? Kind of reminds me of Boxer who Orwell characterized as, "not of first-rate intelligence, but was universally respected for his steadiness of character and tremendous powers of work." Well, maybe the huge horse with the white stripe down his nose killed himself for Napolean and the other "two-legged" pigs of *Animal Farm*, but I didn't see any point in Ralph doing the same for some of the swine who frequent the Presidential. So, after about a month, I finally got through to his gray matter and convinced him to let a caddy or two assist him with getting the clubs on as well as off the carts. Needless to say, I'm paying those guys a few bucks to help him…but let's keep that just between us. Ralph ain't the kind of guy to accept anything like that and I don't want to see him end up in the glue factory. Oh…one more thing…sorry about the swine remark; when it comes to the guests, most of them are pretty fair sorts, so the porkers are definitely a minority.

Anyway, the early morning tee offs are beginning to trickle out of the dining area and are striding toward their horseless carriages. Marcus is going to have to push them out quickly if he's going to find a hole for Dawson, which reminds me, I'd better grab Bottomly's clubs and find something for the child bride, but I'm not going to put a whole lot of effort into this guy. Dawson, like some entertainers I'd rather not mention, is tight. Your tip is the honor of having had the opportunity to render him some small service, but then, there are plenty of generous spenders from tinsel town with the aforementioned Herbert John Gleason, more commonly referred to as "The Great One," being the king of the hill the two or three times a year he plays the Presidential. I mean the guy really spreads the wealth and it seems as if his lust for life just engulfs everyone around him.

And, like I just said, there are other show biz stars, booked to play the main room at the Diplomat, who have yet to pay us a visit. So maybe they play golf; maybe they don't have some guy in their entourage who's supposed to take care of the help…who doesn't; maybe, just like Gleason, they personally enjoy putting smiles on peoples' faces. You never know, but about Dawson we know! Always claims he doesn't carry cash so you gotta see his 'man' who is about as visible as Casper the Ghost. Whatever, maybe the current mare in his stable will toss around some coin and I'm thinking a bottle of Korbel might massage her newly-exalted position in life. Don't jump to conclusions; I'm not about to invest in a bottle of champagne, but that's another story. We'll get to it, but let's take one thing at a time.

*

I'm standing around with my thumbs in my jeans with Marcus, who is pacing out in front of his cubicle, when the Dawsons finally arrive with a medium-sized, nasty looking guy who I'm pretty sure is Charles Sampson, the coal king. We get a lot of kings around this place. We immediately call a halt to our umpteenth, insignificant conversation as the three of them nonchalantly stroll towards us with Dawson's arm clamped around his wife's tiny waist with a less than casual air of possession.

"Hey, who's the starter around here this year?" Dawson growls. For a singer with such a sweet voice, I'm kind of surprised he's so fluent in deep ugly.

"Still here, Mr. Dawson," Marcus responds pleasantly. "And how are you this fine morning, Mr. Sampson?" The nasty guy's eyes light up just a tad, but the look on his face is that of a man who expects to be known by the hired help. I say nothing because I haven't been introduced…and of course, won't be.

"Charles is going to join us today," says Dawson with a slavered air of importance. "We'll need someone to drive my wife's cart and of course some liquid refreshment."

"Is it my understanding that Mrs. Dawson is not playing today?" Marcus asks with his eyes shifting from Dawson to the diminutive brunette who looks to be in her late teens, complete with two little pigtails. Nice going, Marcus, I think to myself. That sure as hell wasn't my understanding, and I spent fifteen minutes trying to find her some spiffy clubs.

"That's right. She doesn't play," Dawson responds abruptly while giving his new squeeze a tight-lipped stare. Subtle as a crutch, right? Five will get you one the newlyweds are gonna have some fireworks down a marriage road that probably won't have too many miles on it when all's said and done.

"Well, in that case, everything is taken care of, Mr. Dawson," Marcus oozes with his best servant's smile as he nods in my direction. "Our course supervisor will escort Mrs. Dawson, and a bottle of Johnny Walker Black and a Bushmills for you, Mr. Sampson, are on the cart. Your bags are loaded, and, also, we thought Mrs. Dawson might enjoy some iced champagne while accompanying you."

Okay then, I'll forgive the Clock for not telling me Mrs. Dawson wasn't playing now that he's bestowed a title upon my humble self. Course supervisor my ass; get real! I paint on a smiley face which is ignored by the three of them as they head toward the two vehicles loaded by Ralph who is just in front and to the right of one of the carts, a perfect gratuity position. He's dumb but he's not stupid. Sampson is an unknown entity and he might be an okay guy with his money clip although his entire demeanor so far suggests otherwise. Ralph offers up a hearty "good morning" with a big wide grin and is rewarded with a couple of grunts and nothing more. Am I a student of human nature or what? I smelled this guy right off and immediately put him on my "stiff" list. I forgot to mention I might also be called the Pirate because I can be a vengeful sonuvabitch and generally do my best to give the non-tippers a moment of frustration. Now this isn't easy because it's a no-brainer that the last thing the Big House needs is a pissed off high roller. The trick is to kill 'em with kindness and screw 'em with an innocent smile, as in, "Who, me?"

Dawson takes the left side on the first cart probably thinking he's the pilot but I suspect Sampson is thinking of him more as his chauffer. My experience to date is that movers and shakers don't think much of entertainers...but sure as hell like to be seen with them. I head for the second cart upon which Mrs. Dawson has placed her petite one hundred pounds, give or take an ounce or two. They say child bride and she really fits the picture: cute little white tennis shorts designed to be tight enough to prominently display the vertical crack that separates her curvaceous cheeks and a halter top that is designed to show off a pair of tits that would make Jane Mansfield look undernourished. Definitely store-boughts! Her hair is jet black and, as mentioned, she has it in two pigtails while no make up and a natural pout complete the youthful picture. I can't wait to hear what she sounds like.

We head for the tenth which is a dogleg par four. It's too early for anyone to have turned the first nine and the two men obviously want lots of space. We roll up to the side of the tee and Dawson and Sampson begin to limber up a bit with some practice swings of their drivers.

"Mrs. Dawson, would you like a glass of champagne or a mimosa or maybe something else?" I ask tentatively. She looks at me slowly and puts her hand on her hip as if she's debating whether or not to speak. Unfortunately, she decides to do so.

"You know," she begins with a sneer, "I've only been married to him for two months, but it seems as if everywhere I go, some joint assigns me their cocksman in residence. Let's get one thing straight; keep that something else in your pants and for the next few hours, champagne is in and stud service is out. You got that, black beard?"

Now, you may recall I mentioned that when I really want something, I screw the pooch. Well, no problemo here. Her hard delivery and harsh tones have quickly and sadly shot the innocent image all to hell and immediately established her as a complete cluster fuck. This I can handle.

"Brown beard, I've got a brown beard with maybe just some red but no black."

She frowns. "I was mistaken. You sound too fucken dumb to be a country club stud; they're usually pretty sharp."

Terrific, so I'll give her my fucken dumb smile, and maybe something I think she wants. "Well, Ron's smart, and he's the man with the ladies, ya know? He's a bartender up in the lounge but he doesn't come on 'til 7:00 p.m. Billy takes the late shift, and he's a nice guy, but he's an old man. Anyway, you want the champagne, maybe like a late wedding present or something like that?"

She seems to be checking me out and pauses ever so slightly when spotting the scar tissue across my forehead and a nose that's obviously been broken more than once. I'd like to believe she's thinking "ruggedly handsome", maybe like Charlie Bronson. "I hear a lot of you guys around here used to be prize fighters. I'll bet you were a boxer; right, brown beard?"

Brown beard! Alright, I'm making some progress here. I'm debating whether to just say I was a ballplayer or to tell her I coulda been a contenda but on da big night my brudda Charlie told me to take a dive for the easy money, when I realize my stage show is about to get the hook.

"Come on, Lena," Dawson bawls from the tee. "Cut the crap with the hired help. I need some quiet here."

She leans toward me, her pout melting away to reveal the first smile I've seen on her youthful face. "Okay, champ, keep the champagne cool until he gets to the next hole."

I turn to the back of the cart to make sure the Korbel is surrounded by ice, some of which has already melted, producing little trickles of water that are drawing curved lines down the side of the black, smooth rubber ice bucket with a silver *P* scrawled on both sides. We don't use any metal ones on the course; they pick up too much heat. Meanwhile, Lena's master and the king of coal hit less than thunderous drives that duck hook and slice respectively after which they start yelling at each other. Like Ben Hogan used to say about the game of golf, "I play with friends but we don't play friendly games!" Terrific, I'm figuring this is going to take the whole fucken morning and then some.

*

I think a couple of hours have gone by and I'm sitting on the cart parked next to some tall trees which line the fairway on the fourteenth hole, a narrow and well-trapped par four. The king of coal's Bushmills is halfway down, the crooner's Johnny Walker is about two inches from the bottom, and the bitch's Korbel is gone. The two dumbshits don't stand a chance of breaking a hundred and twenty and they're so damned gassed I may be out here forever. At this particular moment, they're both standing red-faced in a fairway bunker and for all appearances I think they're digging fortifications in that cat box and may not get out of there until nightfall. I glance back toward the tee checking for irate foursomes who might want to play through and am surprised to see Marcus on a cart heading our way, and waving frantically. Behind him, a huge guy is tapping his wood impatiently on the grass and, from what little I can tell, it won't be too much longer before the big man will either break his club on the ground, break his toe on the club, throw the club into a nearby water hazard, throw himself into said pond, or all the above. Slammen Sammy Snead used to say, "Good golfing temperament falls between taking it with a grin or shrug and throwing a fit" and I can see from here this guy ain't all grins. Marcus pulls up along side me, stomps on the break, and comes to a screeching halt which ain't all that easy to bring off on grass.

"The little lady's mother is on the phone and she wants to talk with her baby and she means now!" he says with a look of concern mixed with a bit of disgust. "You take her on in and I'll see if I can hustle those two along."

I'm guessing his angst is for the baby and the disgust for the semi-comatose golfers although I don't see any reason for the concern part. On second thought, scratch everything I just said. I suddenly recognize the impatient big guy on the fairway, steaming while waiting to play through, and instantly comprehend the real source of the Clock's concern which is now approaching anxiety run amok. John David Robinson. Cattleman, oilman, Texas man! Every waiter in the joint knows he drinks Jack Black on the rocks because when he wants a drink, he doesn't expect you to go and get it, he expects you to have it with you! Definitely the kind of guy who comes home, with maybe three quail in his game bag, and shoots the fucken five thousand dollar bird dog. The word is he divorced his third wife when she screwed up a Cancun vacation by coming down with the flu.

Obviously, he isn't gonna last much longer out here and, just between us, I abhor violence, especially if the violencer is a guy like John David Robinson and the violencee is a guy like me. On the other hand, I wouldn't mind putting up a sawbuck to see him go three rounds with Charles Sampson. This, of course, the Big House would fail to appreciate, so I depress the drive pedal and follow Marcus who is heading for the sand trap. The two men are still flailing away and the Clock is imploring them to get on with it. The baby is sitting on the lip of the bunker and seems to care less that I'm heading straight at her.

"Mrs. Dawson. You've got a long distance call and I'm supposed to take you back to the Clubhouse."

"Why not," she says with a laugh. "This way I can tell the truth and brag that my loving bridegroom broke a hundred." That's terrific, lady. He's got four more holes to go if Robinson lets him live that long.

As she gets on the cart, she laughs again, a deep, hearty laugh. Her tanned skin is just a bit damp with sweat that produces a glowing sheen while her eyes are glazed from the fifth of champagne. She has a certain aroma about her that begins to send little signals from my brain in a southerly direction, but she continues to comfortably giggle to herself, oblivious to my presence. I turn the cart around slowly and, after going down the side of the tenth fareway, I park at the starter's office. She hops off the cart without so much as a nod and takes the phone from Ralph who has dutifully extended it to her. I leave the cart for Gleason's honeymooner look-a-like to park and head for the bag room to make sure the clubs are getting washed and the bags are being put in their stalls. A caddy the guys nicknamed Johnny Red has a bunch of irons in the oversized sinks and flashes me a more or less toothless smile. The sides of his cheeks and nose are a mass of thin, ruptured capillaries, so it isn't too difficult to figure out how ole Johnny Red came by his moniker.

"Hi, D Jack, right on the clubs, see? Thanks a lot for lettin' me work inside today." I give him a high five as he leans back to his work hoping,

I'm sure, that he can walk again by the end of the week. He claims he pulled a hamstring, but I think he's just old and worn out. Sure, I know the monotony of being at the sinks is the pits, but at least at the end of the day he'll have some bread to expend on the evening's liquid consumables.

A few minutes later I'm checking out the starting sheets in Marcus's cubicle when I glance up, straight into the deep brown eyes of the child bride. They're still glassy and her full lips still hold the giggle. She offers her hand and leans toward me. I accept her proffered and somewhat clammy palm and am surprised to feel a crisp bill as she nuzzles my neck.

"Hey, brown beard," she slurs in a conspiratorial tone. "What did you say the name of that bartender was…and when does he come?" Hell, lady, I don't know when he comes, but he starts pouring drinks around the dinner hour.

"Name is Ron, and comes on shift in the Bengal Lounge around 7:00 p.m."

She gives me a sisterly peck on the nose and I gotta tell ya, she looks good and her scent is even better. "Thanks for everything and the champagne," she slurs as her lifeless shark eyes turn away from me. "Be sure to split that with the boys."

I watch her sweet butt wiggle out of the starter's office. Sonuvabitch! I was right, I read her like a book. All that indignation about clubhouse studs she subjected me to was just bullshit. I check my palm, and the C-note quickly soothes my bruised ego. Well, sonovabitch indeed! Now you know what I mean by 'random' services, but then if you divide the hundred spot on an hourly basis and consider all the crapola I had to take from the three of them, in addition to giving away a bottle of champagne, I actually worked pretty hard for it. Split it with the boys? Sorry lady, I'm not as fucken dumb as ya think. I gotta pay the rent, ya know!

I return my thoughts to the business at hand, specifically tomorrows starting times, and can see it's going to get busy as hell. Two more days until Thanksgiving and the sheets are already jammed up from 7:30 a.m. 'til after 2:00 p.m. Then, of course, like I said, a couple of doctors usually come straggling in after 4:00 p.m. but the November early sunsets have pretty well screwed up their late afternoon games. Right now, it's a little before noon and I figure I better get back to the bag room and find a caddy to start loading balls into baskets for the driving range. Truth is, I let 'em stuff extra pails and pocket the two bucks per as a fringe benefit, which makes it easier for me to talk somebody into doing still yet another monotonous chore. I'm obviously preoccupied with this thought, because I fail to realize there's somebody in front of me until he speaks up.

"Do you have a minute?" The voice is somber and I know it in a fractured heartbeat. I look up and am pierced by the harsh blue eyes of Billy, the late night bartender in the Bengal Lounge. His presence is certainly a surprise, and I suspect whatever he has to say won't be pleasant in that he hasn't said a word to me since I started here last year.

"Sure," I respond trying not to be intimidated by his icy glare, "my place or yours?"

"Any of the benches outside will do," he answers. He turns and heads out of the area, moving quickly toward one of the empty benches off to the side of the tenth tee, and I dutifully fall in line. He turns to face me, so I stand there, and he gets right to the quick of it.

"Sam starts work here today. She's going to double the lunch and early dinner shift. Do I need to repeat what I said to you eight years ago?"

"No," I say returning his glare as best I can. Without so much as a nod, Billy turns and heads for the dining room. I wait until he's through the doors before slumping onto the bench, instantly weighed down by a torrent of bitter memories. There are events in all our lives we revisit on a fairly regular basis, and they frequently involve opposite ends of, let's call it, a terrific…terrible continuum. The terrific stuff brings a smile, a feeling of accomplishment, the fifteen minutes of fame thing, but the terrible generates a fervent wish that it never happened, obviously a wish the most powerful genie can never grant. Sometimes I think 'rue' is the worst fucken word in the English language, but unfortunately, ya gotta live with the life you learn with until death clears the slate or a guardian angel intervenes if you're lucky enough to have one but the way things have been going, I think I'd have a better chance with the genie.

I certainly had no intention of serving up this dish, but Billy hasn't given me much of a choice. So, here it is, and with it, my neat guy image takes a hike down a pot-holed gravel road heading south. To begin, let me tell you about Billy. Bar none, he is head and shoulders above every ex-jock in the place because he is the only one in the world who could do what he did, which sets him apart from even the great Ted Williams. The Splendid Splinter was once asked how he wanted to be remembered, and he replied, "All I want out of life is when I walk down the street folks will say, 'There goes the greatest hitter who ever lived.'" But unlike Williams, Billy was the *only* guy who ever played his game and that game was fire-to-fire high diving. Sure, you've seen Jim MacKay talk about the high divers on the cliffs of Acapulco on *Wide World of Sports*, but if you ever saw a guy climb a ladder 110 feet high, set himself on fire, and do a back layout somersault into a tank of water fifteen feet in diameter and six feet deep, with the water also on fire, then you saw the one and only Diving Sensation which was how he billed himself. He used to kid that most people came to see him miss and he enjoyed disappointing them. He did hit bottom once at West View Park in Pittsburgh, jamming both legs, and he got some body hair burned off when a sudden breeze flared up at Myrtle Beach, but that was about it.

He called it quits in '63 at Palisades Amusement Park in Jersey on the day a drunk leaned on the guy wires and his ladders to the sky accordioned to the ground killing his wife and one of his two daughters. The irony of it was that Billy had started there with his very first fire dive, and it had been his favorite place with its malt vinegar fries, the world's largest salt water pool, fifty or so rides, and over a hundred attractions, including the world famous Cyclone roller-coaster and the Tunnel of Love that had initiated thousands of America's youth into a world of tactile mysteries. The elderly owner himself had called it quits about five years ago when he succumbed to a check for $12 mil which paved the way for the dozers to level this piece of Americana as a sacrifice on the alter of progress in favor of high-rise condominiums.

As with most tragedies, Billy needed to completely focus on something positive in his life, so he poured all his energy into his surviving daughter, Samantha. She had barnstormed with him as a kid and was a pretty good amateur diver, but now he became devoted to giving her the opportunities he had missed. As nothing much more than a kid, Billy had won the AAU one meter national diving championships and back then, the AAU guys were better than the NCAA guys, more often than not, representing the USA in the Olympic Games. Those were also tough times, so Billy passed on the Olympics and turned to fancy and stunt diving to make a living. He claimed he never regretted that decision but given his focus on coaching Sam for the '68 Olympics, which included moving to Florida to have her compete against Coach Tommy Lamar and his world-class divers at Ft. Lauderdale's Pine Crest High School, I figure he was blowing some smoke on that one.

As a junior, she won the Florida State Diving Championship. I was a senior at the same high school and headed for an equal dose of fame and glory so it seemed natural for the two potential world-class athletes to date and become an item. I think back to that time and can vouch for the fact that Shangri la isn't any utopian imaginary place, but then, after I graduated, I went to Jacksonville, made up excuses for being lonely, and fell victim to the groupies and one particular blonde firebird. That's the way I saw it at the time, but now I know better, thanks to the blessing and curse of that BA and MA in philosophy.

Quite simply, the German philosopher Immanuel Kant told us individuals often compromise their own sense of morality. This obviously implies the flexibility for people to exercise freedom of behavior but he rejected the notion that people should establish their own happiness as the end all be all. Kant believed in what he called categorical imperatives that provided the foundation for his philosophical focus on moral behavior, but, unlike Aristotle, Kant ranked moral excellence above intellectual excellence. For him, these categorical imperatives transcended individuals and served as laws of behavior because they addressed universal societal needs as opposed to individual desires.

Okay, end of lecture, but let's get serious. This all sounds like there might be a need for the big shovel behind the elephants in the parade but not so. It's really good stuff when you bring it down to Kant simply saying you ought to *know* what you ought to *do*…so do it!

I did, but I didn't. Desire won the day with moral behavior not even a close second. I conveniently convinced myself I was involved in a temporary distraction that would end when I got called up to the Mets at the beginning of the following season, hand-in-hand with Sam, but she had a different take on the situation. Maybe she read Kant; hell, I don't know. Anyway, she saw me play that summer at the season opener in April. She was supposed to catch another game or two in Jacksonville for the 4th of July series against the Toledo Mudhens but I was eventually informed that she got to the park early and saw Miss Firebird draped all over me in her '67 Mustang convertible out in the parking lot and that was that. I wasn't quite sure why I hadn't been hearing much from her, so I was really looking forward to seeing her in for the season home closer against the Charlotte Knights. After that game, she met me at the gate and just flat hauled off and slugged me and I mean balled fist and the whole nine yards. Her message was direct; I had betrayed her trust which was more than unacceptable; it was unforgivable.

I did try to see her after the season ended when I was still living with my dad on Jefferson Street in Hollywood and she was with Billy four blocks away on Dewey. I asked her to meet me on the corner of Washington and 14th, figuring it might be neutral territory, but it was the grim-faced Billy who was waiting for me. You heard him refer to what he said eight years ago and it had been short but not sweet. He made no threats, but it was clear that it would not be wise to ever talk to or see his daughter again, and he made it equally clear that he was speaking for himself as well as for her. We had had a pretty solid old-guy, young-guy relationship, and I knew I had no choice but to respect his wishes, and I knew I still would. So, I've got news for you, sports fans; Kant knew what the fuck he was talken about!

Feeling just a little lower than dog shit or maybe as disillusioned as a sixteen-year-old Montana winter wheat farmer coming out of a backwater whorehouse, I head back to the bag room where a pleasant enough looking fellow meets my somewhat functional right eye with a kind of 'I got something on my mind' look on his face. "I'm looking for the guy they call D Jack. I'm told he works down here sometimes."

"He's me," I answer with a half smile that can hardly be seen through the Zapata moustache that just barely overlaps the full beard. "Can I be of some assistance to you, sir?"

"Well, actually, you can't, but a colleague of mine told me you know Pete."

"Right, Pete's a good friend. I see him regularly."

"That's great," the man says in a pleasing tone, "because he's the guy I need." He reaches into the left inside pocket of his blue blazer and out comes a smooth-surfaced, black leather wallet. He casually peels off five 50's and hands them to me. Nothing smug or pretentious, just what appears to be shaping up as a simple business transaction seeing as Pete's involved. Actually, you've met Pete; you just don't know it yet.

"Tell him I need a tee off time tomorrow anywhere around 8:00 a.m. on the Presidential. I'm playing with some bankers and mixing business with pleasure so getting an early morning start will be a big help." He starts to put his wallet back in his sportcoat, thinks for a second, and pulls out another fifty-spot.

"Here's something for your service, okay D Jack?"

"Sure, Mr., ah…"

"Stanchfield."

"Oh, the Chevy guy on all the billboards, right?" I inquire with a grin.

"One and the same. It's good to know the billboards are working. I've got them all over Dade, Monroe, and Broward Counties and I'm selling more cars than all the dealerships in Florida put together."

I think I'm hearing more of a sense of accomplishment than brag. "No fooling. I'll bet Chevy's are pretty easy to move."

"Tell you what, kid. It's just a matter of doing your homework. When I looked around years ago, Chevy had the market and still does. Hell, this year production in the US was about eight and a half million cars. About five million were GM and almost half of them were Chevies."

"How about foreign stuff?" I ask.

"Germany and Japan pretty much match our production, what with turning out Mercedes and Hondas, but the import dollars were only around twelve million or so."

"It sounds to me as if the bankers ought to be pretty happy with those kinds of figures."

"Kid, bankers are never happy. Right now we're into safety factors. There are about five million drivers, give or take, and 40,000 got killed last year." He seems to ponder that for the moment and then smiles. "So, are you in the market for a nice Impala?"

"Four wheels are two too many for me, thanks."

"So you're a biker. Well, keep the rubber on the road, kid," he says as he turns to go. "Oh," he adds, "tell Pete to confirm for me. I'm in Room 1240."

"Gotcha ya covered, Mr. Stanchfield. I'll make sure Pete gets down what you need," I say as I head for the sinks to check Red's progress. Then, I turn and add, "Tell you what, if you need anything else during your stay, you can find me in the Bengal Lounge every night but Monday, when the House brings in a terrific Roberta Flack wannabe. You can generally catch me from 9:00 'til after midnight."

"Drinking man?" he asks with a wink.

"I play backup guitar."

Stanchfield gives it an easy smile. He pays, appreciates, and gives me a knowing nod as he heads for the door and all but knocks a dining room waitress head over heels. I know she's a waitress because I see a blur of black and purple uniform heading for the floor. Stanchfield recovers quickly enough to get his hand under her elbow and upper arm, thereby sparing her from an embarrassing and potentially painful bounce on her ass.

"Sorry, miss," he says apologetically. "Wasn't watching where I was going." Her back is to me, but her composure seems unruffled. The incident is really insignificant, and she plays it that way. Then she turns, and I go into an immediate panic mode trying desperately to come up with something, anything, knowing an electro-encephalograph would show a flat line thereby confirming zero brain activity.

Even from the ten or so feet away, it's as if I was standing three inches from her strawberry-blond hair...which isn't short or long, not too close or too billowy...just kind of cotton candy-like. Her eyes are of the lightest green with streaks of a slightly darker shade 'flashing' outward from her pupils. Her nose is not too straight but has no flaw, her unpainted lips are full and picture-perfect, and her light skin tone with a spray of tiny freckles completes her Scots-Irish appearance.

From the neck down, I'll leave you to your own fantasies because the uniform, as such, allows for a shapely calf and nape of neck, and that's it. The dress is similar to that of a fraulein you might see bussing tables in a beer garden so, all the waitresses look busty. I'd go on, but she's looking at me and appears to be waiting for me to say something; however, I've been so preoccupied with this mental picture, I haven't generated the one line I need. And don't try to help me with a throwaway come on. For the first time, I'm looking at a woman who I knew as a girl, and that woman is Samantha.

"Hi," I say, like a petrified kid going into a drugstore looking for something he isn't supposed to buy: a regular fucken genius, right?

"Hello yourself, Devon," she says with more than just a hint of ice. She looks at me carefully for a few seconds and then adds, "You look different."

"That's what a full beard and a 97-m.p.h. fastball will do for ya."

Without so much as a nod of understanding, she takes out a pencil and pad and looks at it, not me. "I'm supposed to get lunch orders from the guys down here, so what's it going to be?"

"I, ah, I'll have a Reuben, side of fries, a tossed salad with Thousand Island and a splash of Italian, and a slice of Boston cream pie."

"Do you always eat that much for lunch?"

"It's the only meal the house pays for, and I'm not of a mind to buy dinner when they're paying thirty cents an hour," I respond trying not to sound too apologetic. For the record, that's a full two bucks under minimum wage!

"Fine," she says clinically, and without even a glance from her expressionless eyes, she turns for the cart room. "I'm told lunch will be down in about half an hour," she says, giving me her back as quickly as possible.

"Thanks," I mumble to the swinging doors. I knew as soon as Billy said she would be working the shifts it would go down hard, but I have to tell you, I don't have the words to reflect what I'm feeling right now. When it all ended, I was able to focus on being young and healthy, and, my God, I was D Jack and I was going to the Show. But then the hospital in New York threw me into a deep pit that, in retrospect, doesn't even approach what just happened because I've just been reminded this chasm is bottomless. Murphy's Law was optimistic because all things being equal, you lose. If all things are in your favor, you still lose. And, finally, win or lose, you fucken lose. So, what would you do? Me? I go back to figuring out who's gonna put golf balls in baskets.

Marcus walks into the bag room and, judging from the look on his face, it appears as if everything must be running okay. He's gnawing on a plastic swizzle stick that, for you Batman buffs, is extended upwards in the Penguin position. This immediately communicates there are no backups on the first or tenth tees and that he's undoubtedly pleased with the way he has solved the golden throat, coal king problem.

"Lots of bags starting to come back in?" he inquires while his teeth continue to work on the smooth purple stick.

"Everything's under control. Started about half an hour ago and they're beginning to pile up." I point over my right shoulder with my thumb and add, "Johnny Red's holding down the sinks because he's not up to lugging bags today. When things slow down, I'll shoot him out to the driving range to pick up balls."

"That's fine with me. Bye the bye, what happened with Lena Dawson? Is she going to skedaddle back to Mama's skirts already?" Marcus inquires with a chuckle.

Okay, Marcus. It's eat-your-heart-out time. "She asked me when Ron comes on, and I'm pretty sure she wasn't talking about when he gets to work."

The swizzle loses some of its angle as his lower jaw drops a little and his cheek muscles relax their grip on the stick. "You're putting me on! That sweet little thing in pigtails is putting the arm on our swordsman in residence?"

"Now, now, Marcus," I say, as my palms and what's left of my eyebrows head for the ceiling. "Let's not jump to hasty and unwarranted conclusions. Let us not be led to believe that an inquiry from this sweet young lass regarding Ron's presence implies a desire on her part to consummate a physical lust. There are psychological and long-range social ramifications to be considered here."

Marcus removes the swizzle stick from his mouth and gives me his second eye trick of the day. "Don't give me your philosophy crap, D Jack. You can't honestly look me in the eye and tell me that nineteen-year-old child is just going to walk up to Ron and tell him she heard he's the stunt cock around here and she wants to get to know him better? Come on. You don't really buy that," he concludes whining just a bit.

Needless to say, Marcus grew up at a different time and doesn't realize that there are a lot of nineteen-year-old girls who now hunt just like the nineteen-year-old boys who have been on the prowl since time began. "You're right, Marcus. I concede the point. Agreed, although I can't look you in the eye, that isn't what she's going to say. She's going to flat out tell him she wants to fuck, and I've got a C-note says he nails her by noon tomorrow."

"You're on, and you stink!" Marcus says emphatically.

"I stink; therefore I am. I can live with it if Descartes can."

"Dammit it, D Jack, do you know how many plumbers got employed last year?"

"No," I respond curiously, "how many?"

"Twenty-four thousand, that's how many."

"So what's the point, Marcus?"

"Do you know how many philosophers got employed last year?"

"Let me guess." Whoa Nellie…he's hot!

"You don't have to, because the answer is none and that robust number includes your sorry self," he growls as he turns to go.

"Okay, so again, what's your point?"

"You're about twenty-eight or so, right, D Jack?" he looks me in the eye again, but the edge has come off his voice.

"Yeah in a few months…why?"

"And other than having suffered the most publicized sports injury in recent times, what do you have to show for your twenty eight years?"

"I did graduate from ASU you know," I respond with just a tad of annoyance.

"Sure you did and you're putting all that fine college education into hustling high rollers and playing back up guitar in a bar."

"It's a lounge, thank you, and I write storysongs, too."

"Dammit it, man, when are you going to start to do something with your life?"

"I don't know," I respond softly.

"Well, when you get a plan, come back and talk to me, okay?" he says with about a pound of irritation in his voice.

Hell, I don't want him mad at me all day. I've got to get him off this Lena Dawson thing, which is why I figure he's launched into his 'wasted life' speech. Maybe he's heard something about Sam on the grapevine. "Hey, Marcus, you got a minute? I want to ask you something on the serious side."

"Serious? Impossible," he says, "but I'll give it a try…I'll humor you."

"You know anything about the new girl who started today?"

"Not much," he says, "except she isn't new. She's Billy's kid and she started the season in the Diplomat sports bar, but we had an afternoon and evening open so, she took 'em both. You have to figure she needs the cash."

"Is she involved with anyone?"

"I don't know but I did hear she was pretty much unapproachable at the hotel." The redness is starting to leave his face, and the swizzle goes back into his mouth regaining its Penguin position. "Quiet broad," he adds reflectively. "Doesn't seem to smile a lot; definitely not your type, D Jack. Way too serious; way too tough. And don't ever tell Billy I called her a broad." I guess Marcus has been oblivious to the fact that me and Billy don't talk at all, so I let that go by the boards.

"Thanks for the vote of no confidence regarding jobs and women."

"No offense, D Jack," he says with a smile as he once again turns to head out the door. "I'm just providing you with an honest opinion and, like Howard Cosell, telling it like it is."

Honest my ass, you ole sorrowful bastard. Of course, I don't say that because Marcus was a one-woman man from the old school and his one woman died in childbirth twenty-two years ago. He thinks his late-in-life daughter is an innocent senior at the University of Miami, and that's precisely the reason I'm going to win a hundred bucks by noon tomorrow. I really hate to take the money from poor old Marcus but then there's no such thing as a sure bet, so maybe I'm not really taking advantage of his puritanical self. Regardless, I still feel a little uneasy about the whole thing, so I figure I'll buy his virginal Miami hurricane a present or something when I probably win. Check that. Virginal Miami hurricane has to be an oxymoron. Ah, the pangs of the mind, I think, as I return to the balls and the baskets with a distinct lack of enthusiasm.

III

THE CLOAKROOM

the takers and the givers
in a game that always must
come out all but even cause
their ain't no winners in the dust.

Damn! The afternoon went on for fucken forever. It had barely taken a minute of conversation for me to come down with a potentially terminal case of the Samantha blues. Like I shared with you earlier today, we all revisit the terrific stuff that gets sharper with time, but the terrible stuff eventually gets fuzzy. Maybe it's a defense mechanism that kicks in so you can find a way to stop spitten' at the mirror…or maybe it's something like going through a mourning process. You lose somebody and the thought of that person brings tears and sadness, but somewhere along the line, without even processing anything, that someone conjures up a warm memory or a smile. I figure when it comes to death, sooner or later, you make your peace with it and kind of accept the concept of never. Now, you think about that. Never is really a tough word. It's eternal and forever. It ain't tomorrow, next week, or next year. It just ain't! Some things, of course, are easier than others. Sure, I'll never hit another dinger, which eight years ago was catastrophic, but it ain't all that devastating today…maybe. Regardless, it wasn't anything like the way I felt when I lost my dad knowing I'd never see him again; well, at least not in this world. I lost my mom, too, but I wasn't much more than a baby and was way too young to understand what was happening.

Anyway, what I'm trying to say is that some things slide into the past more easily than others, but to be up front with you, it took more time than I'd like to admit to put Sam into a past I could live with, and it has yet to produce a warm memory or even a fleeting smile. Then, in a heartbeat, it's bingo time and I'm being slammed into the real world by a living and breathing Sam so back to the philosophy books for this one. Come on, don't give me that look; these deep thinkers had things to say. Okay then, a compromise; cut me some slack, and I'll just take up a minute or so of your time.

One philosophical school of thought says ideas or concepts are more real than physical objects. Now, that doesn't seem to make much sense, because you can touch, smell, hear, and taste physical stuff. And, unlike me, you can clearly see 'em too. Socrates and Plato were selling this theory, and please don't ask me where Socrates ends and Plato starts. Regardless, I've got to be honest with ya! Over the years, I obviously couldn't physically experience Sam, so she had become something frozen in my mind, and my idea or image of her was that of a teenage girl with those huge dreams of life and love found only at the top of a spiral stone stairwell in fairy tale castles. To really confide in you, I think it was the only way I could handle my thoughts of her. I had to compress my remembrances into that relatively brief period of our youthful euphoria, so that image of her became fixed. For those two old Greeks, permanence was the biggie and that's why they believed ideas were more real than objects which are finite and must sooner or later come to an end.

Now, Aristotle did a U-turn on that kind of thinking. He believed the physical, material world was much more real than an idea or concept because we experience objects by collecting them, grouping them, and drawing conclusions from them. Almost two thousand years after Aristotle analyzed most of the world's known objects which were sent to him by his protégé, Alexander the Great, John Locke put forth his *tabula rasa* which said the mind, at birth, is a clean slate, and all the things we actually observe or participate in get written on it, so experiencing physical things is the real deal.

Okay, end of today's second foray into deep thinking, and I figure you know where I'm going with this. Four hours and thirty minutes ago, give or take a few ticks, Sam the woman, not the teenage girl etched in my memory from eight years ago, was suddenly standing three feet from me. She's was a living and breathing object, and the "idea" of Sam the girl ceased to exist, so out with Socrates and Plato, and in with Aristotle and Locke who were right on the fucken money, 'cause my senses went into overdrive, and, by God, she's physically real and, much to my dismay, impersonal at best and flat out hostile at worst.

I already told you what I saw, and my sense of smell tells me she still uses the same Estee Lauder Youth Dew that lightly dusted the top of her cleavage, which was more than ample even when she was seventeen. I heard her voice that now is more throaty and sultry even with the icy tones.

The taste of her mouth and the security of her embrace are still in the past and will undoubtedly remain there. Yeah, guys, I'm thinking physical things are the real deal, and I just couldn't help hoping I would see her again at lunch, even though I figured it would be an exercise in futility.

But it was Chico, the diminutive light-skinned Cuban bantamweight, who came through the door balancing a huge metal tray on his shoulder. Marcus more or less eats to live, but Ralph can really do big time damage at the chow table. With the house footing the bill, I'm not about to be bashful about eating their groceries as you already know. So, I'm not sure which amazes me more, the fact that Chico can get the food for the three of us on the one tray or the fact that the hundred and eighteen-pounder can hoist the load to his shoulder and lug it all the way from the kitchen to the bag room. Just think what the *Miami Herald* could do with the story if he fell down the stairs.

"Pie Floors Fighter!" they would announce in Times New Roman bold, thirty-six point type. "Ricardo 'Chico' Martinez, a contending bantamweight of yesteryear, met a tragic end during the lunch hour rush earlier today at the Presidential Golf Course and Country Club when he was pinned to the floor by a huge tray of sandwiches, side orders, and rich desserts. His last words could not be discerned due to a large piece of Boston cream pie that had somehow managed to wedge itself between his face and the floor. However, a witness close to the scene believes the victim may have gasped, "At least it could have been a nice piece of flan." Local authorities are considering indicting the individuals who ordered the inordinate amount of food on charges of involuntary manslaughter."

I almost wish he would have tripped without, needless to say, a resulting obituary. I hardly tasted lunch and by 3:00 in the afternoon was ready to pay five bucks for a shot of Pepto Bismol to settle my anxious tummy. I even headed up to the Bengal to yak with Ron in the hope of spotting Sam, but such was not my luck. In the meantime, I had mentioned my bet with Marcus to the stud bartender. After a brief discussion, he agreed to give me what he calls his gallery shot for a fee of fifty bucks which I quickly pointed out was 50% of the wager. He countered by telling me he would not hit me up for additional fees.

"What fees?" I wanted to know.

"Film, chemicals, and condoms if she's fussy," he said.

"Ain't you generous," I remarked. "Can't I get something cheaper than a gallery shot?" I inquired.

"Nope, that's the only one for a deal like this. You see," he said, "when I'm flat on my back and the broad takes a ride with her back to me facing the wall where the camera is hidden behind the mirror, I get all the toys at work in the same shot and those are the things you gotta show for proof, right, D Jack?" he concluded rather clinically.

"Yep, and now that I think of it, you also get proof positive as to whether the collars match the cuffs."

"That's true, D Jack, so more than her hair dresser knows, right? You think that up?"

"Naw, James Bond said that to Tiffany Case."

"Tiffany who?"

"Jill St. John. Sean Connery said that to Jill in *Diamonds Are Forever* which came out about five years ago."

"And did her collars match her cuffs?"

"No empirical data, Stunt. You'd have to ask Bond."

"Fine with me, college man, but personally I could care less what matches and doesn't with Lena Dawson. I get a fifty spot regardless," he concluded with an air of finality.

I could only nod in agreement as I turned to exit the Bengal Lounge. Terrific, Ron gets laid and half of my winnings to boot, but I can't deny he knows what he's doing. His hobbies are screwing and photography in that order, and he's very proud of the way his diversions complement each other. He says he's got pictures of just about every woman he's banged, and I can tell ya there have been plenty of 'em. I mean you'd flat be amazed how many women come to this place and would rather fuck the help than sit around and wait for some deep pockets to get off the course. And make no mistake about it, the word gets around that Ron's the man, and in his defense if he needs one, I've never known him to use a picture on anyone. I'll tell you this though, between his stuff and J. Edgar Hoover's files, someone could do one hell of a lot of damage.

Thinking on the upside, financially it's been a pretty decent day but I haven't been able to really shake a hangdog feeling. Right now it's a little before 7:00 p.m., and I'm sitting in the cloakroom. If you went to grade school in the '50's or more currently in an old school building, you know all about cloakrooms. For the rest of you, the old cloak consists of a wall that extends all the way across the back of the classroom with open passages at either end. The space behind the wall is just wide enough for kids to walk through, has a long narrow bench to sit on, and hooks for hanging raincoats and the like. Naturally, why else would it be called a cloakroom, right? Well, if our old friend Cosell were doing the announcing, he would tell it like it is, meaning it's really more of a 'get-your-assed-kicked' room. Many was the time I had been banished to the cloakroom in the old classic, two-story brick schoolhouse to await a 3:00 o'clock bell and my fate in the form of a paddle, complete with a dozen or so air holes that allowed for a more rapid delivery. I think today if you touch some kid, you might end up doing time for physically abusing a minor.

So now that you know all about cloakrooms, let me tell you this one is a little bit different. Directly behind the counter in the pro shop is one small door which serves as the single entrance to the Presidential cloakroom. Unlike the public school prototype, this one has no hooks and no low bench but instead is spartanly decorated with six stools in front of a long tabletop suspended from the wall by a thick linked chain at either end. The only objects on the entire length of the table are six 'starting times' sheets, six pencils, and six standard white telephones. Also, unlike the original cloakroom of my boyhood, in this place I am the ass kicker rather than the ass kickee. Some explanation is in order, so sit back and relax.

The activity that takes place in this secret spot with its key-lime, pale yellowish walls involves the recording of starting or tee off times for the three courses for the following day. It's really a very simple operation, in principle. The guests of the Complex are informed that if they want to play golf tomorrow, they have to get a starting time reservation tonight, so they phone into the Diplomat complex operators, beginning at 7:00 p.m. sharp, and ask for starting times. The operators proceed to connect them with one of the six telephones, all of which start jangling simultaneously. It goes something like this:

Pete: Good evening, starting times.

Sim : Hi, Pete. This is Mr. Sim in Suite 200.

Pete: Hello, Mr. Sim, where would you like to play tomorrow…and when?

Sim: How about the Presidential around 9:00 a.m.?

Pete: How many in your party, Mr. Sim?

Sim: Four.

Pete: And your clubs?

Sim: Mine are at the Diplomat and the others will use rentals.

Pete: That's fine, Mr. Sim. You tee off at the Presidential at 9:17 a.m with a party of four, and we'll have your clubs sent over from the Diplomat. Be sure to have your playing partners see D Jack in the bag room, and he'll fix them up with some good clubs. Is there anything else I can do for you this evening?

Sim: That's got it, Pete and, ah, I'll take good care of you. Thanks a lot

Pete: You're very welcome, Mr. Sim. Have a pleasant evening and a fine game tomorrow.

Sim: You bet, Pete.

Pete: Goodnight, Mr. Sim.

Like I said, it's all very simple in principle. The six of us all go by the same name, Pete, so no one will know our identities. The management frowns on payoffs, but I think you already know how we get around that problem. Anyway, each of us has a sheet for each of the three courses. The starting times are staggered by nine-minute intervals; that's two more than most places, but like I keep telling you, this place is class. Duplication is avoided because on the Presidential sheet in front of me I have a 9:17 a.m., but the next time on my Presidential sheet isn't until 10:11 a.m. The five starting times in between are on the other guys' sheets. As you could see, the whole process with a guest takes about thirty seconds and, with the six of us working the phones, you can figure out the sheets fill up very quickly. Just to compound the situation, keep in mind that most of the guests who want to play tomorrow pick up their house phones at 7:00 sharp. They've been told to hold because the lines are busy, and most of 'em want to tee off before 9:30 a.m. Finally, in addition to the speed at which we fill up the sheets, a few names get penciled in a minute or so before the phones start to ring.

You remember Mr. Stanchfield, don't you? The Stanchfields of the world are informed one way or another that arrangements can be made with Pete, and that, in my case, Pete can be reached through D Jack. Needless to say, the other five Pete's are also playing the same game. After all, a little capitalism never hurts; it's the competitive American way! Well, if you recall, I told you earlier today that you had met Pete. So, how do you do, again! It's one minute before zero hour, Stanchfield's investment of three hundred dollars for a prime starting time is deep in the front left, square-cut pocket of my jeans, and the generous Easterner's party is on the sheet as promised.

Suddenly, on the dot as the big hand hits the '12', the six phones begin to jammer, and we're off and running. Things seem to be going quickly tonight which suggests some of the other guys have had the good fortune of making arrangements similar to the one I made with Stanchfield. The bomb descends, and the shit hits the phones as well as the fan, about seven minutes after the hour when I pick up for the eighth time.

"Good evening, starting times."

"Is this Pete?"

"Yes sir."

"How is it I get you every night and you never sound the same?"

"I've got a cold," I responding, rasping a little.

"Hey, that's tough. Well listen up, Pete old buddy. This is Jonathon Warfield, and I've got some very important clients coming in tomorrow, and I've got to get off at a good time, know what I mean?"

"Yes sir, Mr. Warfield." What I really know is that Warfield has been in for about three weeks, demands a lot, and spreads no green, so there ain't gonna be any favors for this guy.

"Well, how about something around 9:15 a.m.?" he asks rhetorically.

I look at my sheet and glance at the five Petes who are all grinning and giving me the ole thumbs down, having heard Warfield's name. I've still got a 9:26 a.m. here at the Presidential, but I'm saving that one for what I call my emergency special, and this schmuck just doesn't meet the qualifications.

"Hack him!" says one of the Petes.

Inside stuff, last year, the wise-cracking comedian Buddy Hackett, was playing the main room at the Diplomat, and he heard about the fun and games that take place in the cloakroom, so he sat in one night. I swear to God, the guy actually talks like that for real…ya know, that squeaky nasal stuff the way he sounds on TV and the movies. Well, he was just driving some of the guests of the hotel fucken nuts when they couldn't get their way, so now when we get some volcano head, we just say 'hack him.'

"I'm sorry to have kept you waiting, Mr. Warfield. I've checked all the sheets and the best I can do is a 12:40 p.m. over at the Executive," I say holding my breath.

"What!!!" he yells scoring just under the 8.0 magnitude recorded on the Richter scale around Anchorage during the great Alaska quake of '64. "I pick up the God-damned fucken phone at 7:00, some bitch tells me to wait, and now just a few minutes later you tell me I can't get off until after lunch," What kind of bullshit is this?"

"I'm very sorry, sir," I say calmly. "The phones have been ringing constantly since the top of the hour, and the sheets filled up very quickly tonight."

"That's it, you mutha fucken, cock sucken, son of a bitch!" His rage is literally flowing through the phone, he's starting to breath heavily, and I hope the guy doesn't suffer cardiac arrest or something like that. Check that; I don't really give a rat's ass about this guy's heart, assuming he has one.

"Look," he continues in his chairman of the board tone of voice. "I'm laying out a shit load of dough on this place, and I'm not about to have some pissant like you give me a run around. And my wife is ticked and she's standing right here, and she's good friends with Mr. Charles Berston. You get my drift, amigo?"

Terrific, he's playing the 'drop the name' card. We call Mr. Charles Berston…Charley the Boss… and, you've got it, he runs the whole complex. This is what I've been waiting for, because now I can squeeze his balls with a plumber's wrench.

"I can see how being privy to your concerns would certainly upset Mrs. Warfield," I answer somewhat sympathetically.

"That's it, you prick! I'm going to have your ass!!!" He's gasping now and obviously exasperated. I guess this clown never read a guy named Hutchinson who wrote in the late 1800s that if profanity had an influence on the flight of the golf ball, the game would be played far better than it is. I know; we're not talking about actually playing golf here, but I think you get the point; time to finish him off.

"That will be fine, sir. I report to Mr. Harlan Bottomly, our head pro who of course works very closely with Mr. Berston, our VP for Operations, and I'm sure he'll be more than glad to hear from you. Mr. Bottomly will be out of town for the next few days but he welcomes all complaints from the guests. You can reach him through the hotel operator, but I'll be more than glad to give you his private number."

To say he hangs up simply doesn't do the situation justice. His bellow and the resounding smack of plastic on plastic has my ear ringing, and he's probably shattered one of Western Electric's most contemporary pieces of communications paraphernalia. It happens around here on occasion. Some power broker can't get his way or get you to grovel, so he's at a total loss. I just can't wait for the phone to ring again, and I don't have to. It does.

"Good evening, starting times."

"Hi, Pete, this is Marvin Eubanks calling for a starting time."

"Right, Mr. Eubanks. It's a little late so the best I can do is a 12:40 p.m. at the Executive." Needless to say, I didn't have to pen Warfield into that slot.

"That's not too good, Pete. Are you sure that is the best you have on any of the courses?"

"Sorry, Mr. Eubanks, it's the earliest time available."

"Well, what the hell. So maybe I'll sleep in and the course will be less crowded. I'll take it."

Now this is more like it. I assume Eubanks is on holiday and has the brain power to make the most of it by enjoying himself. I like this guy! "Right, Mr. Eubanks. Who'll be playing with you tomorrow?"

"Just a twosome, Pete, and we'll need to rent some clubs."

"Can do and your confirmed to go. And, hey," I add in a friend-to-friend tone, "when you get your rentals, ask for a guy named John. I'll give him a ring and make sure you get some solid bags."

"That's very nice of you, Pete. I'll ask for him, and I appreciate it."

"Sure thing, Mr. Eubanks," I say pleasantly. "I hope you and the lady have a nice game. Good night." Big duh there, maybe he ain't playing with a lady, but then, what the hey; if not, maybe I flattered his ego.

Things start to slow down, but I get one more call from a guy named Irving who needs to get off early but doesn't get nasty about his 12:58 p.m. tee off time at the Presidential. He's so nice about it that I tell him if I get a cancellation I'll give him a ring. He thanks me, and that's that. By 7:30 p.m. the other five Petes clear out, and I take the single shift. One of us always sticks around until 8:00 just in case of a late call. By 7:55 nothing is happening, so I decide to go with the 9:26 a.m. emergency special I've been saving. After going through the switchboard and getting Irving's number, I punch in the four-digits, and it only rings twice.

"Hello," says a lady with a throaty voice that would be perfect for a receptionist in a classy bordello…I think; I've never called a bordello. I'm not even sure they have phones.

"Mr. Irving, please. Starting times calling."

"Hold on," she says and calls for Irving to come to the phone.

"This Pete?" he inquires hopefully.

"Right, Mr. Irving," I respond with enthusiasm. "We got lucky tonight. I just had a cancellation on the Presidential at 9:26 a.m. I believe you had a 12:58," I add, reminding him how bad things were less than half an hour ago.

"Hey, that's great, Pete." The guy really lights up like we're long lost friends. "Now you won't have to ship my clubs because they are already there."

"That sounds good, Mr. Irving. "You're good to go."

"Hey Pete," he adds with a personal air. "I really appreciate you calling me back. I'd uh, like to give you a little something for your trouble."

"No trouble at all, Mr. Irving," I respond appreciatively. "I'm more than glad to do anything I can and if there's any other way we can make your stay with us more comfortable, just get ahold of D Jack at the Presidential, okay?"

"At the Presidential?"

"Right."

"I'll do that, Pete, and, thanks again. Have a good one."

"You, too, Mr. Irving."

It's 8:00 p.m., and the phones are officially down for the night. Except for the guy who gave his wife a lesson in the ineffective use of vulgar language, everything has gone okay, give or take. Well, not everything; I mean, how much colorful stuff can you handle in twelve hours? So, you can strike the fucken idea of an okay day unless you're on the same page with Billy and his daughter and I guess if you are, I can't blame ya. Off and on I've been thinking about Sam and wishing I could have made some positive impression but there was something in her eyes that told me to not even give it a try. Anyway, I've got less than an hour to wolf down a sandwich and a very large VO, and get my ass into the Bengal Lounge to backup the Moon man. The long day ain't over yet.

IV

CHARLIE MOON AND THE BENGAL LOUNGE

It was foggy out the day, I saw the brilliant ray
of life and love traced lightly on her face
I wanted so to say, the things I felt that day
but somehow something kept me in my place.

Charlie T Moon plays the *Game of the Smiling Fool* out of D minor and he's doing it right now. As usual, I only did the lyrics for this one. Moon likes to hear people's tales, true or otherwise, and then he has this uncanny ability to marry my words with his music. As for this one, I knew a guy at Arizona State who had a chance with a young beauty and he really wanted to make a move. To make it short, he never did, but when they graduated, she told him she wished he had approached her because she was too intimidated to approach him. Ah, and they say only the Bard on Avon's characters experienced true tragedy.

I'd see her now and then, in class or in the gym
or sitting on a bench outside her dorm
the night lights and the breeze
the sighs within the trees
my evening thoughts of her would keep me warm.

T mixes it up with E, F, G minor and an A sharp. It's a bit haunting and somewhat sad which fits right with most of our portrait songs, but then the lounge is usually quiet, and according to the management, the patrons are here for atmosphere rather than entertainment. So, no need for jokes and just a minimum amount of small talk.

The campus life dragged on, hitting the books till dawn
yet hoping for a sunrise when I'd see,
my heart and mind at rest, her soft hair on my chest
our thoughts and hopes joined for eternity.

He's singing it soft and easy, but then Charlie Moon sings everything soft and easy which is a one-eighty from Ike and Tina Turner's rough and hard. I'm backing him with mostly chords and a few short riffs, and barely concentrating. I daydream a lot when I play and I look at the patrons in the room. I watch and I wonder and even fantasize a little. They rarely look my way because I simply melt into the hardwoods and cushions, whereas Moon catches an occasional smile or a light in someone's eye as the music conjures up maybe a warm memory.

She's gone to seek her fate, beyond the college gate
my chance for love had walked around the bend,
her heart could have been mine
a solid path for all time
but the day to start my life came to an end.

Two good-looking patrons in a corner off to my left are looking at Moon in a kind of a dreamy way, and I spy a large college ring on the guy's right hand. Who knows, maybe he had the courage whereas the ASU Sun Devil didn't.

And I wonder why I didn't say
hello to that pretty girl, that day
so I guess that I will always play
the game of the smiling fool.

Moon accepts some soft applause, acknowledges me with a half smile, and lets the room know we're done for the night. I slide off the stool and put the Yamaha in the imitation alligator case. T and the brothers, who back us on bass and drums, head out of the room to cop a final smoke, but the guy with the ring has caught my eye so I amble over to his table.

"How are you doing tonight?" I inquire pleasantly.

"Having a great time," he responds eagerly. "You're D Jack, aren't you? Can we buy you a drink?"

"I am, and sure thing. That's real nice of you," I add as I slide onto one of the two chairs across from the loveseat where he and his lady are sitting, leg-to-leg.

"We're from Columbus, Ohio. I publish *Black and Beautiful*, and we have box seats at Red Bird Stadium. We saw you hit back-to-back homers once and it sure seems as if you always lit up our pitchers when you came to town."

I smile to myself as I think back to all the good times I had in that neato brick and California Redwood ballpark. "Yeah, if I recall the left line was around 355 feet, so I usually tried to go for the right field fence which was a good 25 feet closer. And, when you say I lit up your pitchers, that didn't happen too often if Dock Ellis or Gene Garber were on the mound," I say with a smile as Sal, the raven-haired lounge beauty, appears from nowhere. I love this place. The waitresses are prettier than the rich bitches coming from their daily makeovers. The word is that Sal did a spread in an issue of *Penthouse*, but unfortunately I haven't seen it and know as much about her as I do the guy sitting across from me.

"My name's J. Thomas Washington. Have you ever seen a copy of my magazine?"

He's black. "I can't say that I have, Mr. Washington. Do you compete with *Ebony* or something like that?"

"No, D Jack, I'd like to think I compete with *Playboy*, but with their circulation of five plus million, that's wishful thinking on my part. What I'm trying to do is carve out a new market. *Playgirl* does about 900,000 so I'm trying to give the public the best of both worlds."

"Guys as well as girls?" I say with a smile.

"Why not," he answers with a grin, "but still mostly girls. Have you ever seen a Black centerfold up close and personal?" he asks, glancing across his shoulder at the youthful woman sitting next to him. I nod in the negative although I'm obviously looking at one now and, other than a glazed look, she's stunning with a kind of Caribbean look, maybe Jamaican. Her hair is jet black and shoulder length, her skin the color of Nestle's Quick, and her braless tits are literally resting on the table. Her mocha rosebuds appear to be straining to push through a sheer satin blouse, and her cantaloupe-sized melons have to be pushing forty-four DD. Sal, who appears to be equally voluptuous, minus maybe a cup size, is getting impatient and throws Washington a half smile. "What will it be?" the guy asks me.

"He'll have a VO and water," Sal answers with a smile. "Would you and Mrs. Washington like another round?"

"Sure would," he answers.

"Thank you, sir," Sal says politely as she heads back to the bar to place the orders.

"Do you write as well as play music?" Washington inquires. "I don't think I've heard most of that stuff."

"We do some of our own music, but the Moon man likes to play lots of covers. I think he was doing quite a bit of Chapin earlier."

"Oh, I do love Harry. We saw him on Broadway last year doing 'The Night that Made America Famous,'" says the somewhat spaced and significantly younger Mrs. Washington. I just nod with a kind of grunt. Sal shows up, and the talk gets small. I already know the wealth comes from his magazine empire, and they are enjoying one of their many brief but frequent holidays. I quickly throw down the VO, smile, do the handshake thing, and try to excuse myself.

"I was wondering if you could do me a small favor, D Jack," the guy says almost to my back. "My eighteen-year-old is at the hotel, and I was hoping maybe I could bring him out here around lunchtime, say Thursday, and get you to autograph a ball. He just graduated from high school and was an all-state catcher, and some big league scouts have been looking at him," Washington says with obvious pride. "What do you say?"

"Sure thing, Mr. Washington, around noon I'll be out at one of the redwood benches next to the driving range."

"Can you throw with him for a few minutes? I'll make sure he brings some gloves and a brand new Spaulding ball," he adds pushing it a bit. "It would really be a big thrill for him."

"I'll be glad to, and thanks for the drink," I add with a smile as I turn to go. Every once in awhile I get to chat with someone who's real, maybe a guy like Mr. Eubanks, but tonight doesn't seem to be my night, at least that's the way I feel about it.

I make my way back to the bar smiling the entire distance, not that any one is really looking. Bowls of mixed nuts are scattered along the length of the gleaming hardwood bar, and I select a few pecans, pronounced PEEcans down south. Supper had been a rather lack luster affair. The appetizer was a VO, the entrée a cold half of left-over Reuben. The side was some wilted green leaf lettuce and another VO served as a combo drink and dessert. Ron wanders down my way which is a surprise because Billy usually comes on around 10:00 p.m. for the last shift.

"Hey, D Jack, your backups sounded a little thick in the old throat tonight."

"Swollen tonsils," I say with a fake rasping sound. He puts a highball glass directly in front of me on the polished bar and drops in three small cubes of ice. He then tilts the brown VO bottle and pours until the ice disappears beneath the amber-colored liquor. He tops it off with some water poured directly from a Perrier bottle. No fizz machines in this place! Everything is poured from glass, even things like Pepsi and ginger ale.

"How are we looking tomorrow?" I inquire feeling strangely indifferent. A broad smile dominates his ruggedly handsome face as he flicks a fingernail against my glass, making a soft, pinging sound.

"You can drink to it, Pirate," he says, his smile surprisingly devoid of lechery. "Dawson tees off at 9:00 a.m. with Sampson, and the little lady should be knocking on my door about the same time dumb shit and the coal king will be digging their way out of the tenth fairway bunker. I should have the photo to you by 11:00 or so," he continues. "You want something special other than the gallery shot?"

I sort of sneer at him but I think I'm really directing that look on an inward path. It just seems like a shitty thing to do to ole Marcus the Clock.

"Now that you mention it, stunt, just keep it simple, and can you make it sort of artsy or something? This deal is going to blow the Clock's mind, so I don't want to gross him out more than I have to."

"Sure, if that's the way you want it, just as long as I have the photo of me and Lena Dawson back and the dollars in hand by Thursday, right?

"You'll have 'em both, Ron."

He nods in the affirmative and then checks the patrons and sees the last few looking our way while Sal patiently waits for him at the opposite end of the bar with some cash in her hand. I lean back and take a slow sip of my VO and take a long, casual look around the room. It's getting late, the clock chimes, the music's done, and the lounge is emptying out. The guy with the ring and his Harry-loving lady are gone and two guys in the corner are getting to their feet while one couple is still exchanging intimacies. Check me on that, as they like to say on Monday night football when Frank Gifford, Howard Cosell or Alex Karras blows one. I look at the couple again and the guy has a bandage halfway around his neck with swollen veins running the length of the naked side of his throat. He appears to be on the verge of losing control while tears are flowing from the bloodshot eyes of the attractive young woman sitting across from him. They've been in since around 10:00 p.m., and I suspect they've run up a healthy tab and the alcohol is dialing up the emotions. This bothers me 'cause the Bengal Lounge just isn't the right place to be unhappy. These unpleasant thoughts are interrupted by Ron, who is back after making change for Sal, and is slipping me a folded piece of paper.

"Can't see what she looks like," he says, "but some broad slid into the booth in Station 15, and Sal just handed me this note."

"Thanks, Ron," I say as I drain what might not be my last drink of the evening. Station 15 includes a love seat and two chairs tucked into a cozy corner with little to no lighting. If you were in a plane above five thousand feet, you could join the mile high club with enough privacy to try out, at the very least, the Yawning and Variant Clasping positions of the Kama Sutra. Curious? Just look for the banned book section in your local library. Anyway, the note says, "I'll buy you one drink" and isn't signed. Interesting…how come just one? Let's you and me go find out.

I'm really feeling kind of tired so it's with a lack of electricity that I head for the corner prepared to do my hired help act for the last time. "Hi, how are you doing tonight?" I inquire while trying to inject a modicum of enthusiasm into my strained voice.

"I'm okay," she says without turning, and for me, it's the second bingo time today because Samatha's voice is etched forever on the blank slate Locke says I was born with. I walk past her, moving toward one of the chairs across from the loveseat as she turns to face me.

"Sit down, and I'll buy you that drink. That will give us more than enough time to cover the last eight years," she says in an expressionless tone.

I face her, pause, and bite my lower lip. "I can't do that."

"Yes, you can. Daddy knows I'm here. It's okay."

"Why?" I'm still standing and for whatever reasons, I feel very apprehensive. You've got to remember the last time I saw her, other than this morning, she belted me, and I don't ever want to get hit that hard again, whether it be fists or words.

"You still don't say very much, do you? I'm curious, aren't you?" she responds.

"No," but I sit down anyway on the chair across the table from her and figure I better say something because my response was pretty blunt. "You didn't go to the Olympics, did you?"

"No, I didn't, and it's another reason Daddy hates your guts." Sal ambles over before I can inquire as to that opening shot, but obviously it isn't sounding too fucken good. Sal smiles at Sam and then turns and looks at me.

"We're closing down, D Jack, but I can get you and the lady a round. After that, if you want, you can take care of yourself, okay?"

"I can do that, Sal. A double for me and, ah, you still drink Bacardi and Pepsi?"

"Yes," Sam responds looking up at Sal. "A large glass but light on the ice, okay?"

"No worries," Sal responds with a warm smile and then turns her full attention to Sam. "Say, didn't I see you working up in the dining room early this evening?"

"Yes. I just started today. Billy's my dad."

"No shit," Sal says wide-eyed. "Oops. Sorry. I didn't know Billy had a kid. He's really a neat ole man. Oops, sorry again," Sal adds sheepishly.

"No need," Sam says with a smile. "You're right. He is a neat ole man."

Sal grins with relief and heads for the bar where Ron is about to fill the last orders of the night. We look at each other across the table. I have no idea what's coming down, but I'm not about to start a conversation because, like Sam just said, that's never been exactly my strong suit. And to tell you the truth, I'm kind of apprehensive in that anything I say is probably not going to be received with a tremendous amount of warmth or understanding. Okay, you're right. Where is it written that I should be on the receiving end of warmth and understanding?

"I hit the diving board about the same time the papers said you were heading to Mexico to play winter ball," she begins, without emotion.

"You'd hit the board before."

"Not doing a forward tuck somersault."

"How the hell did you manage that?" I say somewhat incredulously.

"Daddy says I lost my concentration."

"That happens once-in-awhile."

"He said it was happening all the time, thanks to you."

"Was it?"

"Probably, but I was hurt pretty badly. I took the flip straight up, and when I came down, my back depressed the board, and when I slid off, the board whiplashed upward and slammed me in the back of the head. I ended up in the water bleeding and screaming like a harpooned whale, but Daddy just stood there and made me swim to the side of the pool. I had a concussion, stitches, and it was a month before I got on a board again."

"And?"

"I walked out to the end of the board, looked down, turned and came back. I haven't been on a board since." Her look tells me her mind just left the room, so I say nothing.

"I know I was afraid," she continues reflectively, "but I also know that, for whatever reasons, when the fire went out for you, it took the diving with it. I tried to convince Daddy it was fear, but he never bought it. Whether you meant to or not, you broke some hearts, Dev, but then I doubt you know much about having your heart broken," she adds, with bitterness creeping into her voice.

"I think I do," I say somewhat defensively.

"No, you don't. You only think you do, but taking a baseball in the face doesn't break a heart. People break hearts." She's dialing it up. "So who do you think broke your heart, Miss Firebird or some other bimbo?"

"I think you're wrong; losing a dream can do it," I answer, avoiding her eyes.

"Don't give me that self-serving bullshit!" she says, her voice climbing half an octave and her green eyes afire. She suddenly looks around and takes a deep breath. She always used to do this if we got a little loud in public and were on the verge of embarrassing ourselves. She seems to be thinking about something and then returns her gaze to me.

"Free choice, Dev. People make choices and decisions and as such bear the consequences. But I had no choice. I was on the receiving end of your decisions. But I learned. I swore I would never put myself in a position again where I was not in control and be at the mercy of some son of a bitch like you," she concludes in a lowered, venomous tone.

The words are hurting more than the fists, because I know it's true. The one thing I do remember is that Sam had this knack for mixing sharp thinking with common sense. Hell, I doubt she even realizes she's throwing existentialist freedom of choice right in my face. Now, why in God's name did I think of Sartre and his band of French thinkers at a time like this? Check it again. What God?

Sal returns with the drinks, places them in front of us, and is gone with a goodnight smile. Sam immediately sips her Bacardi while I take a slug of the double VO.

"I guess you've said what you came to say," I proclaim as I get to my feet and finish what's left in the tumbler. "Thanks for the drink and the trip down memory lane. Tell Billy ya done good," I conclude turning to go.

"Before you leave, will you bring me some cashews and stay for just a few more minutes?"

Whoa Nellie! Keith Jackson wasn't invited back to the Monday Night Football party after the first season, so why am I being asked to do an encore after being on the receiving end of her name calling? I'm not too sure I'm up to much more of this, but I do as requested and go behind the bar to grab the fifth of VO that is displayed along with dozens of other bottles in front of a huge glass mirror. I pour the Canadian whiskey into the tumbler to about half way but then decide I'm going to need more before I face her again, so I splash in another ounce, some Perrier, and drop in a few cubes. The cashews are in the same fancy black bowls as the pecans; no peanuts in this joint, so I take a bowl and head back to the increasingly stressful Station 15. I settle myself back into the chair and immediately put lip to glass rim and notice Sam has not reached for any cashews.

"Dev," she begins suprisingly softly, while looking at her left hand which, I suddenly realize, is adorned with a thin, gold, wedding band. "What happened to you?"

I don't know why, but that wedding band hits me like a slammed door and I suddenly feel there is nothing I want to say. "Not much. My father wanted me to be a big league ballplayer, but it didn't happen."

"Like you would say to me, you had your moments," she says, still not looking across the table. "You even had more than the standard fifteen minutes of fame in Shea Stadium," she adds somewhat sarcastically.

"I didn't stay at the Show. He worked all his life to be able to say to the guys at the hotel that his son was playing in the Majors."

Finally Sam is looking at me; she's probably thinking of my father because she liked him. "He must have been pretty upset with the way things ended," she says with a tad of sympathy.

"He never knew it," I respond. "Unlike what you're telling me about you and Billy, he didn't have to suffer a broken heart. About the same time you were swimming to the side of the pool with a bloody head, he died," I say in an emotionless tone. Don't get me wrong. I still love and miss my Dad to this day; it's just that this damn conversation is sending frost up and down my spine.

"What happened?" she asks with obvious sadness.

"It was probably just another day. Knowing him, he got up around 6:00 a.m., shaved, and put on his one light-blue suit, buttoned the white shirt he ironed the night before, and produced a perfect full Windsor with his dark blue tie. He probably had a glass of orange juice, a piece of dry toast, and a cup of black coffee. I'm sure he kissed the picture of my Mom, thanked God for another day, and walked the seven blocks to Hollywood Boulevard to catch the beach bus. Then he hopped the southbound and thirty minutes later was pressing pants at the Monte Carlo hotel on North Beach."

"And?"

"Then he went home and died. I was lacing up my spikes and playing for the Campeche Pirates in the Mexican Southeast League when the manager told me I had a phone call. It was from the Hollywood police. My father had never missed a day of work in his life, and after two days, the hotel called the cops. They found him in bed with a piece of writing paper and a pencil. That letter was addressed to me, but other than my name, there was nothing on it." Now I'm the one whose thoughts have left the Bengal Lounge, but just for an agonizing flash into the past. God, I wish he was still here so I'd have someone to be with and talk to.

"I was told I could take a few days off, but I decided to suit up," I continue. This one's for you, Dad; makes for good movies. Luckily everything into left was routine, but I struck out looking four times."

"I'm sorry he's gone, Dev."

"I'm not," I say returning my complete focus to our conversation and, judging by the shocked expression on her face, taking her by surprise with the bluntness of my response. "His guardian angel was with him. He never had to pick me up at the airport when the Mets sent me home or hear about you."

"You mean you never told him what you did to…"

"Right," I interrupt. "I never told him about us. You were second on his list of dreams."

"And then?" she says, still looking at me.

"I sold the house and went away. And now I'm back. You asked what happened to me; like I said, not much."

Sam gets to her feet. She's wearing a pleated lavender skirt, a white mock turtleneck sweater to keep out the November chill, and is looking foxier than ex-*Playboy* centerfold Stella Stevens who was the neat broad in the Poseidon Adventure.

"I'm going to get myself another drink. You want one?"

"No, thanks, the bike isn't gonna drive itself away from this place." She doesn't respond and heads for the bar. I pull out my tin of Kodiak smokeless wintergreen and wedge a healthy load of the nicotine rich tobacco between my right cheek and gum. As you already know, I chew, but a big cheek of leaf just ain't appropriate in certain settings. Sam returns and eases back onto the loveseat while I check my glass which is empty again; I don't even remember draining it. She takes a sip of the Bacardi and then eyes me thoughtfully.

"You're right, Dev," she begins. "You haven't changed much. Apparently, you still ride bikes, slug VO, and load up with Bart the bear smokeless rough cut."

"The joy of creature comforts," I say with a shrug. "I saw his little brother Bret in the Baltimore Zoo one time. He's not as famous as his big brother." She could care less.

"Well, I have changed, and I want you to know it!" she says with what appears to be sparks in her emerald eyes, but like I said, it's kind of dark so the sparks thing is probably just my imagination.

"So that's why we're here, a little small talk about me and to set the record straight about you. Fine, go for it."

"I went for it eight years ago, Dev, more or less after I got rid of you." Her opening salvo is somewhat bewildering so I just nod. She takes another sip of her drink, a bigger one this time, and seems just a bit nervous, but then I'm probably reading something into nothing.

"To start with, the captain of the cheerleaders married the quarterback of the football team."

Okay, that cat's out of the bag. "You married Dolph Frederickson?"

"Well, not in high school."

Dolph Frederickson…neat guy. He was a junior when he got to number one on the quarterback depth chart. Our coach was old school and one of the last guys to run the full "T" backfield. The fullback was a big, hard-running Italian sonuvabitch who got most of the handoffs. So, at left halfback, I didn't get my hands on the ball more than half a dozen times per game, sometimes more, probably because I was a senior and I really think Dolph wanted me to get some extra carries. In my last season I actually scored five times when he called the old twenty-four trap. In that play, I was the two back running through the four-hole over our right tackle. Our left guard would pull across the line to his right and nail or trap the defensive player to spring me loose. Dolph would actually grin at me when he shoved the pigskin in my gut as I headed for a hole you could drive a Peterbilt through. I've gotta tell ya, I really liked him.

"He earned a full ride to the University of Florida, and I followed him," she continued. "I completed my Associate of Arts Degree, but we decided to get married so I dropped out of school and did the books for the *Gainesville Daily Sun*."

"Career girl, huh?"

"No Dev, mother. The bookkeeping was part time, and the twins were full time."

Whoa. This is all coming pretty fast after eight years of an image frozen in time. "Boys or girls?" I ask with some interest.

"I have two girls, Jesse and Rebecca. We named them after Dolph's parents who were both killed in a private plane crash while I was pregnant."

"My God," I say, feeling genuine for the first time in the past few minutes. "It's sad that they never got to see their grandchildren."

"Not as sad as Dolph," she says with some bitterness. "He was always competing with you and your God-damned ghost which cast a shadow over everything. I told him time and time again that you were dead and long gone for me. Maybe he could have handled things better if he hadn't ridden the bench during his four years. But," she continues with obvious pride, "he was a Colonel of the Air Force ROTC and went straight to flight school after he graduated, then, to Viet Nam. He'd only been there three weeks when the Huey transport helicopter he was piloting took a direct hit," she says softly but still looking directly at me. "So, I took the girls home to Daddy, and we've been at Dewey Street ever since."

There's really nothing I can say. In the space of just a few minutes, Sam has gone from girl to woman, to wife, to mother, to widow. That's just too much to digest. Her gaze seems to be growing cold again.

"I don't suppose you served your country, did you, D Jack?"

Damn, no Dev or Devon; that's a bad sign. "The recruiting officer at Arizona State told me to go back to the dorms."

"Why?"

"I've got screws holding together my right shoulder after surgery on all four points of my rotator cuff and and I also suffered a ruptured appendix."

"That shouldn't have been enough to keep you out," she says skeptically and sarcastically if that's possible.

Okay guys, I hadn't intended to be this specific with you, but she's backed me into a corner. "I'm just about totally blind in my left eye, and the right one is kind of marginal. That hit in the face, as you call it, did more than splinter bones and end a dream."

Sorry again, I wasn't completely candid about the extent of the damage, so that's why I wear sunglasses all the waking hours of the day. The right tinted lens is prescription to help my impaired vision, but the left one is simply a piece of glass painted black. Anyway, that piece of information seems to stop her dead in her tracks, and frankly, I've had enough. For the second time, I get to my feet.

"I don't mean to be impolite," I say, a bit on the apologetic side, which I really am, "but it's been a long day, and I think we're up to date if that's what you wanted."

She's not looking at me, so I turn and head for the door before she can offer any kind of response. So far today, Lena Dawson has called me stupid, Marcus told me I stink, Jonathon Warfield has called me a mutha-fucken, cock-sucken prick, Samatha has called me a sonuvabitch, and Charley "the Boss" Berston hasn't even taken his shot. Tomorrow's got to be a better day. Fuck it! Check that for wishful thinking. It's already tomorrow!

Tomorrow!

Tomorrow D Jack's gonna catch some shit; the Pirate's gonna catch some shit; and Pete's gonna catch a whole lot o' shit. The season is nothing much more than one fucken endless shitty tomorrow.

And tonight?

Tonight, what's left of it, I'll be *driving along, billboards on the fly, heading for home, and another day gone by.*

V

FERDIE, WILLIE, AND THE BOYS

Of course there's a difference
I will go far,
cause when all's said and done
I'm better than he are.

"**W**here you been all morning, D Jack?" Marcus inquires.

"Out on the course," I reply with a sigh and slump of shoulders. "These convention guys'll kill ya. How long's this group staying anyway?"

"They'll be pulling out tomorrow and should be eating their Thanksgiving dinners soon, so the worst is definitely over."

Right now, it's about 11:30 a.m., and all the bags for the afternoon lunch bunch are lined against the beige, textured walls of the cart room. The rounds of golf will probably be hard and fast because, as Marcus noted, most of the guests will be eating and celebrating later in the day.

"There's another crowd coming in Sunday," Marcus continues, "but I doubt they'll play much and will probably just hit us up first thing Monday morning."

I hoist myself up onto the bag room counter and place my hands on my knees as I continue to do my slump act. A three-second exhale punctuates my chagrin. "These guys are really something. I spent ten minutes in the woods looking for a ball, and another guy, some vice-president or someone like that, had me in the pond next to the seventh green. I've probably popped three cases of Michelob and used up half a dozen bottles of Jack Black! Is anybody getting any action from these very important ball breakers?"

"Not a cent, D Jack, typical convention crowd. Maybe we'll do better when the smaller second shift shows up. I think they start arriving around 2:00," Marcus says, and then pauses and kind of looks down at his brown and whites. "I guess you haven't heard about Ferdie, huh?"

"No. Did something happen to Ferd?"

"Hans Schmedler ran him over this morning," Marcus says with a hiss and a sneer.

I wrinkle up my face and stare at Marcus with an air of complete disbelief. "What do you mean, Schmedler ran Ferdie over? What the hell kind of remark is that?"

"It means what it says, D Jack!" Marcus shouts. "You know how it is with Schmedler. Every morning his cart has to be ready at 9:15 sharp, bags loaded, and ready to go. You know the way he marches to his cart with his back straight up like he's got a rod from his ass to the base of his skull, mounts the thing like it's an armored half-track, and then burns rubber. Hell," Marcus continues quietly as he runs his hand back across his temple through his sparse brown hair, "Ferdie was down from the cart loading a second bag on his shoulder when he lost his balance and stumbled onto the cart path just as Schmedler took off. I swear the bastard went straight at him, like going for an armadillo in the middle of the highway, and just flat ran over his left leg."

"You're shitten' me!"

"Cold blooded, D Jack. I swear he intentionally aimed right for him."

"And?"

"Ralph took him to the emergency room at Memorial Hospital in Hollywood, and they fixed him up. Fracture of his left ankle." Marcus is still looking at his brown and whites and appears to be very reflective. "I just can't understand why somebody would do something like that, and he didn't even turn around or bother to stop or anything," he concludes with a sigh.

I wait to catch Marcus' eye, but he continues to look at his shoe tops and it's obvious he's really upset. He'd gone out on a limb to get Ferdie into the caddie's pen at the Presidential. Lots of caddies are hard cases, and the management is pretty tough on who hoists the bags around this place. He was known as Ferdinand the Bull and was a light heavyweight contender a few years before Willie Pastrano showed the world what the sweet science of boxing was all about. Actually, the nickname was a misnomer, because Ferdie, like Willie the Wisp, was a classical boxer who rarely put a guy down. As the story goes, he supposedly got drunk in a small Mexican border town and tried his hand at bullfighting, and somehow Ferdinand the Bullfighter became Ferdinand the Bull. He was ranked No. 2 after beating Paddy Young and the even more popular Joey Maxim, and was on the verge of getting a title shot in '62 against Harold Johnson, the 34-year-old warrior out of Philly. The way to Johnson was through the Argentine heavyweight champion, Gregorio Peralta, but the man from the Pampas beat the holy hell out of Ferd and sent him into instant retirement. That paved the way for Pastrano to take the title from Johnson in Las Vegas in '63, but in that same year, Peralta decisioned Willie in a non-title fight which led to the Argentinian getting his shot at Willie's crown in '64 when the "Wisp" took him out in the 6th round in front of his adoring neighborhood fans in New Orleans. Ironically, Willie and Ferdie shared the same fate. In '65, Jose Torres put Willie down in the 6th at Madison Square Garden for the first time in his fourteen- year career and beat him up so badly that the Wisp couldn't answer the bell for the 10th. So with the light heavyweight belt and the title gone, he called it a day. Like Willy used to say, anyone who makes a living in the ring has to be crazy!

As for Ferdie's future, the ring doctors had no idea how much damage he had sustained from the fists of the wild man from the Pampas but knew he had suffered brain injuries which had resulted in permanent disabilities that would only get worse with time. It was really tragic because Ferdie had been a popular and articulate fighter. Then, in a heartbeat, he was out of the ring and couldn't even talk right. Unlike Willie, no banquet circuit for ole Ferd, and it took less than two years for him to degenerate into a seasoned barfly ex-pug. Somewhere along the line, Marcus engaged in a successful reclamation project, got the Bull clean and relatively sober, and Ferdie has been hoisting the bags ever since.

"Where is he now?" I ask with concern.

"Ralph took him downtown to that roach nest he calls home," Marcus says, his voice as flat as his eyes.

"Will he be able to walk again, with the bags and all?"

"Ralph told me the doctors said it looked like a clean break and that he'd probably be okay with some rehab. Other than a questionable liver, they seemed to think he was in pretty good shape."

"And how about his hospital bills?"

"Hell, Pirate," Marcus moans. "Ferdie's got zip, hand-to-mouth like most of the caddies. The bill, so far, is one sixty, and I have no idea what he's living on, rent, food, stuff. To say nothing about what the damn rehab will cost. Hell, I don't know."

I put my hand on the old man's shoulder and give him a smile but his eyes are still on the floor. "We can handle it, Marcus. All the guys can chip in some, and we'll float him for awhile." I know the kind of guy Marcus is: he feels; he hurts. I doubt if he'll ever get over the tragic loss of his wife. I think because of that he transfers so readily to the problems of others. Suddenly, a terrific idea leaps into my brain. Stunt had given me the topside photo of Lena Dawson Wednesday, but I'd really been struggling with the idea of collecting the C-note from Marcus. Now I figure I might as well kill two birds with one stone, meaning I let Marcus off the hook and get some cash flow in the direction of our injured caddy.

"Oh, by the way," I say offhandedly as I dig into the front pocket of my jeans, "Stunt didn't do so good with Lena Dawson last night so here's the hundred I owe you."

Marcus is still deep into this thing with Ferdie, but he seems to lighten up a little. "Good," he says as a smile of satisfaction spreads across his face, "and you still stink," he adds with some phony hostility. "This will take care of most of the hospital bill," he announces as he folds the C-note while I return his smile, the bait taken.

"Tell you what, Marcus, how about a Ferdie fund? Let's get the guys to agree that what little we make off this convention bunch goes to Ferd. I figure the take over the next few days won't be a whole lot but should be enough to get him through this. Whadda ya say?" I ask with rampant enthusiasm.

Marcus seems to mull it over for a few seconds before responding. "Well, I'll buy into it, and I'm pretty sure Ralph and Stunt will go along. But like you said, the tips are pretty slim pickings. What do you think about the Turk?"

"He's a good fella; he'll buy in, maybe even get some track money into the kitty. Just relax, Marcus. It's gonna come out okay." He seems to be lightening up a little probably because we have a plan and he sees some brightness at the proverbial end of the tunnel.

"But," I say, trying to sound ominous which really doesn't take much acting at this point, "there is definitely something else that needs to be done to make this right. I think we have to even the score with Schmedler so I assume you won't object to me arranging a little something special for the sonuvabitch."

Ah, finally the old man smiles. "Okay, D Jack, you can put on your pirate face and do him a little something…but don't let it get out of hand and be really careful. This guy comes down for two or three months and is good for a couple of thousand."

"For the House, maybe," I say sarcastically, "but as far as we're concerned, this guy is as tight as a flea's asshole."

"Not a very scholarly remark, college man, but you're right. He's tough on us, and so is his wife, for that matter. I heard she threw a glass at one of the girls yesterday, a regular lady, huh?"

I fleetingly wonder if Sam was on the receiving end and really hope she wasn't. "I guess so, but one thing that won't take any guesswork is that her old man's going to experience a very significant moment of frustration in the immediate future which, hopefully, will communicate to him that he's not superior to everyone else on the planet," I answer with a nasty air of finality.

Marcus heads for the door of the bag room but turns and gives me what I call his fatherly look. "Just be careful, D Jack. And remember, this guy is big money. Oh yeah," he adds, "and I almost forgot why I came in here. Speaking of money, Charley is giving us a bit of a Thanksgiving bonus this afternoon up in the Bengal. He's going to let us swap off with a skeleton crew and fete us with hors d 'oeuvres and free drinks from 5:00 to 6:00. And I heard Willie's in from New Orleans, so he'll probably be around. I've never seen that guy pass up anything around here."

Now isn't that a coincidence? We were just talking about Pastrano. Well, not really. The Turk had mentioned the Wisp might be around today, and that's why I gave you some background a few minutes ago. "Why should he pass up a freebie, Marcus? He earned it, and you should know better than anyone else that he was the best greeter this place has ever seen. Sure wish Ferdie could be around to swap stories with the champ; might be good therapy. Do you think he'd be up to it if Ralph could lug his busted body up here?"

"I'll find Ralph and see about it. But don't forget," Marcus says over his shoulder as he heads out, "that bastard is big money, and the House is going to scream if you do something that can be traced back to us."

"Forewarned, Marcus," I say to his back.

Money…money?

Nope. It isn't money that's going to hurt this guy. He's got too much of that, so it's going to have to be something else, something that will really make him rip. A glimmer of an idea pops into my devious mind and I'm thinking maybe interrupting his fucken sacred time schedule might be the key. I've got to put some energy into this, but first things first; I need to get the Ferdie fund up and running. That should be a no-brainer, because the second wave of convention creeps will be descending upon us in a few hours and they might provide some entrepreneurial opportunities. I know you'll wish me luck on this one; after all, it's for Ferdie, and trust me, he's really a prince of guy even if you can't understand a fucken word he says.

I grab a couple of bucks from the Arturo Fuente cigar box, in its usual spot under the counter. After snagging a few bottles of club soda from the lounge, I head for one of the redwood benches on the driving range. I've intentionally been in the bag room as little as possible the past few mornings figuring Sam would be taking lunch orders, and I just didn't want to be around. Anyway, my appetite seems to have gone south. Late at night, after work, I've been sitting on the beach hoping the whispers of the waves and the warm breeze blowing off the Gulf Stream, which is less than a quarter of a mile off shore, might calm me down, but so far, no luck. I keep replaying Tuesday night's conversation, hoping maybe I missed something that was a little bit positive, but it's become an exercise in futility. It's pretty obvious that Sam loathes me, and Billy all but gives off a morally offensive odor, so I guess the two of them have had plenty of time to seal those emotions in cement. I know, this shouldn't come as any huge awakening, but like it or not, I'm human. Just like everybody else, I'm entitled to dream a little, even when there's no sane reason for doing it. But, being square with you, I'm just not a conflict kind of guy, and I just kind of wish these wounds hadn't been reopened. Maybe I ought to call in sick one day and just go swimming.

There's something unbelievably tranquil for me about the ocean which is all of fifty yards east of my place; a three-story stucco that was built around 1947 on the corner of Surfside and Buchanan. Even this time of year, the Atlantic is relatively warm, and there seems to be a limited amount of seaweed and not too many dreaded jelly fish, or worse yet, the Portuguese Man-o-War with its poisonous tentacles. The green water is relatively shallow for the first twenty or thirty yards, but then you literally cross a line into the blue water of the Gulfstream which then drops off quickly to a depth of about twenty feet. The first reef is about four hundred or so yards out from the shoreline. Although the march of progress is doing its best to kill the living rock, tropical fish still call it home and you can find an occasional red snapper or clawless Florida lobster. But all this has to go on the backburner, because my immediate concern is Ferdie. Truth is no one around here will take a day off until the season more or less ends around the 15th of April.

All the benches are empty, so I can eat the bagel I pocketed off the breakfast buffet in some privacy. Thanksgiving, like most holidays at the Presidential, is a day of quality rather than quantity, meaning fewer guests, but they generally up the ante on the tips. Ask any waitress around and she'll tell you that Mother's Day, New Years, and most of the holidays are big paydays, probably because the patrons feel lucky not to be on the job at those special times, a kind of 'I'm glad I'm not you' thing. Even though the money is good, there's clearly a down side, because working the holidays is psychologically tough, particularly one when families get together and have a feast. The problem is, if you're working, you're on your own, and even if you're not working, if you don't have family, you're still alone. I always hate to see some old guy in a restaurant having Thanksgiving dinner by himself; maybe I'm not old, but I'm starting to feel like I'm well on my way to becoming one of those guys.

A few guests are working on their short game, hitting approach shots with their wedges and a well dressed, forty-something woman is off to my left on the putting green. I'm just about through noshing on lunch when I notice a big hunker of a kid heading my way, and, whoa Nellie, Mrs. J. Thomas Washington is matching him stride for stride. I had forgotten I agreed to throw with the kid today. And right on time, here he comes complete with a black Wilson catcher's mitt with a bright orange border around the pocket, a fielder's glove, and a ball. I get to my feet primarily to greet the *Black and Beautiful* centerfold.

"Hi, D Jack," she says as she extends her slim-fingered hand with a radiant smile. This is the first time I have seen her on her feet, and she's got to be five ten easy. She's giving the world the same tit show she did Monday night; I'm not sure how she got into the tight, black leather skirt that barely covers the sacred terrain where her long legs converge and pave the way to her navel studded torso. Damn if it doesn't look like a diamond wedged in there. Holy cow, I've never seen anything like that!

"Hi, Mrs. Washington," I respond as I quickly shift my eyes from the jewelry to the kid, communicating to him that I know he's there. "You must be the all-state catcher," I say with a grin as I extend my hand.

"Yes, sir, name's Gregg. It's really cool to meet you. I hope my Dad didn't push too hard," he adds sheepishly.

"No such thing, Gregg. I love to throw some every chance I get," I answer as I reach for the fielder's glove. "Let's head on down to the side of the range away from those two guys hitting balls, and you go pace off sixty-one feet. Then, you can call some signals, and I'll show you what I got," I say with a laugh. "You want some H.B. Scott leaf tobacco or would you rather load up with some Kodiak smokeless?" I ask kiddingly.

"I chew bubble gum, D Jack," Gregg says pointing to the lump in his right cheek.

Terrific! I think the kid's in trouble already. Seeing as he doesn't chew the real deal, there's a chance he's one of these clean-cut kids. God forbid he doesn't smoke, drink, say fuck it everyday, or chase broads either … because if that's the case, he doesn't have a fucken chance of playing pro ball.

"New breed of ball players, Mrs. Washington," I say with a shrug.

"Boys will still be boys, so have fun," Mrs. J. Thomas responds with a twinkle in her eye as she deposits her rounded cheeks on the redwood bench and demurely crosses her legs. Well, maybe just a little too slowly on the crossed legs part to qualify as demure, because there was just enough time for her to intentionally flash her beaver, so now it's really going to be a challenge to throw this kid some strikes.

Gregg has already dropped the ball on the side of the driving range and has jogged about 60 or so feet down the line. I lean over and pick up the cowhide, noting he's already in a squat position with his cap serving as home plate. He grins and gives me the ole Number 1, the fastball.

"Come on, Gregg," I protest with a grin. "I've got to warm the wing a bit, so how about starting with some off-speed stuff."

"Okay by me," he says as he gives me the sign and then taps the inside of his left thigh. Some kid, he's demanding control too. If we had a right-handed batter up there, he'd be asking for an off speed pitch on the inside corner. Not too shabby. I give it a half windup and let it go, maybe around seventy, I'm guessing. The ball produces a respectable 'pop', and the location is on the mark. The kids grins, nods, and sends it back: hard, fast, and flat. Over the next ten minutes, I shake him off at least a dozen times, staying with the off speed, before I agree to the lone forefinger. This time, I go for a full windup and send it down the pipe, and the 'pop' is more like a 'crack', so I figure it has to be more than ninety. Gregg stands up, takes off the mitt, and looks at his hand.

"That one really had some zing, D Jack. I've never seen a heater come at me that hard." He gets back into his squat and gives me the ole Number 2 and pats his inner right thigh, a curve, low and away. I give him what he wants and he struggles with it just a tad. I guess he was anticipating a big sweep and drop but my curve just kind of jinks and jives; today's guys would probably call it a slider. After about another ten minutes, I wave him in, and he jogs up to me with a big grin.

"That was something," he says with obvious pleasure. "How come you ended up in left field?"

"It's more fun to play every day, Gregg. Pitchers are sitting on the plank and watching four out of five games."

"Yeah, that's why I like catching. I mean, you were playing every day, but in left you were standing around a lot, but when you catch, you're in on the action with every pitch."

"Good point kid, but you don't exactly just stand around. You've got to keep your mind in the game, where's it going, who's on the bags, what's the play, right?"

"Sure, D Jack thanks for going easy on me. I'm kind of curious…how do you grip your fastball?"

"I like to extend my forefinger and middle finger right across both stitches, because feeling those rough edges in two places just seemed to give me a better release. I think today they're calling it the four-seam fastball."

"Well, I'll bet you can still really come with the total heat," he says with a big toothy grin. "Even the few you threw, I was getting the feeling you're probably holding back a little."

"Not so, kid," I say as I roll up the right shoulder sleeve of my ASU t-shirt and expose a scar that runs from the top of my shoulder down to my bicep. "Rotator cuff and some ruptures, Gregg. Don't go there if you can help it."

"You bet, D Jack," he says seriously as we head back to the redwood bench where Mrs. J. Thomas has been basking in the sunshine. She hands Gregg a pen which he extends to me along with the ball. "You don't mind, do you?" he asks.

"My pleasure," I say as I sit on the redwood bench and scribble, 'Swing at the strikes…and good luck, D Jack, #10.' I hand him the ball, and he nods his appreciation.

"Can I ask you something, D Jack?" Mrs. J. Thomas inquires.

"Sure."

"We think Gregg is good enough to get a full ride at Ohio State, being a hometown kid and all, but we're not sure what would be the best school for him to attend?" she says, looking serious for a change. I look over to the strapping young man who is still standing in front of the bench.

"Straight up, Gregg, what's your priority?"

"I've got dreams like everybody else and some scouts have been looking at me pretty closely but I know the chances of going to the Show are tough, so I need a good education. But," he continues with an infectious grin, "I really do want to make the Bigs. You made it right out of high school, didn't you?"

"Yeah, after playing one year of Triple AAA ball. That's a tough decision you'll have to make with your folks, but if you're thinking about college, you might also consider Southern Cal or Arizona State as well as OSU."

"Why do you say those two, D Jack?" she inquires. "There are some solid schools in the mid west and Big Ten Conference."

I'm still looking at Gregg. "Academically I'd agree, but they're not big time college baseball schools like USC and ASU, and those two are also pretty solid when it comes to the academic side of the house. And there's something else, Mrs. Washington. For whatever reasons, the Trojans and

Sun Devils have been highly successful in recruiting top Black ballplayers from all over the country."

"And why is that?"

"Well, California is California, and that speaks for itself. As for Arizona State, do you remember the Olympics in Mexico City in '68?"

"No, but I've seen pictures," Gregg says. "Black power, raised fists on the podium."

"Black gloves, Tommie Smith and John Carlos," Mrs. J. Thomas adds reverently.

"That's right, and those guys came from San Jose State. In the fall, after the Games, San Jose's football team played Brigham Young University and the boys from Provo, Utah decided to show the world how they felt about Black Power, so they beat the San Jose boys up pretty well. Then, a few weeks later, BYU went to Tempe to play the Sun Devils who decided, in turn, they would teach the white boys a lesson. Complete with black arm bands, they saw to it that many of the BYU players didn't finish the game: it was really ugly.

"What I'm saying is USC and ASU are relatively color-blind. I know that Ohio State and the Big Ten are too, but, like I said, the Trojans and the Sun Devils are highly reputable universities, and between the two of them, they've won almost a dozen NCAA baseball championships. Either one would be worth your consideration."

"Thanks a lot for the rundown, D Jack," Mrs. J. T. says as she turns to Gregg. "Why don't you head over to the dining room and get us a table, baby. You can order me a lobster salad and a glass of BV Chablis and I'll be along in a few minutes," she adds.

He nods and offers his hand. "Thanks again, D Jack."

"I'll be looking for you in the sports pages, kid," I say, returning his strong hand shake and trying to conceal my grimace as he turns and heads toward the clubhouse.

"Nice kid," I say looking back into the dark eyes of the woman I assume to be his stepmother at best. She reads my mind. "I've only been married for about a year or so. His mom was Number Two, I think. I'm Number Five."

"Quite a stable."

"More than you know. I might be Wife Number Five but I suspect I'm Girlfriend Number 500."

"So?"

"He's a nice guy and treats his women with class. He's also low maintenance, so he does his thing and I do mine. And, if his track history means anything, the severance package will be a doozy!"

"Sounds like a terrific arrangement," I say as I get to my feet while offering the lady a hand. She takes it, stands, and gives my palm an extra squeeze. "I'd like to give you something for taking some time with Gregg?"

"Naw, that's fine, Mrs. Washington. I really don't get a chance to throw all that much, and it was fun, although I've got to admit I'll be washing down a lot of aspirin over the next few hours."

"I've got a few percs if you need them," she says seriously.

"No, thanks, when I was injured, I got addicted to pain killers, so I'm kind of paranoid about that stuff. The aspirin with VO chasers will be fine."

She slowly looks me in the eye and I get a feeling she's doing her Number-One seductress number. "The best tit fuck you'll ever have will work faster than pills and Canadian whisky."

"Excuse me," I say dumbfounded as my eyes unconsciously gravitate to her exposed cleavage, which could easily swallow up the thirteen-inch 'wadd' of John Holmes, the king of porn.

"The stretch limo is in valet parking and has all the creature comforts we'll need."

"What with your stepson going into the dining room, getting you a table, ordering a lobster salad...and trying to convince a waitress to serve up a glass of white wine to a minor, don't you think your absence is going to be noticeable?"

"D Jack, for one day, you were the best at what you could do, but I'm the best at what I do everyday. Trust me," she says with a killer smile. "You're not going to last long enough for Gregg to miss me. And you can call me Gail after you try to catch your breath."

*

Whew, what can I say, Gail was a bona fide seer! She had predicted two things: one dealing with the penultimate quality of the experience and the other dealing with the duration of that experience, and, like me with my one day in Shea Stadium, she batted a thousand. After that, it's all I can do to face the early afternoon wave of conventioneers who have descended upon the bag room, but only a few of them have clubs. I can see how the Ferdie fund is going to grow rapidily. Once again, I take a deep breath to make sure I can get focused on these bozos.

"Hey," says a red-faced burly guy as his palm slaps the counter top. "You take care of the golf clubs around here?" He laughs, at what, I don't have a clue, and his equally rotund partner joins in the revelry.

"Yes, sir," I say. "The name is D Jack."

"Well, Mr. D Jack, me and Don here need to rent some clubs."

"Sorry, sir," I respond apologetically. "All the rental bags went out this morning with your convention buddies. I guess some ought to be back in by around 4:00 so you still might be able to get in a few holes."

"Aw, shit," he grunts, his red face now sweating a bit. This guy has to be a "multiple martinis for lunch" man.

"Tell you what I can do, though," I say, dropping my voice for a conspiratorial effect. "I'll rent you my personal clubs, and your friend can use my brother's. Cost ya twenty-five bucks per bag, and I've got to tell ya," I add quickly, "I don't do this for just anybody."

"Aw, shit," he repeats as he reaches for his wallet. "What the hell. I'm just gonna pass it on as a business expense anyway." He forks over five ten-dollar bills and adds another ten spot with a big smile. See how much fun this is; the guy just tipped me for taking his fifty bucks. So, with money in hand, I head back to the wooden stalls and get Miller and Marginhoff's bags. These two guys are lawyers and they did their standard late afternoon, mid-week back nine yesterday. Oh yeah, I probably forgot to mention, although the Presidential is owned by the Diplomat, we don't cater exclusively to the guests of the hotel. For a price, a big one, the Millers and Marginhoffs can have the privilege of announcing to the world they are 'select' members.

After removing their membership tags, I deliver the impressive bags to the two perspiring insurance execs with a look of concern. "Now you guys take good care of these, and don't tell anyone, okay? You know how it is. My brother would have my ass if he knew I was letting his clubs go out on the course. You got it?"

"We gotcha, D Jack, whatever the hell that stands for," the money dude says as he shoulders one of the bags. "We'll take good care, don't you worry." The other fat guy hoists his newly-acquired rental, and they head out the door as I reach under the counter for my Fuente cigar box. The Ferdie fund is on its way.

Over the next hour or so, I rent out my supposed clubs and my non-existent brother's clubs eleven times and the take has been over three hundred dollars. Now, don't get sore at me, because the truth be known, all the rental bags actually did go out this morning, and I've mentioned to

Bottomly, somewhat half-heartedly, that the House could use a dozen or more rental bags. So, I'm just providing a service, right?

A small, thin caddy, about the size of a jockey, which he was, comes into the bag room bent over by the pressure of a huge, maroon-hooded golf bag. "Here you go, Pirate. Mr. Schmedler wants to take a lesson at the Executive this afternoon so ship his clubs over there, okay? Said he also wants to play back here tomorrow at his usual time. You take care of all that?"

"Can do, Carlos," I say to the diminutive Panamanian, whose career ended with a hoof to the head during a stretch run in the Florida Derby at Gulfstream Park a few years ago. "I can surely handle that," I say as a light goes off in my mind with a blaze of excitement. "How about waiting for just a second while I tag his clubs?"

He nods in the affirmative and I write, "Immediate delivery to the Executive" on a heavy cardboard tag which has a hole in one end with a string through it. I tie the string to the grip on Schmedler's bag and slide it back to Carlos. "Thanks a lot. You saved me a trip."

"Sure thing, Pirate," he says with a smile. "Glad to help out," he adds as he once again bends under the weight of the bag and heads out the door. Hot damn! A couple of phone calls here and there and ole Schmedler is going to have himself a post-Thanksgiving to remember. But first things first, I need to throw it into high gear if I'm going to be able to avail myself of the Boss's Thanksgiving generosity.

*

It's just a few minutes after 5:00 p.m., I'm all caught up and on my way upstairs, and I can hear Pastrano holding court in the Bengal Lounge a good ten feet before I enter the upscale bar. As hoped for, the patrons have pretty well cleared out and just about everyone on staff is filling up plates of finger food and swigging iced bottles of Michelob. I get a wave and a grin from Willie who is sitting on the small stage with a large tumbler in his hand.

"Okay, Willie," the Turk shouts with a laugh. "You said you wanted to wait for D Jack, so let's have the speech."

"Yeah," everyone chimes in enthusiastically, "da speech, da speech!"

Willie gets to his feet and slowly measures the staff with his boyish grin that has probably 'killed' more ladies in his home town of New Orleans than here in and around Miami Beach. He holds up his hands and is greeted with immediate silence, and, if you haven't figured it out yet, you are about to become privy to Willie's ritual.

"I know all you boys and girls have to eat Charley's food and drink his booze as quick as possible, so I'll give ya the really short version 'cause I'd rather drink with ya than make speeches. So," he begins, "I look at ordinary people in their suits, them with no scars, and I'm different. I don't fit with them. I'm where everybody's got scar tissue on their eyes and got noses like saddles, just kinda like D Jack here, even though he played a non-contact sport and never got in the ring like a real man, but then he still looks pretty good, and maybe he can be a movie star like Bogey or somebody rugged like that," he says with a laugh, which is matched by everyone in the room as they look my way. "Anyway, I go to conventions of old fighters like me," he continues, "and I see the scar tissue and all them flat noses and it's beautiful. Galento, Giardello, LaMotta, Carmen Basilio. What a sweetheart Basilio is. They talk like me, like they got rocks in their throats. Beautiful!!!"

The room erupts with laughter and applause as Willy the Wisp spreads his arms and graciously bows. He steps down from the stage and comes over to me for a handshake and a hug. "How ya doin, kid?"

"Everything's Jake, Willie. Are the ladies being kind to you?" I ask with a grin.

"They don't know any other way," he responds modestly. "Let's go sit and chat some. I don't even haf ta buy ya a drink." We slide into one of the corner booths; in fact, the same one where Sam did her number on me Tuesday night. Sal is quick to wander over with a VO and water. Willie eyes her briefly, and her smile lets him know she's enjoying the once-over before heading back to the hors d'oeuvres table.

"Are you in town to spar with the Champ?" I ask.

"Naw, I taught him all he knows when he was still Clay. I think he's slowen down now after goin with Frasier and Foreman, so Angelo probably doesn't want me to beat 'em up," he concludes with a grin. The legendary trainer, Angelo Dundee, had been in Pastrano's corner pretty much throughout his career and had frequently used Willie to spar with Muhammed Ali in order to expose "the greatest" to the pure art of boxing, rather than the more common blood-and-guts style of most of the heavyweights. Pastrano was always up on his toes and dancing left while snaking out a jab, often tripling it, and Ali still likes to kid that Pastrano is "almost as pretty as me."

"So then, you're just in town to catch the fights and relax some?"

"That's about it, D Jack. I've been worken a few joints out in front of Bourbon Street, and I'm just taken a break."

"Nice, if you can get it," I say raising my glass in a toast. He shifts his gaze over my shoulder, so I turn slightly and am surprised to see Sam heading for our table. Always the ladies man, Willie gets to his feet while I remain seated, figuring it doesn't much matter because I'm thinking this table might have a curse on it. He extends his hand along with his A-Number-One boyish, charming grin.

"Samantha Frederickson, meet Willie Pastrano," I say politely.

"My pleasure, Samantha," Willie says as he takes her hand and gives it a squeeze. She looks at me, rather than Willie, which immediately communicates something to the ex-champ. "Do you mind if I sit down for a few minutes, or am I interrupting?"

Willie answers quickly before I have a chance to respond to her question. "Naw, little lady, we was just tellen some lies and wondering why any guy in his right mind would do something knowing he could get hit in da head. Course some guys are smarter than others, like me, 'cause I was in it for the money where D Jack was in it for the glory. Ain't no glory," he says with a half smile, "but seeing as I'm already on my feet, I'm gonna just cruise for awhile. Nice to meet ya," he adds with a wink in my direction as he shuffles toward the bar.

Sam settles into the corner loveseat across from me and slowly looks up from the drink she was carrying. But she seems hesitant to say something, and my comfort level is worse than it was Tuesday night. If this is round two, she might be going for the knockout, and I'm thinking I'd be better off getting in the ring with the Wisp.

"I figure right about now Billy is wondering what you're doing," I say trying to break, what for me, is an uncomfortable silence.

"He's pretty busy at the bar keeping the troops happy for Charley, and I just need to talk with you for a minute or two."

I'm thinking maybe I can head her off. "I guess I ought to apologize for walking out Tuesday night but the truth is, other than maybe being rude, I'm not sure what I'd be apologizing for unless it's the past. And I think we've already covered that piece of ground."

"That's not why I came over. It's been pretty easy for me to get awfully damn mad every time I've thought about you, but I never considered much about what might have been going on in your life. Even though you got hurt, I just assumed everything was peaches and cream."

"I pretty much told you the other night that not much worked out but it really doesn't matter," I say in an emotionless tone.

"I think it does, and I doubt you said much more than you thought you had to." She pauses. "I shouldn't have gotten so nasty."

This is confusing me. "Sam, let's not fool ourselves, okay? You have every right to be as nasty as you want," I say in a matter-of-fact way, "and for what it's worth, just like everyone else, I live with a past that, among other things, includes you."

"You lied, Dev," Sam says responds matching my clinical tone.

"About what?"

"You said Tuesday night you hadn't much thought about anything but over the years, I think you have."

"Maybe I meant I try not to think about some things."

"Why not?"

"I try to avoid pain, Sam. It's a human instinct."

"Was the past you're talking about the one before or after Shea Stadium?"

"Why do you ask?"

"Before Shea, you lost me and you lost your Dad, but you still had the true love of your life, the game. But afterwards, you didn't have anything."

"Weizut eizar yeizoo dizoo eeizing?"

Carney talk! Billy's standing right behind me, and I'm not about to turn and look into his steely blue eyes. Sometimes, the two of them would converse in Carney talk just for the fun of it, but his voice is clearly confrontational, and Sam doesn't have joy written all over her face.

"Eeizi neeized teeizo teeizalk teeizo deeizvee feizor jeisust eeisay feeizew meeizinueitzets, deeizadeeizee. Eeizeveyei theeizing eeisiz feeizine," she says her eyes just a bit dewy.

"Okeizat," he says, his tone softening.

It's quiet, and she returns her gaze to me so I figure Billy has gone back to topping off drinks and popping bottles of Michelob. "That was a short, private conversation," I say casually. "What was it all about?"

"He wanted to know what I was doing here sitting with you, and I told him everything was fine. He's just concerned, that's all."

"What's he concerned about?"

"I told him about our conversation Tuesday night and that I felt badly about the way it ended," Sam answers as her voice trails off.

"And?"

"And that I wanted to talk to you again."

"Why?"

"Because I couldn't deny that I felt something. Not much," she adds quickly, "but something."

Oh boy, this is really coming at me right out of the blue, and I'm not sure what's going on. For all appearances, it seems as if Sam is opening a door, maybe just a wee crack but opening it just the same, and I suddenly realize that I'm being overwhelmed, more by a sense of discomfort than joy.

Let me put it to you this way. I once lost a prized black cowboy hat that had a band made of braided leather. Well, I didn't actually lose it; I quaffed too many brews and left it at a greasy spoon after playing an exhibition game in Chattanooga. But deep down, I knew I had seen the last of it. I don't know why we played a second exhibition game against the Lookouts later in the season; they weren't in the International League. But I was hoping I might get that hat back; no such luck. Hoping for something so slim was just an exercise in futility and a waste of time, just like trying to hit a dinger dead away in Engel Stadium. The 325 foot left field fence angles out sharply to the alley in left center which is 425 feet and then a sharp incline; that's right, I said *incline* that leads the way to the deepest center field in pro ball: 471 feet! Sure, I know we're not talking about a hat here, or hopeless dingers for that matter, but I can't help feeling the same way, ya know, the 'let dead dogs lie' thing.

"Where are you, Dev?"

"I was looking for my hat in Chattanooga."

"Still a smart ass! Seriously?"

"Okay, seriously, I think the question is where are you, Sam, not me?"

"I'm sitting at a table with a man who used to be the boy I was in love with," she says pensively, "and now I'm not sure he's the person I thought he would be."

"And what were you expecting after all these years?"

"I didn't expect you to be different. I've only been at the Presidential for a few days and the people working here seem to think you're one hell of a guy; a carefree, no problems kind of guy, who everyone seems to like and who, I'm told, seems ready to dig into his pockets, followed by a smile and a pat on the back."

"Who told you that?"

"Sal did."

"So?"

"I know we were just kids, but we had three years together, so I know the other side."

"The all consuming baseball side I suppose," I say with some bitterness creeping into my voice.

"No, I remember the quiet side. I remember all those guys you played with in school and then some of the Suns who resented D Jack, the superstar. I used to think sometimes you stayed extra close to me because of their envy. Actually, I never saw you be a part of the group, one of the guys. I don't think I realized until Tuesday night that all you ever had was me and your dad."

"What we had were dreams, Sam. Two little kids, just teenagers, all caught up in their dreams to be the best of the best."

She noticeably stiffens, and her look becomes very serious. "Take off your sunglasses, Dev."

"No."

"Are you that self-conscious?"

"Well, like Pastrano kind of said, 'I just ain't as bootiful as I used to be.'"

"I don't think you're afraid of scaring me away. I think you don't want me to get into your mind, do you?"

"No, I don't."

Like I've told you, Sam always knew how to get to the quick of it, and still does.

"I don't have to see your eyes, Dev. Even though you still don't say much, I can feel it," she says with just a hint of sadness, "I think you only had one dream and dreams are important because that's all there is. But it's the sharing of dreams, and hopes and fears that bring and keep people together, and if you can't do that, then you're out there by yourself."

"I don't mind being out there by myself, most of the time," I say defensively.

"Then what have you shared recently, and with whom, Dev, and I don't mean the small stuff?" she says in the more hardened tone I heard during our last conversation.

"You already know my dad is gone so you've made your point, Sam, but how about you?" I ask, trying to shift the focus away from me."

"I have my dad, my girls, and my cousin's son. I have dreams for them which are also mine. I share with them that today's a good day, and tomorrow will be better," she says fervently. "I try to make the outside reflect the inside, and I don't have to work very hard at it."

"Well," I say taking a deep breath, "maybe you're not sitting across from the boy you used to know, but I'm certainly sitting across from the girl I used to know."

" Meaning?"

"Meaning among other things, you've buried your mother, your sister, and your husband, none of which has broken your spirit. You're still the eternal optimist who doesn't even look for the silver lining because you're so damn sure it's out there."

"Maybe that's why I wanted to talk to you tonight, Devon."

"Come on, Sam. After Tuesday's little chat in the lounge, what's left to talk about?"

"I don't really know, but if you recall, I was never really comfortable with unanswered stuff," she says almost defiantly.

"I'm not sure I see the point, and anyway, Sam, we haven't talked for eight years. I'm not that nineteen-year-old ballplayer anymore."

"If you were, I wouldn't be sitting here. I loved that ballplayer with all my heart, but I'm not looking at him. I'm looking at you, Devon, and I want to know who you are and then I can close the book on the past," she says somberly, "so I want us to talk somewhere else, privately. Would you be willing to have dinner some where close Saturday night before your first set with T Moon?"

Although the edge has come off her voice a wee bit, her expression still seems kind of serious or maybe pensive, whereas you think a woman would smile if she really wanted to go out to eat with a guy.

"That's a hell of shift, unless you figure you might as well enjoy a last supper while you close the book as you say. Why don't we just do it now and be done with it?"

"I was wrong about the one drink a few nights ago. I thought it would be quick and simple but it wasn't then and it isn't now."

"Why isn't it?"

"Because I figured it would be easy to tell you to go to hell: end of story."

"But you said you want to close the book on the past?"

"I do, but the past is the past."

"I don't get it Sam. Like I said, I can see you're still the eternal optimist and I guess I'm still a pessimist, but I'm really not sure what you're optimistic about here."

"I'm not sure either. But like you used to say, you can't find out if you can hit low and away unless you swing at it. So?"

"So, what's Billy going to say?"

"He won't like it but I'm asking you anyway."

"Where do you want to go?"

"The Forge would be nice."

"I don't know. It is way down around forty-first street in Miami Beach so we probably wouldn't have time. I'm scheduled to work Saturday night in the cloakroom before hitting the Lounge."

"Can you try to change shifts?"

She seems intent on going to the Forge probably because it was the last first class establishment we visited before going our separate ways. I'm not comfortable with this; it sounds like Yogi's *deja vu all over again*. What the hell. "I'll see what I can do."

"Thanks," Sam says as she gets to her feet with a swirl of her purple and black cocktail uniform. "Back to work, Mr. Berston's only generous to a point, and, even though I asked you out, you're picking up the check, right?" she asks rhetorically. And with that, she's gone while I sit back trying to comprehend what has just taken place. But that's going to have to wait because Stunt is waving in my direction.

I head over to the corner of the bar where he seems to be taking a break, while Billy is keeping pretty busy at the other end of the lounge. "Where's my picture, D Jack? You've had plenty of time to collect from Marcus."

"True, but I couldn't bring myself to do it. Hell of a shot, though, Stunt, even if there's no way to tell if the collars match the cuffs."

"Well," he says with a laugh, "maybe they do. I didn't expect to see a French girl with a shaved snatch. That's just never gonna fly in the skin flicks and porn mags."

"How did you know she was French? I didn't pick up an accent or anything. So how did you find that out?"

"I casually asked her why she was two-timing Dawson and she said something like right and wrong are determined by each person and she didn't think she was doin' nuthin' wrong. Then, she said she was born in Paris and said something else about some French philosopher.

"Jean Paul Sartre?"

"Sartre! You got it, D Jack. What did he actually say?" Stunt asks with what appears to be genuine interest.

"He's kind of a shining light in the French existentialist movement and has lots to say about his belief that things like truth and right and wrong are subjective and determined by each of us."

"You mean what's good for me is good for me and doesn't have to be good for you? And that's okay?"

"You got it. And what's good for you might change as you change. One of the basic deals with existentialism is that your existence precedes your essence which constantly evolves."

"You lost me on that one, D Jack."

"Well, Sartre and his French compatriots believed that you exist first, you know, you get born and you're just kind of nothing, but as you live your life, you get your essence, which means you grow and experience things, and you spend your whole life becoming who you are."

“I gotcha ya, so I was born with a dick, and over the years I’ve got it working better and better, right?”

“Flawless thinking, Stunt,” I say with a big grin. “Abso-fucking-lutely flawless. But when it comes to being a philosopher, stick to bartending!”

“All well and good, and you stick to hustling. But where’s my fifty bucks?”

“What fifty bucks?” I respond. “I told you I didn’t collect from Marcus, so I didn’t get any winnings. Half of nothin’s nothin.”

“That wasn’t the deal, D Jack. The deal was that I get a fifty spot to loan you the photo. You see it as half your winnings; I see it as a rental.”

“How about giving me a discount?” I say imploringly. “After all, I’m the guy who set you up in the first place, a service for which I will graciously waive all fees. Now, where are you going to find a pimp willing to do that?”

“We never talked fees, and I sure as hell don’t need a pimp,” he says indignantly.

Damn if he isn’t right, I say to myself, as I fork over a fifty along with the photo I’ve been keeping in the back pocket of my jeans. Fucken ‘A’ if Lena Dawson hasn’t cost me a hundred and fifty bucks. “Is it 6:00 yet, Stunt?”

“Nope.”

“So, Charley’s still buying?”

“Yep.”

“So pour me one more!”

He does and I return to the corner table which now may or may not be a bad luck spot. It’s funny sometimes how you know things, but you don’t apply them to yourself, I think, as I stretch out on the inside of the booth. Here I am filling in Stunt on the basics of existentialism, what with existence and essence and all of that shit, and just a few minutes ago, Samantha Frederickson…boy, that last name sounds strange…is suggesting I’ve evolved into something I wasn’t. And now she’s got me thinking about maybe who I was and maybe who I am. I guess you might have some thoughts on this, but let’s talk later. I’ve got to find some Thanksgiving dinner before hitting the phones.

VI

SCHMEDLER'S MISSING CLUBS

Walking in sand, wading through the foam
closing my eyes, feeling all alone,
look at the shells, pieces all around
back goes a wave, I wonder where she's bound

I've got a headache. I know you think I drink too much, but I generally stretch things out and make sure I nibble on something on and off throughout the day. I just nurse a few when backing T, but the room was pretty empty last night, thanks to the various Thanksgiving celebrations that had been organized for the guests throughout the complex, so I got a little too deep into my cups. The problem is I've come to intensely dislike holidays and don't think I'll ever get used to being alone at special times, like birthdays and stuff like that. It's not like I miss the big family get-togethers, because it was always just Dad and me.

On Thanksgiving Day, he would put on his one suit, but rather than his white hotel shirt, he would wear his special powder-blue shirt and his holiday tie that had very dark blue stripes. I'd still wear blue jeans but I had a short sleeve dress shirt and would also slide into my special event penny loafers. Late in the afternoon, we'd hop the beach bus down Collins Avenue to Sunny Isles and hope to get one of the turquoise-colored booths in Wolfie Cohen's Rascal House. More often then not, we sat at the counter that ran right down the middle of the restaurant with about fifteen seats on either side of the long, narrow service area just big enough for the waitresses to cruise up and down. Just picture a nice little cozy '50's diner and then multiple by ten, or maybe even twenty, and then you've got the mother of all kosher delis!

Dad would always have the stuffed cabbage, and I would gross everyone out by asking for a corn beef on white, and fatty, not lean. This always brought an "oye vey" or something like that out of one of the waitresses, all of whom wore pens pinned to their white uniforms with pink and violet flowered hankies somehow magically attached to their shoulders…and aghast looks from any patrons who might have overheard my unorthodox request. We always took stuff home because we filled up on the breadbasket and the free bowls of kosher pickles, cucumbers in vinegar, and cole slaw that we washed down with Dr. Brown's crème sodas. I went back there last year for the first time and actually got as far as being seated before the wave of melancholy swept over me and I quietly departed the friendly and boisterous premises.

Yesterday, after the hoedown in the Lounge, Chico had been thoughtful enough to rustle me up some white meat and stuffing, and I had eaten the meal on the run in the bag room right before putting on Pete's hat and heading for the phones. I guess you're thinking an exercise in self-pity? Admitted, but don't get too rough on me. When's the last time you spent a holiday by yourself? See what I mean? Aw, forget it, the phone's ringing.

"Presidential bag room, can I be of assistance to you?"

"I need a little information, please," says a heavy, yet sultry, feminine voice of indeterminable age.

"I'll be more than glad to help out if I can," I answer pleasantly.

I hear a masculine voice in the background groan, "Rhoda! Don't ask him when he gets off the course. Just ask him when the earliest he can…." The rest is muffled, and I assume the lady has covered the receiver. She comes back on the line.

"Well, I've got to make a doctor's appointment for my husband this afternoon, and in order to do so, I need to know when he will complete his round of golf. I believe he is going to tee off sometime around 9:00 a.m. this morning."

She sounds a little nervous, and I'm not sure I believe what I'm hearing. Did the guy in the background say "he" or "Hans"? Wow! Maybe we serve up a quiniela today.

"Please hold the phone for just a moment, ma'am. I'll get right back to you," I say as I stick her on hold and punch in the four digits for Marcus in the starter's office.

"Starter's office, this is Marcus speaking."

"It's D Jack, Marcus. Tell me something?" I ask with obvious excitement. "Do you know Mrs. Schmedler's first name?" I inquire as I cross my fingers.

"Yes. It's Rhoda. Why do you ask?"

"Just curious," I respond with a sigh of relief. "I'll get back to you in a few minutes."

I punch back into the line on hold. "Sorry to keep you waiting ma'am. I just wanted to check with the starter to see how the morning traffic is getting along. I'm sorry to tell you that we're really busy this morning, and things are going to be pretty slow all day. I would venture to say, if your husband teed off around 9:00, he most likely will be out on the course 'til as late as 2:00 or even 3:00 this afternoon, so it would be a good idea to get him a late afternoon doctor's appointment. If you give me his name, I could get a message to him, if you like."

"Thanks very much," she purrs, "but that won't be necessary. I'm sure I'll be able to reach him," she says as she hangs up. I just sit there, phone still in hand, and grin. Wow! Between his old lady and the scheme I've already put in place, is Schmedler gonna have a day to remember or what? Hang with me. This is gonna be fun!

*

The nasty little bastard doesn't disappoint us. At 9:15 a.m. sharp, he approaches his golf cart, marching along in that upright, stern manner of his. Schmedler doesn't realize his huge, maroon bag isn't on the cart until he's already placed himself behind the driver's yoke. The expected explosion comes quickly.

"Where are my clubs?" he shouts at Ralph.

Ralph begins his customary scratch of his head, his ever-present bewildered look painted across his broad, somewhat flat face. "Gee, you played at the Executive yesterday, I think. I guess your clubs haven't come back yet."

"What do you mean they haven't come back yet, you dummy? I told them explicitly to send my bag over here today so I could tee off at my usual 9:15 time!" If possible, Ralph's confusion appears to be increasing while Marcus, who has heard the ruckus and has come down from his office, looks equally lost.

"What seems to be the difficulty, Mr. Schmedler?" Marcus inquires in his soft-spoken way.

"I don't have one!" Schmedler bellows. "You do!" His face is turning beet red, and he looks as if he is on the verge of coming apart. "And the difficulty, as you put it, is finding my customized clubs, and you dumb bastards better not have lost them because it would take two months to replace them."

"Where are they supposed to be?" Marcus asks, while working hard at maintaining his nonplused, Irish composure.

"Right here, you simple fool!"

I don't like the way the Clock is being treated so I amble over to him. He turns to greet me with panic written in his eyes, and I'm sure he's wondering what the Big House is going to have to say about all this. He did warn me, if you recall. "D Jack, do you have any information about Mr. Schmedler's clubs?"

I look directly at Marcus, thereby avoiding the glare of the increasingly irate Schmedler. "I tagged them and sent them to the Executive yesterday."

"Did the tag call for a return this morning?"

"Absolutely, but I haven't seen them, and they're hard to miss because we have very few maroon bags in the stalls right now," I say with a look of innocence. "So when I didn't see the bag, I called George over at the Executive bag room, and he assured me he put them on a bus."

"Well then, call John in the bag room at the Diplomat and see if somehow the clubs got put on the wrong shuttle," Marcus says as he turns to encounter the withering stare of Schmedler. "If you'll follow me up to the pro shop, Mr. Schmedler, I'm sure we'll be able to outfit you with some fine clubs until we locate yours."

Schmedler measures Marcus and his face reeks with disgust. "You think I'm going to play golf after all this shit!" he shouts and then takes a deep breath. "Now, I'll tell *you* what I *am* going to do. I'm going back to my suite, and I'm going to sit by my phone and the damn thing better ring by noon, and my bag better be on this cart at 9:15 tomorrow morning, or you'll be on the street at 9:16," he says, glaring at each of us.

Marcus assumes the role of spokesman. "Yes sir, Mr. Schmedler. I'll call by noon and make sure the back nine is clear in the morning." Schmedler turns his back and, with his precise military gait, majestically strides toward the pro shop. Marcus turns and quietly eyes me from nose to toes.

"Okay, Pirate. You got under his skin. Now, where are the guy's clubs?"

I puff up my cheeks and raise my eyebrows toward the few clouds in the blue sky. "You'll never believe it, Marcus, but I don't really know where they are at this precise moment."

"Bullshit! Enough is enough. You've had your fun, and we'll let Ferdie know that Schmedler got some comeuppance." Marcus is slowly adopting his classical, ominous appearance, but I continue to shrug.

"Look, Marcus, I tagged the clubs and sent them over to the Executive. Like I told you and Schmedler, I called George this morning, and he told me he had put the bag on a bus. At 6:30 this morning, Charlie

Shoe hauled the bags down from the front door and Schmedler's weren't in the bunch."

Marcus gives me a look of disbelief, "So, if I buy that, the clubs got misplaced somewhere between the shuttle and the bag room, right?"

"I've told you what I know, Marcus," I repeat with as honest a look as I can muster.

Marcus finally seems to be realizing there is little to be done other than checking the shuttle and the driver and maybe calling John at the Diplomat just in case. "Boy," he says with a half smile, "that guy is sure used to having what he wants and when he wants it. I'll bet he's going to be a regular sweetheart by the time he hits his suite."

My sides begin to ache as I contain my laughter while Ralph and Marcus both seem bewildered by my grin and lack of solemnity. "Guys…you don't know the fucken half of it."

"We don't know half of what?" Marcus responds, suddenly worried. "You mean your comeuppance called for more?" he says as his mouth drops open.

"Well, a second comeuppance wasn't in my plan," I respond innocently. "You know all the times you go to the movies and the bad ass gets away with it and ya kinda hope God knows what the deal is and that God's gonna square it? Well, if I was going to pull the religious bit on you guys, I'd say the Big Fella is giving it to Schmedler with a fist up the ass."

"What do you mean?" Ralph asks as he continues to scratch his head.

"Marcus, do you remember this morning when I asked you what Schmedler's wife's name was?" He nods, curiously.

"Well, I got this call, and this dame wanted to know the earliest her old man could get off the course. I heard the guy in the background call her Rhoda, and you know as sure as the world is round the guy is boning this broad. Thinking ahead, I figure when Schmedler finds out about his clubs, he's gonna hit the roof and probably won't want to play. If I was right about that, I reckoned I'd suggest he go back to his suite so we could reach him when we found his bag, but the sonuvabitch made that decision himself. How's that for irony!" I'm now on the bridge of hysterics. "Right now, ole Rhoda thinks she's gonna get laid when the truth of the matter is, she's about to get screwed!"

Ralph begins to howl and even the straight arrow Marcus seems amused. "Don't get delirious, D Jack. Maybe Schmedler doesn't care if someone is tapping his wife. He doesn't appear to be the loving sort."

"Love," I repeat with a groan. "Marcus, you've got a one-way frame of reference. Love doesn't have a damn thing to do with this. You gonna tell me Schmedler isn't the most possessive bastard around? That's the part that's gonna fry his ass."

Marcus half smiles again. "You've got a good point on that one, D Jack. I guess Mr. Schmedler is going to pay the price today," he concludes, but his smile rapidly fades. "I don't know about the clubs," he says contemplatively, "but I do think this thing with Rhoda is a little shoddy."

"Hey," I respond defensively, "I didn't do anything. A lady asked me if her husband had teed off and when he would get off the course. I told her the truth. If Schmedler hadn't gotten so pissed, he would have taken you up on your offer for some replacement clubs and he'd be on the course, where he's supposed to be, rather than on his way to the great enlightenment, right?"

"Okay, D Jack, I'm convinced. You're a regular prince of a guy," he says as he pauses, and then gives me his ole eye treatment. "Just one more time though. What really happened to Schmedler's clubs?"

I shake my head from side to side, painting a somewhat disappointed look on my face. "Come on, Marcus. Out of one side of your mouth I'm a nice guy and out of the other side you question my honesty. For the last time, ya ole fart, I told you all I know. George said he put 'em on a bus, and that's that!"

Marcus shrugs and smiles at me, so I interpret that as belief and return the smile as he turns and heads toward his starter's office up the hill. Ralph is still scratching his head with that kind of blank stare of his. "Well gee, Pirate," he mumbles, "if George put 'em on the bus, where do you think they are?"

"Got me, Ralph," I answer, holding back my grin, thinking about the final destination of that mysterious bag. I wouldn't mind sharing it with you, but I think maybe we need to get to know each other just a little bit better, so maybe later, huh?

*

Speaking of give and take, that's pretty much what the afternoon had served up. It was the last day for the insurance convention guys who gave up as little as possible, in the form of tips, so I took as much as I could, falling occasionally below the "less than legit" line. Right now, Moon's eyes are shut, and he's deep in some lyrics I developed from another one of my tales of woe:

and the wind whips up the white caps and the foam
like me the mighty ocean softly moans,

and she says to me, a mere whisper in her breeze,
take your feet from my sand, and go see what you can be.
Moving again, wading down the shore
looking in vain, for an open door,
I see her now, sitting by the dune
red hair in salt spray,
her face a radiant moon.
I've seen her here and there from time to time,
sitting by her side would be so fine,
I remember the night, that she nodded my way
but she wasn't alone,
so I lost another day.
Now that she's here, what will I say
if I offer my hand, will she turn away
My heart's beating fast, now the final trial
I looked in her eyes, and she kissed me with her smile.

It's been a typically good Friday night crowd, and T shoots me a wink as he receives the warm applause. Like most things people write, there's often an autobiographical element. I've already shared with you that I've got a thing for the peace and solitude of the beach, but that sense of calm is interrupted when I'm startled to see Sam in the corner booth. She couldn't have been there five minutes ago, because the room's been emptying out and I would think I'd have spotted her. Moon has already departed the small stage, so I lay the Yamaha on the black leather padded stool. With the ever-present VO in hand and Kodiak between cheek and gum, I head for the table where Sam is quietly looking at her drink. As I reach the booth, her eyes come up to meet mine and fiction bridges on fact. I look at her face and let a few seconds pass before I realize my lyrics in T's last offering have not come to be, not that I expected a truly warm kind of reaction from her.

"I think I know a little something about that last song," she says.

"His music, my words, and one of our short interludes," I admit as I take a seat across from her.

"But it wasn't on the beach. If memory serves, it was at Doria's Orange Bowl on Federal Highway and Hallandale Beach Boulevard."

"That's true and you were having pizza with some kid who probably couldn't believe he was out with you."

"And the mighty Devon Jameison came by to say hi, and I asked him if he wanted to sit down."

"And I said, 'Three's a crowd.'"

"And you took me out to dinner the very next night, which is why I came back tonight after Daddy got off shift."

"I think I'm missing something here," I say quizzically.

"Well, last night I asked if you were paying for dinner tomorrow, and I don't recall that I got an answer."

"So whose fault is that? You're the one who turned and left the room."

"So?"

"So what?"

"Are you buying?"

"Sure but not the Forge."

Her features take on a pale, somewhat serious look. "Too heavy?" she asks. We had exchanged rings at the Forge, and the waiters had treated two kids to a very special night.

"It's nothing like that, Sam. The Forge is still the place for celebrations and special occasions and that's why it's booked to the hilt. But I played Triple AAA ball with a guy named Johnny Morgan and he's got a nice little steak and seafood place up on Biscayne Boulevard, so I thought that might be okay. It's got beautiful models of tall sailing ships, thick Delmonico steaks, good salad bar, and as fine a wine selection this side of Bern's Steak House in Tampa. And he does a killer shrimp newberg."

I think she might be a little relieved that the past isn't immediately going to bite us in the ass and pleased that I remembered she loves newberg. "But you're still are going to buy, yes?" she asks pleasantly.

"Sure. So, did you like the song?"

"Well, I do think it was kind of interesting the way you took the Orange Bowl thing and worked it into your love for the beach."

"I'll take that as a yes."

Her green eyes are finally looking at me with a sadness I think I spotted last night. "How far did you go with our short story and when did you share it with Moon?"

"What you heard is all he got. The sharing took place last summer after I went up to Lake City to get inducted into the Florida Sports Hall of Fame."

"No kidding? I hadn't read about that. You're rubbing elbows with some pretty famous athletes," she says with pride, obviously referring to Billy, so I gloss it over.

"I haven't been front page news for a long time but the *Herald* did give it a play with a photo on Page D2. Anyway, I figured I was pretty close to Jax, so I spent a day or so cruising around and ended up at Crossroads down at South Ponte Vedra Beach."

"Is that better than Hollywood Beach?" she inquires.

"Different," I answer. "It has sand dunes and lots of sea oats and you spot gulls and pelicans and maybe even an osprey now and then. But here I like the way the ocean breezes rustle the palm trees right on the beach, and I like the memories."

"Which suggests you don't like your memories of Ponte Vedra?"

I think I know what she's assuming here. "I always went there by myself, Sam. It was just me and the pelicans, my quiet place."

"And Hollywood Beach was our place?"

"Sure…plus a hundred other kids on Sunday afternoons at Johnson Street who couldn't drink legally. So can I freshen' yours?" I ask, having become uneasy with another trip down memory lane.

"Same ole, same ole," she answers as she sticks up two fingers in the direction of Sal. I also hold up a few fingers and look at them. "Not too sore tonight," I say with obvious pleasure. "Sometimes I still don't like to touch things after two or three hours of playing, particularly if the strings are steel. That's one of the reasons I play with cat gut."

"You've got to be kidding, right?"

"Well, actually nylon, which is a lot easier on the fingers and produces a soft sound. That's what Charlie wants in this place: mood music, folk, that kind of stuff."

"Don't you get awfully tired at times, Dev?"

"Sure, I drag around plenty, but after awhile, you adjust to it."

"That's only part of what I meant," she says, her eyes squinting ever so slightly. "I also meant, don't you get tired of being 'on' all the time…I mean with the guests?" she adds quickly.

"I think maybe so but not too often. Most of the rich and famous as well as the pretenders who come here are decent enough and treat you okay, as long as they get what they expect. Even the non-tippers seem to accept the fact that we're human, but then there are just enough nasty ones to produce unhappiness on a fairly regular basis."

"You mean like Hans Schmedler?" she says with a smile. Much to her surprise, I get serious. "That's an isolated thing, Sam. I'm not judge and jury or anything like that, but I just get teed when somebody gets the idea that the hired help have no feelings. Sure, guys like Schmedler expect excellent service. And God knows they pay a whole lot of money for it. I don't expect to make a few bucks off every guest, but when some of these

SOB's start kicking people around, someone has to step up to the plate and provide a moment of humility," I conclude with a little too much heat.

"And you're the best ballplayer in residence, right?"

"You bet he is," Sal says to Sam as she serves up Sam's Barcardi and Pepsi and then places the "Big Dawg" tumbler of VO in my outstretched hand. "I couldn't help but hear you two on the way over, and I loved the way you squared things for Ferdie and me."

"I squared things for you?" I ask.

"Absolutely, I'm the one Rhoda threw the glass at," Sal answers with a smile. "The whole little story of that little incident, plus the missing clubs, is going all around the place. I don't think we'll see that bitch in here again," she says, laughing as she turns and heads for another station. I take a solid hit on the drink and notice Sam does the same. "So, what was it you were accusing me of?"

"I really wasn't accusing you of anything, Dev. I was just curious as to how you feel about what goes on around here; I mean sometimes I wonder how you maintain your sanity?"

"Sanity is the ability to cope with insane conditions," I say with a broad smile.

She returns the smile. "I'll bet you didn't think that up?"

"You're right; I'm pretty sure it was some lady poet, but to answer your question, I guess when all is said and done, it's a bottom basement paycheck with under-the-table benefits, but it's pretty much like what G.D. says up at the front door."

"I see him every day," Sam says with a touch of sympathy and possibly a hint of fondness. "Why do you call him G.D.?"

"We call him G.D. because he's always mumbling, 'God damn! Dis gotta be the lass season.' I'm sure he means it, probably like just about everyone else around this place, but he'll still be here next year."

"How long have you been here?"

"Two years and this is definitely my last season." She responds with a bit of a giggle, and her whole self seems to radiate a little warmth, but only momentarily.

"What?" I inquire.

"I was just thinking about what you were saying. I agree that most of the guests are pleasant, but there always seems to be one or two on a daily basis that make things kind of tough. Sometimes it just gets so God awful hard to focus on the nice things and just overlook the bad, right?"

"I'm surprised. That holds even for you?"

"Even for me, although this place is easier than the hotel. More relaxed, I think."

"Maybe so, but there's more action here."

"Like Schmedler? Come on, Dev. The whole place is dying to know what happened to his clubs."

"First of all, action comes in the form of money and I'm not gonna get a dime outta that guy. And secondly, how the hell would I know what happened to his clubs?" I respond innocently.

"I've got it, get Moon to compose the Ballad of Schmedler, and you can write a tale of the clubhouse Robin Hood getting even with the notorious nobility while championing the cause of an injured, down trodden peasant. What do you think?" she asks expectantly.

"Hey, that's pushing it a bit. I'm not crazy about this place, but I do have to eat, so rubbing Schmedler's nose in it would be pushing Charley the Boss to the edge. I'd prefer avoiding the unemployment line."

"I'm sure you could do something else." She pauses and then adds with that same serious look, "You could do something else, couldn't you Dev?"

"I have a Bachelors and a Masters in philosophy, and Marcus has assured me it's a career box canyon. And, as he likes to add, I just don't have the brains to be a successful plumber."

"You're pulling my leg," she says in a kind of wonderment. "The kid who could barely figure out my biology homework to get me out of the house on weeknights is a philosopher?"

"Degrees from Arizona State don't make me a philosopher."

"I didn't know you were a Sun Devil."

"I didn't know you were a Gator."

"So, what is it you philosophize about, and how do you go about it?" she asks with just a hint of curiosity.

"I could answer the first part by saying that, according to Sir Francis Bacon, 'knowledge is power.'"

"Can you elaborate please?"

"The guy who knows where Schmedler's bag is has the *knowledge* which strips Schmedler of the *power*, no matter how many millions he's worth."

"Okay that takes care of the *what*," Sam says sounding satisfied. "And the *how?"*

"Just like you, Sam, I speculate."

"About?"

"About what happened to Schmedler's clubs, which says that I don't have the knowledge and I don't have the power."

"Not," she says. "Maybe I can only speculate too, as you say, but I think you really know where they are."

"This is really a vote of no confidence. How many times do I have to deny any knowledge of what happened to the guy's golf clubs? You got a Bible, 'cause I'll put my hand on it and swear that as of this moment," I check my watch, "it's 12:32 a.m., and I don't have a clue where that bag is."

"Okay, enough is enough. You're not going to tell me, but I'm going to find out, sooner or later…but," she says, returning to the topic at hand, "I'm still not sure why you're here," she says straightforwardly.

"Bottomly rescued me from the funk of semi-pro ball and, surprisingly, I'm hustling a lot of money, but what I really enjoy is collaborating with Moon and playing in the Lounge. I guess the only thing that's bothersome is that there isn't anything down the road."

"How could you be playing semi-pro if you couldn't see?"

"I guess my instincts kept me from being a complete embarrassment and the most of the pitches were slow and predictable but I knew it was a dead end."

"I kind of feel that way now," she says somewhat quietly. "I often think it would be nice to have some direction or goal rather than the day in, day out."

"Like you said, you've got the kids, and you could always go back to being a bookkeeper."

"Not really. Daddy's not in the best of health, and I need a job that lets me tend to him as well as the kids, so I guess I'll just have to stick with short-range goals for the moment."

"Me, too," I say supportively, "and the shortest-range goal I can think of is dinner tomorrow night at Morgan's. Let's drink to that," I say as I offer my VO tumbler which is immediately met with a clink from her Bacardi glass.

"To Saturday," she says. We both take sips of our drinks and she looks at me over the lip of her glass. Things seem to be less icy than our last couple of conversations, so I send one up the flagpole.

"Did you just *kiss me with your smile?"*

"I don't think so," she replies without missing a beat.

Well, it could have been worse. She could have just flat out said no. Bottom line…bad move, right? You bet, and I can't imagine what the fuck I was thinking about.

VII

WEEKENDS AND FROZEN HORSES

Hey, we seek out the thrill of a pleasure or two,
but we milk it dry, then there's nothing to do.

Weekends are the worst and this one is off to an even more lousy start what with the way Sam and I had gone our quiet and separate ways after the fizzled conversation in the Lounge last night. Yeah, I know we're going to have dinner but I'm apprehensive about this close the book thing. Anyway, just to throw some salt in the wound, I'm watching a commercial that's telling me how AMF makes weekends more fun. I don't know why they even run the damn spots on the weekend. Maybe you can figure it out for me. If weekends are supposed to be for fun, then we should be somewhere having fun, right? Preferably with an item mass produced by AMF, right, like maybe an Earl Anthony bowling ball? I'll bet you're wondering what AMF stands for. Okay, maybe not…but I got curious once and looked it up. Actually, it stands for American Machine and Foundry and that sure as hell doesn't sound like a business that would make bowling balls and recreational equipment.

The company was started by a guy who invented the first automated cigarette machine but after World War II, it was grow or die…so he perfected the automatic AMF Pinspotter which turned bowling into the most participative, competitive sport in America. Then he got into bicycles and all kinds of stuff. So, how's that for a piece of trivial entrepreneur bullshit? Well, it's 1:00 p.m. on a bright and clear Saturday, and the black and white thirteen-inch TV I'm watching is made by Panasonic, not AMF.

My point is that in order to see the commerical on what a fun-filled weekend is you have to be sitting on your ass in front of a television set. Maybe a bar, you say? Okay, so when's the last time you had a glass of AMF beer? A 'nooner' you ask? Sure, and I suppose your bedmate had those three small, AMF red letters tattooed in some strategic spot! Hell, I don't know everything, but then I'm sure you've figured that out by now so maybe I'm wrong. I guess AMF could install a four-inch battery-powered set on top of the combined speedometer/tachometer on my Yamaha Verago, and then I could have fun on the weekend while AMF reminds me to have fun on the weekend, and so on and so on.

Finally, the commercial being piped through the Panasonic, which is on the far end of the bag room counter, fades to black, and Keith Jackson appears and informs us that Alabama has a first and ten on Auburn's twenty yardline. One of the 'good ole boys' rivalries is once again underway on a sunny autumn day and, as usual, the Crimson Tide is really putting it to the other guys. I say other guys because Auburn has had the unique distinction of changing names three times in recent years. At first, they were the Plainsmen, which is easy to understand when viewing the panoramas that surround the small, sleepy college town sixty or so miles east of Montgomery. Then, they became the War Eagles, which might have had something to do with the Choctaws who dwelled in the general area but who are now clustered around Philadelphia, Mississippi. No matter, the grayish bird in that large cage on the campus seems to dispel that particular theory. Finally, today, the War Eagles from the plains of Alabama call themselves the Tigers, and I'm at a total loss to explain that one unless they just flat had to get away from anything controversial like the Stanford Indians who are now the Stanford Cardinal. To return to my original point of departure, the "other guys" have had little success with the five-time defending SEC champs and today isn't going to change that trend.

Like the song says, "*We seek out the thrill of a pleasure or two*," so the way I survive Saturday, without AMF, is to play the football pool and also get down a few bets upstairs with the Turk on the ponies and the dogs. More or less, the pool is recreational, but the racetrack is serious business. A lot of equine owners frequent the Presidential, and rather than hit us with folding green, they give us some inside dope which, surprisingly enough, pays off on a fairly regular basis as long as you don't get too greedy. The tip is generally the same, and it's simply that the owner's horse is out to win that day. Ya see, there are a lot of reasons horses run a race, and they don't always involve trying to win, unless the race is one of the biggies like the Kentucky Derby or the Preakness. Sometimes a trainer wants to see how his horse runs on the rail or from the outside or in the mud or in traffic. Maybe he wants to see if the sleek thoroughbred can come from behind or if he can hold a lead down the stretch. The thing that's important is when an owner tells you he's instructed the jockey to do his best to win the race you've got a better than fighting chance to cash a winning ticket.

With the dogs, you have a completely different ballgame, because now you have to think in terms of losing, not winning. I know, you're confused but hang with me on this. Let's say a Class A dog is doing pretty well but not winning, so the owner wants to drop him to Class B. To do that, the dog is going to have to get beaten badly a few times, so the trick is to slow him down so the stewards will drop him a class. Okay, after that, you get the hound back up to full speed, so he can murder the competition in just one Class B race and the owner can make a killing at the ticket window. All's well and good, but how does one slow a dog down and get him dropped into a lower class, you ask? Very simple! If you want the dog to have a bad run, just let him jump the ladies all afternoon. The jury seems to be out on the question of human athletes engaging in sexual activities prior to a physical contest of skill, but if you let a greyhound mount and hump all day, chances are it's going to take a lot of the play out of him.

Now, if you're not overly concerned with his pleasures or don't happen to have any bitches in heat on hand, the easiest thing to do is throw him in a pool and let him dog paddle for a few hours. Unless he's one hell of an animal, doing that all but guarantees a slow time for the evening's race. All this inside information is great, but truth be known, this season the dogs have cost me about eight hundred bucks, and I'd like to think I'm about even on the ponies. It's just a shame that these little 'pleasures' designed to get one through the weekend have to be rationalized as investments in maintaining one's sanity.

A roar goes up from the Panasonic, and Keith Jackson is drowned out by the allegedly neutral crowd stuffed into the stadium in the Vulcan city of Birmingham. The Crimson Tide has scored again and all but assured itself of another Iron Bowl trophy, so I mentally put the game in the "got right" column. But it's not going to win me the pool, because no one was going to pick the Plainsmen/War Eagles/Tigers to upset Bama today. Maybe Georgia's gonna end their streak. Even Florida was making some noise up 'til last month when late in the game against Georgia in the greatest outdoor cocktail party in the world, held annually at the Gator Bowl in Jacksonville, the boys in orange and blue went for a fourth and one on the Dog's twenty-nine yardline. Well, as the saying goes, hindsight ain't worth a plug nickel and that play cost them the the game, giving the Ray Goff- quarterbacked Dogs three in a row over the hapless Gators who are just flat never gonna win an SEC Championship. So the Dawgs are gonna have to keep trucken' between the hedges in Athens to halt the legendary Bear Bryant.

The same thing goes for the current winning streaks of Southern California in the PAC-8, Arizona State's dominance of the WAC, and

Oklahoma's jinx on the Big Red Cornhuskers from Nebraska. So the trick is to play about seventeen or eighteen favorites and then go for two or three upsets. Well, so much for the science of sports gambling, because Marcus has just come into the bag room and is smiling ear-to-ear which is very unusual for him.

"Don't tell me," I say before he can open his mouth. "The weatherman is calling for a freak storm, and everyone can go home."

"Better," he says, looking something like Sylvester the Cat who's hoping Tweety gets careless while perched on the top of his cage.

"A rich widow wants to buy you a drink?"

He shrugs and nods his head from side to side. "Not even close."

"Okay, then," I continue, "I'll throw out the widow, concentrate on the 'buy' part, and figure it has something to do with money. Yes?"

"That's the way to think that one through, D Jack. That old college brain of yours does work occasionally."

"Is it a share-the-wealth kind of deal?" I inquire excitedly.

"Absolutely," he responds like a father about to do a wayward son a grand favor. He takes a deep breath and wraps his fingers around the sides of his open windbreaker. "D Jack," he says gleefully, "I'm pretty sure I've got the tip of all tips. We are simply going to clean up today. As a matter of fact, I might even leave this place for a brief skiing vacation in Breckenridge," he concludes with a smug, uptown air.

"Bullshit! You can't ski and you hate the cold. But speak to me, Marcus, speak to me, man!" He moves behind the counter top and sits down on the one redwood lawn chair I keep for really slow times while I assume my more customary seat on top of the polished counter. His hands rest comfortably on the wide arms of the chair, and he crosses his legs in such a way that the flared blue trouser cuff of his left leg is resting across his right knee.

"You've heard of Edson Wainwright, I assume," Marcus begins.

"Sure," I nod knowingly, "inherited money, playboy, friendly type, horses. He doesn't pass around much cash, but he's pretty free with…the word!" I say as I come alive. "Is that it, Marcus? You got a hot one from Wainwright?"

"The best and hottest you can get, Pirate," Marcus answers with that cool air of someone who knows something someone else wants to know or put in another way, the "I know some shit you don't" syndrome.

"Fine," I say as the corners of my mouth turn down in a futile attempt to exhibit indifference. "So you gonna spill or play games?"

His hand comes off the arms of the lawn chair, and he clasps his fingers around his left knee. “I wouldn’t kid you with this one, Pirate. This is the honest-to-God big enchilada.”

“That’s the second time I’ve heard this, and I’m really glad that lady luck has bestowed on you her warmest smile,” I say impatiently, “but, for the last time, are you going to get to it or what?”

Marcus still has this shit-eatin’ grin on his face. “Here’s what happened,” he finally says. “I was just looking over the sheets in the office about a half an hour ago, and Wainwright comes up and asks me how I’m doing. I guess he had just finished his round and was on his way to lunch. I gave him the usual crap about how it was a nice sunny Thanksgiving weekend, you know, just small talk and stuff. Then he says I’ve been treating him really well so far this season, and he wants to give me a tip on the ninth at Tropical Park. Then he tells me, with a wink, that Garlido is going wire-to-wire.”

“Isn’t that the name of a cigar?”

“I don’t know but who cares? Don’t interrupt! Wainwright tells me his horse has never run better than seventh in his life and that he hasn’t even been involved in a stretch run. He just winked again, so I’m figuring this is going to be Garlido’s one shot at fame,” Marcus concludes.

“Fame or the glue factory, huh? Did you check it out with the Turk?” I inquire.

“Yes, Garlido’s on the rail and the early afternoon line has him going off at one hundred ten-to-one.”

I whistle with an open jaw, which is one hell of a trick, and grip the sides of the counter feigning dizziness. “You’re putting me on!” I say with my shielded eyes wide open. “That would be a veritable gold mine if he comes in. How much are you putting down?”

Marcus uncrosses his legs, stretches, digs into the front right pocket of his beige windbreaker, and brings out a wad of bills. “Oh,” he says nonchalantly, “I think I’ll go a couple of hundred on the nose.”

“Wow! That’s a little steep for me,” I mumble thinking ahead to tonight and Sam, and Morgan’s, figuring I might want to spot her a Grand Cru Graves like maybe a Chateau Carbonnieux. Okay, smart ass, don’t even ask how I know about something as cultured as French white wine vintages; however, I’ll simply remind you that there was a time when I, ever so briefly, traveled in high circles!

I ease off the counter and reach under it for my Fuente cigar box, then rifle through the bills, and come up with four tens and two fivers, which I hand to Marcus. “How about getting this down for me also on the nose?”

Marcus takes hold of the arms of the chair and pulls his slender frame to his feet. "Will do, D Jack. I just don't want to hear from you, at least for a few days, that I never do anything for you, okay? But," he adds, "I will have to charge you a small fee."

"You do that, and I'll rat ya out to the Turk, who wouldn't be too happy with the idea that someone else around here is getting some money making book," I say jokingly.

"You know that I wouldn't dare step on the Turk's toes. I just thought for my services you would inform me of the location of Schmedler's clubs!"

"Choke on it, Marcus," I say reaching for my fifty bucks. "I didn't know yesterday morning, and I don't know today, but now that you mentioned it, have you heard anything?" Marcus puts up his palm and, with the other hand, slides my hard-earned dollars, along with his own cash, into his windbreaker.

"I'm just pulling your leg, D Jack. The word from the hotel is that Schmedler stormed out of the lobby early yesterday afternoon, and no one has seen him since. The big black Lincoln limo and the poor slob who polishes the damn thing twice a day have been noticeably absent from all the valet parking lots, so we're thinking he might be on his way back to San Francisco."

"And Rhoda?"

"No one has paid the bill, and last night she was sipping drinks poolside with a guy half her age and twice Schmedler's size."

"No glass throwing, I assume?"

"I'm told she looked very happy, D Jack. So maybe, you think, it's her last hurrah?"

"Could be, Marcus, but I'd be more inclined to think that, seeing as he's gone and she isn't, Hans may have married into Rhoda's money."

"You know, I'll bet you're right. And just think," he continues as he scratches his head, "none of this would have happened if he had been a half-way decent human being after running over Ferdie. There is definitely a God in heaven," he concludes.

"We'll talk about God after the ninth at Tropical, even though I have a hunch that we're not gonna need Him. You got any ideas as to how this one might be in the bag?"

"I don't have the foggiest, but I sure felt pretty good with Wainwright winking at me when he said Garlido was going to take the one good shot at it. But I just don't know," Marcus says apparently lost in thought. "They've got to have the 'fix' in this thing somehow." He suddenly lifts his head and his eyes return to their normally bright condition. "Well, I better get upstairs and get the money down with the Turk. I'll tell him the two fifty is all mine, so he doesn't think too many of us are getting in on the action."

I look at Marcus and give him a sarcastic smile. "Sure, you always lay down two and half C-notes on a nag." He doesn't seem to hear me, and I gather he's lapsed back into wishful thinking. "Garlido," he mutters as he heads for the door, "I sure hope this horse can smoke."

I expect him to laugh with his play on words but am surprised to see him maintain that faraway look as he heads out. I guess the thought of ten grand can make most people trip out but not the Edson Wainwrights of the world. That kind of money probably represents little more than a Saturday afternoon something to do, a minor distraction, but I doubt AMF can compete with that kind of recreation. Speaking of distractions, it occurs to me there's some grumbling coming from the back of the bag room.

It's Johnny Red, and he's still bent over the sinks, even though most of the clubs have come back in and been stored in the wooden stalls that run the length of the sidewalls in the bag room. Red had hoped to be walking by Thanksgiving and actually went nine holes Thursday but his legs gave him a lot of trouble and he's been back at the sinks. At the moment, he seems to be cursing a three wood full of sand. Imagine some clunker out there trying to blast his way out of trap with a three wood. Of course, maybe it didn't happen that way. More than likely some guy hooked or sliced a fairway shot and, in a rage, hurled his club into a bunker, because golfers just have this thing about throwing clubs after a lousy shot. I heard somewhere that some pro was asked why he was using a new putter, and he answered that his last one didn't float too well.

Anyway, it just amazes me that the longer I'm here, the more creative the players are when it comes to venting their frustrations on club heads, and shafts, and even grips if they really blow their cool. All in all, I find that most of these poor bastards don't have much fun. I'll never understand why people pay lots of good money to be unhappy, and that goes double for those who watch rather than play.

Let me put it to you this way. I sure hope you're not one of those kind of people who goes to the ballpark, and your home team is on the short end of the stick, so you yell and scream and get red-faced, and your chest starts to hurt and your dog and beer don't taste so good, and, God forbid, you go home and take a swing at somebody! Ya know. I just can't begin to tell ya how much of this I saw when playing away games. We were good and more often that not won on the road and it was okay if the fans were heckling me, but all that yelling and screaming directed toward the hometown boys just never made much sense. I mean I don't think AMF owns a sports franchise, but those people do have it right when they tell you to get out there and have fun, rather than get headaches and bellyaches and go home shit-faced with your day ruined. What I mean is that sport should be a pleasant distraction, a fun diversion, not something that rings your bell and drives you to your local pharmacist or worse yet your sympathetic psychiatrist. Speaking of rings and bells, the phone is making noise, so I'll leave you to your own thoughts on fan behavior.

"Presidential bag room, can I be of assistance to you?"

"Is that you Devon?" Even if I didn't recognize her voice, I'd know it was Sam because only she and my dad have ever called me Devon...and Billy, but he doesn't count. "Hi Sam, are ya having a busy day?"

"Yes, I am, but I'm due for a break and I thought I might come down for a minute or two. Is that okay?"

"Sure. It's pretty slow right now with people resting up for a hot time Saturday night. You know how it is over the weekends at the Big House. You rather I come up?"

"No, I'll come down to the bag room. There are too many people up here having fancy lunches and early afternoon drinks."

"Terrific, I'll lay out the silver and fine china."

"Silly," she says as she hangs up. I grab some change out of the cigar box and head over to the cart area where there are half a dozen vending machines up against the wall. I pop in an assortment of coins and head back to the bag room fortified with a bottle of pop and a bag of nuts. I reach under the counter and retrieve two six-ounce tumblers and am just placing them on the counter when Sam comes through the door, her black and purple uniform swirling just a bit.

"Hi," she says quietly. "I hope I didn't interrupt one of your transactions?"

Ya know guys, I think it's about time I try to lighten up. "No problem at all, little lady," I respond with my best W. C. Fields, "and just to mark the occasion I am prepared to demonstrate my expertise in the fine art of mixology. You can have a VO, water, and ice; a water with some VO; or some ice and VO. In the event none of the above appeals to your delicate palate, I offer a shot of VO and ginger ale, and, of course, to complement this libation, I offer a fine selection of nuts, nuts, or nuts."

She smiles and shakes her strawberry-blonde hair. "You seem to know about all these things so I'll leave the selection to you."

I hear a chuckle behind me, so I turn to face Red who is at the sinks, grinning from ear to ear. "Hey Red, ya want a boost?"

"That would be real nice, D Jack," he says with the look of someone who knows he's intruding but has risked it anyway. I reach under the counter for a third tumbler and splash in some VO, knowing Red likes it 'neat' when he doesn't have to foot the bill. I walk to the sinks and receive an appreciative nod before heading back to the counter where Sam has decided to try her hand at mixing the drinks.

"I've got a supper shift ahead of me tonight, so I thought it would be better if I mixed my own."

"Some deal," I say a little dismayed. "This is the first opportunity I've had to mix you a drink, and you throw me a vote of no confidence."

"Maybe you can mix me a drink Monday night."

"What's this Monday night stuff?" I ask confused. "Why not tonight before we head out to Morgan's?" Her face seems to cloud over as she adopts an air of concern. "That's why I came down. Daddy's not feeling well, so I'm going home right after my shift. Ron said he'd close for him, so that worked out okay."

Again, mass confusion on my part, because I can't get a feel for whether I'm relieved or disappointed. I gotta tell you that I just can't shake this hangdog notion that Morgan's might be the designated place for the final chapter in this less-than-epic saga. Now don't get in my face on this. You have to remember that I knew Samatha as well as a person can know somebody, and among other things, she believed tomorrow was always a new day, which she ushered in by finding a certain mental equilibrium. That may sound a bit like engaging in compromise or even selling out, but make no mistake about it; she's very capable of playing hardball and, in baseball savvy, knows how to line up the barrel of the bat with the cowhide. Need I remind you that I all but took the count when she leveled me in Lakeland eight years ago? To this day, I still can't fathom the emotion that was behind that punch. I know this girl and, if you remember, just a few nights ago, she said she wanted to close the book. Yeah, I know, I seem obsessed with beating a dead horse here.

"So, you want to go to Morgan's Monday night then?" I ask

"I was hoping you'd say that because I asked and know Moon doesn't play in the Bengal on Monday nights."

"Yeah, they have this terrific Roberta Flack wannabe who is knocken the socks off the room. But on Mondays I have a standing racquetball game with Charley the Boss. We play some singles but more often play doubles together and whack some guests of the House, but we're usually done by 9:00. So, we could catch a late dinner if you like."

"So you and Mr. Berston are pretty good?"

"We won the state open doubles title last year," I respond modestly.

"What does open mean?"

"It means the players can be any age."

"And you two won that?"

"Yeah, and went on to the nationals in Seattle, but we got hosed in the quarter finals."

"How are you able to compete at that level?" she asks seriously.

"Charley's damn good, that's how."

"That's not what I meant," she says as she looks at my sunglasses.

"I'm right-handed and play the left side which helps with the vision problem. Charley's left-handed, so it's easy for him to take the right side and also play everything down the middle."

"Oh," she says, although I'm not sure she soaked up my explanation, "so maybe if I can finish my side work in time, I can come watch the two of you play before we head out for dinner. Will that be okay?"

"Fine with me," I say agreeably. "There are glass walls so you could sit outside and watch the games."

"That will be nice. Dolph and I used to play three-wall on the old outside courts in Gainesville, but it will be nice to see what the pros look like."

"Whoa," I say palms up. "I'm no pro. But now that I think of it, I usually get paid if I'm lucky."

"I should have known. Another bet."

"Not if it's just me and Charley, but generally, when it's doubles, the guests want to put a side bet on the action."

"And you? That's all you ever do? Play ball for money, I mean?"

Terrific! I just told her that Charley and I just play for the pure joy of it. So, why is it that when a conversation with her seems to be going okay, another zinger comes into the picture? "Not so, Sam, yeah, I got paid to play baseball, but all I ever wanted to do was just be a part of the game. The last time I laced up my spikes, like I told you, I was playing in Miami Stadium for chump change and free beers, and I'd do it tomorrow if I could. Wrapping my hands around a good piece of Louisville lumber beats the hell out of handing a driver to some pretentious captain of industry."

"Oops, I hit a nerve. Sorry."

She seems genuinely apologetic. "So," she continues, "are you and Mr. Berston going to win?"

"Can't miss," I respond with confidence. "Tell you what. Not that we ever ate it, but do you like duck?"

"With cherries, not orange sauce," she responds. "Why?"

"Fine, with cherries, because if we win, that's what I'll order for you at Morgan's. But if we lose, you have to buy me a Delmonico steak."

"No deal. You're supposed to spring regardless."

"True enough, but you can't blame a guy for trying to bend the rules. Anyway, I'll see if I can avoid the last shift on the phones so maybe we could have a drink beforehand." I look down at the two untouched six-ounce glasses and hand her the obviously watered-down cocktail. "Here's looken at you, kid," I say in a better-than-average Bogie.

She takes a sip of her VO and ginger and wrinkles her nose. "That's not my fav," she says as she gets to her feet. "I've got to go back upstairs," she adds as she puts down the glass and turns to go. "See you Monday."

"Okay," I say to her back.

Maybe I should have asked her if anyone had told her about our little TGIS party, but for some reason decided not to, probably because I think on a 1 to10 conversation scale, we started at a 1 with our initial chat or, more accurately, our confrontation. But since then, things don't seem to be getting any higher than maybe a 4 or 5…but it's better than a stinken' 1!

Not to change the subject, but now that I think of it, I forgot to mention that on late Sunday afternoons, when things are slow, we have a "Thank God it's Sunday" fling. But you'll be there tomorrow if you like so enough said for the moment. Anyway, how do you think I'm gonna do with Garlido? If you want my opinion, I'd say I'll do about as well as the Plainsmen/War Eagles/Tigers, meaning…Keith Jackson is doing a wrap-up and the Tide has done a number on Auburn. Gotta go; phone's ringing.

"Presidential bag room, can I be of service to you?"

"Not really," Marcus says. "I just thought you might want to know the race goes off at 5:05."

"Thanks much. Did the Turk say anything to you when you put down the dollars?"

"He gave me a strange kind of sly smile. I guess he must be in on it, too."

"God, I'll never make it to the 6:00 track news on Channel 4."

"You won't have to, D Jack. I saw Wainwright in the dining room, and he beckoned me over to his table. He said a friend was going to call him immediately after the race and give him the blow-by-blow. Soon as I get it, I'll hit the bag room or find you somewhere...but it'll be easier if you're in the bag room."

"That's great Marcus. I'll just hang here after 5:00 and help Red finish up. Then I'll start polishing a large bag, so we'll have plenty of space to store all our winnings." Marcus rings off, and I start wondering how I'm going to kill off the afternoon.

*

Nothing worked! I cleaned clubs, picked up balls, did some gofer stuff with the conventioneers, but nothing worked! Every time I looked at one of the big clocks around the place, they all seemed broken. You know what I mean, the God damn big hand on a clock never moves when you're counting time?

Well, somehow it must have moved because Marcus has just come down into the bag room. I'm eyeing him from his sparse hairline down to the tops of his brown and whites, and I just can't read a thing. It's almost as if he's practiced total neutrality for this potentially glorious moment. No elation. No despair. Nuthin!

"Give me the words, Marcus," I plead. He shakes his head and holds up his hands. "I'm going to give it to you exactly the way Wainwright shared it with me."

My blood pressure must be approaching a dangerous level. "I don't care how you do it," I say with clenched fists, "just get on with it!"

"Well," Marcus begins, "Garlido broke on top and was leading into the first turn by a neck. Coming onto the backstretch, he opened it up and widened it out to about four lengths running smooth and easy. He led through the turn and at the top of the stretch was still ahead by three big ones. The pack started to close him down a bit, but at the sixteenth pole, he still had 'em by two full lengths." Marcus pauses, still completely neutral.

"And then? And then???" I'm not begging, but I'm getting close. Marcus mumbles. I can't hear him. "What did you say?" Now I'm begging.

"I said he finished seventh as usual," Marcus utters as his body slumps with the effort of the last few words.

"Seventh!" I bellow. "How the fuck can that happen? How can a horse be leading by two lengths at the sixteenth pole and finish seventh?"

"I'll tell you how it happened," Marcus says, finally showing just a flash of emotion. "What happened was that his legs thawed."

Sheer disbelief, what can I tell you? "His legs fucken what?"

"They thawed, dammit all. They thawed!"

"What kinda shit is that?" I explode venting my anger at Marcus, but the old man returns to his calm state and seems resigned to our bitter fate.

"Wainwright told me the reason the horse never runs well is because he has a lot of pain in his legs, something akin to shin splints. So they wrapped iced towels around his legs for a few hours, and the jockey was instructed to hit him wire-to-wire."

"So what happened?"

"What happened, D Jack, was that it was seventy-five degrees out there, high humidity, and wet. The track was a quagmire. The best I can figure out is that somewhere around the sixteenth pole, Garlido's legs thawed out, he felt the pain, and he just flat quit. And that is that," Marcus says and leaves without so much as another word.

I want to say something, to the walls, to you, just something, anything, but I'm just totally wiped. All I know is that AMF is entertaining the world and I just dropped fifty fucken bucks on a fucken frozen, thawed-out horse! Where's a God-damned bowling ball when you need one!"

VIII

DRUNKS ON THE FAIRWAY

A thought, a sound, a thing
emoting, orchestrating, conducting,
perceptions of reality…..

Do you know how I *perceive reality*? No? Okay, so I'm posing the big 'what is real?' metaphysical question; ya know…the heavy stuff. If it's real today, will it be real tomorrow? Is it real if you can't see it or hear it, like a tree falling in the forest? Is something that's real for you equally real for me? Now if you're a postmodernist, you might just say, fuck it; who cares? Well, I'm not a postmodernist and I care, so I'm gonna give you the real deal on this thing. In its simplest form, reality ain't real! I'm not even gonna buy into the pragmatic point of view that reality, with regard to an idea, or maybe an object, is relative and practical, and only holds up for as long as it has any value and can withstand the test of consequences: if it works, it's good or true; if it doesn't work, it's bad or false. The reason I reject this bullshit is because at this very moment, I'm up to my ass in alligators trying to perceive the reality, or unreality, of the situation confronting me, namely, a dozen guys and half that many women clamoring for rental clubs.

"Excuse me for just a minute," I say with clenched teeth as I dial Marcus' extension.

"Starting times," he says pleasantly, which I'm not about to return because I'm really heated up. "Marcus, I thought you told me the next convention group wouldn't be in until Monday." His groan seems designed to enlighten a wayward child.

"That's not what I said, D Jack. What I said was that they would be in on Sunday but *probably* wouldn't hit us until Monday. I guess some of them have jumped the gun and decided Sunday is a day to spend with a driver rather than a prayer book."

"Some of them?" I exclaim. "I'm looking at four or five foursomes down here. This is unreal! How are you gonna get 'em all out?"

Marcus reeks with confidence. "Nothing to it, the first tee has been clear for the past forty-five minutes and the whole front nine has been slow since around 1:30. You just fix them up with some clubs, and I'll help Ralph get the carts ready. And don't forget to see how many drinkers and walkers you've got."

"Grand," I reply, wishing he could see the smirk on my face as I hang up the phone. "Red, gonna need ya for a few minutes." Johnny leaves three or four irons in the sink and grabs a towel in order to dry his hands and forearms. He rolls down the sleeves of his frayed, long sleeve shirt, which has yellowed with age, and carefully buttons each cuff. Hey, we may be brokendown ex-jocks, but you're not going to find any intentional slobs around the Presidential. Red gives me a smile, thereby announcing he's ready to engage in whatever task I'm about to send his way. I know he hasn't been thrilled about being here, but as long as I can make it worthwhile, he continues to cooperate, and I can't ask for more than that. I turn to face the boozed-up mob on the other side of the bag room counter.

"Could I have your attention for a moment please?" I say loudly. No response; on to request two. "Anybody in here want a drink?" The noise and yells are all in the affirmative, just like a bar scene out of a B western movie filmed in Old Tucson.

"Okay then," I say feeling just a bit like a varsity cheerleader, "and it's all on the company as soon as we get you out on the course. First thing is the bags. How many of you need rentals…ladies first?" Two hands go up. "How many of you are southpaws?" The two hands, which collectively sport about six or seven awesome diamond rings, remain in the air. I look over my shoulder and ask Johnny Red to go get two ladies bags, both left-handed, and turn back to face the VIPs.

"Now, how many of you gentlemen need clubs?" This time eight hands go up. "And how many of you are lefties?" No hands go up. I paint on a "Phantom of the Opera" smile and head off to help Red with the remainder of the rentals, and then write one slip that charges two hundred and fifty bucks to the company.

"How many of you are walking and need a caddy?" It doesn't surprise me that there are no takers, because this group gives all the appearances of being fat and boozy. "So, we need maybe ten golf carts, right? One last thing, what are you people drinking today…Michelob, champagne, bourbon?"

A barrel-chested guy with a ruddy complexion yells at me so he can be heard above the din of his colleagues. "Just bring it all, mutha fucka!" he yells, and laughter and shrieks immediately follow his guttural command.

"The name is D Jack, sir," I say with a grin that now makes the phantom look like Howdy Doody.

"That's great, mutha fucka," he repeats with a wise-ass tone, his mouth twisted open. "Just let's have D Jack hijack us a whole load of booze." The laughter swells with his perceived witticism, so I figure this guy must be the company clown. I can just imagine the havoc he bestows on stewardesses and waitresses. Fuck all of 'em…I don't ruffle.

"Okay everybody. Grab your clubs and out the door and to the right." They're all laughing and shuffling along like a herd of Arizona scrub cattle, so it takes a few minutes for them to clear the area. I turn and look at Red who is frowning. Like a lot of guys in his situation, as well as mine, the frivolity of the spoiled and obnoxious well-to-do is just a bunch of cheap shit. The pleasures of life are few and far between, and it's pretty well understood that for most of us, the glory times are long gone golden memories of the diamond, the ring, or the saddle. The reality of our situation is that we had those moments and can still relish in them with an exaggerated satisfaction that meant going "beyond the gusto" in the Schlitz ads. But like that Milwaukee brew, the head goes flat pretty quickly while the perceived reality for these convention executive cluster fucks is that life is great and the glory days are here and will last forever.

I glance over at the black and white TV just in time to catch the NFL halftime scores flashing on the screen. "Well, I'll be damned, Red. The Tampa Bay Bucs are up by seventeen." Another score hits the screen, and I am equally amazed to see that the Giants are two touchdowns ahead of the Cowboys. So I figure I'm dead in the pro football pool today, but don't you be getting the idea that between football and a fucken frozen horse I'm a genuine loser or some poor soul who has been crossed by some shooting star. Let me quickly insert a tidy piece of information that will not allow such a perception to become a reality on your part. It just so happens I won the college football pool yesterday by picking six upsets, including Arizona State's second consecutive victory over non-conference Southern Cal, and the take was two hundred bucks more than my setbacks on Garlido and Lena Dawson. Loser my ass!

Speaking of which, I might get that part of my body kicked if I don't get the booze cart filled up and rolling. Generally, the sponsoring organization picks up the tab for the boozers on the course, and the pseudo-urbane executives, who enjoyed heckling me a few moments ago, expect to be treated in such royal fashion. I grab the phone, dial in four familiar numbers, and await the customary two or three rings.

"Bengal Lounge, this is Ron."

"D Jack, Stunt. I need to get the booze cart loaded up, so can you get Chico and a couple of the guys to run some stuff down here?"

"Name it, D Jack. I'll write up the tab and send it over to the office."

"Great. Give me three cases of Michelob, two bottles of Korbel, three fifths of Jack Black, two J&B, and two bottles of VO. I think maybe a case of Perrier and lots of ice will do and maybe a couple bottles of pop."

"You sure you need two bottles of your favorite Canadian whisky?" he asks jokingly.

"Hey, come on; these guys are from Toronto. I think they're entitled to their national drink of choice."

"My ass, but give me about fifteen minutes. Why don't you have one of the guys pull the cart up to Marcus' office and make it easier for Chico and the boys?"

"We'll take care of it, Ron. By the by, have you seen anything more of Lena Dawson?"

"I'm pretty sure her sugar daddy is still playing the Main Room, but I haven't seen her bare ass since Wednesday."

"You were that bad, huh, Stunt?"

"Naw, but she was. I mean she stripped like she was in the lady's lockers after a tough tennis match and just stretched out on her back and spread her legs. Pointed to her shaved snatch without even breaking a smile and then just put her arms to her sides. You could smell the weed she'd been toking from twenty feet, and I figured I was going to get about as much movement as a thirteen-year-old introducing himself to a knothole. But I knew I had to get that topside shot, so I just picked her up and sat her down. Then I asked her if she wanted to wiggle around or grind or do something, for God's sake. Even though she was in la-la land, she managed to mumble, "Why?" Hell, once I knew I had the photo, I faked a coughing spell, and by the time I got out of the can she was totally zonked. Naw, Pirate, I didn't even get a chance to be lousy. Haven't seen her since and don't want to."

"I guess you just can't beat those hot-to-trot nineteen-year-olds, can you, Stunt?"

"Yeah, and she was French, but then, give me a horny forty something broad anytime and to hell with where she comes from. Anyway, I'll get the booze going, and I'll catch you later at the TGIS."

"Thanks much. I'm really gonna to need to kick back after I get through playing bartender for this crowd."

"Start before you get here," he suggests.

"That's a done deal!"

*

After listening to Stunt's less than erotic sexual adventure with Dawson, I got the herd up and running and have been playing nursemaid for the first seven holes. Right now I'm sitting off to the side of the eighth that's a long par five with a dogleg left. The turn is at the top of a hill so the golfer has to tee off looking at an incline and usually tries to get the shot up and over with a bit of a hook. There are no bunkers but the fairway is lined with trees and underbrush. The center and front right of the green is nestled behind a small pond that gives the golfer second thoughts about trying to drive the green in two. Even Bottomly plays it up short and then likes to use a wedge to "butterfly it with sore feet" close enough for a solid attempt at a birdie. I've never seen anyone drive it in two, so you have to get the iron shot in for an eagle. To the best of my knowledge, no guest has ever done it. The way these bozos have been playing that statistic will certainly not fall today. Among other things, the air is heavy with humidity, the moisture is slowing down the flight of the ball, and there's a chance of thunderstorms later today. Of course, if it really gets ugly, the players can invoke the Trevino principle. For as Supermex once put it, "When I'm on a golf course and it starts to rain and lightening, I hold up my one iron 'cause I know even God can't hit a one iron."

I'm sitting on the booze cart next to Ruby who fought in the post-war era and was one of those tough Jewish fighters who competed in the welterweight and middleweight divisions. Although he was one hell of a campaigner, he had a rep for hitting the canvas in the later rounds, and for some weird reason, the referee who usually counted him out at the Garden in New York was Ruby Goldstein. And you thought his tag had something to do with precious gems.

"Come on, boychick," he growls. "Let's cut through da path and see if that other group is okay." His voice is hoarse and gravelly, something Pastrano would love; his lips are thick and, eventhough he undoubtedly shaved this morning, they're already surrounded by light-gray stubble that covers his sandpaper face.

"I think we better stay with this foursome, Ruby. One or two more drinks and then we'll probably be able to forget about 'em for the rest of the day."

"Where are deez guys from anyway?" Ruby asks.

"Some group called ORGAN."

Ruby squints and his cheeks all but cover the narrow slits of his eyes. "What's that?"

"ORGAN," I repeat. "The Organization of Ranchers, Gardeners, and American Naturalists, which I'm wondering about because I think they're from Canada."

"What da fuck does that mean? Anyway, deez guys don't look like ranchers to me."

"They're not. The rancher part just gives them an excuse to wear hats and boots."

"Ya think so?"

"How the hell do I know, Ruby?" I answer with a laugh. Hesitantly, he joins in, looking rather perplexed. Regardless, the two ORGAN execs and their ladies, currently under our scrutiny, have all teed off, and the bulky, ruddy loudmouth and his wife are heading toward us down the right side of the fairway. The other two have hit long, and their shots crested the rise. The obnoxious guy's lady hops off the cart about twenty yards from us, takes out what looks like a four wood, and actually tees up the ball while the slob grunts his disapproval. Much to my surprise, she gives him the finger, turns her back, addresses the ball, and hits a slider which undoubtedly has caught the rough over the hill to the far right side on the turn of the dogleg. The guy grabs a three wood and, without so much as a practice swing, drives his shot a little longer but in the same general vicinity. Then, both get back on the cart, head over to us, and all but create a fender bender upon arriving.

"Hey, mutha," he commands. "Put two ice cubes in a glass and fill it with scotch. Then do the same for the lady here."

I hop off the cart, swing around to the tail end, and quickly put a few cubes into some tumblers, splashing in a healthy dose of J&B. I move towards the lady, but loudmouth reaches in front of her, grabs one of the drinks, downs it in two gulps, and then grins at her as if he just conquered Mt. Everest. She returns the equally stupid-looking grin and holds her hand out to me without so much as a look my way. So I hand her the other drink, and she matches loudmouth's feat, takes a deep breath, and drops the tumbler on the finely mowed fairway. "Shall we?" she purrs. He floors the pedal and the electric cart lurches up the incline and off to the right side as I lean over to retrieve the empty tumblers.

"Doze other people waving at us through da trees," Ruby says as I get back on the cart and head left to take the shortcut on a path through the underbrush to get back on the fairway on the other side of the hill. This couple has been very polite, even though they too have been drinking. However, I figure they must really be able to hold their booze, because the lady hasn't done anything worse than a single bogey and the guy has two pars and a bird. As we pull up to them, the guy is wiping sweat off his brow with a small hand towel.

"What do you think?" he asks sincerely. I barely hesitate because his tee shot was a real boomer.

"Two iron with little slice. The wind down there is blowing across from right to left, and the way you hit, I'm pretty sure you can carry the distance."

"Makes sense," he says approvingly as he takes his iron out of the bag and addresses the ball. He takes a few easy swings and then freezes like a brown and white Lewellyn Setter coming onto a covey of quail. After about five seconds, he takes a long, stiff backswing and follows through very smoothly, eyes down. The ball takes to the air on a straight line and seems to want to go off to the right. But as predicted, the wind is holding the line of flight, and it drops about ten yards short of the pond, dead center. His lady takes out her four-wood and all but repeats his shot, except she gets a few yards closer to the water hazard. She isn't nearly as big as her old man so I figure she must have some awfully good wrist action to hit that distance, even with a wood. She looks like the type that takes a lot of lessons while hubby is showing the boys at ORGAN how to turn a dollar.

We follow them down to the two white balls that stand out clearly against the green grass which is so beautiful you'd think it's been shot through with food coloring. We go off to the left side in order to be out of the way when the other two hit off the top of the hill, but they still aren't in sight…must be struggling with the trees and underbrush up there, looking for their wayward Wilsons.

"Can I get you something, ma'am?" I ask with a polite grin. She returns a smile that seems warm and natural on her face. "A glass of champagne would be very nice."

I slide off the seat under which I have placed a half-dozen fluted glasses in a tightly packed, reinforced cardboard box. One bottle of Korbel is gone, so I do a little dog-and-pony show while opening the second bottle and slowly pour the effervescent liquid into the tulip-shaped glass.

"Thanks," she says, just a tad on the husky side.

"And you, sir?"

"Nothing for me right now, thanks," he says as he looks back up the hill. "I wonder what the hell is keeping those two?"

"Probably lost der balls," Ruby grunts, and out of the corner of my eye, I see the lady suppress a laugh, but her old man is getting hot and has missed the humor of Ruby's unwitting remark.

"Maybe Ruby and I should try to hustle them along."

"Good idea. You fellows go on up there and see if you can help them out," the guy says, as pleasantly as possible given the circumstances. "If another foursome comes along, we'll stay here and let them play through."

"That's fine. We'll be right back and if we can't find their balls pretty quickly, we'll get them to drop two new ones and get on with it," I say as the guy nods appreciatively.

I join Ruby on the cart, and we head back down the fairway and up the incline toward the empty cart which is sitting right on the edge of the rough. I pull up, and Ruby gets off quickly. "You go into the trees a little to the left, and I'll go a little to the right. Okay, Ruby?"

He nods, and we start off in our separate directions, each of us holding an iron with which to beat some underbrush. Within twenty seconds, I've come across one of the balls that I'm sure they are playing and am amazed they couldn't find it just sitting there in plain view on a clump of sawgrass. My confusion is interrupted by Ruby softly calling my name from the direction of a small cluster of trees, so I head over there. Upon arriving at the spot where Ruby is standing, I'm taken aback by a huge white bare ass with little tuffs of black hair.

"What the fuck!"

"Whadda ya think of that, D Jack?" Ruby whispers, as if someone might overhear us.

"I think the dumbshits passed out," I answer, still not believing my eyes. The guy's pants are pushed down between his knees and golf shoes, both toes aimed toward China. The bare, clean-shaven legs of his ole lady are spread-eagled beneath his bulk, her gold shoes pointed in the direction of the cloud-speckled blue sky. He's face down, his hands at his sides, and under his right shoulder I can see a mop of hair that, other than her bare legs, is all that is visible of the woman. Absolutely nothing is moving.

"Whadda we gonna do, D Jack?" Ruby asks, seemingly more embarrassed than perplexed.

"Let's see if we can bring 'em around."

I walk over to the guy, lean over, and shake his shoulder, but he doesn't respond, so I shake more vigorously, but still nothing happens. It suddenly dawns upon me that the broad could suffocate under this heap of lard, so I lean Loudmouth's head to left and quickly note her golf skirt is covering her face. I push it down to her neck and am relieved that she's still alive; breathing deeply, and totally zoned out…but alive.

"Hell, Ruby, it would take a crane to lift this guy up. They seemed pretty friendly with that other couple, so let's go see if they'll help us out."

"Shouldn't we do something about them first?" Ruby asks.

"You're right. You roll the guy off the broad and get both of them straightened away; make it look like they just casually passed out. I'll go down and get the other couple."

Ruby nods and sets to work rolling you-know-who's fat ass off the drunken carcass beneath him. As I turn, I catch a glimpse of her dark-haired vee but continue to head for the cart. For maybe the second time in all my life, and no inquires about the first time, please, the voyeur in me says no way. It takes only a few seconds to reach the fairway, hop on the cart, and head down the hill, noticing a foursome lining up their approach shots and playing through. I look behind me and, seeing no one, drive the cart across the fairway towards the other couple. The guy is milling around a bit and I figure he's just about out of patience. I pull up just in time to hear the guy say, "…and if George didn't drink so much he would have found his God-damned ball by now."

The woman looks at him with growing annoyance and says, "You do realize, of course, that your wife has been known to hit the bottle pretty hard before the sun goes down." Her tone softens as she adds, "I guess we shouldn't have split up today; you should have stayed with Jill, and I should have played the round with George."

Holy shit! This lady's husband is up there banging this guy's wife, and if Ruby puts their clothes on backwards or something equally obvious, we're going to have one hell of a cluster fuck on our hands.

"Ah, excuse me, but we have a little bit of a situation." They both look at me with narrowed eyes, but I continue on. "You know those two were drinking kind of heavy, and they, uh, well, they just flat passed out. Ruby's up there to make sure nothing happens, but it's going to take some doing to get them off the course without some embarrassment."

The guy shakes his head in disgust while the woman seems more concerned, but I get the feeling this is not the first time Loudmouth has presented her with a difficult situation. "Let's go see what has to be done," the guy says resignedly.

They get on their cart and I immediately set sail for the top of the hill. I've got to beat them to Ruby and tip him off that we have a multiple case of marital infidelity on our hands. I arrive at the top of the hill about ten seconds ahead of the couple, leap off the seat, and head straight for the clump of trees. Ruby has done a good job, slumping the guy up against a tree with a tumbler next to his outstretched hand while curling the woman into a fetal position about six feet away from Loudmouth who we know now is George. I quickly grab Ruby by the arm.

"We got problems, D Jack," he mutters.

"You just ain't blowin' smoke. Look Ruby, that couple behind me are not married to each other. They're married to the two on the ground. You got that?"

"Ah, yeah," he says slowly," but we still got trouble."

"What, man?" I say excitedly as the other couple comes into view. Ruby looks all confused again.

"I can't find her panties."

"What a cluster fuck!" I gasp just as Mr. Jill and Mrs. George come into the clearing and take in the scene with what appears to be a mixture of amusement and revulsion. "Well, one thing's for sure, they're really out of it," the guy says. The woman picks up the pace. "I know and if I had a buck for every time my dumb-ass husband passed out, I'd go to Bermuda…by myself! I'm a little surprised at Jill though."

"Probably the heat as well as the alcohol," I speculate, trying to make up excuses for the broad, although she hasn't been much nicer than George. Just as I conclude my observation, Jill begins to move, and it appears as if she is going to roll over. I hold my breath, because if she stretches and her dress hikes up, her bush is going to hit her ole man right between the eyes, and it ain't gonna take two and two to figure out what's been going here. I release my breath as Jill curls up again and the crisis passes.

"We can't just stand here," Mrs. George says nervously, her embarrassment growing.

"Right," I say, sensing that I'm going to have to take the lead and come up with an action plan. "Ruby…go see if you can get the guy on the cart." I turn to Mr. Jill. "He'll probably need your assistance, sir. I'll lift the lady and take her back on the cocktail cart with me. I also think it will be less conspicuous if the two of you finish the eighth and ninth before coming back to the clubhouse. There are a few cots in the back of the cart room, and one of us will just stand watch until you come off the course."

Everyone nods in approval, realizing there are very few options. The guy and Ruby head for the load propped up against the tree and then lean down, drape one limp arm around each of their shoulders, and start to hoist George to his feet. I make sure the lady is watching intently before approaching the one known as Jill, and carefully tuck my arm under her skirt or dress or whatever the hell it is and press hard against the back of her legs to make sure the apparel stays in place. I put her left arm over my shoulder and gently lift her off the ground, staggering under the load. Hey, I'm no weakling, but when's the last time you tried to lift a totally zonked human being? It's a lot different than working out in the weight room, I can tell you that. I carry her towards the booze cart and note that George is being urged into a walk/drag act. The two guys get him squared away as I lower Jill onto the seat.

"You better hold onto his collar or something, Ruby," I say over my shoulder, "or he's going to fall right out on you." I look at Mr. Jill. "I'll just put my arm around the lady, if that's okay?" The husband gives me a more-or-less indifferent look and shrugs. "I'll be happy if you just get her back there in one piece without to much commotion."

"We'll do our best." I look back toward the tee and see no traffic. "Why don't you leave just a little ahead of us. He nods in agreement as he and Mrs. George start down the hill toward the two white balls that are just short of the pond and awaiting them. I ponder this whole fucken thing for a few seconds making sure they are out of earshot.

"Ruby, get back in there and see if you can find her panties." He props George against the back of the seat, waits a few seconds to make sure he isn't going to flop out, and heads back to the clump of trees. He emerges a few minutes later, puffs his cheeks, and blows out air slowly.

"I don't know what da schmuck did wid 'em. Maybe he ate 'em." I start to laugh but quickly realize Ruby probably isn't aware of the fact that Madison Avenue is currently hyping such a product.

"Why don't you smell his face?" I say facetiously and am surprised to see Ruby ramble over to George, bend, and take a deep breath.

"Well?" I inquire with a laugh.

"Booze, all booze, and boy, does he stink." I look at Ruby's worn facial expression. "We've done the best we can. Grab ahold of good ole George, and let's get them back to the clubhouse."

I put my arm around Jill and depress the oblong metal throttle. She immediately leans a little to the right as we lurch away from the rough, but I'm able to hold her with little to no effort because she's about as petite as Lena Dawson with maybe a plus ten pounds. Ruby also seems to have things under control as he follows me down the hill toward the eighth tee. Fortunately, the cart area appears to be empty as best I can tell, and I spot Ralph up front at the starting office undoubtedly shooting the breeze with Marcus. It must be after 4:00 so most of the caddies have left for the day, but the TGIS crowd will be descending upon the area shortly, so I figure we have a pretty narrow window.

I steer through the entrance of the cart shop and make an easy left turn. Twenty or so feet later comes a sharp right as I lead Ruby down the side of the area where the vending machines are stacked against a wall. Further down, there are about three or four cots just in case a caddy needs a few winks. Our luck is still holding as I stop near the empty cots and hear

Ruby pull up behind me. "Hold on to that guy for a minute; I'll get this broad on one of the cots and then come help you with that bum."

I turn, not waiting for an answer, get off the cart, head around to her side, and repeat my pickup procedure, making a mental note to keep my back as straight as possible. Everything is just as awkward as the first time I hoisted her dead-to-the-world body, but I have no difficulty getting her to the cot and putting her on her back. She quickly rolls on her side, emits a soft moan, and draws up her knees. I head back to the second cart and wrestle George to his feet while Ruby gives him a bear hug from behind. Loudmouth is just a load of dead meat, and it's all the two of us can do to drag him over to the second cot and unceremoniously dump him face down. Both Ruby and myself are breathing heavily with both the exertion of the past few moments and probably some relief, knowing our part in this ghastly play is about over. I go back to the booze cart, pop a Michelob, and hand it to Ruby. As for me, a stiff jolt of VO seems appropriate; in fact, let's make it two swigs back-to-back. See what I mean; is this fucken reality or what?

"Boy, whadda slob," Ruby grunts as he scratches his sandpaper face hard enough so that I can hear his nails scrapping against his one-day growth. "Kind of funny a bum like dat having a pink handkerchief," he says somewhat reflectively.

I almost choke on that last swig of eighty-six proof Canadian. "What pink handkerchief?"

"The one in his front pants pocket. I saw it when I propped him up against the tree and just tucked it down. I thought it was kinda weird having it in his pants, but you told me ta make sure everything looked natural-like, so I stuffed it down."

"Which side?"

"I think maybe da left."

I go over to the cot and reach my hand into George's left front pocket, and my fingers are immediately met with something silky and somewhat wet. As I gently ease my hand out of the pocket, I grip both sides of the garment, and spin around to face Ruby who is still running his hand across his stubbled jaw.

"Ta da!" I proclaim as I display Jill's string bikini panties.

"Gee," he says big eyed. "I never saw nothing like dat."

Maybe in his world, everything between a woman's legs has been 100% white cotton. "Come on, Ruby, no time for gawking. We have to get this thing on her before the other two head back in. Grab an arm and roll her over on her back."

Ruby takes Jill by the shoulder and gets her flat on her back with her arms hanging down over the sides of the cot. If it wasn't for the fact that she's warm, I'd figure she was dead for sure. I push her golf shoes about a foot apart and hold her panties up so I can make sure the label will be at her ass, and then stretch the left leg opening so I can slide it over her spikes. "Lift the shoe slowly so I can get her panties under the heel, Ruby." He does as instructed so gently you'd think he was working with an accident victim.

"Now let's do the other side." We both look down at our handiwork that has successfully placed her panties around both ankles. "Okay, now comes the fun part. You lift both legs straight up, and I'll slide em down to her ass."

Ruby positions himself between her legs, puts one hand under each thigh, and lifts until his arms are extending toward the ceiling, resulting in her dress falling up and onto her face. This, of course, gives us a very graphic beaver shot, and as I lean over to push her panties on, my senses are immediately, but fleetingly, assaulted by her manicured hair and erotic aroma. I say fleetingly, because I am also aware of the fact that if anyone spots us, we're going into the slammer for rape at worst or molestation of an unconscious drunk at best. The fact that I am having trouble getting her panties past her thighs returns me to the "reality" of this situation.

"We're almost home now, Ruby," I say breathing hard more from the tension than the physical effort. "Just give it all you've got and get her ass off the cot so I can slip these things under her cheeks."

Ruby grunts again as Jill's buttocks clear the cot by about two inches giving me just enough space to slide the panties under her hips. Being a string, I don't have to worry about getting them up to her waist. I quickly nod to Ruby who eases her back down onto the cot. As he brings her legs down, I pull the front of her panties up, the stretched translucent fabric quickly flattening her hair. Then I pull her dress back down, roll her on her side, and as before, she immediately draws up here knees. Instinctively, both of us check the cart room to see if anyone has witnessed this comedy of horrors. We're relieved to see nothing more than forty or fifty impersonal golf carts…whoa, Nellie, if golf carts could talk!

"You want me to head back out and check on da other two of 'em?" Ruby asks with a heavy dose of sweat pouring down his face.

"Sure, but check with Marcus first, and leave me the booze cart so I can reload and head back out to see what's left of this group. Most of them are probably off the course by now and those that aren't must be too gassed to know the sun is still shining."

I walk to the cart and take note of the liquor left: four bottles of Korbel champagne, almost a case of Michelob, one fifth of Jack Black, and the 2nd bottle of VO that I never made known to the members of ORGAN because I kind of see it as my fee. I reach into the cart and pull out the bottle of Jack Black, walk over to Ruby, and hand it to him. "This is for you, Ruby. You're one hell of a man in a crisis."

He smiles and obviously feels good about himself. "Gee, thanks, D Jack. Dis is awful nice of ya."

"Just take it home and keep it to yourself, okay? I don't want either of us getting into any trouble. After you tell Marcus about checking out those other two on the eighth, you might as well kick back for awhile, and I'll look after these two until their spouses get here."

Ruby looks at me and seems relieved to know the episode has come to a successful conclusion. He gives me a broad smile, a slap on the shoulder, and heads for the front of the cart room. The click of his heels on the concrete slab echoes throughout the large, rectangular area and slowly fades as he approaches the entranceway. I look back at my drunken wards and figure Demaret had it right: golf and sex are about the only things you can enjoy without being good at it.

It seems that only a few minutes pass before Ted and Alice, or whatever their names are, ride into the cart room and head down the back wall towards me. I suspect the heat, the booze, and the fun and games of their mates have taken their toll because they appear to be pretty worn out. "Everything okay?" the guy asks as he brings the cart to a halt.

"We had a few minor problems but nothing to be concerned about. They're as docile as lambs."

They slide off the seats, and the lady heads towards the cots. To my surprise, the guy offers his hand, and I return his strong grip. "You're the one they call D Jack, aren't you, the guy who played for the Mets?"

"Yes sir."

"Well, I'd appreciate it if you keep this incident to yourself," he says as he releases my hand with a solemn nod and then takes out his wallet and gives me a "go away and forget it" look as he extends two fifty dollar bills. "Make sure the guy who grunts with the busted nose gets one of these. I don't want this situation to make the rounds," he says forcefully.

I take a step back, clearly rejecting his largesse. "That won't be necessary, sir. Ruby might look like a tough used-up pug but he once killed a guy in the ring and for the rest of his career, he gave the widow half of all his purses. If I had the opportunity, I would have done the same…so thanks, but no thanks. I'm glad we could help you out."

A look of sadness quickly paints itself across his face. “I’m sorry. I truly am. I’ve offended you and your friend…but in my high-powered corporate world,” he says with some bitterness, “too many would have take advantage of this situation, or worse. Just like today out there,” he adds, and I get the feeling he pretty much knows what’s going on between his wife and fat George, “I’ve had too many people disappoint me.”

“You won’t have to add me and Ruby to your list, sir…and anything else I can do, just let me know,” I say sincerely.

He smiles weakly, clearly embarrassed, and moves towards the cots. I figure that’s almost a first for me…turning down a gratuity, but I got to tell ya, I feel pretty good about it.

I hop on the booze cart and slowly head around the back of the cart room toward the one connecting door to the bag room. It only takes a few minutes to stash the VO, champagne, and beer in a large cardboard box beneath the counter, so now you know how Lena Dawson got her Korbel wedding gift, and you also know how ORGAN, through my good offices, is going to partially sponsor our TGIS. Like I told you, conventioneers rarely tip, but then again, they do manage to unwittingly supply a lot of goodwill and liquid cheer for the staff.

IX

TGIS AND THE EXISTENCE OF GOD

Play what you want to play
see what you want to see,
do what you want to do
and be what you want to be.

"**H**ey, Mon, what chu got?" Chico is smiling from one cauliflowered ear clear across to the other.

"Tonight's specials," I respond, trying to match his infectious smile, "include scotch whisky, Canadian whisky, domestic champagne, and the best of Ed McMahon."

"Who ees dees Meekmon?"

"Skip it, unless you want a Michelob. So, whaddle it be, Mr. Donahee?" I say with a horrid Gleason accent.

"Me llamo es Cheeco," he responds indignantly.

"I know. I know. I was just kiddin' around. What would you like to drink, amigo?"

"Por favor…dee scotch weeskie," he responds with his broken-toothed grin repainted on his scarred face. I drop a few cubes into a tumbler and pour him a solid three fingers of J&B. He nods his appreciation and heads toward the back of the cart room where some of the others have arranged some not very first class lawn chairs that are used by the caddies who aren't walking on any given day, along with a somewhat lumpy couch purchased from Goodwill Industries. We generally have some late Sunday afternoon drinks to celebrate the end of our unique work week, which of course, never really ends. The standard TGIF doesn't exist for the Presidential's staff who work seven out of seven, so I had instigated a TGIS or "Thank God It's Sunday." The booze is donated by anyone who has had some success scrounging but I'm generally the person who provides the libations, thanks to conventioneers and drunken celebrities. Lots of coins go into the vending machines for assorted bags of junk food, and Stunt brings nuts from the Bengal Lounge. But every once in awhile, we get lucky when one of the girls contributes some untouched morsels from the dining room which, of course, is against the rules of the dining room as well as the Florida State Department of Health.

You might be wondering about this drinking on the job business. Frankly, I think Charley the Boss is a very enlightened guy who didn't go to college to learn all there is to know about industrial psychology and personnel relations. I haven't really told you much about the Boss, but his official title is Executive Vice-President in charge of operations. He's a dapper little guy, with a vested suit always draped on his hundred and forty pound frame and has been in the "make the vacationer happy" business for the better part of his life. He's also a field man who has experienced every aspect of the complex except, oddly enough, golf! Like many hard-driving executives, Charley has very little leisure time, so the few hours he allots himself each week are spent on the four-wall, indoor racquetball courts which were ingeniously incorporated into the clubhouse proper of all three country clubs by a very enlightened architecht...and it didn't hurt that the guy with the creative sliderule was an amateur nationals champ in one of the senior brackets. As you know, I've got a standing game with Charley every Monday night and I've got to tell you that for a fifty-five-year-old guy, he's awfully tough to beat when we're playing singles. But the Boss is not unique in that respect. Go down to any YMCA in a large city and you'll see lots of "seniors" giving the youngsters lessons in athletic humility. Over the past two seasons, Charley has surely given me a few too many, but lately, I've been able to take him down a few times. A ceiling shot to his backhand; that's his weakness, but believe me, he has very few of them, on or off the court. In fact, his game reflects his management style; most of the time he appears to be soft and maybe a little deceptive, but if you put yourself into a negative set-up, he's likely to kill ya. When he gets really desperate, he plays to my left side, but it even surprises me, now and then, how much my impaired right eye has compensated for the left one over the years.

So, now you know a little more about Charley, and now you can figure out why he lends his unspoken blessing to TGIS. With the seven-day week, he knows the boys and girls have to have a bright spot somewhere along the line, and late Sunday afternoon is traditionally dead around the Clubhouse. Most of the patrons are checking in or out and staying close to the hotel, dining rooms, and shows. Many is the time we just close down the Bengal at 11:00 on a Sunday night and just sit around and jam for our own pleasure. However, don't get ole Charley wrong. He's no laissez-faire guy, because the unwritten conditions for TGIS are that no one gets sloshed and that we cover each other so that the few guests at the Presidential at that time of day still get the service they expect and to which they are entitled. What the hey…nothing really new here. The guys on the line in the breweries get their beer breaks. Enough! This is starting to sound like an apology; I've got better things to do than trying to justify some R&R to you.

"Hey, D Jack," comes a yell from the rear, "how's about some Philosophy 101?"

That immediately gets a roar of laughter as I approach an empty seat in the hastily arranged semi-circle. "Sure, Ruby," I respond as I grab an iced bottle of Perrier from a cooler chest before plopping down on the chair. My six ounce tumbler is already half full of VO and some ice, so I splash in the pure water and am ready to go. "Whatcha got in mind?"

"Let's get heavy," he answers with a grin, "how bout God?"

"What about God?" I respond while making no attempt to match his smile.

"Let's go for the biggie, D Jack," the Turk chimes in. "I'm posting five-to-one that says God is just a figment of man's imagination and He doesn't exist." That gets some more laughter and a resounding "Boo" from the assistant pro, Bobby "sticks," who likes to tell everybody on a regular basis that he's a good Southern Baptist, so he's all over the Turk like stink on a skunk.

"What's this *He* shit!" Sal chimes in defiantly. "Where is it written that God is a He?"

"Well taken, Sal, but bad move anyway, Turk," I say with a frown.

"Why so?"

"Of all people, you ought to know better than to ask if God exists. You're pissen into a headwind! You need to play the odds."

"Meaning?" he asks with a touch of curiosity.

"Meaning, a very wise man was once asked if he believed in God and he responded, 'Of course,' which stunned his audience. 'But how does a man of your intelligence possibly believe in God?' one brave soul ventured. 'Quite simple,' he responded, 'I'm playing the odds. If I say I don't believe in God and, when I die I find I am right, no harm done…but if I am wrong, I'll be in very deep shit!'"

"Not good enough, D Jack," the Turk responds above the laughter of the ten or so who have gathered for today's cool down. "You're gonna have to do better than something Don Rickles probably said on stage in the main room at the hotel a few weeks ago."

"Yeah, D Jack, go for it!" Greenie yells. "Make us happy and prove that God exists." Greenie is a salad chef on the line and rarely appears to need some cheering up, in that most of the time he's smoken things he isn't about to add to your romaine, anchovies, and garlic-butter croutons.

"All righty, boys and girls," I begin, followed by an immediate double gulp of VO. "I really appreciate this challenge you have afforded me, seeing as the great philosophical minds of the world have been unable to provide a sufficient response beyond that of speculation."

"Stop stallen and cut da bullshit, D Jack!" Ruby yells as he launches his empty beer bottle in my direction. Fortunately, the glass missle is coming at me on my right side…his aim is as bad as his uppercut was when he was a promising middleweight…so I casually snatch the hurled projectile as it attempts to sail past me.

"Okay, I'm on the job." I stand and push the lawn chair in front of me, resting my hands on the metal-framed back. "I want all you guys to think of Fred Flintstone."

I'm immediately met with a chorus of 'yabba-dabba-doos.' "Great," I continue, "so you know who he is. But let's think of him as a real cave man without his foot-powered car and all his other wacky inventions and contraptions, and gadgets. Tell me what he did with himself."

"He didn't have ta do nuthin with hisself, because he was dragging da broads around by da hair and they did the doin," GD utters, which immediately generates some exuberant applause and a pronounced hiss from Sal.

"Maybe so, GD, but what do you guys think his day was like?"

"He had to eat," Marcus says with a tone that suggests he's getting into it.

"Had to stay warm," the Turk adds.

"Had to get laid," Stunt remarks.

"Not like you, huh, Stunt?" Sal says sarcastically, accompanied by a very lecherous smile. The laughter is hearty, and the goodwill in the cart room is infectious. "Stay on the page, boys and girls. What else did he do?" I prompt.

"Siesta," Chico says.

"Right you are, Chico, and where did he sleep?"

"He sleep on dee, how you say, *el piso*, de ground, de floor."

"Why didn't he sleep in a bed?" I ask

"He's no got de *los muebles*, de furniture."

"So, he sits on the ground too, right?"

“Sí,” Chico says as he nods in agreement after a healthy pull on his J & B.

“Okay, but after awhile he gets tired of having his ass bruised by rocks and such, so what does our caveman eventually do?”

“Obviously, D Jack, he builds a bed to sleep in and a chair to sit on,” the Clock says very seriously. “But what does this have to do with the existence of God? I think you’re over your head and blowing smoke, college man.”

More chuckles, they sense major squirming ahead. “I’d be in good company if I’m over my head, but let’s stay with it a little longer. My point is that up until the Clock’s immediate ancestor built a chair, it didn’t exist, right?” My reference to the Clock’s family tree is greeted with more laughter.

“You got it, prof!” Sal says.

“So, how did a chair come to be?” I ask

“Marcus’s great great granddaddy got an idea,” Stunt shouts with a laugh.

“What do you mean by an idea?” I say in a probing fashion.

“Well, he figured if he built something that had a back and legs and he could sit in it, it would be a hell of a lot better than having his bony ass on the ground.”

“Are you saying a bony ass runs in my family?” Marcus asks indignantly. More laughter.

“Bet your bony ass that’s what I’m saying,” Stunt responds.

“Let’s stay focused, class,” I interject with a sigh. “So, what came first, the idea of the chair or the actual chair itself?”

“No-brainer, D Jack,” Stunt says as he finally appears to be getting serious. “The caveman had to think about it before he could build it.”

“Do we all agree with Stunt?” All the responses are in the affirmative with the expected amount of expletives. “Fine, so the first thing to come was the thought or the idea; another word for that is a concept. A chair is a concept, and it has characteristics which, among others for a chair, include a back, legs, and you can sit in it or on it, right?” Again, the chorus is positive.

“And I could predict that a chair in the lounge upstairs has a back, legs and I can sit in it, even though I can’t see it, yes?” More agreement.

“So,” I continue, “did man dream up a chair?”

“You bet,” Ruby says apparently pleased with himself.

“And does a chair exist? Is it real?”

“Of course it is,” Marcus says.

"So then, a chair started out as an idea or concept, a figment of man's imagination, I think that was your phrase, Turk, but we all agree that a chair does exist, right?"

"Oh no, D Jack," the Turk chimes in quickly. "You're saying man dreamed up a chair and it's real, so if man dreamed up God, He's real."

"Why not," I counter. "Man needs a chair, so a chair exists. Man needs God, so God exists."

"Big flaw, D Jack," Marcus says confidently. "If I follow your argument, you're suggesting man created God."

"Marcus," I say softly looking at my companions in crime who have become suddenly quiet at this point, "as far as this discussion is concerned, it really doesn't matter whether God created man or man created God. The question the Turk offered for our 101 discussion was simply whether or not God exists, not how He came to be or if He's always been. You know what Abbott's law says: If you don't like the answer, you shouldn't have asked. Anyway, I leave it to the jury, and…I need a drink!"

"What about next Sunday, D Jack?" Stunt asks. "Can we stay with cosmic kinds of stuff?"

"Why not, Stunt? There's a pretty new theory about the origin of the universe going around called the Big Bang that basically suggests first there was nothing…and then it exploded. Go figure! How does one get an explosion from nuthin?"

Right or wrong, true or otherwise, Philosophy 101 concludes with laughter, applause, and slaps on the back. Even the Turk gives me a thumb's up because he posted the line but no money got put down, and he's always gracious when he doesn't have to pay off. Marcus is nothing but grins because he is a very religious Catholic, although I suspect I am going to hear about the chicken and egg dilemma before the day is out. I notice my glass is empty and head for the bag room to celebrate the fun with my special stash of TGIS Crown Royal.

The big royal blue golf bag in Stall 200 is where I keep the sculpted bottle figuring if I get a little confused, the color should tip me off that the little bluish-purple bag is concealed in the big blue one, whose owner is some brigadier general no one has seen so far this season. He's probably got a comp membership or something similar to the deal General Omar Bradley had here in the early 60's, or so I'm told. Anyway, I splash in the upscale Canadian whisky and, thinking I need some more jingle change for the vending machines, I turn to get my Fuente box under the bag room counter and am surprised to see Sal sitting atop the smooth, polished surface with her purple and black cocktail dress tucked under her knees.

"I really enjoyed the monthly 101, D Jack, but I must admit all the God stuff is a little heavy for me. As you would say," she continues with a grin, "I'd like to perception check myself, so let's run through a more tangible concept."

"Okay, Sal," I respond anticipating her challenge. "You pick it."

"I was hoping you would say that," she answers, the grin still painted on her face, "how about pussy?"

Cha ching!!!! Now what? Think fast and help me out. She's got that 'I sandbagged you' look all over her face. Too late, but thanks anyway…I'll take a futile stab at it.

"Sure, Sal, that's easy; four legs, four paws, whiskers, and extremely uppity.

"Nice try, but no cigar. Try beaver."

"Flat tail, big teeth, structural engineer."

"Strike two, D Jack. We're talking the human thing here."

So much for cats and dam builders. Whoa, Nellie. Definitely not anticipated, and the look on my face can't conceal my reaction to her choice. She's still grinning and loving every moment of it.

"Let's see what the philosopher can do with something a little earthy, D Jack. Come on, I think you're supposed to begin with, ah, the characteristics of the concept, right? I mean, my pussy is a concept, isn't it?"

"Well, technically speaking, yours is a unique and individual example of the concept."

"So, what you are saying is that if you've seen one, you *haven't* seen 'em all,"

"That's pretty good, Sal," I say as I take a deep swallow of the Crown which fails to remove a growing discomfort in my throat.

"Don't patronize me, you one-day wonder Met," she says with her wide grin melting into something more on the sly side, "and don't let my photo layout in Penthouse as one of the 'Noles' girls fool you. My degree in psych from FSU reads summa cum laude so get on with it: a characteristic please?"

"All righty," I say, impressed, and somewhat chastised, as I lean to the task. "Although I deeply regret not having seen your photos, the first obvious characteristic would be a soft, light brown triangle."

"I'll chalk that up to subconscious personalization…and let it pass. What you're really saying is that a characteristic of pussy is a geometrical shape with hair?"

That's one hell of a paraphrase. "You're absolutely right."

"What if a girl is conscious of her bikini line?" Sal responds impishly.

"The characteristics of a concept don't have to work at the 100% level," I answer with just a hint of sweat starting to build under my ASU t-shirt.

"Agreed, okay, how about another one, prof?"

"Let's student-center the exercise," I answer trying desperately to turn the tables.

"I can do that," Sal says as she leans on her left elbow sideways across the counter with her hand cradling her cheek. Then she extends her legs from beneath her dress, just below the "flash zone," which seems to communicate a physical sense of comfort as opposed to anything of a seductive nature. "Another characteristic would be the physical part of a woman's body that makes guys do stupid stuff."

"If you say so," I say in as neutral a tone as possible given the nature of the discussion.

"I do, and it's also the physical part of a woman's body that often makes it possible for her to secure financial security," she says and then adds, "whether she be a mistress or a wife."

"Yup, although that doesn't say much for romance," I concur reluctantly.

"Okay then, if it's romance you want, if she's really good with it, I mean what you guys generally refer to as a terrific piece of ass, and maybe even in love with a guy, it's the one sure thing that's going to keep him in her bed because it's the closest thing to heaven the guy will ever know," she concludes.

"I'd say you did a very thorough job, Sal. You want a grade?"

"One last thing, D Jack," she says, ignoring my comment as she regains her sitting position on the counter. "You concluded in the cart room that concepts have predictable value, right?"

"Yup." It seems as if my speech pattern is being reduced to that of Gary Cooper at this point.

"Okay, so whether you meant to or not, you predicted my pussy would have a light brown triangle. So shall we validate your prediction? Ya want some empirical data? I mean, isn't that what we need to bring the exercise to a useful conclusion?"

I simply nod in the affirmative because words have clearly gone into hiding in my brain. "Fine," she says, obviously pleased with herself, "but keep in mind, this is just research and will be limited to visual verification."

"Meaning nothing personal," I say in as unflappable a fashion as possible. I mean, normally, I'm not all that good with this kind of stuff, but deep down, Sal has my undivided commitment to the task.

"Of course, there's nothing personal, D. Jack. Being a temporary barmaid, and I stress temporary, I don't get a chance to exercise my mind too often and this looked like a fun opportunity. Anyway, according to Bob Guccione, more than five million satisfied Penthouse subscribers have seen me stark naked, so other than a philosophical exercise, I'm just saving you the cost of a magazine. No more, no less."

With that, Sal keeps looking me in the eye as she slowly lifts her cocktail dress above her thighs and even more slowly spreads her legs ever so slightly. She then slips a finger into her black lace panties and pulls them to one side.

"As you can see," she says clinically, "you were right."

End of class! Field research, for you, is optional; there definitely won't be a test!

*

I'm having a real problem with some buttons! No not my fly thank you. My immediate problem is trying to secure Chico's white jacket in the general area of my navel, and no beer gut jokes from you, please. My abdomen is washboard flat, but I outweigh the diminutive waiter by about sixty pounds which makes him a svelte one twenty-five or so. Chico is in the process of downing his third scotch "weeskie" so I'm gonna bus tables for him upstairs in the dining room until he hits the staff showers. Right now he's in a corner engaged in deep conversation with Marcus and is shrugging and nodding in the negative. I assume that Marcus, once again, is trying to pry out of him the greatest black beans and rice recipe in the world and, as usual, the old man is not succeeding. So I wave to their backs as I head around the corner. "I'll be back in about half an hour, so sober him up, Marcus."

Marcus just nods without a reply and is obviously committed to pursuing his futile effort. I hope he doesn't try to get at the secret by getting Chico drunk. It doesn't work. I know, I've tried it, and maybe I don't know much of anything these days, but I'm relatively sure the south-of-the-border man will take that recipe to his grave. I sure wish I could make book on that one with the Turk.

I walk up the asphalt path, climb a few stairs and slowly head into the dining room with a distinctive lack of enthusiasm directed toward the upcoming bussing of tables which ain't exactly one of my favorite pastimes.

I can see the soft, orange-colored lights from the dusky sunset through the panes of glass and note the room looks relatively empty. I'm not two feet through the doors when a sartorial-looking, silver-haired, middle-aged gentleman in a burgundy blazer waves to me, so I paint the ever-present smile across my face and walk over to his table.

"May I help you, sir?" I inquire pleasantly.

"I left my cigar case in the hotel," he says politely, and then pauses with the look of a man who is about to ask for something but knows his request doesn't have a chance of being met with a positive response, so he gears himself for the expected disappointment. "Does the House have any decent cigars?"

Now I know why they call me the Pirate, because it's just plain lucky the way I stumble across bountiful situations. "I think there might be some Dutch Masters or Antonio y Cleopatra's up in the lounge, but I'm not too sure."

The guy gives it the 'I thought so' number as he glances at the two really fine looking women on the other side of the table. One looks to be late forties or early fifties, being neither cute nor a beauty, but more of the kind of woman who from head to toe might be called handsome. The other one appears to be somewhat younger and flashier, but, to my surprise, it's the older one who smiles at the man in an attempt to ease his displeasure. I figure I've given him enough time to accept his plight which should make an unexpected reward all the sweeter.

"However," I say as I reach inside Chico's white waiters jacket, "I'd be more than glad to have you try one of these," I say as I hand him a cellophane wrapped, seven-inch Claro cigar. "It's a Santa Clara 1830 III, Mexican, one hundred percent tobacco with a Cuban seed wrapper."

The guy really comes alive, I mean to tell ya; it looks like I just made his whole fucken vacation. I'll bet I even surprised you: hell, there are always a few players who are desperately in need of a $5.00 cigar so I always keep a few handy. And yes, the return, one way or another, always exceeds the outlay!

"May I cut it for you, sir?" I say with a smile as I take out a silver and rosewood guillotine from my right front pants pocket. Now the guy is looking at me in awe, and for a fleeting moment, it's almost as if he's wondering why he didn't bus tables for a living. If he could maintain this smoking habit without the corporate hassle or whatever, wowie, but then his look melts into one of curiosity.

"Mind if I ask you a question?" he says as he hands me back the cigar cutter.

"No objections, sir, but as Johnny Carson likes to say: 'Entitled to one luxury in life, no matter what.'"

Okay, guys, this is pure bullshit on my part. I don't smoke cigars because, as mentioned, they're so fucken expensive. "So your one luxury in life is a cigar, not that I'm being critical," he hastens to add. "It's a damn good one."

"Not really. I just keep a few on hand for special occasions."

The man has yet to take his eyes off the Santa Clara, and I figure I've really made his night, but the handsome-looking woman is sending a very warm, almost maternal smile in my direction. Her eyes seem to be shining with some kind of recognition. "Howard, I'm not sure but this young man looks vaguely familiar," she says with her eyes still locked on me.

I don't have a clue as to what's going on but agree with her that Santa Claus could have given Howard the cigar without an acknowledgment; however, she seems to have stirred him out of his reverie, and he takes a good hard look at me.

"No, Lillian, I don't think so but we did hear from Charley Berston that he works for the Diplomat. Young man, do you know Devon Jameison?"

"Yes, I do."

"Do you know how we can get in touch with him?"

That won't be necessary, sir. You're looking at him."

"I'll be damned!" he says as a broad smile engulfs his entire face while he gets to his feet and pumps my hand. "Lillian, no wonder we didn't recognize him what with the sunglasses and beard. Great to see you, D Jack. Have a seat."

"I appreciate that, sir, but Mr. Berston doesn't look too kindly on the staff sitting at a table in the dining room," I say somewhat bewildered by this unexpected how-do-you-do.

"No problem, kid. Charley will be pleased we found you. Just a few weeks ago, I enlisted him in a business venture and during a casual baseball chat, he mentioned you were here," he says enthusiastically as he points to the empty chair next to the younger of the two women. "We want to hear what one of our family's favorite ballplayers has been up too since that Saturday night at Shea."

I take a seat and start to wonder what this guy's interest is. "You remember that?"

"Hell, kid, we were there, all of us were there. Truth is, D Jack, I'm still a minority owner, and we'd been drooling over your stats in Jacksonville and the way you picked right up at Norfolk. When they called you up, it was like Christmas, New Years, and a birthday all rolled into one. Between your potential and Seaver and the way some of the other guys were coming along, we figured it was going to be the year."

"And so it was, Mr..."

"Sheridan. Howard Sheridan. True, we took it all but who knows what you could have accomplished during a long and healthy career. Don't you ever think about that?"

"I guess I'd be blowing smoke if I said it never pops up, but I try to keep everything in perspective. And," I add with a smile," I keep up a rapid supply of fun and games, even if I'm usually the only one playing."

"We saw you on the Carson show, and your fun sense of humor was great even though it seemed as if your injuries hadn't completely healed," the handsome woman says. "We had a dinner celebration with the Met's players after the Series and one of the coaches had mentioned you had gone out to Arizona State. We wrote and invited you to the victory celebration and got your note saying you couldn't make it because of your injuries, and then we lost track of you."

"Until we saw a small article in the *New York Times* about your induction into the Florida Hall of Fame," Sheridan adds, and then Charley mentioned you were working at the Presidential and here we are."

Although I'm surprised the *Times* actually mentioned something I'm somewhat befuddled. "You mean you actually came here to dig me up?"

"Well, not entirely. It's kind of a combined business trip. I've got the rights and FCC approval to start an ABC television affiliate here in Miami, so we're dotting all the i's; we're also looking into building a home on one of the small islands in Biscayne Bay so we can be close to the new enterprise."

"And enjoying the sunshine and the beach," the young one adds with a smile.

"Bad form on my part, D Jack. I'd like you to meet my wife, Lillian, and my sister-in-law, Antoinette." I get warm smiles from both women with the older one being the wife, as predicted, and return their smiles with a nod.

"Anyway," Sheridan continues, "we'll be celebrating Lillian's fiftieth birthday on the 23rd of December and seeing as you weren't able to come to our home back in '69, we'd like you to be our special guest at her party."

"Gee, Mr. Sheridan, that's really nice of you to be so generous, but I..."

"Don't misunderstand, D Jack," he interrupts with a serious tone. "We aren't interested in parading out the 'one-day wonder' or having you on hand as a celebrity jock. And we're not just another wealthy couple into one-upsmanship. We sincerely want you to join us and have a relaxed, wonderful time."

"I appreciate your offer, but it's almost Christmas time and all."

"Do you have a family?"

"Not really; just a friend or two."

"So if you have a significant other, bring her with you or a buddy if that's the case."

"No," I say with a half smile while looking at Lillian who continues to extend an air of warmth I haven't experienced for a while, "no significant other, but I am concerned about Mr. Berston."

Sheridan smiles, "I already talked with Charley, and it's fine with him; in fact, he'll be coming. As I mentioned, he's involved in the television station as well as another fledging enterprise. This is the way I operate, kid, just like the lawyer I was in my previous life. I make sure I've got all the answers to my questions before I ask them."

"Then obviously I'm coming. So where's the party?"

"Aspen."

"Aspen, Colorado?"

"Well, it isn't in New York, although we do have a brownstone in mid-Manhatten, but we only use that for business. Aspen is home. Ever been to Colorado?"

"Yes, once when I was coaching at ASU. We had a road trip one spring and played the University of Wyoming in Laramie and then dropped down to Ft. Collins to play CSU. I think I liked Wyoming more?"

"Why so, kid? Colorado has all those fourteeners with their snow-capped peaks, although Wyoming does have the Snowy Range Pass in the Medicine Bows. Who can pass up skiing in good ole Jackson Hole? My good friend, Spence, still lives there, complete with his fringed coats. Not your typical lawyer…you just have to love that guy," Sheridan concludes reflectively.

"I was thinking more about the people and their genuine live and let live attitude. I went back a few times over the summer of '70 and just really enjoyed the relaxed atmosphere and the slowed down lifestyle."

Sheridan nods in agreement. "You're pretty perceptive to pick all that up in just a few visits, but you nailed it right on the head, D Jack. I was born and raised in Cheyenne, and Lillian says that's what's kept my feet on the ground for thirty years."

"Speaking of feet on the ground, I've got tables to bus and maybe some cigars to light," I add with a big grin as I stand up. Sheridan stands too, and we again shake hands. "You can chat with Charley, and he'll make all the arrangements for you."

"And don't go out and buy anything," Lillian adds pleasantly. "Just bring what's on your back, okay?"

"Can do, Mrs. Sheridan, and thanks so much."

"D Jack, the name is Lillian," she says with a pleasant smile.

I nod in appreciation of the informality, and after taking Lillian's extended hand which is warm, and surprisingly firm, I turn to Antoinette who says, "It was nice to make your acquaintance, Pirate." Her eyebrows arch, and her pupils shine with recognition as her mouth paints a hint of intrigue. She's obviously heard my clubhouse nickname, and her expression tells me what she's heard might not be all that bad. I nod in response and quickly turn and start moving toward the kitchen doors. Once inside, I pick up a huge metal tray and head back out to the dining room to bus some tables. I start cleaning off what was apparently a table for six; the food must still be pretty good, because there's little more than a few snips of assorted meats and sauteed vegetables.

It's kind of funny the way the world works sometimes. The corporation called ORGAN unknowingly provides succor, the wet, alcoholic variety, for our weekly social; I supply the set-ups and the chairs; Chico and the gang supply themselves; Sal provides a platonic exercise in philosophy and anatomy; Howard Sheridan forgets his cigars; and I get invited to a party in Aspen. When all's said and done, this sequence of spontaneous events and coincidences produced a group of relatively happy people, and why the hell not! It's TGIS, and everyone's got a right to feel pretty good once in awhile, yes? You damn sure better agree with me on this one!

I glance around the all but empty dining room as I head for the kitchen with the load of dishes and glasses piled on the tray that I'm balancing on my upturned right palm. A few of the girls are busy setting up for the morning's traffic and I realize I haven't seen Sam. But tomorrow night brings her and Morgan's Inn, although tonight I still have Moon and the Bengal Lounge in front of me. Who knows? Maybe pretty soon I might *play what I want to play, see what I want to see, do what I want to do, and be what I want to be.*

X

JIMMY "BLUE EYES" AND JILLY "THE ICE"

Fifty years at my desk
always gave them my very best
now they have given me the door,
So I'm hanging around my home
never hobbied, never roamed
and I'm wondering what my life's been for.

"**I**'d like to speak with Charley," I say politely.

"One moment please. Who should I say is calling?"

"I'm returning his call. It's D Jack."

"I'm sorry, I didn't hear that."

"Just tell him D Jack is on the line." A button puts me on hold so I take a look at the sheets. It's Monday the 29th, and we're heading for December, so it's going to be back-to-back golfers out there until 5:30 p.m. every day; the season generally gets into full swing right after Thanksgiving. The elevator music on the line is interrupted as well as my dismal train of thought.

"Hello."

"This is D Jack, Charley."

"Right, you didn't have to tell me it's you. The broad on the phone said it was you. What do you think I pay her for? Don't answer that." He rushes on…"You mind some extra action on the racquetball court tonight?"

"Who…and how good are they?"

"A couple of guys from upper New York State want to take us on, best of three, hundred bucks, what do you say?"

"Have you seen 'em play a game or two?"

"All defense. Both lefties, one with a fair corner kill, so we'll play them down the middle with lots of ceiling shots. Can't miss," Charley concludes confidently.

"I don't know, Charley. I got a late date tonight, and I can't risk dropping that much."

"Since when does an ugly bastard like you get a date? You and Ruby and some of the guys going to quaff some brewskies in that sports dive on 163rd street?"

"I'm taking Samatha Frederickson out for dinner."

There's dead silence. "You're taking Billy's kid out for dinner? You gotta to be kiddin. Last year he told me to tell Harlan not to hire you, kid. I mean, I gather he hates your living guts."

"You've got that right, but it's too long a story to tell. Bottom line is we're headed for Johnny Morgan's after our game and that's gonna cost me my boots and my ass."

"Okay, so I'll spot you a few, but that's just being academic because we're gonna smoke these fellas. 8:00 p.m. on the button, kid. See you then."

I'm nodding to myself as I hang up, and within three seconds the phone is ringing. Terrific, I can't wait to be sweet to another irate guest. "Presidential bag room, can I help you?"

"Pirate, get your ass up here on the double. We've got big trouble!!"

"Settle down, Marcus, I'm on my way." I hang up the phone and doublecheck the sheets to make sure no problems are on the immediate horizon. I walk out of the bag room briskly because Marcus rarely sounds petrified and I can't for the life of me figure out why he's so bent out of shape. I'm just approaching the open door to the starter's office when a chill, no, a fucken frozen stalactite complete with pointed tip, runs down the length of my spine. Marcus is trying desperately not to look into the piercing gaze of Vincent Alo, aka "Jimmy Blue Eyes."

"Good going, D Jack," Marcus says with relief, although his glazed look evaporates less than a millimeter. "You're just the one we need. Have you met Mr. Alo?" Thank God, not professionally, but I'm able to conjure up my weakest, most humble smile. "No sir, but good morning to you."

He quietly nods and then lays those steely, brilliantly-colored eyes on me. What a way to start a Monday or any other day for that matter. Vincent "Jimmy Blue Eyes"Alo! If you didn't know any better, you'd just think you're looking at a smallish, almost fragile and somewhat reserved kind of a guy wearing some nice clothes and sporting a slight shadow on his sculpted chin, but when you know you're looking at Meyer Lansky's "chief-of-staff" and a guy who held hands with the Boss of all Bosses up in New York, your mind just paints him as ominous as all hell. The word is that he's a "made man" but the only official stuff is that he did time in Sing Sing for armed robbery and ran Lansky's gambling operations up in Hallandale along with the pre-Castro Cuban stuff. Growing up on Jefferson Street in Hollywood, I was only a few blocks away from his stucco home on South Lake Drive which was allegedly some shrine to his ole lady, but kids were always scared he had shooters around the place, so we fished somewhere else. Same went for Lansky's brother, Jake, who lived on Harrison Street, but on the sheer fright meter, he didn't even come close to another Jake named Jacobi who lived five houses away from us.

Marcus interrupts my brief journey into the primeval forest of the underworld. "We've got a problem here, D Jack. Mr. Alo's clubs seem to be missing. Is there any chance this situation is similar to Mr. Schmedler's?"

"Not a chance, Marcus," I say flatly as I turn and once again encounter the chilling stare of Alo. "I'm not familiar with your bag, Mr. Alo. Can you describe it for me?" He takes me in slowly, his face expressionless except for those cobalt eyes that I think are giving me a message that I interpret as one of doom.

"I just got the bag a few months ago," he says quietly. "It's a big black bag with my name in gold letters. You can't miss it." He pauses and looks at me as if he is evaluating my worth, or possibly my right to live another day! "Look, kid, I come over here today to get a lesson from Bottomly and I go out to the range, right? See? No bag. See? Now, let's find the bag, right, kid?"

"Yessir, Mr. Alo. I'll get on it right this minute," I say as I start to turn but am immediately subjected to the pressure of one of his hands as he takes hold of my shoulder.

"I'm coming with you, right kid?"

No asshole! You're gonna sit here for an hour and lose the first round of jacks. "Of course, sir, let's check with Ralph to see if he has your clubs."

The two of us head down the path toward the cart room where Ralph should still be busy setting up the morning players with the bags that have been lined up against the outside wall. To say the least, it's with a sigh of relief that I spot Ralph right where he's supposed to be.

"Hey, Ralph, how many players you send out this morning?"

"About thirty or forty I guess. Why?"

Now comes my stupid question, but I've got to do something with Jimmy standing somewhat below my shoulder with a watchful eye. "You send out any big black bags today that might have come over on a shuttle?"

Ralph removes his weather-beaten baseball cap and, as usual, scratches his head while he attempts to process this highly intellectual inquiry. "Gee, D Jack, I guess a few were black. I wasn't watching that close. Gee, I can't honestly say."

I walk over to the wall feeling those blue eyes boring a hole through my back. "Come over here and help me for a minute, Ralph. Let's check all the black bags against the wall to see if any have gold lettering across the stitching. We're looking for Mr. Alo's clubs."

If this were a Vincent Price movie, upon my pronouncement of Jimmy's name, eerie gothic sounds would be bouncing off the walls of the movie house. Well, it's not a movie house, but I'm hearing those sounds anyway while Ralph, obviously, isn't sharing my aural experience and doesn't seemed ruffled one single bit. It's hard to believe he's never heard of Alo, but then being Ralph, he's generally oblivious to what's going on around the Clubhouse or the world for that matter. It takes only a few minutes to check all the bags and, as predicted, no luck.

"Is anybody not walking today, Ralph?"

"Paddy's back on one of the cots."

"How about rousting him and getting him to run a check through the bag room, okay?"

"Sure thing," Ralph replies as he starts for the rear of the room and I turn toward one of the empty carts. "Mr. Alo, I'm gonna head for the front door and see what's been happening with the shuttles."

Again, my shoulder becomes his personal property. "I'm coming with you, right kid?"

God's truth, I'm too afraid to even look at him now, so I just nod and head for the nearest cart. Once I'm seated, he slides onto the cushioned space next to me, and I head down the asphalt path that winds around the side of the Clubhouse and points its ebony finger up the hill towards the front door. The silence is approaching ten on the wretched meter scale, and I begin to wonder if anyone has ever been "taken for a ride" on a golf cart. And what if it's all lies? What if Jimmy Blue Eyes is as active now as he was supposed to be in New York? What if I'm destined to be tomorrow's leading headline.

"Pirate Walks the Plank at Clubhouse," the *Hollywood Sun Tattler* would say in thirty-six point courier type. "D Jack, the Pirate, Jameison was found early today at the bottom of a scenic pond fronting the large, yet difficult, eighth hole green at the Presidential Golf Course and Country Club. His body was tied to a large, black golf bag, the hood of which had been placed over his head.

"Authorities were notified shortly after lunch when, according to a Mr. John Red, some of the staff became concerned when Jameison failed to appear for his customary fat corned beef on white with mayo. Between bites of his own sandwich, Red went on to say that Jameison had last been seen in the parking lot of the Clubhouse.

"Police are still investigating the cause of death, although a small, cobalt blue tee was found imbedded at the base of his skull and preliminary forensic evidence indicated it was hammered into the ex-ballplayer by a broad instrument. The Broward County Coroner has notified authorities to be on the lookout for someone who shanks with a driver.

"A Mr. Marcus Clock added he was sure Jameison died a happy man in that he was very fond of the par five, dogleg eighth that had never been eagled by a guest. After a large bite of what would have been Jameison's strawberry cheesecake, a Mr. Turk suggested that it was about five-to-one on finding the perp. Clock then added that, with Mr. Charles Berston's approval, all pin placements would be symbolically centered on each green and that flags would be flown at half-mast for the remainder of the day."

Enough! We arrive at the front door, and G. D. is sitting on his stool with his usual blank stare. I slide off the cart and walk over to him while Alo's eyes take in every movement. "Hey, G.D., you remember any large black bags coming over on the shuttles from the Diplomat or Executive this morning?"

He returns my inquiry with that vacant look of his, and I'm suddenly aware of something large and sticky crawling up my esophagus. Now I really know why the guys call him GD. He doesn't know a God-damned thing, and my ass is going to be in that water hazard if something doesn't happen pretty soon. I turn to walk back to the cart and avoid looking at Alo who is gazing out at the parking lot. Just my luck…and the lump is now in the back of my throat as my decent eye focuses on a large caddy limo, and I picture myself being tied up and thrown into the trunk for a one-way trip out to the eighth, the hood already in place over my head and the bag lashed to my trembling body.

The bag! The trunk!! Could it be? Is it possible? Am I saved from this horrible fate? Will I deprive the boys from feasting on my sandwich and dessert? Hot damn! Stay with me, guys. I think there's gonna be a tomorrow!

I slide back onto the seat and hold my breath. "Ah, Mr. Alo, did you drive over here today by any chance?"

"Yeah, I've still got Flo's wheels," he says quietly

"What are you driving, sir?"

"I'm driving that jet-black '76 Mark IV Lincoln Continental over there."

"She's a beauty."

"You bet, kid. That machine set me back more than eleven thousand."

I quickly head for the parking lot and steer past a dozen or so cars before coming to a slow stop at the back of the Mark IV. "May I have the keys, sir? I'd like to check the trunk. Do you think the bag might be in there?"

"According to my best recollection, I don't remember."

Terrific, the guy is recalling that he doesn't remember, and I hate thinking about what this guy has convinced himself he's forgotten. Regardless, he gives it a slight grunt as he digs into his front pocket and seems just a little annoyed as he forks over two keys, one square and the other round. I take the round one, move off the cart, and insert the key into the slot and then hear a click as the trunk parts a few inches. I take a deep breath and exhale, slowly emptying my lungs like a weightlifter who is about to jerk ten pounds over his best effort, and decide to go with the Bandaid approach, the ole quick rip. I hurl open the trunk and it immediately flies back down and smacks the tops of my wrists, but I feel no pain. In fact, I feel absolutely nothing at all during the three seconds it takes my brain to tell me I'm looking at a large, black golf bag, complete with hood and gold lettering. I take my time, allowing my system to return to a state of normalcy before hauling the bag out of the trunk and taking it over to the golf cart where I'm greeted by a half smile from you-know-who.

"Not bad, kid. I like a guy who can get the job done."

Sure, but what about a guy who doesn't? If Alo figures G. D. should have taken the bag out of the trunk, it might be the ex-pug headed for the water hazard. I think it's time for damage control. "Simple mistake, I'm sure, Mr. Alo. G. D. hasn't seen you play all that much and probably assumed you were here for social or business reasons," I say with a light but cautious smile.

"Yeah," he says reflectively, "I guess you're right."

After securing the clubs with the black nylon crisscross straps to one of the two upright stands at the rear of the cart, I get behind the driver's yoke, and once again, his hand engulfs my shoulder.

"Tell you what, kid. I'm going to be out on the range with Bottomly getting my lesson for about an hour, and then I might putt around a little. Tell your boss I want to meet you in the lounge for drinks around noon, and you're paying, right?" he says with that sinister half smile.

I nod in the affirmative. So what would you do big stuff? Tell him you've got a fatty corned beef on white with mayo waiting for you? Yeah,

I'll bet you would for sure. Anyway, I wind my way back down to the entrance of the cart room, pull to a stop, and hop off. "Just keep the cart, Mr. Alo. The driving range is down the path off to the right of the tenth tee."

The grin has yet to leave his face. "Right, kid," he says as he slides across the seat and positions himself behind the yoke. "By the way," he adds as he extends his hand with a bill in it, "when you pick up the tab, make sure you keep the change."

"Thanks much, Mr. Alo. I'll see you at noon."

He nods, depresses the accelerator, and heads out toward the driving range. Finally, my nervous smile melts into a broad grin as I look at the hundred dollar bill in my hand. Actually, the tip is just a bonus, because it's great to still be alive and vertical on a Monday morning, and unless Jimmy drinks up the whole C-note, I'll have some extra cash for Morgan's tonight. In either event, the story holds true: the "goodfellas" are very generous with their ill-gotten gains.

*

I'm sitting in the Bengal Lounge making small talk with Ron when Blue Eyes walks in. I glance at the ultra-modern Scandinavian clock behind the bar and notice the time is twelve o'clock high, so he's right on the button. Jimmy appears to have taken a shower and looks pretty sharp for a guy who has to be in his low seventies, but if I thought he was scary, hold the phone! He's got a guy with him who appears to be a scaled-down version of Walt Disney's giant in Jack and the Beanstalk. He looks to be about six four, but he's slumping along and bent over so he probably runs closer to six six, and he's got to be well over four hundred pounds. He has no neck, literally, and his bowling ball head appears to be balanced on the top of his shoulders. His face is completely dominated by one thick, black eyebrow that travels the entire width of his forehead about three inches above his lips which would be more at home on a goldfish, and his hair is sparse and gray which is not surprising in that I figure this gorilla is older than Jimmy. Whoa, Nellie…he's got to be Jimmy's bodyguard even though Florida is designated as neutral turf meaning nobody's supposed to get whacked down here. That's why all these guys…Blue Eyes, Meyer (also called The Honest Gambler), the two Jakes, and Frank "The Prime Minister" Costello (who holes up over on 15th and Hollywood Boulevard)…all live in the neighborhood. All these guys have nicknames; ain't it a gas!

Yup, it's Jilly the Ice in the flesh. The word is that he's retired from the trucking business, and even though he's never been in a court or in a jail, everybody knows about the cargo Jilly used to ship. Last year when Ron gave me the profiles of the guys from New York, he said Jilly was known to work throughout the country, although the City was his home base and the East River was allegedly his main warehouse. It's odd how sometimes a guy can look the role, meaning it doesn't take much to think of Jilly wrapping his massive hands around some poor bastard's throat, just smiling him away. You think this guy looks sinister? I can't even begin to tell ya.

The two of them sit down in one of the corner booths, and Jimmy beckons to me. "Hey, kid, over here. It's not dignified for men our age to sit at a bar, and bring a couple of Chivas on the rocks with you." Ron puts together the drinks and I carry them over to the table and sit down in the red leather chair placed at the outside of the polished oak table.

"No trouble with the boss man, I assume?"

"No sir. Would you like to have one of the girls bring you a sandwich or something?"

"No. Thanks. I'll get a bite later at the hotel. I'd like you to meet my associate, Mr. Marinski." Jilly just grunts, so I don't bother extending my hand.

"I want to ask you a question, kid," Marinski begins. "I was in the lounge here last week and you guys were playin' a song about a guy who couldn't work anymore. I asked the good looker with the big chest where you got it from and she said probably you guys wrote it. Is that right?"

"Yes sir. I knew an old man once who worked most of his life for the same company, and they just laid him off one day. The guy was still sharp as a tack, but they just wanted a younger guy who they could pay a lot less, so they showed him the door. So I wrote the lyrics and T Moon put it to music a few months ago."

"Well, seeing as it's yours, do you think you guys could put it on tape for me? It's got a lot of meaning, a lot of similarity. Know what I mean?"

"No sir, Mr. Marinski. Not really."

"Well, give me some of the words, kid. What do they go like?"

"It begins, *looking into my morning glass, wondering where my life has past, sixty-five and I am gray, much too old to work another day, that's what they say, he's old and he's gray, got to send him away.*"

Marinski's eyes take on a withdrawn look and he appears to be deep into himself, while Jimmy is looking at him with a mixture of concern and sadness. Jilly then sighs, his barrel chest rising and falling slowly. "Just like me, kid. I was in the trucking business and I can tell you one thing. I knew my work, I mean no loose ends. You know?"

I don't say a word. Do you think I'm really supposed to respond to a question like that? What would you say? None of the bodies ever surfaced? But he's right about one thing, he was good at what he did…so they say.

"But then, all of a sudden, the company said goodbye, just like that," he adds in a sad voice. "No more Jilly. This old man, the song says he turned to painting, right? Don't your buddy Moon sing that?"

"Yeah, and I did write it like that. It goes, *so I looked and I finally found, on the block I kept walking around, the flowers and trees set me free, now my mind and hand both toil, with the brushes and the oils, maybe a whole new world for me."*

"So he paints, and he's hopeful, right?" Jilly asks optimistically.

"Not really, Mr. Marinski. That part's not true. We like to end most of our songs on an upbeat note, but that old man in real life doesn't really do that, he doesn't paint. He just walks around his block waiting to die."

Ooops-a-daisy! I pushed the wrong button. Jilly looks flat-out totally pissed, check that, indignant. "That ain't gonna happen to me, kid. That's why I took up golf. Imagine that! Seventy-six years old and I'm taking up golf and watching my waistline too. What do you think of that?"

What do I think? How about exercise, eat right, and die anyway which sooner or later applies to all of us? Well, I'd obviously be nuts to tell him that, but I'll share with you that I think he's blowing smoke up his own ass, that the day he breaks ninety he'll quaff some Chivas and forget to play the back nine, and that he's walking around that old man's block.

"I think that's great if that's what you want to do, Mr. Marinski."

"Aw shit, what do I know?" he says with what might pass as a smile as he takes a hit on his scotch. "Just put it on tape for me, okay? I've got a lady friend who does calligraphy, and I'll have her do it up so I can frame it and hang it in my den. Just give the tape to Charley, and he'll see that I get it." He then brings out a money clip, peals off a fifty, and lays it on the table.

"Deals a deal; I'm supposed to pick up the tab," I say looking over at Jimmy who has observed this whole scene very quietly. But his expression is pretty serious, and my chest immediately freezes. "We're honorable people, kid," he says. "As agreed, this is on you."

"That's a fact," Jilly adds as his huge lips spread into a grotesque smile, "so you're definitely buying the drinks, boychick. The bill's for the tape, right?"

Once again, I give it my weak smile. The two of them get to their feet, and Marinski adds, "After I get it framed, I'll send you guys a photograph, and you can tell your friends that Jilly Marinski has class, a collector no less." He laughs at this joke on himself as he turns to leave.

"You're a good kid, D Jack," Jimmy Blue Eyes says. I never got to see you play but heard you had all the skills. And if you ever need something, like a little favor or two, you just let me know." I smile, his comment appreciated.

I wait until the two of them have departed the lounge before I resume breathing. Collector! I'll say. Boy, have those guys done some collecting in their day. On the other hand, Alo, more often than not, is seen around town taking Meyer Lansky's mentally retarded kid, Buddy, to all kinds of places, so who knows? I reach across the table, scoop up the bill, and head back to the bar where Ron has been watching the whole scene.

"What the hell was that all about?"

"Funny, Stunt. I guess you just don't think much about guys like Jilly retiring. I always thought they stayed in business till they died, naturally or by other causes. Maybe Jilly's the exception to the rule."

"So now he's all fucked up, because he never planned for retirement?"

"I guess so," I say, somewhat lost in my thoughts. "I mean, how do you feel sympathetic for someone like that, and whodda thunk these guys actually get melancholy?"

Ron just shrugs, so I head for the door as I find more of my lyrics cruising through my head. *Came one day I was feeling low, Doctor said it ain't much though, you ought to rest a week or two, when I got back they said I was through, sorry man but it's true, and what we've got to do, is find one younger than you.*

It must be a bitch growing old, ya think? But, as the expression goes, it beats hell out of the alternative.

XI

MORGAN'S INN

and sitting alone, with a fire burning bright
a liter of wine, a book and an endless night
this ain't the way to spend the joys of youth
I hope my mind won't accept the awful truth
what a burden to bear
when you're going nowhere….

"See ya, guys," I said with a smile and a thumb's up as I headed out the door of the cloakroom and past one of the counters in the pro shop. The phones had provided little conflict and therefore no humor, so it had been a pretty slow time. Mr. Irving had checked in with me earlier in the day to see if I could contact Pete and arrange for a prime tee-off time the following day. You remember Irving, don't ya? I had given him the emergency special a few days ago, and now he was back for additional services. He'd gladly parted with fifty bucks which I wouldn't need for Morgan's because, as predicted by Charley, the guys from upstate New York were game but just didn't have the shots. Sam had called to say she was going to be hung up on some side work, so she had missed the drubbing we had given those two guys on the racquetball court, which was okay with me because, as usual, Charley had pretty much carried the show.

Right now, it's about 9:30 p.m. and having showered and undertaken a little beard trimming, I head into the dining room to see if I can spot Sam; don't see her, so I make for the lounge to check with Ron, but don't have to inquire. In the soft light of a ceiling spot, I see her strawberry-blond hair silhouetted by the reddish beams, and I note she seems to have adopted the corner booth as I walk towards her with a comfortable look on my face.

"Hi."

"Hi yourself," she responds as she glances at a small, round-faced watch on her left wrist. "It's 9:30, right about when you expected to get finished. How did you and Charley make out?"

"We took 'em two straight, but they were nice guys…none of that mano a mano stuff. One guy was a lifelong Mets fan, so he even asked for an autograph. Can I buy you a drink, or do you want to head out?"

"It's a little late, so I just as soon leave now if that's okay with you."

"That's fine."

She picks up a small black purse, comes to her feet, and smiles. "Shall we?"

I answer with a nod as we head out of the lounge, hang a right down the foyer, and then push through one of the huge, wood-stained doors. We're met by a cool breeze that I hope is signaling a pleasant evening. Amber lights ring the circular driveway and illuminate some of the beautiful flowers that line the approach. G. D. is sitting on his customary perch next to a board with a few dozen sets of keys hanging on hooks. Sometimes, I wonder if this guy actually has a place to sleep.

"How's it goin tonight, G. D.?"

"God-damn lass season," he mumbles, his eyes not leaving a small piece of wood at which he's hacking away with a two-inch penknife. He always seems to be whittling something or other, although I've never seen him finish anything and don't have a clue as to what he's trying to carve. The grapevine has it that G. D. is in someway related to Charley the Boss, but to date, no one has ever confirmed that theory.

"Have a nice evening, ole fella," I say as I glance at Sam whose mouth forms a smile but whose face clearly exhibits a certain amount of sadness. We head down the hill toward the employee's parking lot, and I'm very conscious of the fact that she stays on my right side and holds her purse near her left leg, so making some attempt at holding hands doesn't appear to be an option at this early stage of the evening. That's okay, because I've pretty much decided that if any of that is going to happen, she's going to have to initiate it.

"G. D. was a prize fighter, wasn't he?" she asks quietly.

"Yeah."

"What happened to him?"

"Lots, and now he's on Queer Street," I respond in a matter-of-fact way which stops her dead in her tracks, and she looks at me with that same fire in her eyes that I saw in Lakeland eight years ago and in the Lounge more recently.

"That's a hell of a note!" she says, her tone matching her expression. I stare at her, somewhat bewildered, and then suddenly realize the problem.

"That doesn't mean what you think it does, Sam. That's just boxing lingo. Queer Street means he got knocked out too many times, so now he thinks slowly or can't figure things out. He confuses easily and doesn't know where he is half the time. That's all it means."

"Are you sure? You're just not making that up are you?"

"I'm sure. I wouldn't kid about what getting hit in the head does to a person, okay?"

Her eyes are still staring at me, but the blaze has been replaced by something else, and she seems a little misty. "Okay," she says, barely above a whisper. The silence that follows is somewhat uncomfortable, but both of us seem determined to get back on sound footing as quickly as possible.

"So, what are we driving tonight?" she asks curiously.

"Why don't you pick between a Lincoln, BMW, Mercedes, or a Jaguar?"

"You forgot to include the seat on the back of a bike or none of the above."

"Skeptic," I say, pointing to the XK-120. "She's more than twenty years old and already a classic. What with Detroit saying they're going to discontinue the production of American convertibles this year, who knows what she might be worth someday?"

Sam grins as we approach the sleekest of all Jaguars. I think it sold brand new in 1954 for about $4,200 but God only knows what she's worth today. "She's a beauty and in great shape, but how did you manage to acquire a Jag?"

"The Mets didn't want me to go home with empty pockets, so this was where I invested most of my severance package. I hang out with a guy named Pahnke who likes to recondition foreign cars, so in the off season, we work on it now and then."

Sam approaches the front of the Jag and runs her hand across the long, curved, cream-colored fender as she admires the brown leather workmanship of the cockpit. I suddenly realize that I haven't seen her in street clothes and that, once again, the cute little girl I knew has truly matured into a stunning woman. And having kids surely didn't hurt any. She's wearing a kind of white jersey that accentuates her full breasts and covers the top of a light blue pleated skirt that appears to be made of a heavier material. The skirt falls above her shapely calves and her white, soft leather heels. My eyes come up, and I realize she's watching me, so I might as well tell the truth.

"I always used to think you had the edge over lots of other divers just because of the way you filled out your suit," I say sheepishly. "If there was any truth to that, you'd still win anything today, hands down."

She seems to shrug it off with a kind of "I could care less" look on her face as she turns to the door of the car. "Where's the handle on this thing?"

"No handle," I answer as I reach inside and pull the leather strap that opens the door. Without a word, she gets in, and I head around to the driver's side and lower myself into the bucket seat. My legs are fully extended as I press the starter button and depress the thick, rubber-padded clutch pedal. Then I wrap my right hand around the short leather-encased gearshift which is inserted into the floor between the two bucket seats and glance over at Sam. "Ready?"

She nods, finally exhibiting a little bit of excitement as I let out the clutch slowly and depress the gas pedal. The Jag turns a corner in the parking lot, and we head up the hill and then hang a left to cruise past the flower lined entrance approach. The wind tousles her hair, and although she hasn't said much, she seems content and relaxed, so I flick on the radio just in time to hear Thelma Houston cranking out "Don't Leave Me This Way" with an electric bass setting the driving disco beat.

"Have you seen the movie *Bingo Long and the Traveling All Stars and Motor Kings*? It just came out this year?"

"No, why?" she asks.

"Well, I'll admit it's about a baseball team, but it's got a terrific sound track, kind of a cross between Dixieland and Blues, and Thelma Houston did the vocals. She's the one you're listening to."

"Who was in the movie?"

"Ah, let me think on that. Bingo was the pitcher, and he was played by Billy Dee Williams. James Earl Jones was the catcher, and Richard Pryor was the goofball who tries to pass himself off as a Cuban."

"So I guess Pryor was the left fielder," she says mischievously. I don't think she's after a response here or trying to get a rise out of me, so I just let the music fill the void. The drive to Morgan's Inn is uneventful but positive because, at least when it comes to the issue of supper, I know where I'm headed. Once there, I park in the lot to the back left of the front door, secure the Jag, and hop out. Sam waits for me to come around and open her door. I discreetly avoid looking at her, because the way the damn car is built, she has to lift up and out of the passenger seat and is undoubtedly exposing lots of leg. I don't want to get caught doing the schoolboy thing twice in one night. Her purse is still on her left side so I casually take her arm and head for the front door.

Once through, we are in the foyer that has an array of sailing ships on pedestals bolted to the mahogany paneled walls. The bar is off to the left, but it's late and it's Monday, so there are no patrons killing cocktails while waiting to be seated. John Morgan is standing at the entrance to the main room and is holding large black, leather encased menus under his arm, looking pretty different from his baseball days at Norfolk when he was on the way down and I was on the way up to my brief appearance in the Show. The position and his stature remind me of Charlton Heston holding the tablets in *The Ten Commandments,* but Heston was in some kind of robe and John is decked out in a midnight blue tux. He turns, sees us, and smiles.

"How are you doing, D Jack?" he inquires in his finest old friend tradition.

"Just fine, John. I'd like you to meet Samantha Frederickson." His look is one of obvious pleasure, maybe one notch or so below lust. Hell, ballplayers are ballplayers.

"Very nice to meet you, Samantha, although I can't say I agree with your taste in guys." He's probably expecting a cute smile or something like that, and when she barely acknowledges his remark, he moves into the dining room and heads toward a table in a dimly lit corner diagonally across from a red brick fireplace. A couple of logs are warmly and merrily crackling away, producing a romantic aural as well as visual atmosphere; I think this may be one of the only eating establishments in South Florida that has an honest to goodness fireplace. John seats Sam and then comes over to me and leans over my shoulder.

"Nice, D Jack," he whispers, "very nice, but I put her close to the fire. Maybe it'll warm her up some." He then slaps me on the shoulder and, smiling all the way, ambles back to his station at the door. Sam appears to be taking in the room while her eyes adjust to the light level. As for me, the ambiance is pretty much lost, what with the sunglasses and my impaired vision.

"It's a very charming place, Devon. Did he make all those boats himself?"

"His dad made most of them. Took him the better part of thirty years to build this collection, and I think the old man has been offered quite a few bucks for this stuff, but he doesn't want to part with it. John did say that he donated a clipper ship to a maritime museum down on the waterfront on Factor's Walk in Savannah, but then got pretty sad about it, so everything stays here now. He sure has some beautiful ships, and this establishment is damn near a nautical museum all its own."

"I was wondering where he gets some of these things, like that glass table over there that looks like an old portal or something. And our table looks like what they use to steer the ship."

"I think John once told me there are some neat places up in Charleston where they buy most of the stuff. You want a drink?"

"Yes, thanks."

Like magic, a waitress is at my elbow asking if we are interested in a cocktail before dinner, and I nod in the affirmative, looking at Sam rather than the fine-looking, long-haired brunette.

"I'll have a White Russian and he'll have a double VO on the rocks with a splash of water," she says as the waitress simply grins and turns, figuring maybe it's kind of cool that the lady is placing the order.

"I don't remember White Russians?"

"Daddy makes them for me along with an occasional Brandy Alexander, but I assumed you're still a creature of habit when it comes to drinking."

"True, you picked up something from Billy, and I picked up something from my father. Always drink the same stuff and make sure it's the best quality…but then he didn't drink much which was a good thing because he obviously couldn't afford expensive liquor."

The dining room is relatively empty, so it only takes a few moments for the waitress to return and place the drinks on small embossed nautical cocktail napkins in front of the two of us. Sam takes the narrow-stemmed glass in her hand and seems to hesitate, but I doubt seriously that a toast is in order unless it's going to be pretty impersonal. I grasp the tumbler, shrug and smile, but my mind is almost a total blank, so without thinking, I offer up Bogie's famous line, "Here's looken at you, kid," and am somewhat relieved that she answers the classic line with a half smile. We both sip our drinks, and Sam replaces hers on the napkin and looks downwards at the mocha-colored cocktail topped with a sprinkle of nutmeg.

I decide to get right at it. "Okay, like you said, Billy didn't extend the invititation, so what's on the conversation agenda?"

"Why don't we talk about Mr. Schmedler's clubs?"

"Can't talk about something I don't know anything about," I respond lightly.

"So I guess that leaves out politics, too, huh?" As they say, in Pirate talk, that sounds like a shot across my bow, and like most Pirates, I think I'll ignore the sarcastic part of it.

"We're college educated; we can talk politics if you like, but I'm not sure there's that much to talk about."

"You didn't find last month's election interesting?" Sam says seriously.

"Well sure, it had its moments. Carter comes out of Georgia with nothing on the national scene to speak of and actually runs against Nixon, making morality in politics his issue. Ford's a nice guy who can't avoid Tricky Dickey's paintbrush…and of course, the fact that he pardoned him, so he takes the deep six and goes back to tripping and playing golf. So, which outstanding candidate did you vote for?"

"I helped Jimmy win Florida by more than a million votes because I think he has a little more substance than you give him credit for."

"Such as?"

"Such as draft dodgers. I don't say it often because I lost Dolph, but I think his life was wasted, so among other things, I think it's right that Carter says he'll pardon the men who went to Canada."

I can't tell whether I hear bitterness or sadness in her voice, but she seems pretty passionate on the issue so I move on quickly. "And?"

"And I like his stance on equal rights which I think needs to be addressed, because once Nixon went to China, foreign policy seemed to become the focus, and domestic stuff got pushed to the side."

"Anything else?"

"Well, I don't think we can ignore Cuba forever, so I like what he has to say about at least opening up official channels of communication with Castro's government."

"You seem pretty up-to-date on the big issues."

"I am. A person should know why they vote for a candidate. How about you? Who did you vote for…and why?"

"I voted for Ford."

Sam looks at me and appears to be more dumbfounded then curious. "Why?"

"I think California generally votes the right way and the polls predicted he would win there, and he did."

"And that's it?"

"Well, how about I think Rosalynn is the real genius behind the peanut farmer? She'll make a terrific pillow talk advisor, but she wasn't on the ballot."

"You're not serious," she says with a definite hint of annoyance.

"Right, how about Ford played football for Michigan, and I have a soft spot for nice ex-jocks?"

"Okay, enough of politics, because I don't know if you are being serious or just being a wiseass, but I can see how you could relate to half of what you just said, the ex-jock part," Sam says, obviously omitting the word "nice" and throwing out the second zinger of the evening…and yes, I'm keeping score. So, do I take the pitch or swing away? You probably think I ought to wait her out, but I'm going for the fences because I think I've had enough of the early innings in this game.

I take a solid pull on my VO and look straight into her green eyes. "Okay, Sam, you're implying I'm not nice. So why did you come here with me and why am I buying you dinner?"

"Because I asked and you said yes."

"Why did you ask?"

She matches my serious look, but her voice is soft. "Because for a long time I've thought you weren't nice, which is one hell of an understatement, but after the last week, I'm not so sure."

"Great, maybe, finally, I'm a nice guy. "So, what do you want?" I ask off-handedly. She seems confused because I'm looking over her shoulder, but then she figures it out and smiles as she turns to the waitress who has come up slightly behind her.

"I'll have the newberg." The waitress jots down nothing, which is the way they do things at Morgan's, and then looks over to me.

"Last chance for the duck, Sam, or are you hoping I'll order it?"

"You're a meat-eater, Dev," she says as she turns to look at the waitress. "He'll have the ribeye, medium-rare." The brunette nods and seems to be increasingly amused that the lady has also ordered the gentleman's dinner as well as the drinks. She turns and heads for the kitchen.

"Okay, Sam, you ordered the drinks, and you ordered the dinner, so you're clearly in control, right?"

"Right," she responds defiantly.

"What is it you want to be in control of?"

"Whatever might happen between us."

"And that's what you're not sure about?"

"Dev, we didn't see each other for a long time, and all of a sudden, here we are, working at the Presidential, whether we like it or not," she says, pauses, and then seems to be reflecting about something. "Have you thought at all about how it was with us?"

"I'd be a liar if I said no, but then I just say to myself, it was yesterday and we were kids, at least I was, and fairy tales only exist for the naïve or the truly pure."

"I agree, but there are those that say the past is the past but you can learn from it."

"True, but there are also those who say when history comes in the form of the written word, white-out doesn't make things go away."

"Still the pessimist, aren't you, Dev?"

"No, I'm a realist."

"Then let's get real."

"About what?"

"We work in the same place, Dev. So do we ignore each other, be pleasant....?"

"Have dinner again?"

"You mean a date?" she says cautiously.

"What if we just call it an occasional friendly get-together?"

"Why would you like to befriend a widow with two kids; my cousin's son, who is my ward; and a dad who hates your guts?"

"The same reason you might be willing to spend some time with a guy whose glory days are behind him."

"I've said it before, Dev, there's more to life than the game."

"And there's more for a woman your age than being a widow," I say, getting in my two cents' worth.

She drains her drink and appears to want another one, so I try to catch the waitress's eye. She nods my way, and I hold up two fingers, after which she smiles and heads for the bar.

"Who are you, Devon Jameison?" Sam says somberly.

"That's tough, Sam. How much time do I get?"

"I'll give you one sentence."

"Well, off the top of my head, I was the golden boy who had it all, and now I'm a disillusioned guy who pretends life is still worth living. And you?"

Sam still looks serious. "I'm forever the incurable optimist, Dev, and I know my tomorrows will be better and brighter, and I intend to seek them out."

"Then you haven't changed, and if memory serves, that's a good thing."

"And maybe you have changed, and if memory serves, that might also be a good thing."

"So, does that mean you want us to get somewhat reaquainted?"

"Yes, I'm still curious but I think it will be difficult because we knew each other pretty well, so if we are going to try to get to know each other again, it's going to have to be a very slow process."

"I think I understand what you're saying. But let's make sure I know what you want or don't want, so spell it out, Sam."

"Do you remember what I said to you on our first date at Dania Beach when I was sixteen years old?"

"You said you didn't really think there were submarine races going on out there in the Atlantic Ocean."

"Okay, then the second thing, wise guy."

"No French kissing," I respond with a laugh.

"That's right, Dev. No kissing."

Okay, boys and girls, I've got the message. "Good enough. Are there any other ground rules, ump?"

"That will do for starters. I'll let you know if and when others are needed."

"Agreed, but keep in mind that ground rules are put in place to make the game fair for both sides."

"As you would say, meaning?"

I look at her a little more seriously and would like to take her hand, but I don't. "I'm just like you, Sam. I don't need the pain, and I've had my fill of hurt."

"Me too, but lovers hurt people, Dev, not friendly acquaintances."

Okay, sportsfans; that was number three, and the drinks arrive, thank God. Whether she meant it or not, that last statement is a clear reminder that we were lovers and I was the bad guy. It's clearly a heads up that the "getting to know each other again" process will be very contemplative at best, and between you and me, I think the Turk would go about 6-1 this thing will end with a handshake. You got any small bills you whanna put down? Anyway, once again, I ain't about to bite on that one, so it's time to change the subject.

"So, tell me about your ward. How did that come to be?"

She takes a sip of her White Russian and smiles, and I suspect the smile is from thoughts of her ward as opposed to the soothing effect of the cocktail. "His name is Sean and he's eight. My cousin in Camden got pregnant, and the guy took off. To her credit, she tried to raise him, but the single mom stuff was pretty stressful, and she started drinking heavily. Two years ago she overturned her car on a highway ramp out on the Whitehorse Pike and was killed."

"So you went to Camden."

"Yes, I went to Camden. Despite her weaknesses, she was devoted to Sean, and he's a great kid."

"I'm sure he is," I say with the glaring awareness that she has people in her life and I don't. It's something you try not to dwell on too often, but it can smack you in the head. "Just make sure you don't adopt him," I respond lightly, trying to change my own mood, "because if the U.S. follows India's lead, parents will be penalized if they have more than two kids…and China is even worse"

"So, you *were* being a wiseass; you do keep up on what's going on."

"I do, but apparently not as much as you do. Truth is, I would have voted for Carter, but everything went south on election day, and I never made it away from the Clubhouse," I admit with a tinge of social irresponsibility. "So," I hurry on, "do you plan to adopt him?"

"That's a tough nut to crack for a single parent. I don't think I could have even gotten him down here two years ago without Daddy also being related."

"Is he going to be a diver?"

"Right now he's an outfielder on a T-ball team."

"Maybe he should be a diver, or a football player like Dolph. You know what they say about ballplayers."

She ignores my self-directed shot. "Well, that's pretty far down the road, but Saturday isn't."

"What happens Saturday?"

She takes another sip of her drink and looks at me a bit apologetically. "You asked me earlier why I wanted to have dinner with you tonight, and actually, I've kind of sandbagged you."

"Meaning?"

"Meaning I'm the team Mom, and Saturday we're having our winter clinic and picnic at Jefferson Park. And," she runs on quickly, "I mentioned to the coaches I found out you live here, and they asked me if I could get you to work with the kids for a few hours."

Well sportsfans, so much for a rekindled interest in me, right? "Saturday is usually pretty hectic as you know, and I doubt Charley would let me off," I say, needing an excuse for a bruised ego.

Now her look is just flat sheepish. "I already talked with Charley, and he thought it would be good PR. He said the guys could cover for you until noon, and don't tell me you don't still play some, because I saw you having a catch with a big kid last week."

She's got me boxed in, but I feel the need to take a last stab. "True, but I haven't had much experience with the little ones, Sam, and Little League parents can be just flat nasty if I recall."

She hesitates and looks genuinely remorseful. "I'm sorry, Dev. This isn't fair, and I'm being selfish. You really have no idea how famous you still are around here, and it would have been so special for the kids as well as their folks. Honest, I just wasn't thinking about you, and I should have realized it might bring up bad memories or just be difficult for you to go back to where it all started."

She's got a point. Jefferson Park was where it all started. I was ten years old, and Hollywood had one Little League team, and you had to try out. Twelve kids got 100% wool uniforms, and the rest went home and cried. I figured I didn't have much of a chance against all those eleven-and twelve-year-olds. But my Dad pushed me and one day after school, I rode my used red Schwin bike the three blocks from Hollywood Central School to Jefferson Park. That afternoon I was given my first uniform, and three weeks later opened the season on the mound. That first year, I went 8-2 with a 2.03 earned run average, batted .437, and hit two dingers, one of 'em a grand slam. Yeah…they kept stats on the kids, because Little League baseball in Florida was big time and still is. I was clearly on a roll right from the gitgo, and the train stayed on the track, full steam ahead, right down to the Saturday night wreck at Shea Stadium. Damn, I was good!

"I really am sorry, Dev," Sam says, breaking into my thoughts of what most people would probably view as a glorious youth. Funny how early the envy began and how quickly I had retreated into being a loner. Maybe so, but I sure as hell have some memories I think, smiling to myself.

"What's the grin for?" she asks, sounding a little relieved.

"I was just thinking I had some great baseball moments."

"Would you care to share a few of them?"

"Okay. You were around for two. The first is when I threw the no-hitter to win the state championship, and the second was when I signed my contract with the Mets."

"Even though you got hurt," she says seriously, "I'm surprised you didn't include playing in Shea Stadium. Obviously, I wasn't with you, so maybe it was bad luck."

"I don't think so, Sam. Now that I think about it, you weren't with me for what was probably my best moment."

"I read in the papers you went two for four with a dinger and three runs batted in in your first game against Toledo. Was that it, because you knew you could play at that level?"

"I'm surprised you knew about that, but nope, that wasn't it."

"So what was it?"

"You got me thinking about Jefferson Park and I think maybe my best, not greatest, but best moment was when I got my first Little League uniform. You had to be between ten and twelve years old and they only handed out about a dozen uniforms. And they were really bad ass uniforms: solid red with black baseballs on each shoulder and the team name in black letters across the chest. I was only ten, and nobody who was ten made the team. But there I was, with my bad-ass uniform," I conclude with a grin.

She gives me a warm smile. “So,” I continue, “it’ll be okay with me, Sam. I guess the rich and famous won’t notice I’m missing for half a day. What time does the practice start?”

“Nine in the morning, but are you sure?”

“Yeah, I’m sure.”

Fuck, what else am I supposed to say? I’m trying to think of something to add to take her off the hook, but fortunately, a waiter is approaching the table holding a butcher block cutting board on which is a beautiful black-handled knife and a blood-red tender loin of beef.

“Good evening, sir. I believe you have dined with us before?”

“Right, cut me about ten ounces and I’d like it medium rare…and, ah, the lady is having the newberg, so we’d like a bottle of Chateau Carbonnieux served with dinner.”

“Very good, sir.” He carves the meat with one clean slice and displays the cut on the board for my approval, which he gets with a nod and a smile. “Help yourselves to the salad bar and have a nice evening,” he says pleasantly as he departs.

As soon as he moves away from the table, Sam gives me a playful smile. “That was very impressive, Devon. The Chateau Carbonnieux with dinner. I had no idea I was being escorted by such a cultured gentleman.”

“The rich like to occasionally be seen in public with a jock, so every once in awhile I got a shot at some five star restaurants.” We both push back from the table, getting to our feet. “Well, not too cultured,” I continue. “The fact that it’s a white wine and goes with seafood makes it a solid choice even though I’m having red meat. Some would call me uncouth, while others would champion my selection as that of a dedicated individualist. Needless to say, I would hope that you agree with the latter point, but I figure you’ll enjoy the wine either way, right?”

“Let’s eat, smart-ass,” she says as we head for the extensive salad bar.

*

The next hour passes rapidly as we relish John’s butter-soft steak and velveteen newberg accompanied by twice-stuffed baked potatos with real bacon bits and fresh chive grown in the small garden behind the establishment. The coffee is superb, maybe a hint of chicory, but somewhat anticlimactic after the wine. No room for desserts. We engage in some small talk that includes little stories and recent anecdotes that allow us to become a little more familiar with each other, and then say our goodnights to host Morgan.

The drive up Biscayne Boulevard is quiet but comfortable. It's been awhile since I've been to Hollywood this way, because I usually just take the causeway over to A1A and then go about fifteen miles north to my apartment on Hollywood Beach. I note that Doria's Orange Bowl pizza joint is still in business in its same location a few blocks north of Gulfstream Race Track. About half a mile north of the restaurant, the Hollywood Kennel Club still has a full parking lot even though the night's card must be about over. I've never really enjoyed the dog track that much. You get twenty or so minutes to handicap things, and then the race goes off for about thirty-one seconds. I go another five or six blocks up the road and then hang a right-hand turn on Dewey Street and drive past houses I haven't seen for a long time.

"Dev, I'd like you to just let me out in front of the house."

"No gentlemanly walk to the door?" I ask lightly, figuring all along she sure as hell wasn't going to invite me into Billy's house for a nightcap.

"I don't think Daddy is up. He did know I was having dinner with you tonight but he wasn't overly happy about it. So just in case, I'd rather not upset him by having him actually see us together."

"There's together, and then there's together, so there really isn't any reason for Billy to be upset, is there?"

"No, I guess not."

Terrific, I was thinking I might suggest a place for our next rendezvous, but the timing seems off to me. "So then, I'll see you at the baseball clinic, right?"

"Yes," she responds. "And thanks again for doing it," she adds as she retrieves her purse from its spot just behind the gearshift. The Jag slowly cruises to a relatively quiet stop in front of her house which was built in the mid '40s, about the same time as the Jefferson Street house. She quickly pulls the leather strap and is out of the car in a heartbeat. "For what it's worth, I didn't expect to relax as much as I did," she says with a half smile, and with that, she turns and heads for the front door.

Well, that was a record, I think to myself as I slowly drive down to 14th avenue, hang a left, and head for Hollywood Beach Boulevard. I mean there were times we sat out in front of her house in Billy's Chysler and made out for an hour, after which we would lean against each other at the front door for another fifteen minutes. Those thoughts have me feeling pretty melancholy as I turn right on the Boulevard and head east for the Hollywood Beach Bridge which was actually built by a chain gang and spans the Intercoastal Canal. But deep down, I know what the problem is, and it bothers me that I see it as such. When I said to her just a few minutes ago that Billy didn't have any reason to be upset, she agreed, and I was hoping she wouldn't. So now I'm really thinking dinner was a mistake and I ought to just lay low, but then I've committed myself to working with the kids on Saturday, and I can't back out on that.

You wouldn't, would ya?

Great, we finally agree on something! See ya tomorrow.

XII

ANTOINETTE AND REDWOOD BENCHES

Sitting on a redwood bench
and making up my rhymes
thinking of a crooked path
and headed for bad times

The applause is soft and seems to be coming from all the corners of the room. It's been a pretty good Wednesday night crowd with most of the patrons lending at least half an ear to T's solos. The applause, at the moment, is for Moon's covers of a medley of Chapin's *Taxi*, *Cat's in the Cradle*, and *Greyhound*. There is somewhat of a mystery going on worth sharing. Howard Sheridan's foxy sister-in-law has been sitting by herself for over an hour and has apparently done little more than sip drinks and people-watch. With the medley over, which usually completes Moon's second set of the night, I place the Yamaha on top of its case, slide off the stool, and make my way toward Antoinette's table. As I approach, she looks right at me and gives me kind of a 'come on' smile, so I'm thinking coyness doesn't seem to be her thing. I'm about to give her my A-1 friendly hello but she beats me to the punch.

"You back up the Moon-man with some nice sounds, D Jack," she says, the smile still painted broadly across her cutie-pie face. Her picture-perfect teeth kind of remind me of a toothpaste ad that was made at Slippery Rock in Oak Creek Canyon which was one of my favorite getaways during the Arizona years. I also note those even, pearly whites are surrounded by blood-red, moist lips. "Buy you a drink?" she adds.

"I'd rather buy you one. I've got some pull in this place," I respond as I sit down without being formally invited and note out of the corner of my eye that Sal is already on her way. "What would you like, ah…?"

"You can call me Antoinette, D Jack, and a CC sour will be fine." Sal places a VO in front of me, which of course is a no-brainer, and I order Antoinette her Canadian Club whiskey sour.

"Hope you don't mind if I don't wait." Antoinette's smile tells me no problem so I take a deep pull on my drink. She eyes me slowly, the smile still painted on her face.

"You play guitar about as well as you clip expensive cigars," she observes in a very relaxed manner. "Given what you used to do in the ballpark, I'll bet there are a lot of things you do rather well."

"I do some things a little better than others. Doesn't take a whole hell of a lot of talent to play back-up acoustical guitar or put one end of a cigar into a cutter and snip it." Okay, she's obviously on the prowl, so give me some elbowroom here and let's see where this goes.

"I was very attracted to you Sunday night," she continues, "because you seem to be candid, I mean an honest, trustworthy sort of guy."

Trustworthy sort of guy! What kind of bullshit is this? I definitely smell a rat. A woman only calls a guy trustworthy if she wants to trust him about something, and I doubt seriously I'm the something. Sal interrupts my thoughts as she places the sour in front of Antoinette and quickly moves on to another table after giving me a very fast and curious look. Antoinette takes a sip of her drink and sensuously licks some of the foam from her cherry lips.

"I have a problem, D Jack. I live with a very possessive, wealthy man who basically married me for my connections and who needs to have a good-looking woman on his arm at social affairs which more often than not turn into business affairs. Those are about the only times he wants me around, and unfortunately, I have a very high sex drive," she adds with a look I can't even begin to describe. Hell, lady. Sympathy you ain't gonna get…help maybe but sympathy, no.

"It makes things a bit difficult as I am sure you can imagine," she adds. Lady, you can't even imagine what I imagine, but I give her a supportive look.

"I'm very careful about these so-called indiscretions, primarily because I don't want to cause Howard any embarrassment by being the wayward sister-in-law. That's why I wanted to talk with you. I've been told by a few friends who have stayed here that if I needed something, anything, you were the one to see."

"I do my best to provide for the needs of the guests," I say seriously, once again, assuming I won't be the one filling her needs.

"I'm glad we understand each other," she purrs.

"Is your husband in town? And if so, is he conducting any business while you're here?"

Again, the full relaxed smile but this time there seems to be an extra shine or light in her eyes. "He'll be in an executive meeting, three-way telephone conference call, 10:00 'til noon tomorrow."

"Is he in business with Mr. Sheridan?"

"No way, Howard despises him. And speaking of Howard," she says as she reaches into her purse, "here are two flight tickets for your trip out to my sister's birthday party in Aspen on the 23rd. He got you an extra just in case you want to bring someone with you. There's also an itinerary and some other information in there."

As I take the envelope from her manicured hand with fingernails that match her blood-red lips, for some reason I'm relieved to know Sheridan is not associated with the husband, probably because I think Sheridan seems to be a nice guy, and I'm about to aid and abet his kin. "Thanks…and what we were talking about…nothing to it, Antoinette. We'll just arrange for a putting lesson during his conference call."

She start's moving around just a tad and seems unable to control her hunger; I mean she seems to be showing her appetite for physical satisfaction. "That's perfect. I'll be taking a lesson from you," she says as she takes another hit on the sour. "Now, how do we work out things with Ron?"

Ah hah! Da cat is out o' da bag! I don't know how he networks these things, but his prowess doesn't seem to be the best kept secret at the Presidential Golf and Country Club. "I assume you mean the guy over there tending bar?"

"Are there any other Rons working here?"

"No, so I'll tell you what. Rather than play cat-and-mouse games, how about I just go over and get him and introduce you? I can handle the bar while you two get acquainted. Okay?" I say mechanically.

"Fine," she says and, after pausing, reaches over and takes my hand. "On second thought, why don't you come back to the hotel tonight and make love to me?"

Uh oh, she seems to have picked-up on my business-like tone for not being the anointed one. Maybe I ought to take her up on it, but just between you and me, a sympathy screw has never been high on my list of favorite things to do.

"Antoinette, do you make love to your husband?"

"The few times he's around and wants to, yes."

"So you're saying you hold him in your arms, whisper affectionate words from your heart, hit him up with slow, wet kisses, and then afterwards fall asleep in the warmth of his embrace?"

"You know damn right well that's not what I'm saying," she says, eyes down, as she lets go of my hand and takes a sip of her cocktail. "Have you slept with a lot of women, D Jack?"

"I've never kept count."

Her eyes come up to meet mine, and the smile returns to her face. "So the super-jock lost count, huh?"

"I'd say a hell of a lot less than you'd think."

"And by your definition, how many women have you made love to?"

"One."

"And did she love you back?"

"I'd like to think she did."

"Well then," she says with a hint of sadness, "I guess you have me by one but let me rephrase my earlier question. Would you like to come back to the hotel tonight and bed me?" she asks with what appears to be some make-believe enthusiasm.

"Antoinette, tell me your husband is a self-centered sonuvabitch so all of this with Ron seems right."

Okay. You've got me and that was really embarrassing because I know you've heard that one in the movies, but I'm just trying to inject something into this thing that might make her feel okay with all of this, not that I'm really sure it's necessary. Who really knows what's right or wrong, good or bad…or maybe it's just a matter of justifiable retribution as opposed to some deep extra-marital ugly going on here. No matter, all of it falls under that stuff called ethics which I pretty much avoided at ASU, much to your delight, I'm sure. Agreed, this ain't the time for philosophical speculation, or bullshit as I suspect you would more commonly label it. Anyway, this also ain't the time to be chatting with you because that half-interested look is still painted across her face.

"Sorry, Antoinette, I didn't mean to pry."

"That's okay, but I want you to know," she offers quickly, "I'm not a whore. We haven't been man and wife for years, and I mean about as much to him as that cigar you cut for Howard. It's nothing more than an aristocratic marriage…coexistence, that's all, and for the last few years I simply have refused to co-exist on his terms. But of course, he doesn't know that and I doubt he would care." She pauses, waiting for some sign of understanding, so I just give her a supportive nod.

"So," she continues, "you didn't respond to my restated offer."

"No response is a response, Antoinette."

"You know how to take a girl off the hook, D Jack, and thanks for the drink," she says with an air of relief and a half smile. "Now, how about that introduction we were talking about a few minutes ago?"

Just as fast as it came, her smile fades as she glances away, and there seems to be nothing left to say, so I just nod again and head for the bar. One thing is for damn sure...Ron is about to get himself one of the best photo ops of his lusty life and, who knows, maybe more.

*

For once I'm going to surprise you. I'm actually living my lyrics and sitting on a redwood bench, and frankly, I'm not sure if I'm on a crooked path or not. A number of these benches are under large shade trees set farther away from the driving range and putting green. It's a nice spot to be munching on my Friday lunch of hot pastrami on rye with brown mustard, and washing down bites with a hot cup of coffee. Needless to say, this kind of lunch would get nods of approval rather than *oye veys* at Wolfie's. I usually don't drink coffee other than for breakfast, but there's a distinct chill in the air and a warm-up brew seems to be the order of the day. I'm just sort of daydreaming when I notice Marcus walking my way, carrying a bottle of Schlitz and smiling as he approaches the bench.

"Private party?" he inquires pleasantly.

"Just having some lunch in the sunshine; my bench is your bench."

Marcus sits down and rubs his forearm across some little beads of sweat that have accumulated on his brow. Funny, he shouldn't be sweating on a day like this, so I wonder if he's feeling okay. He then runs his hands through his brown hair, twice, three times. I knock down the last bite of sandwich and take a deep swallow of the dark Columbian brew.

"So much for lunch," I announce as I glance over at the driving range and check a few guests hitting with woods. Truth is, this place is beautiful, and it would be great to just be able to enjoy it for more than a few minutes.

"You've been pretty quiet the last few days, kid. That's unusual for you. Are you feeling okay?"

"Ginger peachy keen, other than pimping for Antoinette and setting her up with Ron last night; how about you?"

"Fine," he says in a too matter-of-fact way, "but I know you better, so let's not do the 'worry about me syndrome' because I've seen you like this less than half a dozen times since you started here...but then I guess you're going to keep your record intact. You've never said anything serious in the past, and you probably won't say anything serious now, right?"

"Well, yes and no Marcus. Your understanding of people sometimes is uncanny, so I owe you this much. You're the guy who said Sam is the one who is way too serious for me." I turn to face the old man. "You remember that?"

He returns a look of surprise. "Sam?"

I nod and look down at the ground and watch some red ants scampering about with an apparent lack of direction. Very funny, red ants really know where they're going, and I'm the one who's kind of aimless. Marcus is obviously waiting for me to continue. I have a strong liking for the old man and don't want to push him aside. Most of the old ones need to be needed, don't they?

"She was a junior in high school when she put all her apples in one basket, and the whole thing went to hell."

"What was the basket?"

"Me."

"And why did it go to hell?"

"I screwed the pooch."

"So the problem is in the past," Marcus concludes. "Today's a new day and so is tomorrow, and there will be lots of tomorrows."

"No, Marcus, the problem isn't in the past. The problem is now, and the future, too."

Marcus seems to sense some concern on my part and takes a few swallows from his Schlitz. "Seeing as you said Sam was in high school, that was maybe seven or eight years ago, and you're both different people now. It's amazing how simple it is to really get to know someone if that's what you want to do," he offers supportively. "I know she was married and has kids. Is that it?"

Good ole Marcus, old-fashioned to the end. "No, Marcus, it ain't her or her kids. It's me, because I screwed up and sometimes you just let it go, but other times, if it's a royal cluster fuck, you want to make it right."

"So, what did you do to make it right, back then I mean?"

"Nothing," I say with a shrug. "I tried to see her once, and Billy blew me off, so I figured I'd never see her again."

"So now you see her, and you want to make it right?"

"Yeah, I do."

"For you or for her?"

"It's kind of one and the same, Marcus," I respond thoughtfully. "There's a theory about equilibrium that says we all try to find an orderly balance in our lives, and we can't be healthy or happy unless we achieve that balance."

"And how do you go about that? I mean, if you had a bad experience, how do you get back your balance, or equilibrium, or whatever you want to call it?" he asks.

"What did you do when you lost your wife, Marcus?" My inquiry clearly sends him into his world of memories, and from the look on his face, I immediately regret having posed the question.

"I was lost, devastated," he replies somberly. "But then, I put all my energy into my daughter, and life went on."

"And what was the quality of that life?"

"Raising her and now seeing her at the University of Miami has been fulfilling. So yes, I've had a good life."

"What you did, Marcus, is you adapted; you adjusted your experience by creating a new plan or scheme, and by doing so you regained your equilibrium."

"Okay, college man, I see what you are saying. But the question still remains, for you or for her?"

"And like I said, it's one and the same. The only way I can regain my equilibrium is to resolve my past with her, and if it's a good and equitable resolution, then whatever is in her gets resolved too."

"So, what's your plan?"

"That's the rub. The only game in town, if there was one, didn't seem to provide much peace of mind. Basically, I think she was just curious to find out who or what I turned out to be, and I think she found out and I think that's the end of it."

"Do you think she thinks you're better or worse?"

"Better."

"So, then wouldn't that be some kind of equilibrium for her?"

"I guess so."

"Then we're really talking about you, aren't we?"

"You gonna bill me by the quarter hour for this?" I say, trying to inject a little levity into the conversation.

"You bet, but I promise it will go into the Ferdie fund. So?"

"So I guess there are some wrongs you can never right, and if I accept that, I can give it up and move on."

"What do you mean by move on?"

"I was thinking of asking Charley if I could work the patio pool bar at the hotel."

"D Jack, how many scars do you have, seriously?"

"Well, we'll count everything above the neck as one, so the shoulder is two, the gut is three, and the knees are four and five."

"Do they hurt?"

"I know they're there sometimes but not really."

"So, would that be kind of a physical equilibrium or balance or whatever you call it for a guy like you?"

"You're a crafty ole bastard, aren't you, Marcus?" I say with a grin. "Carry the scars but not the pain?"

"That's right, unless you have a better plan."

"No plan is a plan, Marcus."

"Fine, then you can stay here, show Sam you're a nice guy and, if that's all it's going to be, reconsider being a plumber rather than a philosopher. So, what do you think?"

"So, what yourself," I say with mock irritation. "If you're gonna be so pushy, get off my redwood bench."

Marcus gets to his feet with an equally phony show of indignation. "Okay, I'll leave you to ponder your future. But just remember," he adds pointing a bony finger at me, "it isn't your redwood bench. It belongs to the Presidential." He then pauses and puts a hand on my shoulder. "Don't blow this thing off," he says paternally. "Maybe this is the best thing that could happen to you and maybe this time next year you'll have had a plan and will have put it into play…*comprende, amigo*? Think about it."

I smile and put my hand on his extended arm. "I'll think about it, Marcus; I really will."

Marcus returns my smile and starts back toward the Clubhouse, and right out of the blue, I think to myself that so much in life seems to be like cigarettes. There are millions of smokers in the world, and almost all of them will tell you not to smoke. But now Marcus says I can't do this all my life. But look at him and the millions like him who set out to do something on a temporary basis and then suddenly wake up one morning to find out it's been too many years and there's no changing course. Hell, Marcus was an attorney before his wife died, and I guess he gave up that grind to take care of his daughter. I don't know, maybe he doesn't want me to follow in his footsteps, but I've got to tell ya, I hope like hell that I don't have to play his role thirty years from now. You don't think much of my chances? I'm starting to get worried 'cause we're agreeing too much. Truth is I'm not too optimistic either.

XIII

BASEBALL AT JEFFERSON PARK

...moments of knowing truth
those brief times at the helm
are clouded by my lapses
into unimportant realms

I see lots of cars, including two brand new Plymouth Voyagers, the extended body versions that seat fifteen people, so I decide to park the Yamaha at the northeast corner of the park at Jefferson Street and 16th Avenue and walk the fifty or so yards to the field. It really hasn't changed much since I was a boy although the infield itself has been repositioned in the center of the block that made possible an outfield fence and metal stands down the first and third baselines.

It's Saturday, the 4th, the first weekend in December and, like yesterday, there's still a bit of nip in the air, so I'm wearing jeans, sneakers, and an old, maroon Arizona State sweatshirt with gold lettering. As I approach the field, it appears as if the coaches have put the parents and kids in the stands and are sharing some information. A big heavy guy in a black and red Hollywood Optimist sweatshirt points my way and everyone turns and greets me with applause. Sure, I'll bet they had to give these kids a short biography, 'cause it ain't exactly like I'm Morgan or Bench or any other members of the Big Red Machine who are sporting the most current World Series Championship rings. I walk up to the big guy who extends his hand and then turns to the twenty or so parents and about a dozen kids sitting in the first two rows on the third base side. He gives me a smile and addresses the small gathering.

"Moms, dads and players, as you know, Annie, me and the boys just moved here five years ago, so we didn't actually see D Jack play Little League, high school, or Legion ball like a few of you did. In fact, unless I'm mistaken, weren't you teammates, Rusty?"

Now that really gives me a jolt. I'm getting a big smile and the ole thumbs up from Rusty Hillen who caught me during the two championship high school seasons. I return his thumbs up and suddenly realize, as I scan the moms and dads, that I went to school with a number of them, including a redhead named Trudy who dated me once and dumped me so she could tell her friends that I was no big deal. Other memories start flooding in, but I shut them out quickly so I can concentrate on the guy who appears to be the head coach.

"D Jack, I'm Jack Henshaw, and I got roped into being the coach this year," he says with a laugh as the parents and kids join in and clap their hands. "It's a real thrill and a pleasure to meet you and, on behalf of the parents and the team, I want to extend to you our appreciation for your willingness to come out this morning and work with the kids." Again, he gives me a very genuine handshake and motions for me to say something to the group. I wander from face to face and spot Sam and a good-looking kid in a ball cap sitting to the far right next to another couple who's vaguely familiar to me.

"First, let me say that it's good to be back in Jefferson Park where I threw my first pitch and hit my first home run, although I have to admit there was no fence to hit it over. The field used to be down in that corner on the other side of the park, and I hit a hard grounder down the third base line just inside the bag, and when it got past the left fielder, it just kept going. Today, with this really neato kazeato facility you have, I guess I would have only gotten a double out of it, so you kids have it a lot harder than I did." I hear laughter…I think I'm going to be okay!

"Before we hit the field, I'd like to thank all of you for inviting me to work with Coach Henshaw and his staff, and for giving me the opportunity to throw some with you. I know you kids probably don't want to hear this, but I'd like to work with you on the fundamentals this morning. Baseball is really a very simple game. When you're up, you hit, you run, and you slide. When you're in the field, you catch and you throw. And you know what, kids? You never stop working on the basics. My first day, right here, when I was ten years old, I worked on shagging fly balls and getting a good throw back to the infield. I did the exact same thing on the last day I played in New York for the Mets. So, Coach, if it's okay, I'll work with some of the kids in the field while maybe you and your staff get the others in the cage for some batting practice."

"That'll be great, D Jack. And again thanks. Okay kids, Sean and Charley and Bobby will start with D Jack out in left field. Sammy, get on your catcher's gear and the rest of you take positions in the infield, and we'll take some batting practice. How much time do you want to work the players, D Jack?"

"How about twenty minutes or so for each rotation, Coach?"

"Sounds like a plan. We'll rotate about every twenty minutes, which means you parents in charge of the picnic can have us set up to eat around 11:30." He pauses and turns to face me, giving me a kind of sincere look. "I hope you don't mind that we asked the kids to bring a ball or bat or jersey or something, figuring you might be willing to autograph them during the picnic, and I think all the kids brought your Mets baseball card."

"Be my pleasure, Coach," I respond and am greeted with some whoops and hollers.

"And one more thing before we begin, D Jack. If everyone will turn to the announcer's booth behind home plate, we have a little announcement. The Board of Directors of the Hollywood Athletic Association have decided it would be appropriate to honor the best ballplayer and only major leaguer to come out of Hollywood, and to that end, we are retiring the number 10 he wore all the way from Jefferson park to Shea Stadium. Coach Billingham will show us where the jersey with his number on it will be permanently displayed in front of the press box, and the official ceremony will be the highlight of our spring banquet. Congratulations, D Jack!"

The applause seems sincere enough, and I'm kind of moved when I think of that short-sleeved, woolen red jersey with jet black lettering across the chest. Needless to say, this is not what I had set my sights on years ago, but I guess in this pretty thankless world, you take what you can get.

"Thanks, Coach, and thanks to the Board for their kindness." I pause and things seem awkward, but Henshaw senses the same thing and jumps right in.

"Okay, everybody knows what to do." The kids cheer and come out of the stands and head for their stations. I notice Sam has given her ward a hug and remained seated, so I just slowly head out toward left as three little kids run up to join me.

"Hi, guys. Who's Sean? Who's Charley? And who's Bobby?" The boys in turn identify themselves, and I give each a handshake. "Okay then, get in a line and face me." After they do so, I ask them to put on their gloves, and I do the same after noticing all three of them are right-handed.

"Today I'm going to teach you fingers and thumbs, and it's really simple. If a ball is coming at you and it's under your belt, the little finger of your glove should be touching the little finger of your bare hand. Go ahead and do it." They follow my instruction with little grins, although the one called Sean looks pretty serious.

"Okay, guys, now if the ball is above your belt, the thumb of your glove hand should be touching the thumb of your bare hand. Go ahead and do that." Again, my instruction is attended to immediately. "That's it, fellas. Now all we have to do is practice, practice, and then after that, practice some more. I'm going to throw a ball at one of you so be ready at all times. Again, below your belt or on the ground, finger to finger; above your belt in the air, thumb to thumb. Here we go."

I must be having a good time, because before I know it, the last rotation is scampering toward the picnic shelters and the aroma of burgers and dogs is in the air. I walk toward the third base stands to greet Rusty who appears to be waiting for me. By his side is a fine-looking blonde who I recall he went steady with in high school, but I can't remember her name.

"D Jack, how you been?"

"No complaints, Rusty. It's great to see you," I say as we give each other a somewhat brotherly hug. Truth is, because we were battery mates for three years, we spent some time together, unlike the way it was with my other teammates, but then that too was only on the field, so I never really got to know him. I don't mean to sound immodest or anything like that, but truth be known, Rusty was only about a notch below me. Honestly, I mean, have you ever heard of a catcher who batted third in the order? He was really one hell of a contact hitter and got on base more often than not, and with me batting clean-up, I got a lot of RBI's bringing him around to the plate. I'm sure he could have played at least in the minors, but I heard he knocked up his high school sweetheart, who could be the blonde he's with, and was man enough to take on the responsibilities of providing for a young family.

"I guess you don't remember me, D Jack," the young woman says with a very pleasant smile. "I was a junior on the cheerleading squad when you and Rusty were seniors."

"And Barb was homecoming queen," Rusty adds with a smile. "We got married when she graduated. I never did go to college, but I'm a master electrician."

"And he still catches in the men's fast pitch softball league," she chimes in with a solid dose of pride, "and actually did some coaching in the semi-pros."

"Sounds great, you've got me beat all around. So, which one of the budding all-stars is yours?"

"You guess," Rusty says with a big grin.

"Got to be Sammy, the catcher, right?"

"You got it, D Jack. What have you been up to?"

Here comes the part of the day I haven't been looking forward to. "I've been just doing a little bit of this and that. Hey, those burgers smell good. Let's hit the chow line, okay?" I say as I start for the picnic shelters before they can answer but they fall in with me, chat some, and then head for the picnic area, so I figure I haven't been offensive. I'm not overly surprised to see Trudy approaching me as I near the pavilion.

"Hi, D Jack, it's good to see you after all these years, sunglasses, beard, and all."

"It's nice to see you, too, Trudy."

"Charley is my oldest, and I've got another son who will start playing next year. So, what have you been doing with yourself?"

"I think no hits, no runs, and no errors would probably sum it up."

"I would think you would have been in a position to make a lot of errors," she says with a foxy kind of look. "Anyway," she continues, "just one error for me," she says. "I got divorced three years ago from Ben Wilson. He played football with you but was younger and rode the bench, so you probably don't remember him. You want to have a drink sometime?"

Wow. She gets right at it. "I'm pretty much tied up every night working at the Diplomat Hotel, and if memory serves, our last date was rather short."

"I admit it. I figured it would be fun to hang out in the Mercedes you were driving."

"So when I told you I was just turning over the SL-190 for somebody who was in Mexico for a week, it was goodbye, D Jack."

"Well, you weren't exactly the most social guy or biggest catch on campus, even though it looked like you might be headed for the pros."

"I guess I never had much to say, huh?"

"Mimes talk more than you did, D Jack, but then Samantha must have found someway to communicate with you. Did you know she married Dolph?" she says in a digging rather than informing way.

"Sam done good," I respond seriously, not taking the bait. "He was the best of the best."

"Yeah, well, I'm in the book, so give me a ring if you feel like it," she says nonchalantly as she heads for one of the tables. Shit, that wasn't any fucken fun. I see Sam sitting with Sean so I figure he must be her ward and they already have their plates piled with dogs, beans, and slaw, so I head in that direction.

"I think the kids had a good time," she says as I take a seat across the wooden table from her and the boy. "Sean says he learned a lot."

"The finger to finger and thumb to thumb thing is real easy to remember and it works!" the kid says with enthusiasm.

"It never let me down, Sean. I always felt I was better in the field than at the plate."

"Yeah, but Mom says you could really sock the ball."

Mom, what's this 'Mom' thing? I look at Sam curiously, and she just smiles. "Both of us are more comfortable with 'Mom' than with 'Aunt,'" she says, having picked up on my quizzical look. "So," she continues, "are you eating hamburgers or hot dogs today?"

"I'm not sure," I say as I get to my feet. "I'm going to have to circulate and do the autograph thing, because I need to get back to the Clubhouse. You working the dinner shift tonight?"

"Yes, but I don't have to be in until 5:00. I hope you don't think retiring a Little League jersey was silly," she adds quickly. "I guess you've been gone so long you don't realize that you're some kind of hometown hero."

"I don't know about that, but I have to admit it's one of the nicer things that happened over the past few years. Who knows? Maybe this ball field was my moment of truth, and I never knew it," I answer as I reach over and extend my hand to Sean who actually gets to his feet as we shake.

"Thanks for coming, D Jack. It was really great to meet you. Maybe we can throw sometime."

"I'll look forward to it, Sean. I'll toss up a few, and you can nail 'em and maybe Mom can play the field."

He gives it a big smile and she gives it a half nod, so I guess it's a done deal but then it also might be a "Let's do lunch sometime" thing. Sam has been pretty neutral, but maybe that's because her ward is here. Naw, truth is, she ain't been nothing but neutral. Anyway, I give the kid a "high five" and head off for the chow line.

Once there, a pleasant-looking woman hands me a paper plate and some plastic dinnerware, and I proceed to get a dog and then make it disappear under some catsup, mustard, relish, and a little mayo. I'm about to look around for an open spot at a table when I feel a slight nudge against my left shoulder and have to kind of swivel around so my right eye can spot someone who obviously wants to say hello, and she does.

"Hello, D Jack."

"Hi, ah…"

She laughs. "That's okay. I didn't really expect you to remember me. I'm Jayleigh, Jayleigh Burney Smith."

Well, I'll tell you straight up, sports fans, maybe I didn't recall her name right off the bat, but I can assure you that Jayleigh Burney Smith is someone you sure as hell couldn't forget. How about 5'11", jet-black hair down below her shoulder blades, large eyes that match the color of her hair, and a stunning bronze-colored face complete with high cheekbones and full lips? Ya got the image? If not, just think of probably the most gorgeous Lakota Sioux in the whole world. Anyway, she knows I'm just taking her all in, so I return her laugh.

"Hi, Jayleigh, It's nice to see ya."

"It's nice to see you, too. Are you eating lunch with anyone?"

"Not really, but the end of that table is open unless you've got someone to sit with."

"No, my nephew is off picnicking with his friends so that would be fine," she says with a smile.

I nod and head over to the end of the table and let her sit down first so I can take a seat opposite her rather than sit by her side.

"How have you been, Jayleigh? Or maybe more to the point, what have you been doing since you graduated from high school?"

"Funny," she says. "Even though everyone knows what you did right out of school, I feel as if I should be asking you the same question."

"You first," I say and then take a bite of the hot dog.

"Okay then, the short version. I got an athletic scholarship to play basketball and volleyball at the University of Georgia."

"Somehow, I get the feeling you were pretty good."

"I was first team, all SEC, in both" she answers, somewhat modestly, and then continues. "I earned a BS in broadcast journalism, but I guess the southern radio and television stations weren't ready for someone like me... and they're still not. So, I went back to school and graduated cum laude with a BA in Education. Then, I got a teaching position on the Pine Ridge Reservation in South Dakota for three years. That didn't work out as well as I had hoped, so I got an opportunity to come back here, and now I'm a 2nd grade teacher at Hollywood Elementary School. Did you go to school there?"

"I did but my second grade teacher didn't look anything like you, and the 3rd, 4^{th,} and 6th didn't even come close."

"What about your 5th grade teacher?"

"He was a guy."

She smiles. "That's very flattering from someone who I recall had very little to say to me when we were in high school," she says softly and pleasantly.

"Well then, you recall I didn't really have all that much to say to anyone. I've already been told once this morning that my social skills were zip to nil."

Jayleigh laughs in an almost supportive way. "That must have been Trudy. When we were all cheerleaders, I remember she used to really rag Samantha about what she could possible see in you other than the fact that you obviously were one hell of an athlete. By they way, I saw you sitting with Samantha. Are you two dating?"

"No," I respond rather abruptly. "She started working where I'm at a few weeks ago, and that's the first we've seen of each other since being in school. She really didn't know I was in the area, so she asked me to come out today and work with the kids. Speaking of kids, which one is your nephew?"

"He's Bobby, my half sister's boy. I think you worked with him at the beginning of the day."

"Yeah, I think he was in the first group with Charley and Sean."

"Okay then, D Jack, it's your turn, and like me, you can do the short version if you want to."

"Well, Jayleigh…"

"It's just Jay, D Jack," she says with a comfortable air of informality.

"Well then, Jay, I went to Arizona State for about five years and last year came back to Hollywood, and I work at the Presidential Golf Course and Country Club. How's that for a short version?"

"I was hoping for just a little more, seeing as you were kind of famous, even if it was only for a brief time."

"Like you said, Jay, it was a very short time, and that's about it."

"No wife, no kids?"

"No, Jay. No wife, no kids, no divorces, and not even any serious girlfriends. And you?"

"I'd say your situation mirrors my own. How come no one has been able to take you off the market?" she asks somewhat seriously.

"You're asking that about me? Speaking of mirrors, I'm sure you look into one every morning, so how is it no one has been able to take *you* off the market?"

"I think one or two guys actually wanted to try until I met their folks. Ethnic differences don't sit well with most of the people down this way."

"Were you sorry?"

"No, hurt maybe, but not sorry."

With that remark, both of us seem to concentrate on our food but I'm thinking she's reflecting on the past few years, and I guess I'm doing the same, and the silence is a little awkward.

"Would you like to go out for a drink sometime?" she says hesitantly with a half smile. "I think someone this morning said they thought you lived on the beach, so maybe the Flicker-lite would be convenient."

"I think that would be nice, Jay, but the Presidential is seasonal; I'm on seven days a week from 6:00 a.m. 'til after midnight, and that's going to last until somewhere around April 15th.

"I'm not going anywhere," she says with a full smile and a kind of sparkle in her eyes.

"Me either. I'll look forward to it," I say as I return her smile and get to my feet, "but for now, I promised the coaches I'd make the rounds and sign some balls and stuff."

"You made a lot of kids happy today, D Jack," she says and gives me a little wave goodbye as I head off to be a no-name celebrity. I mean, who's kidding whom here? The parents have told their kids I was somebody before they were born, so they have convinced themselves that an autographed ball or baseball card will be special. Now that's what I call a moment of truth, even though, for me it doesn't feel so good, because I just can't let go of the fact that I could have been special, I mean really special. Even to this day I could have been playing in left field in Shea with the glint in my eyes and the big smile I saw on so many of these kids this morning.

So, what the fuck is there to feel good about? Well shit, once again I better come up with something, because this ain't getting me anywhere. To paraphrase me and the T, *I had some brief times at the helm but now I'm clouded by my laspses ino unimportant realms*. Okay, I've got it. Maybe these kids will feel good for a few days about getting my autograph, but I can feel good forever because I've got a ball the Mick signed. I'll bet you don't have one of those, but I sure hope you have something you feel good about…and I mean that, I really do!

XIV

A MIDNIGHT PICNIC ON THE GREEN

The afternoon comes, and I head for the beach and the bars
I check all the joints, but always from afar,
because my mind never travels to these scenes
my body's there, but my thoughts are in my dreams,

It's about 4:30 p.m. on a balmy Saturday when I hear a loud noise from outside the front of the bag room so I head out through the doors just in time to see a hulk of a man heading away from Marcus in the direction of the dining room. As I approach, I can see that the ole man's face is flushed, and he appears to be scratching his head in bewilderment.

"Hey, what was all that about?"

"Boy, are some guys stupid," Marcus mumbles, apparently to himself.

"What guys?" I inquire. Marcus looks at me and seems to realize I have asked him a question, but the look on his face tells me he didn't hear it.

"What guys are stupid?" I repeat.

"Where have you been?"

"I've been signing baseballs."

"Oh, yeah, I forgot Charley let you off this morning."

"Fine, what guys?"

"You know D Jack, when it comes to a dumb contest, I don't know which one of these guys would finish first, Hargraves or Sammy Peaball."

"Sammy Peaball, I know," I say as a picture of the muscular ex-jai alai player comes to mind. A few years ago he was one of the big draws up at the Dania Jai Alai Fronton which was the second such sports facility to open in the U.S. about twenty-three years ago. The word is that he could hurl the pelota out of his woven *cesta* at almost 180 m.p.h., and I'm pretty sure his nickname has something to do with that rock hard ball. Rumor is, the mob got to him, and he was eventually booted for throwing games with some of his fellow players. "So, who's Hargraves?"

"Clothing store king, Philadelphia."

Gee, another fucken king. “And?”

“He aced Number Five this morning. First time he’s ever had a hole-in-one, and I gather the guy is pretty serious about his game. Apparently, he’s been watching too many tournaments on television,” Marcus says with a big smile, “so when he got to the green he didn’t see the ball and figured he’d holed it but wasn’t going to believe it until he saw it. He ran to the cup, scooped up the ball, and just like on CBS, he threw it in the air.”

“And?”

“What a schmuck,” Marcus mumbles. “The ball landed right smack in the middle of the water hazard in front of the green. Word is, he got right on his cart and headed straight for the bar.”

“Wonderful, but what’s that got to do with Peaball?”

“At the bar, Hargraves shared his sad story with Stunt and announced to the world that he’d pay good money to get the ball back.”

“How the hell is he going to know it’s the right one?”

“You know, D Jack, sometimes I think these things are made in heaven.”

“Which means?”

“Which means this guy plays monogrammed balls, and he’s got his initials on each and every one. Burgundy colored no less.”

“I think I’m beginning to get the picture,” I say breaking into a broad smile. “Was that Hargraves who just stalked out?”

“Yep.”

“So, how did Sammy screw the pooch?”

“The word was all over the place this morning, but you weren’t around. Anyway, Sammy put all his brains to use, went to Hargraves’ bag, pulled out one of the balls, soaked it in some muddy water, and majestically presented it to the mass-producing clothing king of Philly.”

“How was Hargraves able to tell it wasn’t the real deal?”

“He’d cut a ball earlier in the round,” Marcus says, “and he obviously took a good look at Number Five, figured he might not clear the water, and rather than risk a good ball, he just teed up the cut one. There’s no way anyone is going to be able to fake that ball.”

“So he got mad, and let you know about it.”

“Yep, he’s a regular King Kong. I think his temper is about the size of his waistline.”

“What do you think he’ll pay, Marcus?”

This statement is greeted with a laugh. “Come on, Pirate. You couldn’t find that ball in a million years. It’s got to be the needle in the haystack at the very least.”

"That's not what I asked you, Marcus. I asked you how much you think he'll pay for the gettin' the ball back?"

"No idea."

"Okay then, I'll bet you twenty bucks he pays a hundred or more," I say confidently.

"You're on," Marcus replies quickly, "but it's like what you say all the time; it's hypothetical, and I don't think it's going to happen, so I'll bet you another twenty you don't even find the ball."

"Pessimist," I respond with a sneer.

"Not so. I'm just assessing the skills of the individual who plans to retrieve said ball. How's that for an educated way of putting it, college man?" he concludes with a grin.

"Very impressive, even though it's inaccurate. Wish me luck."

"The hell, I need the money."

I laugh, turn, and head back down to the bag room. I'd like to think my situation with Marcus is about the same as the one with the horses. After countless wagers since coming here, I may be about even, but the last few weeks I think he's been hosing me so I need this one to get back some wagering equilibrium with him. I did nail a football pool last weekend, but that's been my only breakthrough what with old dogs and horses with frozen legs. Then, of course, we had the infamous picture where my ethics got in the way and cost me, but there was also Blues Eyes and Jilly the Ice and Pete raking it in. But then those weren't bets, so I can't put them on the plus side.

Nope, the fact of the matter is I need to pull this one off to be ahead and get back some respect. Sounds like it's important to me, huh? Well, you're right on that one. I guess you've figured out by now that finding ways to get motivated around the Presidential can be a bit difficult and that betting and trying to stay in the black is critical to my day in, day out mental health. Okay, no jokes about my mental health. You look in the mirror lately?

Once into the bag room I'm surprised to see Sam sitting behind the counter hurriedly swallowing a bite of something or other. "Hi," she says with a proud smile. "I sold two baskets of balls while you were out."

I walk behind the counter and notice she has a plate with a half sandwich, some potato salad, and a pickle. I pull over the other lounge chair and sit down next to her, kicking my legs up onto the counter. "Great, as long as you let them go for two bucks each."

She points to the sign on the wall that announces the rates for bag rentals, balls, and other services. "I've got a long night ahead of me, so I thought I'd just grab a sandwich and say hi and thank you for working with the kids this morning. I think Sean was pretty taken with you."

"Well, one out of two ain't bad. It was fun," I quickly add before she can respond to my quip. "So, how long do you think you'll be on tonight?"

"I'm on the late shift and then will have to do side work when the room clears out, so I probably won't get finished until at least midnight."

I give her my A-one lecherous sneer. "How would you like to take a late night ride on a dark golf course?" Her look is pensive, unsure of my intent. I laugh.

"Not to worry, girl, it's just another bet."

"A bet about me?" she says indignantly. "I don't think I'm going to..."

"No, this guy Hargraves..."

"Oh, I heard about him. He's the one who got a hole-in-one and threw his ball in the lake and...oh, Devon, you're not serious! You really can't be," she says, her eyes fueled by the humor of it all.

"Yup, I'm headed for a moonlight swim in the fifth water hazard. Care to join me?"

"I obviously don't bring a suit to work and don't care to enter a wet t-shirt contest."

"You'd win," I say and am surprised that she doesn't seem offended by my remark which obviously reflects my past knowledge of what is concealed beneath her purple and black uniform.

"Of course I'd win. I'd be the only one in the contest."

"What about me?"

"I'd win, but paddling around in that lake in the dark is out."

"Well, will you just stand by the side of the water and protect me with a three wood?"

"Protect you from what?"

"Poachers, Sam, poachers. Do you think the people around here are simply going to allow me to retrieve that ball and walk away with it? The moment I wade to shore in triumph, the multitudes will descend upon me and strip me of my hard-earned prize. Only you can fend them off with well-placed drives and such. And," I add benevolently, "your efforts shall not go unrewarded. You shall share in the profits."

"What profits? And how much will I share?" she asks, her eyes narrowing.

"I'll go forty percent of forty bucks."

"Sixty."

"We seem to have settled on fifty percent which I don't really think is equitable, seeing as I'll be the one getting wet."

She smiles, "But as you said, I'll be there to protect you, so it's a deal."

Now I think I can hit her with the hidden agenda. "Seeing as you're so generously willing to share the profits, are you also willing to share possible losses?"

"What do you mean? What kind of losses?"

"Marcus is betting twenty I don't find the ball," I say sheepishly, "and he's betting another twenty the payoff from Hargraves will be less than a hundred bucks."

She slowly runs a forefinger across her lips as she looks at the ceiling. She then nods her head having made her decision. "I'm in," she says with a sigh, as if she has gone the wrong way on this one.

"Atta girl!" I say with gusto, ignoring her possible vote of no confidence. "So, how much time do you have left?"

"None," she says as she hands me the half sandwich. "You eat this, I get the pickle, and that's that." I look down at the sandwich and fold back a corner of the white bread."

"Corned beef with Miracle Whip!" I say aghast. "My God, we're incompatible."

"That should come as no surprise to you, Devon," she says in a tone that suggests her comment is not necessarily a dig as she gets to her feet. "I'll tell Daddy not to wait up. And," she continues, "I'll be the one in the purple and black."

"I'll be the one in the t-shirt, the only t-shirt," I respond somewhat loudly. She shakes her head and quickly moves through the door. My mind stays with her for a few seconds, thinking this is the first time we seemed to have had a fun conversation. But then I change gears and focus my attention on the problem at hand. How the hell am I going to find that damn ball? You're probably like Marcus because you don't think I'm going to find it either, do you? You know, I'd think by this time you might be a little more supportive, but I guess that's your struggle and I'm willing to take your money too. So, you want to put a twenty on it? Done!

*

On the second ring, I take the receiver off the cradle. "Presidential bag room, D Jack speaking."

"Oh, good, I caught you before you went up to the lounge. I tried earlier, but I guess you were still working the phones in the cloakroom," Sam says somewhat breathlessly. "Have you eaten anything yet?"

"Nope."

"Can you hold out until you finish your gig in the lounge? By the way, when do you figure to get finished?"

"I should be done by midnight. T Moon has changed things abit and wants to go without backup on the third set for the rest of the season, so no more 1:00 a.m. stuff. He told me he might have an offer to go solo at a neato wine bar on Hollywood Beach, so he wants to try out his stuff here. I guess I could hold out on some chow if I go easy on the VO and load up some extra Kodiak, because I sure can't afford to get smashed up there drinking on an empty stomach. Is something up?"

"I've got a surprise and thought we might have a midnight picnic."

"Sounds terrific," I respond enthusiastically. "Are you still going to meet me in the bag room?"

"Yes, and you better bring the liquor cart because it's going to be a very large picnic." Without waiting for a response, she hangs up, and I begin to wonder just what's in store for the two of us out on the fifth green. I open the two top buttons of my shirt, rough up my hair a little, and start for the lounge and a three-hour stint playing backup chords for T.

*

You know how it feels. Like I said before, when you're anticipating something, time just drags by. Right now, the lounge is full which is common for a Saturday night, and the patrons seem pretty receptive to Charlie's music, although I really haven't been monitoring things that closely because I've been too preoccupied with the midnight hunt for the ball and whether or not my plan to find it will work. The hands on the clock finally inch their way toward the vertical overlap of the large and small hand, the Moon-man finishes his Chapin medley, and I immediately leave the Yamaha on the stool and head for the bag room. As promised, Sam is standing at the counter, still dressed in her uniform.

"I would have changed, but I really didn't have much time." I notice a large serving tray on the countertop with the outline of four metal containers of food covered by large squares of white linen.

"Is that supper?"

"You better be hungry," she says with an expansive grin. "I really hit the jackpot tonight, and it couldn't have come at a more appropriate time."

I move behind the counter and reach underneath for a couple of irons and a metal bicycle basket I had borrowed earlier in the day. Most of the caddies can't afford cars, so they ride the bus or bike it. "Be with you in just a minute." I move behind one of the many bag stalls and slip into some navy blue gym shorts I keep around for quick changes for racquetball games with Charley the Boss. I return to the counter, place a bottle of VO in the basket, and push it and the clubs toward her.

"You take this stuff, and I'll carry the tray." She nods and we get everything, plus a few towels, and head out of the bag room. Ralph had left the booze cart for us at the entrance to the cart room, and we put our stuff in the large, wood-framed box behind the cushioned seat. I head over to the wall and get three cans of ice-cold ginger ale from the vending machines. Sam is sitting on the right side of the golf cart, so I assume I'm the designated driver. I hop on the seat, press the accelerator against the metal floor board and the cart jerks to life as we head out of the cart room in the direction of the first tee. I then steer down the side of the fairway and about halfway to the green cut to the left on a cart trail through some of the foliage that separates most of the fairways. That puts us on the sixth, so I head towards the tee. Fortunately, the full moon is providing enough light to avoid hitting palmettos or trees. Off to the left, behind the sixth tee, I point us toward the side of the fifth green.

"Where do you want to eat, Sam, the fairway, the green, or the bunker?"

"Well, the bunker is definitely out. Sitting on sand used to be nice, but this stuff is more like dirt. How about the fairway and some soft grass right next to the pond?" she offers. "That looks pretty level."

I nod in agreement and head up the small rise near the green for about eight or so feet, steer around the water, and stop near the edge of the hazard. I slide off the seat as Sam comes around to the back, takes a large tablecloth from under the tray, folds it once, and sets it on the grass. I start to lift one of the linens covering the containers when she taps my wrist.

"No peeking. Mix me a drink and I'll tell you the story."

"Fair enough," I say as I reach for the VO and cans of pop and then realize I haven't brought anything to drink from. "Oh, nuts," I say, disgusted with myself. "I forgot to bring some cups."

"I took a page from your own book, Devon. Don't drink from plastic unless you absolutely have to," she states with a smile as she produces two highball glasses, both engraved with a **"P"** from under the linen.

"I'm impressed…and very relieved," I say jokingly. I then bring the stuff over to the tablecloth, which serves more as a blanket, and sit down cross-legged. "Okay, I've brought the drinks. Now it's story time."

Sam sits down next to me kind of sideways, tucking her legs underneath her uniform. "Around 8:00 p.m." she begins, "I get this party of four. They were really gassed when they arrived; all I did was bring drinks for almost and hour. Like I say, they were smashed but insisted on ordering dinner anyway."

"Don't tell me."

"Yep, I served four entrees and not a single fork ever left the table. The tab was almost three hundred dollars and one of the guys left me a fifty dollar bill. Of course," she continues, "as you well know, we're not supposed to take any food, but this was just too good a deal to pass up, even hygienic. So," she says as she reaches over to the tray and lifts the first cover, "would you like the Steak au Poivre?" She then lifts the other covers, "the Filet of Sole Marguery, the Steak Bernaise, or the frog's legs?" Her look is one of pure pleasure while I'm simply in awe of this feast, although I am wondering what some of it is.

"Boy, this was worth the wait, but I'm not sure what to try first because the truth is, I don't really know what's under some of those sauces."

She looks down at the gourmet meal spread before us and glances from dish to dish. "Be an adventurer, Devon, you go first."

I agonize for a few seconds. "I can't do it. Let's just share and taste everything, split it down the middle."

"Just like old times," she says with what I perceive to be maybe a hint of fondness.

"Yeah, but back then we were sharing two different kinds of grilled cheese sandwiches, fries, and onion rings."

"Well, not total sharing, Devon, you never did like tomato in your grilled cheese sandwich." I nod in agreement as I lean over, take the two highball glasses, and quickly prepare a mixed drink for her and a half glass of VO for me.

"Speaking of old times," Sam continues, "I saw you sitting with Jayleigh after the practice. Did you two have a nice chat?"

"Yeah, she's a sweet kid."

"Sweet, is that the best you can do? Come on, Dev, she's drop-dead gorgeous."

"Yeah, she is."

"Did you know Jayleigh had a crush on you in high school?" Sam asks mischeviously.

"No, I didn't know that. What makes you think she did?"

"Because she told me so, but she said she knew we were dating and she wasn't the kind of girl to make a move. Of course, when we called it quits, you were already on your way."

"We didn't call it quits, Sam. You called it quits."

"That's water under the bridge, Dev. Anyway," she continues, "you're back."

"What's that supposed to mean?"

"It means I wouldn't be surprised if Jayleigh tries to strike up an acquaintance of sorts."

"Okay then, you ain't gonna be surprised that she asked me if I wanted to meet her for a drink at the Flicker-lite on the beach."

"And how did you handle that?"

"In a very polite way, I said no thanks."

"Why?"

"I haven't really been out on a date with a woman for quite awhile and I've been in a comfort zone that fits me just fine."

"So, you don't consider going to Morgan's Inn being out with a woman?" she says quizzically.

"That wasn't a date, Sam. I think we both agreed we're just having friendly get-togethers."

"Yes, we did. So, I suppose all you've had are lots of one night stands with baseball groupies." She pauses and bites her lip. "I'm really sorry, Dev. That was a cheap shot."

"There were hardly any before Shea and I was nothing but yesterday's news after, Sam, so let's leave the dead dogs alone for awhile and get after the reason we're out here with all your stolen food," I say, trying to sound as light as possible as I lift my glass and beckon for her to do the same.

"Here's to golf balls," I pronounce as we clink glasses.

She takes a deep swallow which surprises me; I've never seen her do that. Maybe she wants to change the subject as much as I do. "How much time are you going to spend in that waterhole before giving up?" she asks with a girlish giggle.

My right eye opens wide, although she can't see it; my chin drops; and I throw a pound of disappointment in her direction. "Give up? Right in front of me is a fine meal and a full moon. All the signs are here and our success is virtually assured." I rise to my feet and stand ramrod straight like Ahab on his deck and peer toward the clouds clearly outlined by the solar reflections from the moon.

"I shall not fail. I will do what others have been unable to accomplish," I proclaim as I gaze intently at the water hazard. "Beneath those depths, the white one patiently awaits my coming." I take a deep breath and, without even a glance in her direction, thrust an outstretched right arm in Sam's direction. "Ishmael…hand me yon harpoon! It's time to engage my fate."

"What it's time for is a hot supper, you oaf. It won't stay warm forever."

For whatever reasons, I'm relieved that both of us seem intent on getting past still yet another conversation which had the potential to turn ugly. "I won't be gone forever, and furthermore, what about eating and suffering abdominal cramps in yon sea?"

"Your sea is probably less than five feet deep, Devon, so just stand in the mud if you get a cramp."

"And stir up the bottom! The quarry will be lost for all time, and poor Sir Hargraves will naught but a tale to tell--aaaaaaargghh!!"

"Devon," she says with the look of a mother humoring a child, "this is all new to me. When did you develop such a blue streak of literary bullshit?"

That brings me up short, but I hang in. "Then again," I continue reflectively, "whoever goes into battle on an empty stomach could be in peril, so I therefore accept the immediacy of your offer of sustenance."

I sit back down on the makeshift blanket, finish my VO, and accept the plate of food that Sam thrusts in my direction. I pour another drink for myself and offer her one which she declines by holding up her half-filled glass. "Have you had a few too many tonight, Devon?"

"You think I'd be doing this if I was cold stone sober?"

"You really like clowning around, don't you? I mean you really seem to get a kick out of being half over the bend. I think I just realized that you never seemed to laugh much; you never seemed to relax. It was like you were always waiting for something to happen, like for a shoe to drop, or something like that."

"Maybe you're right. Things did happen, but now I just try to keep everything in its proper perspective and focus on the easy stuff."

"But everything's not easy. You have to be serious once in awhile."

"Meaning?"

"Meaning, Devon, people can't look for lost golf balls all their lives." Her look is sincere, and I don't have a response, so I reach over to a casserole of something or other and with a large spoon, dig out a generous helping of maybe the Filet of Sole and chew it slowly, savoring the delicately blended ingredients.

"Definitely some shrimp and mushrooms in the sauce. Good."

Sam takes a sip of her drink and begins to nibble on one of the frogs legs. She's obviously waiting for me to say something but seems patient. I take another hit on the VO and then say, "I'm not avoiding that last comment, Sam. I just don't know how to answer it."

"I'm not sure I know how to answer it either," she says as she empties the highball glass and extends it to me for a refill. This brings me up short, because, just like the deep hit on her highball, I don't recall Sam being a two-drink kind of girl and of course what we're drinking ain't her fav. Nevertheless, I mix it and top off my own before returning the glass to her. The moonlight is shining on her face, and the trees are silhouetted behind her. There's a gentle breeze rustling some palm fronds, and my thoughts return to the frequent nights we spent sitting on a bench on Hollywood Beach, holding hands and sharing our dreams.

"You're still not going to take off those sunglasses, are you, Devon?"

"Nope."

"Well, you certainly can't see much at night."

"I can't see all that much during the day, so it really doesn't make a big difference," I say, hoping that piece of honesty will put the issue to rest.

It does. "So, what were you thinking just now?" she asks changing the subject.

"I was thinking I'm not used to this kind of situation."

"What kind of situation is it?"

The conversation seems to be heading down another serious road and once again, I feel apprehensive about that road and just flat don't want to go there. I smile. "This unusual situation involves two working people eating food they can't afford, so they'll undoubtedly eat it all and then pay the price."

She seems to sense my desire to keep the moment light, returns my smile, and again, to my surprise, extends an empty glass. "Are ya sure?" I ask with some concern. "I'm not exactly on Billy's list of favorite people, and he's going to be pretty put out if I have to carry you home."

"I'm not a little girl anymore, Devon. Pour."

"That's a fact, Sam, and I'm no little boy either."

"I'm not sure you ever were a little boy."

Well, guys, I guess I read that one wrong; here we go again. "Really, now what's that supposed to mean? Who do you think I was?"

"You were D Jack, and you were going to be the best of the best. But I've been thinking the game was never fun for you. It was a quest, a mission, an obsession. Little boys laugh, Devon, and I rarely saw you laugh."

"That's pretty heavy, Sam."

"No, now that I really think about it, that was who you were and all you were. After it was over between us, I always thought of you as being selfish because baseball was all you focused on, but then I was an athlete, so

I guess I thought it was okay. But Dev, now I don't think you were selfish. I don't think you really had anything to give. You were one dimensional."

She takes another deep swallow of her VO and ginger as if she's in need of fortifying whatever has encouraged her to say things that may have been in her for a long time, so I might as well let her get some more of the venom out of her bloodstream.

"I guess you're waiting for me to disagree with you, but I can't do that. You're right," I say matter-of-factly. "I was, as you put it, one dimensional, and when that one dimension ceased to be, I couldn't find anything to fill the gap."

"Not even in Jacksonville?"

"The only thing for me in Jax was playing in Wolfson Park, and if you really do believe that all I could ever see was the game, you'd have to admit that everything else, in Jacksonville or anywhere else, was nothing more than a fleeting distraction."

"So then you're saying that I was nothing more than a fleeting distraction, too?"

I pause because I know her question has the potential of putting an end to anything that may have been going on for the past few weeks, and as I have learned since leaving the diamond, or at least I hope so, an honest answer is usually the only way to go, even if it might be perceived as being hollow or, worse yet, a bunch of bullshit.

"One thing a few schools of philosophy have taught me, Sam, is that nothing is absolute. There are exceptions to everything, including, in my case, distractions."

"Exceptions are plural, Dev."

"For me the exception was singular. You were the only person in my life who wasn't a distraction."

"If that was true, Dev," she says quietly, "you seemed to have lost sight of it."

"You're right. Yes, I did,"

Okay, sportsfans, I may have just played my last card. She seems to be trying to internalize what we've been saying. I've got to tell you I feel a certain sense of dread because I've tried to tell her something I would have told her years ago if it had been her on the street corner and not Billy, but now I figure the horse is long gone from the barn.

"I saw the photos in the newspapers, Devon. I sat down to write you twice, but the words wouldn't come," she says with what sounds like just a tad of remorse. "But then it really wouldn't have mattered, because I didn't have a clue as to where you were."

"Well, it's a little like now, Sam. Sometimes people don't know what to say, and sometimes there isn't anything to say, or do, for that matter."

"What do you want to do now, Dev?"

"I think the question is more about what you want to do, Sam."

She actually takes my hand, which I realize is the first time we have had any kind of physical contact. "I don't know, Dev," she says very softly. "I really don't know."

It's time to try to lighten up. Again I get the feeling we're both wearing out, and it's increasingly evident that nothing is going to get resolved on this moonlit night. "Well, for the moment I want to find that damn ball!" I say emphatically as I get to my feet and head over to the cart to retrieve the irons and bicycle basket. As I come back to the tablecloth, Sam is quietly sipping, not swilling, her drink, and she eyes me inquisitively.

"Quite simple," I say as I take out the roll of duct tape I had placed in the basket earlier. "I'm going to stick one iron into the top corner of the basket and stick this iron into the other corner. Now I'll tape the irons to the basket like so and tape the club handles together also." I hold up my makeshift scoop. "Ta-da," I intone. "Now all I have to do is to drag this thing along the bottom out in the middle of the water hazard and up comes the ball. You want to come watch me work?"

She laughs. "Nope, but I'll bet you might want to kiss my hand for good luck before you dive into that pond," she says mischievously.

"You'd lose your money," I respond seriously.

"Why?" she says with the first hint of a slur.

"Because you set the ground rules at Morgan's, and if I recall the past, when you lay down the law, you stick to your guns. So if there's going to be any of that, even on the hand, you're the one who's going to have to initiate it."

"In that respect, you're right; I haven't changed, Devon." The mischievous tone is gone, and she makes no move towards me.

"In that case," I say lightly, "it's time for my midnight swim."

Her mood shifts rapidly, probably because she's on her third drink. "I'll stay here and cheer from the sidelines just like when we were in school and, of course, scare off anyone who comes looking for your prized ball," she concludes with a cocky nod of her head. I strip my shirt and throw it at her and she snags it just short of making an error. "Thanks. If I change my mind and decide to take a dip, I'll use your shirt for a suit."

I give her a thumbs-up and head for the side of the lake. Slowly extending one foot into the water, I'm relieved that it's not as cold as I had anticipated…but mud immediately swirls up from the bottom and, to invoke some of my own lyrics, *if my feet haven't exactly been on the ground for the last few years*, right now they're about three inches into the thick and slimy bottom. I quickly realize, with relief, as I move toward the center of the water hazard that the muck is turning into smooth sand, so I decide to let the lip of the basket penetrate the bottom a little so I can drag it along its relatively level surface.

The hard part is going to be staying afloat because if I put my feet down I'm going to have trouble. Holding the basket by my side, I begin a slow breast stroke with one arm towards the middle of the lake which is about the size of a Little League infield. The moonlight clearly illuminates the sides of the lake, and I have no difficulty estimating the approximate center. When I get there, I tread water with my left arm and lower the basket until it touches the bottom, the water level about six inches from the top of the leather grips. I give the basket a gentle push downward and slowly begin a one-armed sidestroke in the direction of the green using the pin as a line of sight. After about fifteen feet or so, I move a little to the left, head back and swim past what I think is the center of the lake, and then repeat the process, moving from side to side, back and forth, about twenty times.

My fingers are really shriveling, and I figure I've been in the pond for at least half and hour, so I slowly head away from the green toward the fairway edge of the water hazard. As I approach the grass, I let my feet down and quickly sink a few inches into the cool mud. I walk the last few feet, hauling my booty onto the fairway, and much to my amazement, the basket is loaded down with balls. I figure there must twenty or thirty packed down in the wire enclosure. I make my way up to the cart and drop the basket and clubs into the box behind the seats, and after grabbing a few of the towels I had thrown in the back, I head for the makeshift picnic area where Sam has curled up on the tablecloth, the left side of her head resting on both hands. As I approach, I can see a slight smile on her face and her eyes are closed. I quickly note the VO bottle is about half gone, and I know I've only had three drinks so, after toweling down, which doesn't do all that much for my chilled body, I drop down next to her and gently shake her shoulder.

"Okay, girl, nap time is over. Wait 'til you see the haul. That ball has got to be in there somewhere." She opens her eyes, leans up on one arm, and looks at me with a dreamy expression in her eyes.

"Devon," she says with a throaty laugh, "you're all wet."

"Water or personality?"

"Water, silly. Here," she says as she takes one of the towels from my hands. "Let me help you."

She begins to slowly rub the towel in a circular motion across my chest. I feel her hands exert pressure as she pushes me down on my back. Then she sprauls across me and presses her face into the side of my neck. I can feel the warmth of her body and the fullness of her gently moving against me. Whoa, Nellie, I know she's boozed up but still, what the hell's going on and what am I supposed to do now? As I wrestle with my confusion, the problem at hand resolves itself, and I emerge from my mental haze with the realization that she's no longer moving. She's breathing deeply but her journey toward wherever she was going has been aborted.

"Sam?" I whisper as I begin to rub her back between her shoulder blades. "You okay?"

No response. Her breathing continues to be deep and restful, and I'm now conscious of her weight, so I lay quietly, thinking, resting, and frankly, giving my blood pressure time to return to a normal level. After what seems like a few minutes, I ease her off of me onto her side and then hold her in my arms. I figure she'll never know it so I kiss her eyes and the tip of her nose, which used to be a ritual after we made love, and then lean back to look at the peacefull state reflected in her face. Beyond her, I can see that most of the food is still on the plates and I suddenly realize that I'm really hungry. I figure she must have been waiting for the picnic and tossed down those highballs on an empty stomach; hence, crashville.

I ease my arm out from under her, making sure she's comfortable on her side, and move across the tablecloth in order to pick up the steak. After taking a couple of big bites, I realize I'm still pretty cold and, worse yet, nervous, so I take a straight slug from the VO bottle and the smooth whiskey warms a trail down my throat and begins a controlled fire in my gut. I take another belt, sit up straight, cross my legs, and gaze contemplatively at Sam. I figure it's got to be after 2:00 a.m., and I recall she said she was going to call Billy and tell him not to wait up. With some luck, I might be able to get her into her house without that nasty bastard trying to kill me. Boy, I think with a grin, I'll bet this girl is gonna have some questions tomorrow.

Bet! Holy shit! The ball! That's what brought me out here in the first place. I look thoughtfully at the cart and the basket of balls and realize that going through all of them is just going to have to wait. It's first things first, although the first thing isn't going to be that critical to this operation. It's the afterwards that's going to tell the tale. I'm going to have to keep this thing light and simply tell her that she had a few drinks and took a nap. Oh well, fuck it, upward and onward.

I pick up the bottle and glasses, take them over to the cart, and put them in the corner of the box. One return trip gets me the tray, tablecloth, and the empty pop cans. Naturally, I save the toughest for the last, and with a grunt, pick up Sam and start for the cart. Her eyes flicker and her arms tighten ever so around my neck.

"Are you the pirate?" she inquires in a somewhat sultry tone. Terrific, when did she hear that rarely used nickname?

"Yeah," I grunt, the exertion of lugging her limp body quickly taking its toll on what little strength I have left after my moonlight swim.

"Are you abducting me?" she says with a giggle, but when I don't answer, she seems content to carry on.

"You can abduct me, but you can't have me," she continues with a marked lack of authority. "You see," she whispers conspiratorially, "I think I might be falling in love with somebody else."

"Wonderful," I reply as I reach the cart and gently lower her onto the right side of the cushioned seat. I move around to the left and as I sit down she nuzzles against my side and drapes her left arm over my shoulders. With her weight against me, I figure all is well so I start for the Clubhouse. The ride is smooth, with Sam leaning against me in the moonlight, which again silhouettes the beauty of the golf course. I experience a fleeting moment of melancholy as sweet memories of the past whisk through my brain. However, they quickly disappear as I steer around the cart room and head up the asphalt path toward the employees parking lot. It's completely empty except for the Jag which I fortunately drive to the course on Saturdays, figuring it's a good thing to turn her over about once a week. I pull up to the passenger side of the car, ease her off the cart, and have little trouble getting her comfortable with her legs extending along the long floor of the interior and her head leaning against the spot where the rounded seat all but meets the door.

I'm uncomfortable with the thought of leaving her alone for a few minutes but I have no choice. She seems to be breathing heavily but peacefully, so I drive the cart back down the path and park it in the front of the cart room in the spot where Ralph had left it for us. I quickly unload what's left of our picnic and stuff everything beneath the counter in the bag room. Then, off come the shorts, which I throw into one of the washtubs, and on come the jeans, sweatshirt, and sneakers. I check to make sure I have my wallet and keys and, after pulling down the garage doors that secure the area, quickly sprint the couple hundred yards back to the Jaguar. I'm relieved to find that Sam hasn't move a muscle and the relaxed look is still painted comfortably on her face. Once into the car, I realize I'm low on gas, and the round clock on the dashboard reads 2:45 a. m. I turn on the radio to a soft, all-night station, push the starter button, and head out of the lot.

The only thing that changes on the way to Dewey Street is that Sam moves from the door over to my shoulder, which makes it tough to get into fourth gear, so I spend most of the time in third…no problem for the XK-120. She'll turn around seventy in second and a tad over ninety in third when she's tuned up which, frankly, ain't no easy task; she's beautiful but temperamental as all hell. As I approach Sam's house, I suddenly experience the heart in the throat trick. The God-awful lights are still on. So, here's the big question? Did Billy leave some lights on for her, or is he waiting up? And did he know she was with me? As I drive past the house, I quickly figure I can't take the chance and decide to drive around for awhile, hoping the cool night air might revive her.

Fifteen minutes later, there's still no response from Sam. I spot a Wendy's. Fortunately, it's one of the few fast food joints open all night. I guess the swimming and the tension of the situation has really taken it out of me, because hunger pains are raging from my abdomen to my throat. I decide to park in the lot and leave Sam momentarily in order to go into the men's room to get a couple of wet, brown paper towels. Then I return to the car and place one at the back of Sam's neck while running another across her forehead and cheeks. Nothing, absolutely nothing, zonked! I hop back into the car and drive down the side of the building around to the drive-in window where a skinny, dark-haired guy leans out, and gives me a greasy smile.

"You having a little trouble with the lady, bud?"

I look at him tight-lipped. "Three in the morning seems to be an okay time to sleep. Give me a burger and two cups of black coffee."

"We got all kinds of burgers, buddy, in fact two hundred and….."

"Look, Jack, it's been a long day, so get me one piece of meat, two pieces of bread, and put some mustard on the side of your choice. You think you can handle that?"

The guy shrugs and turns away. I can't say as I really blame the guy for being in poor form. The graveyard shift is no fun, and speaking of graveyards, it suddenly dawns on me that I have to be at work in three hours. No doubt about it. By late morning, I'm gonna have to see the Turk for about 15mg of Dexedrine. I hate to do that and don't make a habit of knocking down uppers, but one has to accept one's limitations. There's no way I'm gonna last 'til midnight tomorrow which, come to think of it, is already today.

The guy returns with the burger and coffees, and I hand him five bucks, holding up my palm so he knows to keep the change. "Sorry, Jack, the day's been worse than most."

"Yeah, me, too," he says with a tired smile. "I went heavy on the mustard, okay?"

We exchange weak grins, and I head the Jaguar off to the side of the parking lot. The burger is gone in four bites, and the coffee finishes off what little chill remains from the pond. I try to get Sam to take a sip of the brew, but she's not having any of it and seems to be too deep in her dreams to react to anything. I crank up the car once again and head back towards Dewey Street. I seem to relax a little on the way and am rewarded by the absence of lights in her living room as I approach the house. It's now past 3:30, so I figure Billy threw in the towel. Maybe he was just restless and settled back in for the night or maybe one of her kids was up.

Whatever, I kick off the engine, put her in neutral, and glide to a stop at the curb about twenty feet down from her front door. I figure I better get it opened before I bring Sam in, so I fish around in her purse which yields a set of keys. After reaching the door, the second key turns the lock. I leave the door slightly ajar and return to the car. To my surprise, she looks up at and smiles. What a relief! Maybe she can walk.

"You're home, girl, time to call it a night." Her smile remains intact, and after I open the door, she speechlessly moves out of the car, my arm around her waist. She's a little wobbly but moving under her own steam, so I just help her along and through the front door. The place seems different from what I remember; I have no idea where she sleeps.

"Where is your bedroom, Sam?" I whisper apprehensively, waiting for the sudden glare of a light to smack me in the face, possibly followed by Billy's fist. Her head leans against my shoulder, but she doesn't reply.

"Where do you sleep, girl?" I implore in a controlled way, if that's possible. It must be the desperation in my voice because she replies, "With the babies."

The first door to the left is open and yields the jackpot. It's a long room that I remember as a family room. It's big enough for me to see two small beds placed end-to-end down the far wall and perpendicular to another bed that goes across the back wall of the bedroom. Fortunately, the room is big enough to accommodate still yet another twin bed across from the two little ones. I lead Sam into the bedroom and sit her down on the edge of the twin bed. A small orange night light is plugged directly into a wall socket and surprisingly provides a hefty enough glow for me to see the two girls sleeping in the little beds and Sean in his bed at the far end of the room.

Now what? I'm not sure how Billy is going to react if he finds Sam in her sweaty and rumpled uniform and I sure as hell know she'd get out of her outfit. So maybe I better get her under the covers in some night things. I know you're not going to believe this, but with lust having nothing to do with my decision, I undertake a rapid reconnaissance through a simple chest of drawers which quickly produces a full-length, black nightgown of a silky material. I return to Sam who hasn't budged from the side of the bed. After being as sure as possible the kids are in deep slumber, I hold her uniform just below the neck and draw the front zipper down to her waist. In the deathly quiet of the night, it sounds like a freight train going clickety-clack through Memphis which was on the route of the *City of New Orleans* train. And, just like the song, if something goes wrong here, it's going to be "*goodnight America*" for me.

I bring the sleeves off her shoulders and push the uniform down to her waist. Fuck it…things have already gone wrong, because Sam ain't wearing a bra. My first reacton is that I'm surprised at the shapeliness of her, as I glance at the twins a few feet away. Sam's somewhat bustier than I remember, which one would expect after having two kids, I guess, but her smooth rising curves are still high and youthful. Enough! Contrary to what you're probably thinking, I'm totally numb or maybe even dead below the waist. I quickly slip the black nightgown over her head, straighten the thin straps and the bust line, and lean her back across the bed. I then ease off her uniform, and holy shit, now the *City of New Orleans* is really wailing away, 'cause she ain't wearing panties and, through my hazy field of vision, I see a strawberry-blonde contrast against the alabaster hue of her Scots-Irish skin. I'm dumbstruck; however, I only linger in the past for a moment or so, because what immediately comes to mind is that those two little girls sleeping across from her are Dolph's. Anyway, don't get after me for taking a cheap shot because when we were kids, she always wore a bra and panties. So, how the hell could I know there was nothing under the purple and black?

As for me, I don't know what's going to give out first, my lungs or my heart. I slide the covers out from under her, nudge her head up on a queen-sized pillow, and put the covers back across her restful body. The uniform ends up on the single chair in the room, and then I survey the place to check for last minute details. Everything appears to be okay, so I quietly exit the room and tiptoe out the door, holding down an urge to sprint for the car, rev the engine, and squeal around the corner.

I honestly think I'm a solid two miles from her house before my lungs fill with air, and then my mind becomes a mess. For one thing, I don't recall anything about her shoes. For another, the ache in my lungs is spreading to my brain, which is starting to think about swimming under water, golf balls, and whether or not this long night will yield some success.

It's after 4:00 a.m. by the time I approach the Presidential. I figure I've got to get that basket, and it doesn't make much sense to go to the efficiency at this hour. After a drive that could have earned me a minimum of five moving violations, I screech into the lower parking lot, leap out of the car, and head for the bag room. Within seconds, all the balls have joined my gym shorts in the washtub, and I begin to rinse off the mud in search of Hargraves' cut, burgundy-monogrammed ball. Five minutes later, I have my answer.

Whadda ya think? Well, I'll tell you what. You owe me twenty bucks, that's what. So, it's going to be twenty from you, twenty from Marcus, and if I get more than a hundred from Hargraves, another twenty from Marcus. So what do you have to say about that, you skeptic? At the very least, you've got to admit it's been one hell of a day, and it still has about twenty hours left to go. Will Hargraves kick in over a hundred? Will Marcus pay his debts? Will Sam split the money or even talk to me after wondering how she ended up in her bed in a nightgown with her uniform on a chair? And what about the missing shoes? Stay tuned. I've got to hit the cot and get a few hours of sack time. See ya at 6:00 a.m…or maybe you ought to sleep in; fine with me.

XV

HARGRAVES AND THE GREAT WHITE BALL

But seeking out a life of worth
can cause a lot of pain
with her love striving to be
and trying to maintain
an even keel or better yet
a smile upon my face…..

Ah hell! I'm too tired to be thinking about my lyrics; in fact, I'm just way too tired to even give it a half smile. The few hours of sleep hasn't dented the depths of my exhaustion, the dexadrine is barely keeping me vertical, and I doubt seriously I'm even going to be able to keep up with you on this rather bleak Sunday morning…but thanks for hanging in. At the moment, I'm doing a pitiful shuffle-butt towards the cart room when Marcus sticks his head out from the starter's office and yells at me.

"D Jack, you have a call on two. You can take it here if you like." I head over to the window and Marcus hands me the receiver, releases the hold button and pushes in number two, both of which are bracketed by a third button, all of which are lined across the bottom of the flesh-colored receiver.

"This is D Jack, may I help you?"

"I think you've probably helped too much. Guess who?"

"Sounds like my financial partner in the lake excavation business."

"Oh my God, I forgot about the ball. How long did you stay out there last night before quitting?"

"Thanks for the vote of confidence," I quip. "And we stayed out there until I found the ball, that's how long."

She laughs. "You actually found the damn thing? For sure?"

"I'll show it to you around 3:00 p.m. if you can get a break. Hargraves is playing the Presidential today, and I figure to find him in the dining room or lounge after his round. That way both of us can give it to him and you can get your 50/50 split."

"I think you should do it yourself," she says a bit on the quiet side. "I really wasn't much help."

"Sure you were; you brought the food."

"Devon, I have a few problems with last night," she responds self-consciously.

"No, you don't, Sam. I found your shoes this morning and nothing to speak of took place during your, uh, nap."

"Did you put me to bed?"

"I did."

"And I didn't take off my clothes did I?"

"No, you didn't, but I figured Billy would scratch his head if he saw you dressed. He had to be sleeping, and your kids were zonked, so no problem."

Moments pass. "I'm sorry, Dev, really I am."

"Why? "I respond innocently. "We had a nice meal under a Florida sky, complete with stars and moonlight on the pond, and we found the ball to boot. Who could ask for more?"

"And nothing happened?"

"No, absolutely nothing, not even a goodnight handshake," I say seriously and forcefully.

"And no fleeting glances either, I suppose?"

"Well, after I got over you not having anything on under your uniform, I categorically deny lingering and emphatically deny leching. But I will admit to fleeting which was sufficient to note the addition of a few stretch marks here and there, but I guess those are the rewards for having two kids."

"That's not fair," she says, "and you're right, they *are* rewards. But there are still a few gaps you're going to have to fill in for me."

"There aren't any gaps, Sam; end of story. Anyway, I have to work for a living and have to get back to mingling with the rich and famous. Your shoes are under the counter, and maybe when you pick them up you can leave me a corned beef on fresh wheat, no toast. You hear that? No toast. And Dijon mustard, *no* Miracle Whip."

"You're right," she says with what sounds like a sneer. "We are incompatible, but I'll see what I can do anyway."

"Thanks. I'll hope to see ya in the Lounge at 3:00 p.m." She hangs up, and I notice that Marcus has a funny look on his face and realize he has overheard the entire conversation.

"What's with the funny look, Marcus?"

He shakes his head from side to side and the corners of his mouth are turned down. "You're not actually going to tell me you found that ball out in the water hazard on the fifth, are you?"

I paint a big shit-eatin' grin on my face, slowly remove the ball from my front pocket, and turn it in such a way as to allow Marcus to see the small half-moon cut on the pimpled surface just below the burgundy H. He just flat stares at the ball with utter disbelief. Then, with a cynical sneer, he says, "How do you know you put the cut in the right spot and that it's the right shape?"

I place the ball back in my jeans and return his stare. "Okay, enough fun and games, and I don't want any of your sore loser bits. Pay up. I get the first twenty for just finding the ball if you remember. That was the deal."

Marcus begrudgingly reaches into his pants pocket and pulls out a wad of bills. He peels through a load of singles and some fives and tens before sliding out a rumpled twenty that he meticulously tries to straighten out. Just like him to have a double-thick wad arranged in denominational order. Hell, when I haul in the bills, I just stuff 'em in my jeans and then periodically unload 'em into the Fuente box. Part of the fun is sorting them out at the end of the day, just to see what they are and what the grand take has been for eighteen hours of toil, sweat, and hustle while bowing and scraping.

"Don't spend it just yet, Pirate. We've still got twenty on whether Hargraves comes across with a hundred or more or even certifies it's the right ball. If not, I want the same bill back plus my earnings." As an afterthought, he takes the bill from my hand, takes a black ink pen from behind his rather small right ear, and draws an 'X' across Jackson's face. Then, he returns the bill to my still outstretched palm. "You got that? The same damn bill."

"Sure thing, but don't forget to have another one of these ready at 3:00...and you can even mark it the same way if you like. It spends regardless."

Marcus returns my hostile expression. "Never!" he says with a certain air of finality. "You'll never collect forty bucks off of me in the same day. That will just never happen. Understand? Never, meaning not today, not tomorrow, or not ever. And if memory serves, I hit you up big time recently I believe," he concludes with his own shit-eatin' grin which easily surpasses mine.

My thoughts go to Lena Dawson and the picture Marcus never saw. I figured I had done the right thing, but now the crusty ole bastard is rubbing my nose in it. I wonder if Stunt will rent it out again, so I can nail Marcus's scrawny ass to the wall, instantly knowing it ain't never gonna happen. So I smile weakly, throw my hands in the air, turn without saying another word, and head for the cart room entrance to pick up the mobile bar which has already been loaded for a few executives from Prudential.

As I get to the cart, I notice just a few bottles of Schlitz and a single bottle of Charles Krug Beaujolais. It looks like an easy afternoon, because the booze is on the light side, and the bags aren't rentals. That suggests this twosome wants to enjoy the course and play some serious golf; frankly, I wouldn't mind being a part of it for a change.

*

For once, I was right. The two execs finished the first nine just before noon and decided to break for lunch. One guy was two over par, and the other guy was three over so the golf had obviously been pretty good. My expertise had been sought out a number of times with positive results, particularly on my old friend, the eighth. The better player of the two had not realized that his second shot would be mostly downhill on the dogleg and had selected too much club. After I quietly pointed it out to him, he went with my suggestion, changed his club, and put the ball down just in front of the water hazard, after which he chipped up within ten feet of the pin and holed out with a solid putt, giving him his only birdie on the front nine.

Right now, I'm heading back to the bag room after agreeably settling on a one-hour lunch break. I quickly note Sam's shoes are gone, and she has replaced them with a thick, lean corned beef on rye accompanied by two large kosher pickles. I'm about to take my first bite when the phone rings, so I dutifully pick up the receiver.

"Bag room, this is D Jack, may I help you?" I like to change it around once in awhile.

"D Jack, it's Turk. Where you been?"

"I've been out on the course with a couple of guys from Prudential. What's up?"

"The news is all over the place," he answers excitedly, "all the staff, waitresses, caddies, everybody. All three courses too," he continues hurriedly, "and even some of the people in the hotel, a couple of horse players."

"What news?"

"You finding Hargraves's ball, that's what," he says impatiently as if I should be the last guy he has to tell about this grandiose event.

"So?"

"So, everybody's putting money down with me. I mean the joint has gone totally bananas," he continues dropping his voice about an octave, "I've had more than fifty betters in the last two hours and must have more than a thousand bucks going on this thing. I'm giving four-to-one that Hargraves doesn't come across with a hundred or more."

"You got the hundred dollar figure from Marcus, I suppose."

"Yeah, I did."

"Fine," I say with a glow. "I'll take some of that action."

"No you won't, Pirate. You've got your bet down with the ole man.

"Hey, wait just a minute," I say sharply. "Do you want people to think you run an exclusive service? If I want to lay down some cash, you've got to pick it up. That's the law in bookie land, man."

Turk's tone turns to a cross between hurt and beg. "Aw, come on. I was just pulling your leg."

"Right, Turk, so put me down for a fifty-spot that Hargraves will come across with the C-note."

"I got you down, man," he says and immediately breaks the connection. I proceed to eat my sandwich, after which I pick up the Prudential boys at 1:00 p.m. sharp and head for the tenth tee that, strangely enough, is clear. Looks like a good omen…and it is. I thoroughly enjoy the golf and the small part the execs allow me to play in their game. Nothing pretentious and no bullshit, just two guys relishing in their athletic hobby and having no difficulties adhering to the Jimmy Demaret Law that says: "Golf is based on honesty; where else would you admit to a seven on a par three?" Anyway, they're dead even after eighteen, and because they're running late and the course seems to be clogged-up behind us, I suggest they putt out again on the final hole from about ten feet. Both of them sink the shots and decide to call it an even day. Each shakes hands with me and slips me a couple of twenty dollar bills along with some friendly smiles. Who says there aren't any winners at the Presidential?

I'm making my way back to the bag room, after parking the booze cart, and am confronted by a zoo. Stunt, Marcus, Ralph, Turk, Red, and half a dozen others all stare at me as I approach the counter.

"Where the hell you been?" asks the exasperated Turk.

"I've been out doing my job which makes me wonder who the hell is running this place with all you guys gawking behind the counter. If Charley is in the building, some of you slobovians will be out of work."

"D Jack," Marcus says patiently, "at the gong, the time will be quarter to four, and it's all we can do to keep Hargraves in the bar. You do remember Hargraves, don't you?"

"Hargraves? Oh yeah, Hargraves. Okay, let's go see him, but first I've got to get Samantha. She kept my back on the great white ball hunt, so she's in on the deal."

"She called me and told me she couldn't get away but would try to find you later if she got a break," Marcus says and adds, "and she wished you good luck."

Needless to say, I'm disappointed that Sam won't be in on the finish, but it's a grand procession of working stiffs that I lead from the bag room upstairs to the dining room and over into the Bengal Lounge. The room is fairly empty, so it's easy to spot Hargraves. I walk over to his table where he's sipping something on the rocks while a guy with him is working on a tall draft in a pilsner glass. I stop directly in front of Hargraves who looks at me in a somewhat curious way, like "what the fuck do you want?" Feeling the presence of half a dozen bodies over my shoulder, I face Hargraves who probably figures this might have something to do with the ball, but he's obviously waiting me out.

"Uh, Mr. Hargraves," I begin as I dig into my pocket, "I believe I have something that you threw into a water hazard." He immediately paints a frown across his face as I retrieve the ball and extend it to him. He's pissed!

"It's already been tried, kid, and it's getting to be a pretty lousy joke," he says as his eyes dismiss me and he returns to his drink.

"No joke, sir," I say politely as I push the ball toward him. "I went into the pond at number five last night and found it just about smack dab in the middle of the water hazard." He looks up with an even nastier expression and takes the ball from my hand. He then slowly rotates the ball, and in a flash, his eyes and mouth erupt as he spots the moon-shaped nick just under the monogrammed H.

"By God! You really did find it. Well I'll be a sonuvabitch! SONUVABITCH!!" he repeats as he slams his palm down against the dark-colored mahogany table. "This is great kid, just great. You can't imagine how much I've wanted this damn ball. Just great," he repeats like a seven-year-old who's just spotted his first birthday bike. "And I'm going to show you my appreciation, too." He reaches for his billfold and you can cut the tension with damn near any somewhat sharp object. It's the bottom of the ninth with the home team down by one, one guy on, and two outs; it's fourth and inches at the goal line; it's the glitz of Oscar night, and someone's about to open the envelope. Hargraves opens the folds of rich, brown leather, reaches in, and with thumb and forefinger, brings out a small white card that he passes over to me.

"That's my business card, kid." I take the card, noting the same large burgundy H in the middle with his name and address printed just below it. All of us are bewildered and have to concentrate as Hargraves continues.

"That's the address of my downtown store. So the next time you're in Philadelphia, just drop in, and you can have any suit in the place. How does that strike you?" he asks with a satisfied smile.

"Gee, Mr. Hargraves. Thanks much. It's very kind of ya, and I'll look you up in Philly." I give it a weak smile as he shakes hands and follows it up with a slap on the arm. But his eyes never leave the ball and I get the distinct feeling I've ceased to exist.

I quickly turn, and the guys, who have been hanging back, follow me out of the Lounge except for Ron who drifts back behind the bar. The others continue to troop silently behind me as we head for the bag room. Upon arriving, the silence continues until Turk takes the lead.

"I guess all bets are off," he says dejectedly. Check that…depressed is closer to the mark. No one responds, and after a few seconds I snap my fingers as my face radiates a mixture of enthusiasm and potential victory,

"Let me summarize the situation," I begin."The bet was that Hargraves would come across with one hundred or more, right?" I catch nods in the affirmative, so I continue. "Okay then. Hargraves tells me I can go into his main operation in downtown Philly and take *any* suit in the place. So, if he carries suits over a hundred bucks, I win. It's as simple as that."

Ralph looks at me quizzically with that old scratch of the head confusion of his. "Yeah, D Jack, but how we gonna know what they cost?"

"Ma Bell," I reply as I retrieve Hargraves's card while glancing over at the Turk who gives it a "why don't you try it" look, so I head over to the phone and check the operator for the area code for Philly. She quickly informs me the area code is 215, so I dial the long distance information number and ask for Hargraves downtown. After about twenty seconds or so, a clinical voice gives me 1-215-923-5190. I quickly dial the numbers and beckon Turk to come over next to the phone to verify the impending conversation. After a few rings, a young pleasant male voice informs me that I am talking with Hargraves of Philadelphia.

I clear my throat feeling a bit of apprehension beginning to close in on me. "I just moved to town and was told I can get a nice suit for the money at Hargraves."

"I'm sure we can fit you, sir. We have many sizes and styles."

"Can you give me a price range?" I inquire gingerly as I hold my breath.

"Our suits start as low as thirty-nine ninety-five and go up to eighty-nine ninety-nine." The Turk smiles, curls his fist, and playfully shakes it at the assembled crowd.

"Are those sale prices?" I ask, grasping for straws.

"Those are our everyday prices, sir."

Another light bulb barely flickers, but it's worth a last ditch effort. "Are those prices for two-or three-piece suits?"

"Oh, those were standard suits, sir," he responds. "We do carry three piece suits, however."

"And how much do they run?"

"All of our three piece suits are ninety-nine ninety-nine." The smile on Turk's face seems to fade a bit. "That's fine," I say with a grin. "Thanks much. You've been very helpful."

I hang up the phone and look at the Turk. "You heard the man, Turk. Just throw in sales tax, and that means Hargraves's deal is worth more than a hundred bucks. I rub my hands together, stare at the bookie with my best "Oil Can Harry" look, and pretend to curl my moustache letting him know in no small way that I have just increased my investment fourfold at his expense.

"Not so quick, D Jack," the Turk whines. "Let's be honest about this thing. Hargraves didn't give you a deal worth a hundred bucks, because the truth of the matter is, the bastard stiffed ya!"

"You want to explain that?" I ask, somewhat annoyed and the Turk suddenly seems more confident. "I'd be more than glad to. He says next time you're in Philadelphia, you should drop in and get any suit off the rack, right?"

"That's right."

"But the truth is, the guy figures it will be a cold day in hell before you're in Philly, so the only thing that ball cost him was his business card which sure as hell ain't gonna turn into a voucher for more than a hundred bucks worth of merchandise, or even ten cents for that matter."

I smile benevolently and put my hand on the Turk's arm. "Nice try, ole timer, but it just won't wash. He gives me the card, he says take any suit in the place, and the salesman clearly prices the suit, plus tax, in excess of a C-note. It's payday, Turk."

"Hold on just a minute, Pirate," says Marcus. I've wondered why the old man has remained silent up to this point, and it appears as if I am about to get my answer. "The deal was that Hargraves was supposed to hit you a hundred or more, right?"

"That's old ground, Marcus, but I think it's fair to say it's a hundred or its equivalent." To my surprise, Marcus nods his agreement. "Okay, a hundred or its equivalent, but that's the worth to Hargraves, not to you. Hargraves does the paying out, so the only important thing is the worth of what he's paying out. Don't even raise your eyebrows, D Jack. There's no way you can argue it."

"Okay. So?" I ask already knowing where Marcus is going with this, and I'm furiously trying to stall for time in order to dredge up a response.

"So, Hargraves surely doesn't pay anywhere near a hundred bucks for a three-piece suit. He's a bad businessman if he's paying more than half, and you can check that with Murray the Thief downtown or Saul over at David Alan's on Lincoln Road if you want. No deal, D Jack," Marcus concludes with a smile. "You lose. Give me my twenty bucks back, and like I said earlier, I want the same one."

I give it my A-one show of indignation. "Well, if you insist on getting so damn picky about it, the fact is that Hargraves has to shell out more than just the cost to him for the suit. He's got a lot of overhead that has to be thrown in like lights, air, salaries, deliveries, tailoring, shoplifting, back-door rip-offs, defective articles, etc., etc., etc. Hell, man, you just can't say the worth to him is his dollar cost for getting the suit in the store."

The Turk breaks the deadlock. "You two can bitch and moan all you want, but the rest of you guys know I run a fair and clean board. When I have to make a decision on a local wager, I make it the best and fairest I can. Now I see no way to resolve this thing, so I simply declare that all bets off; your wagers will be returned, and that's final." He turns his back and strides away followed by everyone except Marcus. I get in the first punch.

"You heard the man, Marcus. All bets are off; no winners, no losers, so I'll just keep the twenty you lost when I found the ball.

"Where's your code of ethics, college man?" Marcus asks with a strong dose of dissatisfaction. "You know as well as I do that number one, Hargraves stiffed you, and number two, even if he didn't, there's no way you come out over a hundred dollars."

I stick to my guns. "You heard the Turk."

"I agree with the Turk, but that has nothing to do with *our* bet. This is between you and me and was a private deal until the whole joint got in on it. God, so much action, people around here will bet on anything."

"And by the way," I say, trying to move off the main issue to something truly superfluous, "whose fault was that?"

Marcus looks at me big-eyed and open-mouthed. “Well, don’t blame me if you get loud when you talk to your girlfriend.” His face suddenly takes on a look of concern. “Samantha is your girlfriend, isn’t she?”

“You’ll have to ask her about that, although I think the answer is no. And anyway, it’s none of your damn business, and don’t try to change the subject on me,” I answer with an overblown irritation regarding his inquiry into my private life. Nonetheless, even though I think I’m just being a goofball, I screwed up, because Marcus seems to take my comment to heart.

“Ah, hell,” I say with a sigh as I reach into my jeans for the defaced, crumpled bill. “Here, ya crusty ole bastard, take the twenty.”

He shrugs and waves his hand from side to side, his head down. “I don’t want it. You keep it,” he says. “After all, you did find the ball.”

“Well I don’t want it either.”

“Well that’s tough, so you just keep it.”

“It’s yours,” I say with a smile, “and we both know it, because it has a great big ‘X’ right across Jackson’s ugly mug. So you got to take what’s yours. House rules, right?”

Marcus looks up and realizes I’m laughing, and he slowly breaks into a broad grin. As they say in collective bargaining, it appears as if we are about to avoid impasse.

“I got it!” I say.

“That’s what I’ve been telling you all along,” Marcus concludes but I blow off his comment. “The Ferdie Fund, that’s where it goes,” I say to him as he finally accepts the bill. “It goes to the Ferdie Fund which is probably about due for a few bucks. Right, Marcus?”

The old man nods his head as his smile tightens with the thought of Ferd who is up but barely hobbling around. “Good show, D Jack. It goes to the Ferdie Fund.”

Marcus seems lost in thought; I’m sure he’s concerned with whether or not Ferdie is going to be able to weather the storm but a smile returns to his face, and he says, “So, not to change the subject, but are you ever going to tell me what happened to Schmedler’s mysteriously absent golf bag?”

I shrug and nod in the negative. “I know what I knew yesterday, and I know what I’ll know tomorrow. They were put on the bus.”

He gives me a “you still ain’t coming clean” look and then puts the bill in his wallet. Needless to say, it shouldn’t surprise you or me that he doesn’t add the bill to the wad he keeps in his pocket. I mean, let’s face it. You’ve been along for awhile, and you surely have the feel of Marcus’s character, right? In fact, let’s be honest. You were never in my corner on this Hargraves thing, were you?

Confident? You bet I'm confident; in fact, I've got an unmarked twenty that says I'm right. So, what's it going to be this time, play or pass?

XVI

LATE NIGHT FISHING WITH BILLY

Have you ever been down
have you ever been out
have you ever been told, my friend
that there's no doubting……

"**Y**ou look a little green," I say, sliding into the corner seat that appears to have become our rendezvous in the Bengal Lounge. It's just after 11:00 p.m., and I'm through; Moon only wants to do two sets on Sunday night, and he's doing the second one solo. Sam has been in for about fifteen minutes and appears to be sipping some clear kind of soda pop. She gives me a somewhat weak but brave smile.

"I think I must have poisoned myself last night. I hoped I would be feeling better by now, but it's been a pretty tough day with two long shifts."

Her look tells me she might be about to start in on some kind of apology, so I quickly deflect that possibility. "Maybe this will make you feel a little better," I say pleasantly, handing her a ten-dollar bill.

"What's this for?"

"It's your half of the deal. If you recall, you were a silent partner last night, and I did find the ball. We agreed to split the winnings down the middle, so I got twenty off of Marcus. Here's your take."

Yeah, I know and you know that I didn't get squat from Marcus, but a small grin slowly creeps across her face, so I think it's a worthy investment. "I heard all about that suit business, Devon, and it's my humble opinion that you've been had."

"You're going against me on this, too?" I say aghast. "I thought at least you of all people, my partner in this escapade, would support me." I contemplate the situation for a few seconds, chewing the inside bottom of my lip after pushing a load of Kodiak back toward my molars. After a sparkling idea, I return my fuzzy gaze to Sam.

"I'll show all you guys. Just to prove I wasn't stiffed, I'll be wearing a three-piece suit courtesy of Hargraves no later than Friday."

"Fine, and if you do, we're still partners. So, do I get the jacket, the vest, or the slacks?"

I return her bit of a grin and glance at the beer garden bustline of her uniform. "You being five-six, the slacks are out. The vest won't have a chance, so you can have the jacket, figuring you might be able to button a forty-four regular."

A blush barely makes its way through her tired, off-color complexion. "So, you really did glance. That's not fair," she says, somewhat hostile.

"Yeah, I know, that's the way I felt too."

"What do you mean?"

"I mean it wasn't fair that you got so sleepy out on the green."

"You mean loaded."

"Let's compromise and call it tired," I say, hoping to find some middle ground.

"And if I hadn't been so, ah, tired as you say?"

"Are you talking about the picnic or your house?"

"I don't remember you putting me to bed, but I vaguely remember giving you a hug on the course," she says.

"I wouldn't call going to sleep against me as a hug." She seems somewhat surprised, so I doubt she really remembers much of what she said or did.

"The question remains," she continues. "What if I hadn't been drinking?"

"We've been over that, Sam. You're the one who's responsible for the rules so any decision has to be yours. And you weren't exactly in a position to make one. Anyway, I'm glad nothing happened, because it wouldn't have been good for either of us."

"I drank because I was nervous, because we have a past," she admits.

"No need to be," I say in a matter-of-fact way. "Sure, we once knew each other but now we don't really know much about who we are. We've had a pretty long hiatus, during which I've tried to re-create myself and you fell in love, got married, and had twins. You probably won't believe this, but I don't think serious things should happen between people who really don't know each other," I conclude in a very somber and, hopefully, sincere way.

"Then how do people get to know each other again, Dev? How did we get to know each other in high school?"

"If I recall, very slowly at first, but I think you have to have something in common that eventually accelerates things…and we did. We shared knowing how damn good we were and how damn good we were going to be."

"Do you think we have anything in common now?"

"Well, you're the one who says I'm one-dimensional and obviously that one dimension is long gone. And if we put the past in the past, no, I'm not aware of anything that's happened to suggest we have anything in common."

"As you say, not that you're aware of, but maybe if we just talk and spend time together, we might discover things we don't know."

"Why would you want to do that?"

"I'm not sure and frankly it scares me a little. That's probably why I drank too much last night. It was kind of cowardly of me to put you in that situation."

"I hope it wasn't some kind of test," I say cautiously.

"Honest, it wasn't," she responds sincerely.

"So then, what is it that scares you?"

"You know the old cliché, Dev, once burned…."

"That person is gone, Sam. He died on a Saturday night at Shea Stadium."

"That's pretty dramatic," she says, but not critically.

"I know, and self serving as you said a few nights ago, but I guess the real sad part is it's pretty accurate."

"Maybe not as much as you think," she says softly. "I know you lived and breathed baseball, but I think there was some warmth in you, for me, and I know you loved your father very much. In your own quiet way, you were kind, and I've seen a lot of that kindness extended to a lot of people over the past few weeks."

I'm not comfortable with her pointing out a few pluses. It's almost like she's trying to convince herself, not me; time to once again, change the subject. "Let's talk about you, Sam. What happened to you?"

"After you and the diving were over, I picked up the pieces and got on with my life. Dolph was sweet and in love with me so it seemed like a good thing."

"That sounds to me like something was missing."

"There was, but it was my fault. I still wanted the fairy tale, but that wasn't fair, and God knows I didn't want to disappointment him."

"People don't disappoint other people when they care about them and try to go the whole nine yards."

Sam gives me a long hard look. "You wouldn't have said that when we were younger, and I don't think you could have thought it either. How did you learn that? Somewhere along the line, did you have the whole nine yards?"

"No, Sam. Somewhere along the line, I realized I should have really shared myself and and maybe I could have grabbed the brass ring."

"With me?"

"Yeah," I respond somewhat bitterly and then add with a half smile, "but that's spilt milk…and anyway, it ain't like I actually had the opportunity to choose a path in the fork of the road. Billy took care of that."

"Yes, he did," she says in a matter-of-fact way. "So, what happens now?"

I pause for only a second before answering her with obvious concern. "I don't know. Is something supposed to happen?"

I notice for the first time that her eyes are wet, but the moisture seems to have washed some of the hardship of last night from her cheeks. Her soft blush has returned, and I get the feeling that something is transpiring between us but don't know what it might be. My thoughts are interrupted by a tapping on my shoulder, and I reluctantly turn to see Sal standing behind me. "Sorry to break in on you, D Jack, but T is about to start his last set. You told him you'd spot him a capo, and it's not in your guitar case."

"Right, Sal," I say as I reach into my pocket and bring out the silver metal-bar that goes across the neck of the guitar. As I hand it to her, she gives me a look that suggests her timing was bad but she had no choice. She then gives Sam an almost sisterly smile before heading back towards the bar where I notice a new guy washing highball glasses.

"Where's Billy?" I inquire.

"He's only working part time now, Wednesday thru Saturday."

"Why so?"

"He's feeling a little more tired, and the full schedule is too hectic for the two of us, what with the kids." Her eyes are now dry; apparently the serious moment has passed. I'm left wondering what to do now and figure I need to get light, but she beats me to the punch.

"So why do they say 'the whole nine yards'? That's obviously one short of first and ten."

"That's the length of a machine gun belt, so when things really got hairy during the war, the gunners held down the trigger and fired the whole nine yards."

"Thanks for *sharing* that tidbit," she says with a smile, as I note her emphasis on "sharing." "So," I ask, "do you want a drink?"

She also seems to pick up on my attempt to back off as she points to her glass. "I have a 7-up and I'll be more than glad to share it." Okay, guys…second use of "share" so ya think maybe she's got some kind of agenda here?

"I'll take a pass on that, thank you. That would be almost as much fun as drinking salt water."

"Oops," she says, "salt water reminds me that Daddy told me to tell you he wants to go fishing tomorrow night when you get off the phones. He knows you don't work the lounge on Mondays."

"He wants to what?" I ask, absolutely dumbfounded.

"I know, it's right out of the blue, but he really wants to do this. So don't make me have to twist your arm, okay?"

"Sam, I don't want to go fishing or fighting with your ole man and that's what it'll come down to."

"I don't think he wants to fight, Dev, so do me a favor and go."

"This doesn't make any sense. He's barely said a word to me since I started here. I don't see the point; he's got nothing to say I'd want to hear and I've got nothing to say at all."

I sense some anxiety in her and don't want to pile anything on top of the events of the past few days. I figure the bastard ain't gonna kill me, so what the hell. "Okay, but will you owe me one?"

"I will, but within reason, Dev."

"How is it you always get to set the damn rules?"

"Because we agreed it's my ballpark."

"I don't remember it being exactly that way, Samantha."

"You don't remember a lot of things, Devon."

"Well, I did get hit in the head if you recall."

"Do you play that card often?"

"Only if I think it'll work."

She gets to her feet. "Well, it won't work with me, so you better get yourself a new deck of cards," she says, giving me a smile as she leaves.

Okay, I know you're pretty sharp and realize the stuff in common thing was left up-in-the air and that absolutely nothing was resolved during the conversation. This open-ended kind of thing seems to be the way our conversations end and it's starting to wear me out…and probably the same goes for you.

*

I'm heading east on Van Buren which dead ends at the Intercoastal Canal. This was an interesting place for me because I used to fish with Billy during the week and make out with Sam at the same spot during the weekend. She used to laugh about it and was always joking about what would happen if her ole man showed up unexpectedly with his tackle box. As I approach the end of the road, I drop the Yamaha into second and take a right turn off the asphalt onto a gravel cul-de-sac that's surrounded by brackish water. Billy's '54 red and black Chrysler sedan is already parked, and he's sitting on a lawn chair with rod and reel in hand. I lean the bike on the side kickstand and slowly ease myself out of the saddle. Off come the helmet and padded jacket and then I head toward the empty chair Billy has provided a few feet from himself. A rod and reel are propped against the chair, and I can see he's attached a plug to the line.

"Is anything biting yet?" I inquire as pleasantly as possible, picking up the rod and sitting down on the lawn chair. I'm still clueless as to why he wants to have this conversation.

"Had a pretty good strike a few minutes ago so I know they're here. Want something cold?"

Eight years ago I would have said yes because he was always buying. But it was Ballantine Ale, and I had to work at getting used to it, but not now. "No, thanks, I figured it was going to be chilly out here so I packed a little anti-freeze."

"Times change," he replies somberly.

"That they do," I offer as I cast the plug into the middle of the Intercoastal. Then I just stretch out my legs, reach for the half pint of VO wedged in my back pocket, and take a hit. This is the way I like to fish. Throw the line out, take a swallow, and let a fish decide if he wants to get caught. All that reeling in and casting out is too much work. A pretty good-sized yacht, all lit up like a huge Christmas tree, is puttering around just short of the bridge about fifty yards to our left, because Hollywood Boulevard is a main thoroughfare, and the wood-slatted drawbridge only goes up on the half hour.

"So, what do you want to talk about? I figure this ain't a social visit and you have something on your mind, so let's get at it."

"The last time we sat here you would have waited for me to start the conversation."

"I'm not an eighteen-year-old kid anymore, Billy.

"Yeah, it shows."

"Fine, that's one for you. So?"

"So what's going on between you and my daughter?"

"There's absolutely nothin' going on between me and you daughter."

"Okay, then let me put it another way. What's your relationship with her?"

"I don't have a relationship with her," I say bluntly.

"But you can take her clothes off, huh?" he retorts sounding really nasty.

No sense ducking that one so I decide to match his nastiness. "She was sweaty and a bit messy, and it's not like I saw something I've never seen before."

"I know that."

"What do you mean, you know that?"

"I know it, so just leave it at that. What I really want to know is how can you say you don't have a relationship if you've talked with her a few times and even taken her to dinner, to say nothing about moonlight swims at midnight?"

It would seem as if Sam has been sharing stuff with Billy, which doesn't surprise me because it's been just the two of them since the ladders collapsed at Palisades Park. So I know I have to play this straight, although there's really very little to say. "I know you and me used to play chess, so in this case Sam is white and I'm black."

"Tell me something I don't know. She's the good guy, and you're the sonuvabitch. No argument from me."

"No argument from me either, but that's not what I have in mind. What I'm trying to point out is I'm sure you remember that white always has the first move and black has to react. At the Grand Masters level, if white doesn't screw up, he should win, and black is always doing little more than playing for a tie."

"Of course I remember; I know all that so what's your point?"

"The point is that Sam has come into the Bengal Lounge to see me a few times, she asked me to take her to dinner, and she brought a huge tray of food out to the fifth green," I say employing the ole half-truth. "I've initiated nothing, and absolutely nothing has transpired between us, clothes or no clothes. That's why I'm telling you there isn't a relationship here; there's nothing. Okay…ya happy now? Can I go?"

"I'm not so sure. I know Charley and everyone around the Presidential thinks you're okay and I know my daughter. I'm seeing and hearing things out of her and I'm starting to wonder."

"About what?"

"The most obvious is she knows how I've felt about you over the years, and she seems to be trying to soft-pedal any conversation about what she may be thinking or feeling."

I feel a slight tug on the line, but figure at best a snook is just having some fun, so I take another swallow of VO and decide to go head-to-head with him. Hell, it isn't like I've got something to lose here. "Then I'm not your problem, Billy. If there is one, which I seriously doubt, you'll have to talk with her. So don't give me your short 'stay away' speech; I've heard it."

"If you really loved her, you wouldn't have fooled around with some broad in Jacksonville, and I wouldn't have had to meet you on a street corner!" he says just short of rage.

"That's a two-edged sword," I answer with more than a hint of irritation. "Maybe if she really loved me, the two of you would have given me at least a chance to say I fucked up. But then, I suspect you were perfect, huh? The world famous Diving Sensation never had groupies doing what ever it took to get an autograph and then some, right?"

That seems to stop him cold, and he appears to be reflecting on something or other that produces a look of sadness. "It was more complicated for me."

"You bet; it's always that way when a guy's talking about himself."

"Her name was Suzanne, and I used to see her every day when we played Cedar Point up at Sandusky."

Whoa, Nellie! What the fuck's he talking about.

"She was married, and obviously so was I. It took years for Katherine and me to get past it; things were never really the same," he says, "but thank God we were able to patch it up as best we could before she was killed at Palisades Park."

Sorry, guys, I'm gonna have some trouble with sympathy here. "Well, you're one sanctimonious sonuvabitch! You were a family man with something serious on the side while I was a wet-nosed teenage kid having bimbos throwing bras and wet panties in my face. And I can see how things were complicated as you say. You can hate my guts all you want, Billy, but there's only one adulterer trying to snag a snook here."

The look on his face tells me that comment has hit him like a dagger. "I've known that all along but I'm Sam's father and when it came to you that made it different at least that's what I've thought over the years."

"So what really happened is that you didn't want me to hurt her like the way you betrayed her mother? After all this, that's a terrific explanation, just fucken terrific, but why are you even bothering to tell me now?"

"Because there are times I still don't like myself, but I've hated you so much that I only process anything that confirms you're a louse. But now, I hear stuff, like the Ferdie thing, and I'm having trouble making it fit. You know what I'm saying?" he asks as he reaches for his can of ale.

"Actually I do," I respond reflectively. "People take stuff that fits comfortably into their brains and use them to reinforce what they already think."

"Yeah, Sam told me you went to Arizona State. Who would have dreamt a dumb jock like you could go to college? Too bad you tried to play baseball first. You didn't do so good, did you superstar?"

Terrific, he's right back to being a nasty bastard. "I guess I was good enough to be inducted into the Florida Sports Hall of Fame," I respond defensively.

"I don't see why they put you in. All you had was one good year in the minors and one day in the Show."

"You're just having one hell of a good ole fucken time aren't you? Sure, I know. You were a one-of-a-kind and I was a one-day wonder. I'll bet you don't miss the diving, do you?"

"No, why do you say that?"

"Because you were the best in the world, and it's probably easier to walk away from something when you know you're at the very top."

"You're bitter, aren't you," he says rhetorically.

"You're fucken-A right I'm bitter," I say, raising my voice. "I might have been damn good. I might have done it all, and that ain't brag. That's because I believed in myself and brought it off at all levels; Little League, high school, Legion and the minors. I was going to do it, and not for the wet panties or maybe even a couple of thousand grand…and then, in a fucken heartbeat, it was all gone and I'll never know. And you'll never know or even have a fucken clue how that feels. And the fact that Katherine took you back and stayed with you just the same; you'll never have a clue about that either. And don't tell me about losing your wife and daughter. When I lost my Dad, I not only lost my father, I lost the only person in the world who believed in me, because you and Sam sure as hell had taken a hike."

"You drove her out of your life."

"Bullshit! She never gave me a chance. I don't know if she sent you or you did it on your own but it was her loving dad who met me on a street corner in the middle of the fucken night."

"How old are you, Devon?"

"I don't want to hear it, Billy. I get that speech on a regular basis from Marcus and even now and then from Charley Berston."

"You can't play baseball anymore, son."

"I'm not your son, and I'm fucken aware of what I can and can't do!"

"Take a look at that yacht out there and tell me what you see."

I look toward the bridge where the yacht, probably a Chris-Craft, is just idling in the water. My attention is drawn to all those lights that are shining on a very long-legged blonde in a red bikini leaning up against a shiny, metal railing. "Just like the old days Billy. I see a sexy broad impatiently waiting for the bridge to go up and I know what you're going to say next."

"Yes, you do. She probably doesn't look as sexy sitting on a toilet seat."

"You always liked to blow the image of a foxy broad, but that was because I was dating your daughter and wasn't supposed to look. That's obviously no longer the case, so what's your point this time?"

"The boat's idling because it can't control the bridge and has to wait before it can move on."

"So you're saying I'm dead in the water, but I should wait for the bridge to open and then get out of Dodge?"

"That's what I'm saying," he confirms as he takes another long hit on his Ballentine Ale can.

I decide to haul in my line, having lost interest in a snook even though I had little interest to begin with. "I'm really curious, Billy. You basically haven't talked to me since I started at the Presidential and now I'm getting a speech; why even bother?"

Billy checks his wristwatch, and he too brings in his line and an empty plug. "I'm hoping you'll move on to something, anything, so you're not around Samantha. I'm hoping you won't come by the house now and then because I don't want her to watch you and me stare at each other. Maybe I remember the son I thought I was going to have, until you broke my daughter's heart," he concludes as he packs down his tackle box, stands up, and folds his lawn chair. "But what I do know is that I feel sadness as well as bitterness, and I'm getting towards the end."

I get to my feet, grip the chair with one hand and the rod with the other, and follow Billy to the Chrysler. After loading everything into the humongous trunk, he turns and faces me, waiting for a response. "So, is that what this was all about?" I ask. "I'm just supposed to sail away to make you happy?"

"I all but ran out of time once and almost lost everything. Samantha's all I have and I don't want to run that risk again."

"Baseball, Billy. In baseball, you never lose; you just run out of innings, so don't worry. You might run out of innings, but you'll never lose your daughter."

The old man says nothing. As far as I'm concerned, I've tried to reassure him of Sam's love for him, and have received nothing in return. I figure he just wants the damn bridge to go up and so what if it does? There's just the same Intercoastal Canal on the other side. Yeah, I know, once a pessimist, always a pessimist; ya don't have to remind me!

Billy heads for the front door of the sedan, so I move off toward the Yamaha. As I swing my right leg over the saddle, I hear the Chrysler's engine kick in and the soft crunch of the gravel as he slowly drives away. I gaze across the water at the motionless yacht and the blond-haired babe still leaning against the rail, but I'm preoccupied with what has transpired and she's more out of focus than usual. That's what happens when I get tired. And if I'm really tired, the vision in my right eye gets even worse with what the doctors sometime refer to as a kaleidoscope effect.

So whadda ya think? Billy obviously is after some peace of mind, but why? Assuming Sam has satisfied her curiosity and that's that, why did he need to have this hostile chat? Can it be that he's concerned that his only child is looking at me in a different light after all these years, and he's afraid he might alienate her if he continues to voice his disdain for me? Personally, if I had to choose, I'd place my bets with the Turk on the 'hostile chat' thing. Sam might be looking at me in a different light, but if so, that light is no more than a flicker as opposed to the blinding variety.

What a fucken night! To be honest, and I really have tried to be all along, I'm tired and I don't think I have the energy to ponder this thing anymore. My gaze returns to the Chris-Craft drifting toward the cul-de-sac, now close enough for the blonde to smile my way. At least I figure so, but like I said, things are pretty blurry at that distance. I guess she's been standing there all this time, and I'd like to think she's been looking my way all the while. She then stands away from the rail she's been leaning against, arches her back, and slowly removes her bikini top after which she seductively cups her small, shapely breasts and gives them a slow, seductive squeeze.

You know, on second thought, she really would look pretty damn good sittin' on a toilet seat!

XVII

HARLAN BOTTOMLY V. JOHN DAVID ROBINSON

You never will place
you never will win
thrown in the towel, old man
you might as well begin…..

“**H**ello, D Jack, buy you a drink?”

“Thanks, Mr. Bottomly,” I respond enthusiastically as Hammering Harlan Bottomly waves to Sal. I think I’ve shared a little with you about Bottomly, but to recap, good but not great, so the years have treated him pretty well. He’s got to be in his early sixties, but his tan is deep and his eyes are clear. A few wisps of hair remain and are combed across his head while his rounded shoulders have barely diminished his original six-four, well maybe an inch or so. He has a great smile but one rarely sees it these days unless he puts on his “greetings” game face for the patrons. To be honest with you, I really think he suffers from a terminal case of boredom being in the twilight of his life as head pro and one of yesterday’s personalities. It’s probably too much management and not enough time on the course that dials up his occasional down-in-the-dumps look. He usually stays around the Presidential but cruises the hotel now and then, so Bobby Sticks…you remember him, the assistant pro…gets stuck with most of the lessons other than the high rollers who insist on Bottomly. Truth be known, he’s soft spoken and one hell of a nice guy.

“Still drinking Canadian whiskey?” he asks as Sal approaches the table.

“What can I say; I’m a creature of habit.”

“Three fingers of Grand Award on the rocks for the left-fielder, my dear,” he says with a pleasant smile to Sal, “and I’ll have my usual dry Beefeaters.”

Sal matches the friendliness of Bottomly’s tone. “Can I get you some cashews or macadamian nuts, Mr. Bottomly?”

"Cashews will be fine, Sal, but just a few," he adds as he pats the slight bulge beneath his waistline. I'm lost for the moment, anticipating the rarely tasted and peerless whiskey the man has ordered for me. Just in case you're not familiar with this smooth Canadian distillate, Grand Award is made by Hiram Walker. It's a twelve year old with a boost up to ninety proof. If you can find it, be prepared to shell out as much as sixteen bucks for a fifth, and for God's sake, don't put water in it or ginger ale or anything else, for that matter. Bottomly interrupts my mental, alcoholic revelry.

"It's good to see you, D Jack. It's been awhile since I bought you a libation."

Before I can respond, a guy at the table next to us, whose back is to me, wisecracks, "Probably can't afford it," and the smile quickly fades from Bottomly's face as he stares at me, his head cocked to one side. The guy turns to face the head pro and adds, "Just in case you didn't hear me, I said you probably can't afford to buy that guy a drink, but then I suspect the House picks up your tabs, right?"

I place the guy quickly. John David Robinson, cattleman, oilman, Texan man. You remember him; he was the guy who threw his club in the lake when Lena Dawson and her playmates were getting smashed in a fairway bunker a few weeks ago. I heard the guy was impatient, but now I mentally add obnoxious to his personality folder. Bottomly quietly measures the jerk and responds in an unemotional tone.

"What is that supposed to mean, Mr. ahh…?"

"Robinson, John David of Fort Worth, and what that's supposed to mean is that, based upon your golf game, you don't have too many bucks to throw around to busted up ballplayers and the hired help."

Gee, I should be flattered; he knows who I am, or was, but then he all but spits out the reference to me. I just glare at the bastard, but I'm a non-entity so he fails to be on the receiving end of my venomous expression.

"Oh, I don't know," Bottomly says evenly, exhibiting no redness of face or malice of voice. "I still pick up a few dollars here and there."

"Yeah, in the pro shop maybe," Robinson retorts as he continues to press the situation.

Bottomly is unruffled. "Yes, as well as on the golf course; I'm still pretty consistent from tee to green."

Robinson warms to his increasingly obvious task. "Not consistent enough to beat me, I'll wager!"

My man doesn't even blink as he picks up the challenge immediately. "How much would you care to wager, Mr. Robinson?"

"Say a thousand, or is that too steep for a washed-up pro?"

"Let's just agree on two thousand, sir," Bottomly says as he smiles for the first time.

Robinson bores on with his dead serious approach. "I've got a five handicap, and I'll take two more strokes because it's your home course."

"I haven't played the Presidential in six weeks."

"That's what you say, Bottomly," he replies with a sneer.

Our man is unruffled. "Mr. Robinson, being from Fort Worth I assume honesty comes high with people down your way. I didn't question your five-handicap, and I consider it an insult that you question my statement."

Robinson shrugs off the comment. "Fine, I'll take six strokes and meet you on the first tee at 9:00 a.m. on Sunday morning. Make sure that Marcus starter guy arranges it."

"I always enjoy a good game with a guest of the hotel," Bottomly responds politely.

Robinson gets to his feet, drops a bill on the table, and begins to stride towards the door. After he takes a few steps, he stops, hesitates for a moment, and then turns back our way. "Oh yeah, and one other thing, old man, we walk." A shit-eatin' grin makes its way across his leathery face as he turns and exits the Bengal Lounge. Everything is quiet for a few moments before Bottomly breaks the awkward silence.

"Sweet man, I wonder what ever happened to the notion of southern hospitality, or worse yet, was that it?" Bottomly says.

There seems to be no point in responding so I take a sip of the Grand Award that has mysteriously appeared on the table, and Bottomly follows suit with his martini. He seems very contemplative, and I'm not sure whether or not I should eventually say something. He solves my dilemma as he returns his glass to the table.

"Do you know anything about this fellow, D Jack?"

I think back to the brief episode with the Dawsons and the King of Coal and realize that my sole experience with John David Robinson from Fort Worth, Texas tells me very little about the man. "Not much, although I think his burning point might be a bit on the low side. I can make a few inquiries if you like."

"I think that might be a good idea," he says reflectively. "I have a sneaky suspicion that this fellow might be giving me the hustle. And," he adds with a hint of disappointment, "I appear to not only have taken the bait but upped the ante," he concludes, shaking his head slowly from side to side. As far as I know, the two thousand will be about the highest stakes the head pro has played for in quite awhile, although the truth of the matter is that in most big time country clubs, two grand ain't that big a deal. But in this particular situation, the stake might be sizable.

"I don't like this guy, Mr. Bottomly; in fact, I don't like him so much that I want to get some money down on this thing. How about you let me cover some of the action? And I think some of the guys might want a piece of it, too."

Sometimes one's ideas are not too rational or, shall we say, philosophically pragmatic, but I get the gut feeling that Bottomly is going to need some support both in terms of his morale and his wallet. Additionally, my intuition tells me Robinson might be a hothead and can be had. Like Bobby Jones once said, "Competitive golf is played mainly on a five-and-a-half-inch course, the space between your ears."

"How much do you want to cover?" he asks with what I perceive to be a slight sense of relief, well-masked, of course.

"Say a thousand."

"Why are you willing to cover so much?"

"Why not," I respond with a smile. "A hunch, naturally, but to tell you the truth, I've got to get back some of my losses after that fiasco with the frozen horse that forgot to run down the stretch at Tropical Park."

Bottomly doesn't blink on that one, so I guess he wasn't around and isn't aware of Garlido's thawed legs and run in the mud. "How are you going to cover that much?" he asks with some concern.

"I'll spread some of the action to a bunch of the guys: fifty here, fifty there. Hell, I'll be lucky if I can hold on to a couple of hundred for myself. After all, we're going to war, and you're the champ, right? The guys are gonna back you," I conclude confidently.

"No promises, D Jack," he says seriously. "I don't want to play this guy and have to worry about some of the staff giving up some dollars, and that includes you."

"No problem, just another betting day at the Presidential. I'm sure the Turk will be licking his chops. Hell, Sunday's the pits except for the pro games; so the match will give us something with which to get through the day."

Bottomly gives me a broad grin. "Something with which to get through the day? What kind of English is that?"

"It's the correct kind, big guy."

"I should have known better, but it's hard to look at your busted up face and remember you earned a couple of degrees at Arizona State. Normal people would simply say, 'This will give us something to get through the day with', not 'something with which to get through the day.' But then you've never been playing with quite the full deck, D Jack."

"What's this busted up face stuff?"

"Well, obviously you're not as pretty as you used to be, but then I guess the ladies still find you handsome in a non-Hollywood kind of way."

I measure the man quietly with a fake grimace. "Well, thanks for the backhanded compliment, but in the immortal words of Sir Winston Churchill, 'This is something up with which I will not put.'"

He slugs down the last of his Beefeaters, which seems appropriate given my reference to Britain's Renaissance man, takes down the green olive in one bite, and throws up his hands. "Enough! I plead ignorant as usual," but then his tone quickly changes to a much more serious note. "Don't forget to check him out, okay? At least we'll know what we're up against. I'm hoping you'll carry the bag and call off the distances for me."

"I'll go anywhere for you, sir," I respond with a laugh.

"I won't!" declares a booming voice resounding from the roughly two- hundred-and-fifty-pound frame of Jackie Gleason who comes into the lounge and strides towards our table while Sal magically materializes on the scene and extends a double scotch on the rocks to the Abdominal Showman. Gleason flashes his boyish smile in Sal's direction, takes down half the drink and, as expected intones, "How sweeeet it is!"

"Good to see you, Jackie. Take a load off," Bottomly says.

"Can't do, my friend, I just came in for a pick-me-up before hitting the links with a few producers."

"That sounds good. Seems to me you haven't made a film in awhile," Bottomly says in an inquisitive tone."

"That's a fact. I doubt today's generation has even seen *The Hustler* or *Requiem for a Heavyweight*."

"I've seen em both, Mr. Gleason," I say supportively.

"Yeah, that's because you're not normal, D Jack, and while I'm at it, your straight pool game needs some work if I recall our friendly little game a few months ago."

"Fast Eddie I ain't," I respond pleasantly.

"Yeah, but you coulda been the next Mick, kid."

"Thanks, Mr. Gleason," I say sincerely.

"Anyway, what's this about a new movie, Jackie? Academy award stuff?" Bottomly asks.

"You gotta be kiddin'," Gleason responds. "Burt Reynolds wants to do a film about a southern cowboy type who runs interference for a semi hauling illegal Coors from Texas to Florida or Georgia or somewhere."

"And who do you play?"

"I'm a redneck sheriff chasing him all the way. Not much, huh? But with Burt being a matinee idol, maybe it will make a few bucks. Anyway, I got to go. No travelin' music, huh, D Jack?"

"I'll try to whistle it if you want, Mr. Gleason."

"Save it, kid," he answers as he nods, extending his hand to Bottomly. "How about we go eighteen holes next week, Harlan?"

"That will be my pleasure, Jackie," Bottomly responds as he takes Gleason's hand, getting to his feet. Gleason finishes the second half of his scotch with one swallow, smiles, and heads for the door. "And awa-a-ay I go!" he says, his voice surpassing his boisterous entrance.

"It seems he's always going somewhere," I observe with a laugh.

"I'm glad you said that, D Jack, because I all but forgot why I was looking for you. Charley needs a favor, and I think it involves going somewhere."

"Where does Charley want me to go?"

"I don't know, but pick up a house phone and call him. He's waiting to hear from you."

"Terrific."

"Get to it, kid, and don't forget to do some homework on Robinson," he says pleasantly as he turns to go.

I simply nod as Bottomly strides away from the table, his John Wayne gait taking him towards the one public exit/entrance to the lounge. It worries me to note that his head is tilted ever so slightly downward, and I figure there isn't much I can do for him for the moment. The only thing I can do is to research the John David Robinson problem. My mind begins to sort out possibilities but this is going to be a tough one, so feel free to offer suggestions at any time.

I head over to the far end of the bar, pick up the receiver on the red house phone, dial in Charley's numbers, and am greeted with the sweet voice of Charlene, his administrative assistant. "This is Mr. Berston's office. May I help you?"

"Hi, Charlene, it's D Jack. I think the Boss is waiting for a call from me."

"You're just in time, D Jack. He's about to head out of town. I'll put you right through."

After a short pause, Charley comes on the line and roars, "What the hell took you so long?"

"I was just having a friendly chat with an important individual and I'm fine, Mr. Berston. Thank you so much for asking, and how is your sorry ass today?"

"Well I hope that individual you were shooting the breeze with is a high-paying guest of the hotel because I don't want you socializing on my dime."

"Hey, Charley," I finally get in with lots of 'whoa there' in my voice. "Lighten up. I know I'm just an employee around here, but I think it is incumbent upon me to inform you that the tone of your verbal interaction definitely communicates to me…that you have a hair up your ass. Anyway, Bottomly needed a favor, so I think that was important enough. And now I hear you want a favor, too. Ain't this my lucky day."

"Very astute, D Jack, very astute, so I'll cut you some slack on Harlan but it isn't a hair up my tail; it's more like a thorny stem without a rose. The truth of the matter is that I've got a problem, and I think you're just the guy who can handle it."

"Well, you're sure going about it ass-backwards. You ain't exactly endearing me to your cause, whatever the hell it might be."

"Don't give me any shit. It's been a bad day, in fact, a bad week."

"Spare me, Charley. I'm not up for how tough it is at the top, okay?"

"Okay.We'll call it even and cancel all the hostilities. Are you familiar with a guest named Major Rollstone?"

It only takes a second or two for my cardex brain to settle on Rollstone's mental folder. "The few dealings I've had with him have been pleasant, but nothing special. He's a good tipper and just a downright nice guy, best I can tell. One of the big guns I'd say."

"That's him, and just about the biggest, D Jack. He probably dumps more money on this place than anybody else, and he stays the whole season, too."

"So you've got to treat him really special, huh, what's he want?"

"Hold on to your ballcap, D Jack. To begin with, Rollstone is from South Dakota and is big in sheep ranching up in the northwest corner of the state. He's also pretty much cornered the dairy market in the southeast where he lives, sixty or seventy miles from Sioux Falls."

"So what does the South Dakota king of sheep and cows want already?" I ask impatiently, adopting the questioning pattern of Jilly the Ice.

"They've got a sheepdog they dearly love, and right before they came down for the season, the damn dog was run over by a baling machine or something like that and had its back end pretty much crushed. The dog was flown to the Auburn Vet School for treatment, and they got word yesterday that he's ready to be discharged."

"They discharge dogs?"

"Okay, so he's ready to go home. Is that better?"

"Yeah…and?"

"I told him I'd fly the dog down here because I know they're really anxious about putting the mutt in the baggage compartment of a commercial jet."

"That doesn't sound like much of a problem to me; send your Captain John and the hotel Lear jet."

"No can do. Charlene has me booked for the next three days to fly off and meet with each of the Board of Directors to chat face-to-face about some expansion plans."

"And you can't just pop the damn dog on Ozark Airlines or whatever flies out of that part of the country."

"I already explained that, and you're missing the point, kid. These are wealthy and somewhat eccentric people. I don't think they have any kids or they're grown and gone or something like that, and the way Rollstone tells the tale, you'd think his ole lady carried the dog herself for nine months."

"Only about sixty days for dogs, Charley."

"I don't need shit like that, D Jack. Point is, she's not about to let anybody stuff that dog in the baggage compartment of a 707, and that's the only way the airlines will take an animal that big. They only make exceptions for yappy little lap dogs or medical companions or something like that."

"Well then, how about the train or maybe even the bus?"

"They would still have to cage him, and the Major says that's out of the question."

"So?"

"So I chartered a Cessna and got my hands on a licensed pilot who can't fly the plane *and* deal with the dog, so you're elected."

"Are you telling me I'm supposed fly to Auburn, Alabama in a single-engine plane for a fucken dog?" I ask incredulously. Charley doesn't respond. "What about the weather? Those little planes are dangerous," I say with the feeling that I've played my final card.

"Clear and sunny for the next five days and the Cessna 182 will be ready to go at 9:00 a.m. Thursday morning out of Ft. Lauderdale. I'll send some credit cards over to you on the next shuttle. Just charge whatever you need, but don't go ape shit either, okay?"

"I guess you've covered all the bases, huh Charley?"

He chuckles and I know the sonuvabitch is smiling ear to ear. “You bet, kid. That’s why they call me….”

“Yeah, I know, Charley the Boss.”

“You got it, kid. But you know I always balance the slate, right?”

“I can assure you, I’ll think of a beaut, Charley.”

“We’ll talk about it when both of us get back, but I think there’s a little something in this deal for you already.”

“Terrific.”

“Okay then, Buck Rogers, have a good flight, take care of the damn dog, and I’ll see you next week, weather permitting,” he says laughing as he hangs up.

I place the receiver in its cradle and fleetingly recall an overnight pre-season bus ride from Jax to Montgomery with the capital city of Alabama being about sixty miles west of Auburn, and just like so many other bus rides, I really never saw much of the countryside. But then if it had been daylight, I would have been looking out the window and not seeing anything anyway.

On the way to games, some guys would sleep; others would play cards while others would swill a six-pack. Me, eventhough it was just spring training exhibition games against the Barons, I’d still just stare out the window and see nothing but an opposing pitcher, and I’d try to remember what kind of stuff he threw, or maybe the quirks of the left field fence, or just maybe the overall hostility of the damn place. Whatever, no matter where we were, I was always “lost” on the team bus. Those memories fade quickly as I return to the pressing issue of the day that, as I am sure you would understand, has nothing to do with a fucken broken down sheepdog in Auburn, Alabama. Whoa, Nellie, what to do about Hammeren Harlan Bottomly and Mr. John David Robinson?

*

I figure it’s about late afternoon in Fort Worth when I dial the long distance information numbers and hear two or three rings go by before a male voice grunts something or other at me, so I wait and he repeats himself.

“What city please?” he asks with just a tad of irritation. Nice service, right?

“Fort Worth.”

“This is Fort Worth information, sir. What number would you like?”

“I need the number for the Colonial Golf or Country Club. I’m not really sure how it’s listed.”

After a brief pause, the guy comes back on the line. "That number in Fort Worth is 926-4671."

"And the area code is 817?"

"That is correct, sir."

"Thanks very much," I say indifferently, but I've already heard a click and the guy has gone on to be unhappy with someone else. I immediately place the call, and it rings a few more times before a much more pleasant, feminine voice comes on the line.

"Colonial Golf Club, this is Marsha. May I help you?"

"Sure, Marsha, can you connect me to the head man in your bag room?"

"I'll ring that extension for you, sir."

"Excuse me, Marsha, but do you happen to know off-hand the guy's name?"

"I don't believe I know his last name, sir, but I'm pretty sure his first name is Pete." Small world, huh! A golfing fraternity of Petes!

"Thanks much."

"You're welcome, sir. I'll ring that number for you now." After just one ring, I hear the phone come off the hook.

"Bag room, this is Pete. What can I do for you?"

"Hi, Pete, my name is D Jack, and I'm calling from the Presidential in North Miami Beach."

"No kidding," he says with surprising enthusiasm. "Are you the same D Jack who played for the Mets for one day?"

"That's me."

"Full name's Peter Bogdaglio from Queens. I guess we were able to win the World Series without ya. Sorry about that."

"They were a great bunch o guys and deserved the whole enchilada, right?"

"You bet. So what can I do for you?"

"To level with you, Pete, we have a bit of a situation down here and I thought you might be able to help us out. But it's somewhat delicate, so I'll just put it to you straight away, and if it's offensive, bite my head off, okay?"

"That sounds fair enough. Shoot."

"You familiar with a member named John David Robinson?"

Pete responds with a bit of a choking sound. "Who isn't? He's absolutely the biggest prick in Fort Worth and maybe in all of Texas."

"Glad to hear it," I say with a sense of relief. "Now things aren't too delicate."

"That's enough mystery, D Jack. What's going down?"

"You ever hear of our head pro, Harlan Bottomly?"

"Yeah, I've heard of him. Pretty good in his day, but I would guess he's long in the tooth by now and pretty faded."

"He still hits a pretty good ball, but that's neither here nor there. This guy Robinson challenged him to a game, and anything you have on him might be of some use."

"Well," Pete begins and then pauses before continuing, "I've already filled you in on his basic personality and aside from that there isn't a whole lot I can add. Our fifth hole down here has the rep for being one of the toughest in the whole country. It's a four hundred fifty-nine yard par four, narrow and trees from the tee to a green that's about the size of a peanut and ringed with three deep traps. To make a long story short, the prick pars it like clockwork and picks up an occasional bird, so that pretty well tells you about his game."

"Fine, Pete, but what about him, you know, when he's on the course?"

"Again, not much I can help you with, but I can tell you he's tightfisted as all hell and the muthafucker hates to lose. And maybe he's a big hitter, but he's an impatient sonuvabitch. That screws him up once in awhile. That's about the best I can do, D Jack. So how much is on the line?"

"Nothing monumental, just a couple o' grand," I say nonchalantly. "You want in? It's on our board in the backroom of the men's lockers, and I could wire you the winnings."

"Sure, it's worth fifty to me just to bet against the bastard."

"Gotcha," I say and then suddenly remember one of the major things I wanted to ask if all went well with the conversation. "Pete, there's just one more thing. What's Robinson's handicap? Do you happen to know off-hand?"

"No. They keep that information up at the pro shop; it'll just take a sec, so I'll stick you on hold." He doesn't even wait for me to say thanks before the drone of a low buzz comes into my ear. Only a few seconds pass before he's back on the line.

"According to the boys in the pro shop, he's got a handicap of two. What did he tell you, five or six?" Pete asks sarcastically.

"Let's just say that little piece of information gives us the right to play some games of our own, yes?"

"All's fair in love and war, D Jack, and you can double it when it's war. So go for it, 'cause the best you can hope for with this guy is to just even the slate. Getting a leg up on him is gonna be tough, understand?"

I comfortably smile to myself. "I hear you Pete. Sounds like this guy went to the Paul Harvey School of Scorekeeping whose motto is that golf is a game in which you yell 'Fore', shoot six, and write down five. Now I won't have a guilty conscience, no matter what we try on this bum. Thanks loads."

"So when are they playing?"

"They tee off Sunday morning."

"And I can expect you to wire the winnings on Monday then?"

"I think we can take care of it Sunday night, Pete."

"So tell me," he asks curiously, "are you the greeter at the Presidential?"

"Not exactly, but I do get to rub shoulders with the movers and shakers now and then."

"I guess you never played ball again, or not that I ever heard of, huh?"

"You got that right." So," I say quickly changing the subject, "hang in there and keep your sinks empty."

"Will do," he says pleasantly and hangs up. I immediately dial up Marcus who answers with his usual identification and job title. "Marcus, D Jack here. I've got something in the hopper and I need some help. Can you zoot on down here for a moment or two?"

"Let me check the sheets," he answers, and I hear the ruffle of papers in the background. "It looks pretty clear for awhile. I'll be right down."

I spend the next few minutes trying to figure out how we can even things a bit with the Texas liar, hit on a few good ideas, and hope they'll be enough to serve as equalizers. But the problem is that my few schemes have that uncontrollable factor called luck! Marcus comes through the door with a somewhat negative expression on his face.

"Okay, what's this going to cost me?"

"Hey, wait just a minute," I say defensively. "You haven't heard me give you the raspberries over that damn 'sure thing' you got us into at Tropical, have you," I respond rhetorically. "I think I was super gracious about that one. You cost me a bundle…and now you come down here and don't even give me a chance to explain the deal. Worse yet, you all but accuse me of hooking you into something that will go south, thereby wasting your money even." I shake my head and throw up my hands, adopting a look of disgust. "Not only that," I continue disapprovingly, "but friends are involved."

"What do you mean 'friends are involved'"? Marcus inquires. Obviously my tirade has had no apparent effect on him whatsoever.

"A friend named Hammering Harlan."

"H. H. Bottomly, I can't believe you've got him involved in one of your, how do you say, 'projects.'"

"I didn't get him involved in anything. He got himself involved, and anyway, it isn't a project or a scheme or anything. Why does everything I do always have to be seen as something shady and underhanded?"

"Because that's why some people around here call you the Pirate, dumbwad!"

"No shit," I say with a mixture of surprise and disappointment, "and all along I've thought it was because I'm a clever kind o' guy."

Marcus smirks and sighs at the same time, a trick he has learned to co-ordinate so effectively that it usually leaves very little room for further conversation. "That's enough of this. How does Bottomly figure into this venture or whatever it is?"

"I didn't think you were interested," I say in a tone suggesting I'm blowing him off.

"Get on with it," he replies, approaching a state of exasperation.

"John David Robinson challenged him to a match. We were sitting in the Bengal having a drink, and that obnoxious sonuvabitch really tried to get his goat something terrible."

"How did he handle it?"

"He stayed cool, but I'm not so sure he figures he can take the guy."

"What's the bet?"

"Bottomly upped the ante to two large."

Marcus lets out a low whistle as he runs his hand back through what's left of his brown hair. "I picked up a thousand of it," I continue, "because I don't think he can cover the bet, and he seemed pretty relieved. I'm going to try to parcel out some of the action through the Turk later today."

"When's the match?"

"They go off at nine Sunday morning and Trash Mouth made a point of telling Bottomly to get ahold of you to make sure that tee-off time was firm. Either you can do it, or if you want, I can handle it on the sheets when we hit the cloakroom and the phones Saturday night. So, do you want some of the play?"

He looks at me; it's obvious the conversation is about to become serious. "Can he win?"

"That's what I want to talk with you about."

"What do you mean?"

"I checked with Robinson's home club in Fort Worth a few minutes ago. He's a prick and a liar."

"Say more."

"The guy in their bag room told me he carries a handicap of two. Robinson told Bottomly his handicap is five and then hustled an extra stroke because he's playing our man on home turf."

"So you're saying Bottomly gave him six strokes when the guy should only have two, right?"

"You got it," I respond emphatically.

"And am I to assume you want to chat about how you might put things in their rightful order?"

"You got it again," I say with a smile. "Not too shabby for a middle-aged, straight-arrow starter at our rich and famous Clubhouse."

"Thanks a lot," Marcus says nonchalantly, "so how do you figure to go about it?"

"Well, to begin with, in order to place things in their proper perspective, from what little I've picked up, Robinson has two things we need to turn against him. One is physical, and the other is mental. The physical is that he's a long-hitter, a real boomer. The mental is that he's impatient as all hell. We've already seen that up close and personal with the Dawsons, and Pete also verified that."

"Who's Pete?"

"The bag room guy at the Colonial in Fort Worth."

Marcus nods his head. "Okay, so he can smack the crap out of the ball and he's a schmuck…now what?"

"Now we figure out how we can use those things against him and cut four strokes off his game which will equal things up. Then Bottomly will have to beat him fair and square."

"Does Harlan know anything about this?"

"Nope, and he won't. All he did was ask me to check around, and all I'm gonna tell him is that Robinson is a long-ball hitter with a temper. The fact is that's all we do know about his game. Bottomly won't know he lied about his handicap; we'll just have to create some circumstances to carve off the bogus strokes."

"You, ah, have any circumstances in mind, my bearded friend?" Marcus asks with a conspiratorial grin that I return with my most devious smile. "That's why I asked you to come down here. Are you sure you're in?"

"I'm in," he says with some steel in his voice.

"Are you putting some money in too?"

"Yeah," he says with a little less confidence, maybe thinking he might be wasting some hard-earned bucks. I figured all along the money thing with Marcus wouldn't reel him in but hoped being a part of sandbagging the

Texas liar might entice him into being a player in this game. I figure by now you're getting to know Marcus pretty well and realize he has a deep feeling for fair play. But we also have to figure that he isn't going stand on the sidelines and let John David Robinson screw our man out of two grand, right? And more importantly, steal some pride, as Frank Gifford keeps reminding us throughout the pro football season. Cosell keeps talking about pride, too, but then Howard never played anything I know of, so he doesn't have the credibility Frank has, at least, not with me.

"Okay then, Marcus. As they say at General Motors, let me run a few things through my brain and then send them up the flagpole for your consideration."

"I hope those things don't turn out to be a bunch of Edsels," he mumbles.

"Edsels were made by Ford."

"Okay, okay, get on with it already. I'll sit, and you think."

"I'm on it," I say as I lean back in the lawn chair and prop my boots up on the countertop. That's just like Marcus, he's gonna make me do all the brainwork here. I got to be up front and tell ya my ideas are a little shaky at this point. I know you haven't taken me seriously in the past when I've asked you for some input, but if you think you have something that will work, I'm all ears. Okay? I mean Bottomly is a worthwhile cause, ain't he? Thanks tons…in advance.

XVIII

CESSNAS, SHEEPDOGS, AND THE 'Y'

I've been out in space
in a world spinning round
for over two years
my feet never touched the ground

I can't remember exactly what I was referring to in that particular ballad but, just a few nights ago, *my feet may have never touched the ground* because I was deep in muck and trudging through sand. Anyway, as directed by Charley the Boss, it's Thursday morning, my Yamaha is up on the kickstand in the long-term parking lot, I'm walking down a very long corridor toward the far west end of the Ft. Lauderdale airport, and within the hour my boots are going to be about 10,000 feet off the ground. There's only one gate at the end of the concourse so I head in that direction and approach a middle-aged guy decked out in a starched white shirt and a red skycap.

"How are you doing?" I inquire pleasantly, eliciting an equally cheerful response and a smile. "I'm supposed to get on a Cessna headed for Auburn, Alabama and was told you could point me in the right direction." The guy comes out from behind his counter and leads me over to a large window next to an opened door.

"Just go through that door, down the stairs, and it's that blue one off to the right with the number 9218 on it. See it?"

"Got it, thanks much." We exchange friendly nods, and I follow his directions down to the tarmac, hang a right, and head for the single-engine, high- winged airplane. The right side passenger door is open, and as I approach, a shapely leg, the knee barely covered by a blue pleated skirt, extends through the door and…whoa, Nellie…it's Samantha!

"Hi, Dev, Mr. Berston told me the first thing I should say is 'I'm your surprise.'"

Surprise, my ass, this is a total shock! "You're the licensed pilot?"

"I'm not here to serve coffee, tea, or milk."

"When did you learn to fly?" I ask, still taken aback. That's the only thing that's come into my addled brain.

"Dolph taught me and I soloed when we were in Gainesville."

"Do you fly much?" I inquire as she steps out of the plane and ducks under the wing.

"Not really, it's too expensive."

"So when was the last time you were up?" I ask with noticeable anxiety.

"You don't want to know, Dev. But I'm really very good and I'm sure you'll be a wonderful co-pilot."

"You mean I've actually got to do something?"

"Can you read, I mean with your eyes?"

"I know what you meant and yes, I can read."

"Then we'll be just fine. Come on, let's get going."

Sam gets back into the plane which affords me a terrific view of the bare back of one thigh before she settles into the left-hand seat. I obediently follow and go to school on her buckle-up routine. She then points to a headset which I dutifully put on and am greeted with a thumbs-up. There's a little bit of static, but I can hear her very clearly. I notice the windshield is very high so I can't see much. Being severely visually impaired, this whole thing is going to be even more frightening.

"Central ground," Sam says, "Cessna niner two one eight golf at Ft. Lauderdale International, taxi to depart northbound."

I wait for the response from the control tower and look over at Sam who is grinning at me as if she was a female John Wayne in the movie, *The High and the Mighty*, the thought of which immediately brings to mind exploding planes and crashes. "Taxi to runway one three," a calm, male voice responds. "Winds one one zero at seven, altimeter two niner niner seven."

"One golf, two niner niner seven," she repeats and adds, "roger." She then releases what I assume to be the brake of the blue and white trimmed Cessna, pushes in the single throttle, and manipulates something with her feet to direct the nose wheel down the center line of the taxiway.

"Having fun?" she asks.

"I'm not sure yet," I answer apprehensively. "I think I'm too used to big jets and silver-haired fatherly types assuring me over the intercom that all is well. I don't think I'm afraid of flying, but I don't really think I'm gonna have fun as you say."

"Relax, Dev, piece of cake. The flying conditions are good, and it's a beautiful winter morning with a cool clear sky all the way, so the weather guys tell me. A veritable pilot's delight," she concludes with a smile as she does something with her feet to bring the high-winged plane to a gentle stop just short of a broad, yellow painted line that runs across the width of the runway. "Reach into the glove compartment on your right and get out the checklist, and we'll do a run up. What's first?"

"What's first? You mean you don't know?"

"Of course I know, silly, but you never take things for granted when you fly, so read them off."

I retrieve a laminated page and start from the top. "Check controls for free and correct movement." She pulls back the yoke and turns it while looking out the window to make sure the alirons and rudder are moving properly.

"Okay. Next?"

"Check trim for take-off setting," I say, trying to be very matter-of-fact.

"Check."

"Engine run up to seventeen hundred." On a gauge off to my left which says "Manifold Pressure," I watch the needle climb as the plane begins to roar and rock against what I assume is some kind of brake. Once the needle hits seventeen hundred, she checks the two magnetos to make sure the engine is firing properly…at least that's what I think she's doing because I read it in a novel somewhere. Having satisfied herself that all is well, she reduces power and starts to check various flight gauges on the instrument panel in front of her. I do recognize such things as compass, artificial horizon, and altimeter. I figure we are about ready to go after I see her adjust the flaps and note she has turned on the strobe lights at the tip of the wings, but I'm really not sure.

"Should I continue, Sam?"

"Yup."

"Flight instrument check?"

"Got it," she says. "Seat belt tight?" I must look a little nervous because she flashes me a bit of a grin. "Honest, Dev, I'm really good at this," she adds confidently. Just between you and me, I'm glad to hear it, but I'm still not doing cartwheels thinking I'm going up in the air in this cracker box. These unhappy thoughts are interrupted by her voice coming through my headset.

"Central ground Cessna niner two one eight golf ready for take-off on runway three."

"One eight golf," the faceless voice responds immediately. "Clear for take-off."

She releases what is obviously a hand brake and pushes the throttle forward enough for the plane to rock somewhat awkwardly, maybe like a turkey, onto the runway. I can only hope this damn thing will fly better than it can taxi. She then gives the Cessna full throttle and what appears to be maybe some right rudder to offset the torque which is causing the plane to veer slightly to the left. Simultaneously, she eyes the runway and watches the air speed indicator as it approaches sixty-five. She then pulls back somewhat on the yoke to get the weight off the nose wheel. Out of the corner of my eye, I notice Sam bites her lower lip as we experience an elevator-like sensation and the small four-seater takes to the air.

It suddenly occurs to me that I'm focusing on her every move. As she releases the pressure on the yoke, the plane immediately adopts a nose high attitude; a gauge tells me we're doing about one hundred and ten. She then reaches over toward the center of the instrument panel, takes off the flaps, and reduces power by pulling back on the throttle.

"Are you still with me?" she asks lightly. Well, what the hell are my options? Gradually, a sensation of exhilaration replaces my intial anxiety.

"It's a little different than sitting in a seven twenty-seven, but you sure don't get this kind of view," I answer, sounding like a kid with a new toy. She doesn't respond and appears to be concentrating so I figure I better keep quiet. I keep watching the gauges and notice she's reduced the RPM's to around twenty-three hundred. We're at about four hundred feet when she banks into a gentle, climbing turn. She seems to be less occupied at this point so I chance an inquiry. "Does the engine ever quit on these things."

"Dev, look at the RPM's, the damn thing's hardly working."

"So if it's hardly working, what's all the noise I'm hearing?"

"We're climbing, that's all. Hey," she adds quickly, "what's the tachometer on your Jaguar read when you're doing about eighty-five miles per hour? I'll bet when you're spiffing along, the tach is four thousand plus, and here we are cruising at about twenty three hundred. See," she concludes with a big smile, "like I say, the damn thing's hardly working." Maybe so, sports fans, but she didn't answer my original question, did she? Hell, I don't even know what the original question was, do you?

The Cessna is just about at ninety-five hundred feet when Sam begins to level her off, and I can feel the pressure due to the plane's tendency to rise. She must be feeling it, too, because she rotates a wheel located on the floor between the two seats which immediately relieves the pressure. After a few minor corrections, she checks the instrument panel and turns my way with still yet another grin.

"That's it, Dev. Now we just follow the flight plan to Auburn." I try to return her grin but it falls short. I look out the side window down at the ground and try to enjoy the view of many things I'm sure you've seen from the air. The big difference is that I'm a lot closer to them, and the cockpit is noisy as all hell. Looks like things are going to be boring for the next few hours if I'm lucky, so let's let Sam fly the plane and we'll find something to do for awhile, okay? Like close our eyes and pray?

*

I find Sam at the Hertz counter where the black-haired, chunky female rep is handing her some keys. "It's the blue Ford parked in number ten," she says. "Go out the door to your right; it's in the first parking lot." Sam turns as I reach her side.

"Everything set?" I ask.

"Ready to go," she responds. We head out the doors of the small Auburn airport which also serves the nearby town of Opelika. As I mentioned before, this sleepy college town is only about an hour or so from Montgomery, so the big boys don't fly into this place, just the puddle jumpers and the private stuff.

"Did you get us some directions?" I inquire as we head toward a short row of rental cars.

"The lady said we turn west on Glenn which will take us downtown and then we go south on Gay Sreet, then west again on Magnolia. Do you mind driving?" she asks. "I'm bushed. It was a longer haul than I thought, and the ride was just a little bumpy."

"Tell me about it, you and your clear skies," I say as she hands me the keys. I head for the driver's side, insert the key, and open the door. Sam slides gracefully onto the front passenger seat and then pushes it back as far as it will go so she can stretch out. I crank up the engine which sounds pretty well tuned, and head out of the parking lot. Almost immediately we turn onto the highway we were told would take us downtown, maybe ten minutes away. We travel in a westerly direction before bending south where I run the Ford up to the maximum posted fifty-five miles per hour speed limit. The sun hangs low in the December sky, the rays coming directly through the passenger window, causing Sam to move away from the door.

"God, this whole place has the odor of cow manure," I exclaim, peering out the window and looking at what appears to be miles and miles of brown, flat pastures. Maybe it's green in the summertime, but I don't think I want to come back to verify that possibility.

"It's not exactly offensive, but then it's not exactly pleasant either. I prefer it to the lumber mill air pollution around Gainesville though."

"Maybe so, Sam, but it reminds me of the damn feed lots and stockyards in Phoenix, and that's an aroma I can do without."

"If you say so," she says with a yawn. "I'm pretty beat, so I'm just going to close my eyes for awhile."

"That's fine with me." She doesn't responsed. It's just like when we were kids…Sam can drop off in a second. I'm thinking she should have been in the Army because she certainly has mastered the power nap.

I have no difficulty finding Gay Street which seems to be one of the main drags. But I know Auburn is a sprawling university, and I don't have a clue where the small animal clinic is located. A quick stop at a 7-11 solves that problem as well as my desire for a cup of black coffee. Sam is just sitting up when I return to the car and is gently rubbing her eyes. "Are we lost?"

"No. We're in Auburn, Alabama, the United States of America. Okay?"

"So we're lost."

I open the door and slide in behind the wheel. "The people at the airport told us how to get to the university, but I wanted some specific directions on how to find the small animal clinic." I crank the engine, get back on the main drag, and head in the same direction we've been traveling until intersecting Magnolia where I hang a right-hand turn. Within minutes, we encounter the huge campus, double-check a map in a vertical glass case, and head for the clinic. Once there, we pull into one of the spots designated for visitors and head for the front door. I'd brought a windbreaker, but I quickly realize the weather is really cold here and I'm in for a chilly time. Fortunately, Sam seems to have brought a pretty warm coat so I guess she'll be okay. Who would've thunk! I mean this is Alabama, but then I realize the only time I've ever been in this part of the country was when I was playing for the Suns and, of course, it was springtime. We go through some glass doors and turn left to a reception desk, behind which sits a rather stern-looking middle-aged receptionist/nurse.

"May I help you?" she asks stiffly.

"We're here to see Dr. Ernest Lyle and we're supposed to pick up Major Rollstone's sheep dog."

"I'm sorry, he's not here right now and neither is the dog," she answers briskly.

"That's it? Lady, we flew up here today from Ft. Lauderdale to get this dog, and we were told the vet knew we were coming."

"That's correct."

"So why isn't he here?"

"Apparently some complications set in and Dr. Lyle wants to make sure the dog is okay, so he took him home."

"Okay, so now what?"

"Dr. Lyle instructed me to tell you that you can drive to his home, and he will inform you of the dog's medical condition."

Sam seems to sense that my ability to remain polite may be in doubt, so she gently nudges me and then pleasantly addresses nurse ogre. "We'd appreciate it if you could give us directions to Dr. Lyle's home and call him to let him know we're on our way."

"He already knows," she says, addressing Sam in the same frigid tone she directed toward me. "When I saw the two of you get out of the car, I assumed you were here to get the dog and called Dr. Lyle. Just go down Wire Road about two miles and look for a red doublewide on the left side. He drives a white pick-up truck." She then turns her back on both of us so I guess we'll find Wire Road on our own.

On the way back to the car, Sam stifles a laugh and says, "Southern charm?"

"Beats me, you're a woman so maybe you have some insights into her not so friendly ways."

"It's probably the beard and jeans, and of course your damn sunglasses, Dev. She thinks you're a hippie."

"Well, you don't exactly look like a country girl, Mrs. Short Skirt."

"Touché." She then gets a serious look on her face, and all I can think of is that maybe my reference to her as 'Mrs.' has brought back some memories, so I figure I better put that one in cold storage. Speaking of cold, I'm shivering so I turn the dial on the heater to high and hope Ford makes a damn good one. She warms up pretty quickly, and better yet, we find Wire Road without even looking for it. It's a two-lane job which seems to be heading southwest towards I-85, and I know from the map that the interstate highway is about a dozen or so miles down the road. True enough, just a few minutes pass before we spot the doublewide with the white truck out in front. I pull off.

"You sitting or coming in?"

"I'm a south Florida girl, and you bet I'm coming in. I wish we had known it was going to be this cold up here. Maybe you haven't noticed it's starting to snow."

She's right. It's very light and you can barely see it, but little white things are starting to hit the windshield. I nod in agreement, and as I open the door, a cold gust of wind drives through my windbreaker and cuts a shivery path down my spine. Small clusters of white stuff have already started to accumulate at the base of a few trees, and you can hear the wind howling. We hustle ourselves to his three-step black metal porch and knock on the single, wood door. A big guy, maybe six four with lots of blonde hair and baby blue eyes, opens the door. I mean a really big dude, probably played football for the University of Siberia. “I guess you’re here for Rollstone’s dog. Come on in. I’m Ernie Lyle.”

As we walk into his small living room, I realize the face and the name seem vaguely familiar to me, but I can’t place him. Anyway, the good news is he didn’t drop the ‘Dr.’ on us. “Here, let me take your coats.”

“No thanks,” Sam says pleasantly. “I didn’t expect the cold, I’ll keep mine on.”

“Me, too,” I add.

“So then, you two want something to drink?”

“Would I offend you if I asked for anything alcoholic?” I ask.

“Drambuie or Budweiser, take your pick.”

“Way too cold for beer, so I’ll take the Drambuie, neat, and thanks.”

“Me, too,” Sam chimes in, “but I’d like lots of water and a little ice if that’s okay.”

“No problem,” Lyle says as he moves around a countertop that separates the living room from the even smaller kitchen and gets busy with the drinks. I look around and note the place is furnished as if he hasn’t been out of school very long, although he does have a pretty classy stereo sound system that he appears to have tied into his 25 inch television. He returns with our drinks and a bottle of Bud for himself and slowly checks out Sam.

“I don’t mean to be forward,” he says casually, “but have we met somewhere, Miss?”

“I don’t think so, but sorry, we forgot the introductions. I’m Samantha Frederickson.”

“No kidding,” he responds with a smile, “Damn if I wasn’t sure I’d seen you somewhere. You married Dolph Frederickson? I played football with him at the University of Florida. Well, kind of, we both warmed the bench most of the time. How’s he doing?”

“He was shot down and killed in Vietnam in ‘72,” Sam replies gravely.

“Damn,” Lyle replies. “He was a hell of a guy.”

“Yes, he was,” Sam says and it gets kind of quiet.

I offer my hand. “I’m Devon Jameison. It’s nice to meet you.”

Another grin from Lyle. "Boy, it sure is a day for the small world thing. I didn't recognize you what with the beard and sunglasses."

"You've got me. I'll admit when you opened your door you did look familiar, but I can't place you. I use a hit in the head as an excuse," I add with a lame smile.

Now he's grinning. "I played defensive tackle in high school for the Flying L's, and one of my most memorable moments was when you guys ran a twenty-four trap and I nailed you."

"Now I've got ya; that has to be the toughest hit I ever took."

"You'd never know it. I remember you just got up, never said a word, and went back to the huddle."

"You were too scary to say anything to, and if I remember, they called you Big Ernie."

"Just Ernie now," he says with a grin as he takes a hit on the long-necked bottle.

"Well, I also didn't say anything because I couldn't breath," I say with a grimace, "but then if I recall, I got even with you."

"Yeah," he says sheepishly. "I also played 1st base for the L's, and in the two games we played against you, I struck out eight times."

"I remember the time we climbed your fence and painted your outdoor basketball court," I say with a huge grin.

"Sure, but I remember the time we broke into your school and stole your cement bulldog."

"That was illegal."

"And defacing private property wasn't?"

"Having fun, guys?" Sam interjects lightly. "I would like to see if we could fly the dog back today, okay?"

"No can do, Mrs. Frederickson," Lyle responds with a definite air of finality. "That dog suffered an oblique transverse fracture of the distal femur, and there were complications."

I recognize the word 'femur' but the rest of it's Greek. "You mean he got his leg broken, right?"

Lyle nods.

"What kind of complications?" I inquire.

He sighs. The whole thing seems to be a huge pain in his ass, and I get the feeling this quick and easy trip is about to go south on us. "The dog got his leg caught in an old coyote trap, and in addition to the broken femur, he suffered multiple lacerations of the quadriceps and the semi-tendinosis and the semi-membranosis and…."

"Whoa, Ernie, we were told he got hit by a hay baler or something like that."

"I don't know where you got that story from, but he'd probably have come off better if it was a piece of farm equipment."

"So, what you're saying is that the muscles of his hind leg got torn up?"

"Yeah, and based upon the amount of dried blood and the overall condition of the dog, I'd guess he was in that rusty trap for maybe twenty-four hours, which ain't all that good. I've really been hard pressed working on infections, and pinning the bone was pretty tricky."

"You mean the rusty trap and tetanus and all of that?" Sam asks finally getting into the conversation.

"Right, that and also osteomyelitis which is an inflammation of the bone in the area of the break. I'm really sorry because I thought I had him ready to go, but he's running a low-grade temperature. I shot him up with some antibiotics, and I'm pretty sure I've got the situation under control. But then," he continues, apparently talking more to himself as opposed to us. "I've been worried all along about intestinal stasis because of the loss of blood and obvious pain, but I'm figuring I've got him past that now."

I chalk up the last potential complication to medical jargon and let it pass seeing as he doesn't seem too worried about intestinal whatever. "Might be some damage to a branch of the sciatic nerve but we won't be able to tell for awhile," he adds as an afterthought.

"So," I say as pleasantly as possible, "why can't the dog leave?"

Lyle finally looks me in the eye, and I realize this guy is really tired. I guess that's what happens when you have the pressure of dealing with a sheep and dairy king from South Dakota. "I think you can figure by now this dog has had a pretty bad time of it. And I'm sure you can appreciate the fact that I don't want to take any chances with Major Rollstone's pride and joy, so I need to make sure those antibiotics take hold. Assuming everything goes okay, you can pick him up at the clinic tomorrow morning around 9:00 a.m.

I start to say something, but Lyle holds up his hands. "Sorry, man, that's it, non-negotiable."

"Terrific. Then I suppose we'll have to fly him back for a check-up or something like that."

"No," he replies unruffled. "I used an internal open reduction procedure which means I inserted a pin in the medullary cavity. I'll let Rollstone know when it needs to be removed, and any vet can handle that. Look, I'm really sorry to screw you two up," he continues, "but Rollstone promised if we could save his dog, the clinic would receive a sizeable endowment, so they've really had me under the gun to get the animal healthy, okay?"

I nod, smile and give it a "what the fuck" shrug. Sam goes over to Lyle and extends her hand. "I'm sure he'll write a big check, and I hope the people here at the vet hospital appreciate all you've done," she says warmly.

"Thanks, and I'm really sorry about Dolph."

Sam just nods, and I figure it's time to go so I finish off Edinburgh, Scotland's 'drink that satisfies' and extend my hand to him. "So now I know how you flattened me on that twenty-four trap," I say with a grin. "Nobody was big enough to block ya."

He shakes my hand firmly and returns the smile. "I guess not, but then, nobody could touch your fastball, so why did they take you off the mound and put you in the outfield in the pros?"

"They were more interested in my hitting and wanted to play me every day."

"Yeah, well anyway, I'm sorry it all ended so fast for you."

"Thanks. So we'll see you in the morning?"

"No," he says as he moves toward the door. "I'll be over at the large animal clinic working on some prize bulls."

"Bulls, like plural?"

"Yeah, like in five of them. Bulls today are too bulky for their hind legs so when they breed, it's not uncommon for a hind leg to just snap, which is one hell of a price to pay for them getting their rocks off. If the ranchers keep this up, artificial insemination will be the only way to go."

"Too bad for the bull," I say.

"Not much fun for the cow, either," Sam adds with a sly grin. With that exchange, we're out the door and walking briskly toward the car which now has a dusting of white powder on the roof. Once in the car, I turn over the engine and let it idle in order to get it to blow some heat at us.

"What now?" Sam asks as she tucks her legs under her body in a futile attempt to get warm.

"I guess we start motel huntin' seeing as we're in for the evening."

"I saw a Tomahawk Motel on this road just when we left the university, and it seemed okay."

The Ford's engine has been going for a minute or so. When I flick the heat switches on the dashboard to high, a warm flow of air finally begins to make its way into the front seat area. I put the gearshift in reverse and slowly back away from the doublewide. Some snow is beginning to accumulate on the highway, but it looks as if the driving conditions will be safe for the time being. "I've had a bad feeling about this trip," I say, unable to mask some bitterness.

"Could be worse," Sam responds.

"How many times did I hear you say that in days gone by?"

"Lots of times, and if you recall, my track record was pretty good."

"Well, unless you haven't noticed, it's starting to snow harder, and we're not exactly dressed for the dead of winter," I say as I turn right on Wire Road and head back toward town. After a few minutes, I see a long L-shaped motel whose sign proudly announces it's the War Eagle Tomahawk Motel. "So, that's where you want to spend the evening, huh?"

"It looks quaint enough, and it's got a restaurant so we won't have to go out until tomorrow," she says.

"Speaking of which," I ask hesitantly, "can you fly in this stuff?"

"I'm instrument rated, but I'd rather not. Let's just hope the sun's shining and we get lots of blue sky."

"Terrific. I better check the weekly rates."

"Pessimist," she says with a smirk.

"Yup, makes it easier to deal with disappointment."

"Or maybe move in line with your expectations?" she inquires.

"Too much thinking going on here, I just want to get out of the cold, thank you." I turn the Ford to the left off the highway and park at the office which is located at the end of the long arm of the L. "I'll just be a minute, Sam."

I hop out of the car and go into the office as quickly as I can without taking the chance of slipping on some ice and breaking my ass. I'm greeted by a pleasant-looking woman who glances out the window, sees Sam in the car, and gives me a smile. Being a college town, I figure the youth of America check into this place on a regular and probably brief basis.

"I'd like two rooms, please," I say not waiting to ask if I can be helped. She seems confused, maybe because I have asked for two rooms, and then her look turns to one of sympathy. Okay, so I'm not gonna get laid. So what?

"I'm awfully sorry, sir, but we're full. The university is hosting a holiday basketball tournament, and we're booked through Sunday."

"I guess everything else is socked in, too?" I ask more in the way of a fact as opposed to a question. Not surprisingly, she nods and confirms my suspicion, so I mumble some thanks not knowing why and head back for the car."

"Sorry, Sam," I say as I join her quickly in the front seat. "No rooms."

"Well, Dev, we could just get one room, but two beds, and you can't sleep buck naked like you used to when we camped out on the beach."

"You're missing the point, kiddo. This ain't a ploy. When I said no rooms, I meant no vacancy."

"So what's Plan B?" she says with concern.

I put the gearshift in drive, head up to the highway, and hang a left toward town. "Well, let's lick our wounds over some coffee and chow and see what we can come up with."

She just nods, so I continue down Wire Road that ends just short of the campus and then turn right as directed by a sign that says "Business District." After a mile or so, we intersect the main drag that extends two or three blocks in each direction. Near a corner to the north, I see a green restaurant sign topped by a derby hat, so I head for it simply because there's a parking space right in front and I sure as hell don't need a walk in the increasingly ice-cold, dense, and needle-like Wiregrass that's common in this part of Alabama. After parking the car, we quickly exit the Ford's warmth and scurry through the single glass door into the toasty air of Auburn's "World Famous Derby House," at least that's what the sign in the window says.

I'm immediately struck with how clean the place is. She's a keeper with white tile floors and counter seating in front and to the left of the door. Across from the counter and paralleling long plate glass windows set in a brick foundation are nine green booths, so we head down to the far booth and shrug out of our coats. I hadn't noticed Sam had a scarf around her throat under her light-weight coat which she removes, folds, and places on top of our winter gear. A young waitress, probably a co-ed, immediately approaches the table with two steaming cups of coffee.

"How did you know?" I ask, feeling suddenly warm, both physically and psychologically, for the first time since arriving in Governor Wallace's beloved state. He's quite the survivor. Tries to stop Blacks from going to school, runs for the Presidency a few times, gets shot, gets re-elected governor in '72 with the support of the Black vote, and he's been running the state ever since out of a wheelchair. Yeah, the man is truly a survivor.

"I didn't know," the cute, smiling co-ed says, thereby returning my thoughts to my present whereabouts. "The worst that could happen is that I would be wrong and I'd take them back, but in this kind of weather, I'm right ninety-nine percent of the time." Her teeth are large but even, her light brown hair is long and fine, and she's a few pounds overweight, but cute anyway.

"Do you have any Sweet-'N-Low?" Sam asks. The waitress digs into an apron that's white with green trim and hands Sam a half dozen of the small, pink packets after which she hands us two black menus. "I'll give you a few minutes," she says as she turns and heads back towards the counter.

Sam pours what appears to be a solid two ounces of cream into her coffee, thereby causing an immediate overflow. What with all the cream and sugar, I used to call it 'mocha delight.' When she barnstormed with Billy as a kid, he felt she was too young to drink coffee, but with all the drives through the night to get to another show, her job was to chatter away and keep him sharp. So when he'd pull into a truck stop, he'd prop her up on a stool and allow her to drink half coffee and half all the other stuff. Obviously, she's still drinking her coffee the same way.

"Wouldn't it be easier if you just asked for a half a cup of coffee?" I ask with a laugh. She nods in the negative. "That would take the challenge out of it," she answers as she tears off a corner of one of the pink packets and pours the artificial sweetener into the cup. I smile and open the menu which surprisingly, offers dinners and not just sandwiches. There's an extensive breakfast listing also, so I figure eggs and such must be the specialty of the house. We quietly sip our coffees and peruse the menus until cute and chubby returns.

"Decided yet?"

"How about giving us some recommendations?" I answer, placing at least myself in her hands.

"The blue cheese dressing is homemade and great on the tossed salad. I like the corned beef a lot if you want dinner, and the egg salad is the best sandwich. Hash browns are tops," she concludes, flashing her ever-present white teeth and wide smile. I look over at Sam who opens her eyes wide in a "Why Not?" expression.

"Sounds good, the lady will have the egg salad on fresh white with some mayo mixed in with some sweet relish and a side of hash browns." I hesitate and then give her the true test of the greasy spoon aficionado. "Can you smother those browns well for her?"

"Sure thing," she responds without missing a beat.

"Thanks, and I'll have the hash but hold the egg, and let's go heavy on the blue cheese with the salad, okay?"

"That's fine." She pops her pencil back into her apron and heads back to the counter with our order. We continue to sip our coffees while looking out the window at the increasing swirl of snow now beginning to form powdery banks against the curbs and other immobile objects.

"Thanks for asking for the relish; it makes me feel good that you remembered. And while I'm thinking about it, you don't seem as tense as you used to be when things weren't going well."

"Simple," I reply, "I found the secret years ago. Have you noticed I usually wear t-shirts?"

"Not really."

"Well, that's the key, Sam. People really come apart…blow their cool and all of that…when they get hot under the collar. So, it logically follows that if one doesn't wear a collar, one has nothing in which, or under which, to get hot. Most of the great truths are rather simple, you know. For example, did you ever hear of cavemen having to consult shrinks? Of course not, because they never wore collars."

"Isn't that a little like snapping your fingers to keep the elephants away when there aren't really any elephants?" Sam says with a twinkle in her eye.

"Poor analogy, I'm talking something profound here, a new secular philosophy. I'm talking Collarism, and I'm the founder of the Collarist movement, the father, if you will. I figure since I'm in my late twenties, I ought to be fathering something by now. And when you put an 'ism' on something, it immediately takes on an air of profound importance. I think I'll even start to organize study groups and maybe start knocking on doors and do a little proselytizing."

"So that's what your degrees in philosophy have done for you," she says, and I'm surprised that she seems somewhat serious or maybe even sarcastic where I figured she'd be laughing at my instantaneous creation of Collarism. "Then I guess you weren't wearing a t-shirt when you and Daddy had your little chat a few nights ago," she continues, "because obviously I asked and he wasn't specific, but he told me you were really bitter about a few things."

"He's the one who initiated the conversation and I understand he ain't exactly doing cartwheels what with you being around me a few times. But I didn't think it was his place to give me any advice and I won't deny I resented it," I say matching her serious tone.

"What did he suggest?"

"Basically he said I can't play baseball anymore and I ought to get on with it. And of course, he wants me out of Dodge and away from you."

"And you don't think that's a decent suggestion, Devon?"

Fuck it, we're back to Devon. "You're missing the point, Samantha. When it comes to getting on with what to do with my life, I've heard the same song from Berston and Marcus, and I have no problem with that because I know they're sincere. But it's just flat out bullshit coming from your old man. He couldn't give a rat's ass about what happens to me; all he wants is for me to take a hike."

"It's more complicated than that," she says, taking the edge off her voice.

This is the second time I've heard about complications, not including Big Ernie, but I figure I better take it down a notch. "Sam, I don't know anything about complications, because when he asked about our relationship, I flat out told him he we don't have one and that you would be his daughter forever. And I can assure you there was no bitterness in me when I said that to him. I only got hot with the advice thing."

"Well, if there is a next time, maybe you could try to make it less confrontational."

"You know Sam, Billy has summoned me twice and both times he's laid me out. So I'm not interested in a next time and I intend to avoid him all-together…and when you said he had a decent suggestion, if that included staying away from you, you need to say so." I pause, knowing I'm putting it on the line, but I've been in limbo too long and it ain't a healthy place to be.

Bad timing; Miss Auburn arrives with the chow. The sandwich is overflowing with egg salad, the corned beef hash looks nice and meaty, and the blue cheese dressing is full of chunks, but the hash browns appear to be the piece de resistance, chock full of onions and cooked down and crispy. Sam pours a little catsup on the side, and we both pick at the potatoes with our forks. The food is quickly disappearing while the coffee cups are being refilled without asking. A few minutes later, the waitress checks us one last time, puts the check on the table, and says thanks.

Sam dabs her lips with a napkin and finally looks at me. "I'm sorry it's taken me this long to say something."

"Sometimes silence says it all."

"I need some time, Dev."

"I'm not sure what that means?"

"It means I never thought I would see you again and after all these years, here you are, and you're not who you were. Or maybe I never knew who you were back in school. It's hard; I never expected this."

"You never expected what?"

"I never expected you to come back into my life and I need time to figure out what to do about it."

"Are we back to Billy; he sure as hell doesn't want me back in your life?"

"No."

"Is it your children?"

"No, it's me," she says, eyes down.

Damn! This hurts! After all these years, the last thing I want is to bring more stress or pain or whatever you want to call it into her life; she's got too much on her plate already so I think it's time to take her off the hook.

"Sam, I hate to pull baseball on you but sometimes when I'd dig in at the plate, I could feel the tension building up between me and the pitcher, so if he took too long or was glaring at me, I'd ask for time and step out of the batter's box."

"And that gave you more time to figure him out?"

"Not really; it gave me time to relax."

She gives me a long look; I think she gets the message. "Thank you, Dev," she says with an expression that communicates relief…but from what? I keep coming away from these conversations totally bewildered. Once again, I've had enough; it's time to move on.

"So," I say lightly, "you just never know if or where you're going to find a bright spot in a cold, winter storm. Maybe we should eat breakfast here tomorrow before picking up the dog."

Sam nods her approval as she takes the last bite of her sandwich and a final swallow of coffee. "Was this Plan B or Plan C?"

"I think it was B but I saw a Holiday Inn sign at the airport, and it's on the road to Opelika so let's give it a try. The lady at the Tomahawk seemed to think everything in Auburn is booked."

Sam leans over for her scarf and coat and I fish a few singles out of my pocket and lay them next to my empty coffee cup. I then pick up the tab which totals a delightful seven-fifty, grab my windbreaker, and head for the cash register which sits at the near end of the counter. A thin guy with a pencil thin mustache takes the ten I offer and hands back the change. "Thank you, sir, and have a nice evening."

I smile as I put the change in my pocket. "Great groceries; we'll be back in the morning for breakfast." The guy nods and smiles appreciatively.

Sam meets me at the door and we negotiate what is becoming an increasingly treacherous sidewalk. Fortunately, it's only a few yards to the car, and it's gotten chilly but not freezing. I crank her up and head north on Gay back toward Glenn. It takes us about fifteen minutes to find the Holiday Inn which is about five or six miles northeast of the airport. I park at the entrance and suggest to Sam I'll only be a minute, trying not to sound too anxious, but it's obvious the parking lot is full, it's getting colder, and the situation is getting down toward the last gasp. I hop out of the car with the engine still running and quickly walk in to a warm lobby with fine aromas coming from the dining room which must be nearby. Hell, maybe all those cars just brought people out for some good eats.

I walk up to the front desk with rejuvenated spirits and am met by a dour little fellow complete with bald head and wire rims perched on the tip of his nose. He peers up at me and gives me a look suggesting I've just brought the bubonic plague into his establishment.

"I hope this isn't going to be ugly," he says with a frown.

"No problems with me," I reply cheerfully, ya know, that kill 'em with kindness bit again. "Need two rooms, but if you're crowded, one will do with double beds, and I'll pay with cash," I conclude as I optimistically reach for my wallet.

"No you won't."

"Fine, so if you want a credit card, I'll give you a credit card."

"You won't do that either, mister," he says with what I perceive to be a hefty dose of sadistic pleasure. "We're booked solid. No rooms. Nothing," he says with a small, thin-lipped smile.

I give him my bewildered look. "Hey, I've already tried everything in Auburn, but that's ten or fifteen miles away. So how is it that you don't have any rooms?"

"There's a basketball tournament going on, and basketball's big down this way, so I'd suggest you keep driving because all the other establishments in Opelika are full, too."

I start to say something, but he holds up his hands and doesn't give me a chance to get going. "There's no point in discussing this. I know what you're going to say, but a nice gentleman and his lady came in fifteen minutes ago; I called all our sister hotels and I couldn't find him a thing. The management says we have to try, and I tried. So there isn't any point in doing it again. There wasn't anything for that gentleman, and there isn't anything for you."

"Maybe someone's had a cancellation."

"Like I said, fella, it's a big basketball tournament, and all the rooms in all the establishments required pre-payments."

I think I'm in trouble here. Fifteen minutes ago there was a gentleman in here and now I'm being referred to as "fella." Maybe Sam's right about the beard, and I guess the sunglasses ain't doing me much good either. "Hey, man," I say in my best buddy-buddy kind of way. "I've worked the hotels myself and there's always a room or two tucked away, so how about it?"

"I knew this was going to be unpleasant. I could feel it when you walked through the door," he mumbles to himself as small beads of perspiration form on his pate and his grimace shows some concern, probably in terms of how he's going to get rid of me. He goes for the friendly approach. "Look, fella, if there was something I could do, I would. But facts are facts. The simple truth is even my own room is being used by my brother-in-law and his girlfriend, so I'm really sorry."

"Yeah, I can see you're really broken up."

"I think there are a few open tables in the dining room, though. We have a special on prime rib tonight."

My look tells him what he can do with his prime rib and clearly communicates my intention to live up to his ugly expectations, but his dour expression returns and he merely dismisses me by turning and walking into a back room. I trudge out the door literally with beard on chest. This whole damn day seems to be a test of my mental fiber. For the umpteenth time, I get into the Ford, feeling a sense of hopelessness. Sam has to know from my expression that we've struck out again but she gives it the brave upper lip trick.

"So, two rooms, or do we have to put a board down the middle of a king-sized bed?"

"Holiday Inn is on my shit list forever."

"No rooms then, I gather?"

"Worse. No rooms here or in Auburn or in the confines of greater Opelika. By the time this thing's over, I don't know who I'm going to dislike the most: Rollstone, Charley, Lyle, hotel clerks, or all the above. I think it must be some kind of Alabama curse; I never did like playing in Montgomery."

"Maybe so, but I heard through the grapevine the few times you played there, you lit up their pitchers," she says, trying to inject something pleasant into the conversation. "Did you ask him about an emergency special?"

"Yeah, but he claims his brother-in-law and girlfriend already have it."

"He said it was his brother-in-law and girlfriend, not his sister?"

"Hell, we're in Alabama, what's the big deal."

"Okay, what plan are we on now? I think we must be down to D or maybe E. Come on, Dev, crank out an idea."

"Well, Plan D I think would have been to sleep in the airport, but I saw a sign at the ticketing counters that said the damn place closes at 8:00 p.m. Have you ever heard of an airport that closes, Sam?"

"Like you said, Dev, we're in the deep south. Next?"

"Next would have been to find the police station and ask them if we could sleep in an empty lock-up. I did that once, but with you along I don't think that would be a good idea."

"What's wrong with that?"

"Well, because that experience was in a little town like this one in Arizona, and the lock-up was a big square room with four steel cages where they put the hard cases. I slept on a bench in the big room and during the night they brought in a drunk who had gun-whipped some poor slob, and actually bent the trigger guard on the guy's head," I add reflectively. "I never did find out what happened, but he wailed all night and I didn't get much sleep."

"Gee, and I was finally considering sharing a room with you."

"Very funny, but things are getting pretty desperate, so I guess we could try it."

She nods, so I head out of the parking lot and get on the highway that leads back towards Auburn. Once downtown, I just cruise around some before I spot a policeman writing a ticket for a car parked in front of a fire hydrant. He's on the opposite side of the street and I don't want to throw a U-turn, so I pull over to the right side and park the Ford.

"I'll just be a second," I say to Sam as I get out of the car and walk across the street to talk to the officer who's sitting inside his cruiser. He sees me coming and seems amused maybe by the sight of a shivering, bearded guy walking across a cold and windy street wearing little more than a windbreaker. He takes his window down just a crack, eyes me, and says nothing.

"Evening, officer," I say pleasantly but with my hands in view just in case. "I've got a bit of a problem." He continues to look at me in an expressionless but attentive way which encourages me to continue.

"We're from out of town and we were supposed to fly back home tonight, but some complications set in and we're stuck here." He now looks curious, so I continue on with my sad tale.

"As you probably know, there's not a room to be had here or in Opelika, and I was hoping we might be able to use a few bunks in the city jail."

"I wish I could help you out, sir, but the jail is full, mostly college kids and some boozed-up teenagers. So our job is to try to sober them up and keep them off the streets."

"I guess it just ain't my night," I grumble.

"Why don't you try the 'Y'?" he offers. "They might have a couple of empty cots or something."

I point over my shoulder towards the car. "I've got a lady with me and that might make it awkward."

"Well," he shrugs, "that's the only suggestion I've got. It can't hurt to try. If you do, keep going down the street for about three blocks, and you'll find the 'Y' on the left corner at the intersection with the first red light you come to. It's a big, square old thing with an outside staircase up to the front door. You can't miss it."

I start to say thanks but his eyes have already returned to his ticket book and he's closing his window, so I turn and retrace my steps across the street and hop back into the Ford.

"Good news and bad news," I announce as I settle into the seat and let the warmth from the heater slowly permeate my thin coat and jeans. "The bad news is that the jail is full of youthful drunks and the good news is that there's a 'Y' down a few blocks. We might be able to spend the night there. You know," I say thoughtfully, "I'm beginning to think this whole thing is some kind of test. If this 'Y' thing falls through, I think the only thing left will be to crawl into the trunk and hope our body heat keeps us warm," I say with an air of finality.

"I've also got some good news and some bad news," she says somewhat humorously. "The bad news, maybe for you, is there's no way you're going to get me into that trunk."

"I wasn't about to get me in that trunk either, so is the good news body heat at the 'Y'?"

"I'll consider it if it's a matter of life and death."

"You know," I say jokingly, "the way things have been going, it just might come down to that."

Having uttered that point of view, I steer the car away from the curb, head down the street a few blocks, and quickly spot the large, ominous looking 'Y' on the corner. This time I do throw a U-turn and park directly in front of the outside, cement staircase. We exit quickly from the car, climb the concrete steps, and push open the old-fashioned, wood-framed door that welcomes us with a noisy creak. We're confronted immediately by an old man, with wisps of gray hair who is pushing a mop around the wood floor in front of another staircase leading to an upper level. The guy is paper-thin; only his tattered suspenders keep his drab, baggy pants from falling to the floor. He is clean of face, and his yellowed shirt appears to have been ironed recently. His look is one of suspicion and immediate displeasure, and I'm thinking he might be related to that creep back at the Holiday Inn.

"We've got a real problem, sir," I begin, "and we were hoping we might be able to spend the rest of the evening here. Do you have any space at all?"

"No females allowed upstairs," he says with disdain. But then his eyes spot Sam's wedding band and he adds, "I mean there's a rule that says ladies just aren't allowed."

"You mean they can't even come in the building?"

"No, they just can't go upstairs."

I look off to the right of the staircase and notice what appears to be a reading room. "How about if the two of us just go in there and settle into a couple of chairs for the evening? Do you think that would be okay?"

The old man is giving me the once-over, and I keep thinking the beard and sunglasses have caused a lot of grief today. "Honest, mister," I implore. "We've tried the hotels, motels, and even the jail, and this is the last thing we've got going. I can assure you we won't be any trouble. You see," I say, lowering my voice, "our, ah, traveling companion, who had to stay with the doctor, has a horribly mutilated leg. The distal femur was broken in six places, the semi-tendinosis and semi-membranosis may never heal, and there might have even been some damage to the sciatic nerve. He might never even walk again. Furthermore," I add solemnly, "he might actually have intestinal stasis." I shake my head from side to side and drop my eyes to the floor, figuring if I look at Sam we'll both bust out laughing. The silence is deadly, the only sound being the swishing of the mop which has continued throughout the brief conversation.

"Well," he says begrudgingly, "I guess it won't hurt if you two go on in there. Just make sure if you read the magazines or anything, you put them back, and if you use that bathroom down the hall, make sure you leave it the way you found it."

Sam steps up to the stooped old man, and before he can move or try to protest, she gives him a kiss on the cheek. He says nothing, turns, and continues to mop the wood floor behind the staircase. Hell's bells, he's doing better than me; when it comes to a kiss, he's one-for-one, and in the affection game I haven't even gotten off the bench.

We head through the double doors into the reading room where there are a number of over-stuffed chairs and one old sofa. Sam quickly surveys the room, looks at me with a half-smile and says, "Well, at least the price is right. Do you think the stuff on the dog sold him? And, while I'm thinking of it, how did you remember all that medical mumbo jumbo?"

"It's a skill I picked up trying to remember all the big words of dead, white Western philosophers. Obviously, we didn't understand any of Lyle's diagnosis so neither does mop man. So I think he just gave up. So, you want to flip for the sofa?"

She gives me a big smile as she turns and heads toward the two-cushioned, rumpled old couch. "No coin flips," she announces as she takes off her coat, stretches full length on the sofa, and places the coat over her torso. "Dev," she says, "do you really have any idea what happened to Rollstone's dog?"

"I think he's got a broken leg and some torn muscles, but I don't have a clue about the nerves and intestines stuff."

She doesn't reply and I can see that her eyes are already closing. This time it's going to be a lot more than a power nap. I've always heard that flying a plane is more stressful than it looks, and of course, the day's events have undoubtedly amplified her exhaustion. She rolls over on her side and rests her head on her folded hands. Damn, how many times did I used to see her in this peaceful state thinking maybe I had something to do with it. I'm still wondering if time is ever going to help me let some of this go.

Okay then. My immediate problem is where the hell am I going to sleep, but I quickly solve the problem by getting two of the over-stuffed chairs, which are approximately the same size, and pushing them together thereby providing me with a makeshift loveseat. I settle in and take one last look at Sam whose expression hasn't changed, so I figure the kid is really deep into it. But then I realize, for the umpteenth time, that she's a mother of two…yet I keep thinking of her as a kid, or maybe more accurately, a vivacious young woman. Maybe those things aren't mutually exclusive. I really don't know; for one thing, a mother has never kissed me. They kiss janitors maybe, but not me.

Fuck it! This really isn't helping much, and if I'm going to get any sleep at all, I better start thinking of Sam as a damn good pilot. 'Cause if tomorrow is anything like today, she's either gonna have to be an ace or her guardian angel is gonna to have to work overtime for the both of us; mine hasn't been around since '69. Yeah, I know you're still not in my corner, and you figure I don't deserve a guardian angel anyway. Even though I haven't seen any cracks in Sam's ice, I'd like to think at least *you're* having some second thoughts about my dubious character. I really must be beat because why the hell should I care what you think or, on second thought, why are we even having this conversation? Anyway, I'll catch up with you back at the Presidential… if the creek don't rise and the plane don't…well, you know!

XIX

THE MATCH

And I have been there many times
it ain't a place to be
a broken mind all shot to hell
and eyes too blind to see….

"**I** see you brought the brokendown ballplayer with you, Bottomly."

The sneer is still painted across John David Robinson's face, and I'm beginning to wonder if he was born that way and if that look stretches across his features in his sleep. You'd think eventually the bastard would get a cramp or something, but I'm not about to take his shit all day so I give him some of his own.

"No sense trying to rile me, Mr. Robinson. All I'm going to do is lug the bag and give Mr. Bottomly a ride to the bank after the game."

"And call off the distances. Don't hustle me, Jameison. I figure you know this course a lot better than left field in Shea Stadium; after all, you've been here more than two hours."

That one hurt. Sweet man; about a one-eighty from Major Rollstone who had been overwhelmed with relief when I took the sheepdog up to his suite a few days ago. His wife had been understandably upset because the dog was pretty thin and even his eyes were bloodshot but I assured them that Dr. Lyle said he was really doing great and was confident he would recover completely. Of course, I also shared with them the flight back had been bumpy, and the dog hadn't liked that at all. Hell, just between us, that's one fucken understatement. The long, white-haired sonuvabitch beast had gotten airsick, tossing his breakfast all over the back two seats. The stench was so nauseating that Sam had to put down somewhere in North Florida to have us clean up the cockpit or else she probably would have gagged at the controls and Rollstone would have sued the Presidential for killing his precious mutt. But all's well that ends well, and he give me a five hundred dollar bill which, of course, I'll split with Sam when I see her. Both of us have been up to our asses in alligators since getting back Friday, and I'm kind of hoping to bump into her at TGIS later today or maybe in the Bengal Lounge this evening after the phones. Maybe we'll be able to figure out what to do on that first so-called date we haven't had yet. Anyway, my mind returns to the fact that Texas obnoxious has just reminded me of my one day in the Bigs, and again, I'm not about to let this prick get under my skin.

"Tell you what, Mr. Robinson. I'll be more than glad to consult with your caddy at any time regarding distance and club selection, okay?"

"Fuck you and go to hell, wise guy."

"As you mentioned, that was taken care of at Shea and as for going to hell, most of us will, thank you, sir."

I immediately turn my back on Robinson, not caring whether or not he tries for the last word and hoping that he's not used to having this kind of conversation with the worker bees at the Colonial. Obviously, part of our plan of attack is to get him pissed as quickly as possible. Apparently he's lost interest in me because I hear nothing as I take a driver from Bottomly's expensive bag which, if you recall, is the same one Schmedler wasn't interested in. Our man appears to have been indifferent to the verbal exchange that has just taken place as he calmly accepts the club and takes a few practice swings merely for the purpose of limbering up. Bottomly is definitely from the Julius Boros school of golf; you just tee up your ball and whack it, period.

"You're the guest of the hotel, Mr. Robinson," Bottomly says politely. "It's your honor."

I don't expect Robinson to take issue with that invitation, and he doesn't disappoint me. He strides to the middle of the tee as if he had the right all along to tee off first. A good move by Bottomly because from this point on, the Texan is going to have to earn the honor.

Robinson places his ball pretty high on an orange wood tee and takes three quick practice swings with his driver before laying the club head on the grass about a half inch behind the white ball. Everything freezes for about three seconds, and then he begins a very slow, deliberate back swing that terminates well over his head. The club comes down a hell of alot faster than it had gone back and hits the ball squarely with a resounding smack. The flight of the ball is dead center down the fairway, the arch resembling more of a line drive as opposed to a Texas League blooper. You'd think with that line it would take a couple of big bounces, but the ball hits, takes a relatively short hop, and settles into the finely trimmed grass. Ruby (you remember him from the missing panties episode, don't you?) reaches out to take Robinson's driver while grunting his approval, but his lordship seems somewhat miffed with the shot.

"I hit that bastard square on the money, and it should have gone further, dammit!" Ruby continues to smile, but the Texan ignores him and starts to walk off the tee in the direction of the fairway, so Ruby reaches out and taps him on the shoulder. "Ah, Mista Robinson, Mista Bottomly hasn't hit just yet."

Robinson stops but doesn't turn and seems to be impatiently waiting for the ole pro to address the ball. Bottomly walks slowly to the right side of the tee, places his ball on an equally colorful piece of wood, takes a slow, almost sluggish three-quarter back swing, and brings his club through in an effortless fashion. The direction of his drive is about the same as Robinson's but the flight is higher and his ball lands a good twenty yards short of the Texan's. He extends the club to me with a smile, and the two of us head up the fairway. Robinson, of course, has not even waited to see his opponent's shot but has simply begun his march to his ball the instant the sound of Bottomly's club head meets his Wilson #4 golf ball. A good beginning, I think to myself.

The first hole is a not-too-tough par four, dogleg left around three hundred and sixty-five yards. There are two fairway traps on the inside turn and a trap to the front left and rear left of the rather large green. Today, however, just to make things more difficult, the pin position has been tucked into the front left side of the green. Bottomly is away, around a hundred and forty yards, so I hand him a seven iron. He quickly steps up to the ball and hits it without the customary practice swing. The arch is very high and the ball plunks down in the middle of the green. Thanks to his undercutting the ball, it rolls backwards and stops about five feet away from the hole. I've got to tell you sports fans, it was his short game that kept him in the hunt and high up on the leader board. It's uncanny the way the man can get the ball to do his bidding whether it's a pitch-and-run, backing it up like this one, or just getting it to drop dead.

I see Ruby hand Robinson an eight iron and I cross my fingers, because this shot is going to tell us a lot with regard to the potential success of our simple yet potentially masterful strategy. He takes what appears to be his customary two or three practice swings and then freezes once again. He hits the ball squarely and keeps his head down for that single yet critical second. His blank features adopt an instant frown as he realizes he's gotten too much club into the ball which hits the back of the green and rolls to a stop ten feet from a small tree. With little apparent emotion, he drops his eight iron on the fairway and walks toward the green, leaving Ruby to retrieve the club and shuffle after him.

Bottomly and I casually pull up the rear, and we're approaching the green as Robinson's pitch-and-run hits the rough edge of the green and rolls up a good fourteen feet short of the hole. We figure we're in for a long day when Robinson sinks the tricky putt, but our man gets down in one for a birdie and we're a quick plus one; so far, so good.

The second hole, a five hundred thirty-eight yard par five is even and uneventful. Robinson's two fairway shots outdrive Bottomly but not by substantial margins, and the ole pro's approach shot again serves as an equalizer. They both two-putt for pars, and my only observation to this point is that everything seems to be dead serious. I had expected Robinson to engage in lots of wisecracking, but whatever is going on is staying between his ears. As for Bottomly, he's usually light and chipper, but it's increasingly obvious that there's more than money on the line this bright Sunday morning. By God, you're right, Giffer; pride is a factor. Yeah, Howard, you're right, too.

The third and fourth are also uneventful, and believe it or not, the par four, three hundred eighty-eight yard fourth has nine, count them, *nine* fairway bunkers, but both players continue to hit the ball straight and the sand traps present no problems for either of them. On the par three, one hundred and eighty yard fifth hole, we strike a bit of a mother lode. After a brief discussion which I prolong much to Bottomly's curiosity, he selects a two iron and lays the ball down a mere seven feet from the pin which again is set close to the front of the green only twenty or so feet from a huge pond that separates the green from the fairway. You remember the fifth, don't you? Well, if not, let me refresh your memory by referring you to midnight picnics, muddy water hazards, and monogrammed golf balls. In fact, now that I think of it, I'm proud to share with you that I've been immortalized because that body of water has been named the 'Pirate's Pond' in honor of my having retrieved Hargraves's ball.

Getting back to cases, Robinson goes to school and, because he's been out-hitting Bottomly, probably should have gone with a three iron, but the sight of the mammoth water hazard and the pin placement intimidates him and he also selects a two iron, so he gets too much club into the ball and he puts it into a bunker behind the green. One out and two down gives Robinson his first bogey of the day and this, coupled with Bottomly's sweet putt for his second birdie, puts Robinson down three strokes so we're almost half way there. If our man can just maintain his nice even game, Mr. obnoxious is going to be writing a big check.

The important point is that Robinson continues to be pissed off about the lack of distance he's getting on his drives and Bottomly continues to stay abreast of his opponent with sterling approach shots. They both routinely par six and seven and then swap birds and bogeys on eight and nine. However, it's Robinson who bogeys the par four ninth, which is a short, dogleg right with, would you believe, *ten* fairway bunkers. Now Robinson will have the hour during lunch to ponder the bitter taste of the last hole that cancelled the bird as well as the momentum he had picked up on the eighth. As we head for the Clubhouse, well behind Robinson who has stalked off the green, I give Bottomly a cautious smile.

"It's looking pretty good at this point, Mr. Bottomly. Not only do you have him by three strokes but, more importantly, you're one under and looking solid."

He appears to be apprehensive. "I don't know, D Jack. This guy looks awful good for a five handicapper. Consistent as hell," he adds reflectively. "A little fade now and then but generally right down the slot, and if it wasn't for the fact that he's using too much club with his approach shots, we'd be about even."

I smile to myself and say nothing regarding his analysis of Robinson's game. We walk up to the entrance of the cart room, and I dump the big bag against the long, concrete wall. Robinson is striding away, and Ruby appears to be headed for the pen. The Texan then suddenly stops, turns, and waits for Bottomly to approach.

"Don't forget old man, we agreed to start the back nine at 1:00 p.m. sharp."

"That's fine, Mr. Robinson and, just to make sure, I'll be in the pro shop." Rather than wait for a reply, Bottomly turns the tables on Robinson. "Why don't you drop by and pick me up on your way out of the dining room?" he says as he slowly strolls past the big man and up the path. The Texan just stares for a second or two with that totally blank look in his eyes before making his way toward the dining room. I head for the starter's office to file a report with the anxious Marcus who sees me coming and all but hangs across the lower door. I give him a big smile that quickly communicates to him that everything is under control.

"I gather we're okay up to this point, yes?" he inquires, eyes big and brows arched.

"Our man is one under and Robinson is two over." On the 'sigh scale,' Marcus hits about an eight. "Not bad," he says, "but we've got a long way to go. How is the strategy working so far?"

"I'm not sure," I respond somewhat quizzically. "The guy is holding his temper a little better than we had hoped for, but the back nine is going to try his patience a little more than the front. Watering down the fairways last night was perfect; his drives haven't gotten any big bounces and that has him pissed. As hoped for, he figures he isn't hitting as hard as he normally does, so then he's using the wrong irons to approach the greens and he's hitting long."

Marcus smiles, "yeah," he says very pleased with himself. "That coupled with the way we had the pins placed toward the front of the greens must be causing him some trouble."

"True, but I think he's adjusting pretty well and the sun is drying out the fairways, so that part of the plan is pretty much over and done with."

"Those pin placements on fifteen, sixteen, and seventeen should still give him trouble," Marcus adds hopefully.

"Maybe," I mumble, "but what I'm really counting on is that the guy is just going to blow his cool. The 'physical' has won the front nine for us, but the 'mental' on the back nine is going to have to carry the day. Are our 'players' ready to do their thing?"

"As far as I know," Marcus says, "but like you've been saying, there's that element of luck that's going to dictate some of the action. Have you figured out yet how you're going to get Bottomly and Robinson into the pro shop?"

"That's already taken care of by our unwitting pro."

"What do you mean? How did it happen?"

"Robinson gave the ole man some shit about being at the tenth on time, and Bottomly calmly told the bastard to come by the pro shop and pick him up at the appointed hour."

Marcus's eyes gleam behind his glasses. "Perfect. The schmuck played right into our hands on that one. I guess the rest will just have to fall into place, right?"

"You've got it." I change the subject. "Have you seen Ferdie today?"

"He's doing fine, D Jack. Limping around but grateful that's he on his feet and working the bag room for you, seeing as Red is back lugging the bags. It's the first day he's really been up, and he's sober, too. Even seems to be chatting some with the guests. A few people have heard his name, and they've been asking him questions about his career in the ring, so maybe he's starting to feel like a minor celebrity. Thanks for letting him work the bags and the sinks."

"I'm just following the pirate lore, Marcus. Captain Blood had his Jeremy Pitt, and I've got Ferdinand the Bull."

"Who was Captain Blood?"

"He was the hero of Sabatini's classic pirate yarn about adventure and romance," I answer unpretentiously. "Hollywood made it with Errol Flynn, Olivia deHaviland, and Basil Rathbone, you know, when movies were fun and all of that."

"Maybe I'll read it or try to catch it on a late movie on TV sometime," Marcus responds self-consciously although that surely wasn't my intent. I feel a little uncomfortable, so I put my hand on his shoulder.

"Ferd can have the bag room for as long as he likes and for a bonus, I'll throw in the club rentals which ought to bring him some extra bucksfor as long as the conventions keep sending us their execs."

Marcus grips my hand which is resting on his shoulder. "I know you're doing this as much for me as for Ferd, D Jack, and I appreciate it. I really do."

"I'm doing it because it's the right thing to do."

We look at each other, and I'm thinking that Marcus has been a pretty positive influence and maybe I should be more attentive to his redwood bench speech. "Well, I'm off for a bite of lunch, a sip of the grape, and, hopefully, the successful orchestration of this afternoon's events. Wish me luck, ole man."

"Ole man, my non-bony ass. Anyway, you don't need luck. That's why we call you the Pirate."

"Gee, and all this time I thought it was because I was a schemer and a robber and a black marketeer."

"Well, now that I think of it, when all is said and done, you probably did steal Schmedler's clubs and sold them to some guest."

"Not so," I respond innocently.

"Get out of here, dumbwad."

"Now that's more like the Marcus I have come to know and love," I say with a grin as I head for the lounge.

*

"Let's go," Robinson growls impatiently as he approaches Bottomly who is standing behind the counter in the pro shop. The round Simplex clock high on the wall above a display of colorful golf bags reads 1:00 p.m. right on the nose, and I'm sitting in a chair next to a rack of assorted sport shirts, hoping my next planned event goes off better than the on-time travel record of Amtrak. I still have my star player in the wings, and he's assured me he knows what to do, but I'm not too sure of the supporting cast. Check that, I breathe a sign of relief as the two of them fly through the door right on time.

"Who's the head man around here?" says one of the unbelievably statuesque blondes. Her tone is that of unadulterated and open hostility, but Bottomly still manages to paint on his most pleasant smile. "I'm the head pro, ma'am, but I've got an appointment and my very able assistant, Mr. Wilson, will be with you momentarily. He'll be more than happy to be of service."

She turns to her identical twin sister. "Did you hear that, Sally? This guy says he's the man, but his *boy* is going to help us out. Am I wrong or didn't I ask for the head man, Sally?"

"That's what I heard you say," Sindy answers as she heads straight for Bottomly with her mammoth tits bouncing all over the place under her white t-shirt; you got it, no bras for these girls. "I think if my sister wanted your flunky she would have asked for him, but she didn't. And we only want to go through this once, pal," she concludes with her rack pressing up against Bottomly's neck. If you recall, you've met Sally and Sindy, but the fact that they were working each other over in the sack probably means you wouldn't have noticed the two of them go about six foot five.

"If you give us your *boy*, we're just going to have to do it all over again, so let's get at it, okay?" Sindy asks in a rich bitch snotty tone.

Bottomly looks over to Robinson, and the Texan quickly addresses the situation. "Get Wilson in here, Bottomly. We agreed to a 1:00 p.m. tee-off on the back nine, so let's get to it."

Sindy, at least I think she's Sindy, casually strolls over to Robinson, gets about two inches from his face, and looks the Texan squarely in the eye, which also means he's got to be feeling the pressure of her chest against his. "Do you run this place, asshole?"

Robinson's jaw drops. Nobody, but nobody talks to him this way, and I doubt seriously he's going to take anything from the buxom blonde twin. "I mean, are you the owner or President or Chairman of the Board of the Diplomat Complex or something like that?" she continues, dripping with sarcasm without giving him a chance to say anything, "or are you just some loudmouth with a big stupid looking cowboy hat? Where are you from anyway, the back lot of a Hollywood sound stage? I mean you've got to be in the movies to look that dumb. Real cowboys sure as hell don't look like this asshole, do they Sally?" she asks, addressing her sister with a smirk while she continues to stare Robinson down.

Sally picks up the cue, ignores Robinson, and looks at Bottomly. "You know we can buy and sell this whole fucken place, right?"

Bottomly knows no such thing because he doesn't have a clue as to who they are and, much to my relief, has obviously never been to strip clubs in the Gables, although I had been concerned he might have spotted them in Miami Stadium one night. After all, you could easily pick out these two even in Times Square on New Years Eve. Bottomly continues to smile but can't seem to find any words.

"Well, what's it going to be? Are you going to hear us out on this thing, or are you going to run off and play games with the phony cowboy schmuck?" Sally asks indignantly as she jerks her thumb over her shoulder in the direction of the increasingly red-faced Robinson who is really struggling with being treated in such an abusive fashion by two apparent bimbos no less.

"I'm very sorry, Mr. Robinson," Bottomly says. "I'll have to attend to these young women's needs, but I'm sure I won't be more than a few minutes."

Sindy steps away from Robinson, puts her hands on her hips, and tilts her head just a tad. "Yeah, stupid, he's gonna attend to our needs," she says with a snarl, noting Robinson seems to be transfixed by the outline of her soft nipples under her t-shirt. "And what are you staring at?"

"You're the one showen 'em off, bitch."

"Looking is one thing, staring's another. Keep it up, and I'll have the man call security and slap a harassment charge on you."

"Fuck you."

"Not in your dreams, asswipe!"

Robinson takes one last look at Sindy's tits before turning to glare at Bottomly. I guess he senses the futility of the situation, so the obnoxious Texan just stalks out of the pro shop and heads for the cart room.

Twenty minutes elapse before I've got Bottomly's bag on my shoulder and the two of us are heading for the tenth tee where we can see Ruby leaning against a golf bag while Robinson paces back and forth between the men's and lady's markers. "By God!" the ole pro exclaims with a rush of exasperation. "All that over two pair of golfing shorts that had defective zippers?"

"No big deal," I say with a supportive smile. "They might have started off like tigers, but they both ended up like pussycats. I mean, after all, you ole fox, they do want to buy you a drink after the match and, ah, make amends. You can never tell about amends. I really think they like you, and the way they demonstrated the broken zippers was pretty nice too, don't ya think?"

"I don't think they were wearing panties, D Jack."

I'm suddenly concerned that some fantasies about Sally and Sindy might screw up his game. "Oh, I think they just wear some skimpy stuff. Didn't I hear Charley say that Frederick Mellinger has a penthouse at the hotel?"

"Now that you mention it, Charley told me we've comped that guy for all the shows and his golf while he's in town, but his name doesn't ring a bell."

"You're not putting two and two together, you know, panties and Frederick?"

"You mean he's Frederick of Frederick's?"

"You got it, and those two have been seen with him, so either they're his top models or maybe his nieces, ya think?"

"Could be," Bottomly answers. "Okay, then I'll leave it to a drink and a pat on the ass, which any young thing is willing to grant an old man."

I sigh with some relief as he appears to dismiss thoughts of Sally and Sindy and refocus his mind on the irate Texan. Whew, thank God Ron had told me he had nailed one of Frederick's models and knew the lingerie and undergarments king was in town for some kind of promotion. Stunt says the guy started making stuff by himself in some upstairs place in Manhatten just after World War II and then went to Hollywood where the movie stars went ape-shit over his creations. Damn, I love self-made kings, but I'll bet you ten bucks Robinson ain't one of em; he stinks of inherited money.

"I don't think anyone would get annoyed with you being nice to them but first things first," I say, making absolutely sure he has his mind back on the game as we approach the tenth tee. "You need four strokes in nine holes and that ain't gonna be easy, unless this guy's game collapses, which I seriously doubt."

"Do you have any suggestions?"

"One little thing, now that you mention it. Do you remember when I took some extra time on the fifth?"

"Yes, I was curious about that."

"Well, let's just slow things down a bit. I know you like to step up to the ball and fire out, and that's okay because we don't want to monkey with your swing, but let's take a little more time with club selection and stuff like that."

"To psych him out?"

"Let's just say I think he's going to be anxious to get his strokes back as quickly as he can or just to break even, so I think we want to keep him as frustrated as possible."

"Is this kosher, D Jack?" he inquires with some possible misgivings.

"I don't know much about kosher so you'll have to ask Ruby about that, but come on, ole pro, since when has psyching out your opponent not been legit in any sporting contest.

"But betting is involved here."

"So Ali psyched the shit out of Liston and Foreman, and no one bets on the heavyweight championship of the world?"

"That's a point well taken."

"Well, I'm glad that load is off your mind," I say as we walk up the slight incline to the tenth tee. "Now let's go for the gold."

Robinson picks up that last statement and echoes the words loudly. "Yeah, old man, let's get on with it. You sure as hell took your time with those two bimbos. Did they finally let you fondle their tits?"

Bottomly blows off Robinson's attempt to get under his skin as he takes the three-wood I've taken out of his bag. "All the guests of the hotel are entitled to the best services the employees of the Diplomat can provide, and I am sorry it took longer than anticipated."

"I'll bet," Robinson snorts cynically as he approaches the center of the tee and leans over to place his ball.

"I believe you had a bogey on the ninth, Mr. Robinson, so it's Mr. Bottomly's honor," I announce flatly. The reminder of Robinson's unsatisfactory ninth hole earns me still yet another sneer as the big man moves aside. Bottomly peers down the fairway and seems to be debating as to whether he should try to drive over the narrow stream stretching the entire width of the fairway or play up short. I get my answer as he turns, calls for the driver, but then seems to change his mind as he reconsiders the three-wood. Out of the corner of my eye, I note that Robinson is clearly annoyed. The ole pro sure is a quick study.

"What do you think, D Jack?"

"Little bit of headwind. You'll really have to pop it to clear the stream, so I think you should play up short. I'd still use the driver but just take a little off it."

"Sounds good," he says as we finally swap the three for the driver. As per his game, Bottomly quickly addresses the ball and hits a picture-perfect shot just short of the stream. Robinson quickly strides to the middle of the tee and crashes the ball a good ten yards over the water. Once again, however, our man's approach shot with an eight iron equals Robinson's easier use of a wedge, and they both par the hole. I detect just a tad of erosion in Robinson's composure and assume he wants to make a quick move; maybe he hasn't considered the par to be sufficient. What a jerk! We still need four strokes, and we're down to eight holes. The arrogant bastard is too blind to see he's winning. Something better happen fast and it does.

On the one hundred seventy yard par three eleventh, Bottomly gains two strokes as his deadly two-iron puts him within eight feet of the cup, while Robinson's tee shot picks up the bunker on the left side of the green. We had intentionally placed the pin on the far right side of the green due to the large lake which surrounds that side and all but parallels the entire fairway. In fact, the back nine is often referred to as the "water" nine because of the two large lakes and more than half a dozen streams that crisscross many of the fairways and go around some of the greens. In the hope of Robinson putting one in the sand trap, we figured he'd have to play up short for fear of going across the green and into the water and getting a little long, and so it was. The increasingly unhappy Texan was way short and had to two-putt for another bogey, while the ole ice man calmly rolled in the eight-footer for a bird and suddenly we're five to the good.

More importantly, Robinson is starting to show that he might be a good golfer, but he sure as hell isn't a pro. The pressure and the delays are starting to take their toll as have the watered-down fairways and super difficult pin placements. The delay situation gets progressively worse as we are slowed on the twelfth, thirteenth, and fourteenth by two guys who are obviously duffers. They're just barely staying ahead of us, and Bottomly is slowing his game to compensate for theirs. The old man is picking up his pars nicely, but it's increasingly obvious that Robinson is struggling for his equalizers. Nevertheless, he hangs in and the fifteenth and sixteenth are also played even. Upon approaching the seventeenth tee, we are surprised to find the duffers have yet to tee off even though the fairway is clear.

"Come on already," one says to the other with a crystal clear New York accent. "It's only a hundred and fifty or so and ta hell with the fucken stream, already. Use the four-iron and smack da shit out of it already," he concludes in a huff.

"I think I'll just bang da shit out o' it with da five," the other guy responds, sounding definite but then continuing to scratch his sparse gray hair with apparent indecision. Robinson quickly strides up behind the rotund man and tries to nail him with his most dictatorial tone. "Come on, you dumb bastard. Either hit the God-damned ball or let us play through. I've been looking at your fat ass since the twelfth, and I'm getting pretty damn fed up with you and that other fucken clown you're playing with," Robinson says, barely containing his frustration as he literally hurls out the last few words.

The significantly older man seems not to react at all, but after a few seconds of being motionless, he turns very slowly and measures Robinson with his thick, black unibrow and goldfish lips which appear to be twisted into an evil, or at the very least, ominous grin. Remind you of anybody we've met recently? Like maybe a guy who watches the back of a smaller, even more dangerous and powerful person? I swear to God, if a no-neck monster from *Cat on a Hot Tin Roof* ever existed and grew old, I'm looking at him right now.

With apparent ease, Jilly the Ice jams his hands into Robinson's armpits and lifts the tall Texan so that his pointy snakeskin boots are a good four inches off the ground while the hazel eyes of the retired New York "trucker" seem to pierce Robinson's face with what I interpret to be sadistic memories of his Hudson River warehouse days.

"You speaken'to me, Mista?" Jilly inquires forebodingly. Like a stalked animal, Robinson senses he's in mortal danger, and, after a three-second eternity, he quickly licks his lips and nods in the negative, so Jilly allows his boots to return to earth.

"That's nice," Jilly says with a less than benevolent smile after which he turns to address his playing partner as if nothing has transpired. "I'm definitely gonna hit da shit out o' it with da five. So whadda ya think?"

His partner nods. "So get on with it already!"

I look around and for the first time since the match began, Robinson is sitting down on one of the benches placed off to the side of the tee next to a ball washer. His face is flushed and his eyes are down, and although his hands are holding each other, he can't mask the trembling that's cruising through his body. I smile and look over at Bottomly who returns my gaze but seems somewhat bewildered.

Must I say more? Unless I miss my guess, the match is over. And over it is! Robinson refuses to tee off until he can see that Jilly and friend have departed the seventeenth green and then immediately plunks his first truly rotten shot in a water hazard and takes a double bogey. He's too shook up to recover and suffers another bogey on the par five eighteenth. He then approaches Bottomly after the "ole man" drops a ten-footer for a par and merely informs him that his personal check for two thousand dollars will be delivered to his office before the day is out. I may be taking some liberties here, but I get the distinct impression that the Texan feels two grand ain't that much when considering the joys of another sunrise.

"Nice game, Mr. Bottomly," I say with a smile.

"Did you know Marinski was out on the course in front of us?" he inquires suspiously as we walk toward the Clubhouse.

"I'd seen the sheets, and I knew he was going off the tenth sometime in the early afternoon."

"So you had Marcus set him up nine minutes in front of us?" he asks, sounding annoyed.

"Come on, Mr. Bottomly. Some might think I'm a bit of a schemer but even I'm not that clever. If you recall, we were more than twenty minutes late just getting out to the tenth thanks to the blonde amazons. And if you further recall, Marinski was not in front of us when we began the back nine. Robinson couldn't control himself, so he went after a minnow and ended up with a mouthful of Great White shark. Hell, man," I add quickly, "you beat him fair and square."

"Yeah," he says softly, "I guess I did at that. As a matter of fact, I played a damned good round," he concludes, sounding very pleased with himself.

"Two under ain't exactly something to be ashamed of," I add with gusto. We arrive at the cart room door and I ease his bag off my shoulder and lean the clubs against the wall knowing Ferdie will give them a good washing.

"Do you have to make your payoffs tonight?" Bottomly asks.

"Not really. See if you can cash his check tomorrow and get me the thousand so your backers can celebrate."

"Just out of curiosity, D Jack, how many votes of confidence did I get from the boys?"

"My lips are sealed, sir. Let's just say you made a lot of guys happy to see James Bond take out Goldfinger and make a few bucks in the bargain."

"I didn't read the book and I didn't see the movie," he replies as a small smile starts to form at the corners of his mouth.

"Well, do one or the other and then you'll know what that golf match was all about," I say as I glance towards the starter's office. I don't see Marcus, so I start for the cart room which of course, connects to the bag room.

"We'll see about the movie and I'll catch you later," Bottomly says over his shoulder but then turns and adds, "and thanks for everything." I nod with a smile, give him a friendly wave, and continue on my way towards the clubs and sinks where I find Ferd rubbing some mud off a three wood. Now I ask you, how does one get mud on a three wood on a sunny day like this? I'm continually in awe of Sunday golfers and what they try to do and can't, no matter how hard they put their minds to the task.

"Hey, Ferdie, how's it going?"

He looks up from the sink with a grimace. “Leg hurts. First day I been up on it.”

I walk around behind the counter and join the ex-contender at the sink. “Why don’t you knock off and I’ll finish up? I’ve got a few hours before I have to hit the phones and do some crap catching,” I say with a grin.

Ferdie nods appreciatively and then wipes off his hairy, muscular forearms with a towel. “I put all the tips and stuff in the cigar box, just like you said,” he says, sounding like an elementary school kid looking for a loving pat on the head.

“Good going, Ferdie. We’ll both toss in whatever we get back here and split it down the middle when the sun goes down. But today’s different; you did all the work, so you get to clean out the box.”

“Ain’t that a little tough on you, D Jack?”

“Not so, Ferdie, I had a few other enterprises going for me, and today I just hit a big one with Bottomly,” I say sounding like a Vegas high roller and then throw in a wink, which further suggests it was a really big haul. He grins, rolls down his sleeves, and begins what appears to be a painful walk towards the door.

“See ya in the a.m.,” he grunts.

I turn my attention to the few clubs in the sink and am busy washing and drying them when Marcus storms into the bag room. “I just saw Ferdie limping out of here and figured you must be back,” he says breathlessly while looking a little pale around the gills. “Did all of it work? Did Bottomly ace him?”

“In answering your inquiries in order, it all went off like clockwork, and the ole man took him down with a two under card. I think the final difference was about eight strokes, and I’m positive Mr. John David Robinson was happy to get off the course alive.”

“So Marinski put the arm on him?”

“He didn’t just put an arm on him,” I respond with a belly laugh, “Jilly lifted his whole sorry ass off the ground and said less than ten words to him. I guess the only thing that really surprised me was that Robinson was able to finish the seventeenth and eighteenth at all. But I’ll tell you one thing,” I add with the utmost sincerity. “I never really imagined how unbelievably sinister Jilly could be, and it almost scares me that I went to Jimmy Blue Eyes and asked him if Jilly could do us a little favor. I’ve got to tell you, Marcus, I was a dozen feet away from him and you could smell death, I mean, really smell fucken death! Like some British columnist once said, ‘Golf is not a funeral, although both can be sad affairs.’”

Marcus chuckles. “When did you catch up with him?”

"I think around the twelfth or thirteenth, I'm not sure. He probably let the two foursomes you put between us play through in there somewhere. I had already asked Bottomly to slow his game down, so it was just a matter of time before Jilly would stall like I asked him to and Robinson would blow his cool."

"And Bottomly has no idea?"

"I don't think so. I convinced him we couldn't have rigged it because of the incident in the pro shop."

"My God, D Jack, I saw those blonde twins come out of the pro shop! I haven't seen that much meat on the hoof since I worked on a Brahman bull ranch in Ocala a few years go. Where did you find them?"

"The three of us met at the ballpark last year. Let's just say we're old friends."

"I'll bet those two are really something to see."

"They're perfect, and if you really want to know, they strip in some upscale joint in the Gables, but you better take your nitro pills if you go. Knowing you, you really shouldn't go at all."

"Ah hah, gotcha!" he says ignoring my remarks. "You once told me you'd never pay for that kind of thing."

"I didn't," I answer unable to suppress my grin, "and if their bodies are perfect, our plan was even better, if that's possible. I mean, it was just what we needed to get Robinson riled up and off on the wrong foot. And it didn't hurt either that Sally and Sindy fed Bottomly's ego. That really helped. Everything helped, and I'll bet that Robinson *has a broken mind all shot to hell.*"

"Yeah," Marcus nods in agreement, "ain't it a shame? But just out of curiosity, where did you get the idea that all this would work?"

"Well, he didn't play golf that I know of, but Lou Gehrig once said that the ballplayer who loses his head and loses his cool is no ballplayer at all, so maybe there is a place for some philosophy in real life. It sure as hell worked on Robinson."

But, I think to myself, one thing is for sure; the Iron Horse never lost his cool on or off the diamond. Playing ball is one thing, but the way he dealt with his fate with such dignity was just flat off the charts! I need to think of him more often.

"Maybe so," Marcus says, "but I still think you should seriously consider being a plumber in your next life," he concludes with a smile as he turns to exit the bagroom.

"I will if I find out that all the porn flicks about plumbers making *service calls* are true."

Marcus pauses for just a second and then continues on his way. Damn, I love getting in the last word. Yeah, I know, I haven't pulled off that trick with you yet, but I'm working on it!

XX

AN OFFER IN ASPEN

...guess I'll see ya around
but it might not be so
pullen up stakes
and headen for a new show

"You want A or B?"

"Excuse me?" Sam responds.

"Do you want the window or the aisle?"

"I'll take the aisle, thanks. I really don't like looking out the window, and anyway I'll probably have to go to the bathroom once or twice. How long is the flight?"

"I think it's about two hours from Lauderdale to Atlanta," I answer as I slide into 16A and place my small, black carry-on bag under the seat in front of me. "Then it's something like three or more out to Stapleton Airport in Denver, and I'm not sure about the puddle jumper to Aspen. But, not to change the subject, I'm curious about something. How is it a pilot doesn't like to look out the window?"

Sam settles herself into 16B and reaches for one of the safety belts wedged under her seat. "When I fly, I'm in control, but that obviously isn't the case here. Anyway, this thing will cruise over 30,000 feet, so there isn't much to see. And not to change the subject as you say, but isn't Eastern the airline that lost a plane in the Everglades a few years ago?"

"I hope not," I answer with a little bit of anxiety creeping into my voice, knowing it's too late to reconsider this trip. I really hadn't been all that enthused about going to Colorado, but Charley had mentioned he was also heading to Aspen for the birthday party and that Howard and Lillian Sheridan had been pretty insistent on me making the trip. If you recall, Howard is a minority owner of the Mets who had a cigar crisis, and Lillian's little sister is the hot-to-go Antoinette. When I had approached Sam with the idea of keeping me company, she hadn't seemed all that enthused either because of Christmas Eve and being away from her family, but I assured her we'd be going out on the 23rd and starting back early in the morning on the 24th. She was still uncomfortable with not having been directly invited, but Charley took care of that and told her Lillian's sister Antoinette said she could share her bedroom suite on the 3rd floor of the family mansion. No, I haven't shared Antoinette's bedroom at the Diplomat, but Ron sure as hell has and added he was very surprised at the intensity of her affection because for him, the ladies generally just screw and leave. Anyway, back to cases, I did put Sam on a guilt trip, saying she had taken me flying and it was only fair that I return the favor; after all, we were supposed to have a date, but it had gotten serious when I jokingly suggested maybe she just didn't want to go out of town with me. She had quickly responded that she would enjoy my company but felt awkward because she had not been formally introduced to our hosts. So here we are and now I'm the one feeling awkward because we haven't talked much and, like she said in Auburn, I assume she's still trying to figure things out.

"So, what do you want to talk about?" I ask lightly.

"I brought a magazine because that way I won't think about somebody at the controls."

"Then we're not going to talk at all?" I ask, disappointed.

"Now's okay, we're still on the ground."

"So, what are you reading?"

"It's cultural anthropology stuff. I really got into it at Gainesville, and there's supposed to be a neat article in here about Mary Leakey who just this year found eight adults and three kids in Tanzania who are more than 3.5 million years old."

"You mean like the remains of a human family?"

"Sounds like it."

"That kind of beats the hell out of the Book of Genesis, doesn't it?"

"I'm not so sure. I've heard an obscure philosopher recently proved the existence of God," Sam says, looking me right in the eye with a wise-ass grin. "I guess he could take a crack at what God was doing in Tanzania a few million years ago."

"That sounds too complicated. The wannabe philosopher you're referring to would cop out by saying they were really animals and were better off that way."

"Why would they be better off if they were animals as opposed to being human?"

"Because animals have these advantages over humans: they never hear the clock strike, they die without any idea of death, they have no theologians to instruct them, their last moments are not disturbed by unwelcome and unpleasant ceremonies, their funerals cost them nothing, and no one starts law suits over their wills."

Sam stares at me wide-eyed. "You didn't dream that up on your own, did you?"

"No, I didn't; that's Voltaire."

"And you know it by heart?"

"You bet. I realized very early on at ASU that if I could just regurgitate all kinds of quotes and aphorisms, I could pass most of my exams in philosophy with ease."

"You mean they never encouraged you to use critical thinking or do things like that?"

"Like what?"

"Like undertaking a concept analysis of the female anatomy," she says with a grin. I immediately feel my face flush but figure the Stetson, sunglasses, and beard are hiding the obvious.

"How did you find out about that?"

"Sal told me. We were having a drink in the lounge, and I told her I thought you were probably hard to rattle, so she shared her little intellectual exercise with you."

"And she wasn't embarrassed?"

"Dev, you know a million guys have seen her in the buff, so it wasn't exactly like she was sharing some intimacy, and it sure as hell wasn't personal."

"Isn't that what I was trying to tell you after putting you to bed a few weeks ago?"

"Are you kidding me?" she says, dumbfounded.

"Well, I'm going to assume a million guys haven't seen you nude, but it wasn't intimate and wasn't personal."

"Dev, if you undressed me a thousand times, it would still be intimate and personal."

"Can we get serious for a moment, Sam?"

"I thought we just did."

"Okay then, is there anything we've done during the past month or so that you've enjoyed, anything different from when we were kids maybe?"

"I think so," she replies as she shifts a little to face me. "I'm seeing things I would never have predicted. It's almost like I'm proud to be around you, like when you were teaching the kids how to play ball or throwing with that high school catcher."

"You saw that?"

"Yes, and I made a point of getting their table for lunch that day. You made that young man feel like a million bucks, and it's something he'll never forget. You inspired him and gave him the confidence that he could go to USC or ASU, but he said he wanted to go to ASU because you'd been there."

"Yeah, I was there but not as player."

"That doesn't matter, Dev. He just wants to be the next D Jack…but it's not just him. It's little things, like letting the vet know he rang your bell in a football game or helping Ferdie realize that he has some dignity, or at least starting off and trying to be polite with Daddy even when you know how he's felt about you all these years," she says somberly.

"How much of that conversation did he share with you?"

"Most of it, I guess, but more about the way you felt about being out of the game."

"Yeah, I know he saw the bitterness about not being able to play," I say with a pause and then add, "and other things too. I usually keep things to myself," I say reflectively, "but I guess he said a few things that kind of took me over the top."

"Are you referring to Suzanne?"

"He's told you about her?"

"No, Dev. I think he's always hated himself for that. Mom told me the whole story before she died because it was so obvious he was constantly trying to make up for it."

That brings a silence for both of us as I realize, and figure she does too, that Billy's scenario applies to us as well, but not really because all I did was get blindsided. Yeah, you don't have to tell me; I'm splitting hairs…and I know you don't have to be married to betray someone. Ah hell, this is way too heavy, so I gotta to change the subject and break the silence.

"Did he share the babe in the red bikini too?" I say in attempt to inject some levity into what's become a horribly serious conversation.

Sam seems to sense the same need to get past the moment. "Dev, have you two ever gone fishing when there wasn't a babe in a bikini?"

"They're getting skimpier. You'd look good in one, Sam."

"You're forgetting my stretch marks, aren't you?"

"Like you said, badges of honor or something like that." On that supportive note, I figure it's time to change the subject again. "So, what are you wearing to the party tonight?"

"Last week I asked Charley what he thought would be appropriate, so he sent me over to the boutique at the hotel, and his assistant Charlene picked out a nice outfit for me."

"I didn't mean for this little day trip to cost you some bucks," I say apologetically.

"That's okay. Charlene said we'd work something out and that I should check with Charley when I get back, whatever that means. How about you? What are you going to wear?"

"I'm in it."

"I hope it doesn't include that stained windbreaker you've got on. How come you're traveling in what you're going to wear?" she asks in what sounds like a critical tone.

"I don't like to check luggage; I guess it's also a carryover from my playing days. Jeans, some socks, and a toothbrush in a small black bag always got it done for me."

"I don't like to check things either. I just brought a carry-on bag that the stewardess hung up. So what's under the jacket?"

"I've got on black wranglers, white long sleeve, pearl button shirt, and a black vest."

"Complete with black boots, sunglasses, and your standard black cowboy hat," she adds.

"Not standard. I gussied up the Stetson with my Saturday night porcupine band."

"Don't you think you're just a bit ominous-looking for a birthday party?"

"Mr. Sheridan told me to dress comfortably, and this is as comfortable as I can get without looking like I'm revving up a Harley and looking for a tattoo parlor. Anyway, I've never seen you in black and figured you would be wearing something colorful, so we certainly won't clash. If memory serves, you'll be the one in lavender, right?"

She nods as the pilot starts to rev the two engines mounted one apiece on the wings with a third mounted in the vertical tail. The plane starts to vibrate somewhat and it quickly becomes apparent they don't call the Boeing 727 the noisiest aircraft around for nothing. "It's magazine time, Dev. Have a nice flight."

"Do you want to hold hands, or something?"

"It takes two hands to read a magazine, Dev," she replies without looking at me.

Great…I feel like I just struck out on a wild pitch, so I look out the window and see a guy in hiking boots, shorts, and an orange flack jacket waving a baton to let the pilot know he's clear as the reverse thrusters kick in and the plane slowly backs away from the gate. I can see the airport's omnipresent palm trees blowing gently in the wind, and those green fronds immediately take me back to the countless hours of tranquility I shared with Sam on Hollywood Beach. We would stretch out on a blanket, and I would run my hands through her hair as she leaned against my chest. Our kisses always started out soft and tender and then went far beyond what casual lovers commonly exchange. Sometimes we wouldn't say anything and just listen to the Gulf Stream breezes caressing the trees and foam crested waves. Sometimes, a full moon illuminated a silver border on the tops of thin-layered clouds, and in those clouds I would only see the game and Sam. Thinking about it now, I know I was in love with both but obsessed by only one. I've got to admit to you that Sam was right; baseball had been a quest, and when it was over, I was left with nothing more than an empty glove and bittersweet memories. But unlike Cervantes' Quixote, my never-ending quest had come to an abrupt and sudden end whereas I'd like to think he pursued his dreams into eternity.

I look back to Sam who has wrapped herself in her magazine and her self-announced attempt to block out her discomfort with being a passenger. Okay, so let's get right to it and see what you think. She said some positive things about me, right? But then, a psychiatrist will tell you some nice things too but that doesn't mean you're gonna get to dance; in fact, you can bet about ninety-five dollars an hour and the thirteen-cent stamp on the envelope that you don't have a prayer of getting out on the floor. So maybe she wants to play pop psychologist so brokendown Devon can go after a new windmill, ya think? Or maybe, just maybe, she's wondering if we can go back to the beach and listen to the ocean breeze, smell the salt air, and wiggle our toes in the cool sand. Anyway, I think maybe you figure the books aren't closed on this thing, but you have to admit we've been traveling this slightly bumpy road for almost a month or so. Without even thinking about it, the words of Deng Ming-Dao, absorbed in Graduate Philosophy 616-The Eastern World, come to mind: "The time to contemplate the ending…is before the ending."

Did you ever do that? I sure as hell didn't. I figured me and Sam and baseball were in it for the long haul. So, who says philosophy has no practical value? Let's do some contemplating, okay?

*

"D Jack, good to see you. Did you have a nice flight?"

"Just fine, Mr. Sheridan. Thanks a lot."

"I'm sorry the plane had to put down in Eagle and you had to put up with a two hour drive, but the airport here was socked in all morning."

"Actually, it worked out for the best," I respond with a smile. "That drive through Glenwood Canyon was awesome, and just a few miles out of Glenwood Springs there were at least a dozen big horn sheep right on the side of the road. We stopped for lunch at Doc Holliday's Saloon, and that place was something else. We really appreciated the unexpected road trip."

"I'm glad you enjoyed the scenery," he says sincerely. "Is everything okay with Mrs. Fredrickson? Antoinette was supposed to be here when you arrived."

Mrs. Fredrickson…that still sounds so damn strange to me. "I think your housekeeper was helping her out, and anyway, we're pretty low maintenance, Mr. Sheridan. Everyone, particularly your chauffeur, has been really friendly; I guess it was the butler who showed us where to put our stuff. This is some place you have here. I didn't think you could build something this size on the side of a mountain. And," I continue enthusiastically, "that's one hell of a view you've got looking down into the town and across to the ski slopes. By the way, there seemed to be an awful lot of security at the gate."

"There usually is because quite a few celebs live in the Starwood subdivision, what with all the beautiful mountain views. But it's even tighter now because Spider Sabitch was living in a stone A-frame chalet up here. I assume you know what happened to him?"

"Sure," I respond, not realizing the world-class skier had lived in Aspen. "Didn't Andy Williams' ex-wife shoot him or something like that?"

"Yes, it was something like that," he says skeptically. "Her name is Claudine Longet, and she and her three kids had been living with Spider up here for about three years. We think she's staying with John Denver and Annie, but we're not asking."

"I don't recall hearing about what happened to her?"

"Nothing has happened yet, D Jack. That's why there are security men and hordes of media people all over town. Her trial is set for January 10th."

"So, what are the betting odds?"

"There are no odds on a Hollywood celebrity, but who knows? She could get ten years or she could walk. Either way, lots of people around here think she shot him in cold blood, so she's not exactly greeted with open arms. We'll see," he concludes. "But you are right," he says, changing the subject, "it is one hell of a view up here, isn't it? Again, I regret we couldn't be here to greet you; we had to go down town to get some last-minute fun stuff for the party," he says with a smile.

"If you don't mind me saying so, you seem to really enjoy yourself, Mr. Sheridan."

"That I do, D Jack, and I think I know what you're saying. You see plenty of movers and shakers at the Presidential and the Diplomat, don't you?"

"Yup."

"And would you say most of them are having fun?"

"Well, some of them are. I read once that high-powered people take short holidays because they're afraid to be away from the switches. I know some are down for the season, but I hear they often fly back to their corporate headquarters or whatever to check up on things. Bottom line is I don't see a whole lot of relaxed people. Pretending maybe, but not really relaxing."

"And me?" Sheridan inquires with a half smile.

"Is the host putting one of his guests on the spot?" I answer with my own grin.

"Just curious, D Jack; you see, I don't think it has a whole lot to do with wealth. I think it's a matter of being able to simply enjoy the hand you're dealt rather than living in a constant state of aggravation or stress, whether you're about to pioneer a television station in Miami or helping Bottomly win a grudge match that Charley told me about."

"I wouldn't disagree with that," I say, feeling pretty satisfied knowing that little story has made the rounds.

"Good because you would be disagreeing with yourself. It's your insight I'm talking about. You knew Bottomly could beat Robinson because the game wasn't going to be fun for the other guy."

"Well, it's not always fun and games. You've got to get serious once in awhile."

"Agreed," Sheridan says with a grin. "So you got serious about giving Bottomly a leg up?"

"With a round of two under, I'd say the ole pro beat him flat out, but actually, yes," I respond seriously. "I'm sure that's true for you, too; I mean, situations arise that call for putting the toys in the attic for the moment. And I did get serious about offsetting Robinson's lie about his handicap."

"And it was the right thing to do, as long as those toys don't stay there too long, D Jack," he says as the grin leaves his patrician face. "A person isn't going to be very happy or healthy for that matter if he doesn't retrieve those toys or find new ones," he concludes.

Okay, boys and girls; I think this clearly falls into the realm of fatherly advice, and he's certainly communicating an air of sincerity, but I don't know where he's coming from or why he's interested in counseling me. So I need to find a quick way out without blowing him off. "I'll bet you've been doing that for a long time."

He laughs. "Put it on the board with the Turk and take it to the bank, D Jack," he says with a smile as his hand leaves my shoulder.

"You pretty well know what's going on, don't you?"

"Like I mentioned a few weeks ago, Charley is involved with launching the station, so he shares the good stuff over drinks. But now, as you might say, it's time for me to put on my game face and be the charming host."

"I'd wager you don't have to work at it."

"And you'd win again. Lillian and I have a very simple philosophy when it comes to entertaining. If our friends want to come, they come, and if they want to have a good time, they have a good time. If not, that's their choice. We're not interested in overseeing a party; we're interested in being the two people having the most fun."

"Any hints for me? I haven't been to this kind of shindig since being wined and dined as an up-and-coming ballplayer."

"Just have a good time, D Jack. Lot's of our friends are really looking forward to meeting you, and if you start to run out of conversation, just keep Mrs. Frederickson on your arm because no one is going to focus on your ugly mug if she's standing next to you."

"I'll let her know you said so."

"No need, D Jack," he says as he turns and heads for one of two spiral staircases on either side of his marble-tiled living room. "I've already shared that view with her, but of course, I limited my remarks to your ugly mug," he says, but I don't really hear him because my brain is totally focused on Sam who is coming down the right staircase; heavens to Betsy if she doesn't look flat-out stunning.

Sheridan is still chuckling as he walks away and I wait for Sam. She comes up to me with a smile and then, without a word, the two of us head out of the tastefully resplendent room into a more informal living area that has lush wall-to-wall carpeting and a huge fireplace in which a number of ponderosa pine logs are merrily crackling away. Charley is sitting in a plush loveseat, drink in hand, and seems to be relaxing, which is a rare event for a guy whose energy level always seems to be off the charts. I steer Sam in Charley's direction and let her know that I'm headed for the wet bar. It looks like a miniature replica of the resplendent appointments found in the J Bar in the Hotel Jerome where we had an afternoon drink earlier in the day after arriving in Aspen. Then we cruised one or two beautiful side streets, window-shopping in some really unique western stores on Cooper Avenue.

The Aspen watering hole had really been first rate but not as neato keazeto as the aforementioned Doc Holliday's with its four, short Doric columns supporting three dark, hardwood arches which held mirrors that reflected the old brick wall across from the bar. Harnesses, reins, and all sorts of homestead paraphernalia were hung from the bricks along with portraits of Doc and his "sporting woman" girlfriend, Big Nose Kate. According to the story, Doc had come to Glenwood Springs for the healing waters found adjacent to the Colorado River and the majestic Colorado Hotel, but the sulfur fumes aggravated his advanced tubercular condition and he didn't last very long. Legend has it that he actually sat at the bar that had been built for the mining town of Leadville, Colorado, but for some reason was shipped to the Glenwood Saloon on Grand Avenue…which was eventually named for him. Again, it wasn't as ornate as the one in Aspen but was a lot more fascinating due to its history.

Anyway, Sheridan's bar is fully stocked, and the barman generously fills my requests for a Crown Royal and Bacardi and Pepsi, both of which he serves up with a few cubes of ice in cut glass tumblers. Needless to say, there's no tip jar in sight. I head over to Sam and Charley who appear to be having a friendly and very animated conversation. "What's going on?" I ask as I hand Sam her drink and receive a nod of thanks.

"I'm trying to explain to Mr. Berston how Daddy didn't hit the bottom of the tank even though it was only six feet deep."

"That's what you're doing with the straw, huh?"

"Yes, I'm showing him how Daddy would draw up his legs as soon as he touched the water and do a backward spin in a tuck position," she says, bending the thin red plastic tube.

"Well, it obviously worked, right Charley?"

"He's still making customers happy in the Bengal Lounge with all his war stories, D Jack, and I think he really enjoyed the laminated poster we placed in the lockers showing him doing the fire dive."

"I'm sure he appreciated it, Charley. But does that mean you're going to put up a poster of Ruby flat on his face or Ferdie with a closed right eye?"

"That might be a good idea. Unlike you, I suspect most ex-jocks love to relish in their glory years, and it doesn't hurt for our patrons to see we have some pretty famous people on the staff."

"Always marketing, huh, Charley? Remind me next time we play singles to hit you square in the ass as hard as I can."

"I'm not worried. Your eyesight stinks, and your aim ain't that good."

Sam gets to her feet and gives us both a shrug but seems somewhat surprised about Charley's reference to my vision. But since we're both smiling, I guess she figures it's just fun and games between the two of us. "If you two gentlemen will excuse me, I think I'll have that nice man over there freshen up my drink." Wow! She downed that one pretty quickly.

We both give her lame smiles as she heads for the bar, and again, I realize how gorgeous she is. Her lavender, pleated skirt has a matching sport coat, or whatever you call a coat on a woman, with a white blouse that shows just enough cleavage to be sensuous without being trashy. Other than her ever-present wedding band, her jewelry is limited to an ankle bracelet and a delicate gold necklass with three gold beads attached to a thin chain.

"Nice kid, huh, D Jack? I know you two knew each other when you were on your way up."

"Yeah," I say reflectively turning to face Charley who has lifted his slim body off the couch. "We were both starry-eyed kids and were going to set the world on fire."

"So, what went south for the two of you? Did she have trouble adjusting when you went down for the count?"

"It was over by then, Charley, although I didn't know it at the time. When I caught the plane home, she was in Gainesville working on a degree and a marriage."

"That was bad luck, D Jack."

"Nope," I say with a feeble smile. "A tough break and a healthy dose of stupidity is a lousy quinella."

"That's pretty insightful. How long did it take you to figure it out?"

"I'm still working on the stupidity part," I conclude with just a bit of a grin. Charley returns the smile and gives me a shot on the arm. Both of us then look toward the formal dining room where the noise level seems to be increasing, because a number of guests have started to arrive. "Charley, isn't that John Denver?"

"Sure is. I'm told he lives here year-round with a bunch of other interesting Aspenites."

"What do you mean by interesting?"

"You now me, D Jack, I'm just a simple nuts-and-bolts kind of guy, but *Newsweek* recently referred to the residents of this place as being very 'rich recluses, hip hedonists, mellow cowboys, and cocaine-snorten' vegetarians.'"

"So where does Sheridan fit into that scenario?"

"He doesn't. He and Lillian just like the convenience of having a place next to some great ski slopes. Anyway," Charley concludes, "it's time to circulate, D Jack, but I'll be back soon with some close friends. Until then, have a good time," he says as he turns and walks away.

I turn to see if Sam is still at the bar and am pleased to see she's just leaving and is on her way back to where I'm sitting. Sometimes it's really difficult for me to realize we used to go to bed together, but it was so long ago that it's like looking at a picture of my rookie card without remembering where or when the photo was taken.

"You've barely touched your drink, Dev," Sam observes as she sits down next to me on the loveseat.

"Tell you the truth, I'm a little nervous."

"About?"

"I don't know. I'm just apprehensive about being asked a lot of questions about getting hurt. That always seems to be the main topic of conversation when people meet me."

"I saw your interviews with Johnny Carson and Joe Garagiola, and you seemed to have your sense of humor working overtime. Was that just for show?"

"Well, you know, you try to be light and positive and project the image that something neat is just around the corner."

"Devon," she says in a serious tone, "do you think in the last eight years you've even attempted to walk around a corner just to see what was there?"

"Not a good question, seeing as it's party time"

"That isn't exactly a denial. Maybe we can talk about it on the way back to Florida tomorrow morning."

I paint a goofy grin back on my face. "Not if you're going to read your damn magazine all the way. You ain't exactly the world's best traveling companion."

"I'll try to make an exception, but for now, I can serve as an excellent companion. So what's our story, and what would you like me to do?" she says with a mischievous glint in her eye.

"How about you conjure up the story part?"

"Okay, we're old friends who recently bumped into each other and are pleasantly getting re-acquainted. Do you think that will work?"

I laugh. "You think anybody really cares?"

"Absolutely not, but you're the one who seems to need a story. So, having settled that," she continues, "do you want me to behave like the sweet bimbo of the month on your arm or somebody serious in your life?" The glint hasn't left her eye.

Ain't that terrific, sportsfans? She's just tossed out another bimbo reference. "First of all, I don't think we can pass Mrs. Frederickson off as a bimbo because you're not dressed for the part. And secondly, being serious with a wedding ring might not fly."

"Easily solved," she says as she slips the gold band from her finger and hands to it me. "I don't have any pockets, okay?" I look at the ring, realizing what it has symbolized for both of us and quietly slip it into my Wranglers.

"Okay, Sam, you smile and be charming and run interference for me and we'll just be friends."

"We've been friends before, Dev, so that part should be easy."

Yeah, I think, and we've been lovers, too, so where in the hell do we go from here, if anywhere? Thankfully, my deep and somewhat depressed thoughts are interrupted by Charley who appears to be escorting three guys over to where we're sitting.

"D Jack, I want you to meet some good friends of mine. This is Sam Peterson of Philadelphia, Myron Goldsmith of New York, and the guy with the suntan is Alton Marks of La Jolla. Fellas, this is Devon Jameison."

I get to my feet and after grins and handshakes, Goldsmith says with a note of seriousness, "It's really great to meet you, D Jack. You look a lot better than the last time I saw you."

"In Shea, I suppose, but it's nice to know that little incident didn't mess up my Adonis-like appearance," I respond lightly, hoping that will be that on the good ole end of the good ole career. The smiles and soft chuckles suggest that dog has been put to rest.

"So," he continues, "who do you think are the best players in the game today?"

"Well, Mr. Goldsmith, you being from New York, I can go with Munson in the American League. And Schmidt, of course banged out almost forty homers last year in your hometown, Mr. Peterson, but I'd have to go with Joe Morgan in Cincinnati."

"No votes for anyone from the coast?" Mr. Marks asks pleasantly.

"Well, Randy Jones won the Cy Young, but I think you're gonna have snow in San Diego before you get an MVP from that part of the world, unless it's for fishing. I think twenty or so years ago somebody bagged a fifteen hundred pound Black Marlin off the coast of Peru, so maybe one of 'em will swim north."

I seem to be doing pretty good because Charley is smiling, and I figure he's my barometer. "Do you see fishing as a physical sport, D Jack?"

"I got to tell you, Mr. Marks, I think I'd rather step into the batter's box against somebody like Jim Palmer than try to boat that Marlin. But then I guess it must take more than brute strength because I think I heard somewhere that the world record for a bluefin tuna was set by some lady, so there must be some real skill in there somewhere."

"What about things like golf and tennis or maybe Indy racing?" the guy from La Jolla continues inquisitively.

"Tennis, I think, is awesome, and we're gonna get a lot of thrills out of watching Connors and Borg. Sure, maybe golf doesn't put as many guys in the hospital as say football, but I'd be hard pressed to argue that a guy like Nicklaus isn't one hell of an athlete."

"And what do you think about Indy racing?"

This has all the appearance of a third degree, but I'm not sure why. "I figure guys like Rutherford, Foyt, and Andretti have forearm strength that could take a baseball downtown to the tune of six hundred feet or so, and the thought of driving a car around a track two hundred times at 189 miles per hour for five hundred miles about six inches from some guy's rear end is just flat-out frightening. You bet they're jocks, although I'm not sure they wear 'em."

After a few chuckles, the guy from Philadelphia changes gears. "What do you think about sports movies, D Jack?"

"I think they're fun and mostly fantasies. I know Rocky jumped up and down on some steps in Philly and has been big in the movie houses," I say with a smile, "but just ask some of the guys at the Presidential Country Club in North Miami Beach, like Ferdinand the Bull or Willie Pastrano, how many shots you can really take square on the jaw or just how much blood you can put on the canvas before a ring physician tells you you're through. I'm hoping," I add sincerely, "that one of these days Hollywood makes movies that really show you the life, like maybe something about the minor leagues with overnight bus rides, greasy spoons, and the mixture of thrill and fear in every young kid. That's something I'd really like to see."

"What I'd really like to see is some dinner," Charley says after giving me a slap on the back while his three buddies nod in agreement, "and maybe afterwards some competition on Howard's snooker table or maybe some rotation," he adds. "Are you up for that D Jack?"

"Depends upon how much money you guys are going to put on the nine-ball. If you want the stakes to be as high as Jackie Gleason's are, even when he says he's just giving me a lesson, then you can count me out," I say with a grin that's matched by Charley's pals.

I'm really hoping those last few remarks have pretty much put an end to this grilling and am relieved to see Lillian Sheridan and a middle-aged woman, conservatively but tastefully attired, approaching us. Their impending arrival seems to also signal a departure for the men, who start for the dining room.

"Gloria, may I introduce Devon Jameison and Samantha Frederickson who came all the way from Florida to be with us this evening. Gloria's husband is also a minority owner of the Mets," Mrs. Sheridan adds.

Sam gets to here feet. "It's a pleasure to meet you, D Jack, and you too, Samantha," Gloria says pleasantly. "I've heard so much about your ball-playing skills. I was hoping the two of you might sit next to me during dinner."

"That would be our pleasure," Sam responds, taking my arm and leading us towards the dining room. Most of the guests have already been seated, and three waiters decked out in white dinner jackets and black slacks are bustling around the room making sure everything is as it should be. We appear to be about the last ones to be seated. My thoughts are interrupted by the clink of a piece of silverware against a glass, and I notice Howard Sheridan has gotten to his feet. The small talk quickly fades to silence as Sheridan holds up both his hands and grins at everyone in the room.

"Before we dive into some of Lillian's favorite dishes, I'd like to thank all of you on behalf of Lillian and myself for joining us for her special birthday. I'm sure no one is surprised that there are just twenty or so of us here, because you know the two of us like to celebrate with those dear to us and we consider everyone in this room to be family. Those of you who were able to get here last night know that I have already bestowed presents upon my beloved birthday girl, and tonight I would simply like to say what you already know. Lillian," Sheridan says, turning to his wife and taking her hand, "a man can only have a few valuable things in life, and I believe those things are the true love of a woman, children, and a career of worth…and, yes, in that order. And as I have done many times during our lives together, I want to thank you for the first two and for making the third fun all the way." With that said, he kisses her gently on the mouth to the soft applause and genuine smiles of all those gathered.

"There is something else Lillian and I would like to do this evening before we eat," he continues "and we've been looking forward to it for quite some time. I hope you've had a chance to meet Devon and Samantha, and I'm sure you're familiar with his fleeting exploits in professional baseball, although only a few of us ever saw him play. Lillian and I were in Shea Stadium when D Jack went three for three, snagged one at the fence, and took one off his shoe tops to throw out a Cardinal at the plate. And then in a single moment, it was over for a man who had the skills to possibly be one of the best players in the game. We'll never know."

Terrific I'm thinking; ya could hear a fucken pin drop!

"So how good was D Jack?" he continues. "One week before that Saturday night, the decision was made to bring him to the Show. The Monday of that week was a traveling day for the Mets, and the Triple AAA team in Norfolk was playing a night game. So Gil Hodges decided he wanted to see the kid play, and we flew to Norfolk together. I'll never forget Gil, may God rest his soul, just staring at D Jack most of that night. He played errorless ball, went four for four including two home runs, stole third twice, and accounted for most of the runs in the victory. Gil never said a word, but on the way to the airport around midnight, he said he had read the scouting reports but thought they had to be overblown. 'But now,' he said, 'I saw it but I don't believe it. The kid runs like Mantle, plays the outfield like Mays, can hit the ball like Aaron, and has the eyes of Williams.'"

Sheridan pauses and then says reflectively, "So who knows what might have been," and then he sighs and shrugs his shoulders. "Anyway, many of you were in this very room in early November of 1969 when, as minority owners, Lillian and I hosted our World Champion Miracle Mets. We invited D Jack to attend, and he wrote us a letter declining the invitation." Sheridan pauses with a serious look on his face as he reaches into his coat pocket and brings out a piece of paper. "I still have his note and, D Jack, I don't mean to embarrass you, but I'd like to share what you wrote."

Well, if he's kept the note all this time, who am I to say no? So I just nod with a weak smile.

"Dear Mr. and Mrs. Sheridan," he begins. "I deeply appreciate your invitation to come to Aspen and participate in the victory celebration you have been so generous to sponsor. However, I regret that I will be rehabbing for quite some time and am not really up to traveling at this point. I would like to say that without the generosity of you and the Mets organization regarding my medical treatment, the success of my rehabilitation would be in doubt. On a more serious and honest note, I must share I didn't contribute anything whatsoever to the championship year, and obviously never had the opportunity to become a part of the team. Again, thanks for the invitation, and I know the party will be deeply appreciated by the players. I'd like to close by saying that my dad always hoped I'd be a Major League ballplayer.

He has passed and obviously my playing days have come and gone…but I'll always be grateful to you and the Mets for making his dream come true. Sincerely, Devon Jameison."

The room is very quiet, and I'm looking at my glass because I really don't want to be looking at anyone after that somber speech. But then as usual, the ever-present sunglasses shield me from the people at the table.

"D Jack, it gives me a great deal of pleasure to tell you that you were wrong," he says with a gentle smile. "You're wrong because you contributed something vital to that miracle season. No one talked about your accident for almost two days because you were in pretty serious shape. Then, Gil told me later that he addressed the team in the clubhouse and told them the good news was that you would be okay but the bad news was you would never play ball again. He then told them simply this: 'This season, I only want one thing from all of you. You saw this kid walk into a major league ball park and in two hours set the world on fire. In that one day, he went out and played his heart out and tried to make his dreams come true. Let's keep that spirit in the dugout, and every day each of you takes the field, I want you to do your best and make our dream come true.'"

Many of the guests turn from Sheridan to look at me. I do the best I can with a shy smile as my discomfort level soars towards the wood-beamed ceiling.

"So you see, D Jack, you did contribute, significantly contribute, to the team. I know you're not the kind of person to think I would dream this stuff up, but just in case," he says with a twinkle in his eye, "I've kept something else over the years in addition to your note. At the end of the season, the team approached the owners and told us they wanted the Mets organization to present you with an honorary World Series ring," he says as he leaves the head of the table, walks toward me, and takes a small blue box out of his pocket. I stand up, and without a word he opens the box, removes the ring, and hands it to me. It takes a few seconds for all this to dawn on me and realize that everyone in the room has come to their feet.

"I regret it has taken this long but the circumstances never seemed quite right. This is undoubtedly an unexpected moment for you, but I'm sure all of us would appreciate a few words or thoughts." He then whispers, "Meet me in the study upstairs right after dinner, okay?" I nod and Sheridan then returns to his place at the table and puts his arm around Lillian who is standing and seems to have shed a few tears. I'd love to look at Sam, hoping she's beaming all over the place but figure I better get at it, so I settle my gaze on Sheridan and his wife, both of whom regain their seats along with all the guests. I thank God for my sunglasses because I'm starting to feel that knot in the throat you get when you're really stressed.

"I'd have to say 'unexpected' doesn't quite get it done, Mr. Sheridan," I begin slowly and softly. "But let me say that having had the pleasure of getting to know you and Mrs. Sheridan just a little bit and having heard your toast just a few minutes ago, I'd gladly swap this ring for a wedding band and what it's meant to you." That gets me huge smiles from my hosts and oohs and aahs from their extended family.

"You know how to punch the buttons, don't you D Jack?" Sheridan says with a laugh and is immediately joined by all in the room. Fortunately, that seems to break the seriousness of the moment, and I feel a sense of relief.

"Tell us about the good things that happened that night in Shea, D Jack, and then I'll sing for my supper," John Denver says enthusiastically.

"That would take way too long, Mr. Denver, so let me share just one thing quickly so we can get back to the reason we all came here tonight."

"Good form, D Jack," Charley says supportively.

"Praise from the guy who signs my paycheck is a nice way to start," I say to Charley and that gets something just short of belly laughs from the guests. "Anyway, if you live long enough, you remember things that changed your life, and hopefully you focus on the good and not the bad. When I think back to Shea, I remember my most neato keazeto home run ever. Some guys like to think about taking one downtown about five hundred feet and I came close a few times, but that's the one you know is gone from the instant it dings off the sweet spot on your bat. I used to like the ones I wasn't sure about, the ones where you put your head down and ran like hell for first and you didn't look up till you rounded the bag and headed for second. At that moment, you realize either it's a fly out or the ball has hit the fence, and ya got to try to leg out a triple or hold with a stand-up double. Or she's gone, and you just kind of lay back into what I used to call a *professional* trot."

"I haven't heard that expression, D Jack," Charley says.

"Well, on my first day with the Triple AAA Suns in Wolfson Park in Jacksonville, I put one out in left that I found out later crossed the street and ended up in the parking lot. Hell, I was only eighteen, and I guess I celebrated too much because the batting coach, a grizzly ole veteran whose name was Pepper Kwalchek, took me aside and told me the pitcher I dinged worked just as hard to get there as I did and I needed to respect him…so from that point on, when I took a pitcher downtown, I just made sure to be professional, tag all the bases, and keep the celebration inside.

"So how did you feel when you hit the homer in Shea, D Jack? What made it different?" Sheridan asks.

"What made it so special was I never played in a minor league park with left field bleachers, and the only way I knew the ball was gone was if I saw the left fielder slow down and look back toward the infield. But in Shea, when I rounded first and looked up, there were people out there going crazy, and I think I even saw some guy raise his arm with the ball. And I'd never seen anything like that before. Anyway, that's what I remember but it took awhile to put the rest of it away. In fact, I only realized last year that I only had fun playing baseball once," I conclude reflectively.

"But I always hear that baseball players are just little boys having a good time," Antoinette says seriously. "It wasn't fun for you?"

"I think what a professional athlete feels is satisfaction and a terrific sense of accomplishment, but I've got to tell ya, the stress is out of sight. You worry that if you get hurt and can't play for a few weeks, you'll lose your position. For ballplayers, if you really get into a slump, maybe the organization will send you down or cut ya, and you sure better hit low and away curve balls once in awhile or that's all you're gonna see.

"So when did you finally have fun, D Jack?" Antoinette asks sounding genuinely curious.

"A year ago summer I got conned into playing for a semi-pro team in Miami. Somewhere in the first game, I dove for a fly ball and ended up flat on my belly. I held up my glove for the ump to see the ball, but guess what? No ball! E-7, sports fans, and that means an error on the left fielder. And what did I do for the first time in my entire life? I laughed, I just flat laughed. But I did more than laugh. I learned that laughing is okay, and I'd like to think I've been doing it ever since, much to the dismay," I add, turning to Charley the Boss, "of my current employer."

"That's true, D Jack," Charley says with a phony dose of annoyance. "I guess you're still laughing, but I really do want to know what happened to Hans Schmedler's clubs."

"Come on, Charley; why talk to me? I've got an alibi. The last time I saw that sweet man's clubs was a full twenty-four hours before they vanished. You can check it out. Ask Marcus, or Ralph, or Ron, or the Turk. And while you're at it, give George a call over at the Executive bag room. I'm pretty sure he's the last guy who saw 'em."

"Inside story, everyone," Howard Sheridan quickly interjects. "As the tale goes at the Presidential golf course, a rather arrogant industrialist ran a golf cart over a caddy's leg and broke it. The next day or so, the industrialist's clubs mysteriously disappeared, and all fingers pointed to D

Jack who has maintained since then that they were put on one of the Presidential's Mercedes shuttle busses."

"You know about that?" I say aghast.

"Like I told you earlier this evening, you'd be surprised what Charley has to say about you over a glass of Johnny Walker Black."

"There's some truth to that, D Jack," Charley says, "and I think you had fun settling the score, as you say, with Schmedler, so I'm still not buying your story that the last time you saw those clubs was when they were put on one of the shuttle busses."

I slowly look in Sam's direction, and her expression suggests she once again is aching to know what happened, so I figure I might as well spill the beans…two thousand miles away from the crime. I return my gaze to Charley. "I don't recall ever referring to the bus as a 'shuttle,'" I say with a big grin.

Huge pause and Charley's jaw drops. "Are you telling me you put his clubs on a commercial bus?" he retorts matching my grin."

"I believe that's what a Greyhound is, isn't it?" The 'family' is starting to chuckle, and most seem to be thoroughly enjoying this tale of retribution.

"And may I also assume it wasn't headed for Schmedler's hometown of San Francisco?"

"I've always heard the Scots invented golf, so I thought someone in Halifax, Nova Scotia might enjoy them. And with that, I hope you won't call the cops or fire me; at least not before I can take my seat and have all of us continue to honor Mrs. Sheridan," I conclude with a slight bow to my hostess as I plop down to hearty applause.

"Well done, D Jack, on all accounts!" Sheridan says with gusto. "Let's eat!"

*

I walk into the study that looks to be something like six hundred square feet and about twenty-five feet high. At the far end of the room, a very tight spiral staircase leads to the second level. About half way up, there's a six-foot wide walkway that goes entirely around the rectangular room, that's paneled with a dark cherry-like wood against which are stacked hundreds of books. What I assume to be the west wall of the study houses an irregularly-shaped fifteen-foot high window through which I can see down into the lights of the skiing Mecca and across to the snowy runs of Aspen Mountain. Sheridan is comfortably seated in a large overstuffed leather chair and beckons me to join him in the matching piece of furniture which is about three feet away, separated by a small marble-topped coffee table adorned with two brandy snifters and a humidor with a carved sailing ship on the lid.

As I approach, he smiles and says, "You once offered me a fine cigar so I thought I would return the favor." He opens the cedar-lined box as I take a seat and select a Don Diego Churchill that's about the size of a Little League bat. Sheridan continues to grin as he extends to me a silver cutter. "I know you're a Canadian whiskey man, but I figure a fine cognac will serve as a decent substitute."

I pick up the snifter, swirl the liqueur, and, inappropriately, take a little bit more than a sip. After cutting the cigar and twirling it into the match Sheridan has extended, I sit back and take a deep breath. "I know this has been a very special night what with you celebrating Mrs. Sheridan's birthday, but I have to tell you it's been a long time since I had a night like this myself, and I really want to say thanks."

"We wanted it to be a special time, D Jack, and you were a part of that plan. As I said," he continues with genuine sincerity, "I regret that it took this many years to present you with the ring, but we had difficulty finding an appropriate time and place. And then, life isn't always roses. Lillian had a double mastectomy five years ago, and we're hoping she's out of the woods. To be quite frank, you stayed off our radar screen during that time."

"As it should be, and that's wonderful news that she's in remission, Mr. Sheridan," I say sincerely. "I guess it's pretty tough not knowing what tomorrow's going to bring."

"I don't think you have to guess, D Jack," he says seriously. "I think even at your young age, you've probably spent too much time on just that issue yourself. Am I right?"

I contemplate this inquiry briefly and then answer, "I'd like to be able to deny that, but when all your life you just think you're going to play ball and then it suddenly disappears, it's kind of hard to shift gears."

"And there was no one to help you find your way?"

"My mom passed when I was too young to even remember, and my dad raised me. He died when I was playing in Jacksonville."

"And Samantha?" he inquires softly.

"Charley does talk a lot," I respond in an annoyed tone that surprises me; I mean, after all, this guy has flown me out here, but I can't see where this is any of his business.

"I can understand your reaction to that, but don't blame Charley," he hurries on. "We're business partners, and I asked him to tell me as much about you as he could. He told me you and Samantha were very close in high school but the relationship ended when you went to the minors and she got injured diving."

"That's true. And if you have to know, I did something that was stupid and thoughtless, so the answer to your question is that I didn't have anyone. In a period of six months, I lost the game, Dad, and Samantha. The first two weren't my fault, but sometimes I think that was the price I was supposed to pay because the situation with her was my fault and was inexcusable."

"You don't pass the buck, do you kid?"

"No, sir, I don't."

"That's to the point and pretty impressive, D Jack."

"It wasn't meant to be impressive, Mr. Sheridan. But speaking of points, and I apologize for being so blunt, what's yours?"

"That's a fair question, man-to-man. I'm sure you're pretty ticked, and I would be too if I was in your place but I think the next few minutes will clear that up," Sheridan concludes, as he sips his cognac and takes a deep puff on the Diego. The look in his eyes tells me he has something to say, so I simply nod and take another "slug" of the warmed liqueur.

"We didn't bring you out here just to join Lillian's celebration and present you with a ring, even though that was very special for us."

"I'm glad you said that, because I was wondering what was going on when Charley's buddies gave me the twenty questions and third degree on sports in America."

Sheridan laughs. "We just wanted to see how your sports knowledge and communication skills would hold up in an informal setting. Charley has watched the way you handle yourself around the Presidential," he continues more seriously, "and I'm not patronizing you when I say that the staff and guests think you are one hell of a guy. Well, some of the guests," he adds with a smile which I return, "and you know sports inside and out, and you have a great sense of humor. I mean a guy who can laugh at himself on the Carson show just after what happened to you is a pretty special."

"Most of what I did and said was an act."

"Sure, D Jack, but good acting and that's the point. So let me get right to it. As you know, I'm starting up a television station in Miami in October, and as you also know Charley is a major player in this venture. We want you to come on board as sports director in addition to anchoring the prime time sports slot." He pauses, looks me straight in the eye which, of course, he really can't do thanks to the sunglasses, and takes another sip of the cognac. "What do you think?"

What do I think! Whoa, Nellie! Obviously, I've never thought about going into television and, as I am sure you've figured out by now, I've never much thought about doing anything.

"I'm not sure what to think, Mr. Sheridan. I've never really thought of myself as a TV person or celebrity or anything like that."

"But that's just who you are, D Jack," he responds excitedly. "People have heard about you, you're highly intelligent with an uncanny sense of humor, and best of all you were an outstanding athlete. That gives you instant credibility, and whether you believe it or not, maybe people in Boise, Idaho or Erie, Pennsylvania only know you as a baseball footnote, but people in Florida know and admire you.

I smile. "Mr. Sheridan, I really appreciate all your kind words, but this comes right out of the blue and it's something I've obviously never thought about so I'm going to have to kick this around for awhile."

"That's fine with me, D Jack, but I've got more for you to think about. As you already know, I'm big into sports, and I think the Dolphins have really started something in Miami. I'm hoping one of these days this city will be able to land an NBA franchise as well as a major league ball team. And when that happens, I intend to be involved not only as an owner but I want our TV station to be Miami's flagship sports station."

"I hope you're right, Mr. Sheridan. I think Miami can support professional teams, and it would be great for the station to be a major player in reaching fans."

"I'm glad you agree, D Jack. So to kind of kick things off, you may or may not have heard Miami is getting a Double AA team this year."

"Actually I did hear about that; they're gonna play in a new stadium being built in downtown Miami."

"You're right; it's almost finished. At the beginning of the year, we'll announce the team will be the Miami Mets and that I'm the sole owner."

"Wow," I say with genuine surprise, having heard nothing about his involvement, "that's terrific! Congratulations."

"Thanks," Sheridan says with a grin, "and now we're back to square one. I know most of the people in this area know who you are, but you'll need more exposure before the station goes on the air, so I want you to manage the team."

"You're kidding," I say somewhat aghast. "I don't know anything about managing."

"You know people and you know the game, and more importantly, I think you respect both."

"Mr. Sheridan, I've got to be honest with you. When I went out to Arizona State, I not only went as a student but as a hitting coach, and I was flat-out miserable."

"You mean you think you weren't a very good coach?"

"I figure I did okay with the coaching part of it but I was miserable because I wanted to play. That's all I could think about."

"That's understandable. It was too soon, but it's been half a dozen years since you suited up."

"I just don't know, Mr. Sheridan."

He takes a sip of the cognac, and really feeling the need, I knock down more than a taste. "I kind of anticipated your reaction, D Jack, so let me add a few things to see if I can allay your apprehensions. First of all, I once asked Hodges why managers were called managers and not head coaches like all the other major sports. He said the job of a coach is to instruct and refine the skills the players already have. The job of a manager is to manage: manage the game and that entails attending to line-ups; making decisions during a game such as using relief pitchers and pinch-hitters; knowing what to do when the game is on the line; and motivating and getting your guys to play as a team. And eventhough you have to be a PR man on occasion, particularly after a game, all the off-field decisions are more often than not made by the general manager. Finally, seeing as coaches do the coaching, we've already brought on board some talented guys who will be there for you right down the line so, again, as Hodges said, stay out of their way and let them deal with the X and O stuff."

I grin. "You come loaded for bear, don't you Mr. Sheridan?"

"Yes I do," he responds with his own smile.

"Ah, who are you talking about?"

"Well, I told you that Charley is a partner in the TV station and he's also going to be President of the ball club. But the day-to-day operations will be undertaken by our general manager, your old hitting coach, Pepper Kwalchek. Also, the semi-pro team you played with a few times is going to fold but the guy you played for, Leo Blake, is a top-notch baseball man and he's excited about being your bench coach."

"Wouldn't that be kind of awkward for him?"

"He's been around the game for a long time, and if everything goes the way we hope it will, we've told him he'll manage the club next year when you move on to the station. I've got to add that all three of them figured you would be hesitant to do this, so not only will they give you all the support you need, but they agreed that you could pick a coach or two to help you, if you knew of a few that might be up to the task. But they have to be good because we want this first season to be highly successful."

"You're right, Mr. Sheridan," I say with enthusiasm much to my surprise, "and I can think of one who is in the area."

"Okay, fill me in."

"I know this is going to sound daffy, but the best high school kid I ever played with was an all-state catcher who I really think could have made the Bigs. The guy was a natural at the plate, and I think he could be a solid hitting coach and I just saw him a few weeks ago, and I think he might have coached some at the semi-pro level. His name is Rusty Hillen."

"D Jack, generally I don't go along with things that are sight unseen, but I've got confidence in your judgment, so let's add him to your incentive package. Will you do it? I mean all of it?"

"Like I said, Mr. Sheridan, this is all coming at me pretty quickly; I really do need a day or so just to soak it all up."

"And as I said before, that's fine with me," Sheridan responds, getting to his feet and extending his hand, "but if I don't miss my guess, I don't think it's premature to welcome you to the family."

I return his strong handshake and turn to leave as he sits back down to finish his cigar and cognac with what appears to be a very satisfied look on his face. Once out the door I walk down one of the spiral staircases and head for a hand-carved swing that's sitting on a beautiful redwood deck. As agreed upon at dinner, Sam is already waiting there, enjoying the evening sky. With an elevation of just under eight thousand feet and little in the way of city lights, the sky is ablaze with millions of dots of light with Venus very prominent in the western sky and the Big Dipper clear as bell and low on the horizon to the north. Well, not really clear for me, because everything up there looks fuzzy as hell, but I know for others the Dipper is sharp as can be. I take a seat next to Sam on the swing and spend a few moments somewhat in awe of the vastness of Colorado's domed, starlit ceiling.

"Some view, huh Dev?"

"It sure is, and very peaceful. It reminds me of Arizona State when I was a henchman at a guy's wedding up on top of Camelback Mountain."

"What's a henchman?"

"It's like being the best man. Sure was different…a full-blown Druid ceremony."

"Really," she says enthusiastically. "What was it like?"

"Well, think of a wheel. The hub of the wheel is where most of the ceremony takes place, and the rim is formed by the guests who make a circle, leaving an open space at the north, south, east and west ends."

"And what happens in those spaces?"

"Let's see if I can remember," I say thinking back. "I believe at the north the high priestess asks for the blessing of the great bear and fruitful earth; the south is the great stag and the fire of the sun; the east is the hawk of dawn and the pure air: and, I think the west is the salmon of wisdom and the sacred waters but I don't remember which one she went to first."

"So it's all nature and stuff?" Sam says with obvious interest.

"Oh yeah, and you invoke things. One of the fun parts of being the henchman was when the high priestess went to each direction and asked for the blessing and bowed. Then I was supposed to hit a hammer on an anvil."

"Not so!"

"Absolutely, and I did things like meet the high priestess and the couple at the south end, which was fire, and ignited some flammable stuff in a cauldron."

"Wow! What else?"

"Well, the groom wore a kilt and carried an eight-foot sword that he held aloft. That's when I said to the gathering that they could object to the wedding, but I pointed to the sword and suggested it might not be a good idea."

Sam laughs. "So it's like a celebration rather than a serious religious ceremony?"

"Yeah, it's more like a Jewish wedding where there is some serious stuff but lots of laughter, as opposed to a Catholic ceremony that's very solemn."

I notice Sam getting kind of quiet and figure she might be thinking about her own wedding ceremony, so I figure it's time to change the subject. "We sure don't get views like this on Hollywood Beach, do we?"

"Nope, but we had some pretty moonrises over the ocean," she answers reflectively. "So, what was the chat about?"

"I guess you know Sheridan and Charley are starting a major TV affiliate in Miami next month."

"Yes, I've heard about it."

"Well, if I take the job, you're looking at their sports director."

She turns to face me with a big grin. "You're putting me on."

"Is that the best you can do?" I say with a frown.

"Oh, come on. You know what I mean. I assume you said yes?"

"Not yet, there's more."

"What?"

"Sheridan is also bringing a Double AA team to town in a few months, and he wants me to manage the team for the first season to get some exposure before taking on the sports job."

"That's great," she says enthusiastically. "But again, how come you didn't accept his offer?"

"Because both jobs are things I never thought about, and I just want to mull it over for a few days."

"What's there to mull over, Dev?" she says with enthusiasm. "You'll do great. People know who you are, know you were a pro. Besides, you know all kinds of sports trivia. But now that I think of it, that would also qualify you as one hell of a bartender, certainly better than Ron or Daddy, because as the saying goes, I think as a bartender you'd be more than a pharmacist with a limited inventory," she concludes with a giggle.

"Thanks much."

"No, really, you were made for something like this. You've got all the right stuff to do both."

"That's pretty much what Sheridan said. He also thinks lots of people know who I am probably because of the Hall of Fame thing and the sudden end of my career but, hell, it's been more than half a dozen years ago since I was in the public eye."

"No, it wasn't, Dev. It was last week," she says seriously.

"Last week? What are you talking about?" I ask totally perplexed.

"When I was talking with Charley earlier this evening, he asked me if I had seen the latest issue of *Sports Illustrated*. I said no, and I guess you haven't either."

"No. I haven't. What about it?"

"For on of their last issues of the bicentennial, they did a feature story on the five most tragic sports figures in recent times."

"And I'm on it?"

"You're Number Five," she answers solemnly. "The article said it was because the others were all champions in their own right. It went on to say you had all the skills to be great…and it was tragic because you were deprived of the chance to try to make it all happen."

Fuck! Here it comes again. I'm figuring you know by now that I struggle with all of this, and it just won't go away. It seems as if every time I make some progress tucking the whole thing into the past, something comes along and revives it. "Okay," I say with a sigh, "who's on it?"

"Herb Score was fourth. His injury was kind of like yours although he still played for a few years. As I'm sure you know he was the Indians pitcher who got hit in the face when Gil McDougald of the Yankees hit a line drive back to the mound during an All-Star game. Number Three was Benny "Kid" Paret who was killed in the ring.

"I assume Charley filled you in on all these details?"

"He did. Roberto Clemente was two. The article said he may have been the most famous of all, but he was killed in a plane crash rather than during a game or event," she says quietly.

"And Number one?"

"Bill Vukovich was Number One because he won the Indianapolis 500 in 1953 and 1954 and was actually leading the race in 1955 when he was killed."

We both get quiet and the peacefulness of the beautiful sky seems to evaporate. "So, what are you going to do?" Sam asks, returning us to the task at hand.

"I don't know. I'm not sure what's going to go through me if I step onto a ball field."

"So," she repeats with a look that obviously tells me she's prodding me on. "We both know you can't play again, but at least you can get back into the game for a little while," Sam says in a more serious tone.

"Maybe so," I say with a shrug.

"Well, at least you're not making jokes about it."

"What's that supposed to mean?"

"It means I think you have a tendency to deflect serious things with humor or, if not, just make a game out a situation."

"Like what?"

"Like what you were saying about Gerald Ford. Or the whole Schmedler thing as well as diving for golf balls and seeing what Hargraves would pay for it…and how about that whole thing on Collarism when we were talking about you and Daddy?"

"And I suppose you figure that's the wrong approach, right?"

"When is comes to serious matters, yes."

"What would you do if you were me?"

"I'm not you."

"That's a cop-out, Sam. You sound like political candidates trying to get incumbants out of office. They only say what's wrong but never have an answer or solution when it comes to what to do."

"You're right," she admits, "I'm sorry." She gently bites her lip and then continues. "When I think about what you wrote in your letter to the Sheridans, you probably weren't even twenty and it seemed like you had lost it all. Maybe keeping everything at arms-length or frivolous is the right thing to do; maybe it enables you to maintain your mental health."

"What about your mental health? You lost more than I did?"

"You're right again, but I've had Daddy and my kids. You've only had you."

A few moments pass and the conversation has come to a dead stop. It's like when we were kids; if things got heavy, the two of us just clammed up.

"There you two are," Antoinette says, interrupting what was quickly lapsing into a two-ton somber moment. "Samantha, a few of us girls are going to have some after dinner drinks and swap some gossip and lies upstairs, and we were hoping you would join us."

"I'd really enjoy that, Antoinette, but this guy is kind of helpless on his own," Sam says as she points in my direction.

Whoa Nellie. Was that some kind of throw-away line or was she summarizing our conversation. And if it's the latter, are we in the end game or is she going to embark on a reclaimation project? Damn!

"He'll be in good hands. I've also been asked to inform you, D Jack, that the presence of your company for brandy and cigars in the billiard room has been requested by Charley, which means, of course, that you are to join them immediatley."

"When the master calls," I say with a shrug as both Sam and I get to our feet. "I hope you only share the good stuff, Sam," I say half seriously.

"And I hope you run the table like you used to do with Daddy," she answers as she gives me a tap on the shoulder.

Oh well, I think as I head for the boys and the pool table. With her or without her, I guess I might be...*pullen up stakes and headen' for a new show?*

XXI

SOMETHING IN COMMON

I've been out in space, with my head spinning round
for over two years, my feet never touched the ground
but now's about time, to banish all my doubts
get a light in my eye, and getting me up and out

"**H**appy New Year, D Jack," Ron says jubilantly from his ever-present station behind the bar in the Bengal Lounge. "You looked pretty spiffy cruising around in that monkey suit all night."

"Sure, and you tending bar in a tuxedo ain't exactly shabby either."

"Agreed, but I still had to work while all Charley wanted you to do was just wander around and smile at people."

"That's a fact," I say as I slide onto a bar stool and beckon the husky barman to serve up a nightcap, "but it's still being on the clock and, just like you, no dancing or partying. And the bicentennial went its way without anyone special giving me my first 1977 kiss, right?"

"That's the way of it, D Jack," Ron replies as he puts a six-ounce cut glass tumbler in front of me, plops in a few ice cubes, and tops them off with some Crown Royal. "That's what we get for not having family like Marcus and Ralph and even the Turk. Those guys sure were happy to be heading somewhere special tonight I guess," he adds with a tinge of melancholy.

"Maybe next year, Ron."

"You never know. I think I'm actually dating someone."

"Are you fooling me?" I ask somewhat astonished. "Do I know her?"

"Probably, it's Charlene."

"No shit! Charley's administrative assistant?"

"Yep, that's her."

"And she knows she's dating a male prostitute?" I ask with a wry smile.

"I'd rather think of myself as the person around here who provides therapeutically appropriate services for women in need," he responds with his own grin. "Truth is I'm pretty sure she's one of Charley's early reclamation projects, so we might be even in that department."

"Sounds like a match made in heaven."

"Only time will tell. Speaking of which, I need to clean up some glasses and get my ass out of here. When are you leaving?"

"I figure I'll polish off this nightcap and head for the mattress for a few hours of shut-eye. Big day tomorrow what with the high rollers usually feeling sorry for the hired help on New Year's Day."

Ron gives me a knowing smile and then looks over my shoulder, so I slowly turn and see Sam coming into the Bengal Lounge. "I was hoping I might catch you before you left," she says as she walks across the room and beckons me in the direction our personal corner table.

"You want me to bring you something?" I ask surprised but pleased to see her. Actually, during the unbelievably hectic week from Christmas Eve 'til tonight, we had done little more than exchange smiles and pass in the night, although I had gotten the distinct impression that she was feeling increasingly relaxed around me and that as soon as things slowed down, we might actually spend some time together.

"A Bacardi and Pepsi will be fine, thanks." Ron quickly builds his last drink of the night and gives me a wink as I carry it over to the booth.

"Have a good night?" I ask, placing the drink on the table and sitting down across from her.

"You know New Year's Eve. The only day that's better with the tips is Mother's Day."

"Yeah, but mothers shouldn't have to work on Mother's Day, don't you think?"

"I'd rather have Christmas off, which I did, thanks to Charley. Have you talked with him since Aspen?"

"Yeah, we agreed my last day would be February 10th which will give me some time to get acquainted with how things are going to work with the ball club."

"Are you anxious?" she asks somewhat curiously.

"Kinda. The whole idea of launching a career of sorts is a little scary but then I was always a little nervous at the plate, so I figure it's an okay thing."

"See you guys," Ron says as he heads for the door. "How about knocking out the lights and closing up when you leave, okay?"

"Can do, Ron, and happy new year," I reply as Sam gives him a goodnight wave.

"You look pretty dapper in that midnight blue tuxedo, Dev, although the sunglasses are a little out of place," she says seriously. "Why don't you take them off?"

"You already know I'd be uncomfortable without them."

"But I want to see your eyes."

"Why?"

"You know what they say; the eyes are the windows to the soul, and," she adds lightly, "I want to see if you have one."

"Is that a prerequisite for anything you have in mind?" I ask with a smirk.

"Maybe I just want to see if there's any little boy left in you."

"You'd probably be better off looking into the eyes of your own kids."

"I don't think so," she says and then pauses. "I don't remember where, maybe at Morgan's Inn, but you told me we had nothing in common, right?" she says rhetorically, changing the subject. "But we do have something in common, something very important."

"I guess you're talking about the past but for the life of me I can't think of anything else."

"Nothing at all?" she responds with a disappointed look on her face.

"Okay," I admit. "This is going to be shaky ground for me but there are times over the past month or so that I got a glimmer of hope and thought maybe there was something and we could try again, you know, be close friends or something like that, but I've just kind of held myself in check."

"Why?"

"Maybe because the sages say you can never go back. It's kind of like a jigsaw puzzle," I say, thinking back to my all time favorite puzzle of Dumbo sitting in a tree while the crows are laughing their asses off.

"Say you've got this favorite puzzle and maybe it's got a hundred pieces and maybe you put it together three or four times. But then somewhere along the line you lose just one piece and the puzzle can never again be complete or whole; it's ruined, but you can't throw it out. So you put in way back on a top shelf in a closet and you quit on it." I pause and note the seriousness in her eyes. "With wrongs," I continue, my tone matching her expression, "you can't throw them out, so you stick them as far back into your brain as you can, and then it's not much of a step before you start to give up and not really hope for much of anything."

"I don't believe that, Dev. Whether you want to admit it or not, and lots of people don't quit on the missing piece of the puzzle; they keep looking for it. But when it comes to life, they often just have to try to find something that fits." She sighs. "Have you ever considered that things could be even better than they were for us when we were just wet-nosed kids?"

"What could have been better than you going for the gold in Mexico City in '68 or in Munich in '72 and me actually *earning* a World Series ring in '69.

"Even if those things had happened, I'd be out of diving by now and you'd be at least halfway through your career. And when you finished, then what? What were you figuring we would do when we were thirty-five or forty-five or sixty-five?"

"You know the answer to that, Sam," I say quietly. "I never thought about any of those things."

"I didn't either," she admits candidly, "but now here we are with our whole adult lives ahead of us, so again, what are you apprehensive about, Dev? Is the thought of holding hands with a widow with kids too much for you?"

"I'm confused. In that restaurant in Auburn, you're the one who said things were complicated and you needed time to figure things out."

"Yes, I did, but I wasn't referring to maybe you and me dating. It was something else."

"Fine," I say, "then to answer your question about holding hands, I don't believe in that baggage stuff, but if anything, it's obvious if we tried to have a go at it, you'd be the one taking on the baggage. And for both of us, the past and its eight hundred pound gorilla will never go away."

"I know," she says with half a smile, "but over time, that gorilla can lose weight if we work on it together."

Ya know, guys, I'm kinda surprised she seem's to be pushing for some kind of a relationship; I mean, this is really coming out of the blue.

"Maybe so," I respond thoughtfully, "but there's together and there's together. I guess it's all a matter of degree. Other than my dad and a few years with you, I've been alone all the way, and the idea of things like picnics in the park, going to the beach, maybe even a dance recital at school some day are experiences I never thought about; I mean, you know, like doing neato keazeto things with someone special, and her kids, too," I add quickly.

"And maybe having a catch? As you love to say, would that be neato keazeto?" she adds with a nervous grin as she reaches for her Bacardi and Pepsi.

"Obviously," I say as I feel some color come into my face.

"Is there anything else while you're speculating?" she inquires, seemingly to urge me on.

"Well, the ballplayer in me would say having a catch with my own kid would be toward the top of the wish list, so if we ever got to be more than good friends maybe down the line that could be a dream come true."

I quickly look down at my drink. "Sorry about that," I hurriedly add self-consciously. "That's pretty personal, but you're the one who asked."

Sam replaces her drink on the cocktail napkin and takes both of my hands into both of hers, and I notice her eyes are misting. "You can do that now."

"Do what now?"

"Have a catch."

Have a catch now? Am I missing something here? You've gotten to know her. Do you have any idea what she's talking about? "I think what you just said went way over my head, Sam."

"You talk about getting personal," she says, her voice full of apprehension as she inhales deeply. "I've been trying to find the right time and, like I said, figure things out, because I knew I was going to have to tell you this sooner or later, and it's really going to be hard, but I think this time is as good as any. Do you remember the gold chain I was wearing at Sheridan's party?"

"You mean the one with the three gold beads?"

"Yes. Do you know what the gold beads on the chain stand for?"

"No."

"Each one represents the children I've had," she says as she exhales very slowly."

I mull over that statement for a moment and realize I'm not surprised that she would include Sean along with the girls. "I think it's wonderful that you think of Sean as one of your own. I can't imagine how important it is for him to have that kind of acceptance."

"I don't just think of Sean as one of my own," she says, her eyes now wet with tears. "What I'm finally sharing with you is that we do have something in common, Dev, and it's the missing piece of the puzzle. Sean is our child…he's your son."

Oh my God! Whoa, Nellie!

There are times in life, although I think few and far between, when you're just flat speechless, so I just sit there and look at her because so much in the past becomes instantly and abundantly clear to me. No wonder she belted me so hard in Lakeland that last time I saw her. No wonder it was Billy who met me on a street corner and still hates my guts. No wonder she quit diving. No wonder she seems intent on some kind of a relationship. WHOA NELLIE!!

"Why didn't you tell me?" I ask incredulously.

She squeezes my hands. "Devon, how was I going to tell a teenage superstar he was going to be a father? I knew where your focus was, your passion, your life. I couldn't bring myself to interfere with that."

My mind quickly shifts to Rusty Hillen having a kid but only for a fleeting moment. "But you never gave me a choice, Sam" I say dejectedly.

"That's true . I had no intention of putting you in a position where you had to make a choice."

"And your diving injury, did that actually happen?"

"It did, but I was pregnant so it was time to stop."

"And did you really have a cousin in Jersey?"

"I did and I do. She's alive and well, I'm happy to say," Sam responds with her first genuine smile of the evening. "I gave birth to Sean in Camden and she agreed to keep him until the time came that I might be able to take him home. After Dolph was killed and the twins got a little more manageable, I concocted the story and went to Jersey to get him."

"Did Dolph ever know?"

"No, I figured sooner or later I would have to tell him but I've told you what our relationship was, so I just put it away. Then we obviously ran out of time."

"I assume Sean doesn't know I'm his father? God," I say with a strange mixture of sadness and awe, "I think I'm still in shock just thinking about this, and you, and him."

"No, he thinks his folks died in Jersey. He doesn't have a clue that I'm his mother either, but I think we can change that if it's what you want."

"I'd rather not," I say seriously, still trying to process such an unexpected revelation, "at least not about me, not now."

"Why do you feel that way?"

"Because all I would be is his biological father, and I think he's probably too young to handle the fact that his dad is just his mother's friend."

"You said you'd be surprised if we could ever be more than friends. Why did you say that?"

"I think you can answer that for yourself, Sam."

She takes her hands from mine and takes a sip of her cocktail while appearing to consider my response. "Okay, we've already agreed an eight hundred pound gorilla is in the room, and honestly, it would be difficult to totally commit to you right now," she says candidly, "because I'm not so sure a person can have complete faith and trust in a person more than once," she concludes.

"And I'm not sure I could completely commit to a person who'll probably never truly be in love with me again," I add, matching her matter-of-fact tone.

"So where do we go from here?" she inquires softly and then adds contemplatively, "I guess if we didn't have Sean, the answer would be simple."

"Do you really think so?"

She fiddles with her drink for a few moments. "Not really," she admits. "We share a bitter-sweet past, but some warmth has started to overcome the coldness I've felt up until the last month."

"And?"

"And I really don't know, Dev, but I do think I learned with Dolph that people can care for each other without necessarily being romantically in love with each other. Do you understand what I am saying?"

"What I understand, Sam is that you seem to be suggesting there's a pretty fine line between caring and loving. Do you care about or do you love your dog, your car, or a sunrise? And even if you do love those things, none of them can return any kind of emotion."

"You should listen to yourself, Dev."

"What do you mean?"

"As I've said before, you're only true love was for the game, and she gave you nothing."

"I've got a few good memories," I respond defensively.

"Are they enough to offset the fact that she robbed you of your youth and blinded you from seeing how wonderful our future could have been?"

Suddenly, Sam seems to shudder and quickly, once again, takes hold of both my hands. "I'm so sorry, Dev," she says in a whisper. "I didn't mean to say anything about your being bli…."

"That's okay, Sam," I say quickly. "I know what you meant."

Things get quiet, but I'm kind of surprised that she's still holding my hands in hers. "Your Baseball Queen abandoned you at home plate in Shea, and when it all was said and done, you had played your heart out and, like Pastrano said, there wasn't any glory," Sam says softly. "She left you alone, didn't she, Dev? And like you said, you've been alone to this day."

"My choice…since then I haven't seen the point to reaching out to anything or anyone."

"So all the people around here haven't seen the real Devon Jameison, have they?"

"They've seen as much as I'm capable of."

"That sounds like my dad," Sam says with some sadness. "After he lost Mom and my sister, all the guilt that had welled up in him seemed to just wash away any feelings of love. So all he's been capable of showing me over the years is that he cares for me. But I still love him. So," she continues, challenging, "how about love for a parent who really cares for you but doesn't love you back?"

"Point well taken but blood sustains that relationship, and that's obviously something a man and a woman don't share."

"So, in your opinion, can something take the place of blood?"

"I think you've already answered that one; faith and trust can do it, but I'd add passion. That's what I really think being in love is about, and it's not logical or rational. I don't think you can create it or make it happen."

"So you're saying you don't think a man and a woman can have a successful relationship even if they really do care for each other?"

"Not indefinitely."

"Maybe so, but I've always believed tomorrow is a new day and anything is possible."

"Tomorrow can also serve up a load of regret, Sam," I say cautiously.

"For you?"

"Maybe, maybe not...but then, other than me, I suspect you don't have any regrets, do you?"

"You don't have a monopoly on making mistakes, Dev," she says with that little bit of fire in her eyes.

"I hope you're not referring to Sean," I say anxiously.

"No, I'm referring to Dolph."

"I don't agree with that. Dolph was a fine person; you married the best of the best, Sam."

"Yes, I did marry the best of the best, but he didn't. After you, I was obsessed with being my own person. It wasn't fair for me to marry him because, like you say, the passion wasn't really there. So I guess I wasn't truly in love with him, but then I really think it was all about me being paranoid, about being dominated by anyone again. I deeply regret all that and the really sad part is that I think he knew it. So I guess he just figured he would take what I was willing to give and call it happiness or love or, like I said, caring."

"And, as you also like to say, everything is measured in degrees," I say, feeling somewhat uncomfortable with her confession. "So, how much weight do you think the gorilla can lose?" I inquire, trying to get us back on track. "Or put in another way, what do you really want?" I ask sincerely.

She barely pauses. "I want to be a full-time mom. I want to put the kids to bed and take Sean to school. I want to sit at a breakfast table and go shopping and take care of Daddy," she says and then quietly adds, "and, at least for Sean's sake, I want us to try to make some kind of go of it, not the way it was when we were kids but with things like respect and trying to attend to each others wants and needs."

"I think I can do that," I say quietly without hesitation.

"She simply nods in agreement, takes her hands from mine, and then finishes her drink. I do the same and get to my feet. "Shall we?" I say supportively.

Sam stands up and I take our glasses over to a stainless steel sink behind the bar and then meet her at the door of the Lounge. I throw the light switches and secure the room, after which the two of us hang a right and head for the entrance. Once through the double doors we are greeted by an unseasonably warm evening with the ever-present breeze rustling the palm fronds. I figure the sky is crystal clear and I'm thinking, or maybe wishing, the three massive stars that I used to see in Orion's belt might be relighting our way. I suddenly remember something and reach into my pocket for the ring Sam had handed me at Sheridan's party.

"Sorry, I forgot to return this to you," I say, extending the gold band to her.

Sam quietly takes her wedding ring, but rather than slip it on her finger she puts it in the side pocket of her uniform.

"Take off your sunglasses, Devon."

This time I do as I'm told, and she looks into my bad eye, complete with a total lack of focus as she runs her finger across what's left of an eyebrow that's little more than scar tissue. She then shifts her attention to my right eye, seems to realize that that one is less than perfect, and repeats her caress along that equally sparse line of hair.

"What?" I ask with a smile

"I can almost see a little boy," she answers and then, after pausing and looking hard at my souvenirs from the Show, she asks, "Do you still have pain?"

"Some now and then," I respond self-consciously, more from her gaze than her question.

Sam stands on tiptoe and gently kisses one eybrow and then the other. "Do you think that might make it better?"

"I hope so," I answer, somewhat hesitantly.

"You see, Dev," she says with a grin, "you said you don't believe in hope, but deep down you do. And who knows? Maybe those dreams will be our dreams."

"And deep down, what might those dreams be, Sam?"

She pauses to deliberate, her eyes reflecting something from within. "Do you want to kiss me, Devon, softly and tenderly?"

Okay, if you recall, those wonderous moments with her on Hollywood Beach often began with soft and tender kisses, so maybe things won't be as platonic as it sounds. And yeah, I promise to try hard not to invoke some philospher's view of life all the time. But I think you know Sam by now and realize this is probably a big step for her; hell, I guess that goes for me, too. And I know I'm 0-1 when it comes to being *kissed by her smile* but her grin tells me I might have a chance of batting .500.

"That's not the right question, Samantha. When we were out on the fifth green for our midnight picnic and you wanted to bet that I wanted to kiss your hand for good luck, I said you would lose because of your ground rules. So the bottom line is…do you want to softly and tenderly kiss me?"

Rather than reply, she steps towards me and slowly closes her eyes…while just a few feet away I hear G.D. mumble, "Dis gotta be da lass season."

**

BOOK II

THE MIAMI METS

I guess more players lick themselves that are ever licked by an opposing team. The first thing any man has to know is how to handle himself.

Connie Mack

I cannot get rid of the hurt from losing, but after the last out of every loss, I must accept that there will be a tomorrow. In fact, it's more than there'll be a tomorrow, it's that I want there to be a tomorrow. That's the big difference, I want tomorrow to come

Sparky Anderson

I

GOODBYE TO THE PRESIDENTIAL

There's nothing greater in the world
than when somebody on the team
does something good,
and everybody gathers around
to pat him on the back.
Billy Martin, Manager
Minnesota Twins/Detroit Tigers/Texas Rangers
New York Yankees/Oakland Athletics

It's been about two months since we last chatted, and I'm not sure you remember Charlie "T" Moon. Just in case you need a refresher, he's one hell of a story song man and musician who plays acoustical guitar in the plush Bengal Lounge at the Presidential Golf and Country Club. Hopefully, you do remember I've been playing back-up guitar for him since November along with two neato keazeto brothers, one of 'em plays bass and the other one is on drums. Right now, it's about 1:00 a.m. on a Saturday night. Well now that I think of it, it's actually Sunday morning, February 27th, if you really need to know. Anyway, Moon just finished the last set with one of our new ones. The lyrics are about a guy packing his bags and moving on to a new show, so it's pretty obvious this story song is about me.

I look around the dimly lit room and smile at the few patrons who are closing out their bar tabs. I catch Charlie's eye, and he just gives me a wink and a nod as he heads for the door. For a guy who writes such terrific music, and some occasional lyrics, it's surprising that he's never been one for words, now even more so, because I think he's really not into the goodbye scene. He said earlier in the evening that he was getting a regular gig at a place called Sketch on Hollywood Beach, and really wanted me to sit in with him on a regular basis; he thinks we could do well enough to pay the bills. Truth be known, I'd love it, but my immediate future is pretty well set, so I figure the books are shut on that one.

The two brothers give me big hugs and even a couple of kisses on the cheek which doesn't come as any big shock. They're both warm and affectionate kind of guys, and on Saturday night they usually do some extra weed between sets. They finish off our last hurrah with big grins and then set about stowing their equipment. I take my classical Yamaha G-51, place it in my fake alligator case, and step down from the small stage located in the back right corner of the lounge. Then I head for the long, mahogany bar which is graced with elegant cut-glass bowls of cashews, smoked almonds, and walnuts. I guess I never shared much with you about the bar, but now that I'm leaving, I'm seeing it in a different light. There are about eight or ten plush barstools in front of the bar itself. Behind it, you can find every brand of hard alcohol and liqueurs known to mankind, well, and womankind too, given the social acceptability of sexual equality when it comes to bending the elbow. Anyway, the bottles appear to be endless, thanks to all their reflections in the etched, wood-framed mirrors that rise to the ceiling of the lounge. The rest of the upscale room houses small red leather-backed, couches with deep-cushioned, matching seats and a few large sofas bracketed by mahogany hardwood end tables. It goes without saying that the lighting is soft and the room is just flat out romantic...but I'll say it anyway.

Ron, my favorite bartender, is standing behind his 'work station.' He gives me a big shit-eaten' grin as I plunk down onto one of the barstools. Then, he places a glass in front of me, pours about four fingers of VO Canadian whisky, and drops in two or three ice cubes.

"That's your last one on the Presidential, D Jack," he says with even a wider grin if that's possible. "From this point on, you're nothing but a paying customer."

"Ah, the pangs of losing fringe benefits," I say with a moan, and then proceed to down half the drink.

"So then, this is it?"

I slowly look around the room and think about the good times I've had playing with Moon. Then my thoughts settle on the love seat in the dimly lit back corner of the lounge where, if you recall, me and Mrs. Samantha Frederickson had our first confrontation, after more than half a dozen years of not seeing one another. Man, that 'Mrs.' still sounds awfully weird.

"Yeah, Stunt Man. This is the bottom of the ninth for me in this place."

"You almost sound melancholy, D Jack. I find that surprising. After all, you know what G.D. up at the front door is always mumblin."

"Yeah, I do. He's always mumblin 'dis gotta be da lass season.'"

"And that's what most of us are always hoping for, so I see it as you being one of the lucky ones."

"I guess I ought to feel that way, but I've got lots of good memories of this place…and I made some damn good friends, too," I add reflectively.

"Moving on isn't always the perfect thing. But, again, the way I see it, you've got some really exciting irons in the fire. That ought to be your focus, right?"

I grin.

"What?" he asks with the smile still on his face.

"Stunt Man, I've known you for a few years, and this is the first time you've pulled the wise ole bartender shit on me."

"And I ain't even gonna charge you a fee."

"Well, that's a relief. The last time you did that was when you loaned me that photo of you nailing Dawson's French wife. Hell, I didn't even get to use it to collect my bet with Marcus."

"Those days are done, D Jack. No more Stunt Man."

"You mean you and Charlene are pretty serious?"

"You may find it hard to believe, but yes. The two of us really are having a fine time, and we're thinking about sharing some rent."

"Way to go, Ron."

"What about you and Samantha?"

"What about me and Samantha?" I respond, wondering what kind of rumors are flying around the Clubhouse.

"Well, everybody knows the two of you flew up to Auburn to pick up Major Rollstone's sheep dog and that she went with you out to Aspen for Mrs. Sheridan's birthday party. So, you know. People talk."

"Really," I say sounding vaguely interested. "And what are they talking about?"

"Ah, hell, D Jack," Ron says sounding like a kid who just got caught with his hand in the cookie jar.

"Come on. Bring it, Ron"

I got to tell ya. That "bring it" used to be one of my favorite expressions, but that was when I was playing for the Suns in Jacksonville, and trying to stare down a pitcher. Well, for the Mets too, up in Shea Stadium, but as you know, that was a one night stand.

"Okay then," he says with a sigh. "The word is that the two of you used to date in high school and you haven't seen each other until a few months ago when she started a double shift here and…you know."

"No. I don't know. You tell me." Now I'm getting annoyed.

"That's really about it. But some of us are pretty curious as to what happened. Knowing you, we figure back then, she dumped ya," he concludes with a friendly smile and a soft chuckle.

"Well, you got that one right, Ron," I say taking the edge off my voice.

"I'll bet it was up in Jax when you were playing for the Suns. Weren't you the rookie of the year, or the MVP, or both or something like that?"

"You're right on all counts. I guess I got too full of myself and really got stupid."

"So what did Samantha do?"

"She got married and now has two kids and a ward."

"She does, really? I can't recall, but I don't think she wears a wedding band. Did she get a divorce or what?"

"Sadly, it's the 'or what', Ron. I knew the guy, and he was top-shelf. He was a helicopter pilot and he got shot down and killed in Nam in '72."

"That's too bad," he says somberly. "I was there in '68 in the Tet Offensive. It was a shitty time, D Jack," he adds quietly.

"I never knew that."

"Well, I don't talk about it much, and try to think about it even less. Okay then, wise guy," Ron continues trying to lighten things up. "I'm still not getting anything out of you as usual. Are you and Samantha dating?"

"Uh, I think so, but I'm not sure."

"What the hell kind of answer is that? Either you is or you ain't."

"Not so. I think it's a definite maybe. Last month, in fact, it was New Years Eve, we agreed to see each other, but since then she's been totally preoccupied with Billy."

"Yeah, I was wondering about that. Her old man is okay, and I enjoy bartending with him, but he's been kind of scarce lately."

"I know. His doctors had to run all kinds of tests on him. He's been losing weight, lots of fatigue, stuff like that. Just a few days ago Sam told me he's been diagnosed with diabetes, so that really explains things."

"She really loves her Dad a lot, doesn't she?"

"As far as I know, she thinks the world of him."

"And he's pretty tight-lipped, but he's slipped a few times. I gather there sure as hell's no love lost between you and him."

"You're batting a thousand tonight, Ron."

"The stupid stuff, huh?"

"It's a little more complicated than that. But, yeah, the stupid stuff."

"I know D Jack. I've done some stupid stuff too, but when the horse leaves the barn, there's not much of a fucken thing you can do about it," he says with what almost sounds like some bitterness in his voice.

It gets quiet, both of us lost in our own thoughts, but Ron decides to get us past the moment. "So, how do you feel about going back out on the ball field?"

"I'm pretty anxious about it. After Shea, I coached a little at Arizona State while I was going to school and actually tried to play a little semi-pro down here last year, but it all went south."

"I can't even imagine what that must have been like," Ron responds empathetically. "Charley and Bottomly say you had the whole package and could have been something out there."

"Well, nobody really knows when he's playing his last game," I say with a shrug, "such is life." On that note of finality, I knock down the rest of the VO and get to my feet.

"I guess it's time to call in the dogs and piss on the fire, D Jack."

"I don't think I need the dogs, Ron. I get the feeling a number of fires are going out on their own." I extend my hand, "let's keep in touch, you know?"

"Sure thing, man," he says, giving me a firm shake and a genuine smile. There's really nothing left to say, so I head for the door that leads out of the Bengal Lounge and into the Clubhouse's spacious foyer.

Obviously, it still looks the same with its leather couches and cherry-wood end tables, all sitting on plush, brown, shag carpets that run wall-to-wall. Just like the bar though, when you look at something for maybe the last time, it just seems different. I hang a right and exit through the double-paneled, wood-polished front doors. Rather than head for the employees' parking lot, down and off to the left of the huge cinnamon brick circular driveway bordered by red, yellow, and blue flowerbeds, even though we're in the middle of February, I turn to the right and head down the stone path. Once past the pro shop, I walk up the small hill toward the redwood bench that sits on the side of the putting green. For the better part of the past year, as you may recall, this bench has been my special place, a place of solitude and deep thoughts. Well, maybe not so deep.

By now I figure it's got to be well after 1:30. Maybe it's a good omen that a full moon is high above the two shade trees that frame the bench. A soft breeze rustles the leaves, although it's unseasonably warm with the temp probably in the low 70's. I plunk down on the bench, stretch out my legs, and lean back with my hands clasped behind my head. I'm a bit surprised that my thoughts focus on tomorrow, because it's been a long time since I've done little more than live day-to-day.

And eventhough those days at the Presidential were kind of boring, sometimes almost depressing, there was something secure in all of it. I mean, I know I wasn't going anywhere, and was just spinning my wheels, but there was a certain comfort in it; no stress and nothing on the line. Sure, Marcus was always kicking my butt trying to get me to 'do something useful' as he so often put it. But now I think about it, deep down, maybe I was happy just being one of the guys.

And speaking of the guys, the farewell scene with Marcus earlier in the day was just God-awful! It was one of those deals when you know what someone wants to say, and you know what you want to say, but neither is able to bring it off. So, there were a few quiet platitudes tossed on the table; a little shifting of weight from foot-to-foot; and a sincere but very quiet, hug.

Ralph and the Turk were a lot easier. Those guys, along with Ron and, of course, Marcus, always made me feel like I was a part of the team. It really made me feel good that each of them, in one way or another, gave me a parting pat on the shoulder.

Speaking of goodbyes, it's interesting that now and then I think it would have been a good thing to have walked away when Howard Sheridan dropped his bombshell on me in Aspen this past December. I mean, the guy swings a whole new career at me with this sports director thing, but that's not until next year, so I agree to manage the new Miami Mets, which is part of the deal. And that's something I really don't want to do. But it all happened so fast. And now, I'm sitting on this redwood bench thinking the full moon above the trees may not be a good sign at all. I guess the long and short of it is…I'm wondering what the fuck I'm doing!

And then, there's Samantha. Over the past few months, I thought she was beginning to see me in a new light. But now, I'm wondering if all of that was just because I'm Sean's father. Well, not all of it. She seems to have warmed up some, but I've just got it in the back of my mind that I'm never really going to shine in her eyes. Maybe that's just the past talking, ya think?

Okay, then. I'm really trying to be up front with you. But with Ron, I wasn't about to come clean about Samantha. Sure, she's a widow and lives with her father and three kids, but I wasn't going to share with him she actually gave birth to all three and I'm the father of the oldest. I also said I hoped he and Charlene might make a go of it. But the best I could muster up for me and Sam was to mumble something about dating. I guess that's because I really don't know. She said on New Year's Eve she wanted to try to make a go of it probably because of Sean. But again, I've hardly seen her during the past two months and when I think about that mental health conversation at Sheridan's place in Aspen, I'm not sure what she wants to do.

We talked some last month and I understand her preoccupation with Billy and his health situation. And I know it's been important to give her the time and space she needs to settle everything down. So, I just told her to get in touch when she was ready. She knew I was heading out Thursday for the Mets spring training camp at the brand new, three and a half million dollar Al Lang Stadium in St. Petersburg.; therefore, I've got to think it wasn't a coincidence that she called me Saturday to see if I could come by her house tomorrow night and take her to the Orange Bowl for pizza.

The "come by her house" thing is really going to be tough. It will be the first time I see Sean knowing he's my son. And it's also going to be the first time I see Billy, knowing finally why he's been mad as hell at me all these years.

And then, of course, the Orange Bowl. That's where it all started for me and Sam back in high school. Those few years were happy ones. I guess the problem is, for lots of us, sometimes we don't really appreciate something until afterwards. Yeah, I know it's the big enchilada cliché that you don't realize what you have until you lose it. Unfortunately, if that's true, it can equally be said that it's human nature to want it back, and ninety-nine times out of one hundred, it just ain't gonna happen.

One thing is going to happen for sure; when the clock strikes 6:00 a.m. this morning, I won't be hopping on my jet-black Yamaha 500cc 4-stroke TX 500, loading up with a breakfast cheek of H. B. Scott leaf tobacco, and heading for the Presidential.

With that thought, I get to my feet and survey the moonlit putting green for the last time. I don't know how you deal with things like this, but when I close the book on a chapter of my life, I try to figure out if something good came from it. Did I learn anything? Did I grow a little bit as a person? Am I better off for the time I spent doing whatever was at hand? So, now I'm looking at the Presidential and processing the eighteen months I toiled for the rich and famous. I'm really racking my brain to find a few pearls, but am settling on the inescapable conclusion that I did little more than tread water, literally, if you recall my midnight swimming escapade in the pond next to the fifth green!

Now, you might say, you *did* reconnect with Samantha, and Howard Sheridan provided you with a golden opportunity and an opened door.

Okay. I understand that. But you already know I'm not exactly an optimist by nature. Yeah, I know that I philosophically bullshit all the time, but this ain't the same thing. You won't find Murphy or his mega-pessimistic laws in any classical philosophy text. But I seem to quote his negative take on life more than the grandiose thoughts expressed by all those great minds.

So, when it comes to Sam, there's reconnect and then there's *really* reconnect. That could mean anything from, "let's spend this life together," to "we tried, see you in the next life." As for Howard Sheridan and opened doors, if you ever read the *Lady and the Tiger*, those doors don't always lead to awesome things.

You know. Maybe the problem is that I've been too passive about what's been going on. I mean, I think I was right to let Sam set all the rules, seeing as she was the aggrieved party. But now, maybe I need to step up to the plate, rather than just sit back and wait for her to tell me what our relationship is going to be, or might be, or isn't going to be. Hell, just like playing ball, I'd rather go down swinging instead of just standing there and taking a called-strike three! That ain't pretty but if it ever happens to you make sure you stay as far away from your manager as possible.

And, seeing as I'm on a roll here, maybe I need to do the same thing with Sheridan, even though he's been one prince of a guy. Up to this point, he's decided what doors to open, but I've got to decide what I'm going to do after I walk through them.

Man, this is exhausting.

I take a deep breath, turn, and make my way back down the hill towards the fork in the stone path. I head for the parking lot with the assurance of knowing where that narrow path will take me. As for the bigger path I'm about to travel, I'm not so sure. But, maybe *the grass will be greener* and maybe, just maybe, *I will find some peace of mind.*

II

THE ORANGE BOWL

People who live in the past…generally are afraid to compete in the present. I've got my faults, but living in the past is not one of them. There's no future in it.
Sparky Anderson, Manager
Cincinnati Reds/Detroit Tigers

I remember being really nervous the first time I knocked on the front door at Dewey Street, in Hollywood, Florida, on a cloudy Sunday afternoon. The Thursday night before, Samantha had quietly approached me at the Hollywood Teen Center just to say hi. Well, I hate to admit it, but by my senior year in high school, I was already trying to alleviate the baseball stress with eighty-six proof. Not a lot, mind you. Just a sip or two, mixed with some H. B. Scott leaf chewing tobacco, to take the edge off, and I always packed a pocketful of mints. Being quiet anyway, I remember mumbling something and then walking away with a half-hearted, "Nice to meet ya."

Anyway, I felt bad about it, because she looked pretty down in the dumps. So, I called her the next day and asked her if she would like to go out Sunday afternoon to play some miniature golf and maybe bounce around on some trampolines. I don't know why I was so relieved when she agreed, but I was. That should have told me something from day one.

I didn't have a car, but we only lived four blocks away from each other. So, after I knocked on her door, we walked down to Hollywood Beach Boulevard and took the bus to a small amusement park in North Miami Beach.

We had fun! I beat her in miniature golf but only by one stroke. And she got a hole-in-one on the eighteenth and won a free game. As for the trampoline, it wasn't even close. I knew Sam was on the diving team but had no idea how good she was. While I was doing little more than jumping up and down, Sam was throwing double flips, twists, and all kinds of stuff. When I took her home and left her at the front door, she was smiling, and I was feeling really good about myself. Off the ball field, that didn't happen very often. Three days later she was wearing my high school ring around her neck. Dad spotted me a few bucks and I got it from a pawn shop.

The point of sharing some past history with you is to explain my current level of nervousness. Here I am knocking on that same door eight or nine years later, and I'm downright petrified! Among other things, how I react to seeing Sam's little girls and Sean is something I can control. But how Billy is going to treat me is entirely up to him, and I'm just hoping he'll keep things civil because of the kids. The door starts to open, and I'm suddenly aware of the fact that I've stopped breathing.

Check that. I'm breathing…and hearing the giggles of the two, five-year-old girls who have answered the door. I wait briefly for a greeting but figure they're not up to it.

"Hello," I say pleasantly with a smile.

More giggles, but they step back, so in I go just as Samantha comes into the small living room.

"Hi," she says softly as the girls scurry to her side. "This is Rebecca and this is Jessica. Say hi to Devon, girls."

More giggles, so Sam gives me a nod which I pick-up as a cue of sorts. "Hello, Rebecca. Hello, Jessica. I'm pleased to meet both of you," I say as I extend my hand. Both move forward and each gives me a soft touch of a hand while they continue to giggle.

"Okay girls," Sam says with what I perceive as a pound or two of relief. "Go into your bedroom and get your sweaters so we can go to Sean's practice."

After the two of them scamper off to the bedroom, Sam hits me with a sweet smile. "Thanks for being so friendly," she says as she comes over and gives me a peck on the cheek. I'm a little disappointed, but maybe the sisterly kiss is because the kids are in the next room.

"They're cute."

"Do you think they look like me?"

"I'd like to make some points here, but I think it's too early to tell. Maybe in four or five years, if they're still strawberry blondes, they'll be pretty close."

"Okay then. Do you think Sean looks like me?"

"The one time I met him, I wasn't looking at him that way. But then, do you think he looks like me?" I ask quizzically.

She quickly turns, probably to make sure the girls are out of earshot. "Actually, I do think he looks a little more like you than me, but…"

"So, what's happening this evening," I say as pleasantly as I can while clearly conveying that we need to move on to another topic.

She smiles so it appears we're on the same page. "We're going over to Jefferson Park to drop off the girls. Sean's practice is over around 7:30, and Daddy will watch the three of them, get some pizza, and then come home."

"You mean they're going to join us at the Orange Bowl?"

"No," she responds still smiling. "We get the good stuff, and they go to the store and get the Totino's frozen."

"That sounds okay to me." Damn, she's drop dead gorgeous, and I think I'll say so. "Uh…you look very pretty this evening, Samantha. I've missed seeing you."

"Thanks, Devon," she replies appreciatively. "It's been a tough couple of months. I'm sorry I haven't been in touch very much."

"Hey, I understand. But at least Billy's got a diagnosis, so now you know what to do, and how to handle things."

"It's more than that, Devon." Her expression clearly shows the strain she's been under.

"You mean with Billy?"

"No. There's just more."

"We can talk about it over pizza if you like."

"I would, Devon. I'd like that very much."

Whoa, Nellie. I don't have a clue what all this is about, but obviously I'm going to find out. The little bit of silence has become uncomfortable, but fortunately, giggle #1 and giggle #2 skip back into the living room holding their sweaters and obviously ready to go.

"So, do you want to walk the girls over to the park or squeeze them in on your lap and go over in the Jag?" I ask.

"We'll squeeze in. It's only a few blocks, and the girls will get a thrill out of it."

"That's fine; ready to go?"

"Yep, let's do it."

Sam takes both girls by the hand and heads out the door towards the car. Seeing the Jag, the girls squeal with delight and tug Sam towards the sleek XK-120. "How about if I get in first and then you can lift the girls on to my lap," she says.

"Sounds like a plan."

Sam reaches over the side of the car and pulls the leather strap on the inside that opens the door. She then lowers herself into the bucket seat, and

I lift the girls one at a time over the door and pass them down to her. It's pretty cramped, but like Sam said, Jefferson Park is only a few blocks away. I move around the front of the long-hooded Jag and then slide down into the driver's seat. There's just room enough for me to manipulate the short gear shift housed in a small leather-covered box on the floor between the two seats. I push the starter button and rev her up to about four thousand rpm's, just for the fun of it.

"Are we ready to go, girls?"

Sam nods, and the girls are wide-eyed. I depress the small, rubber-padded clutch, shift into first gear, and slowly glide away from the house. As the girls squeal with excitement, Sam grins from ear-to-ear. The few blocks go by quickly, but I'm still kind of relieved to pull up at the park on the first base side of the ball field.

I quickly secure the car, get out, and walk around so Sam can lift each of them out to me. They barely touch the ground before running for the stands, having already spotted Billy who is waving at them from the first wood-planked row.

"Looks like they really love their grandfather," I say as I extend my hand to help Sam exit from the low-slung sports car.

"He's really great with them," she beams with obvious pride.

"Is he equally great with Sean?"

"Yes, he is Devon. He loves his grandson."

"I'm relieved to hear that. I really am."

That said we walk toward the stands where Rebecca and Jessica have already found a spot on each of Billy's knees. Once again, I feel the anxiety meter climbing as we approach him. I hang back a step or two so Sam can greet her Dad, which she does by putting her hands on his shoulders and giving him a daughterly kiss on the cheek.

"How's the practice going, Daddy?" She backs away just a bit so I can approach him.

"It's going good, pumpkin. Sean's already been in the cage and got in a lot of good licks." He pauses. "Hello, Devon."

"Hello, Billy."

A few seconds pass before he reluctantly offers his hand. I suspect Sam asked him to do so. I extend my hand as we briefly greet each other, without smiles. "Samantha told me you've had a diagnosis and that you're getting better already. That's good news."

He picks up on the tone of my voice. "The diet is nasty, but I'm coming along. Thanks."

The next few seconds are flat-out uncomfortable, probably because he knows…that I know... I'm Sean's father, and neither of us can come up with any further words. Fortunately, the child in question bounds over to where we're sitting and greets Sam with a big hug and then, to my surprise, hugs each of the girls. This whole thing just feels surreal. He doesn't even know that Sam is his mother and that Rebecca and Jessica are actually his half sisters. Turning to me, he extends a hand.

"Gee, D Jack. It's great to see you. Are you going to help out with the practice like last time?"

I return his *manly* grip. "Not tonight, Sean. We're heading out to the pizza joint."

He doesn't miss a beat. "Our next practice is Saturday. Do you think you could come and throw some?" he asks hopefully.

"I really wish I could, but Thursday I'm heading out for St. Petersburg and spring training."

"Gosh, D Jack," he bubbles over. "Are you going to play again?"

I glance at Sam who eyes me with concern. I'm sure she's apprehensive as to how I'm going to handle this.

"Not this time, Sean. Playing is for young superstars like you. Coaching is more fun, and you don't have to do all those wind sprints," I respond with a grin.

"I didn't know you were going to coach. Why don't you coach us?"

"I think you're really lucky to have Coach Henshaw."

"So who are you going to coach, D Jack?"

"He's going to be the manager of the new Miami Mets," Sam reveals, with maybe just a hint of pride.

Sean stares wide-eyed. "You mean down in that brand new stadium they just built?" he asks obviously excited.

"That's the one. I think it would be great if you all come to the season opener in April."

"Could we really?"

"You bet, Sean. And you can even come into the clubhouse. I'll have all the players sign a ball for you."

"Wow!"

"Okay, everyone," Sam interjects. "We have to get going. So, we'll see you later if we don't come home too late."

After some smiling goodbyes for the kids and another somewhat forced handshake with Billy, we head back towards the Jag.

"Thank you for all that, Devon. Between Daddy and Sean, I'm sure it wasn't easy to be so up."

My silence says it all.

*

I'm surprised to see the Orange Bowl has barely changed since our school days when we used to hit this place after football games. The décor is unchanged: indirect lighting, red and white checkered tablecloths, and Chianti bottles plugged with half-melted, multi-colored candles. Without even thinking about it, we head for the booth in the far corner away from the kitchen and restrooms. We always sat there if it wasn't occupied, because I wasn't much good on the social scene. Like you haven't figured that out by now, right? Sam takes a seat, and I slide in across from her.

"This is going to be memorable," I smile.

"Why so?"

"Because it'll be the first time I drink in here, legally!"

"Devon, you never drank in here."

"Technically, you're right, but the parking lot was also illegal, and even you took a sip of beer now and then."

"That was because you always handed me the can, and I was quick to hand it back. I never cared for beer and," she adds reflectively, "I still don't."

"Me either. The only reason I drank beer when I played ball was because the older guys were buying."

"Were they also buying you Canadian whiskey?"

"No, but there were always fans in local bars, ready to buy the under-aged D Jack a round," I say quietly.

Sam picks up on the tone of my voice, and I know that both of us are revisiting a past that doesn't entirely conger up fond memories. "Anyway," I continue, "now I've got some bucks in my jeans and can afford your expensive tastes. How about I spot you to a Bacardi and Pepsi?"

"I'd love one," she says with a relaxed smile. "And, I guess we can order," she adds as a waitress approaches the table.

"Hi, guys," chirps the short-haired brunette decked out in a checkered apron that matches the tablecloth. "Can I start you off with some drinks?"

"Sure," I respond pleasantly. "Can we order too?"

"You bet. What would you like?"

"The lady will have a Bacardi and Pepsi…and I'll have a double VO on the rocks. For eats, we'll have a small basket of garlic rolls and a medium-sized pizza."

"What would you like on the pizza, sir?"

I grin at Sam, and she returns my expression with a nod. "We'll have some mushrooms, black olives, and anchovies."

"I'll put that right in and be right back with your drinks."

"Thanks." I'm still holding Sam's gaze.

"I'm glad you remembered."

"I'm glad you still like anchovies. It took awhile for both of us to get used to fish with hair."

She looks at me warmly, but to my surprise, the smile runs away from her face. Yeah, I know. Billy Joel's *Piano Man*! But just like John, the bartender in that song, something's bothering her. In the song, he wanted to be somewhere else. I hope that's not it.

"Okay, Sam. You said at the house something about…there's more to it…so let's get at it."

She nips her lower lip, so I figure I better say something else. I'm afraid I'm about to hear some bad stuff so I might as well lay it out there.

"Sam. Are you having second thoughts? You know…about the two of us giving it a go?"

Her eyes come back up, and I've got to think she sees concern written all over me. "No Devon," she murmers softly. "I've really missed you, and I feel badly that we've barely seen each other since New Year's Eve."

"Missed you too," I quickly add with some relief. "But it's obvious you're pretty upset about something, and I'll listen if you like. You know…big broad, ex-jock shoulders to lean on." I try to make it light with an easy smile.

"I've seen that nasty scar from your right bicep to the top of your shoulder. Are you sure you can handle it with just one good arm?" she asks with a half-smile.

"Samantha. I can handle it."

A few tears instantly appear and start to draw a very slow path down her cheeks.

"What?" I say concerned.

"I never dreamed I would hear you say something like that. I always told myself that if I ever saw you again, I wouldn't believe a word you said."

"Fair enough, so how about some of things I've said in the last few months?"

"You know me, Dev. I always try to be positive."

That doesn't answer my question, but I feel I've got to keep going. "Like I said, Sam, I can handle it, and I'm here for you, and I don't mean just tonight. So, go ahead, try me."

Okay, guys. I said I was going to put it out there, and to my surprise, I did but I haven't really put much thought into what might be down the road for us, what with this new career stuff, her ever-loving father, and her kids and…my kid! Whoa Nellie!

"I'm scared."

"What are you scared of?"

"I'm really worried about Daddy."

"I'm sure you are, but now that you know what's ailing him, the two of you can go after it. Does he have some kind of health insurance that can help pay his medical expenses?"

"Yes. Some of the VA hospitals don't have the greatest of reputations, but everything related to being diabetic is pretty much covered. Obviously I'm not, and the Presidential has no fringe benefits. I'm not home enough to take care of him, and I worry that the kids aren't getting what they need. I don't know what I'm going to do if something happens to them, or me."

"You mean about health stuff?" I ask, matching her serious tone.

"I mean everything, Dev."

"What about benefits for widows?" I inquire hesitantly.

"You know what they say about government bureaucracy. I've been told that thousands of pensions for widows are still pending. One official correspondence even noted only one in seven of the survivors of deceased soldiers who likely could qualify will actually receive a monthly check." She sounds defeated.

After a few seconds of reflection, she continues, "For almost five years, I've been struggling just to take care of everyone, including myself, and I don't see any end in sight. I know it's been lucky that nothing has happened, but that can't go on forever. I'm just living hand to mouth. I've got no safety net, and I'm just out there, and I'm alone. So I'm scared, Dev. I'm really scared."

It doesn't take long for her words to sink in. I've wondered over the past few months how she's been able to hold up under the strain of Billy's health, to say nothing about being a working mom with little kids. Well, now I know. I guess I ought to feel good about her letting go, but obviously she's pretty close to hitting the wall.

Miss Checkered Apron arrives with the drinks, and I mumble thanks without taking my eyes off Sam. The waitress is perceptive enough to figure a serious conversation is underway, so she says, "You're welcome" and quickly heads back toward the kitchen. I slide Sam's cocktail against her hand and lift my glass. She gazes up at me with those beautiful misty, light green eyes.

"Glasses up, Sam," I say hoping it doesn't sound like a command. She lifts her glass and clinks it against mine.

"Here's to tomorrow, Devon," she says, doing her best to sound positive.

"Nope, here's to tonight," I respond with some bounce in my voice.

"You're right," she sighs. "Here's to the world's greatest garlic rolls and pizza with hairy fish."

"Wrong again, Sam. Here's to the plan," I say as I knock off half the VO.

After sipping her drink, she asks, "What plan?"

"I think I know how to put your fears in a box and make them go away."

She looks at me very seriously. "I wish you could, but I don't think that's something you can do."

"Well, Samantha Frederickson, I'm pretty sure I can," I declare confidently.

"I hope this isn't going to be some of your Philosophy 101."

She's skeptical. It's time to get serious, sports fans. I know you think this is gonna be absolutely nuts, because we've talked about the near impossibility of being able to right a wrong. But, again, like Quixote, that doesn't mean you don't try. I figure you're going to rate what I'm about to suggest as a minus figure on the plausibility scale, but I'd appreciate it if you'd keep your eyebrows down and just buckle up. Here we go!

"Philosophy is mostly an exercise in speculation. This is reality, Sam, and I have a plan that I know will work."

She looks apprehensive, not knowing whether I might have a bona fide solution or just some hairbrained notion, or temporary quick fix.

"Okay, I'm listening."

I stop breathing for a moment, and then load up on some much needed air. "I'll marry you, Samantha."

She puts down her glass and looks at me. "What the hell are you talking about?"

She sounds shocked. I'll bet you guys are thinking the same thing. You ought to be, I am! This half-baked idea just popped into my brain about thirty seconds ago and, as they say, at this moment, the silence is deafening.

"Take off your sunglasses, Devon," she orders, lowering her voice.

I'm sure you know this is something I don't like to do. The left eye is dull and glassy, and the right one is pretty much out of focus. But she's seen it all before, so I do as asked.

"You're serious," she says cautiously with a hint of inquisitiveness.

"It would solve all your problems, Sam."

Now I'm really thinking off the cuff. If I can't come up with something logical, she's probably going to think I'm dimwitted, or worse yet, that I've got an agenda.

"On New Year's Eve, you told me you wanted to be a full-time Mom," I continue. "Howard Sheridan is paying me a pretty good sized chuck of change to manage the Mets, and the job comes with a completely paid benefits package. You and the kids will be financially secure, and you can stay home. And you won't have to work unless you want, like when maybe you're totally bored after the kids graduate from college," I suggest with a little grin.

She mulls that over before taking another pull on her drink. "All that would be true, Dev, but I'm just getting to know you again." She smiles. "I like where we're at, but I haven't thought much beyond that."

"I know, Sam. So, it would be fine with me if we just continue on and see where it takes us. Just like Yogi says, we'll travel until we get to the fork in the road, and then we'll take it," I say trying to lighten the moment.

"And we're going to do this in a marriage?" she says incredulously. "How on earth are we going to be able to see where it takes us if we're living together?"

"Who says we're going to live together?"

"Well, it'll be awfully difficult for people to think we're happily married if we don't."

I've tossed out this idea so quickly that I obviously haven't had time to process all the ins and outs, but I think this one's pretty simple.

"We'll just tell Billy, the kids, or anyone else that I've still got six months to go on my lease."

"So why wouldn't we be moving in with you?"

"That's an easy one. Five people won't fit into a one-bedroom apartment."

"So why wouldn't you break your lease?"

"We could say it's a great place for the kids to come and play on the beach."

"You think pretty fast for a busted up old jock."

"Well, like I said, it solves your problems, and really wouldn't change all that much, for you and me. We'll have plenty of time to see how it goes, without dialing anything up."

"Like going to bed?" she asks, giving me a half smile, with maybe just a hint of apprehension, or maybe anxiety, I don't know.

"Come on, Sam," I reason, with my own smile. "You've got to be kidding. Since the fates put us in the same work place three months ago, there's been no hand-holding, no hugs, and one kiss. If I was still playing ball, with those stats, I'd be lucky to suit up for a semi-pro team. So no, that scenario ain't in the playbook, and even if it was, guys don't have to ask girls to marry 'em anymore to get 'em in the sack."

"I know that, but I grew up with the notion that marriage is serious, and it's a commitment, and when it comes to making…"

"Don't worry about all that, Sam. Both of us will know why we're doing this. And, the worst thing that can happen is, if it all goes south, I promise I'll still provide for you and the kids if you want an annulment or a divorce."

"Is that an easy thing to do in Florida?"

Okay, guys. It's time to take that concern off the table. "Yes, it's an easy thing to do anywhere, if the marriage isn't consummated. For that reason alone, a judge will grant you either one in a heartbeat."

"But this could go on for quite awhile."

"As far as I know, time ain't a legal factor."

"Do I understand what you're saying? I mean, do you understand what you're saying?" She's totally dumbfounded.

"Hell no," I say with a grin, trying to break the tension, but her look goes from dumbfounded to aghast. I figure I better throw in Philosophy 101. "Einstein once said you don't really understand something unless you can explain it to your grandmother, and if I had one, I sure as hell couldn't explain this, right?"

It works! She gives me a half smile that quickly changes to one of contemplation. "Dev, I have to assume you've had your share of women over the years."

"A lot less than you'd think. If you recall, I never was much with the ladies."

"That was before you became famous."

"It didn't change. And you know as well as I do, if I *was* famous, it was short-lived."

"Judging from what I've heard and seen recently, I beg to differ. So, when was the last time you got a girl between the sheets?"

"Does it matter?"

"It shouldn't."

"Why do I get this feeling you want to see if I'll answer a personal question? Are we revisiting the 'trust' issue?"

"I'm off base, here, Dev. I'm sorry," she apologizes.

I take that as a yes. “Then we’re back to your concern over whether or not we can have an honest relationship, aren’t we?”

“Yes.”

“Okay, I don’t recall circling a date on a calendar, but the sheet thing was long before that day you walked into the bagroom, looked at me with utter disdain, and asked me what I wanted for lunch.”

“I still shouldn’t have asked you about your private life,” she demurs, still somewhat regretfully.

“I’m glad you did. I’ll take any opportunity I get to up your faith in me.”

She smiles.

What the hell; what’s good for the goose and all that shit. “What about you? I know a gentleman isn’t supposed to ask a lady such things, but fair is fair.”

“You’re right; two and a half,” she responds quickly.

Talk about being perplexed. “The two are obvious, but I’m not sure about the half.”

She looks at me with sadness, not remorse, or embarrasment or anything like that. “I’m sure you’ve heard of the widow vulnerable syndrome,” she says. “It was just a casual acquaintance kind of thing, a few months after Dolph was killed. There was some hugging, and kissing, but when we got into bed, I fell apart and just couldn’t.”

“And then?”

“And then he apologized and left. I never saw him again.” She takes a deep breath and sighs. “I guess I’m just old-fashioned, Dev; I have to be married, or at least, very much in love.”

“That’s good to know. It’ll make things easier.”

“How do you figure that?”

“Well, if we go through with this, you’ll be married in name only, and both of us know you’re not in love with me. Maybe I’m a little old-fashioned too.”

“Is that why you didn’t do anything when you undressed me and put me to bed?”

“That was different; you were drunk.”

“And if I get drunk tonight?”

“I’d do the same; anyway, I figure making love to an unconscious woman would be about one step above nechrophilia. So no, it wouldn’t make any difference.

“And what would make a difference?” She runs her hands through her hair. “I’m sorry, Dev. It’s just that your plan, as you put it, is so off-the-wall. I guess I'm worried that your solution, over time, would become awkward…and stressful."

"I prefer to think of it as unconventional or maybe eccentric," I smile. "But to answer your question, I already said both of us know how you feel, or more accurately, what you don't feel. So, the only thing that'll make a difference is if you ever tell me you're in love me. It's as simple as that."

"You're doing this out of a sense of guilt, aren't you? I've picked up little things you've said since that night in the Bengal Lounge. I think, over the years, you've really been down on yourself because of what happened between us. And you didn't even know about Sean. Worse yet, I'm pretty sure you're convinced that no matter what you do or how hard you try, nothing will change. You don't have to do this, Dev."

I think you know she's pretty well pegged me on this one, and we know for sure, guys, she's dead serious about the guilt thing. Maybe she's right.

"I know I don't have to; I want to. And maybe you're right; maybe there is a sense of guilt, but I guess I'm also being selfish. If this doesn't work out you'll probably stick to your original story concerning Sean and sooner or later, you'll get married again…and only your cousin and Billy and you and me will ever know Sean is my son. So, the only responsible thing I can do is be a silent provider of sorts. And, if that's all there is, I'll have to settle for it."

Her eyes open wide. "I know back in high school, most of the kids thought you that your only interest was to make the pros. Maybe that's the way you were. Or maybe you were just quiet, or self-conscious. But now, you almost sound selfless. Is this something recent?"

"I don't think so."

"Did you get it from your dad?" she says with obvious affection.

"Whatever's in me, I got from both my dad and my mom."

"How can that be? Your mom died when you were just a little boy?"

"Yeah, she did. But she was always in the room with us. In most of our conversations, Dad would always tell me what she might have thought about a situation or a problem. And when he did, the love he had for her was just overwhelming."

"That sounds sad to me, Dev."

"It wasn't. When he talked about mom, he lit up like a Christmas tree. I know in books and movies, sometimes there's this thing about true love, like a fairy tale, and you figure it's just fiction. But for Dad, I think it was even more than that. And he shared it with me, he *exuded* it. I know that kind of relationship might be rare, but it can happen, and eventhough I was too young to really understand, I was privileged to see it."

"So, am I to believe you're a romantic?"

"I never thought of it like that, but yeah, I guess so."

"And all that aside, without the romance or passion, you'd still do this?" she asks, bewildered.

"Yes."

Again, it gets really quiet like one of those times when you think you can hear your own heartbeat. Sam downs the last of her drink and motions that she wants another. I turn and wave to the waitress who's been keeping a respectful distance from us. She comes over to the table, smiling. "What can I get for you, sir?"

"Another round will be just fine."

"I'll be glad to, and your dinner should be out shortly."

"Thanks again." She turns and heads for another table.

"What a life," Sam says, as I turn to face her.

I don't have a clue what that's supposed to mean, so I just give it a shrug and wait for her to continue.

"When Dolph proposed to me, I knew I had feelings for him, but I wasn't passionately in love with him. Now," she laughs nervously, "I might get married again, with the same feeling, but this time I wasn't even proposed to. You didn't even *ask* me if I would marry you. You just said *you'd* marry me."

"I didn't want you to misunderstand my intention. If I said, 'Will you marry me?' it would have been different. This way, you don't even have to say something like, 'I will.' If you want to, all you have to say is, 'I think the plan will work.'"

"But what do I say to Daddy and the kids?"

"That's a no-brainer, Sam. When you think the time is right, you tell them I asked you, and that you said yes. It's the ole half truth, right?"

"You know Daddy is going to ask me if I love you."

"I'll leave that response to your creative imagination."

"I'll be honest with you, Dev," Sam says tenderly. "I really have mixed emotions about all this. On the one hand, as you say, it would solve my problems, but on the other hand, I wouldn't be comfortable announcing to world that we're married when, in fact, it's nothing more than an arrangement that benefits me. I mean, what do you get out of it?"

"At the very least, it'll give me an opportunity to help you and be close to my son for awhile so I can get to know him. And come on, Sam, how many marriages involve some kind of arrangement, as you put it?"

"I don't really like your second point, but I can buy the first one…although I'm not sure how the medical thing works with the kids."

"If the medical policy doesn't cover the kids as dependents, I'll legally adopt the girls, and both of us can adopt Sean. Wouldn't that be bizarre; his adopted parents would actually be his biological parents."

The brunette returns with the drinks as well as the basket of garlic rolls and the pizza. After a few pleasant remarks regarding her hope that we enjoy our dinner, she once again heads for another table. Sam reaches for her drink and smiles.

"Is the smile for the drinks and dinner, or for the plan?" I ask hesitantly.

"It's for the plan, Devon, although I don't have any idea how it will end." She pauses, and gives me a big grin. "So, even though you didn't ask me, I *will* marry you."

For the second time tonight, I raise my glass and clink it against her tumbler. "Here's to you, Samantha Frederickson Jameison."

I don't know about you, sports fans, but I think the Orange Bowl has been pretty good to me. Eight or nine years ago, we met here, and maybe we just met here again. And I feel good, because today I sure as hell won something. I'm not sure what, and you probably don't know either. I figure, about now you're scratching your head and thinking I've really gone bonkers with this whole marriage thing. Maybe I have. Check that. It's abso-fucken-lutely insane!

Anyway, I guess I'll just have to be patient and take it one step at a time, while Sam and yours truly inch our way towards Yogi's inevitable fork in the road.

III

DINNER WITH CHARLEY

Well, that's baseball.
Rags to riches one day
and riches to rags the next.
But I've been in it thirty-six years
and I'm used to it.
Casey Stengel, Manager
Brooklyn Dodgers/Boston Braves/New York Yankees/New York "Miracle" Mets

The wedding was…stressful. Check that. It wasn't a wedding. It wasn't even a marriage in the traditional sense. It was nothing more than a legal procedure. And, stressful is not the adjective I should use. Flat-out awful is a lot more accurate! I'm glad you weren't there. Other than Samantha, me, a notary public, and two witnesses, no one was there. No maid-of-honor; no best man. Let me backtrack for you.

As you know, since Sam and I met up again about three months ago, she's pretty much set the tone and direction of our relationship. And given the awkwardness of our arrangement, as she put it, I knew this wasn't the time to become a little more forward in terms of how I might like things to be.

So, over the pizza and garlic rolls, at the Orange Bowl last Monday night, we engaged in ah…well, let's just call it a planning session. When all was said and done, Sam decided she would ask Charley for a two-week leave without pay. Then, at the end of the two weeks, she would tell Billy we were married, inform Charley that she was through at the Presidential, and start being a stay-at-home mom. However, she would also tell her dad not to say anything to the kids, or anyone else for that matter. Her plan was to have the kids get to know me before springing the marriage news on them.

I really didn't have any objections to any of this, because all the perceived complications were on her side of the fence. However, without thinking, I did tell her that I wanted to wear my dad's wedding band. She quickly pointed out that neither of us would be wearing wedding bands in the near future. If and when the time was right, she said, we'd tell the kids, announce to the world we were a family, and start wearing rings.

So, this thursday morning, we drove up to the Broward County Courthouse in Fort Lauderdale. In the anteroom of the county judge, we stood before his notary, exchanged the legally required words, and signed the appropriate papers. In addition to the notary, his two secretaries also signed as witnesses. A simple kiss was followed by half-smiles and we departed as man and wife, having satisfied the laws of Florida.

The drive back to Dewey Street was quiet. I figured Sam was deep in thought, and I wasn't exactly a glowing bridegroom. At first, I had been uncomfortable knowing I was going to catch a plane to St Petersburg later that morning. But in hindsight, it was probably a good thing that we had so little time together.

We rehashed what she would be doing over the next four weeks, and I shared that I had no idea what my role would be at the Mets spring training camp. I smiled and said I would call when I got in. She asked me if I would call her every evening. I smiled again, and said I'd love to.

That was that.

This all sounds pretty clinical, doesn't it? Not really. I would have loved to walk her to the door, give her a soft kiss and a hug, and say tender things. But I didn't, because I knew she would have been anxious about any display of affection, what with the possibility that Billy or the kids might be peaking through the front window.

But I've got to share with you that when we were at the Orange Bowl and I told her the only thing I got out of this arrangement was to be able to get to know Sean, I wasn't entirely up front. The truth is I really think I want to be a part of Sam's life. And I don't know if I'm going to get a second chance, so I'm covering my bets. That's why I was so quick to tell her I would take care of her and the kids, even if things didn't work out between us.

So the long and short of it is I'm pretty sure I want things to work out. But, if they don't, at least I'll still be a part of their lives. Like Sam says, I'm an eternal pessimist.

After dropping her off at Dewey Street, I made one more stop on the way to Fort Lauderdale International Airport. I went out to Taft Street and

Highway 7, and drove into Hollywood Memorial Gardens. I parked the car and walked the fifty or so feet to my parents' gravesites.

There aren't any flowers or benches. There's just a small, flat bronze plate on a piece of grass that says, "Edwin Ethan Jameison, 1921-1968." Right next to it, is a twin marker that says, "Katherine Eva Jameison, 1922-1951." I was born in 1950, so I have no memories of her. But I always talk to both of them, because I'd feel guilty if I only shared things with my dad.

Okay. Don't freak out on me. I have this belief that everyone needs someone to talk with, and if you don't have someone, you talk with someone who has passed on to the next world, a dad, a mom, a brother, a mate. Come on. This shouldn't be so hard to take. After all, if you recall the TGIS discussion at the Presidential, I clearly established the existence of God or, at the very least, how God may have come to be. Okay, let's not go there. Regardless of how you feel about God or the next world, I hope you have someone in this world to talk with. And if you're lucky enough to have that situation, cherish it. Embrace it for all it's worth.

Anyway, I only have one worn, faded, black-and-white photograph of me and my mom. She had short, dark-brown hair and was wearing light colored pants and a matching blouse with dark stripes. In the photo, I was wearing a little white jumpsuit, and she was holding me up, and looking at me with a warm and beautiful smile. And there was love in her eyes. And I was looking at her, with a joyous expression of belonging.

That's why I talk to her as well as my dad. I think had she lived, she would have listened. But about my dad, I'm positive. He was always there for me. He listened. He didn't say much, but when he did, he spoke softly. I never heard him raise his voice or show his disappointment with me, although I always knew somehow when he thought I was off-base. He was all I had and, I guess I was all he had, although I know deep down he talked to my mom just the way I now talk to him.

Like I've said before, *rue* is the worst word in the English language. You already know how I feel about not being able to play ball and, maybe worse, about Samantha. But if I could only change one thing, I wouldn't have been playing ball in Mexico when my dad died, alone. Hell, I don't know. So deep down, I'd like to believe my mother was there waiting for him.

So, before I headed out to St Petersburg, I talked to both of them about my apprehensions, about getting back into organized baseball, and my anxiety about the surreal relationship I had initiated with Sam. Obviously, my Mom never saw me play ball and never met Sam, but my dad had hoped we would marry. Somehow, I don't think this is exactly what he had in mind. But I hope he's smiling now; if not, maybe he will be one of these days.

*

The Yellow cab let's me out in front of Bern's Steakhouse located at 1208 S. Howard Avenue, just south of downtown Tampa at the top of the little peninsula that separates Tampa Bay and Hillsborough Bay. I was here once and remember thinking is was weird the way the outside was pretty simple with its smooth, white walls and slanted tiled roof while the inside décor was totally contrary with red-flocked, velvet-covered walls, and gaudy staircases. I have no idea what an upscale bordello looks like, but I think this place could have doubled for one in a previous era…and oddly enough, I kind of enjoyed it.

Once through the door the maitre d' checks me out and, having barely met the dress code with slacks and a sport coat, he begrudgingly escorts me to a secluded table towards the rear of one of the spacious dining rooms.

"Mr. Berston told me to seat you and that he would be here shortly," the majordomo says with no expression, verbal or facial. I'll bet you'd never guess this guy's jet-black hair is short and parted down the middle, and his clipped mustache is stiff with wax. Anyway, before I can grunt some thanks, he turns and briskly removes himself from my presence. I take a seat facing the dining room, so I'll be able to spot Charley when he arrives.

I've got to tell ya. Eventhough I enjoyed it some, I can do without the fanciness of places like this. You often need to get a reservation a month or more in advance. They want you to select your wine prior to arrival so it can air, decant, or chill, if necessary. Speaking of the wine, the joint claims to have the largest wine list of any restaurant in the world, something like 6500 labels. Okay. I know. I shouldn't refer to such a high-class establishment as a joint. I mean, maybe you really like the atmosphere and trappings that come with fine dining. That might suit you to a tee, and that's all well and good. All I'm saying is that restaurants like Bern's make me uncomfortable.

On the other hand, maybe you'd like a place like the one in Ybor City where I would have preferred to eat. That would be the Columbia Restaurant. Established in the early 1900's, it may well be the oldest place in the country that serves Cuban cuisine, and maybe the world's best paella to boot!

The Columbia is big, noisy, and ethnic, just like Ybor City itself was for so many years. After the turn of the century, Vincente Martinez Ybor set up his cigar factory on forty acres just north of what is now downtown

Tampa. Business boomed, so he built a company town with hundreds of small houses that attracted a much-needed labor force, most of whom were Cuban or Spanish. Clubs, restaurants, and other establishments sprung up to accommodate the hustle-bustle of the multi-ethnic community.

The boom years ended with the conclusion of World War II and the rise of better jobs. By the early 70's, Ybor City had pretty much emptied out with a population of little more than 1,000. But just recently, there's been talk of an urban renewal effort, and I think it would be neat if they can pull it off. And how do I know all of this? I like talking to the locals. I'll bet you've done the same somewhere along the line. Regardless, I'm going to make sure I get to the Columbia before heading back to Hollywood, with or without Charley. Like I say, you want to find out about a place? Talk to bartenders!

A waiter approaches me, addresses me by name, introduces himself, and asks if I would like something to drink. After informing him I would like a double Crown Royal on the rocks, he gives me something between a frown and half-smile, thanks me, and departs. I guess he figures I should have ordered a $200 bottle of wine. Like I was saying, that's the kind of place this is…and I don't have a clue as to how the guy at the front knew who I was, or how the waiter knew my name. Like I've been saying, I would have been much more comfortable with the friendly h*ola, amigo,* greeting at the Columbia.

Speaking of comfort, I haven't experienced much of that today. After flying into Tampa this afternoon, I caught a cab and went straight to Al Lang Field, the brand new spring training ballpark of the New York Mets. And she's a beauty!

The park, located on Bayshore Drive in St Pete, opened just a few a months ago. It can hold about 7,000 fans and has a cantilevered roof that covers more than half the seats. The really neato keazeto parts of the park are located along the foul lines. Down the right field line, from first base to the fence, is a steep, grassy bank with plenty of room for the fans to sit and watch the game. But the third baseline, from the bag to the left field foul pole, is downright spectacular. In addition to a grassy bank, there are hedges and bushes with little white flowers; half a dozen cabbage palms spread their green, finger-like leaves; and behind the bank is a magnificent view of dozens of pleasure boats, docked on the side of a waterway that leads out to Tampa Bay. Hell of a place to watch a ball game, ya think?

Charley had asked me to meet him in the manager's office and, after admiring the park, I found him right where he was supposed to be. He greeted me with a big grin, and handshake, made some small talk, and then griped about all the back-to-back meetings he was locked into. He suggested I get out on the field just to look around and that he would meet me at Bern's around 7:00 p.m. that evening.

So, I made my way out to the diamond and, after standing around the plate for a minute or two, headed for left field. That didn't last much longer; I could feel the ghosts closing in. A bunch of guys in uniform were hanging around the dugout so I headed over, figuring to say hi on the way out.

Bittersweet…Jerry Grote gave me a nod and a smile, obviously not recognizing me what with the beard and sunglasses. I walked over to him and introduced myself, and he gave me a greeting with a whoop and a holler. A few of the guys gave it a smile and a wave and then resumed whatever it was they had been doing. I recognized Dave Kingman, who, last year, had hit 37 dingers for the Mets. And I also recognized Tom Seaver who, in that fateful year of 1969, won 25 games and the Cy Young Award. However, he won only 14 games last season, and the word is that the Mets might actually trade Tom Terrific. I find it hard to believe they might let him go.

Anyway, you might not remember, but in the eighth inning of the one game I played, I fired a frozen rope to Grote at the plate, and he made the tag on a St. Louis Cardinal sliding into the plate. Well, Grote was nice enough to recall that moment, which was cool because I always thought of him as a really classy guy and a hell of a ballplayer. When asked about Grote, Johnny Bench once kidded that if he and Grote were on the same team, Grote would be catching and he would be playing first base. High praise, indeed!

On the way out, I noticed the manager, Joe Frazier, standing at the pitcher's mound chatting with Willie Mays, the Say Hey kid himself! He's one of Frazier's coaches, and the head man is going to need all the help he can get. Last year, the Mets notched 86 wins with 76 losses, which was good for third place, but they were 15 games out, and the big boys certainly want a better season this year. I figure they may have a winner, because Frazier came up to run the big club after managing my old team, the Triple AAA Norfolk Tide, to the International League championship.

What a day.

My mental review of the past few hours comes to a halt as Charley makes his way over to the table. As usual, he's decked out in a charcoal-gray, three-piece suit and looks as dapper as ever. Bad eyes and all, I'm still amazed that the small, trim man used to beat the hell out of me on the racket ball court.

"Good to see you got here on your own," he says with a smile. I stand, return his smile, and shake hands. "Good to see you weren't going to be in meetings all night, Charley. I can't afford this place and would have slinked out if you called and said you couldn't make it."

Having exchanged quips, we both take our seats just as the sommelier magically appears from nowhere. He's the real deal, because he's sporting a heavily braided gold chain around his neck upon which is fastened a small wine tasting vessel. I think this time you can guess that he too, has his haired parted down the middle and also sports a French-styled moustache.

"I believe you requested the 1960 Chateau La Croix Blanche Montagne, sir. A fine selection, if I may be permitted to say so."

Obviously, Charley had called ahead, because the bottle has been opened to do what opened bottles of reds are supposed to do.You know, air, decant, all that stuff. The wine steward pours an ounce or so into Charley's glass…and waits, but Charley simply nods, which I assume is a signal for him to continue to pour the wine. The majordomo's twin does as asked but skips my glass as he sneers at the cut-glass, half-full whiskey tumbler in front of me. Then, he turns and departs without a word.

"There sure are a bunch of fun guys working this establishment. Are they always this cheerful?"

"It's a serious business, D Jack," Charley says as he takes a sip of wine. "I'm told the waiters spend half a lifetime apprenticing here."

"It shows. I guess there's lots of stress when you have to cater to the well-heeled."

"That never seemed to bother you at the Presidential."

"That's because I was confident my employer had my back," I respond with a grin, hoisting the tumbler for another healthy pull on the Crown Royal.

"Enough already," Charley says as he lifts his arms in the air. "Let's order before we get down to business. What do you want?"

"Well, it's a steakhouse, so I'll have a steak. I'll leave ordering the rest to your delicate tastes. I assume you know this place and have your favs."

"True enough."

I think these tables are wired for sound, because no sooner has Charley decided we'll order than the waiter who had brought me a drink, materializes out of thin air.

"What will we be having this evening, sir?"

I suddenly realize no menus have been offered, and Mr. Friendly doesn't have a pad or anything to write with. And what's the deal with this *we* shit? Is this guy going to eat with us as well as serve dinner? Not!

"We'll start with some Russian Imperial Caviar, and also an Oysters Beignets. Then, we'll have a couple of two-inch Delmonico's, medium rare, with shitake sauce and carmelized red onions on the side. That will do for the now," Charley says.

"Thank you, Mr. Berston, and may I say it is good to see you again, sir."

"It's nice to be back in town, Maurice."

I swear to you, Maurice all but gives Charley a bow before departing. "Hell, Charley. At least he didn't click his heels."

"Actually, I think he may have done that once," Charley says with a laugh. "Among other things, you can request a waiter here, so I've seen a bit of Maurice over the past few years. He's somewhat of a snob, but he's an excellent waiter and he's very discreet."

"And that means?"

"That means he doesn't talk about the people I dine with."

"How do you know that?"

"I know, D Jack."

"I'm sure you do," I say with a laugh. My experience with Charley the Boss over the past two years is that he knows everything, and I mean everything!

"But," I continue, "I don't know what you want to talk about. So, what *do* you want to talk about?"

"I want to fill you in on some of the thinking of the organization and chat about your role as the Miami manager," he explains taking another sip of wine before replacing the glass on the table.

"Do I have any input on either one, or do I just nod and smile?"

"'No' to the first; 'yes' to the second; and you can nod and smile for both," Charley answers pleasantly.

"That sounds fair enough, so let's start with the 'no' input, organizational part of it."

Charley looks a little pained. "The ownership had its meetings in late January. In fact, Howard wined and dined them at his place in Aspen."

"Good move," I say, remembering the fantastic atmosphere of Sheridan's home, nestled in the mountains just east of the Colorado ski mecca.

"I agree, but it didn't help all that much. The organization has some big problems, the biggest being Grant, the chairman."

"I remember the name. Wasn't he credited with bringing in Gil Hodges to manage the team?"

"Yes, he did, and you probably saw Willy Mays today. He brought him in, too. Even though Mays didn't have much left, he was great for ticket sales. And then, or course, Gil died suddenly at the start of the 1972 season and that's when things started going south and now are just getting worse."

"They seemed to being doing okay last year. What's the problem?"

"The problem, in part, is the same Mr. Grant. And what's changed is that the co-founder and majority owner of the team, Joan Whitney Payson, died two years ago. When that happened, her daughter assumed the ownership of the team."

"I remember Mrs. Payson. She wrote me a really kind and supportive letter. Wasn't she the President?"

"She was. She served as President from 1968 until she died. And she was really something else. I mean, she was a minority owner of the Giants and was really against the move to San Francisco. So, when that happened, she dumped her stock and went to work to get a new team in New York."

"And, am I to assume that her daughter isn't really 'something else,' as you put it?"

"Well, let's just say she isn't as focused; in fact, she's pretty much turned the club over to Grant."

"So, we're back to Mr. Grant. Again, what's the problem?"

"Among other things, he talks to the press and tabloids more than the players. And, just between you and me and the red walls of this place, he has a real bone in his throat when it comes to Seaver."

"I was in a situation once where there was friction between the players and the brass," I say reflectively. "It made it hard to come to the ball park sometimes."

"Well, that might be where all this is going, D Jack, but it was clear in Aspen that the pressure is really on to be seriously in the hunt this year. And that directly impacts the farm system."

"I'm listening."

"From what I've been told by Howard, he figures that maybe half a dozen new guys might be playing in Shea Stadium this year. Most of them will probably come from Norfolk.

"What about the Double AA clubs?"

"Maybe one or two might go straight up, but I think they'll have to be awfully good for that to happen." Charley takes another sip of wine.

"I'm not so sure I understand why this is supposed to be so complicated." I empty the tumbler of what's left of the Canadian whiskey.

"I suspect you want a refill?" Charley asks rhetorically with a smile.

"Did the Trojan Horse have wooden body parts between his legs?"

"Crude, D Jack. I don't think the Greeks were interested in what was between his legs, but I'll get you another drink anyway."

With that, he nods to Maurice who has been hanging back in a shadowy corner in the room, undoubtedly waiting to be beckoned. Rather than have the waiter trudge over to the table, Charley simply holds up one finger and then points to me. Maurice acknowledges the request with a slight nod of his head, and departs.

"The complications," Charley continues, returning to the task at hand, "include three things. The first is that attendance for Mets games has been tanking and some New York sportswriter is starting to call Shea Stadium Grant's tomb. The second is that Norfolk has won the International League Championship three or four times, but they skipped a beat last year, and the organization is worried about attendance there as well."

"So, the first two involve fans coming through the turnstiles. What's the third?"

"It's the same issue for the Double AA Jackson Mets in the Texas League. It would appear as if the good folks in Mississippi really expect the team to be on top every year, and last year was the first time in quite awhile they nose-dived."

Charley pauses as Maurice approaches the table, places the drink in front of me, and departs without a word. I immediately take down half the drink and look Charley right in the eye. Well, you know me; I *kind* of look him in the eye. "Is this conversation finally getting down to something that involves us?"

"Yes."

Charley empties his wine glass and then pours himself another half glass. "At the meeting in Aspen, it was no great surprise that Grant decided the number one priority is for the big club to compete for the pennant. Right behind that was the same goal for Norfolk and Jackson."

"And where does that leave the new Miami Mets?" I inquire with a healthy dose of trepidation.

"Grant figures the excitement of a new franchise, a new stadium, and the enthusiasm of the fans, for the new manager, among other things, will be enough to get us through a mediocre season."

"I think I can figure out what's coming next, Charley."

"What's next is that Jackson is going to get the prospects the organization thinks can make it to the top, and we're going to get the developmental players who just might show some signs of being able to play ball at a higher level."

"That's just dandy, Charley. How in the hell does the organization, as you put it, think I have the ability to help kids who are marginal at best? I don't have the experience or the technical knowledge of the game to do that."

"They know that, kid," Charley says in a solemn tone. He then pauses and looks down at his glass.

You know, guys, these deadly conversational silences are starting to wear on me. First, it was the one with Sam, and now, Charley is sitting across from me, staring at his expensive wine. This is really turning into a rough, fucken week! Charley finally looks up at me and gives me a smile. I simply nod and shrug.

"Relax, D Jack. It really didn't take much for Howard to sell them on you. They quickly realized the fans are going to welcome you with open arms and, more importantly, you'll be able to relate to a bunch of starry-eyed kids. And they also understand we've surrounded you with some top-notch coaches who will shoulder the instructional duties. Like Howard told you, your job is to manage, not to teach. He also told me that when he got done, the brass was confident you'll make a positive impact on the team."

Well, sports fans, we know better than that, don't we. I doubt seriously that Sheridan shared the whole idea from the gitgo is for me to be a local sports celebrity who gets exposure for the new team…and then transfer that popularity to Sheridan's new television station. Doesn't all this just make you feel wanted and warm and fuzzy all over?

"I know what you're thinking," Charley continues with concern. "In addition to all this, I was standing at the top of the ballpark, this afternoon when I saw you briefly shuffling around home plate. You didn't spend much time in left field either. I figure you're still wrestling with some demons. Howard shared with me that you had some reservations about getting back into organized baseball."

"I'm not going to deny that, Charley. I'm no different from anyone who thinks about what could have been and wishes it would have happened. But, like most people, I guess, you eventually get on with it. The truth is," I continue, "that right now I think I'm more preoccupied with being a greenhorn manager."

"I understand that, but I think I've gotten to know you, and I'm confident you can really accelerate your learning curve. And more importantly, I know you're good with people and that you're going to get a maximum effort out of all the kids the organization assigns to us."

"This is starting to sound like the boss giving the employee a pep talk and a premature pat on the back," I say with a grin.

"I guess it's something like that," Charley replies somewhat seriously.

It's pretty obvious he too is feeling some pressure and, I'm not sure why, but I feel the need to try to take the conversation down a notch. "This isn't going to turn into some kind of group hug, is it Charley?"

His expression softens. "Group hug be damned. When you get back in a few weeks, and you're not on the road with the team, let's resume our Monday night racket ball game. I enjoy kicking your ass, and teaching you things, on and off the court."

"Come on, ole man. You don't outscore me enough to be considered a mentor, and I sure as hell don't qualify as the son you never had," I say lightly.

Whoa Nellie. I just pushed a button. In a heartbeat, Charley looks at me with a pained expression on his face…and here we go with still yet another episode of dead air. I'm not sure whether I should say something or wait to see if Charley is going to respond to my off-handed remark. All I know is Charley looks like he just aged five years in five seconds.

"I had a son, D Jack," he says, breaking the silence. "He had just been elected president of his senior class in high school when he was killed in a head-on car collision."

I've heard of small world things, but this is *outer-worldly.* "That same thing happened in my high school when I was a senior.' I pause, almost afraid to ask. "Was your son Jeff Woodling?" I inquire hesitantly.

"Jeff was my only child," he whispers. Then, Charley looks at me, and I'm sure he sees my confusion. "I was married to a very modern woman. She kept her maiden name and insisted that it be Jeff's name as well." He pauses, takes a deep breath, and says, "We weren't able to lean on each other for the first year so she found comfort with another guy, and I lost myself in my job," he concludes in a matter-of-fact way.

Damn if we don't always focus on life throwing us curveballs. And then, boom! We realize we aren't the only ones playing on that tragic team. Damn!

"I'm really sorry about what I said, Charley," I apologize quickly. "I didn't even know you had been married, let alone been a dad." I think for a moment and then say, "I still miss my dad today as much as the day he died, but I can't imagine losing a son."

"It's just like what you said a few minutes ago, D Jack; eventually you get on with it. You know," Charley continues with a thin smile, "Jeff used to talk to me about you." He's obviously changing the direction of the conversation, making a feeble attempt to sound a little up-beat.

"That's interesting."

"Why do you say that?"

"I say that because I remember talking about Jeff with my dad. I remember he said he was going to go to college and be a Rhodes Scholar. I didn't have a clue what a Rhodes Scholar was, so I asked my dad. He told me that in order to get a Rhodes scholarship, you had to be on top academically as well as a being a civic leader and a pretty good jock. So, I figured he was going to be able to do it. I knew he had the academic tickets and played a great game of tennis."

"He also played some pretty good baseball, too, if you remember," Charley adds with some pride. "He obviously didn't come anywhere near your skill level, but he did play shortstop in the last two innings of the game in Jacksonville, when you threw the no-hitter against Bolles to win the state championship."

"You saw that game?"

"I did. I saw quite a few games. You certainly were a piece of work."

"Maybe so, but Jeff was the whole package and probably the most popular kid in school. All I could do was just play ball. I sure as hell didn't have the skills, as you put it, to be a leader of anything. Hell, Charley, I wasn't even in a club; I hardly had any friends, let alone close ones."

"I'm not so sure of that," he says with that thin smile still painted on his face. "Jeff said you spent most of your time, off the ball field, with the cutie-pie captain of the cheerleaders. If I recall, her name was Samantha."

"You know, Charley. I think you really do know everything," I say as we both laugh at that one. "And now that I know there's a connection to the past," I continue, "I figure it was you, not Bottomly, who brought me into the Presidential." Charley's grin tells me I've hit that nail on the head.

Once again, Maurice materializes as if an illusionist had just conjured him up, but this time he's pushing a small metal cart. He stops at the side of the table and begins to remove the silver lids from the Wedgewood bone-china plates. Charley places a large, cloth napkin across his lap and says, "I know one thing for sure, D Jack. We're about to enjoy the finest steaks money can buy."

"I hope so, Charley, because I'm guessing it took the better part of a years salary to buy em."

With that, I knock down the last of the Crown Royal and sadly reflect that for all the talk about getting on with it, I figure I'm still looking for my father, and Charley is still looking for his son. You might still be looking for something, too. But I guess the bottom line is, when all's said and done, we either find something to fill the void, or we just flat stop looking. I'm not presumptuous enough to speak for you or Charley. But for me, filling the void is the only option. The trick is finding something, or someone, that will do it.

And I don't mean taking up space. It's something that gets you out of bed in the morning with a smile and an enthusiasm for what lies ahead. And even better yet, something you take to bed with you at night that provides you with a sense of accomplishment and peace of mind.

I'm thinking my dad did that with my mom, even though she wasn't physically there. But that's because I'm pretty sure they had something the poets write about. Something so unbelievably wonderful that, in truth, she was with him until the day he died. And still is.

So, I figure my dad had peace of mind, which seems to be no easy trick for me. All too often, I think back to the way things might have been with Sam, or what could have happened if I hadn't been hit with a fastball in Shea Stadium. I can't help it; I still agonize over all of that…and I know I'm not supposed to.

When I took my philosophy degrees at Arizona State, I memorized some of the writings of Kiyoko Takeda who, among other things, said that…*recognizing what we have done in the past is a recognition of ourselves. By conducting a dialogue with our past, we are searching how to go forward.*

But now that I'm older his words should mean more to me than just some saying I once needed to regurgitate on an exam…so I hope I'm ready to get excited about filling that void and going forward. It's about time, right? Yeah, I know: why did it take me so long to get on board with something so fucken simple?

IV

COMING CLOSER

Humanity is the keystone
that holds nations and men together.
When that collapses,
the whole structure crumbles.
This is as true of baseball teams
as any other pursuit in life.
Connie Mack, Manager
Pittsburgh Pirates/Philadelphia Athletics

I'm home.

I wouldn't exactly say the last four weeks were anywhere near as stressful as exchanging vows with Sam, but they sure as hell weren't much fun and games either. That's because most of it, in my humble opinion, was bullshit!

Once the local press got wind of the fact that I was going to manage the new Double AA club in Miami, it became a feeding frenzy. The top brass saw a great opportunity to get all kinds of publicity, so, not only was I instructed to grant every request for interviews and photo-ops; I was also *encouraged* to make the rounds. And to that end, they made damn sure I was invited to everything from mall openings to local beauty contests. I even kissed a few babies, just like some fucking politician! I mean, if I had to do all this crapola in Miami, maybe I could understand it, but this is fucken Tampa. What do they care about who's managing a minor league team in Dade County?

Do you think I might have been uncomfortable with all this? You can't even imagine. I mean, there I was, a one-day wonder, being treated like some baseball legend. You'd think I was some kind of hero.

Terrific! Not!!

Getting hit in head, in the only big league game I ever played, falls short of being heroic, wouldn't you say? And it all ought to be bullshit anyway. Sparky Anderson, the legendary manager of Cincinnati's Big Red

Machine, once said, *"Don't call us [ballplayers] heroes. Firemen are heroes."* And I'd add policemen, too.

As for the actual baseball stuff, my job was to sit in the stands pretty much like a scout, and chart the playing ability of the guys who had come to St. Pete with the same dream I had nine years ago. After the first few weeks, it was pretty obvious who was going to play in the majors in New York or suit up for the Triple AAA Mets affiliate out of Norfolk. It was more difficult to calculate which guys would be the prospects playing Double AA with the Jackson Mets or the developmental guys playing Double AA with us in Miami. The best I could tell the pitchers with control problems and the hitters who weren't very consistent were going to end up in my dugout. But if those problems couldn't be corrected, they'd get shipped down to the high-A team in St Lucie. That road would eventually transport almost all of them back to the farm or the factory or wherever they came from.

So, the days were long. The nights were shorter because I was pretty much out of gas and went to bed early. Sam and I talked briefly each night, with the conversations being more informative than personal. I guess most of the time Billy or one of the kids might have been in the room with her, and she figured early on that I didn't want to talk all that much about the team or what I was doing.

So, what can I tell you? Everything right now seems to be up in the air. Ron, the bartender, had been nice enough to have the Turk drive him up to Fort Lauderdale International to get the Jag and take it back to my apartment on Hollywood beach. I had to get a cab because the flight got in around 6:30 p.m., and for me, driving around nightfall is no longer an option. Anyway, you might be wondering why I keep saying Ron the bartender. The truth is I don't know the guy's last name. But then, when it comes to the Turk, the bookie at the Presidential…well, I don't even know his first name or his last for that matter!

So, again, I'm home.

Well, actually, I'm out on the beach with my butt in the sand, a glass of VO in my hand, and a cheek full of H. B. Scott chewing tobacco wedged into the right side of my mouth. Yeah, I know. Nothing much has changed; I continually seek solace in bad habits. And just like all those nights in St Pete, having done little more than chart player performance, I didn't hit my mattress last night with a feeling of accomplishment. Nor did I arise this morning with any semblance of enthusiasm. That's because I'm headed over to Dewey Street tonight for dinner with Sam and the kids…and Billy.

Like I said, my phone conversations with Sam were pretty much surface kinds of things, but I figure by now she's quit working at the

Presidential and told Billy we're married. I don't know how he's going to handle all this. So, at the moment, I'm flat-out nervous. I figure Sean thinks of me as awesome and, given the circumstances, that makes me a bit uncomfortable; the girls just giggle. That's okay; that's what little girls do I guess. But I know Sam will be anxious about how it goes, so I hope I can push all the right buttons, for her sake. Well, yeah, mine, too.

The moon's low on the eastern horizon and the brilliant, golden orb is illuminating the faded stucco walls of my three-story apartment building. I live on the top floor, and have a great view of the ocean. Maybe the patio is on the small side, but it's a great place to sit late at night. But in the early evening, I prefer being stretched out on the crushed, seashell beach under a few royal palms with their broad, pale-green fronds rustling in a tropical Gulfstream breeze.

I'm pretty sure I've shared with you how much I love the beach and the ocean. It's like it was all designed with the single purpose of providing me with an atmosphere of unsurpassed tranquility. Well, not exclusively just for me, of course, but I always feel this beach is personal…it's mine. I even like it in the dead of winter when the breeze is chilly, and the surf is choppy and full of nasty seaweed, compliments of the Sargasso Sea, almost half a world away. But, obviously, I like it more in the summer when the water temperature is in the 80s and the Gulfstream, only a quarter mile off shore, is a deep, cobalt blue. Some of my fondest memories are right here, but there are lots more of those special memories a few hundred yards north at Johnson Street, where Sam and I spent countless hours gazing at the stars…and each other. We talked endlessly about her hopes of diving in the Olympics and me playing ball in a big league park, like maybe Fenway with its Green Monster or the ivy-covered, outfield walls of Wrigley.

But, now that I think about it, we didn't talk about much else. Or at least, I didn't. So, I guess Sam is right when she says I was pretty much one-dimensional. And she's also right on the money, believing that the meaning of love changes, and it comes in different forms. Maybe I've got to reconsider that our teenage romance was more of a fascination with each other, as opposed to the true love thing. In fact, I'm beginning to wonder if you have to be married, through thick and thin, and make it into your sixties or seventies to really know what true love is all about.

But you might not live that long. So, maybe when we're alone in life, we cherish and embrace those special times in our past, even cling to them. And because they're so important to us, over a period of time we might even distort them by expanding them into so much more than they actually were.

Some might call this an exercise in promoting positive mental health. Others might think of it as a defense mechanism; a subconscious device designed to embellish reality; to make the fuck-ups and, yeah, the loneliness a little more comfortable.

Let's just skip it, okay? I'm supposed to be relaxing out here, rather than trying to engage you in a conversation about the nature of reality. Well, I guess I have to skip the relaxing part, too, and get refocused on going over to Sam's house pretty soon. I mean, this whole thing is so fucking bizarre and, yeah, I know…it's all my doing. Here I am, headed to Dewey Street to have dinner with a wife I don't live with, a son who doesn't know I'm his father, and a father-in-law who would undoubtedly be very happy, nay, euphoric, to see me exit stage left. But you know, guys, I think we need to take Billy off the page, because, regarding him, I think we're just beating a dead horse.

Maybe you ought to just hang out on the beach tonight. I get a feeling dinner this evening may not result in a memorable experience worth embracing or clinging to, for that matter. If that's the case, I can only hope by tomorrow morning enough time will have elapsed to allow for some massive reality distortion.

*

"Come on in, Dev," Sam says anxiously. "The kids and Daddy are out back, and I need to talk to you before they come in for dinner."

With a look on her face, that matches her tone, she turns and heads for the small kitchen off to the right of the living room. "I've got to toss a salad. Can you cut up the lettuce? There's a cutting board under the sink, and the knives are in the drawer."

The kitchen is so small, there's hardly room for the two of us. The sink, cupboards, and drawers are to the left; a side door, leading to the backyard, is straight in front; and the refrigerator and stove are to the right. Sam opens the refrigerator and retrieves a head of romaine lettuce, a cucumber, and two vine-ripe tomatoes. She turns to hand me the lettuce, but I put my hands on her shoulders, and plant a light kiss on her forehead.

"Hi, Samantha, it's good to see you too."

She puts down the lettuce, turns, and gives me peck on the cheek. "I'm sorry," she says sheepishly. "I was preoccupied. I was afraid I wouldn't get a chance to tell you some things you need to know."

"Like what?"

"I didn't tell Daddy we're married. I tried to work you into a few conversations, but his reactions made it clear that he can't handle it right now."

"Is that because he's going through a tough time, getting used to his meds and diet and all?"

"I'm sure that's part of it, but every time your name comes up, he changes the subject. I think it's going to take some time for both of us to convince him you're not who he thinks you are. He's really got a bone in his throat."

"I assume that bone has something to do with Sean?"

"He doesn't say so, but that's got to be some of it. And you know the old expression about once burned. When someone gets hurt, really hurt, I'm not sure it ever goes away."

That's just great. Now I don't know whether she's talking about Billy or herself. Regardless, I ain't going there. "So, you figure he's afraid that if you start spending time with me, history will repeat itself?"

"I think so."

"All that stuff was eight years ago," I say with some frustration.

"I guess you're right, but eight years ago is still today."

"You guess? After the last few months, that's the best you can do?" I'm annoyed. "Are you talking about Billy, or are you talking about yourself."

Fuck it…this ain't going very well.

"I'm sorry, Dev. That was a poor choice of words. If I didn't have some faith in you, we wouldn't be standing here, and we sure as hell wouldn't be married," she says with a smile. "But there's more," she continues.

"I think I can figure out what's next, Sam," I say, dropping my hands from her shoulders and reaching for the lettuce. "If you didn't tell Billy you're married, I suspect you're still working at the Presidential."

"I am. But it's okay, because I know there's a light at the end of the tunnel." She pauses, and then turns to me, and smiles. "Get ready. I just heard the back door open…and I hear footsteps and some joyful belly laughs."

There are definitely giggles. Within seconds, Jessica and Rebecca race into the kitchen and surround Sam. But they're looking at me.

"Hello, young ladies. Do you remember me?"

The giggles are now accompanied by smiles. I take that as a yes. I then realize Sean is standing just outside the kitchen. I told you it was small.

I quickly take a step toward him, and offer my hand. He takes it with a big grin.

"Hello Sean. How are you doing?"

"I'm doing great, D Jack. I'm starting in left field."

I look over to Sam who is watching the proceedings. "You know what they say about left fielders, Sean?"

"Not really," he responds, "but I'm wearing number 10!"

I keep looking at Sam. "Whoa, Nellie, now you've really got some trouble on your hands." I return my gaze to Sean, "How ya doing at the plate?"

"Super!" he says with pure joy. "You get two real pitches before they put it on the tee, and I haven't had to hit it off the tee yet."

"That's terrific, Sean, and you're probably not even eight years old."

"I'm seven."

"That's great; I'm proud of you."

"Thanks, D Jack.

Sam breaks in. "We'll talk more when we eat, but right now, I need you kids to help me set the table. Dev, why don't you go out back and say hi to Daddy. We'll call you in when dinner is ready. It'll only be a few minutes."

"That sounds fine with me. I'll do anything it takes to avoid breaking dishes."

With that, I head into the living room and hang a right into the back bedroom which in turn leads to the patio. As I approach the back door, a feeling of dread begins to come across me. I mean honest-to-God dread!

Once through the door, I see Billy sitting in an old, faded lawn chair that I remember from back when. I'll give him this. He's real handy and has probably rewoven the plastic strips on that chair three or four times. I slowly walk a dozen or so steps toward him and sit down in the matching seat across from him. He hasn't gotten around to this one, but it looks to be in need of his re-webbing skills. A small, round glass table is positioned between us. On the table, there's a blue can of salted Planter's peanuts and his ever-present six-pack of Ballantine Ale.

Billy's already got one in his hand, so I pick up a brew, open it with a church key, and take down about half. I never did like this stuff and never will. But I do like the brushed-gold can, and its three-ring trademark that proudly announces purity, body, and flavor. Billy drank it to chase Christian Brother's brandy, but I haven't been around enough to know if he still does that. It could be that he's off the sauce or the diabetes precludes it. Actually, now that I think of, maybe he still drinks Ballantine because it was the only endorsement he ever had. Years ago, the brewery ran an ad campaign featuring different Ballantine Ale Men. Billy was the first and they ran it for months. The best I ever got was some local stuff in Jax, and I don't remember pulling down more than a couple of bucks for those gigs.

"Hi, Billy, how are you doing with your treatment and the diet?" I inquire trying to sound sincere.

He eyes me suspiciously and thinks about that for a moment. "It's slow," he begins, "but I have more energy now, at least enough to be back on my shifts at the Bengal Lounge."

"That's a good sign. How are Ron and Sal doing?"

"Okay, I guess. We don't talk a whole lot."

"Well, tell them I said hi."

"Okay."

Both of us know that isn't going to happen. He takes another hit on his ale. "How are things going with spring training? Do you like being back in uniform, even if it's only in a manager's monkey suit?"

The second inquiry is obviously a dig, a not-so-subtle reminder that I'm not a player anymore. I sure as hell ain't gonna swing at that cheese. "Basically, all I did was compile scouting reports and chart lots of stats. As for uniforms, I'm still in street clothes."

"Yeah, well, I guess it must have been pretty tough going into the Mets lockers in New York for the first time, and taking off your uniform for the last time on the same day," he says indifferently.

Okay, guys. This one requires a response. "I wouldn't know. The last time my uniform came off, I was in a hospital in Queens."

"That's right. I forgot," he says, blowing it off. "So," he continues half-heartedly, "is Miami going to have a competitive team?"

Hell, Billy, why don't you just fucken yawn or something? "I don't know at this point. We'll carry an active roster of twenty-five, and the organization will start assigning players next week. I know with two Double AA clubs in the Mets organization, the Jackson Mets will get the cream of the crop, so I guess I have my work cut out for me."

"That sounds like a pretty tough assignment, especially for a new manager with no coaching experience."

"It'll give me something to do."

"I suppose that beats hustling people at a country club," he concludes sarcastically.

I've had it!

"That's just fine. I politely ask you how you're doing, and you proceed to rip my ass upside down and backwards. Are there any other topics you'd like to discuss, or should we just go in and pretend to enjoy a big plate of spaghetti? Or better yet, maybe you should just tell me to get out of your house; I figure that's what you want."

"I want more, and I think you want more than a spaghetti dinner. So it's pay back time. Get out of Samantha's life!"

Wow. I always figured Billy had a bone in his throat but now it's obvious he's on some kind of vindictive binge. His steely blues are boring right into me, and for once, I'm doing my best to bore back. "Before you embark on a journey of revenge, Billy, dig two graves."

He laughs. "You sure as hell didn't make that one up."

"Your right, it's a pearl of wisdom from Confucius, so if you're dead set on kicking me out the door," I say raising my voice, "you can explain that to your daughter. And the explanation better be a damn good one!"

He just stares at me, blankly, and I can't read a thing.

"It's your call, Billy. Do what you want. But one thing's for sure. This is the last time I'm going to just sit around and let you fuck me over, Sam or no Sam!"

"Things haven't been going the way I hoped they would," he finally sighs, grimly.

"And just what have you been hoping for?"

"When we went fishing, I hoped you'd just go away, but you didn't. Now I'm hoping Samantha will tell you to go to hell."

"You told me lots of things when we went fishing. But," I say, quickly recalling our late-night conversation on the banks of the Inter-coastal Canal, "now that I think back on it, you've dialed up your own agenda."

He doesn't say anything. He doesn't have to. His look is all but vicious; his feet are dug in. So are mine.

"And what do you think is Samantha's agenda?" he says.

"I'm not sure. I don't really know."

See, guys. I told you. This is why I wasn't exactly relaxed on the beach earlier today. I was clinging to the possibility that Billy might not take off the gloves. But deep down, I think I knew he was going to try to lay me out. Maybe I ought to just tell him I know Sean's my son. Okay, check that. He's already over the top, and I don't want him getting sick. Worse yet, Sam would have a complete cluster-fucked situation on her hands. Okay, thanks for listening, and thanks for not staying at the beach. I'll hold my fire, but I'm through taking his shit.

"Billy, I don't give damn what you're hoping for. But I'll make a deal with you. If the day comes when Samantha wants me out of your house, and out of her life, I'm history. But I'll tell you something else. You know the old cliché: be careful of what you hope for. You might get it!"

It's deadly quiet.

Actually, I don't feel all that bad. I hate confrontation, but sometimes, unlike Yogi's fork-in-the-road, in this case, the active road versus the passive road, one path becomes obvious, or, more accurately, necessary. Of course, you could turn around and avoid the fork altogether, but right now, that's not an option.

He takes another pull on his ale, and I empty what's left of mine. We just sit there. I don't have a clue. He looks tired and defeated. Maybe he's shocked because I've confronted him. Maybe he's confused or concerned about what's going on with Sam. Maybe he's wondering how many tomorrows he's got left. No matter. He looks like he's had enough. I don't know about you, but so have I.

"What's it going to be, Billy, dinner or the door?"

He slowly gets up from his chair, beer can still in hand. "I think Samantha and the children are waiting for us."

*

Dinner was a mixed affair. Sam played ringmaster and did her best to make sure the men were civil. The girls were enthusiastic about telling me funny little stories, and, of course, Sean was talking baseball. I figure I was able to respond with the right stuff and smile at the right time, because Sam kept flashing me approving smiles. The amusing highlight of the evening occurred when I unceremoniously dumped a fork full of spaghetti on my white, Mets tee shirt. Even Billy laughed, but I suspect he had a different agenda. Whoa, Nellie, I gotta start thinking positive.

That part was okay. But then Sam wanted the kids to help her clear the table and do the dishes, so she banished me and her dad to the backyard, again. She said she'd join us after putting the kids to bed. Rebecca and Jessica stood on chairs and gave me bashful hugs. Sean offered a manly handshake. That was the highlight reel, guys. Now it's back to reality.

Once outside, Billy simply walks over to the pool and lights a cigarette. He doesn't offer, and I don't ask. Why the hell should I? I don't smoke. I slump down into the lawn chair I vacated about an hour ago. Out comes my can of Kodiak and in goes a hefty pinch between cheek and gum. At least I've still got my old friend, Bart the Bear. Billy fills his lungs with smoke, takes a seat, and opens one of the beer cans left on the table. As with the cigarette, he doesn't offer a beer either. He takes a sip and then another drag on his Camel.

He looks across the pool. I stare at Bart, looking fierce on the green and white smokeless tobacco tin. We sit. It seems like forever.

It is!

Finally, Sam comes through the back door and walks over to us. Billy simply nods her way, and then laboriously gets to his feet. "Come sit here, pumpkin. I kept it warm for you."

She walks over to Billy and gives him an affectionate hug which he returns. After she kisses him on his cheek, he heads back into the house without another word and without looking back.

Sam sits down in the vacated patio chair and eyes me with concern. "I get the feeling you didn't have much in the way of a friendly conversation."

"That's very perceptive of you, Sam. What leads you to that conclusion?"

"Well, to begin with, when the two of you came in for dinner, you both looked uptight. I know I was doing most of the talking while we ate, but I couldn't help noticing you were totally avoiding each other. And, when I just came out, the two of you were just sitting here without saying a word."

"You're amazing, Sam. Your summary was accurate to the nth degree."

"What happened? You must have had something to talk about?"

"Now that I think of it, the conversation before dinner was similar to two prize-fighters feeling each other out."

"Given the lack of conversation at the dinner table, I assume that didn't last too long."

"You're right on the money again, Sam."

"So, who took the first swing?"

"Actually, I'd say your dad took the first three, all straight, stiff, jabs to the head."

"And I assume you responded with some jabs of your own?"

"No."

"No, you didn't respond?"

"No, I responded, but not with jabs."

"I see," she says a little dejected. "Then I guess it was pretty difficult to be polite, even though you know he's not feeling well."

"I tried, Sam. I really did," I offer, frustrated. "I asked him how he was feeling and all, but he wasn't having any of it. Maybe it's because he's sick, but he just seemed intent on sticking it to me."

"I was hoping it would be different, but I'm not surprised."

She smiles warmly. "Thanks for trying. I know this evening hasn't been very easy for you. But, if it helps any, when I tucked in the kids, they were all smiles and put you in their *lay me down* prayers."

"That does help, Sam," I say with a positive nod.

"So, here we are," I continue, as if I'm making some profound announcement. "The kids are in bed, your dad has left the premises, and it's finally just the two of us. What do you want to talk about? How did things go while I was over in St Pete?"

"It's been all kind of eerie," Sam answers, looking at the palmetto, thatch-roofed chickee, bracketed by two palm trees on the other side of the small, rectangular pool. The moon is high enough in the east to cast its reflected light on two small, bright yellow plastic tubes floating gently on the light blue water. The moonglow also highlights her strawberry-blonde hair and halos her silhouette in its soft light. She's taken off the apron she was wearing and replaced it with a long-sleeved, Kelly-green sweater to ward off the slight chill in the air.

I interrupt my distant thoughts. "It's been eerie?" I repeat. "I think you're going to have to explain that one, Sam."

"I've been thinking a lot about the last few months," she begins, turning away from the trees and gazing at me. "The eerie part is that I realize that we've had less than a dozen conversations, and that we don't really know each other. I don't have any idea what you've been doing or thinking over the past eight years."

"That goes equally for me, but I figure I could take some pretty educated guesses."

"And you'd probably be close, but I can't say the same about you. I'm not sure I'd even be in the ballpark."

"That's an interesting choice of words."

"You know what I mean," she says seriously.

"I do. So, what do you want to know?"

"It's not that easy. The problem is, I don't know *if* I want to know."

"Don't go there, Sam," I say quickly, wanting to nip this one in the bud. "You've said a few times that a relationship has to be built on trust, so if you need to fill in the blanks, you've got to believe that I can be up front."

She waits a few seconds and then the determined look on her face tells me she's made a decision. "Okay," she challenges. "When's the last time you really shared anything of yourself, and with whom?"

I don't miss a beat. "I think you can guess right on that one. It was with my dad. The day I left to play winter ball in Mexico."

"What did you talk about?"

"I told him I was scared. How's that for being honest?"

Her look clearly tells me my response was totally unexpected. "I never saw you scared, Dev."

"Neither did my dad, but I was scared all the time."

"You were scared of what? You were D Jack. You had it all. What could you have possibly been scared of? I have trouble believing that."

I slowly shake my head from side to side, frowning. "That's great, Sam. I mean, we're really off to terrific start on the believing and trusting part."

"I'm sorry. You're right," she adds apologetically. "I wasn't ready for that. It just never occurred to me that you were ever afraid. You certainly never showed it. Gee," she smiles, trying to lighten up the moment, "I used to watch you dig into the batter's box with your spikes almost touching the plate. You were absolutely fearless."

"That's not what I'm talking about. Let me put it this way. Were you ever scared when you stood on the board, about to throw a one and a half somersault with a full twist?"

"No. I was too focused on nailing the dive."

"It wasn't any different for me. I was focused on staring down a pitcher, and trying to remember his patterns, if I'd seen him before."

"So you weren't afraid of being injured?"

"I got hurt plenty of times, but I just picked myself up and got on with it. Being seriously injured was never on my mind."

"What was it then?"

"Right or wrong, I always felt lots of people wanted to see me fail, and I didn't want to make them happy."

"You really believed that?"

"I did. But the worst part was the fear of failing the one person whose whole life was wrapped up in my ability to play ball."

"And, like you've already told me, your dad never saw that happen."

"No. Thankfully, he didn't. But that last conversation with him made him anxious, because for the first time, he heard me talk about wondering if I had what it takes to be a big-league ballplayer. I'd like to think that, somehow, he knows I actually got there, even if it was for only eight innings."

"Where is your dad buried, Dev?"

"He's next to Mom in Memorial Gardens out on Taft Street in West Hollywood."

"I know where it is. My mom and sister are buried there too," she murmurs solemnly.

I can't speak for you guys, but I'm wearing out. I figured I was in for a confrontation with Billy, but didn't anticipate how ugly it might be. And it was, thanks to me, I suppose. Now this serious conversation with Sam is making me somewhat apprehensive, and I don't even know why. Maybe it's because nothing is bridging the gap between us.

"This is all kind of heavy, Sam. Do you want to ask about something else?"

"I think all my questions would be heavy, as you put it. But, talking about your dad, and my mother and sister, makes me realize that at least I have my dad, and of course the kids. It must have been very difficult for you to have been alone."

"What makes you think I was alone?" I tease.

She smiles wryly. "Let's call it an educated guess. I saw you around people at the Presidential, and I think you have an invisible wall or shield around you. I'm not suggesting you haven't had friends over the years, but I'm willing to bet you let no one in."

Okay, guys. You know she's got me on that one, unless I can count some of my conversations with you. But I think I'd have a hard time talking to her about talking with you. It's time for a side-step.

"Well, recently on paper, if you recall, I let someone in."

"And you call a marriage license letting someone in?" she asks playfully.

"I think it's fair to say that's accurate, at least for normal people. But," I continue quickly, "it's more than one piece of paper."

"Dev, now you're going to have to explain that one to me."

"Actually, it's lots of paper. I didn't mention that while I've been gone, all the necessary documents have been approved, and you're now the legal beneficiary of all my worldly belongings."

Her positive glance tells me changing the subject is okay. "And just what *are* your worldly belongings?" she inquires.

"One ivory 1954 XK-120 Jaguar; one jet black 550cc, 4-stroke TX 500 motorcycle; and one ash-blond Yamaha G-50A classical guitar."

"Is that it? Don't you even have a television set?"

"Sure I do. It's a nine inch black and white. I figure it isn't worth adding to the estate."

"Well, as for me," she says with a smirk, "in no particular order, I don't know how to drive a stick shift car, I refuse to drive anything motorized...with only two wheels, and I can't play guitar. You don't have a Jew's Harp, do you?"

"No, but if I did, I could do three of the four."

"Dev, you've lost me again."

"Okay, I'll clarify. I think I could play a Jew's harp, I can play guitar, and my current driver's license says I can legally drive the bike as well as the car. But my eye guy says when I renew my license I probably won't be on the bike anymore, and I'll have restrictions when it comes to the Jag. And he's already cautioned me about driving at night. So, I figure that makes it three out of four."

"But you drove over here tonight, in the Jaguar," she says with a double-dose of alarm.

"There's hardly any traffic between here and the beach. Even so, it's the last time I break the law, that is, when it comes to driving at night."

She sighs. "I really didn't want to toss out anything else, and I'm sorry. But just how bad is your vision?"

"How bad can things be if the Department of Transportation reissued my driver's license a few years ago?"

"But with restrictions," she says, "and anyway your answer was legal, not medical."

"Hey. Speaking of medical, I forgot to tell you something else."

"Are you trying to change the subject again, smart ass?" Sam accuses, sounding frustrated.

"It seems that way, doesn't it. But this is important, and it's good news. How about it? I'm just trying to put a smile on your face."

"I'd feel better if I knew you were okay."

"Sam, the specialists told me the right eye is trying to hold its own. That's all I know."

"That's fair enough," she concedes. "Okay, then. What's your good news? Fire away."

"You and the kids now have health insurance," I say, grinning widely, as I pull out my wallet, retrieve the cards, and hand them to her.

I'm hoping Sam's huge look of relief has supplanted her pre-occupation with me. Knowing she has the financial security to medically provide for herself and the children has to be a huge monkey off her back. However, I'm surprised that she's not doing cartwheels; she's just quiet and seems very reflective.

"I can't begin to tell you how important this is," she says, sounding more beholden than anything else.

I lean very close to her and whisper, "I'm just trying to be a good provider. I think it's what's expected of a newly-wed."

I think she's going to nail me on that one, but we hear a creak and look over to see Billy standing in the half-opened doorway. He's got concern written all over him; hell, I hope he hasn't overheard the last few minutes of our conversation.

"Jessica is having some trouble getting to sleep, sweetie. She's tossing and turning. I think you need to come in." Without waiting for a reply, he turns and closes the door.

I guess he didn't hear anything, but I'm not buying this new piece of bullshit! You know, I'm starting to believe that having a bone in his throat is an understatement. But I guess it could be worse. If we were in Sicily, he probably would have used a lupara on me. That's their weapon of choice, similar to the sawed-off shot gun more commonly used to settle these matters in the Blue Ridge Mountains. In that he's already said things aren't going his way, he still might!

"Do you think something's really wrong with her?" I ask.

"I don't know. She rarely has trouble going to sleep. And like I said, Daddy's not overly pleased we're seeing each other. But," she says as she gets to her feet, "either way, I've got to go in."

"Okay," I say, standing to join her as we head for the door. "That being the case, I'm going home. If we're reading him right, the evening is over."

At the door, she turns, and wraps her arms around me, bringing her face almost to mine. I don't know what it is, but there's something in her eyes, something quizzical and a little confused. She hesitates. Her look changes, the way it usually does when she makes a decision. She slowly closes the distance between us and kisses me, yearningly. After a second or two, she starts to pull away but I draw her to me and return her kiss, softly and lovingly.

"That was unexpected," I say with a smile, "and sweet."

She returns my smile. "Yes, it was."

A second or two passes and then she adds, "You've had a stressful evening with Daddy, and I wanted to make sure you know that I'm here with you."

"Sam. I could never come between you and Billy," I say earnestly. "I'd walk away before I'd let that happen, because I know what he means to you. And more importantly, I know what you mean to him."

"If Daddy could hear you now, he'd begin to see the father of my son in a much different light," she says tenderly. "Just try to be patient, Dev."

She looks up at me with an encouraging smile, although there are tears in her eyes. Obviously, this evening has been tough for her, too. She gives me another hug and, without another word, turns and goes through the back door. I just stand there.

You're probably wondering why all this is so difficult? Well, one thing is certain, it sure as hell is. Every time we start to get closer, a monkey wrench, tonight's hand tool being Billy, gets thrown into the works. You know…the ole one step forward, two steps back.

Check that. I need to be thinking this evening was two steps forward and only one step back. Agreed?

I look across the pool. The glowing moon, majestic trees, and palm-thatched chickee all seem at peace with the world. It sure would be nice to walk over there, plunk down on the wooden platform of the Indian dwelling on stilts, and lose myself in that scene. Like I've been trying to say, it's time to stay on the offensive and make it happen! So, you don't think I can make things happen?

I'm not even going to offer you a bet on this one. It wouldn't be fair to take your hard-earned money. So, for starters, before I head for home, I *am* going to enjoy the serenity of the Seminole house. Or was it the Miccosukee's who built chickees? I don't think it matters. The point is I'm heading for the other side of the pool to think good thoughts about me and Sam, and *that* does matter!

V

WELCOME TO THE MINORS

The manager is by himself.
He can't mingle with his players.
I enjoyed my players,
but I could not socialize with them…
So I spent a lot of time alone
in my hotel room.
Those four walls
kind of close in on you.
Al Lopez, Manager
Cleveland Indians/Chicago White Sox

I'm sitting in my office. That really sounds strange; I've never had an office. And I never envisioned sitting in one, particularly one with carpets and wood paneling. It's just something I never expected. But then, this morning's meeting was something I never expected either.

It took place in the luxurious team offices, situated behind the home team lockers on the third base side of the brand new Miami Park. It began with the team's general manager, Pepper Kwalchek, introducing me as his manager in front of a bunch of coaches who know a hell of a lot more about baseball than I ever will.

Howard Sheridan told me in Aspen at his wife's birthday party he had offered the GM spot to Pepper, who had been my hitting coach at Jacksonville. After that stint, he was elevated to the position of manager with the Class-A St. Lucie Mets, and, after completing three winning seasons, he was promoted to the position of bench coach with the Double AA Jackson franchise. As far as I'm concerned, Pepper ought to be managing the Miami team but, as you know, Sheridan wants me in that position for the first year, primarily for public relations. He figures my so-called celebrity status will get lots of ink, which will also be useful to his new television station in Miami when I move over there next year as sports director. But I think we've been through all of that.

The meeting went well. I'd like to think Pepper was really getting pumped about being in a position he probably thought was years away, if ever. I was concerned that he'd be ticked about me calling the shots on the field. But from the onset, his demeanor communicated his desire to take me under his wing, just like he had done more than half a dozen years ago.

That was reinforced earlier this morning when we had coffee before the meeting, and he offered some managerial advice. He prefaced his remarks by saying a few things had worked for him and maybe they would work for me. He said managing a game had three parts: before, during, and after. Before the game, study the scouting reports and the stats of the opposing team's players. During the game, go with the numbers, but also go with your gut. You've got to continually look at the match-ups, both in terms of your hitters as well as your pitchers. After the game, think about what your players could have done, should have done, or didn't do at all.

His supportive tone concluded with a smile and a pat on the shoulder and continued at the meeting when he directed a few positive words my way. After that, he introduced each of the coaches, training staff, and support personnel. I'm sure you'll get to know them better during the season. As for me, it was helpful that I had gotten together a few times prior to the meeting with the guys I'd be working with on a day in, day out basis.

Just to fill you in, Leo Blake was brought on board to be the assistant manager and bench coach. I played for him, briefly two years ago when I took a futile stab at staying in the game with a semi-pro team in Miami. He's a hell of a baseball man but probably pushing sixty. So, his hope of managing at a higher level has all but gone over the hill. But I think Howard Sheridan told me Leo knows the master plan calls for him to succeed me next year when I shift over to the television station.

Tico Serrano was brought in as the pitching coach. The word is this guy came out of Cuba, but he's pretty tight-lipped about that. Who cares? He threw in the show for 10 years with a life-time ERA of 3.8. Any guy who can hold a team under four runs per game for an entire career really knows his stuff. Fortunately, having pitched before being converted into a left-fielder, I was able to hold my own when we got to talking about four-seam and two-seam fastballs, curves, change-ups, and cutters.

My most relaxed moments have been with Rusty Hillen who, if you recall, caught me throughout our two high school state championship years. I knew he was a gifted hitter, even at that young age, and wasn't surprised to find out he played Double AA ball with the Savannah Braves for two years. However, when we bumped into each other at a Little League practice at Jefferson Park a few months ago, he never mentioned it. Maybe he figured with me being out of the game, it might bother me that he suited up. He eventually said he had to pay the bills and support his family, so he hung up his spikes and got his master electrician's license.

You might recall I mentioned Rusty to Howard Sheridan in December and he agreed to put him on the coaching staff. He probably thought he didn't have the experience for the job but went along with me, figuring I'd be comfortable using Rusty as a sounding board.

After the introductions, Pepper proceeded to inform us he had no intentions of settling for a honeymoon season. Most people, including the higher-ups in the organization, figured we could hold our fan base even with a mediocre year, but he wasn't having any of that. He told us in no uncertain terms that it was our collective job to get the most out of the twenty-five players assigned to us on the active roster. The bottom line was very simple: we're here to win! To that end, he also made it very clear that on the field, it was the coaches' responsibility to suggest; it was my responsibility to decide. Like I said, I certainly never expected anything like this.

Having blown his bolt, he ended the meeting by introducing one of his assistants, a gorgeous statuesque redhead in her mid-thirties, who led us out the door and gave us the VIP tour of the new park.

I've got to tell you, this place sure as hell is no typical minor league ballpark. It's pretty obvious that Sheridan's not going to be content to have a Double AA franchise for long. The first clue is that Miami Park seats more than 10,000 which is the minimum to qualify for a Triple AAA team. Furthermore, other than the large overhang roof designed to protect a significant number of fans from south Florida's frequent rain storms and abundant sunshine, the park could easily be expanded into a full blown major league stadium. I think the tip-off might be the red brick exterior of the park, complete with five white-concrete vertical columns on each side of the grand entrance directly behind the home plate area. That facade sure has the look of a big league park.

Other features not commonly found in the minors include lower and upper decks that wrap around the park from first to third base with, would you believe it, stadium seats! Behind the lower deck, a concourse is lined with eateries that offer everything from hot dogs to Cuban black beans and rice. Souvenirs, team clothing, and a variety of sports memorabilia can also be purchased at what appear to be moderate prices.

The sideline bleachers that run the length of the first and third base foul lines are contoured and made of aluminum, as opposed to being smooth, flat boards. An additional twenty rows of bleachers are behind the right field fence and above them is a two-story edifice that houses a plush restaurant and lounge.

A family picnic area and children's playground is behind the left field fence and is cordoned off by rows of magnificent royal palm trees. There's also plenty of room for dads and kids to play catch. In dead-away center, a small botanical garden sports more palm trees, a variety of indigenous shrubs, and a three-tiered waterfall. Actually, the waterfall is to the right of dead-center, so as not to interfere with the batter's ability to see the pitcher's delivery and eye the ball as it leaves his hand.

So, you bet, this place is a far cry from the rust-buckets I played in. But, you know, some of those rust-buckets had a hell of a lot of character, and they still do.

Well, time to go. Here comes the fun part. The players reported in this morning and were assigned lockers, uniforms, and given a look at the facilities. At this moment, they are in the locker room, patiently awaiting their manager. So, let's go say hi.

My office leads into a larger area with desks and lockers for the assistant coaches. A large alcove that houses stationary bikes, whirlpools, training tables, and other equipment is situated between the offices and the large, rectangular, players' locker room. On each side, there are more than a dozen five-foot high open lockers. Above each is a smaller area for personal belongings. Two smooth-polished benches run parallel to and flush against the lockers. At the far end of the room, a tunnel leads to the dugout. The entire area is covered with a beige carpet made of some kind stuff that appears to be heavy-duty.

As I enter, most of the guys are in front of their lockers in various stages of suiting up for practice. The small talk comes to an abrupt halt as they realize I've arrived. The first thing that hits me is their collective look of anxiety. Welcome to the minors, boys!

"Good morning, gentleman."

Nothing, well, maybe a few grunts, but they just stand there like a herd of deer in the headlights. I wait a few seconds figuring things might loosen up.

No such luck.

They continue to look at me as if I'm their executioner as opposed to their manager. Now that I think of it, I suspect before the season is over I probably am going to end some dreams of playing professional baseball.

I forgot. That's another piece of information Pepper volunteered this morning. It wasn't the first time I heard that telling a player he was through, or going down, was the toughest thing a manager has to do. So, he told me, when the time comes, make it sound like an organizational decision, and don't use kid gloves. In the long run, dashing their hopes and dreams does them a favor, because after it sinks in, they can get on with their lives.

I don't know if I can do that.

"Why don't you guys have a seat and get comfortable. You're only going to have to put up with one long speech from me this season, and today's the day. And really, that's a promise, more to the coaches than to you. They've already informed me I'm not the world's greatest orator," I grin.

It seems to break the ice. I hear a few laughs and notice some of the players exchange smiles as they sit down on the benches in front of their lockers.

I remain standing. "I'm Devon Jameison. Let me begin by welcoming all of you to the Mets and the minor leagues. Each of you is a proud possessor of a professional athletic contract. Like everyone likes to say, it's the first time you're going to get paid to play ball and have fun. So, the purpose of what I'm about to say is not to motivate you; just being here should be more than enough to jack you up."

More laughs.

"All but one of you played college ball, so you're familiar with university admission standards. At the graduate level, for most schools, admission means they fully expect you to graduate and are committed to doing all they can to make that expectation a reality. It doesn't entirely work that way here. The part that *is* the same is that we too are committed to doing our very best, for each and every one of you, to develop your potential, and you *do* have potential. If you didn't, you wouldn't have that contract, and you wouldn't be sitting here," I say in a serious way.

It's quiet. You could hear a fucken pin drop.

"But, even though the organization is making a financial investment in you," I continue, "the reality is the majority of you will never play an inning in Shea Stadium or any other big league ballpark for that matter. Statistically, only a few of you will go the Show. And make no mistake about it. Baseball is most definitely a game of statistics."

I wait a moment or two for that sobering fact to sink in. "Even if you don't make it to the show, some of you will play Triple AAA," I continue, encouragingly. "And at that level, players fully expect to get the call. Maybe you go on a hot streak, or maybe someone on the big club gets injured or just goes into a deep slump. If none of that happens, you still might make a career out of it. There are lots of guys who can't sustain, on a day-in day-out basis, what it takes to play in the majors, but they're good enough to continually play at the Triple AAA level and have a rewarding career.

"The thing is…you're not there. You're here, and Double AA is different. Your chances of going to the next level aren't all that hot, so what you need to do is really set yourself apart from the crowd; ya gotta be outstanding. And unlike Triple AAA, you don't stay here very long, so there are three ways to go: up, down, or out. And I'll be real honest with you. I know this sounds discouraging on day one, but going down to our High A team in St. Lucie is about the same as going out."

I look around the room, and their expressions are pretty grim. It's hard. Like I told you a few months ago, most of these guys have been coddled since Little League, and here at the onset of their professional careers they're being told their chances of going all the way aren't that good. But what the hell, they should already know that. Regardless, Pepper had advised me to lay it on the line from the beginning. But looking around the room, I'm wondering if this was the best way to go.

"I know that's pretty blunt, but that's the way it is, guys. However," I say supportively, "every one of you has my one hundred percent guarantee that the coaching staff here will do everything possible to get you to the next level. And, you might not know it yet, but these men are great teachers.

"So, guess what? We're going to take you back to Fundamentals 101." That remark evokes a mixture of laughs and phony groans. The important thing for me is the coaches are smiling supportively.

"I'm not the first, and I won't be the last, to tell you baseball appears to be a very simple game: you catch, you throw, and you hit. No one plays Double AA ball unless you're pretty damn good at two of the three. But to go up, I mean really up, you have to be better than damn good, and you need all three. That's why we're going back to fundamentals. And when we get through, you might be even better than you think you are. And that's no easy task, because right now you guys probably figure you're great."

That really gets a laugh, and some of them are looking around and nodding approvingly to each other.

"I've shared with you a little bit of the coaches' responsibility to you. But in turn, you have responsibilities too. As I said, baseball appears to be a simple game, but it takes time and experience to be able to make adjustments and lightning-fasts decisions on the field. You have to be able to think on your feet, so I can tell you straight out, you're in for a long season. And it is long. This isn't football. Here, you not only play every day, but you practice every day as well!"

It's getting quiet again. I slowly look around the room, trying to catch the eye of each and every one of them. They might be quiet, but they're attentive.

"Responsibility number one," I begin, "is to play hard and play to win, always! We're going to get beat, hopefully not too often. And you're going to have some bad days. Even so, I never want to see you quit. Don't worry about your last at-bat. Like I said, it's a long season. Bad days and mistakes are useful, if you can learn something, if you can improve. And don't worry about yesterday or today. Play better tomorrow."

They still look pretty serious but are also nodding in the affirmative as if committing to the hard work in front of them.

"As for practice, be on time and bust your ass when you're out there. And," I add with a smile, "laugh it up once in awhile. Twenty-four hour serious will kill ya."

They collectively lighten up with that remark. Man, this has been one hell of a roller-coaster ride.

"As for me, my job is a piece of cake," I say with a shrug. "All I have to do is figure out how to win ball games. To do this, I've got to get the most out of all twenty-five of you and keep everyone on the same page. If you read Jack London's *Call of the Wild*, you'll recall Buck was the hero, the lead sled dog. You need to understand that no one here is named Buck, and there is no lead sled dog. You're on a team, and we play as a team, and we take pride in being a part of a team that wins. That's what we do. You get paid to play; I get paid to win. It's as simple as that."

At this moment, I can't tell if I've scared the hell out of them or if they can't wait to get at it. We'll know soon enough. Either way, I've said my piece; that's all there is, sports fans.

"Before you report to your coaches and hit the field, I want to mention a few organizational matters. If you require any attention from our trainers, you need to be here at least an hour before you suit up for practice or before a game. Jason and Jeremy are always here before as well as after practice. Both of them have degrees in kinesiology from Penn State and are licensed physical therapists. They've been with the Mets since 1973. Get to know them. You're going to worship the ground they walk on. But don't go looking for father figures. They're only interested in keeping you physically fit.

"If you need advice and stuff like that, our traveling secretary, August Stewart is the man to see. Among other things, he's got a degree in clinical psychology, but I suggest you don't go there with him; he'll charge you by the hour." I see big grins and hear solid laughs, the loudest coming from

Stew himself. He's standing near the entrance to the tunnel at the back of the room with Leo, Tico, Rusty, Jason, Jeremy, and the rest of the coaching staff.

"Seriously, if you have any problems, like finding a place to live or something more crucial like locating the nearest Cadillac dealership, Stew's your walking encyclopedia."

More chuckles for the Cadillac thing. "That goes double when we're on the road. Whether we're home or away, you have to be totally focused on the game. So, he's your main man. And, I really shouldn't have to say this, but anything you discuss with him is confidential, if that's the way you want it to be. Stew," I say, raising my voice somewhat to make sure he can hear me at the back of the room, "is there anything you'd like to share with these young men?"

He takes a few steps away from the wall and slowly looks around the room. I don't know if you had a Dutch uncle or, if you did, what he looked like, but August Nathan Stewart sure looks like one to me. His whole appearance is non-threatening: half-glasses perched on a small, straight nose; big smile, mostly bald, and a little pudgy; red suspenders on each side of his rounded belly.

"I think I'll just say, at this time, that my door is always open, but I don't do house calls." The players cheer as one. That's great. I'm guessing some of these guys are going to need a house mother.

"Finally, a few weeks ago," I say loudly enough to get them re-focused, "you all received information about the exhibition game we'll play tomorrow night. We thought about calling it a father-son game, but most of you are way too young, or not in a legal position to be fathers."

Whew. They're still laughing.

"Mr. Sheridan wants the community to know we're here, so admission will be free. Everything else will be two bucks, including guided tours, souvenirs, and dogs and sodas. If you've got buddies coming, tell them beer will go for three bucks with a valid ID of course, because I get the feeling some of your friends have yet to experience a close encounter with a razor blade. Make sure you see Stew and let him know if you have any family or friends who want to participate in the game."

"There'll be sign-up sheets in my office," Stew says from the back of the room. "After that, you'll need to see Jeffrey, our equipment manager, who'll rustle up some game jerseys. Tell those who are going to play that jeans and sneakers will be fine, and if they happen to have a glove or maybe a favorite bat, they can bring them along."

"For about half an hour after the game," I continue," the fans will be invited to join us on the infield so you can sign autographs, not that anyone really knows who you are. It's going to be kind of hectic. After the autograph session, Mr. Sheridan has also arranged a full-blown catered BBQ dinner for players and family in the picnic area behind the left field fence."

One guy yells out, "what if it rains?"

"Obviously, you haven't met the team owner, Mr. Sheridan. There's no way he's going to let Mother Nature mess with him tomorrow. But just in case you're skeptical about his ability to control the elements, the weatherman on WTVJ is saying it will be a perfect night for baseball."

More laughter. I pause, giving them a moment to settle down and process all the information. "I figure you probably have some questions, but I'd rather get you guys out on the field. We'll address anything you think you need to know during the day. If it deals with something all of us need to be aware of, we can handle it when we all get together, briefly, at the end of practice."

A hand goes up. Way up. He's six-six, probably goes around two-thirty or so. He's a left-handed flame-thrower out of the University of Southern California. Fortunately, I've done some homework and matched pictures with bios.

"Denny?"

"Uh, sorry, but I do think we need to know one other thing, if it's okay," he says with obvious hesitation.

"Sure. Fire away."

"Uh, what do we call you?"

The giggles abound, the loudest once again coming from the back of the room.

"Good question, Denny. The coaching staff decided *chief* wouldn't work, even though I lived in Arizona, and I don't have gray hair, which could justify *boss*, so they settled on *skipper*. That's not up for a vote. In fact, nothing is up for a vote. Okay?"

"Okay…skipper," Denny responds with a smile.

"That brings the speech part of the day to an end. Finishing suiting up, hit the field, and report to your coaches. Once again, gentleman, welcome to the minors."

*

I've found my new watering hole! Thanks to the punishing work schedule at the Presidential, I never had time to relax in any of the laidback bars, lounges, or restaurants on Hollywood Beach. Four of the most popular spots are within walking distance of my apartment. I tried all of them a few days after I ended my two-year stint at the country club.

The most popular of the four is Joe Sonkens Gold Coast Restaurant located on New York Street and North Ocean Drive. It's about four blocks south of Buchanan, which is the street I live on. My patronage of this place was short-lived. It was way too big to provide the cozy atmosphere I was looking for. But the clincher was found at a table in a far corner, where Jilly "the Ice" Marinski was holding court with some of his associates. After a few innocent inquiries, directed toward a friendly bartender, I found out the Gold Coast was known as a mob place, so that was that.

The second spot is two blocks north of the Gold Coast. It's called the Flicker-lite, and it's owned and operated by Frank and Joan Capone. And yes, they're from Chicago, but they claim to have no famous relatives in the windy city. I ruled this place out because they do too much business, and it's small, so they're not selling much in the way of peace and quiet. But Joan makes a killer Chicago-style pizza, so I'll go in occasionally to get supper to go.

Number three is the most convenient because it's on the corner of Buchanan and North Ocean Drive, a mere block away from the ocean and my apartment house. This one is Sketch where Charlie Moon plays and it's easily the most atmospheric because it has more than a hint of romance with its indirect lighting, soft carpets, and informal furnishings. I'm not sure what kind of place Billy Joel envisioned in his signature song, *Piano Man*, but I think he might have had something in mind like Sketch even if it doesn't have a piano. There's a small, horseshoe-shaped stage in a corner of the back room and a similar larger semi-circular bar with half a dozen barstools for single patrons who prefer sitting there rather than at one of the dozen or more tables that occupy the larger front room. This was clearly my first choice, but the owner's priority is that of being a wine bar, and his application for a full liquor license is pending. That's too bad; no VO, no go. But I'm sure I'll go in once-in-awhile to catch Moon and maybe even sit in for a gig or two. Who knows? The one time I've been in to hear him play, the 'T' man was pushing me pretty hard to join him on a regular basis.

Happily, after crossing all three off my list, I stumbled on a watering hole on Garfield Street which is about six blocks north of where I live. It's located halfway between North Ocean Drive to the west and the Hollywood Boardwalk that parallels the beach to the east. That's important, because, as you know, I shouldn't drive at night. Speaking of which, I got lucky. Rusty, his wife, and kids, moved over to the beach about a month ago, and he volunteered to drive me to the park and back. I was pretty concerned about transportation, particularly when it comes to night games, and was relieved to have that problem solved.

So, at this very moment, I'm sitting in Ziggy's, my new home away from home. The sun has gone down, and I'm adjusting to a different lifestyle. Among other things, this means having no more than two drinks before dinner, which I actually eat in my own apartment; relax on my patio; and hit the sack before 11:00.

I'm nursing my first VO and reflecting on day one with the team. My first thought is, there weren't any fuck-ups. I had mixed emotions about my talk, but Leo said he thought I did a good job. How about you? Did I do a good job? Anyway, Leo added he might not have been quite as blunt. But, given the fact that I'm not much more than five or six years older than most of the players, he felt it was appropriate for me to lay it out there.

The afternoon had gone pretty well too, other than general disappointment with the decision to forego batting practice until tomorrow. The coaches wanted to get a good look at running, throwing, and fielding. And Tico wanted to get the pitchers and catchers together so he could check out their mechanics.

I went from group to group, and generally adopted a low profile. Pepper suggested it would be a good idea to let the guys bond with the coaches. He cautioned me that, once again, because of my age, some of the players might attempt the buddy-buddy thing. He laughed and added that, regardless of age, in the words of Whitey Herzog, the current manager of the Kansas City Royals, "If they need a buddy, let them buy a dog."

The toughest part of the day came after practice. Everyone had gone, and I was sitting alone, adrift in a swirl of memories.

You know, now that I think of it, I figure I owe you an apology. Yep, you're probably sick and tired of me and my melancholy. Chances are you've dealt with much more serious stuff than me not being able to play ball. I hope not, but if so, I'm really sorry. Honest. This is the last time I'm going to say anything about it. This is the end of it. That's it. You can take it to the bank!

Anyway, Pepper came into my office, and looked at me as if he knew exactly what was going through my mind. I stood up, feeling out of place in my spanking-clean Miami Mets uniform.

"You know, kid," he said as he approached. "I never thought I'd see you wearing #10 again." He gave me a hug and then stood back a step. "I remember when we were together in Jacksonville; you didn't think you'd be able to hit low and away on a regular basis. But, you listened to me, and worked your way through it. Trust me, kid. You can do it again."

He smiled, and gave me a pat on the shoulder, just for old time sake I guess. He lingered only for a moment. Then he turned and headed for the tunnel. I sat back down and thought to myself, he was right eight years ago so, hopefully, he'll be right again. My thoughts are interrupted by Ziggy himself, who wants to know if I'd like some popcorn.

"No thanks, Zig. Now that I have to wear a uniform, I need to be in good shape. No junk food for me."

"So, maybe you would like a healthy nosh?" he inquires with a heavy New York accent and a big smile.

"That would be worse than popcorn. You don't have a clue as to what a nosh is, Zig. Everything Rose puts together is enough to feed an extended family."

"You're right!" he says, his ever-present infectious grin spreading across his face. He pats his excessive tummy, which dominates his five and half foot body. I've seen him do this often; it must be a habit, like tweaking your tie. His bald head is shaped like his belly, with a few tufts of dark hair above and behind his ears. His scruffy, salt-and -pepper beard barely covers his cheeks.

Rose, Zig's wife, is almost his twin physically. All you have to do is substitute lots of henna-colored hair on her head, and a plethora of rouge and lipstick. Oh, yes, add just a hint of a mustache!

I love this place! It's cozy. My grandparents were gone long before I was born, but my dad used to tell me how much he loved to sit in their parlor. I don't know why, but I feel that parlor might have looked something like Zig and Rose's bar. It's very small, only about eight tables. The floor is a lightly-stained hardwood, but the table and chairs are darker, maybe mahogany or cherry. The unisex bathroom is behind Rose's kitchen, which is great, because, for whatever reason, she likes to give me a bear hug on the way to the can.

Another really neat thing about the place is it offers you an olfactory experience. When you walk in, you'd swear from the tantalizing aromas that you're in Wolfie Cohen's Rascal House down on Collins Avenue in Sunny Isles. And, better yet, the guys in that kitchen could take lessons from Rose. Everyonce in awhile I've sampled a half-sandwich. So far, her deli concoctions have surpassed Cohen's world-class, kosher restaurant. And, if I put a little mayo on something, there aren't any "oye veys" uttered by the matronly waitresses. More importantly, there aren't any memories to trigger a feeling of melancholy.

There's something else that isn't in Ziggy's Bar: A bar! There's a small countertop, but there aren't any stools. The counter just serves to separate the dining tables from a three-tiered shelf that holds an assortment of liquor bottles. Unlike the western-style saloons in Glenwood Springs and Aspen, you won't find any ornate woodwork or beautiful glass panels in this establishment.

That's about the best I can do. I hope it's enough for you to get the feel of the place, its warmth and genuine friendliness. There was one thing I certainly hadn't expected; during a casual conversation upon my first visit, I introduced myself, and Zig and Rose knew who I was. It turns out they lived just off Bedford Avenue in Williamsburg, Brooklyn. They were avid baseball fans and, with Shea Stadium being in the neighboring borough of Queens, the Mets were their team. They said they only went to the park once a year but always listened to Lindsey Nelson doing the radio broadcasts. Like most Mets fans, they followed my medical progress for the few days I was a news item. Thankfully, it was a brief conversation that ended with them simply saying they were glad I was okay.

In a way, their fortunes hadn't been much different than mine. The two of them, already married, emigrated from Poland right after World War II. Scores of refugees were flooding into Williamsburg, and for years, Zig and Rose managed to keep busy, and were modestly prosperous. He was a cabinet maker; she was a seamstress. Then, as the war faded into the past, the economy sank, and the township declined into a morass of social ills, drugs, and crime. They scraped together all they could, headed south, and bought the bar about four years ago.

Their beach bungalow is only two blocks away. They don't own a car or much of anything else, as best I can tell, but they're always ready with a smile and a warm greeting. They laugh a lot, and more importantly, they say life is simple, but good.

Things would be just a little bit better, if Sam could join me here once in awhile. But she's still working the late dinner shift, so that's not going to happen until she quits. I just think we could have good conversations in such a warm place. You know, hold hands; the whole romantic thing.

It's been a long day. I'm tired. I'm going home.

Well, actually, I'm not.

I'm waiting for a guy named Daryl to pick me up. Howard Sheridan is having a dinner party for the Mets brass at the Diplomat Hotel tonight, and he asked me to join them. I know he's building a home on one of the exclusive islands in Biscayne Bay, so I figure it isn't finished, given the address of tonight's affair. I also figure Charley told him I can't drive at night.

So, here I am, knocking down my second and last VO and waiting for Daryl. You probably wouldn't mind coming along, but you'll have to settle for my blow-by-blow tomorrow. After all, when it comes to the Mets organization, I'm low man on the pole; extending invitations isn't part of my pay grade!

And while we're at it, I owe you another apology. I mean, I'm taking up more of your time since leaving the Presidential. Over there, I could shoot the shit with Marcus and Ron, and, to a lesser extent, Ralph and the Turk. Here, I'm not very comfortable with most of the coaches, because they know so much more than me. But tonight, I'm going to have a good time regardless. In fact, I'll bet you a twenty spot that my evening will be more fun than yours. Yes? You're on.

VI

THE EXHIBITION GAME

A manager's job is simple.
For one hundred sixty two games
you try not to screw up
all the smart stuff
your organization did
last December.
Earl Weaver, Manager
Baltimore Orioles

The fans are filling up the seats in Sheridan's new ballpark and the exhibition game is scheduled to go off in about thirty minutes. He bet Charley it would be standing room only, and it looks like he's going to win. Speaking of which, you owe me twenty…I think! I don't have a clue what *you* did last night, but *I* had a really good time. That was because, among other things, Howard Sheridan and his wife, Lillian, were even friendlier than they were at her birthday party in Aspen last December.

And then there was Lillian's sister, Antoinette, who pretty much avoided me. I don't know why, but I found that to be somewhat amusing. She was with her allegedly loveless husband and you could just feel the shit going down between the two of them. If you recall, she told me about her marital relationship when I introduced her to Ron in the Bengal Lounge. I figure that wasn't bothering her, because she was very cordial at Lillian's party in December. But her husband wasn't there and he was this time, so that might have been the explanation for her aloof behavior, although she did flash me a smile once or twice.

The corporate baseball men were friendly enough, but deep down I figure they weren't all that happy about a guy in his late twenties with no coaching experience managing their Double AA team. Not to worry; I can live with it.

There were plenty of fun moments. Buddy Hackett was there, and so was Willy Pastrano. Sheridan wanted to have honorary managers for the exhibition game, so he talked Hackett into doing it, and it didn't take much arm-bending for me to pry Pastrano away from Bourbon Street. The two of them joked around, much to the amusement of Sheridan and his guests. Hackett left early for his late show gig in the main room of the Diplomat just before everyone settled down to a prime rib dinner.

That gave me a chance to swap spit and tell a few lies with Willy, who wasn't his usual exuberant self. When the party broke up, we headed for the poolside bar. Over an after dinner drink he mentioned his wife, Faye, hadn't been feeling too good. I've got to tell ya that Willy's really a fascinating guy. Everyone knows he's quite the man with the ladies, but he's also very much in love with his wife and devoted to his kids. The proof was that every time he entered the ring, his wedding band was tied to the laces of one of his lo-pro, split suede-leather, boxing shoes. It never ceases to amaze me that marriage can be very complicated and still work. I'll bet you know a couple or two whose apparently successful marriages don't exactly fit the norm, whatever that is.

Hells, bells! When it comes to norms and marriage, yours truly doesn't exactly qualify; that we know for sure, but, on the other hand, we don't know if it's going to be successful, do we?

So, you go ahead and decide who gets the twenty bucks. I'd share more of the evening, but the noise in the stands is starting to distract me. Sheridan wanted a full house and he's got it, royally. He's really endeared himself to the fans because, among other things, he built Miami Field entirely with private funds, much to the relief of the Dade County taxpayers.

At this particular moment, I'm out in the bullpen behind the right centerfield fence. I told Leo I wanted to get a good look at the pitchers as they warmed up. Actually, I've had a pretty good look, and it's a mixed bag. Two of the starters look solid, but the other two are going to have to improve as the season progresses if we're going to have an effective, four-man rotation. As for the rest of the team, I think we're okay behind the plate, and the infield looks pretty solid, although there's plenty of room for improvement when it comes to turning double plays. And finally, all the outfielders are pretty good gloves, but only the starting center-fielder, Donny Quine, has anything close to a big-league arm.

So here I am, mulling over the talent, or lack thereof, the organization has assigned to me. But, truth be told, I've already done it; I'm just sharing it with you out here, because I don't feel like being in the dugout with the family and friends of the players; that's just too much chaos for me. Now, I don't want you getting the idea that I'm anti-social; I'm just saving up my limited amount of charm for the family picnic after the game.

While we're speaking of chaos, this whole thing is a three-ring circus. Charley pulled out all the stops and even played an equality card or two. Honorary bat boys are a standard thing, and that was a no-brainer. Sean would do the honors for the blue and white squad, my squad, and Rusty's kid, Sammy, would do the same for the blue and orange squad, coached by Leo.

But Charley also wanted honorary batgirls, certainly older than the boys and definitely better built. I suggested Sally and Sindy, but I think Charley might have known about their day jobs stripping in the Gables. He had already made one decision, and it was a natural.

Remember when I addressed the team I mentioned all of them had played college ball, except one? Well, I forgot to tell you the one player is Gregg Washington, the all-state catcher from Ohio. Maybe you don't remember when I had a catch with him last Thanksgiving. But I'm sure you remember his *Black and Beautiful* centerfold stepmother, Mrs. J. Thomas Washington; she was Charley's nominee. This could be interesting.

Not to be outdone, I then recommended the Presidential's *Penthouse* centerfold, Sal, the cocktail waitress in the Bengal Lounge. The fans are going to love it. It's a real toss-up. They're both stunning and sporting racks almost equal to those of Sally and Sindy. Oops, poor form. Now that I'm an ole married man, maybe I shouldn't be talking about women's breasts. No matter, the fans will have to be satisfied with their drop dead looks, because it's a family affair, and Charley insisted on loose-fitting, blue warm-ups trimmed in orange and white.

As I watch the big hunker from USC take some final warm-up pitches, the live organ music amps up and then stops. "LAAAAADIES AND GENTLEMAN," the announcer bellows. "Welcome to Miami Park, home of your new Miami Mets!"

A huge roar goes up from the thousands of fans, whose enthusiasm has been stoked by Sheridan's half-priced dogs and beer. "Please rise as we pay tribute to the United States of America. Our national anthem will be played by the University of Miami 'Band of the Hour' and sung by that famous star of stage and screen, Tony Martin. Ladies and gentlemen: the Star-Spangled Banner."

The crowd continues to make its presence known as the orange, green, and white clad Hurricane marching band takes the field, accompanied by Martin. Like Buddy Hackett, Martin often plays the main room in the Diplomat and was quick to accept Sheridan's offer to perform. I don't know this for a fact, but Ron told me he thinks Sheridan owns a pretty good chunk of the classy hotel on Hallandale Beach.

The crowd becomes quiet as an honorary team of members of the major branches of the armed forces quietly marches to home plate. Sheridan couldn't ask for more: the band sounds great, Martin belts out a straight, traditional rendition of the Star-Spangled Banner, and the crowd sings with gusto, followed by their tumultuous roar of approval. And finally, "PLAY BALL!"

That's my cue, guys. I've gotta go lend myself to the festivities. Hope you enjoy it; I'll catch up with you after the game.

*

I'm standing in front of the mirror in my office, building a half-Windsor knot in my blue tie. I've got on a long-sleeved, white shirt, because the low temperature tonight will be in the 60's. So, let me catch you up on the past few hours.

The game, from my point of view, was successful. No one got hurt, and everyone seemed to have a good time. And, there was a solid balance between the importance of the event and some high jinx.

For starters, the mayor of Miami, the Honorable Maurice Ferre, the first Hispanic to hold that office, took the mike at home plate and welcomed the team to his city. His comments reflected his gratitude that the franchise was providing one of the first jewels in the crown of his newly initiated urban renewal master plan. Rumor has it that, if he can pull off rejuvenating downtown Miami, he'll eventually run for national office.

Ferre was followed by the Honorable Governor of the great state of Florida, Reubin Askew, who threw out the first ball. Although most of Florida votes for Republican candidates, the population centers of Dade and Broward County support Democrats. So, it was no surprise that Askew, one of the few democrats to be elected twice to the statehouse, received a tumultuous welcome.

As for the goofy part, the funniest situation occurred in the bottom of the fourth inning when the backstop umpire called one of Leo's guys out at the plate when he tried to score and plowed into Gregg Washington. Leo ran out and made quite a fuss, but it was nothing compared to the team mascot who got between Leo and the ump, and started jumping up and down and kicking dirt. I thought for a moment the huge cloth baseball that serves as his head, complete with a happy face and blue and orange cap, was going to fall off and roll towards the stands. When all was said and done, the ump ejected the mascot!!!! And, of course, you guessed right; the whole thing was scripted.

There was something else that was scripted. In the bottom of the last inning, with two outs, the crowd started to chant, "We want D Jack!" This went on for a few moments and became even louder when I emerged from the third base dugout and headed for the plate.

I had been tipped off by Pepper that Charley, being the promoter he is, would probably plant a few guys to start up the chant. So, during our standing handball game, a week or so ago, I first hit him square in the ass with the small, hard rubber ball. Then I told him what was behind my intentional abuse of his butt. To his credit, he convinced me that it was probably a good idea, and better yet, he didn't retaliate during the rest of the game.

So, after everyone left the park yesterday, I got in the batting cage against a pitching machine programmed to come in at around eighty. Obviously, I can't see worth a damn, but it didn't take much to get the timing down. It also didn't hurt any that Tico Serrano agreed to throw the last inning with the other coaches and some of their family members backing him up in the field.

As agreed, he wasted a few, and then tossed one high and inside with medium cheese, just like what I'd been swinging at in the cage. I quickly got around on the ball and jacked it downtown, literally. The ball easily cleared the left field fence as well as the family area behind it, and landed somewhere in Mayor Ferre's urban renewal project. I know it didn't even come close to some of the massive explosions that came off the barrel of Mantle's ash bat, but it had to a go a good 420 feet. As I trotted around the bags, the fans got to their feet, and once again, took up the chant, "D Jack, D Jack." They loved it.

You know what? I loved it too! And the best part of the whole thing was I didn't flash back to my playing days and what might have been. It might sound corny to you, but I think it was some kind closure, of finally getting the eight hundred pound gorilla off my back, and putting it in the past, where it belongs.

So, feel good for me. And hey, don't be so rough on me for hitting a setup. It was only an exhibition game. But, speaking of Mantle and some of the tape-measure shots he hit, if you really want some inside dope, it's pretty unspoken, but those in the know believe Denny McLain grooved one for the Mick.

The story goes that in September 1968 at the end of Mantle's career, he was tied with Jimmie Foxx with 534 homers. The Mick came to the plate in the 8th inning against McLain, and the Tigers catcher, Jim Price, called time, and headed for the mound. Both seemed to be smiling when Price left the mound. Some claim after Price took his position behind the plate he looked up and said something to Mantle. Then, Mantle appeared to say something and smiled. McLain threw a few pitches that didn't have much heat on them. Even though it was late in the game, most figured a guy who had already won thirty games that season would have more on the ball. Whatever, Mantle slugged the next pitch over the fence, way up into the right field seats, and McLain actually clapped as Mantle took his victory trot.

Okay, I realize it wasn't an exhibition game like this one, but Detroit was winning 6-1 and had already clinched the American League pennant. So, maybe McLain and Price gave the Mick a grand send-off. What the hell, why not!

My high continued during the autograph session on the field after the game. I figure I signed autographs for a good forty-five minutes. The young kids were all bug-eyed, and the older fans tossed out countless comments, like, "It's good to see you," and, "We're glad you're okay." It was also a good feeling to have Sean standing next to me beaming, as he introduced me to some of his friends. Whoa Nellie, if he only knew he was really introducing his father to his buddies!"

Anyway, that pretty much brings you up to speed on Howard Sheridan's inaugural event.

Leo comes into my office. He's wearing a tie and a short-sleeved dress shirt tucked into his khaki pants. Sheridan wants everyone to look professional, and that includes the coaches as well as the players. "It's picnic time, D Jack. All the guys have cleaned up and headed out."

"What about their families and friends?"

"The guys cleaned up here and the women used the visitor's clubhouse. I figure all of them are about to get their faces into some barbeque, so let's go!"

We leave my office and head for the tunnel at the far end of the players' lockers which leads to the dugout. At the end of the tunnel, about fifty feet or so away, a figure is standing, silhouetted by the lights on the field. As we approach, I recognize Sal, who appears to be waiting for someone.

"Hi, Sal," I say in a friendly tone. "If you're waiting for a player, I think they're all over at the picnic area."

"Actually, D Jack, I was waiting for you," she replies with a smile.

"Okay," I reply cautiously, "What's up?"

"D Jack," Leo says quickly, picking up on her smile. "I'll head on out to the get-together and see you there." Without waiting for a reply, he slides past Sal into the dugout, walks up two stairs to the top, and heads for the left field fence.

Sal comes up to me, puts her hands on my shoulders, and greets me with a kiss. Then, she takes a step back, still holding my shoulders at arm's length, and smiles. "What was that for?" I ask, surprised.

"That was fun…and I always wanted to do it…just once. You always looked kissable to me, but if I kissed you in the Bengal Lounge, I figured you might read something into it," she says pleasantly.

"And what should I read into it now?" I inquire, returning her gaze.

"There's really nothing to read into a friendly kiss. And, I know things. I've had some nice conversations with Samantha. She says the two of you are dating."

"Does she say that with a smile?"

"I'd say she's way beyond the smile stage." Sal gives me another hug but this time, no kiss. "Are you coming to the picnic, Sal?"

"Nope, I have a date, and he's taking me out for dinner."

"And you're going in warm-ups?"

"Are you kidding? If I show up like this, they'll turn us away in a heartbeat."

"The place sounds pretty uptown. It's none of my business, but is it serious?"

"I hope so," she responds wishfully.

"So, where are the two of you going?"

"Well, I asked Sam to name me a place and she suggested….."

"Don't tell me," I interrupt with a laugh. "I'll bet the farm you're going to the Old Forge."

She laughs again. "You don't look like a farmer, but you'd win."

"It's a terrific place, or at least it was eight or nine years ago. Have a great time, Sal," I add, "and good luck."

"Luck has nothing to do with it," she says with a foxy grin. "Oh, and one more thing," she says, more seriously, her grin fading away. "I'm sorry about the beaver flash in the bag room a few months ago. I was just trying to give D Jack, the philosopher, a hard time."

"You damn near succeeded."

That not-so-subtle remark returns the grin to her face. "But then," I continue, "as you said, more than five million satisfied Penthouse readers have seen you, so no big deal."

"Maybe so, but none of them were in the same room with me. And it was a ballplayer I was with, not a philosopher."

"You mean ex-ballplayer, Sal."

"Are you kidding me? That ball you hit an hour ago is half way to Biscayne Bay by now."

"That was just luck. You've got to have the best eye-hand co-ordination in the world, plus great wrist action, to hit a big league fastball. Obviously, that's long gone for me, so I needed something extra."

"What was that?"

"My pitching coach grooved one for me," I say with a big laugh.

She smiles, and then turns to leave. "Have a wonderful life, D Jack."

"Same too you, Sal."

I give her a few moments to go up the dugout stairs and head for an exit. Once on the field, I'm surprised to find Leo waiting for me. "I thought I'd hang around just in case you needed some help getting away from the groupie.

"That groupie, as you call her, has a degree in psychology, ya ole goat."

"In addition to a few other things," he adds with a dopey grin.

"Yeah…in addition to a few other things. I thought you were hungry," I say as I shove him toward the picnic grounds."

"I am," he says, still grinning.

"I mean for food."

"I can do that, too."

It takes only a minute or two to reach the small gate, in the left field fence, that offers an entrance into the family picnic area. Things are in full swing, the picnic benches are totally occupied, and a ton of kids are swarming over the playground equipment. More than a dozen are wearing Hollywood Optimist Little League uniforms. What with Sean and Sammy being honorary batboys for today's game, I was concerned about favoritism and stuff like that. So, I asked Charley if it would be okay to invite Hollywood's coach, Jack Henshaw, and his entire crew to the picnic. I even offered to foot the bill. Luckily, Charley said *yes* to the request, and *no* to footing the bill.

Thanks in part to me inviting people, the picnic area wasn't big enough to accommodate everyone so two large tents had been erected, in left field, immediately after the game was over. Each tent is large enough to house an area for warming and serving food buffet-style. About a dozen round linen-covered banquet tables with seating for eight occupy the rest of the space.

And talk about food! Tent #1 is manned by a crew Sheridan flew in from Bono's Famous Barbeque on Beach Boulevard in Jacksonville. Not to be outdone, Colonel Harland Sanders, complete with goatee, white suit, and black string tie, is holding court and dishing out Kentucky Fried Chicken in Tent #2.

Once through the gate, I look around and quickly spot Sam, who is waving to me from a large picnic table near the playground. As I approach, she smiles and points to the empty seat next to her that she's saved for me. I return her smile and see she's brought me a large cardboard plate full of samples from both tents.

"Thanks for saving me a seat," I say, plopping down next to her. Sitting across from us are Rebecca and Jessica, who both give me sweet smiles before returning to their KFC drumsticks. I decide to start with a half of pork sandwich, inside cut and chopped.

"Daddy told me to tell you he was sorry he couldn't make it. Ron wasn't feeling too good, so he volunteered to take the late shift tonight." Sam looks at me seriously and then says, "I know you might not believe this, but I think he genuinely wanted to come to the game."

"That's fine, Sam," I respond between bites. "Did the girls enjoy themselves, or was it too long for them to sit?"

"Well, they did take little naps but fortunately were awake for all the fun and games with the mascot. And," she adds with a big smile "they did see you hit one out of the park. How come you didn't tell me you were going to take a few swings? I was kind of surprised when you came to the plate."

"I wasn't sure it was going to happen. Pepper tipped me off that Charley was going to get someone to start a chant, but I was hoping he might change his mind at the last moment."

"I'm glad he didn't," Sam admits proudly. "You really nailed it…and the fans loved it. And, I've got something for your trophy case," she concludes, handing me a ball.

"This is the ball?"

"Yup! Coach Henshaw took off with the team, and they found it just short of that construction site out there. Jack figures the shot was around 450 feet. Not bad for a beat-up, ole ballplayer."

"Tico grooved it."

"But, as you would say, you still had to get the barrel on the ball."

"That's true," I respond, happily.

After a few moments, Sam takes my hand. "Are you back at Shea?" she asks full of concern.

I squeeze her hand, gently, and give her a relaxed smile. "No, Sam. I'm not. That was yesterday. This is today, and it was fun."

She looks at me, a sense of relief washes over her face. "So, you'll put the ball in your trophy case?"

"Sam. I don't have a trophy case."

"You've got to be kidding!"

"Well, I do have stuff in a few boxes in a closet."

"Dev, one of these days Sean is going to have to see a trophy case."

"I think I can do that."

"Do you think you could also go get me a chicken breast and some cole slaw?" She asks, giving my hand another squeeze.

"Absolutely," I say, getting to my feet. "Do the girls need anything? Has Sean eaten?"

"They're fine, and so is Sean. He's over at the playground with the other kids. Oh, and by the way, if you see Jayleigh, make sure you say hi," Sam says with an impish grin. "She was asking for you, if you know what I mean."

You met Jayleigh Burney Smith at the Little League practice and picnic a few months ago, and if you don't remember her, something's wrong with you! "Thanks for the heads up. I can assure you I'll be as friendly as can be."

"Not too friendly, I hope."

"I promise I won't let her get between me and your chicken breast," I say, heading for the food tents.

I don't bump into Jayleigh, but it does take a few minutes to navigate my way through some handshakes and small talk with some of the players' family members. Most of the guests are already eating, so I'm only behind a few people waiting for the Colonel's best in tent #2. I've barely been standing there when I feel a tap on my shoulder and turn to gaze into the big brown eyes of Mrs. J. Thomas Washington. She gets right to it.

"Hi, D Jack," she purrs. "I loved the game. You can still give a baseball a ride. Maybe after the picnic, you'd like to take me out for a drink…and give me a ride. I promise both will last longer than our last little affair."

I've got to nip this thing in the bud right now. It's going to be a long season. "That would be a little awkward, Mrs. Washington, given the fact your stepson's career is in my hands for the next five months."

"If I recall, you've had a few other things in your hands," she says, smiling down at her voluptuous assets.

Okay. So I had a brief affair with Mrs. J. Thomas Washington. Check that; a ten minute tit fuck in the backseat of a limo doesn't qualify as an affair. You want to help me out here? I'm at a loss for words at the moment.

"Come on, D Jack. What's the big deal? I'm just talking about a friendly get-together."

"I don't think so, Mrs. Washington."

"It's Gail, if you remember. We're past the *Mrs. Washington* stage. So what's the problem? It can't be J. Thomas; you know I'm nothing more than a trophy wife?"

Cut it anyway you like, sportsfans, it's still adultery on her part, and technically mine, but only technically.

"Mrs. Washington, uh Gail, like I said, I just really think that…"

"Hello Mrs.Washington. Congratulations on Gregg making the team!!" Sam says with a big smile, approaching us with an outstretched hand.

Gail looks quizzically at Sam, but takes her hand anyway. "I'm Samantha Fredrickson. I'm a waitress at the Presidential. Everyone knows Gregg is going to play for Miami this season."

"Of course," Gail responds, turning on her centerfold charm. "Thank you so much." She then looks at me. "Do you know D Jack?"

"Oh yes," Sam says, meeting Gail's gaze steadily. "We went to the same high school."

"Were you high school sweethearts?"

"Well, you know how those stories go; once upon a time, in a previous life," Sam responds with a sly grin. "Devon, I've got to get back to the table. Do you think you can bring me a chicken breast," she asks sweetly, as if it's the first time she's made the request.

"I'd be more than glad to."

After brief goodbyes, Sam leaves. Gail steps back and looks at me in a serious way, rather than the catch-me-fuck-me, and I-won't-run-too-fast expression I was expecting…and dreading. Complications with a player's stepmother is about all I need right now. "I'm sorry, D Jack. I just wanted to have some fun times and wasn't thinking about putting you in an awkward situation."

I just nod.

"Is your name really Devon?" she asks, breaking the ice.

"Yes."

"She's very nice, and quite beautiful, Devon," Gail says with an I-think-I-know-something smile, and then turns and walks away.

"You're right, she is," I say to her back.

After getting myself a couple of pieces of chicken along with the requested breast, I walk out of the tent through the gate and rejoin Sam who is sitting alone at the picnic bench. "What was all that about?" Sam asks as I sit down.

"More importantly, how did you know to come save my butt?"

"I forgot to tell you I also wanted a wing?"

"And I thought it was telepathy?"

"Could be, but you certainly didn't need ESP to figure out what was on Mrs. Washington's mind."

"Do you want the short version or the long version?"

"I probably don't need either. It was pretty obvious Gregg's stepmother was on the prowl."

"Yup," I respond sinking my teeth into a crispy thigh.

"How did you handle it?"

"I told her I was her step-son's manager," I say, after swallowing the juicy morsal.

"And you think that's enough to back her off?"

"Nope," I say, turning to look at Sam, "but you are. Too much competition; she said you're beautiful. Thanks for getting my ass out of the ringer."

"You don't think you could have done it on your own?"

"I could have, and would have, but flat out rejecting her might have gotten ugly. After all, I couldn't take the easy way out," I say leaning over and whispering in her ear. "I'm not exactly in a position to inform her, or anyone else, that I'm married."

"Well, as you would say, Dev, there's married, and then there's married, right?"

I look at her seriously and softly say, "I know our situation is unorthodox, but we *are* married, Sam. I know the ceremony at the courthouse wasn't bells and whistles, but we pledged things to each other, and I intend to honor them."

"Because you think it's something you ought to do?"

"No," I answer quickly. "A philosopher once said it's not too hard to figure out what you ought to do. The trick is *doing* it because it's the *right* thing to do. I messed that up once; I don't intend to do it again."

"You *are* talking about us, aren't you?"

"I am."

Sam reflects on that but only for a moment. Then she smiles and says, "It's been quite a day, hasn't it?"

"It has."

"Yes," she responds with a smile, "it certainly has, Dev."

She's right! You know, when it comes right down to it, it's not only managers who have to try not to screw things up. Sooner or later, everyone gets a chance, in life to either strike out or hit one out of the park. And today I'm figuring, maybe I did more than hit a ball four hundred and fifty feet. Ya think?

VII

GREYNOLDS PARK

What I miss when I'm away
is the pride in baseball,
especially the pride of being on a team
that wins.
Billy Martin, Manager
New York Yankees

It's a beautiful Sunday, and it promises to be a pretty good ending to a fun weekend, given last night's successful exhibition game and picnic. We'll be on the road tomorrow, heading for Wolfson Park in Jacksonville for the season opener against the Suns. As you know, they were affiliated with the Mets when I played for them in '68 and won the International League. Since then, they've been in the Kansas City Royals farm system and are now a Double AA team. Howard Sheridan had hoped to open the season in Miami, but he knew all along the Southern League powers-that-be would keep the legendary Sun's owner, Peter Bragan Jr's., string of home-openers intact.

After three games against the Suns, we'll head up to Savannah to play three against the Braves, and finish the road trip in Orlando against the Twins. So, the bad news is we open the season with a ten-day road trip. But the good news is the guys ought to be settled down for our home opener against the Charlotte Orioles on Sunday, the 17th.

Sam thought it might be nice to spend some time with her and the kids before I left, and I suggested a picnic at Greynolds Park. So, here we are, stretched out on two large beach towels under the same hardwood hammock tree Sam and I carved our initials in almost ten years ago. I think I heard somewhere along the line, the park was originally a rock quarry smack dab in the middle of a mangrove forest. It was probably an eyesore back then, but today it's a beautiful place. Other than the beach, Greynolds was our favorite spot.

So far, the kids have had a ball. We started out with a trek on the moss-covered slabs of the Old Trail that winds its way through the scrub, more or less paralleling the Oleta River. I've always wondered how they name these bodies of water. I mean, a river should at least be wider than a creek, and this thing can't be more than thirty feet across. It's only half that distance when you go over the arched stone bridge, which is the only way you can get to the lagoon that borders the north side of the park.

Once off the trail, we indulged ourselves in a peanut-butter-and-jelly picnic lunch. Then, we hit the lagoon and wore ourselves out taking turns getting all three kids out on the water. Each one got a ride in a canoe, kayak, and paddle boat; if you do the math, you can understand why I've got some aches and pains.

I think we saved the best for the last. After rewarding the kids seagoing bravery with vanilla ice cream cones purchased from a small refreshment center, we climbed the narrow, spiral walkways of the rock fort that sits atop a very small rise in the center of the park. The fort's turret reminds me of the top of a classic rook chess piece. It's made of large stones and rocks held together with mortar, and at the top of the medieval replica, a small American flag flies from a narrow metal pole. Although the grassy, five-degree downward slopes are probably less than thirty feet, the locals laughingly refer to the hill as the only mountain in south Florida. Kids have been rolling down it since the park opened about forty years ago, and I know it might sound silly, but when we were young, that castle and that hill were flat-out huge! Anyway, Sam left the trial runs with the kids to me, but right now they're on their own, easily visible from the spot Sam chose to monitor the action.

"It's hard to believe it's been a dozen years since we've been here" Sam says, as I plunk down next to her on a super-soft piece of Bahia grass next to the hammock trees at the base of the *mountain*. She's sitting cross-leggged with her arms positioned behind her so she can lean back. Her strawberry-blonde hair, rests on her shoulders, and appears even lighter when contrasted against a velvet blue sweat-suit that offers more than a hint of her full body.

She catches me looking at her. "What?" she asks.

"I was just thinking that Charley should have used you as an honorary bat girl rather than Sal."

"Are you kidding me? Have you ever seen Sal's centerfold?"

"Yes, have you?"

"I have, and she's stunning."

"Well, I've seen you too…and so are you."

A slight blush comes to Sam's cheeks. "That was a long time ago."

"No, it wasn't, Sam; it was only a few months ago."

The blush spreads. "I'd still vote for Sal," she murmurs.

"Maybe so, but she isn't radiant. You're stunning…and you're radiant."

"I'm *radiant*? What's that supposed to mean?"

"It means everything about you exudes a beauty that goes way beyond the way you look."

"Dev, you had to get that out of some movie, right?"

"Nope, if it sounds corny, then I guess I'm corny."

"I don't know about corny, but do you think a married man actually says something like that to his wife?"

"If he's totally enamored with her, he does."

"Are you saying you're totally enamored with me?" she asks with a glint in her eye.

"I am."

"Stretch marks and all?"

I remove my sunglasses and try to look her in the eye. "Are you enamored with me, Sam, busted up and all?"

"I am," she replies with a sigh.

I put my sunglasses back on and grin. "Touche'…I rest my case."

Sam takes my hand, gives it a squeeze, and then changes the subject. "Can you believe we actually used to roll down that hill?" she laughs.

"All I know is, just like the trampoline, I could never compete with your gymnastic ability. When we use to come here, I remember flopping all over the place, but you used to roll straight down the hill as smooth as a beach ball."

"You're right," she grins. "I was pretty damn good at it. But then, the one time you put me in a batting cage, I wasn't too much competition for D Jack."

The grin leaves her face, and it's seems pretty obvious where her thoughts have gone. "Are you going to be okay? I mean, going to Jacksonville and all?" she asks seriously.

It only takes me a moment to realize what I want to say. "If you would have asked me that a few months ago, I'm not sure what the answer would be, but now? Piece of cake," I say smiling confidently.

"What's the difference?"

"*You're* the difference."

"I'm the difference?" she says, surprised. "Why is that?"

I pause, and the look on her face gives me the courage to continue. "When Billy confronted me on that street corner, I knew it was over, but something in me refused to totally accept that. So, I locked you up in a tiny space, somewhere inside my heart, and kept you there, until this past Thanksgiving."

"When you first saw me at the Presidential and I took your lunch order?"

"Yeah, but it was like some monster had gotten out of its cage."

"That's not very flattering," Sam says with a phony pout.

"I'm sure you know what I mean. All I could think of that day was that you didn't even hate me; I was just kind of nonexistent. And then, in the Bengal Lounge, I figured you wanted your pound of flesh, and you sure as hell got it."

"And regretted it," she says squeezing my hand again. "You were a memory to me, and some of it wasn't very good. But then, I realized pretty quickly that I really didn't know who you were. Now, I think I do."

"That's because I changed. You didn't have to. My memory of *you* was a good one…and you're all you always were…and more."

"That's kind," she says, with a soft smile, "but I've had to change, too. I don't think life let's you stand still. I think you've got to keep moving and growing, if you're going to be happy."

"That's what I'm getting at, Sam. I think I'm growing…up that is."

"What do you mean?"

"It's taken me far too long to realize that sooner or later, every ball player has to let go of that little boy in him and move on, and live the rest of his life."

"I agree, but you said I'm the difference?" Sam asks.

"My dad is gone and the game is gone, but the reason I can go back to Jacksonville is because you're here."

"And I'll be here when you get back." She pauses; then, another serious look. "Dev, have you ever lied to me?"

"Absolutely!"

"Devon!!!!"

"Well, Samantha, there's lies, and there's lies."

"Oh my God, I think Poseidon just released the Kraken from his undersea cage."

"I'm up on Greek mythology, but what's that supposed to mean?"

"It means you're going pop philosophical on me. So, go ahead. Tell me about lies."

"Okay, Andromeda. To begin with, there are at least three kinds of lies that come to mind: good lies, bad lies, and something in-between."

"There's such a thing as a good lie, Dev? That sounds like an oxymoron?"

"Nope."

"Then give me an example of a good lie, a personal one."

I think for a minute, and then say, "That first night in the Bengal Lounge. Do you remember I said I never told my dad about us, because you were second on his list of dreams?"

"Yes," she says softly.

"That was a good lie. I did tell my father what happened to us. I know you loved him, and that he loved you. I felt at the time, that to tell you he knew we were through would have been tough. I think it would have made you sad."

She reflects a moment on my words. "I think you're right. I think it would have been painful, I agree: it's not an oxymoron. So then, what constitutes a bad lie?"

"I think some people tell bad lies because they're ashamed of some things they do."

"But isn't it better to admit it?"

"Probably, but then you run the risk of, shall we say, dire consequences."

"But if you don't, and you get caught in the bad lie, what happens then?"

"That's worse. Then the dire consequences are all but guaranteed," I say with finality.

"So, then it's better to tell the truth."

"Way to go, Sam," I say, grinning.

"What did I say?" she responds quizzically.

"You find *truth* in tons of philosophical writings; you don't see the word *lie* too often."

"So you like the word truth?"

"It's a hell of a lot easier."

"Truth is easy?"

"Sure. Samuel Butler once said any fool can tell the truth, but it requires a person of some sense to know how to lie well."

"That sounds reasonable, but I don't like the idea there are accomplished liars out there. So," she continues, blowing off the thought of good liars telling bad lies, "what about this in-between thing?"

Again, it only takes a moment to come up with something personal. "This one is kind of gray, but do you remember when you told me Sean was your cousin's son?"

"Of course I do."

“Well, I don’t think it qualifies as a good lie, because the way you felt about me at the time, you could have cared less about sparing me any pain, right?”

“I think so…yes.”

“And I don’t think it’s a bad lie, because I’m sure you’re not ashamed that Sean is your son.”

“You’re right. I’ve never felt anything other than joy for having Sean.”

“And I’m glad about that too, but you didn’t tell the truth either, did you?”

“No, I didn’t.”

“So what would *you* call that?”

“I’d call that in-between,” she says with a little giggle. “But let’s get back to where we started.”

“Where was that?”

“We were talking about you going to Jacksonville, and how you’re going to tell the truth, right?” she asks with even a wider smile.

“I’m hoisted on my own petard. Fire away.”

“Okay. How are you going to feel getting on the team bus and heading for a game you’re not going to play in?”

“Wow, you don’t hold anything back, do you Sam?”

“No, I don’t. I remember how you used to tell me that on all those overnight bus rides, you always looked out the window and concentrated on the park or the pitchers you might face during that series. I know you’re going to look out the window, Dev, so what are you going to be thinking about?”

“You’ve got a good memory, Sam.”

“You bet I do. So?”

“I don’t know. But I think it’ll be different.”

“Why would it be different?”

“I think because, as a player, there’s so much pressure to succeed, and success, or the lack of it, is obvious. Maybe it’s a team sport, but out there, you’re on your own. You hit or you don’t; you catch or you don’t. That was always in the back of my mind when I looked out the window.”

“I think I know what you’re saying, but as a manager, success is just as obvious. Either you win or you lose.”

“That’s true enough, Sam, but in the minors, the job is also to bring out the best in the players and get them as ready as possible to play at the next level.”

"And I think that's the best part of it, Dev, but winning is always going to be the yardstick you get measured by."

"Come on, Sam," I say matter-of-factly. "Both of us know when the season ends, I'm not going to get promoted, re-hired, or fired."

"Does that make it harder or easier?"

"Like I said, it makes it different."

"I think you'll still give it all you've got," she says supportively.

"I know I will, and I intend to enjoy it, too." I pause. "Are we through, or do you have another friendly inquiry?"

"I have one more unless you think I'm being pushy."

"And if I did?"

"I'd ask anyway, because I think it's important for you to be thinking about these things ahead of time. Is that okay?"

"That's just fine."

"Then, how do you think you'll feel when you step onto the field at Wolfson Park?

"Are you asking if I'm going to converse with some ghosts?"

"Maybe, but what I was really thinking about is how you're going deal with the fact that you may have been the best ever to play there."

"That seems like a long time ago, Sam, and anyway, there'll be at least a handful of guys out on the diamond Tuesday with more skill than I ever had."

"I'm not so sure of that, but when you imply all that was yesterday, you've told me yourself that you've struggled with the past…and not too successfully at times."

"I know Sam, but that was before I thought about the future."

"And managing is your future, even though it's only going to be for a year? Or is the TV station the future?"

"It isn't either one. I told you I'll be fine going back to Jax because of you. I'm hoping you're my future, Sam."

Wow! That's really putting it out there, isn't it? Before I can even contemplate the consequences of that admission, Sam squeezes my hand and, like the lyric goes, *kisses me with her smile.* Okay guys, I'm thinking upward and onward.

"So," I say, with an amused look, "now that we've both admitted to lying to each other can we put your Kraken back in his cage?"

"That's fine with me, but only if we can get the philosopher out of Greynolds Park."

"I'm not sure he was here."

"Okay. I'll bite. Why wasn't he here?"

"He wasn't here because alcoholic beverages aren't allowed in the park."

"Devon, what's that got to do with philosophy?"

"Well, Sam, to paraphrase Louis Pasteur, there's more philosophy in a bottle of VO than in all the philosophy books that have ever been written."

She laughs. "Somehow, I think that's a hell of a stretch. Not having any Canadian whiskey didn't appear to stop you from sharing your theory of lies."

"But you'll put the Kraken back in his cage anyway?"

"Yes, I will. Do you want to shake on it?"

"I'd rather close the Greek mythology book with a kiss."

"I don't think so," Sam says, looking over my shoulder, shrugging, and rolling her pretty green eyes. I get the message and turn to see Jessica, Rebecca, and Sean running toward us.

"Wow, I can't even kiss my wife," I complain. "Is this what married life is all about?" I ask thoroughly frustrated. "I mean, does all the romance go away once you put on a ring?"

"Dev," she says, with a laugh, as she turns to greet the kids, "check your fingers."

Hey, sports fans…no ring…there's hope!

VIII

PLAY BALL

We'll head over to the park
in two busses.
The first will leave at 2:00
with those who need batting practice.
The second will leave empty at 3:00.
Dave Bristol, Manager
Cincinnati Reds

I'm not gonna to lie to ya. Not even a good lie. Sam was right. I did look out the window. And I did think about all those countless hours on the Porthsmouth/Norfolk team bus, heading for the two circuits. The first was against teams from Louisville, Columbus and Toledo. The second took us up to New York to play against Rochester, Buffalo, and Syracuse.

The good news is that something kind of weird happened without me even thinking about it. At first, I'll admit I reminisced about the excitement of playing Triple AAA ball, but pretty soon, again without thinking about it, I focused on what was ahead of me as a manager.

I had finalized the starting line-up with the coaches and reviewed all the other stuff that typically gets talked about before a game. Once the bus, I felt pretty good because I found myself dreaming up scenarios, like if it was a tight game, say in the sixth or seventh inning, would I opt for playing small ball, or tell the boys to swing for the fences?

Oops! I know guys. What the hell is small ball? Sorry. It's like manufacturing runs. For example, let's say our lead-off hitter gets a single. Well, small ball would be something like getting him to steal second, if he's got the moves and the speed; bunt him over to third; and then maybe a sacrifice fly to get him in. So, one run on only one hit! Ya got it? Small ball!

I also felt good about talking baseball with a few of the players. When we loaded up in Miami outside the ballpark, I asked the coaches to keep an empty seat next them in the event a kid wanted something or other, and I'd told the kids to feel free to chat if they had any concerns. But I hadn't expected any of them to personally take me up on the offer, and was surprised to have two brief travelling companions.

The first was the big hunker pitcher, from USC, Denny Fisk. He sure as hell had a solid college career. The Trojans won back-to-back NCAA championships in 1973 and 1974, and even though Fisk was only a freshman and sophomore at the time, he was about the best pitcher they had. By the time he finished his senior year, his earned run average was under two runs per game. Guys throwing in the Show would kill for that kind of ERA. Oh yeah, he even graduated!

So, he had walked to the back of the bus. I always liked it back there; I had more space, although being behind the rear axle was sometimes, literally, a pain in the ass. I think they might have put some better shock absorbers on this one; anyway, I hope so.

"Skipper, do you have a minute or two?"

"Sure, Denny. Sit down. What's on your mind?"

Okay, like I really had to ask him? He was far and away our choice to open the season, and tomorrow he's going out to the mound for the first time in his professional life. He was obviously nervous and apprehensive, and undoubtedly had plenty on his mind. He sat down somewhat uncomfortably. I don't know the last time you were on a bus, but there ain't a whole lot of leg room, and this guy goes about six and half feet.

"I've been thinking, Skip," he began slowly, "and I guess I'm a little nervous."

"That's understandable. It's your first game.

"Were nervous before you played your first game?"

"I think terrified might come closer to the mark."

"Gee, I would have never thought that about you."

"Everyone gets really nervous when you suit up for the first time and for lots of guys, it never goes away. It might not be as intense, but there's always going to be some nerves. That can be a good thing, unless you let it dominate ya."

"So, where did you play your first game; not in college…I mean in the pros?"

"I went to the Mets Triple AAA Jacksonville Suns right out of high school. Unlike you, I went to college afterwards and got a couple of degrees in philosophy; you know…useless stuff."

That got a good chuckle out of the USC grad. "Anyway, it was in Toledo, against the Mud Hens. Imagine being called a Mud Hen. I had to find out why they called them that, and some guy told me it had something to do with the town's proximity to some marshlands and the waterfowl that hung around there. He also said they almost got called Swamp Angels. I think I would have preferred being a Swamp Angel to being a Mud Hen."

"Me too, Skip. So, how did you do?

"I hit a double, a homer, and drove in three runs."

"Wow! How did you do the next day?"

"Thanks for asking," I said with some phony sarcasm. "I went 0-4 against Mike Marshall, who was just coming down from Detroit. I guess he was out to show the Tigers they made a mistake."

"They must have. I saw him pitch for the Dodgers when I was a senior at USC, and he looked pretty darn good, but I think he got traded."

"He's throwing for the Braves now and still striking guys out," I said, thinking back to how I felt that day in Toledo. "Baseball is a humbling game," I concluded reflectively.

"Yeah, I guess so."

It's nice the kid has to guess about it. That won't last long. "Okay then, what's on your mind, Denny?"

"Well, Skip, I just keep hoping I can show everybody what I've got out there tomorrow."

"We already know what you've got. And more importantly, so do you. And like I said, being nervous is okay. I think you're going to be surprised tomorrow. When you go out to the mound and get ready to throw that first pitch, you're going to realize you've been there a hundred times. And, just like always, it's the guy at the plate, and it's you and your catcher with seven teammates behind you out there ready to back you up."

He nodded and smiled, "That sounds good, but just in case, any last minute suggestions?"

"Sure. But like I keep saying, it always comes down to the fundamentals. Mix up your speeds, mix up your pitches, stay away from the middle of the plate, and do your best to hit your spots. If you do all of that, you'll get it done, right?"

"Yeah, thanks, and seeing as you got degrees in philosophy, is there something some wise man might have said about playing baseball."

"Sure," I said with a grin. "You won't find him in any philosophy book but Satchel Paige once said his philosophy of pitching was simple: keep the ball away from the bat!"

Denny matched my grin. "Who was Satchel Paige?"

"He's a Hall of Famer who at the tender age of forty-seven was still pitching for the St. Louis Browns so he obviously knew what he was talking about. And speaking of talking, why don't you go up and sit with coach Serrano for awhile if you still want to chat some more."

"I think I'm fine. I'll just go back to my seat."

"And stare out the window," I said with a smile.

"Did you stare out the window?"

"Everybody does, Denny, except for overnight rides when you conk out after playing a game."

Laughing, he got to his feet, and headed up the aisle. His seat was still warm when Gregg Washington plunked down and sat quietly for a moment or two.

"What's up, Gregg?"

"I'm not really sure, Skipper. I can't figure out if I'm nervous, anxious, or just plain scared."

"I'll bet against scared. You've only known for a few days you were going to be our starting catcher for the opener tomorrow. No one expected Persiano to be on the disabled list on opening day. So I figure you're just anxious. After all, it's been less than a year since you were playing high school ball. It's just come on ya kind of quickly. That's all. Get used to it; you always gotta be ready to go."

"I guess so," he said, sounding somewhat convinced.

"Coach Hillen has been working closely with you the past few days. He knows his stuff, Gregg. He was a hell of a catcher."

"I know, Skip. He's really been great working with me on my mechanics."

"I've noticed. Your throws to second have been right on the bag."

"I just hope I can do it tomorrow if some guy trys to steal."

"You can bet on them trying you out as soon as they get a chance."

"How do you know?"

"Gordon McKenzie is the Suns new manager. In the Bigs, he had a brief shot at catching for the White Sox. You can be sure he knows you're not number one on our depth chart, so he's going to test your arm as soon as he can. But don't panic. Fisk has looked pretty good when it comes to holding guys close to first, and he has a quick delivery to the plate. You won't have to rush your throw. Just step out and fire a nice frozen rope to second."

"That sounds good, Skipper. Are there any other little things you think I oughta know?"

"Absolutely," I said with a smile, trying to keep the moment on the light side. "I know I've told you guys time and time again to respect other players, but there is one huge exception."

"What's that?"

"If a pitcher is at the plate and, say he goes for a bunt and drops his bat, never, and I mean never, pick it up and hand it to him. We want pitchers to do everything on their own, even something as simple as picking up a bat."

Gregg laughed. "I'll remember that for sure, anything else?"

"Yeah, don't take anything for granted. I'm sure you've watched big league games on television and know the catcher puts his glove exactly where he wants the pitcher to throw it. But at this level, that isn't going to happen all the time, so you always have to be ready to adjust. And, I figure Coach Hillen has mentioned it, but if they have a guy on third, and Fisk throws one in the dirt, don't try to backhand it. Block it with your body. It probably means a run if you let it get past you."

"Hey, that's neat. Coach Hillen has me practicing blocking pitches everyday."

"Okay then, one last thing. Speaking of Fisk, if we get into a critical situation and you go to the mound, try to go with what he wants, what he's comfortable with, and be positive."

"I will, Skip and thanks," he added, getting to his feet and heading up the aisle. As for me, you got it. There wasn't much to see, but I started looking out the window again anyway.

*

We're in the lockers just behind the visitor's dugout on the 3rd base line of Wolfson Park. I got to tell ya, this is the first time I've been back in Jacksonville, and it's been kind of weird. I'll fill you in as we go because at the moment, I've got twenty-five anxious ballplayers getting ready to open the season against the Suns.

"Everybody needs to take a seat," Leo says. He's just finished making the rounds, providing little tidbits and encouragement for each of the guys. "Okay Skipper, they're all yours."

I get to my feet and walk into the middle of the beat-up old locker room. Like I said, weird; I played in this park for a year but was never in the visitor's lockers!

"When you guys were assigned to us," I begin, "among other things, I promised you only one long speech, and you've heard it. So, before you take the field, I just want to say two things. The first is kind of serious, so I want to get it out of the way. Every guy you go up against, on every team in the Southern League, has busted his ass just as hard as you have, and has the same dream. I know in some quarters it's getting fashionable to gloat over a dinger, or charge the mound if a pitcher throws one at your chin."

I give it a pause. "Now, I'm only going to say this once," I say slowly and solemnly.

I've got their undivided attention. "Any lack of respect out there, and I'll sit you down. If some flame-thrower throws you a heater to back you off the plate…well, that's baseball, boys. Just stare him down and dig in. The league has its own rules, depending upon the situation, but if you charge the mound, you can count on being fined. And unlike the Show, the organization isn't going to pay it for you."

I pause again and slowly look around the room before continuing. "Now don't get me wrong. I'm not saying I don't want you to be aggressive. Being respectful has nothing to do with playing with fire in your belly. So, I damn sure don't want you making friends with anybody out there. And if you play against guys you know and like, forget it. Off the field is okay, but during a game, you go at 'em full bore."

Leo gives me a supporting nod. You may recall during my first week with the Jacksonville Suns, I hit a dinger and did some gloating, and Pepper sat me down and gave me the same speech. I hope it works as well on these guys as it did on me.

"So, the bottom line is, when you take the field today, all of you will officially be professionals, and the coaching staff expects nothing less from you, on or off the field."

It's pretty quiet, but I see nods in the affirmative, so I think I've made my point. It's time to lighten things up a little. "Hell, guys, after today, little kids are going to want you to autograph baseballs, and who knows what some of the ladies might want you to sign!"

Lots of laughter.

"Okay then. The second thing I want to say sounds like a cliché, but I think it's true. It's going to be a long season, so take the games one at a time, and play your guts out in every one of them. If you do that, we're going to win and, as Billy Martin likes to say, everything looks nicer when you win. The girls are prettier, the cigars taste better, and the trees are greener. And, seeing as he's managing the Yankees, he must know what he's talking about."

Even though Martin's thoughts on winning have produced some smiles, unlike the long speech I offered up on the first day of practice, it's just as quiet as it was then, but not nearly as grim. They look focused and determined, like a bunch of thoroughbreds waiting to bolt from the starting gate.

"I do want to add one other thing. You guys are about to play the first game ever for the Miami Mets, just like the guys taking the field today for the brand new Toronto Blue Jays as well the Seattle Mariners. So, gentlemen, it's time to start your engines, get out there, and play ball."

I start to clap, slowly at first, and then the guys join in until we're making one hell of a ruckus. I gots goosebumps, sports fans!

*

"Hello, D Jack. It's good to see you again."

"It's good to see you, too, Ed. How's the tavern business been treating you?"

You guessed it. I wasn't about to come back to Jax without stepping into Brinkman's, the all-time favorite watering hole of my youth.

"I have my ups and downs just like anybody else. How about you? What have you been up to these past few years? Did you ever play anymore ball? I mean, we never heard down here that you did?"

"Not really. I went to Arizona State and did some coaching while I was there and kicked around a little semi-pro for awhile," I say with a shrug.

It gets quiet for a moment. "Anyway," Ed continues, "I was watching Dick Stratton with the late sports on WJXT, so I know you took the opener tonight. It looks like you're still batting .1000! How does it feel to be 1-0 as a manager?"

"Good and I get to go back to the park tomorrow. That makes it even more special."

We both chuckle. "I think it's great, kid. I still have lots of regulars who were here when you played. Quite a few of them were in earlier, and most of the conversation was about how glad we all were to see you back out there. But we thought that interview you had with Stratton before the game was over the top."

"I gotta agree with ya. I felt a little embarrassed with some of the stuff he said. I mean, you don't talk about retiring a guy's number when he only played one season."

"Yeah, but it was one hell of a season, man. There hadn't been that much focus on baseball here since the early 50's when Hank Aaron played for the Jacksonville Tars. He led the league in just about everything, made MVP, and the Tars won the South Atlantic League Championship. Sound familiar? Kind of like what you did with us in '68?"

"Come on, Ed. Give me a break. Lots of guys have a good season and then, who knows? Among other things, I learned at ASU that you really never know until afterwards. And about Aaron, that afterwards has come and gone, and we know. I mean, the guy just hung up his spikes less than a year ago. Nobody is going to top his 755 homers, and sportswriters have him in the top ten of all time."

"True enough, but nobody knew back then just how great Aaron was going to be. The same could be said about you. But I guess your afterwards never came."

"That's past history. Let's just drop any more chatter about greatness and retiring numbers and shit like that. It gets old."

"Fair enough, D Jack," Ed concedes, probably feeling that he gave it his best shot to make me feel good. If that's true, I guess it's kind of nice that he tried, but I really want to change the focus.

He beats me to the punch. "So," he continues, "How about it if the house buys you your first legal drink in this establishment," he asks with a laugh.

"Thanks, Ed. I'll have a can of Schlitz."

He heads back to the bar, and I look around. The place hasn't changed much. Maybe he's added a few more mahagony cases to display his huge collection of beer cans and bottles, but other than that, the place looks about the same.

Anyway, as Ed just mentioned, we won tonight; the score was 3-2. Just before the game started, when I walked to the plate to exchange line-ups and go over the ground rules with the umps and Gordon McKenzie, I got a standing ovation from the fans. Now, that felt pretty damn sweet. McKenize wished me good luck, and I did the same. He also said his bench coach, Jamie Bell, wanted to buy me a beer at Brinkman's after the game. I said sure. The two of us played for both the Jacksonville Suns and the Triple AAA Portsmouth Mets, just out of Norfolk, and it would be good to swap some spit and tell some *good* baseball lies.

As for the game itself, all in all I can't complain, but we had some pretty rough spots. As predicted, they tried to run on Gregg Washington early in the game and, even though his first throw was on the bag, it was late, and the guy beat it. But on his second opportunity, he got his throw off faster, and he nailed the guy trying to steal second base.

Fisk threw seven innings of shutout ball, pretty much limited the Suns to hitting grounders, and only walked two batters. However, our set-up reliever, Ben Streeter, kept us in a state of anxiety when he gave up back-to-back dingers in the bottom of the eighth. Fortunately, I called for George Campbell, our closer, to take the mound in the bottom of the ninth, and he set the Suns down in order, with one fly out and two strike-outs, to earn his first professional save and give us an opening-day victory.

About forty-five minutes after the game, we headed back to the Thunderbird Hotel, which is located just a mile or two east of Wolfson Park across the Arlington Bridge that spans the St. Johns River. The Main Street Bridge to the south and the Acosta Bridge to the west provide the other two main thoroughfares into Jacksonville. It's really convenient being in the Thunderbird, because once you cross the Arlington heading back into the inner city, Wolfson Park is right there next to the Gator Bowl and the Jacksonville Coliseum. All in all, it's a neato sports complex.

Anyway, before heading over to Brinkman's to see Jamie Bell, I met with the coaches for a short post-game skull session in the Zodiak Lounge in the Thunderbird. After each had provided something akin to a scouting report on their assigned players, I chimed in with a few observations.

"We all know the good thing about sliding head first," I began, "is that you can stretch out your arm and slide away from the bag. And some guys think you get down faster. All well and good, but tonight Stuart and Smith both went into second head first, and there were two wild throws from their catcher that went into center field. Needless to say, you aren't going to be able to get up off your belly and head for third. So, from my point of view, we missed two really good opportunities to score.

"I realize Stuart and Smith, and half a dozen other guys have a comfort zone going in head first; they've probably been doing it that way since high school. But I want to try to kick them out of it, and I figure we can convince them to give it a try by emphasizing three things: first, if you go in feet first, you'll hardly ever overslide the bag which you might do if you go in head first; second, if there's a wild throw and you go in feet first with a pop-up slide, you're ready to head for third; and last, middle infielders covering second usually think twice when they see a pair of cleats aimed for their shins."

"That's good baseball, D Jack. I think we ought to work them on it," Leo says. The other guys nod, so I figure I've got the green light on that one.

"Another thing I think we all saw," I continue, "is that most of the guys tonight were swinging for the fences. We all know that power comes with maturity, so these guys have a long way to go. For now, I think we need to work on their bat speed and their hand speed. And, I want to see if we can get them more focused on extending their swing. Good hitters have to do more than just get the barrel of the bat on the ball."

"I pretty much noticed the same thing, D Jack," Rusty says. "I'll start them off at practice tomorrow morning by getting them zeroed in on making contact with the ball, rather than trying to go downtown."

"Sounds good, Rusty." I check the time on the Simplex wall clock. "I know it's getting late so thanks for the sit-down. Tico, everything okay with the bed check?"

"All the babies are tucked in, D Jack."

"Great. I think we're off to a pretty good start. Like Pepper always says, timely hitting and good pitching wins games and tonight we got both." I get supportive nods. "So let's have 'em up for breakfast and in the dining room tomorrow morning by 8:00, and we'll try to load them up on the bus by 9:00. See you in the morning…and thanks again, guys."

After some smiles and handshakes, the coaches headed upstairs and I hailed a cab for Brinkman's. I hope that fills you in on the game. I wouldn't mind sharing a few other things, but Jamie just came into the bar and is heading my way. We didn't get a chance to chat today, but I'm struck with his appearance. He seems older than I expected, and he's definitely walking with a pronounced limp. I get up as he approaches the table, smile, and extend my hand. His grasp is solid, and his smile softens his features.

"D Jack, it's been awhile," he says as we sit.

"I figure it's going on something like eight or nine years. I'm having a Schiltz. Can I get you one?"

"No way, I told you the drinks were on me, and you're not even going to cost me two or three VO's. I'm getting off cheap."

"Then how about I spring for Ed's Big B sandwich? We can split it."

"Not at this hour; you wanna get fat?"

"You're right, no eats." Ed arrives with my Schlitz. "I'll have the same, Ed," Jamie says.

"I thought you might," Ed says smiling, as he places another beer on the table. "Now that I think of it, you were a few years older than D Jack, so at least you were legal when the two of you showed up after a game. But you always ordered two drinks, and I never saw you knock down the second one. Where did it go?"

"I haven't a clue," Jamie says. We all smile.

"Do you guys want something to eat? It's late, but we can still throw something together."

"No thanks, Ed," I say as I look over at Jamie. "My wife is watching out for me tonight."

Oops! More inside stuff, guys. Lots of times, when an older ballplayer looks out for a younger guy, the senior citizen is referred to as a wife. I think it has more to do with being a nag then anything else. As Ed mentioned, Jamie is about three or four years older than me and he was one of those guys who seemed destined to stay at Triple AAA for as long as he played. But that championship year when we played together and won the International League Championship, he flat out went off the charts.

As you know, I played left; Jamie played center. Both of us went to Portsmouth/Norfolk in the spring of '69 and I'm sure the Mets figured the two of us would be patrolling the outfield in Shea Stadium for a long time. Well, we all know what happened to me, but I never saw Jamie's name in a Mets' box score and don't have a clue as to what happened to him.

Ed heads back to the bar and the two of us go to work on our brewskies. "Here's to good times, Jamie," I say, raising my beer can in his direction. He returns the gesture.

"We had a few, didn't we? Just not enough I guess."

"What happened, Jamie? I'm going to guess you never played in the Bigs."

"You're right. It's almost uncanny that the organization had such high hopes for both of us…and it never happened. Actually, I didn't last much longer than you did, but I was competing on a different field," he says solemnly.

"I get the distinct feeling it wasn't in a ballpark."

"It sure wasn't. Three days after you played in New York, I was drafted. Being an athlete and in A-one shape, I went through an accelerated boot camp at Fort Jackson followed by jump school at Fort Bragg. Before I knew it, I was in Vietnam attached to the 101st Airborne Division."

"That was all pretty quick, wasn't it?"

Jamie laughs. "It took me the better part of my life to be a pretty good ballplayer; it only took a few months to become a highly proficient fighting machine."

"You said you didn't last much longer than I did."

"That's right. On May 10th, we started a direct assault moving up the slopes of Hill 937. It took about ten days to capture it, but on day one, I was hit."

"I guess that explains the way you walked in here tonight?"

"Everything below my left knee ain't mine."

"Damn."

"No, D Jack, the damn part is that hill in the A Shau Valley near Hue was of little to no strategic value. Almost fifty guys were killed, and more than four hundred were wounded."

His look is one of remembrance and bitterness. "Worse yet, the Command ordered us to abandon it…and North Vietnamese forces retook it, unopposed."

"You know, Jamie, I might have heard about that. I was at Arizona State at the time, and students, even the newspapers, were up-in-arms about what they were calling, I think, the debacle at Hamburger Hill."

"Hill 937 and Hamburger Hill were one and the same. So, like I said, both of us went down, and I figure we were doing lots of rehab at the same time."

"Maybe so, but what you went through would make what I underwent look like a cakewalk."

"Probably, but the end result was the same. We were both through playing baseball."

"But you must have stayed in the game somehow. A guy doesn't get to be a bench coach at your age unless he's been at it for awhile."

"I don't know about that. You're younger than me, and you're a fucken manager," he says with a grin.

"That's another story. Maybe someday I'll share it, but today ain't the day. So, how did you get back to Jax?"

"It was just slow and steady. Actually, the guy who managed us in Norfolk, Clyde McCullough, put in a good word for me and I started as a scout. Then I got a few coaching positions in D and C ball, managed in A ball for three seasons, and came to the Suns two years ago.

"McKenzie's brand new, isn't he?"

"Yeah, last year he was with the Expos organization in West Palm. He's a good baseball man, really knows his stuff."

"I suspect he's going to be here for a while. Did you have a shot at the job?"

"I thought I did, but at least they kept me on as his bench coach."

"But it's still kind of a dead end, isn't it?"

"I like my glass half full, D Jack. And as the saying goes, I'm still out there."

"Good for you, Jamie."

"Good for you too, man."

We both reach for our beer cans. Ed had arrived with two more cans while we were talking and we didn't even notice him. There doesn't appear to be much more to say, about baseball, anyway. Jamie breaks the brief silence. "Speaking of glasses, eventhough I'm holding a can, I ain't much for beer these days."

"Neither am I. So how about a couple of manly ones after tomorrow's game?"

"I'll try, but after we play you guys tomorrow, I promised to take my kids to a softball game."

"You've got kids?"

"Yeah, I've got a boy, John, who's six and he's got two younger sisters, Edythe and Kailey."

"I remember a drop-dead gorgous brunette. You're not going to tell me a stunner like that married a baseball bum like you?"

"Her name was Jade, and it still is, although her last name is different now. We got engaged before I went overseas, and the really great part is, she married me when I got home, no leg and all."

"That's great, Jamie. I'm really happy for ya, but what's this thing with softball? Why do your kids want to see guys play softball when they got you and the Suns around?

"It's not just softball. We've got a team called Warren Motors and last year they won the ASA National Championship. How would you like to play for a team that went 94-2?"

"You're kidden' me?"

"Nope, and their number one guy hit over .600!"

"Are you making this shit up?"

"Sure sounds like it, but no. Now you can see why the kids like to catch a few games. It's a double-header tomorrow, but I figure I can pry them away from the second game. So yeah, something with ice cubes sounds good."

"Are you sure? Won't your kids be disappointed?"

"It'll be fine. But loser of our game tomorrow pays, so bring some cash. We're gonna take you guys tomorrow. We've got a fireballer named Dan Quisenberry, and you ain't gonna touch him."

"Like hell!"

We both grin. Like I told my guys earlier today in the clubhouse, we're friends tonight, but we'll be enemies in the morning. Some manager once said (I think it might have been Alvin Dark of the Oakland athletics) friendships are forgotten when the game begins. Durocher was a lot more hostile about it. He said something like: you can buy a steak for a player on another club after the game, but don't even speak to him on the field. Get out there and beat him to death.

That's baseball, sportsfans.

IX

BACK ON THE BEACH

Keep your head up
and you may not have to
keep it down.
Joe McCarthy, Manager
New York Yankees, Boston Red Sox

Sean seems to be having trouble making sandcastles with the three different sizes of Dixie Cups Sam gave him. His mind is clearly somewhere else, and I'd like to try to find out where. But I don't have any experience in coaxing info out of kids. This is gonna be interesting.

"Making the turrets of the castle looks like a pain, Sean. How about you digging the moat around the castle, and I'll try my hand at building the turrets at each corner?"

"Okay, I'll do that."

He moves a foot or two away from the center of the castle and starts in on the circular trench, with no sign of enthusiasm. Well, guys, looks like strike one on me. I might as well just go for it.

"What's up, Sean? You look pretty down-in-the mouth?"

"I can't hit," he says dejectedly.

"What do you mean, you can't hit? How do you know that?"

Without looking up, he continues his half-hearted digging of the moat. "We've had three games since you've been away, and in the last one I had to hit the ball off the tee everytime I came up."

"That's not so bad. How many hits did you get before that game when you were swinging at pitched balls?"

"I got on every time," he says, looking up at me.

"That's pretty darn good, Sean. What do you think happened in the last game you played?"

"I don't know."

"Why don't you show me?"

"I don't have a bat."

"Use the plastic shovel over there."

He nods, gets up, walks a few feet away from the castle, and picks up the plastic substitute for a bat; it's about two or so feet long and should do the trick.

"Okay, pretend you're in the batter's box; show me your stance, and how you hold the bat."

He smiles and gets right to it. I notice quickly he's spacing his feet pretty close together, he's holding the bat high and straight up, and he's cocking his right elbow way above his ear. Oops, I guess I should mention the kid is right-handed.

"I'll bet you've been swinging under the ball, right?"

His eyes get as big as silver dollars. "How did you know that, D Jack?" he says.

"I've looked at lots of hitters, Sean. Actually, what you're doing ain't all that bad, but let's make just a few little changes and see if you're comfortable with them, okay?"

He grins. "Okay, coach," he says, giggling boyishly.

"First, I want you to open up your stance a little. Just put about a half step more between your feet."

"Okay."

"How does that feel? Are you comfortable?"

"It feels good."

"Great. Now, bring your bat down so that it'angling away from your ear." He seems confused with that, so I take the plastic shovel, in his hands, and move it where I want it.

"How's that, still okay?"

"Yes, still okay."

"Good. Now when you do that, what happens to your right elbow?" He looks down at his elbow and checks it out.

"I guess my elbow is pointing down."

"You're right. Keep the bat in this new position but lift your right elbow so that both your elbows are level and straight across your body."

I wait for him to do it. "Now, I want you to swivel your body at the waist, and pretend you're in the batter's box looking at the pitcher." Once again, he's a good listener and it's pretty obvious he's thinking up a storm. "Do you feel relaxed?"

"Yeah, but it feels a little weird."

"That's because you're not used to it. When's your next practice?"

"I'm not sure. I'll have to ask Mom."

There he is calling Sam mom again. You talk about weird? Here's a kid calling a woman Mom, who really is his mom, and he doesn't know it. Whoa Nellie!!!! Wait until he finds out Sam's his mother and, blow my mind, I'm his dad! Enough, guys. I've got to get refocused.

"Well, whenever it is, you work hard on that stance and make sure you have your coach help you with it. Okay?"

"Sure thing, thanks loads."

"You're welcome. So, you wanna keep digging the moat or try your hand again with the turrets?"

"I think I want to try the turrets again. Is that okay?"

"It's your castle, young man, go fer it."

He carefully crawls back into the middle of our medieval project and picks up the largest of the three Dixie cups. Then he packs it down with wet sand, turns it over, and carefully places it at one of the four corners of the castle. He removes the cup…and the new turret holds its shape. TaDa! He looks up at me with a beaming smile.

"That's a great turret, Sean. One down, three to go."

As he returns to his construction tasks, I glance down the shoreline to see if I can spot Sam and the girls. No problem, even for me! They're only about fifty feet away, wading through some clean white foam, heading towards us. Fortunately, the Sargasso Sea West is cooperating today; there's no seaweed in sight, and there have been no blue tentacles of an ominous man o'war in the water or even any disk-like, translucent jelly fish on the beach.

"The castle is starting to take shape," Sam says upon arriving, admiring our efforts. Then she plunks down on the sand next to me while the girls go over to help out Sean if he'll let them. And he does. I've noticed the kid is really good with both Rebecca and Jessica, and I suspect handling two little kids at one time is no easy task.

I look over at Sam and check out her bathing suit. It's a one-piece, jet black with vertical white strips about an inch or two apart. "That suit looks good on you."

"Thanks. I'd look pretty silly if I had a two-piece with all the little frills like the girls have on."

"I don't know. It might look kinda sexy."

"Sure, what with my checkerboard tummy and all."

"Like I said before, childbearing scars are well-earned."

"Speaking of scars," she says, somewhat seriously, "this is the first time I've seen you in just a pair of shorts. You're a mess."

"Thanks a lot. Just some extras from playing ball, that's all."

"Not that one on your gut, I'll bet. That looks more like you had an appendectomy."

"The answer to that is yes and no."

"What do you mean, yes and no? That's sounds something like…pregnant almost."

"Well, for the life of me, I can't even remember how this happened, but I got spiked in the abdomen in practice, and they had to do an exploratory to see if there was any internal damage."

"And was there?"

"They didn't find anything serious, but seeing as they were in there, they took out my appendix."

"That's good. Who needs an appendix anyway." Her eyes move from my gut to my shoulder. "What got you that nasty scar?"

"It starts at the bottom with a repaired ruptured bicep and at the top ends with fixed tears in all four tendons of my rotator cuff. They did it with screws or anchors, or something like that so, contrary to popular opinion, I actually have some internal value."

"And it took surgery for you to figure that out?"

"I guess so, but that made it worth getting hurt, right?"

"I doubt it, but what about the scars on both knees? I'll bet that hurt some?"

"Are you referring to the injuries, the surgeries, or the rehab?"

"Physically, I've been hurt, too, Dev," Sam says sympathetically. "For me, by far, the worst was the rehab. The pain is almost as bad as the injury and lasts a hell of a lot longer."

"I assume you're still talking about physiological injury?"

"Not entirely. For me, maybe a month after I hit the board, I knew it was over…and when the dream was gone, and I realized I'd never dive again…I think that mental kind of pain was far worse."

"That surprises me just a little, Sam. Now that I know things, I figure you quit mostly because of"…I glance over at Sean…"you know why."

"That was part of it, Dev, but if that hadn't been the case, I knew from the injury alone, I'd never compete again."

"Sam, I'm really sorry."

"Both of us are, Dev. The same thing happened to you."

She smiles, and quickly changes the subject. "For months I've known you're a mess above the neck, but now, you look worse below the neck. Do you have anything that still works?" she asks with a sassy look.

"I'm not sure. There are lots of things I haven't tried for a long time," I answer, with a wise-ass look of my own.

"Name one," shes challenges.

"Fine, I will." I look over at Sean. "Hey Sean, have you ever body surfed?"

"No, D Jack, how do you do it?"

"You wanna learn?"

"You mean right now?"

"Sure."

"Gee, can I mom?"

Sam looks out at the surf. It's really perfect for a beginner who's just a little kid. A sandbar is no more than sixty feet from shore, and the water at that point can't be more than two plus feet. The waves are breaking right on the bar and are about five feet high; perfect for some shallow water body surfing.

She turns and looks at me. "You're not going to go out too far, are you? There's stuff out there?"

"Only the big, dreaded forty-four pound world's record lobster, but somebody landed that monster off the coast of Nova Scotia last month."

"I'm so relieved, but you will be careful, right?"

"Other than your concern, I have another reason for being careful with him," I respond lightly, with just an iota of seriousness.

"Yes, you do." She turns to Sean. "Okay, let's see what you can do, but be careful."

*

I'll tell ya what. I think the kid is a natural athlete! I guess between his mom and dad, it ought to be a no-brainer. Yeah, I know, but don't get on me for that. Like some manager once said, it ain't brag…if you've got the stats! Anyway, within a half hour, I had him body surfing like he'd been doing it for years. For the first couple of waves, I actually held him up and timed the wave for him. The trick is to get as close to the wave as possible and, when it peaks, swim like hell, right in front of it, just before it breaks. If you wait too long and the white caps come down on ya, you've missed it.

After about half a dozen successful tries, I let him go for it on his own, and he nailed it! Sam had stood at the shoreline and, best I could tell, was aglow with pride. I'd like to think some of it was directed my way for being a pretty damn good teacher. Oh, and by the way, I caught a few solid rides of my own.

After that, she took a few pictures of our monumental castle with her Kodak Instamatic camera. That was a good thing, because the tide was coming in and yours truly had picked a spot too close to the water. I figure more than an hours worth of work would be washed away in about ten minutes. Check that, an hour's worth of fun in the sand and the sun.

Right now, Sean, Rebecca, and Jessica are sitting with their toes in the water, working on some Italian ices that a neat old man sells from a pushcart up on the boardwalk, complete with a green, white, and red umbrella. We're stretched out on a blanket under a palm tree about thirty feet up from the kids. Sam is working on a mixture of coconut and papaya juice, and I'm working on a cheek full of H.B. Scott.

"Are you ever going to give that stuff up?" she asks, wrinkling her nose in disgust. "It's ugly."

"I agree, but it helps me keep my girlish figure."

"That's all well and good, but what's it doing to your mouth?"

"Nothing healthy, I'm sure."

"So?"

"So, I've been cutting down."

"Are you cutting down on smokeless as well? Don't you want to set a good example for your players?"

"Sam, I'm not about to let all those budding ballplayers see me chewing gum. But I do agree with you, and when the season is over, I'll try to kick it all."

"Try?"

"It's a nasty addiction, so the best I can honestly say is that I'll try. Play me, coach, and I'll give ya the best I got."

"Very funny, tough guy; make sure that you do."

"You think *I'm* tough. I'd hate to play ball for *you*."

"Speaking of which," she says, "you haven't said much about the road trip. Could you share a little more? We never had much time to talk on the phone."

"There really wasn't that much to say. Jacksonville was good because we took two out of three from the Suns, but then we ran into trouble against Savannah and Orlando."

"Why do you think that was?"

"I'm really not sure. But my best guess is that the guys don't realize how long a season is. So, when Garmondy went 0-4 in the first game against Savannah, he probably started thinking he couldn't hit. Or, when Ewing made an error at shortstop early in the same game, maybe he started second-guessing his fielding abilities.

"If you think that's it, how do you handle it?"

"There's no rocket science here, Sam. We just practice, practice, and then practice some more. If we actually spot a weakness, then we go after it."

"Give me an example," Sam says, sounding genuinely interested.

"Actually, I can. Fred Clark is our starting first baseman, and I noticed in Jacksonville that he has a habit of striding for the ball a little too soon.

"I'm not sure I understand."

"Okay, let's say the batter hits a grounder to short. Ewing fields it and throws to first. Well, I've noticed that Clark starts to stride towards the ball almost as soon as Ewing throws it."

"And that's bad?"

"It is, because when he does that, and if Ewing's throw goes off to his left or right side, he's in an awkward stance and he may not be able to make the catch and get the putout. We've been working on him to wait until the ball is clearly coming at him, so he'll be able to adjust if he has to."

"And it's been working?"

"It has so far."

"What about some of the other guys? Do you think you've got a prospect or two?"

"I'm not sure about two, but it wouldn't surprise me if Denny Fisk is called up…and maybe Donny Quine."

"Isn't Fisk the big pitcher?"

"That's the guy. He's already 2-0 with an earned run average under one and a half. Tico's doing a great job with him."

"I'm curious. Just what is it that a coach does to improve a pitcher? I mean, either you can throw or you can't, right?"

I laugh. "Sam, would you say either you can dive or you can't?"

She laughs, too. "Okay, you've got me. So, what's Tico doing with Fisk?"

"Some of the things he's been doing are working on Denny's control and his curve. If you're going to pitch in the big leagues, obviously, you have to have a fast ball, but you have to be able to locate it."

"I'm not sure what that means."

"Well, if the catcher calls for a fast ball high and inside, and puts his mitt right there, right where he wants it, that's the target the pitcher has to hit. If he can't do that, he's going to be in trouble, particularly if he puts it anywhere around the middle of the plate. If he does that too often, guys in the Show are going to light him up like a pinball machine."

"And I guess if he throws nothing but fastballs, he's going to be in trouble, too."

"You're right, eventhough a fastball is usually a pitcher's bread and butter." I pause and almost frown. "This is starting to sound like I'm prepping you for a test on baseball terms. Do you really want to hear about all this stuff?"

"Absolutely, I think I've got the fastball stuff down pat; how about the curve?"

"The most important thing about a curve," I say with renewed enthusiasm, thanks to Sam's show of genuine interest, "is you have to be able to throw it effectively when you're behind in the count. Let's say you got a count of three balls and a strike on a batter. Well, if their scouting reports say you don't have confidence in your curve, the batter is going to figure you'll come with a heater, and he's got a pretty good chance of nailing it. That's why a curve is so important, as well as a slider. You gotta mix up your pitches and keep the batter guessing."

"What's the difference between the two?"

"More or less, a curve dips down when it gets to the batter, whereas a slider dips, too, but more from side to side."

"Wow, I didn't realize everything was so precise."

"You'd be surprised. You said if a guy throws just fastballs, he's going to be in trouble. Well, there are fastballs, and then again, there are fastballs."

"Oh, no.This is really getting complicated. Just when I thought I really knew what you're talking about, you tell me a fastball isn't a fastball?"

"Sorry Sam, all I'm saying is a guy can throw fastballs at different speeds."

"How does he do that?"

"If he wants to throw his A-one heater, he throws a four-seam fastball. You know what the seams are, right?"

"Sure. They're the red threads."

"Right, so he puts his forefinger and his middle finger across two seams. Two fingers and two seams make a four-seam fastball."

"I see."

"Now, if he wants to take a few miles-per-hour off the pitch, he only lays his fingers across one seam."

"And that really slows the ball down?"

"Just alittle, but he can slow it down even more if he wraps all four fingers around the ball and palms it."

Sam looks at me with big eyes and raised brows.

"What?" I ask.

"I never realized how many techniques and decisions were involved. And you could hit all that stuff?"

"Not all the time. No one can. I just always remembered that some coach once told me that his theory of hitting was simply to watch the ball as it came in, and hit it. But that's easier said than done."

"You really *were* something, weren't you?"

"I gave it my best."

It gets a little quiet for a moment or two. "So," she says, obviously wanting to move on, "it starts with the eyes?"

"Yup, if you can read the seams like people say Ted Williams could, you're going to be a great ballplayer.

"And you could read the seams?"

"Not if the pitcher really threw hard, but even with those guys, I could pick up the motion of the ball, and that tells you a lot. But that's only the beginning. Then you've got to be able to get all of your body into getting the barrel of the bat right smack on the ball and swinging all the way through."

"Like you were showing Sean?"

"Yeh, more or less, but I'm sure you know all about it, Sam. Baseball's no different than diving; it takes a hell of a lot of work to be good at it."

"Yes, it does."

Sam gets a faraway look in her eyes. "What are you thinking about?" I ask.

"Nothing much."

I'm not buying it, guys. She's chewing on her lower lip, just a leettlebit, and it's obvious she's got something on her mind. But I'm not about to press it.

"Anyway, speaking of work," I say, figuring we've pretty much talked enough baseball and wanting to get her mind on something else, "what's happening with you and the Presidential? I figure the season is all but over?"

"It is. Mr. Pierce made recommendations to Mr. Berston as to who stays and who goes."

"Who's Mr. Pierce?"

"He's the new dining room executive director."

"How do you think it'll shake out?"

"I'm not really sure," Sam says with a shrug. "He asked all of us if we want to stay on or go so if enough want to leave, it will make things easier for him."

"What did you say?"

"I told him I could stay or go."

"What are you waiting for, Sam? You know you're gonna leave."

"I wanted to talk to you about it. I'm wondering what to do at this point," she says, sounding slightly concerned, but I get the feeling her primary concern ain't the job. I'm pretty sure I know where this is going, guys.

"You don't feel you can tell Billy about us, do you?"

"I'm really not sure. His attitude towards you seems different, since your blowout on the patio a few weeks ago."

"Is it better or worse?"

"Better. I've intentionally worked you into a few conversations, like talking about the stuff that's been in the sports pages about your road trip. At times, I think he's almost proud of you."

"Are you telling me there's been good stuff about the way we've been playing? Hell, we're coming home with a losing record!"

"Honestly, Dev, the sports writers have been focusing on the Mets being a very young and new team, and the general consensus seems to be that you're going to have a good season."

"That's nice to know. And," I quickly add, "even better to think Billy might be thawing out some. But there's still too much ice to tell him about us, right?"

Sam checks the children, who are still playing close by on the shoreline, to make sure they are out of earshot. "I think part of the problem is that I'm not sure what I would tell him."

"It seems to me, you have three options: tell him we're married and leave it at that, tell him of our arrangement, or just tell him nothing."

"If I tell him nothing, Dev, I have to keep working, which really doesn't bother me at all, at least, not for now."

"But what if this Pierce guy doesn't keep you on?"

"That's not a problem," she says with a smile. "I seem to have connections in high places."

"Like who?"

"Like you, smarty. It seems that Mr. Berston has this idea that I'm your girlfriend, so he's already told me he'll tell Mr. Pierce to keep me on. And if I'm not comfortable with that, he'll give me a solid recommendation and get me an interview at the Stagecoach Steakhouse on Hallandale Boulevard."

Place your bets, sportsfans; I think this one's a done deal.

"Sam. I've got a ten spot says you're not ready to drop the bomb on Billy, and, remembering the way I used to listen to you talking about special treatment, your comfort level at the Presidential just fell off a cliff. What are the hours at the Stagecoach, and when do you start?"

"It's the dinner shift, and I start tomorrow night." Her grin is almost ear-to-ear. "You've got a good memory. You remember how much I dislike being indebted to anyone. And you're also right about Daddy, but I think that's because of my agenda as opposed to how I think he'll handle it."

"And just what is your agenda? I hope you ain't waiting for your ole man to fall in love with me. That dog just won't hunt."

"Probably not, but just like me, Daddy had very deep feelings for you when we were dating."

I grin. "And how about *you* and the dog; will *she* hunt?"

She returns my grin. "I think she's picking up the scent."

File that one away, guys. Whadda day! I try my best to get Sean to lift up his head, and Sam puts mine in the clouds. Ya know what? One of these days, hopefully soon, I think there's gonna be another carving in that hardwood Hammock tree in Greynolds Park! You can bring the Bowie knife, okay?

X

THE HOME OPENER

Managing can be more discouraging than playing,
especially when you're losing,
Because when you're a player,
there at least are individual goals
you can shoot for.
When you're a manager,
all the worries of the team…
become your worries.
Al Lopez, Manager
Cleveland Indians, Chicago White Sox

This is gonna be interesting. We're in the locker room, and the guys are in various stages of suiting up. Given the looks on their young faces, you could cut the tension with a knife, even a dull one with a nicked blade. Among other things adding to their stress, it's a sellout crowd and the fans are enthusiastically waiting to welcome their new team to Miami Park and the home opener. More importantly, the organization's brass are assembled in the executive suites, and it will be the first time these guys play in front of the select few who wield the pens and sign the contracts, or not, as the case may be. At the moment, I'm sitting off to the side at the back of the room next to the tunnel that leads to the dugout. All the coaches are seated close to me except for Leo, who is making his way towards the front of the lockers.

"This ought to be good," Rusty says. "Do you think the guys are going to listen to somebody they probably never heard of?"

"With Pepper in the room," I respond, "I think our guest speaker will have their undivided attention. And anyway, I hear he's funny as hell."

You may recall Pepper Kwalchek is the General Manager of the Club. A few days ago he'd asked me if I'd mind if he brought in someone to address the players before our first home game. He and Charley thought it might be a good idea to establish a bond with the Mets, you know, some tradition, some history, stuff like that. I certaintly didn't have any problem with it, so they dug up a pretty neat guy from the very first Mets team. More later sportsfans, Leo's about to make some introductions.

"Okay, guys. Grab a seat."

By now, almost all of them have on their uniforms, and they sure as hell have on their game faces. I think I've shared some of this with you before, but I just love it when so many broadcasters say, 'go out there and have fun.' I mean, sure, it ought to be fun sometimes, but there are lots of times, just like any job, when things are on the line. I mean, do you think broadcasters would tell some junior VP to have fun when he's heading for a boardroom to plead his case for something he's be working on for months? And maybe his job is on the line? Yeah, my ass. Again, there are fun times, but *everyday* a ballplayer goes out there, his job is on the line.

I don't know who it was, but somewhere along the line, a ballplayer was being interviewed by a local sportswriter and was asked how he felt about getting paid good money for just going out there and having fun. The player must have gotten pretty ticked because he said something like he never smiled when he had a bat in his hand. He went on to say that's when you got to be serious, so when you get out on the field, it ain't fun and there's nothing to joke about.

And while we're on the subject, let me also throw in…you can't fake it, and you don't get to do it over and over in a game until you get it right. You know, like a movie star who nails a scene…after thirty five fucken takes!

Well, actually, check me on that. There is a situation where, in a way, you do get to do it over. Let's say the starting pitcher for the team you're playing against is throwing pretty well, and he's still in there for the eighth inning. Well, that means you'll go up against him at least three or maybe four times. And, if you know what you're doing, by your third at bat, you've seen everything the guy's got, and you're in a good position to ding him. But other than that, there ain't thirty-five takes in baseball, or in life for that matter. Enough, this is starting to sound like sour grapes.

"Before we hit the field," Leo begins, "our General Manager, Pepper Kwalchek, wants a few words with you. Pepper, they're all yours."

Pepper strides to the front of the room. He looks pretty natty in a blue, pin-stripped suit, although his orange, blue, and white Mets tie ain't exactly a fashion statement. Actually, I've never seen him in a suit. I guess it goes with the new job and the big corner office in the executive suites.

"Thanks, Leo. It's good to be in the lockers again, especially with this being the first professional ballgame in Miami Park. I want you to know that I asked D Jack if it would be okay if we had a guest speaker briefly address you before the game. As you guys well know, your manager loves long speeches."

His pronouncement is greeted with an outburst of groans and then laughter, which seems to break some of the tension in the room. "But," he continues, "after some arm-twisting, he was kind enough to file away his twenty-minute pep talk, and I thank him for that."

"We do, too, Mr. Kwalchek," Denny Fisk says loudly. More laughter.

"I'm glad it's okay with you guys," Pepper says with a smile, "and I'm not going to make a speech either. But I am going to introduce you to one of the original Mets, who suited up for the legendary Casey Stengel in their first season in '62. I know all you guys have heard of Casey, and it would have been nice to actually have him here today. He passed away just a few years ago, but I'd like to think his spirit, his baseball savvy, and his sense of humor are with us today.

"But, I'm please to say, that the man I'm about to introduce you to had just as much desire and devotion to the game and also had one sharp sense of humor. Just like you, he had his start at the Double AA level playing for the Denver Bears. In three consecutive seasons, from 1955 to 1957, he led the American Association in home runs and runs batted in, and in 1956, he was named the league MVP. In 1958, he went to the Show and played two seasons with the Yankees before being traded to Kansas City for some guy named, uh, Roger Maris."

That remark gets some chuckles from all of us. "After a short stint with the Baltimore Orioles, he joined Stengel and the brand new New York Mets. In his first season, he batted .244, hit sixteen homers, and drove in forty nine runs. He also holds the distinction of being the first Met to play in an All-Star Game.

"Was he popular with New Yorkers? Well, at one point, he had a fan club that numbered around five thousand, most of whom wore shirts with 'VRAM' written on them, which happens to be his first name backwards! So, let's give a warm welcome to Marvin Throneberry!"

The guys respond with what I would call slightly more than polite applause. I mean, after all, I figure most of these guys never heard of Marvelous Marv, as he was popularly known during his playing days. But outside of New York, he wasn't exactly a household item of conversation. Anyway, a pretty good-sized guy with a really pleasant smile walks over to Pepper and shakes hands. He's dressed casually, which seems to match his whole demeanor. Pepper comes to the back of the room and takes an empty seat next to Leo who has also joined us.

"It's great to be back in the ballpark," Throneberry begins, "but the first thing I want to do is set the record straight. Maybe I was the first Met to play in an All-Star game, but the league always wanted at least one guy from each team to play in that classic. Now, seeing as we set a major league record that year with one hundred and twenty losses, all I can say is that I was probably the best of the worst. And, while we're at it, it was nice of Pepper to share some of my stats during my first year with the Mets, but he did omit one significant number. He forgot to tell you that my fielding percentage was a record setter: I made seventeen errors at first base. So, the first thing I want to share with you guys is, don't do that!"

We're all laughing with him, not at him, and I'm figuring so far so good.

"Pepper mentioned Casey Stengel, and yeah, he was the first manager of the Mets, and yeah, he was a piece of work. There are lots of stories about Stengel, and, for better or worse, a few of them involved me. Maybe the best one is when we played the Cubs in June in '62, and I hit a triple.The ump called me out because he said I didn't touch second base. Casey went ballistic, but then the ump told him not to argue because he said I missed first base, too! Anyway, the next guy up drove it out of the park. Casey ran out to the ump and pointed at all four bases which he obviously had touched. The fans loved it. Lots of guys called him Casey the Clown, but never to his face."

Our guys seem to be loven' it too. More importantly, they seem to be getting loose, which, in addition to the history and tradition stuff, has to be one of the reasons Charley and Pepper brought Throneberry down here.

"Another story that I'll deny along with the first one, was about the day we threw Casey a birthday party and gave him a cake. I don't know why, but I didn't get a piece of it, so I let Casey know it. He told me they really wanted to give me a piece, but given my fielding skills at first base, they figured I'd drop it."

More laughter, even a few guffaws!

"Well, enough about me. If Casey was here today, I figure he'd give you guys some advice. Among other things, he might have been thinking of me when he said he didn't like players who drove in two runs at the plate but made errors and screwed up in the field, allowing the other team to score more than two runs. So, the message here, fellas, is: if you're going to have a successful career in this game, you gotta be able to go both ways. I know what you do at the plate gets most of the attention, but teams don't win pennants unless they can play solid ball out in the field. And speaking of teams, Casey used to say that finding good players is easy, but getting them to play as a team is another story. I'm sure you've heard this time and again from your coaches."

Almost to a man, the players turn their heads to the back of the room, nod, and grin at us.

"I'd like to finish up," Throneberry says, "with one last thing. Maybe Casey was famous for his quips and maybe he had a warped sense of humor, but he was a baseball man, and when it came to the game, he was always pretty damn serious. I'll always remember one of the first things he said to us. He said he wasn't a very successful player, because baseball is a game of skill."

He pauses and gives them time to focus on that thought. "Obviously, you guys have some skills; if you didn't, you wouldn't be here. But they don't call this the minor leagues for nothing. It's here and right now, that you have to work your butt off everyday and fine-tune those skills if you want to be a big league ballplayer. I'm sure you have the desire, and I know you have great coaches here who'll do all they can to get you there. So, good luck to all of ya."

The guys actually stand up, and give Marvelous Marv a round of applause. Pepper strides to the front of the lockers and gives Throneberry a handshake, a brotherlyhug, and a big smile. Then Pepper beckons me to join him, so up I go. I've never met Marv, but he gives me a big hug too, as if we were teammates or something. I don't know why, but it makes me feel pretty good.

"Do you have any last words?" Pepper says to me.

"The only thing I'd like to say is, today, Marvelous Marvin Throneberry definiteley touched second base…and first, too!" The roar is spontaneous.

"Okay, guys. Hit the field!"

*

"Time," I yell at the ump and then turn toTico Serrano. "Whadda ya think?"

The pitching coach scratches his cheek. "They've got two on and one out. We've got a right-handed pitcher on a right-handed hitter, so that's in our favor. Campbell has only thrown fourteen pitches so I'd like to leave him in and see if he can get this guy out. If he can finish the inning, we can pinch-hit for him in the bottom of the ninth. I just kinda have this feeling that we don't want to go into extra innings if we're going to win this one."

"I agreed." We both think Campbell is going to be our number one closer because he's got more focus and concentration than our set-up guys and he seems to love the pressure, which is a huge plus. "Do we have a scouting report on the guy at the plate?"

"Not enough to tell us what he likes or what he has trouble with; it's too early in the season."

"What's your assessment of Campbell's stuff?"

"It looks to me like his velocity is down some, but his location seems pretty good…and he's pretty much on target with his slider."

"I've seen about the same thing," I say, "and I'm sure their coaching staff has, too. So, the guy on first showed some speed earlier in the game, and the guy at the plate is one of their power hitters. They probably figure we're going to start this guy with fast balls to try to keep the guy on first from stealing second base."

"That makes sense," Tico says. "But like I said, it looks like Campbell's fastball doesn't have much pop."

The ump is walking towards us with his mask off, and he doesn't look too happy. "Come on, you guys. Break it up; let's play ball."

"I'm just on my way to the mound," Tico says starting up the dugout steps.

"Okay, but when you get out there, you better make it quick."

"Can do, ump," Tico replies.

"Tico," I say. He stops and turns to face me. "I know Campbell's not throwing much in the way of heat. But the guy at the plate has been up three times, and he seems to have a consistently long swing. This is his first at bat against Campbell, so let's jam him with a few fastballs, high and inside. That'll keep the baserunner close to first. Then, see if we can get the guy at the plate, low and away, with sliders, and either punch him out or get him to hit into a double play."

Tico shrugs, but nods in the affirmative, so I take that as a green light from the seasoned and savvy pitching coach. "I'll go settle him down some," he says, "and also listen to what Washington has to say. The kid seems pretty sharp and he might have picked up something we missed. Oh, and one last thing. Let's get Haley up and throwing in the bull pen. Depending on what they do, we'll have to use him if Campbell can't close out the inning…or maybe Reynolds. I'm pretty sure Murphy has at least one left-handed and one right-handed guy left on his bench who can pinch-hit."

"Good point. Get em' both up."

"Will do," Tico replies heading for the pitcher's mound.

Just for the record, guys, it's always a good thing to have both left-handed and right-handed pitchers warming up. But between us, I'll be inclined to go with Haley, because he's been more successful so far mixing up his pitches, whereas Reynolds has been mostly throwing fastballs, and he seems to have some control issues.

I take off my cap and run my hands through my hair. It's been a rollercoaster ride, boys and girls. I've really had my hands full trying to outguess the Charlotte Orioles' manager, Mike Murphy, but he's been around for awhile, and so far I think he's been a step or two ahead of me. While Tico's out there talking to Washington and Campbell, let me fill you in on what we have and haven't been able to do up to this point.

To begin with, as you already know, the Orioles have two guys on, more specifically, on first and third. We're in the top of the ninth inning and the score is tied at four. That sounds pretty good, but they've been playing small ball with nine hits, mostly singles; have had guys on base almost every inning; and we've helped them out by making two infield errors. As for us, we only have three hits, and our monster centerfielder, Donny Quine, has two of 'em. And he's got all four runs-batted-in!

In the fourth inning, we got a hit and two walks. So with the bases loaded, Donny hit one into the gap in left-center and drove in all three guys. Then in the seventh, he hit one out of the park in right-center field. Like I told Sam back on the beach, I don't think we're gonna have this guy for very long; same goes for Denny Fisk. Quine obviously hits the ball to either field and plays a pretty good glove out in center and, he's got a rifle for a throwing arm. I think the only question is whether he's going to the Triple AAA club just out of Norfolk or straight up to New York. For the moment, Lee Mazzilli is patrolling centerfield for the Mets in Shea Stadium, and he's only something like twenty-two years old. He's also a fan favorite because he comes from Brooklyn. So I get the feeling Mazzilli's going to be there for awhile.

Anyway, Tico's on his way back to the dugout. Like I more or less said earlier, set-up guys pitch in the seventh and eighth innings, and basically, their job is to keep us in the game. The real pressure is on the closer, who generally only throws the ninth to seal the deal. So, now we're gonna find out what Campbell's made of. Gotta go.

"What's up, Tico?"

I'm standing at the rail that separates the bench from the field when Serrano trudges down the steps into the dugout and joins me. "Campbell says he feels he's on his game, and Washington hasn't seen anything different from what we've seen."

"So what did you say?"

"I told him to throw strikes right from the gitgo. The more pitches he throws, the more the guy at the plate is going to get a handle on him and have a better chance of hitting him. God forbid he goes over a six-or seven-pitch count. I figure Murphy is thinking the same thing and will have this guy taking the first few pitches, so I'm hoping we can get an 0-2 count on him real quick-like."

"I think you're right, but there's a lot going on out there. Campbell's gonna have to hold his concentration and you can bet your ass the guy on first is going to take a big lead and try to distract him."

Serrano gives me a clap on the back. "Don't worry so much, D Jack. The odds are on our side. When I was in the bullpen with the Reds two years ago Big Klu used to say that hitting a baseball was harder than walking through a pitch-black room with new furniture without bumping into something."

The Big Klu he's referring to is Ted Kluszewski who was a great first baseman for the Cincinnati Reds and is currently, I think, their batting coach, or at least he was last year when the Big Red Machine successfully defended their title and took the Yankees four straight in the World Series. "I hope Klu's right."

Campbell circles behind the mound, rubs the ball, and turns to face the plate. He steps on the rubber, leans over, and lets his right arm dangle a little. He says he likes to do this to relieve some of the tension. Then, he looks over to first base and checks the runner. As predicted, the guy's taking a pretty good lead, maybe five or six steps off the bag. Campbell looks back to the plate. He doesn't need a sign from Gregg Washington; the first two pitches were decided when Tico was out there visiting.

Campbell checks back to first. Fred Clark is all but straddling the bag in order to try to keep the Orioles' runner close. Additionally, he's protecting the first base line, because if a ball is hit and gets past him close to the foul line, it's gonna score some runs for sure. Roland Garmondy, down at third, is doing the same.

Campbell turns to the plate, pauses for a second, and fires a fast ball, high and inside, right where it's supposed to go. The runner doesn't break for second; the batter doesn't swing. Clearly, Murphy has the take sign on. I don't think he's gonna let this guy swing at the next one either.

As predicted, the batter watches another heater whiz past him, in just about the same location; so far, so good. On the third pitch, Campbell throws a pitch-out, way wide of the plate, just in case the runner is thinking of stealing second. He doesn't.

Campbell looks confident, maybe because the game plan is working. As suggested, pitch number four comes in low and away. The batter can't chance a call strike three because the ump has established a pretty generous strike zone throughout the game. One thing is for sure in baseball: the strike zone ain't a perfect science!

Their power hitter takes a pretty lame swing at the ball; about all he can do is protect the plate. Even so, he hits it pretty hard toward second base. Jack Hersey fields it clean on one hop, turns, and throws to Buck Ewing who swipes his foot across second base. Almost in the same motion, Ewing throws a frozen rope to Clark on first to complete the double play. In your book, you can score it 4-6-3. We're out of the inning!

The guys come off the field into the dugout, and seem pumped so, as usual, I leave all the rah-rah stuff to Rusty. We've got the number two guy in the batting order leading off. He's our left fielder, Issac Smith, and so far, he's off to a good start with a batting average of .296, and he's got some good speed. He's already stolen six bases this season. The key to any inning is get your first hitter on base, so I walk over to him just as he's starting up the dugout steps.

"Issac, I want you to work the count on this guy. Unless you get behind early, you need to wait for something you really like. I know you've got two homers so far this season, but don't go for the fences; just make solid contact with the ball and get yourself on base."

"Gotcha, Skipper."

I give him a pat on the back. "Go get 'em."

He nods, goes up the steps, and heads for the batter's box. I turn and beckon to Fred Clark who bats third in the order. He strides over, bat in hand. "What's up Skip?"

"If Smith gets on, I want ya to lay one down."

"I can do that."

"I know you can, kid. And don't wait for anything. If the first pitch is in the strike zone, go for it. I think Murphy will have him bring it, figuring you'll watch the first one. Ya got it?"

"I got it."

I've noticed this about Clark. He doesn't say much, but he seems intent as hell anytime I've said something to him during a game. And, so far, more often than not, he's delivered. I get the feeling he really trusts the coaching staff and thinks if he can do what we ask of him, he'll keep getting better. I hope so; that's what I'm supposed to be doing with these guys. And I'm supposed to win, too! Pepper hasn't exactly put it in words, but I know he really wants us to nail this first game in the new park.

Smith digs in at the plate and the Twins' pitcher wastes no time. With the first pitch, he tries to pick the outside corner, but misses. His second one is in about the same spot, and he's quickly behind in the count with two balls and no strikes. Like I keep telling our guys, Henry Aaron says guessing what the pitcher is going to throw is 80% of being a successful hitter, and the other 20% is execution. So, who's going to argue with Hank, right?

I'm guessing fast ball right down the pipe, and figure Smith is, too. The next thing I hear is that sweet crack of the bat that resounds when the barrel nails the ball just right. The ball is between their third baseman and shortstop before either can make a move. Smith heads down the line for first, hits the bag, and turns for second. He quickly sees that their left fielder has already picked up the ball and is about to throw for second, so he turns and heads back to first with a clean single. The crowd is on its feet and it looks like no one has left the park. They continue to clap and shout as Clark heads for the batter's box.

As instructed, with the first pitch, he squares off at the plate to bunt, but their pitcher must be rattled and throws one in the dirt. Their catcher goes to his right, drops to his knees, and blocks the ball. But it skids off a few feet, and Smith heads for second. He doesn't even need to slide; he goes in standing up.

Now, the crowd is going wild. Leo is coaching third base and signals Clark to bunt, which I've already told him to do. I just don't want him to forget what with all the excitement. We need him to be cool and collected, because with Smith on second, Clark needs to drop it down the third base line. It ain't all that easy. If he doesn't get it down far enough for the third baseman to have to come in and play the ball, the pitcher can get to it and cut down Smith at third.

Having just thrown a wild pitch, the guy on the mound is probably going to play it safe, and he does. His first pitch ain't exactly down the middle but close enough for Clark to get some wood on it and bunt it right down the third base line. The pitcher doesn't have a chance for it, so their third baseman has to come in, field it, and throw to first. Easy play and Smith goes into third standing up. With only one out, the winning run is ninety feet from the plate.

The place is going nuts as our big man, Donny Quine heads for the batter's box. He takes a few swings, steps in, and plants his feet. Quine has power written all over him, but Murphy signals his outfielders to come in anyway. He knows it doesn't matter if Quine hits one over their heads, because if he hits it deep, and they're out there to make the catch, they'll never be able to throw Smith out at the plate. If they're in closer, and Quine hits a pop fly, they've got a chance.

Time to earn my pay; I've already told Leo that if we got into this situation, I want him to signal Smith and Quine that we're going for a suicide squeeze. Not to be insulting, but a squeeze calls for the guy on third to lead off the bag maybe four or five steps, but not break for the plate until he sees that a good bunt has been executed. Ah, but the ole suicide squeeze. Well, this requires the guy on third to break full bore for the plate the instant the ball leaves the pitcher's hand. In this case, if Quine doesn't get his bat on the ball, the catcher steps out in front of the plate, and Smith is dead meat! That happened to me once; it wasn't pretty.

Their pitcher isn't using a full windup. He's trying to hold Smith close to third. After he checks him twice, the guy throws a slider, hoping to throw a strike on the outside corner of the plate, and also figuring Quine has less chance of really stroking the ball deep into the outfield.

Surprise! Smith is already on his way to the plate as Quine squares and bunts the ball down the first baseline. Their first baseman isn't playing deep. If he has to field a grounder, he'll have a chance to throw Smith out, but you can tell by the look on his face, he sure as hell wasn't ready for the squeeze.

By the time he fields the bunt, Smith is already sliding into home plate. Quine gets the walk-off bunt single and winning RBI. Game over!!!

The crowd erupts, and our bench empties. All the guys are jumping up and down, and doing everything from back slaps to hugs. Then as one, they converge on home plate to greet Smith, and, before you know it, we've got a full-fledged pigpile out there…and the fans are going berserk, I mean, sheer bedlam! What can I say: sweet music to my ears!

I stay put. It's their win; it's their celebration. Like the Pittsburg Pirates manager, Chuck Tanner once said, "the greatest feeling in the world is to win a major league game." Admitted, this ain't the majors, but I'm feelin' awful damn good just the same. I only wish Sam could have been here but as you know, she just started a new job at the Stagecoach and wasn't about to ask for time off. And that being the case, Sean isn't here either, so obviously, my promise to let him visit the lockers after the game was postponed.

Leo comes over to me and offers his hand. "That was a gutsy call," he says with a smile. "That'll give all the other managers in this league something to think about. And plenty for the sports guys to write about in tomorrow's papers."

"I guess so, but if Smith had been tagged out at the plate, they would have had a field day, tapdancing on me."

"That's the way of it, D Jack, maybe a hero today, maybe a goat tomorrow."

Leo's right, sportfans, but isn't that the way it is with everything? Anyway, for the moment, who cares? Let's just watch those kids rolling around out there, much to the delight of the fans. And if you didn't know it before, now you know why baseball players are referred to as the boys of summer. Ain't it grand!

XI

JILLY AND JAYLEIGH

It's wonderful to meet
So many friends
That I didn't used to like.
Casey Stengel, Manager
Brooklyn Dodgers, Boston Braves,
New York Yankees, New York Mets

Rusty pulls up in front of the Gold Coast Restaurant. As usual, he's been nice enough to drive me home, or rather, on this particular night, close to home. His wife, Barb, is with him. Seeing as there's school tomorrow, they'd gotten a sitter so she could come watch the opener against the Twins. They'd asked me if I wanted to have a drink with'em at the Flicker-lite, but I declined because I have to meet somebody at the Gold Coast.

"Thanks for the ride, Rusty," I say, as Barb opens her door and leans forward so I can get out of the red and white '57 Chevy convertible that's sporting big white-walls, with the rear tires somewhat hidden by half skirts and, of course, the mandatory dice hanging from the rear view mirror. I mean to tell ya, this baby is in absolutely cherry condition. "You've got one hell of a car, Rusty."

"Actually, it's mine," Barb says with a big grin, "but I let Rusty take it to work so all the players will think he's cool."

"Yeah, right," Rusty says. "I'm cool without it," he laughs.

"Of course you are. If you weren't, we wouldn't be married," she says, teasing.

"And we wouldn't need the burgundy slant-six, Dodge station wagon to haul the kids around in."

"You two can continue this married stuff on your own time. I'm outta here. Thanks again," I say, laughing along with them.

"Our pleasure D Jack, and way to go tonight calling that suicide squeeze."

"Thanks. I wanted to send a message to Murphy and the other seasoned managers."

"And I'm sure they got it. You told them you ain't gonna do anything conventional, or play it close to the vest."

"He's just trying to suck up to his manager," Barb says with a laugh, giving her husband a jab to the ribs.

"Why would he want to do that?" I ask. "I know your ole man is going big time after the season."

"Did you tell him, Rusty?" Barb asks with definite pride in her voice.

"Yeah, seeing as that's what we're going to do, I figured he ought to know early on."

What he told me, guys, is that he's heading for the business world and and the big bucks. You might remember at Jefferson Park he said he had his master electrician's license. What he failed to mention is that his father-in-law is the sole owner of Biscayne Electric, which is about the biggest residential and commercial outfit in South Florida. He'll start as a general manager at about $32,000 with, more or less, a paved road to an executive vice-presidency and a corner office. What the hell. Baseball is fun, but it ain't gonna getcha a three-car garage!

"I'm glad you shared the good news, Rusty. I think it's great…and I'm real happy for both of you."

"Thanks, D Jack," Barb says with a smile. "Even though the girls always dissed you, I thought you were a good guy."

Okay, sportfans, she was on the cheerleading squad in high school. You know; that group of sweet young things that always liked to tell Samanatha what a closet case I was. "Thanks loads. Don't spread it around; I wouldn't want to ruin my image."

"What image?" Rusty adds.

I slam the door. "I've had enough," I say, still laughing. "I hope your sitter calls you at the Flicker-lite, and you have to go home early."

"Not a chance. We already checked in, and the kids are sound asleep. So, who are you meeting here?" Barb asks with a cheshire-cat grin.

"You don't want to know."

"Is she pretty?"

"*He* is well over six feet, gotta be a good four hundred pounds, and is the scariest person I've ever seen in my whole life."

"Sure *he* is. Have a good time anyway," Rusty yells as they drive away.

Does my description ring any bells…say, alarm bells?

Before the game tonight, Charley called me and told me that Jilly the Ice Marinski wanted to buy me a drink at Joe Sonkens. Like I told you before, it's rumored that Sonkens has mob connections, and they've got money in his restaurant; that's why I've only been there once. That, and if you remember, Marinski and some of his cronies were holding court. No thanks.

But, here I am, going into the Gold Coast on two feet and hoping I come out the same way. I know that sounds melodramatic, but then who can predict what Jilly wants or why he wants to see me. God forbid he's thinking of fixing baseball games!

Once into the establishment, I glance around and quickly spot him. He's pretty hard to miss. I smile and immediately head for his table, surprised and somewhat relieved to see he's alone. He pushes back a chair, with what has to be a size fourteen shoe, and I plop myself down.

"So, how ya been, kid? I heard ya managin' da Mets. You doin' good?"

Terrific! He knows I'm managing the Mets. I can't wait to see what's coming. Check that. I can wait! "I'm doing fine, Mr. Marinski. How about you? Are you still playing lots of golf at the Presidential?"

"Not too much, boychick. Me and Jimmy been looken to fill our foursome. One of the guys dropped out. I got lots of friends, but don't like 'em enough to play golf with. You ever meet Jake Jacobi? He's the guy that used to play with us?"

Did I ever meet Jake Jacobi? Holy shit! You meet this guy once, and he's etched in your brain forever. I mean, like I told you a few months ago, Jacobi makes Jilly the Ice look like a choirboy.

"I think I only saw him once or twice, Mr. Marinski. Did he decide to give up the game?"

"He decided to give up everything, kid. Last month he crawled into an empty 55 gallon oil drum and commited suicide. Shot himself six times to make sure he got the job done. I don't undertand it. Great looken wife, two little kids…just don't understand why he shot hisself."

Hold the phone, sportsfans! How the hell does a guy shoot himself six times? Ya think maybe he shot off three toes and two fingers, before he stuck the barrel in his mouth or under his chin? I'm thinking maybe Jacobi had a "friend" who helped him. Ya know, a friend to the end kind of thing. Regardless, I thought there was some kind of unwritten rule about offing guys in Florida. I guess the goodfellas must be dialing it up.

"I'm sorry to hear that, Mr. Marinksi. That's pretty tough."

"It got tougher for awhile. Jake's mother's Catholic and, ya know, suicide is a serious deal and you're not supposed to do that; that's Gods job. So, the priest didn't want him buried in holy ground. But Blue Eyes talked to Meyer Lansky, and Meyer talked to the priest … and it all turned out okay. That kinda surprised me," Jilly says reflectively. "I'm pretty sure Jews really look at suicide as pretty heavy; I mean a big sin and all of that. Meyer's a Jew ya know," Jilly concludes, talking to himself, I think, more than to me.

After looking blank for a few seconds, he looks up and smiles, if you want to believe his gnarled lips can form a smile. "Kid, the reason I wanted to see ya is I've got that song you and Moon did. Like I told ya, my friend did the calligraphy, and I'd like ya to sign it. Okay?"

No, asshole, not a chance! Just like the last time with this palooka and his boss, Vincent 'Jimmy Blues Eyes' Alo, I'm going to challenge him to a fucken game of jacks. That's after I get done doing cartwheels in my mind because, thank God he didn't make me an offer to fix a game. "I'd be more than glad to sign it…and thanks."

"No, thanks to you, boychick," he says picking up the picture frame that's face-down on the table. He carefully bends back the small black-metal tabs and removes the cardboard backing. Then he lifts the work from the frame and slides it over to me, along with a soft-tipped pen. As I pick up the pen, he looks over my shoulder and paints a hug grin on his grotesque face. I sign the work, slide it back towards him, and look over my shoulder.

Whoa, Nellie! It's Jayleigh Burney Smith, and she's looking right at us. I wave to her to come over. She smiles and starts for the table. Marinski surprises me again; he gets to his feet, so I do the same.

"Hi, Jay," I say extending my hand to her. Much to my relief, she takes it and smiles. "Mr. Marinski, I'd like you to meet a friend of mine, JayLeigh Burney Smith."

Her hand leaves mine, and she offers it to Jilly. He accepts, clasping it with both of his beefy hair-tuft hands. Gee, such tenderness. "Pleased ta meet ya. Ya wanna sit down and have a drink. I'll be glad to buy ya a Chivas on da rocks?"

"Ah, Mr. Marinski," I say quickly, before Jayleigh can answer. "We're supposed to meet some friends over at the Flicker-lite and we're running a little late…so I think we need to get going."

Picking up my cue, thankfully, Jayleigh nods to Jilly. "Can I have a raincheck?" she asks sweetly.

"Dat would be my pleasure, you too, D Jack. You kids run along and have a good time. And thanks again, boychick."

"You're welcome, Mr. Marinski," I say quickly as I take Jay's hand and lead the two of us toward the door. She gives my hand a squeeze. I don't know why, but I assume it's of a supportive nature. Unless I miss my guess, Jay was in no big hurry to sit down with Jilly the Ice.

Once out the door, I take in a lungful of Atlantic Ocean air, turn to Jay, and release her hand. "Thanks much, Jay. If you hadn't come along, I might not have survived the night."

"That man is kind of scary looking, isn't he?"

"What you see is what you get. And I would be ecstatic if I never lay eyes on him again."

"Speaking of what you see," she says with a drop-dead beautiful smile, "it's good to see you again. I heard you were back in town and thought you might be having a nightcap. There aren't all that many places on the beach, so I tried the Coast first. Do you really want to go to the Flicker-lite, or was that just an excuse to get away from King Kong?"

I'm thinking Rusty and Barb are probably still there, but what the hell. They don't have any idea as to what my social life is, or isn't, for that matter. "Sure, it's only two blocks away."

"You can drive us, if you like."

"I don't drive, Jay. Do you want to take your car?"

"I'm on my bicycle."

"Where do you live? I remember you said you like to hang out at the Flicker-lite, so do you live on the beach?"

"No, I rent a small place on the corner of 16th and Monroe. It's really convenient because it's just a few blocks from Hollywood Central School."

"You're still teaching second grade there?"

"Yes."

"And obviously you ride your bike all the way down here. It must be at least a couple of miles?"

"It is, but it keeps me in good shape."

"That's obvious too, my lady friend."

She let's that equally obvious remark pass. You may not remember, guys, but you met Jayleigh Burney Smith at Jefferson Park a few months ago, and I guess we just missed seeing her at the exhibition game picnic. And like I said before, if you don't remember the statuesque Lakota Sioux, you gotta be brain dead!

"Then I guess we're walking," she says, taking my hand. "It's a nice night for it."

"What about your bike?"

"I can walk the bike. It's just down the street. I'll only be a minute."

She lets go of my hand and walks down the sidewalk towards half a dozen cars parked diagonally in front of Sonken's place. She's wearing a sweatsuit with a bandana around her long jet-black hair. You don't see it too often, but she's the whole package, stunning, athletic, and she's got the smarts because she graduated cum laude from the University of Georgia. Like I said…total package!

She returns with her bike, a racing-green, three-speed gearshift job. I notice the seat has to be up a good eight inches. Going just under six feet tall, this girl does have long legs. She smiles as we start up North Ocean Drive. "I heard on the radio, before I left home that you won tonight. It must feel good to win the first game ever played at Miami Park."

"You're right; it does. It was great to get that first win in front of a full house. I think they even sold tickets for standing room."

"Did it feel as great as the home run you hit in the exhibition game a few weeks ago?"

"Better. Winning tonight was for real."

"And *jacking* one out of the park wasn't" she says, laughing at her play on words. "It sure looked like the real deal to me."

"Come on, Jay. Our pitching coach grooved it. You could have planted that one."

"Maybe I could hit it over the fence, but not out of the park."

"Sam told me you were there, I guess with your sister's boy. I didn't see you."

"Well, I saw you just before the picnic, but you seemed pretty busy signing autographs. Then, I saw you sitting with Sam, so I figured maybe another time."

"You should have come over and said hi."

"Does that mean you and Sam don't have something going?"

Oops, now what? At the picnic at Jefferson Park, she didn't want to intrude, and now, if I read it right, she's sending a signal up the flagpole. Whadda ya think? Too late!

"Do you?" she asks straightforwardly.

"Let's just say we're getting reaquainted."

"And how does one go about getting reaquainted? I could use a few pointers on the subject."

Now I'm almost positive about the flagpole. I've got to figure out a way to take this thing down a notch. I should have done a quick goodnight at the Gold Coast, but I really felt beholden to her for getting me out of the grip of Jilly. The fact that she's gorgeous didn't make it any easier.

"Uh, people can always talk about their past together, if they have one."

That should work; Jayleigh Burney Smith and Devon Conover Jameison most assuredly don't have a past. Oops, sorry, forgot to tell you my middle name is Conover. That was my paternal grandfather's name; he was a Scottish coalminer who came over from Ballingry Parish.

"That sounds reasonable," she says with a shrug, "but if you don't have a common past, wouldn't it make sense to share what you've been doing over the years?"

"I guess you could do that, if you've actually been doing things that are worth sharing."

"Well, I've already shared with you that I was a pretty good athlete at Georgia, got a BS in Broadcasting, taught on the Pine Ridge Rez in South Dakota, and…am unattached."

"I remember."

"Then you probably remember you didn't have much to say, but then, you never did have much to say, did you?"

Ya know, guys, I'm getting tired of all these reminders that I wasn't an A-one conversationalist in high school. I know I was quiet and didn't really say a whole lot, even when I had something to say, but I sure as hell never envisioned myself as some kind of toad!

"You're right. Talking was never my strong suit," I respond indifferently as we approach the streetfront entrance of the Flicker-lite. I don't see the chevy parked in the small lot off to one side of the establishment, so at least I won't have to smile and make small talk with Rusty and Barb. And God knows they would have given me some shit. Jayleigh is about the farthest thing from a *he* you can get.

"It looks like you can leave your bike right in front," I say changing the subject. I hope she wants to talk about something else, too.

After she parks her bike, we walk into the small restaurant, and one of the owners, Joan Capone, immediately smiles and waves to Jay, so I figure she's a regular. The few times I've come here to get one of Joan's killer Chicago pizzas to go, it's been crowded and noisy, and tonight is no exception. However, there is an open table in a corner of the room so we head for it. Joan comes over as we sit down.

"Hi ya, Jay, how have you been? It's the first time I've seen you this week."

"I've been catching up on lesson plans and grading a lot of papers the past few days."

""That's life, kid." Joan turns my way. "It's good to see you, too, D Jack, congrats on the win."

"Thanks. It was good to get the first one under the belt."

"Speaking of belts, what can I get you two?"

"I'll have a Jack Black on the rocks," Jay responds.

"And I'll have a VO, also on the rocks," I add looking across our table and once again confirming that Jay is one of the most striking women I've ever seen. I figure I better say something. Maybe I can steer the conversation in a more comfortable direction.

"So you're still teach second grade at Hollywood Central. How's your year been going? I mean, do you have nice kids and stuff like that?"

"My kids are great, and I really enjoy teaching, but if you recall our conversation at Jefferson Park, broadcasting is my first love."

"I'd think between your success as an athlete and your degree, it's just a matter of time before you can do what you really want to do."

"Not until the culture changes. I just don't think television is ready for women doing sports just yet."

"It's coming, Jay. The popularity of women's sports and the growing numbers of girls playing them is sure to impact the network bosses pretty soon."

"I hope you're right. It's not that I don't love my second graders. I do. But I think a trend is beginning in education that's going to put an awful lot of paperwork and pressure on teachers…and take away from instructional time. That's the part I'm not going to like."

"I don't know too much about what's happening in schools these days. Is there something particular that really concerns you?"

"There sure is. The big one right now is called mainstreaming."

"What's that?"

"It's a way to integrate physically-and mentally-disabled children into regular classrooms."

"That seems like a fair thing to do. When's it going to start?"

"It already has. President Ford signed it into law a few years ago. I think it's called the Education for All Handicapped Children Act or something close to that. Actually," she continues, "it's somewhat complicated."

"What makes it complicated?" I ask with genuine interest.

"Well, there are different categories of integration."

"How many are there?"

"Three. The first simply requires disabled students to be taught at the same school as regular students but not in the same classrooms."

"Are you doing that at Hollywood Central?"

"Yes, we are."

"So, does category two put all the kids in the same classes?"

"No, it doesn't. It just involves social integration like being together in the cafeteria or playing together during recess…and we're doing that, too."

"Then am I to assume that category three puts the kids together in classrooms?"

"Yes, but even that's controversial. Some believe classroom integration should be limited to non-academic subjects like art and music."

"Why is that? What's their issue about integrating the disabled kids into all the classrooms?"

"The major concern," Jay says, skeptically, "is they bring down the level of learning of the regular students.

"Is there data to support that?"

"Actually, the overwhelming majority of the research shows just the opposite."

"Wow," I say, still a little confused, "you're really up on this, and you sound pretty passionate about it."

"I am, because I think it's fair. Most of the complaints don't come from teachers; they come from parents of the regular kids."

"Do you get complaints from the parents of the disabled kids, too?"

"Only a few who are concerned their kids will be ostrasized or become outcasts. But again, the research suggests the kids are being successfully integrated into classroom activities and peer clusters."

"What the hell is a peer cluster?" I ask with a smile.

Jay returns my smile. "That's a label for some of the research designs used to see how kids interact with one another?"

"And most of them show the kids get along okay?"

"Yes, they do."

"Is that what you've experienced so far?"

"I have."

"But you seemed to imply there's a lot of pressure involved and that it ain't exactly a piece of cake?"

"That's because school boards and administrators strongly believe that teachers are primarily responsible for the success or failure of the program."

"Do you agree?"

"In theory, yes, but the most important aspect of the program is the pairing of a regular classroom teacher with another teacher trained in special education," Jay says clinically.

"I get the feeling that ain't happening at Hollywood Central School, right?"

"You're right, it's not happening, because the school board hasn't funded the specialist positions. And I don't think the Federal Government has either. But the thing that really concerns me is I get the feeling it's not going to happen at all. I think regular classroom teachers are going to shoulder most of the responsibility on their own. So now you know why I think it might be time to move on to something else. And I've always had my heart set on getting into broadcasting and doing something I truly love."

"That would be a plus. Not too many have that kind of luxury."

Jay looks at me with some concern. "Does that suggest you're not doing something you love? I would think baseball is near and dear to you."

"Playing was. I'm not so sure about managing."

"Is there anything else you're not sure of?"

Damn! It looks like the school thing didn't work. I think we're back to square one. "Like what?"

"Like you and Samantha. You said you're getting reaquainted. I don't mean to be nosey, but just how reaquainted would you like to get?" She gives it one of her cute little shrugs. "I guess I'm being pretty obvious, huh," she says, her features hardening somewhat. Maybe she's anticipating a response from me she doesn't want to hear.

I'm not sure how you'd handle this situation, guys, but I've been pretty candid with you about just how reaquainted I would like to get with Sam. I think I need to be just as honest with Jay, so she's going to hear it.

"You don't have to answer that, D Jack," she says, beating me to the punch. "It's written all over you. You really want to get back into her life, don't you," she asks rhetorically, with maybe just a smidgen of disappointment. Or maybe not, maybe that's just a male ego thing on my part.

"Yeah, Jay, I really do."

This is fucken surreal. I'm married to a girl I want to get re-aquainted with? And Sam thinks things are bizarre on her end? Holy shit!

Jay interrupts my mental confusion. "Does she know that's what you want to do?" she asks, adopting the ole big sister role.

"I think so."

"And do you think it's mutual?"

"I hope so."

She hesitates, but only for a second. "I do too," she says, her features softening. "All kidding aside, in school I thought I saw something in you that the others didn't. You had a sweetness about you. If you and Sam hadn't been dating, I think I would have fallen for you. Maybe I did back then anyway."

Jay leans across the small table and kisses me on the mouth. Her lips are soft and full. She presses them against me and parts them invitingly. She smells good and tastes better.

I don't respond. Either you do or you don't. It ain't something you have time to mull over. It's one of those occasions when something that ain't planned just flat-out happens. And maybe, subconsciously, in a split second, a light turns red or green. This one, for me, is as blood-red as an Arizona sunset.

She leans back and smiles. "If you kiss Sam like that," she says lightly, devoid of any kind of sarcasm or attempt to be cute, "your reaquaintance is going to be short-lived."

She gently bites her lower lip and ever so briefly seems to be deep in thought. I guess she wanted to give it a last shot, and if that's the case, she knows this ain't goin anywhere.

She looks up at me, having made some kind of decision. "Why don't we have another drink…just between friends?"

"Are you sure, Jay?"

"I am now, D Jack."

I am too, sportsfans, and I figure you know what I'm talking about.

XII

DINNER AT THE FORGE

Nobody's going to be...
perfect.
Bobby Cox, Manager
Atlanta Braves

I'm surprised. After all this time, you'd think the joint would have changed some. It hasn't. And there I go again; the Old Forge is the farthest establishment from a joint you could imagine. In some ways, it reminds me of Bern's. It's elegant and it's plush, but unlike the famous steakhouse in Tampa, thankfully, it doesn't have the bordello atmosphere. Sam wanted to sit side-by-side, the way we did the one time we came here, when I signed my contract with the Mets. But I convinced her it would be easier for me to see her across from me. That being the case, I graciously commandeered the chair that faced the more comfortable, padded, upholstered, semi-circular booth. Right now, I'm just unwinding while Sam's in the powder room doing whatever it is that women do in powder rooms.

It's been a long day, and I'm starting to feel it. We left Birmingham right after the game last night and didn't pull in until 11:45 this morning. In Birmingham, we swept the Barons three straight. It was really neat to have Rickwood Field be so good to us. I had a feeling we'd do well because, like most ballplayers, I was, and still am, superstitious. And that grand old yard was always good to me, maybe because I just liked playing there, eventhough they were exhibition games. It has an old throwback drop-in, hand-operated scoreboard out in left center field with lots of trees over the wooden fences. It's a big park and seats something like ten thousand. The best part, for me, is its five majestic, steel-framed light towers that extend a good seventy-five feet into the air and angle out from the roof. Its unique towers are complemented by the equally unusual gazebo press box, which sits atop the stands, directly behind home plate. And, it didn't hurt any that it's a hitter's park with fences not all that deep.

I can't say the same for Engel Stadium in Chattanooga. Although the ballpark was dolled up just last year and looks pretty spiffy with its fresh green and yellow paint job, it's still a tough yard to play in. At least it was for me; I'm glad I only played one exhibition game there. The outfield grass just didn't seem all that friendly, and I didn't hit a dinger because it's four hundred and seventy one feet to dead center. To get one out of the park, you pretty much have to hit it right down the foul lines, over the left field fence at three hundred twenty five feet or the right field fence at three eighteen. That's where we went after playing Birmingham, and they took us two out of three. But we played well, and the scores were close right down to the last inning.

All in all, I have no complaints. The guys played pretty well, particularly in the field. In two games, they committed one error in each and played error-free in the other four. When you play away games, and you win more than you lose, management is going to tell you it was a successful roadtrip. So, when I got off the the bus this morning, I was beat but generally pleased with how things went.

Speaking of beat, Rusty drove me home, and I don't even remember hitting the mattress. The next thing I knew, Rusty was back, rousting me out of the sack. Fortunately, he's got a key to my place. I'm sure I wouldn't have heard him knocking on the door. I'd slept for six hours and he'd come back to give me a ride to Sam's house. I told him I could take a cab, but he said it was no problem. We'd been on the road for a week, and he and Barb were going out for dinner, so it'd be no big deal for him to drop me off on the way.

By the time we got to Dewey Street, Sam had put the kids to bed, and she was ready to go. Billy was out back doing something or other, so I sure as hell didn't argue with her when she suggested we just get going. The ride down to Miami Beach, in her chocolate-brown, Honda hatchback was quiet but comfortable. I've learned very quickly that Sam doesn't like to talk when she's driving. It's like the time she flew us to Auburn to pick up some rich guy's dog; she talked a little, but when it came to take-offs and landings, absolute concentration was the order of the day. Apparently, she takes driving a car just as seriously as flying a plane. I can live with it.

Sam slides into the booth across from me. "You must have been lost in thought. You didn't even smile when I sat down. Did you order us some cocktails?"

"I did, and I'm sorry, Sam. I think I'm sleep-deprived. One thing is for sure. I ain't gonna miss overnight bus rides for awhile."

"I've seen you look worse."

"I've never seen you look better."

"Thank you, kind sir. Now that we're married, I wasn't sure I would still be on the receiving end of such compliments," she says with a twinkle in her eye.

The twinkle tells me she's being a bit of a cute wise-ass, so I figure I can match her. "Maybe I'm just trying to avoid a divorce."

She laughs. "I'll drink to that. Speaking of which, are you sure you ordered while I was checking out my face?"

"Yeah, I did, but what's wrong with your face?"

"It's a girl thing, Dev. It's what all of us do as soon as we walk into an upscale place like this."

"So, if we go to the BBQ joint in Dania, where the old drive-in theater used to be, you wouldn't go to the powder room?"

"No. In the first place, it doesn't have a powder room."

"Sure it does. It has to. It's the law."

"I know, but I think going through the kitchen into a bathroom with one sink and a toilet doesn't qualify as a powder room."

"Point well taken."

"And in the second place," she continues, "what's the point of sprucing up when you're going to use your hands to eat ribs drenched in Carolina Gold BBQ sauce, piled on bread right out of the Merita bag?"

"Okay. Then there's really nothing wrong with your face, right?"

"You tell me."

"I already did."

"You already did what?" a voice says from behind me.

Sam looks past me and smiles. I'd know that voice anywhere: soft, pleasant, and genuine. I get up and turn. "Mr. Sheridan, it's good to see you. I thought you were in New York?"

Howard Sheridan smiles as he extends his hand. "I was," he says as I match his firm grip. "I just got back a few days ago," he adds, looking across the table and smiling at Sam.

"Ah, Mr. Sheridan, you remember Samantha Frederickson, don't you?"

"Of course I do. It's wonderful to see you again, Mrs. Frederickson. We didn't get a chance to talk very much in Aspen. I hope you had a good time."

"I had a wonderful time, Mr. Sheridan, and thanks again for inviting me to your wife's birthday party. Would you like to sit down?"

"Actually, I came over to invite you to join me for a drink. I have a few guests who I'm sure would enjoy meeting the two of you."

Terrific! My first night back in town, and our quiet little getaway is about to go on hold. Wouldn't it be fun to just say something like, sorry, no can do? But then, as the saying goes, ya can't bite the hand that feeds ya.

"We'd be delighted," Sam says getting to her feet. We follow Sheridan across the room towards a corner booth that's about twice the size of ours but designed to provide much more privacy. Given his two guests, who are chatting about something or other, I'm not surprised.

Jump back, Jack! The guests chewing the fat are Johnny Carson and Mickey Mantle. This is really a shocker. I've always heard Mantle loves the nightlife, but I was under the impression that Carson avoids being in public…but then going out for dinner in a posh restaurant ain't exactly exposing oneself to being in the limelight.

As we close in on the table, they spot Sam and simultaneously get to their feet. "I'm sure my guests need no introduction," Sheridan says with a smile. "Gentleman, let me introduce you to Samantha Frederickson and Devon Jameison. They're both very good friends of mine."

Wow, we've been anointed. When did that happen? Anyway, the two of them offer handshakes to Sam as well as me, mumble some greetings, and sit back down. Sheridan points to some empty chairs, and we do the same.

"Your name sounds vaguely familiar," Carson says pleasantly, "but I can't seem to place you."

"I was on your late show in '69, Mr. Carson. At the time, most people called me D Jack."

"D Jack, well I'll be damned! You're the kid who played for the Mets, and you got hurt in your first game."

"That's me."

"I remember that," Mantle says. "Maybe you only had one day, but it was a damn good one, kid. And you're also the guy they said was going to be the next me," he adds, complete with his boyish grin. I check Sam; she's looking right at him. Who wouldn't; even now, the guy's a damn matinee idol.

"Enough of the past," Sheridan says as a waiter approaches us. "What can I get you two to drink?"

"The lady will have a Barcardi and Pepsi…and I'll have a double VO on the rocks."

"Did you get that, Josef?" Sheridan says, turning to the waiter.

"Yes sir. Would any of you gentlemen like another cocktail?"

The three of them nod in the negative. "And Josef," Sheridan says, "do you see that empty table with the two drinks on it across the room from us?"

"Yes sir?"

"Can you hold it for us?"

"Very good, sir."

"Thank you."

Josef departs, and Sheridan turns to face us. "The reason I wanted the two of you to meet Devon is because I'd like to include him in our plans." Sheridan turns to me. "I'm organizing a fund raising event for the fight against cancer. I'm sure you know why," he adds looking at me.

"I do."

Actually, I really do. Sorry guys. I forgot to share with you that Charley Berston told me he was pretty sure that Sheridan's wife, Lillian, had relapsed.

"I invited Johnny down this weekend," Sheridan explains, "to explore ways to publicize the event with some of the celebrities that regularly appear on his late-night talk show. Mickey is willing to help me with some of his athlete friends and actually wants to get into the thick of it."

"Only if it has something to do with golf clubs," he says jokingly. "That's why I stuck around giving hitting tips during spring training in Fort Lauderdale. This is one terrific place to play golf, and you can do it everyday."

"Because I own the Miami Mets," Sheridan continues, addressing the two of them, "I want to tie the ballclub into the event. Devon manages the team, and he's very popular in this neck of the woods, so it seems a perfect fit to get him and the club involved.

Josef shows up with the drinks, thank God. This is starting to feel really awkward. Aside from the rush, I'm not finding a comfort level here, and Sam has yet to be included in the conversation. It's time to make a move, and I hope I ain't being rude. I stand up and nod for Sam to do the same.

"I hope you won't mind if we take our drinks back to our table, Mr. Sheridan. I just got in from Birmingham and it's going to be an early night. And I'd be more than glad to do anything for the benefit."

"I appreciate that, Devon."

Mantle gets to his feet and comes over to me. "Ya know kid, I was lucky enough to play eighteen seasons and when I retired right before the 1969 season, New York sent me off in style…and Joe DiMaggio presented me with a plaque to be placed in Yankee Stadium's centerfield wall."

"Yeah, but if you recall, you said you thought yours should be just a little lower than DiMaggio's," Carson says grinning.

"I did because it was like the torch was being passed to me, and some thought that maybe the torch might get passed to you, D Jack, even if you weren't going to be in Yankee pinstripes." He pauses, and his boyish grin turns serious. "They tell me you were good. I wish it had lasted longer for ya."

"Thanks," I say quietly.

As if coming into a scene on cue, Sam takes my arm. "It was wonderful meeting all of you," she says, smiling at them, "and thanks for the drinks, Mr. Sheridan."

"You're welcome, Samantha. I look forward to seeing you soon, you too, Devon."

I nod to all of them as Sam steers us towards our table. Upon arriving, I wait for her to slide into the booth before sitting across from her. As noted by Sheridan, when talking to Josef, the drinks I ordered are sitting on the table. That's great. I'm definitely going to need more than the one in my hand and the one on the table. Seeing as we're back where we started, our waiter immediately heads for our table.

"Are you ready to order, or would you like me to return shortly?"

Sam turns my way. "I'm not really hungry, Dev. I think I'll just have a Caesar Salad…and maybe some dessert later."

"That sounds good." I turn to the waiter. "Make that two."

"Very good, sir," he says and quickly departs.

"Oh, I almost forgot," Sam says. "Have you heard from Charlie Moon since you got back?"

"No, was I supposed to?"

"I think so. He tried to get ahold of me at the Presidential, and I guess someone over there told him he could reach me at the Stagecoach. When he called me there, he said he had something in the works he wanted to talk with you about. I didn't have any numbers for you, so I told him to try the Miami Mets business office."

"He might have left a message for me, but I won't be at the park until tomorrow morning. I figure it can wait."

"He sounded pretty excited."

"We've talked a few times about me sitting in for a set now and then. That's probably what it's about."

Sam takes a sip of her drink, and I take a good hit on my VO. "Not to change the subject, but that *was* kind of surreal over there, wasn't it, Sam? Who did you like the most? Don't tell me; it had to be the Mick."

"He was easily the most likeable, but meeting Johnny Carson was really a thrill. He's in our living room every night, for God's sakes. Talk about surreal!"

"Yeah, the whole thing was off the page. But I really don't think Carson was all that relaxed. I was surprised he was here. I didn't think he went out in public that much."

"I've heard the same thing. I guess that says something about Howard Sheridan's influence in the celebrity world."

"More likely the business world, I think."

"Obviously both, but when you come right down to it, Sheridan was the most likeable, relaxed, and genuine person at the table. If not, I think he has Carson beat as a showman. It's interesting how huge amounts of money affect people differently."

"Agreed, and I can also guarantee you that I was the least relaxed."

"I know," she says understandingly, "but you done good."

"All that baseball talk made me really uncomfortable. I mean, it was nice of Mantle to say what he said and maybe I could have been pretty good but then, maybe I would have just been a flash-in-the pan."

"That's the first time I've heard you doubt yourself," Sam says, sounding concerned. "Why?"

"Because there's a huge different between stepping in against minor league pitchers and big league pitchers. Like Pepper used to tell me, minor leaguers throw; big leaguers pitch."

"What's the difference?"

"Throwing is when they wind up and just hurl it so you just dig in and swing at the ball. But pitching is subtle. It's taking just alittle off a fastball, or offering up a slider that breaks a few inches, or getting you to bite on a splitter."

"Why is getting you to bite on a splitter subtle?"

"It's subtle because it looks like an off-speed fastball coming in maybe low around you knees…but just before reaching the plate, it drops like a lead sinker. Nine times out of ten, it hits the dirt and the catcher has to block it."

"Then to be good you have too…"

"You have to be patient, Sam. You have to be able to wait that split second to see what's being served up. It's called pitch recognition."

"Then you must have had it," she says supportively. "In that one game, you ate them alive!"

"Not really, Sam. It was my first game and the guy on the mound wanted to welcome me to the Show. He wasn't pitching Sam; he was throwing. That's why I'll never know…but it really doesn't matter anymore. It's in the past, along with lots of other might-have-beens…and that's exactly where I intend to keep it, along with a few other things."

"What other things?"

"Things like some of my toys."

"What toys?"

"Well, to start with, the bike. When I got home this morning, I decided to give her one last whirl around the block and then put her up for sale."

"I'm glad you're going to sell her, but I'm not sure about you taking a ride."

"I'll be fine, Sam. I'm not going out on any highways or getting into lots of traffic. I'm just going to stay on A1A and cruise the beach. I doubt I'll even get her out of second gear. And I promise not to hit any trees or phone poles."

"That makes me feel a little better. I hope you really enjoy it."

"I will."

Sam leans across the table, gives me a soft, lingering kiss, smiles warmly, and then sits back. She tilts her head, slightly to one side and looks at me. I return her smile but say nothing. I figure something's on her mind and decide to wait and see what it is.

"I'm just so proud of you," she finally says, still smiling.

"I'm glad. What did I do…and when did I do it?"

"I'm not exactly sure when. As for the what, my biggest concern was with your preoccupation with what happened at Shea, and whether you could get past it."

"And now?"

"And now I know you can."

"So do I, but I should have done it a long time ago."

"How long ago?"

"I think more than half dozen years ago when I was at Arizona State. The philosophy curriculum included a course on world leaders, and I read a quote from Gandhi. He said, 'Glory lies in the attempt to reach one's goal and not reaching it.'"

"I think that's great."

"Me too, now, but at the time, I wasn't ready for it. I should have been, but I wasn't. I was too busy feeling sorry for myself."

"We all do that, Dev."

"Even you?"

"Even me; after smacking the board, and being pregnant, too, I think I hated the world."

"What you really mean is you hated me," I say in a matter-of-fact way.

"No, Dev. I never hated you, but just like you, I certainly felt sorry for myself."

"Maybe so, but I know how you think. I remember one time when I had to sit out a few games with a bone bruise I was bitchen up a storm. You said you'd give me one day to feel sorry for myself, and that was it."

"I remember that, too," she says with a laugh.

"So, I'll bet you gave yourself all of one day to feel sorry for yourself, right?"

"Do what I say, not what I do, Dev. I think I actually gave myself a whole week."

I match her laugh. "Gee, a whole week! Seeing as it took me the better part of eight years, I'd say you didn't contradict your philosophy of life."

"Speaking of philosophy, if you want to call it that," she says more seriously, "at Florida, I took a course in comparative religion. I recall the prof said that Gandhi was against Christian religions. Did you ever read anything to suggest he was?"

"Not really. From what little I studied about him, I don't think he was opposed to any organized religion. I just think he felt there were things people did in the name of religion that he wasn't overly thrilled about."

"Can you remember anything specific?"

"Well, not specifically, but when you refer to Christianity, I seem to recall he said he liked Christ, but he didn't like Christians who he thought were so unlike Christ. But I also remember it was more than religion. He was once asked what he thought about western civilization and his reply was 'I think it would be a good idea.'" Sam seems to be mulling that over.

"Pretty heavy, huh?" I ask, hoping we're not going to get into a lot of cultural issues and religious mumbo-jumbo.

"I guess but, as you like to say, I went somewhere else."

"And where was that?"

"Do you remember a week or so ago when we were on the beach, talking about fastballs and curves?"

"Yeah, I do."

"And you asked me what I was thinking about?"

"Yeah…and you said nothing."

"But I was thinking about something."

"I figured as much, but I didn't want to push. So?"

Her look tells me she's about to get dead serious. I'm trying, quickly, to remember what we were talking about, but it seems to me we were just yakking about baseball stuff. Now that I think of it, we also talked about her moving from the Presidential over to the Stagecoach, so maybe it has something to do with work.

"Dev," she begins, and then hesitates. "Did you see any old friends in Jacksonville?"

Okay, guys, that cat's out of the bag. "Actually, I did."

"Really, and were you in Brinkman's?"

"Actually, I was."

"You're not making this very easy. I shouldn't have asked. It's none of my business."

"It's definitely your business, Sam, and I'm sorry. I guess I wasn't ready for that, although I was positive you had something on your mind at the beach, and hoped you'd share it sooner or later."

"Why weren't you ready, as you put it?"

"Maybe I was hoping you'd have enough faith in me not to ask."

"Now it's my turn to be sorry," she says with a frown. "I guess some thoughts are lurking deep down in me somewhere. I didn't ask when we were on the beach because I thought I could handle not knowing anything."

"And now you think otherwise."

"Sadly, yes."

"That's my fault, Sam. I don't want you to feel like you're asking something that's off limits and I know it's going to take some time for you to build up your confidence in me. So," I say with a dopey grin, "I was at Brinkman's because that's where *he* wanted to buy me a drink."

"He?"

"That's right…*he*."

"And just who would *he* be?" she asks with a quizzical look that slowly morphs into a smile.

"Jamie Bell."

"Wow," she says with genuine surprise. "That's a name out of the past. When I went to those few games in Jax, I used to sit in the stands with his girlfriend. I don't remember her name, but she was really sweet."

"Well, now that same sweet girl, Jade, is Mrs. Jamie Bell and, just like you, they have a boy and two girls: John, Edythe, and Kailey."

"That's terrific! Where did you bump into him?"

"At the ballpark; he's the bench coach for the Suns."

"That's great. Good for him!"

""Well, it is and it isn't. He got passed over this season for the manager's position. The organization brought in a new guy, so now it looks like a deadend for any advancement there."

"How long has he been a coach?"

"I think maybe four or five years."

"He must have been pretty young when he started coaching. If I remember, he was a good ballplayer. What happened to him?"

"You've got a good memory. He was a damn good ballplayer. When I went to Norfolk, he did too, and it looked like both of us weren't gonna be there for the whole season. From what little I know, I think the Mets figured the two of us would be playing left and center for a long time. But about the same time I got injured, he was drafted and shipped to Vietnam."

"Obviously, unlike Dolph, he came home," she says with some sadness. "But," she adds, trying quickly to sound upbeat, "you'd think lots of guys just picked up where they left off, wouldn't you?"

"I suspect most of them did, but not if you lost your left leg."

"Oh my God!"

"Yeah, I felt the same way when we talked about it. I felt pretty small when I thought about the way I've handled myself."

"I don't think you should feel that way at all. Maybe you didn't lose a leg, but the result of your injuries was the same as his. You loved the game, it was your whole life, and it would have been hard for anyone to face the fact that they'd never play again."

"I know that, but I should have handled it the way he did."

"You have no idea how Jamie dealt with what happened to him. All you know is that he's obviously doing something with his life now, just like you are. And anyway, Dev, nobody's perfect."

I laugh.

"What are you laughing about?" she asks, sounding a little put out with me.

"You're absolutely right about being perfect, no one should be! I learned that at ASU, too. Perfection is an affront to Allah!"

"Really, I thought you majored in philosophy, not religion."

"Some would argue there's a very fine line between the two."

"And I'm sure you'll share what the fine line is, right?"

"Hmm, is that an invitation?"

"No, it's my acceptance of the inevitable."

"Thanks loads…to hell with it. Let's talk about something else."

"Oh, come on. I can't wait to be exposed to your fine lines."

"Not a chance," I respond with mock hostility.

"Okay, but it's probably because you're afraid I'll shoot holes in your theory. I went to college, too, ya know."

"Oh boy, I think I've just been challenged? Are you throwing down the gauntlet?"

She picks up the humor of it. "I am, Sir Knight!"

"Then I have no choice but to accept. My honor is at stake."

"That's fine. Get on with it."

"Do you insist?"

"I do."

"Okay then. I'm not sure I bought into it, but I took a whole course in something called Sacred vs. Secular Speculation."

"You took a course? Wow! Good for you," she mocks, feigning astonishment. "If this is a joust, I just knocked your ass out of the saddle. You don't even have a theory; all you've got is some lame academic course," she concludes with a giggle, followed by what appears to be a victorious smile.

"Not so fast lady. I haven't hit the ground yet."

"What is it you ballplayers like to say? I think it goes something like, 'the fat lady is clearing her throat.'"

"We also like to say, 'it ain't over, til' it's over.'"

"That sounds like you're about to give it your last shot. So, go ahead. What was it you failed to buy into?"

"It's not about a buy-in. I just thought the whole course was apples and oranges. That's all."

"And what do you mean by that?"

"I mean most philosophy stuff is considered to be a social science based on speculation."

"And that obviously isn't the case with religion, right?"

"Right, most religious teachings are founded on pure faith."

"But isn't there some faith involved in speculating?"

"I don't know, but speculation often provides a foundation for scientific inquiry. Faith starts with faith and ends with faith."

That remark is met with a laugh, bordering on a guffaw. And, just the way she did when she was a kid, Sam quickly looks around to see if she's embarrassed herself. Much to her relief, the patrons around us seem to be totally focused on their own conversations.

"What was that all about? What are you laughing at?" I ask, genuinely annoyed.

"I hate to say it, but I think I'm laughing at you, on second thought, at us."

"Gee, thanks a lot!"

"Dev," she says, amused, "can you imagine us saying such things the last time we sat here, when we were all of seventeen years old? About all I can remember is you talking about your new contract and playing in the Met's organization, and me talking about training for the Olympics."

I think back to that time, and smile. "You're right. Most of our conversations were about sports, sports, and then again, sports."

"Yes, but we did talk about a few other things. Sometimes we talked about how we were going to do it together."

"Yup, so we did. But," I add quickly, "you're absolutely right. We never talked much about stuff that was heavy, and probably didn't have a clue as to what philosophy was."

"Or religion either, for that matter."

"Did you hang out with any kids who were real religious?" I ask.

"Hell, yes," Sam responds with a laugh, but this one is noticeably toned down. "Sometimes I think the only reason I was captain of the cheerleading squad was because half the girls were Southern Baptists and the other half were Episcopalians. They were definitely dancing to different kinds of music, so I spent an awful lot of time just trying to keep the peace."

This is fun. It's almost like we're getting to know each other again; ya know, like dating. I want to keep this going.

"Speaking of music, what kinds of music do you like?"

"Well, given the few times I was working the dining room, and could hear you and Moon in the Bengal Lounge, I'd say I like what you do, but it's not on the top of my list. I hope that doesn't disappoint you."

"Not in the least. I'm not even sure I have a list; I'm kinda eclectic when it comes to music. So, what *is* on the top of your list?"

"Being eclectic, I have to assume you like classical music, yes?"

"Is that on the top of your list?"

"It is. Do you listen much, or do you have a favorite composer or something like that. I mean, is there a classical Harry Chapin out there for you, or maybe a Jim Croce?"

"Hey, that's neat. You did hear some of the music in the Lounge."

"I did, but I didn't recognize a lot of it. I asked Sal once about it, and she said most of it was stuff you and Moon wrote."

"That's true."

"And I liked it."

"That's good to know. Anyway, to answer your question, I don't think I have an absolute favorite classical composer, but I really like Tchaikovsky, and have a soft spot for Rossini."

"I like Tchaikovsky too, but I'm not all that familiar with Rossini."

"I think you are," I say with a grin. "I'll bet you watched the Lone Ranger when you were a kid."

"Didn't everybody?"

"Sure, and I'll bet you loved the theme music?"

She lights up. "Do you mean Dum-ta-da-dum; ta-da-dum-dum-dum-dum-dum-dum-dum-dum-dum; ta-da-dum; ta-da-dum; ta-da-dum?"

"You got it!"

That little ditty does get some people to turn our way, but they just smile and continue on with their conversations.

"And Rossini wrote that? What is it?"

"It's the *William Tell Overture* and he wrote other really neat stuff too. One of my favs is *La Gaza Ladra* which means Thieving Magpie. I thought the guy must have had a sense of humor until I read it was about a French servant girl who was executed for stealing. Then they found out it was a magpie, so it was pretty serious stuff."

"That sounds awfully tragic. It must have been an opera."

"It was although I think Rossini is more famous for his overtures, but I really don't know. I never could get into opera that much."

"Why was that?"

"Like you just said, most operas are tragic and it just seems to me, like someone once said, if something's really tragic, you don't sing about it."

"I think you're right."

"Okay, your turn. I already know you have a list, so who's on top?"

"When I took humanities at Florida, I fell head over heals for Beethoven...particularly his *Fifth Symphony* and *the Ninth."*

Now it's my turn to laugh. She looks mad. "What's wrong with you," Sam says indignantly. "Beethoven is as good as it gets!"

I put up my hands to protect myself, just in case I have to stave off an assault. "I absolutely agree; he's the best of the best. I was laughing because I had a prof at Arizona State who thought Rossini was Beethovan on speed."

Her confused appearance quickly evaporates into a giggle. "You mean like tripping or or something like that?"

"That's what he used to say."

"So maybe he was right. Were all Rossini's works as fast as the Lone Ranger stuff?"

"Most of them were, but a lot of them started pretty softly...and slowly."

"More like Tonto's horse, huh? He always seemed to be behind the Lone Ranger and Silver."

"Hey, you really did watch the Lone Ranger. And you're right. I saw Jay Silverheels interviewed once on a late show and he said he could run faster than Scout."

"Do you know if he was a full-blooded Indian?"

"He said he was, that he was a Canadian Mohawk, but his name wasn't Tonto."

"What was it?"

"Would you believe, Harold Smith?"

"Dev, where do you get all this stuff?"

"I pick up things, here and there."

"So do I and I'll bet I've got a classical tidbit you're not aware of."

"I'm sure you do. Lay it on me."

"Do you remember our high school alma mater?"

"Sure, it starts off…'*neath sun and palms*.'"

"And do you know where the music comes from?"

"No idea."

She grins. "It's a movement toward the end of Jean Sibelius' symphonic poem, *Finlandia*. The movement actually has a name, *Finlandia Hymn*, because unlike most of the work, which is rousing and tumultuous, it's very melodic and calm"

"That's fascinating. I wonder how many alma maters have their origins in classical music."

"Not too many, I'd wager."

I don't repond but quietly look across the table at her. "This is fun, isn't it," I say, realizing there's so much about Sam I simply don't know, or never knew, for that matter.

""Yes, it is. It's really exciting to find out things we don't know about each other. It's a shame," she says regretfully, "that we didn't have more talks like this one."

We both nod and smile at each other. She takes a deep breath, and then slowly lets it out. I get the impression she's just made a decision and, if so, the look on her face suggests she's comfortable with it.

"I'm getting hungry. I hope we get served pretty soon. It's getting late, and I still have to take you to your apartment."

I guess I'm wrong. That doesn't sound much in the way of serious decision making. "If you're tired, you don't have to take me home. I can grab a cab from your place."

"No, I'll drive you, but first I need to make a quick stop at home."

"Why's that?"

"While you were on the road, I came down with an eye infection, and I need to put in antibiotic drops four times a day, the last being right before bedtime."

"I don't like to hear things about eyes. Are you okay?"

"The doctor said I'll be fine. I probably got something in my eye that irritated it. He told me it should be gone in a few days, as long as I'm diligent about putting in the medication."

"So why don't you just drop me off first and then go home."

"That won't work. I'm not going home tonight, Dev."

"Uh, you're not going home?"

"No, I'm not. I'm going to stay with you."

Guys, I'm not going to tell ya I've been taken by surprise. I'm just going to tell ya, I've been *totally* taken by surprise! "Do I have a vote, Sam?" I know, guys, pitiful; why should I even want a vote, right?

"No, you don't" she says softly with a smile, "You've said all along that it's up to me to initiate things, so I'm initiating."

"Ah Sam, aren't you forgetting something?"

"What?"

"The annulment option will go off the page."

"So I'll have to find a reason to divorce you."

"But you won't look too hard, right?"

"I won't look at all, Devon," she says, all aglow, or at least that's the way she looks to me.

Without having seen him approach, I realize the waiter is standing at our table holding a large metal tray on his flat palm, over his shoulder. "Dinner is served, sir."

It certainly is! And the poets have spoken: life is sweet.

XIII

SHOWDOWN AT ZIGGY'S

I just thought you might like to know
that I passed a kennel
on the way to the game.
Your mother is all right.
Ralph Houk, Manager
New York Yankees, Detroit Tigers, Boston Red Sox

What the hell!

I'm sitting in Sam's hatchback, out in front of her house, waiting for her to come out the door, but it's Billy who's heading my way. Here we go with Yogi's déjà vu shit. The last time I expected to see Sam and didn't, it was her ever-loven father on a street corner about nine years ago. That was fucken ugly, and I've got a nasty feeling this is going to be the same, if not worse. I get out of the car as he approaches.

"I'm going to take you to your place, Devon. Samantha's in the house, and she wants to talk with you for a minute or two. I'll be waiting in the car."

Without even giving me an opportunity to say something, anything, he turns and heads for his red and black 1954 Chrysler sedan that's parked on the white-gravel driveway to the left of the house. I walk to the front door that he's left open and go into the small livingroom. Sam is seated on the couch waiting for me. She looks concerned but not totally upset or anything like that. I walk over to her and sit down.

"What's up, Sam. How come Mr. Friendly is taking me home?"

"Daddy said he needs to talk to you."

I figure he sure as hell ain't gonna talk *with* me; probably just wants to insult me some more. "Did you tell him you weren't coming home tonight? Is that what this is all about?"

"No, when I came home, he was waiting for me, and I barely got a chance to even say hello. He simply got up from his chair, told me the kids were sound asleep, and said he was driving you home."

"Do you have a clue as to what's going on?"

"I don't. He didn't sound mad or annoyed or anything."

"That'll probably change."

"Devon, do me a favor."

"I'll try. What do you want?"

"Try not to throw the first punch," she says with a weak smile.

"Okay, I'll just try to protect myself in the clinches," I respond, not with a weak smile, but probably a silly one.

"Thanks. You better get going. I think he's started the car."

"You mean the bell for round one, don't you?"

She gets up. "I hope not."

I get to my feet and give her a hug. She returns the hug and then gives me a kiss. It's almost like I can feel the apprehension in her lips, so I break it off quickly.

"I'll make sure he isn't out late, okay?" I say, heading for the door. Sam just stands there and nods.

Once out the door, it's just a few steps to the Chrysler. Billy has already opened the passenger door for me. Gee, just like Jilly, a regular gentleman. Is it possible our little showdown has begun with some kind of peace offering? Somehow, I doubt it.

"Thanks for the ride. I live over on the beach."

"Before that, I want to go somewhere that's not too busy. Do you know of a place that's open at this hour?"

Surprise, surprise, sportsfans, we're gonna have a chat. I promised Sam I'd cool my jets, so I think the best thing is to go somewhere I don't want to fuck up my image.

"There's a place called Ziggy's on Garfield just a few blocks north of the paddleball courts."

"That'll do," he says, with absolutely no expression.

Like father like daughter when it comes to driving. Billy doesn't say another word all the way to Ziggy's. It's late, so it's easy to find a parking spot big enough to accommodate the huge Chrysler right in front of the place. Both of us exit the car and head for the modest but quaint bar. Billy's walking at about the same pace as me, so I start to hang back in order to let him walk through the door first. He does, and seeing an open corner table, he heads for it. As you know, Ziggy's is pretty small, but it's usually quiet and somewhat intimate. For tonight I can do with out the intimacy. And why is it I always seem to end up at a corner table?

Ziggy is across the room serving something to a middle-aged couple. They're the only ones in the establishment. The few times I've been in at this hour, the place hasn't been doing all that much business, so it's pretty obvious Ziggy doesnt attract the late-night crowd. The short grizzled proprietor heads our way with a big smile.

"D Jack, it's so good to see you. When did you get back in town?"

"We got in this morning."

"Did you win a few?"

"We only took one against Orlando, but we took Birmingham three straight."

"That's pretty good. Who's your friend?"

No comment, sportsfans. "Ziggy, I'd like you to meet Billy."

Ziggy extends a beefy palm. It's nice to meet you, Mr. Billy." Old school.

"You too," Billy says, taking Ziggy's hand without getting up.

Ziggy turns to me. "Rose went home, but I'm sure I can get you something from the kitchen if you want a nosh."

"I'm not very hungry, but thanks for the offer."

"Nothing for me either," Billy adds. "Do you have Ballantine Ale?"

"Sure I do. Would you like a glass, or just the can?"

"A glass will be fine, thanks."

"And what can I get for you, D Jack."

"I'll just take a Pepsi in a glass with some ice."

Ziggy looks at me, confused. That's understandable. It's the first time I've asked for something nonalcoholic. Then, he shrugs and heads for the bar.

Okay, guys, let's get right to it. "What's on your mind, Billy?"

"You don't even want to start with some small talk, huh?"

"You and I don't do small talk. Anyway, it's late. You obviously have something to say, so why not just get at it?"

"You don't sound very friendly."

"Friendly! You've got to be kidding. In the last six months, I think we've had, maybe, three conversations, if you want to call 'em that. You initiated them and, unless I'm mistaken, your intent sure as hell had nothing to do with being friendly."

"You're right. It would be hard to tell someone you want them to go away nicely."

"Fine, so what's on your agenda for this evening? Let's not screw around. I assume you still want me to take a hike, or have you come up with some other plan?" I inquire feeling exasperated, "Just what *do* you want?"

"It's not necessarily what I want. It's what Samantha wants?"

"And what does Samanatha want?"

"My daughter wants you."

"You think she wants me?"

"Yes, she does."

"And what leads you to that conclusion?"

"She told me she's in love with you."

That stops me flat in my tracks; she told him before she told me. It's starting to look like Sam wants us to be truly married, so I think she's starting to prime Billy for the big news. "And what did you say to that?"

"I asked her if she's trying to convince herself of that because you're Sean's father."

"What did she say?"

"She told me she's never stopped loving you."

Holy shit, now what? He sounds more resigned than mad, which is good I guess, but I sure as hell ain't sensing any enthusiasm on his part.

Ziggy arrives with the drinks, places them in front of us, and heads over to see what the couple wants, if anything. Billy knocks down half his brew, and I take a few sips of the Pepsi.

"If you still hoping I'll go away, it's not going to happen," I say, trying very hard not to sound confrontational. "You might as well get used to it. I can't do anything about it if you're going to hate my guts all your life, but I love your daughter and I want to be a good father to our son."

"I don't hate you, Devon."

"Why do I have trouble believing that?"

"You have every right to feel that way. But think back to when you were in high school. I'm not an evil man; I'm not even mean. But when you hurt Samantha, all I could see was red. She's all I had left, and along with my grandchildren, she still is. And then six months ago, you walked back into Samantha's life, and the more she talked about you, the more I had to accept the fact that that's where she wants you to be. That's not easy for me to accept, particularly when it involves the only thing I hold precious in this world."

I know Billy. He's not capable of bullshit. "So where do we go from here? I figure this is painful for you."

"Not as much as you think because if you love someone, and you put them first like you should, you can deal with the rest and it'll eventually go away."

"Like you say, that's not an easy thing to do, and eventually can take a long time."

"Are you suggestioning I don't have that kind of time?"

"Sam says you're doing great, so no. But you know your daughter better than I do. She'd probably say stretching out the inevitable is a waste of time, so why not go for the brass ring. Didn't you do that, Billy? Wasn't that what showbiz was all about?"

"It was, but sometimes that's not all that easy either."

"Who ever promised any of us it would be easy? I know I'm a lot younger than you are, but even at this tender age, I think I've finally learned not to stay at the dance too long."

"For you, that would be a good idea. Samantha used to tell me you were a lousy dancer," he says, feigning a smile. Well, that's better than a sneer, I guess.

"I was and still am."

"But on the other hand, you used to shoot a pretty mean game of straight pool. Can you still do it?"

Now, his smile seems genuine, and this sounds like a peace offering. "I'm not sure. Is Shorty's Billiard Hall in Dania still open?"

"I don't know; I haven't played in years. It might be."

"And you still think you can sink fifty balls before I can?"

"You're damn right."

"Is this a challenge?"

"Why not?"

"Okay then, but this time around, things will be different," I say, returning his half smile with one of my one.

"How's that?"

"I'm not eighteen anymore, Billy. For the first time in my life, when we cue up, I'll have the pleasure of buying you a Ballantine Ale. And I won't even have to drink one; I never did like 'em."

"But you drank them anyway."

"The price was right."

"Well, at least now, I won't have to buy one for you and break the law."

We both laugh.

What a night! Billy says Sam's in love with me…and I'm thinkin' he doesn't want to kill me anymore. Damn, guys, we've got to do some celebrating, and like I just told Billy, I'm buying. So, whaddah ya have? I sure wish Sam was here to see her dad and, uh, her husband bury the hatchet. She'd want a Barcardi and Pepsi or maybe even a White Russian or a Brandy Alexander. How about me buying you something, and you drinking it for her?

Thanks!

XIV

ONE LAST RIDE

They don't realize how tired you get
during a baseball season…
mentally tired…
you need time to unwind.
Lou Piniella, Manager
New York Yankees, Cincinnati Reds, Seattle Mariners,
Tampa Bay Devil Rays, Chicago Cubs

I'm sitting on the only good-sized rock to be found on a gravel cul-de-sac that borders the Intercoastal Canal. You might not remember, but you've been here. It's the quiet little fishing spot where Sam and I used to do some late-night dreaming, among other things. I've probably been around this rock more than a hundred times, beginning with when I was a little kid with a cane pole and more recently when Billy and I had our recent face-to-face encounter.

There's a bit of a nip in the April air, but that's because it's pretty early in the morning. In an hour or two, when the sun gets higher in the sky, I figure it'll be a good twenty degrees warmer, and I'll have to take my black leather jacket off, because by then the last ride on my 4-stroke 500cc Yamaha TX 500 will be history.

So far, it's been just short of exhilarating, kinda like that one E-ride you get when you buy a ticket book at Disney World. But this morning, it's been even better than Space Mountain. Maybe it's because when you know you're doing something for the last time, the excitement just goes off the page.

Anyway, just like I promised Sam, I've avoided the main thoroughfares around town and pretty much stuck to the side roads in Hollywood Beach. I didn't have anything in mind when I cranked her up this morning, but so far the ride has turned into a road down memory lane. After going up and down Johnson Street, which probably still serves as the hang-out spot on the beach for the high school kids, I decided to cross the

Hollywood Beach Boulevard Bridge and head west away from the Intercoastal Canal. I rode for about a mile and then went north towards the high school. I haven't seen it since I've been back and was curious as to whether it's changed much. It hasn't. That's a good thing, I'm thinking.

Then I took a back road up to Dania to see if Jobi's was still there. It was. Sam and I had an ice cream out in front of the place in Billy's car damned near every night. Most of the time we'd just sit there and laugh about the requests phoned into the local rock-and-roll station. They always seemed about the same, something like, "Can you play Otis Redding's *(Sitten' On) The Dock Of The Bay* for Susie?" We always talked about phoning one in for each other but never did.

After that I cruised back down to Hollywood past my elementary school, Hollywood Central. It was grades one through seven, and then you went to the high school for grades eight through twelve. I can tell you for sure, being an eighth grader in high school was damn intimidating.

Jefferson Park is only three blocks from Hollywood Central, so I headed over there and went around the whole thing. It's hard to believe something like fifteen years have gone by since I played in my first organized baseball game. Just for curiosity sake, I stopped at the ballfield to see if they had hung my jersey number on the press box. And, sure enough, there was a red and black jersey with the number 10 on it. That felt good.

My dad's home was east of the park on Jefferson Street, so I just headed a few more blocks in that direction and slowly cruised past the house. I hardly recognized it. Additional living space had been built on the front of the house, so it appeared to be much bigger, and there was less grass between the house and the street. There had been a beautiful royal palm tree in the front yard. I had spent countless hours under that tree, lost in my daydreams. Sadly, the tree was gone; I guess things gotta change.

So, that brings you up to date and I guess I've had my bike ride into a world of nostalgic memories. I better get going. I started early because Rusty is picking me up at my apartment around 10:00 a.m. so we can get to the ballpark at least a half hour before the players show up for batting practice. I straddle the jet-black bike and kick her over which is easy; she's got an electronic ignition system. I slowly steer across the gravel and pick up a little speed after hitting the paved street.

I keep her in second gear and cruise down Van Buren for a block, hang a right on 9th avenue, and proceed for another two blocks before intersecting Hollywood Beach Boulevard. Then I hang another right and head east towards the bridge which is about half a mile away.

Once over the bridge, I lean into the left-turn lane in order to be able to turn north on A1A and head for my apartment. A car in front of me slows for a light that has just turned red. I'm already going slow enough to drop her into first gear and depress my right foot pedal that controls the rear brake. Then, I kick her up a half-step, into neutral, come to a complete stop, and get my boots down on the street.

The Hollywood Beach Hotel is right in front of me on the ocean side of A1A. That really brings back memories. As a senior, Sam convinced me to take her to the prom and…

I hear a loud screech…

BAM! BOOOOM!!

I reflexively check my left rearview mirror. A white pick-up truck is airborne, and the damn thing's coming right at me! What the fu…

XV

HERE WE GO AGAIN

A manager has his cards dealt to him
and he must play them.
Miller Huggins, Manager
St Louis Cardinals, New York Yankees

Everything's black. I mean, it's really black. It seems to me I mentioned Plato's Cave once, but at least there were glimmers of light and shadows in there. You know, just enough to make you think you're seeing things you're not really seeing, or something like that. Well, there ain't gonna be any interpretations here, real or otherwise. There ain't any glimmers or shadows; there just ain't anything.

I'm flat on my back, so I start to roll over on my side, but bump into a metal railing. Great, at least now I know where I'm at. Hospital beds are the same everywhere. That means somewhere around my pillow, there ought to be a gadget that lets me call for a nurse. I hear a door open; I guess I can skip the hunt for the buzzer.

"Good morning, Mr. Jameison," says a pleasant voice.

"Hi, I was just about to call."

"I know. We've been watching you closely and monitoring your vital signs. We figured you were going to wake up any time now. How do you feel?" she asks as she takes hold of my wrist, going for a pulse.

"I'm not feeling much of anything."

"That's because you've been on an intravenous drip since you were admitted."

"So how am I doing? And by the way, where am I?"

"You're doing just fine, and you're in Memorial Hospital. You're not in the ICU; you're in a private room, and you've been here since yesterday morning. You've been sedated; that's why you slept this long. Now that you're awake, I'll track down Dr. Milleckston so he can come in and talk with you."

"And what kind of a doctor is Dr. Milleckston?"

"He's a retinal surgeon, one of the best."

Fuck it! This can't be happening to me. Here we go again.

"Can I get you anything?"

"Some water would be nice, if it's okay."

"Water's fine. I'll be right back."

"Thanks."

I hear her cross the floor and close a door. I reach up to my face and feel pads on each eye and some kind of wrap around my head. Then I check myself out. Everything seems to move and, other than lots of tape around my chest, I don't feel anything out of the ordinary. As for the tape, been there, done that: broken ribs. I'm breathing without any pain, but that's got to be the drip, probably morphine or some relative of it. I hear the door open again and some footsteps approach the bed.

"Good morning. It was very considerate of you to wake up while I'm making my morning rounds," a male voice says lightly. "I'm glad you're awake; it's a good sign, Devon. May I call you Devon?"

"Sure."

"I'm Dr. Milleckston, but I prefer just John."

"Okay, just John."

"Here's the water you asked for. I'm glad you have a sense of humor," he says pleasantly.

"Thanks."

"Do you know what happened to you, Devon?"

"Not really."

"Try to tell me anything you can remember."

I think for a moment. "I was on my Yamaha," I begin, trying to get things in focus, "and I'd just crossed the Hollywood Beach Boulevard Bridge. I got into the left turn lane and stopped for a red light. I think there was one car ahead of me, maybe two."

"That's good," he says encouragingly. "Keep going."

"Well, I kicked her down into neutral and just sat there with my boots on the road. Then I heard a really loud noise. I checked my rear view mirror on my left handlebar and saw a white truck bearing down on me. That's all she wrote. Sorry, there's nothing else…just a blank."

"No, you did fine, Devon."

"Make it Dev, okay?"

"Sure thing, as I was saying, this is good. Sometimes with these kinds of injuries, a patient doesn't recall what happened right before the incident."

Okay, guys, let's get right to it. "What kind of injuries?"

"You suffered a mild concussion, and you've got two broken ribs. You've also got some bruises and road rash, but nothing serious. Actually, you ended up underneath a car that was directly in front of you. If you hadn't been wearing a helmet, we wouldn't be having this conversation," he says solemnly.

"So, what's with my eyes?"

He doesn't say anything, which tells me a lot. "I've been through this before, John, so just lay it out there, okay?"

"Okay, we were able contact the ophthalmologist and neurosurgeon who treated you in New York and they got your charts to us ASAP. As I'm sure you know, when that baseball hit you, you suffered injuries to the retinal blood vessels in your left eye which resulted in poor blood flow to the optic nerve. That caused an acute atrophy of the nerve. It's clinically referred to as ischemic optic neuropathy. I suspect, you've still been able to see light but very little else."

"You're right on the money."

"Well, Dev, that won't be the case anymore, I'm sorry to say. This accident finished what the baseball started; you're totally blind in the left eye."

Shit, one down, one to go. "How about my right eye, it's bandaged too?"

"You asked me to lay it out there, so I won't pull any punches. You've suffered vascular disturbances in your right eye which has resulted in the onset of the deterioration of your optic nerve fibers." He pauses and then continues slowly. "The process is irreversible…and there's no treatment. I'm sorry, Dev."

"Do I have any vision now?"

"It's going to be similar to what you experienced with your left eye, probably a little better."

"How long will it be before I'm totally blind?"

"I can't say."

"Not even a ballpark guess? I won't hold you to it."

"I think maybe a year ir two, maybe more…but probably less."

"Thanks. I know it isn't easy for you, but I appreciate you telling me what I'm up against."

"I know this isn't going to help any, but Howard Sheridan brought in a specialist from Mt Sinai…and he corroborated my diagnosis."

"Actually, it does. You know how everyone wants a second opinion when the news isn't so good. You can't help hoping someone else might have a different take on things."

"There's always hope. Sooner or later, medical science is going to beat this thing."

"But in my case, it sounds like it's going to be a lot later than sooner."

"I'm afraid so," he says. "Do you have any questions?"

"Not at the moment, but do you have some idea how long I'll be here?"

"Actually," he says, sounding upbeat, "you're really in solid shape, and you didn't have to undergo any procedures. We'll continue to observe you today to make sure you're okay, and if all your vitals are good, there isn't any reason we can't release you early tonight."

"Terrific, I get to enjoy a hospital supper."

"I'll take that as humor as opposed to sarcasm, right?"

"You got it. Is there anything else?" I ask, trying to maintain a chipper fascade.

"I'm going to want to see you for some follow-up in, say, three or four days. My office will make an appointment for you, and let you know before you leave. Is there anyone who can, uh, help you?"

"I'll be fine, John. Thanks for asking."

"Okay then, I'll check back with you later today before we release you. There are a few people anxious to see you. Are you up for it?"

"Is one of them a good-looking strawberry blonde?"

"I'm sorry to say, unfortunately, no. I assume you're referring to Samantha?"

"You've met her?"

"I have. She was here yesterday but I knew she was worried about her children, so I told her there was nothing she could do while we were keeping you sedated. I told her I would call her as soon as you were awake."

"I guess she asked a lot of questions, huh?"

"She did, but Dr. Etting, from Sinai, was still examining you. I've got to tell you, Dev, you're going to have a very concerned and frightened young woman on your hands. I did my best to settle her down."

"I appreciate it, John. As for the others, can you say I'm sleeping or something like that? I need a little time alone."

"I understand. I'll take care of it."

He lays his hand on my shoulder, and I grip it with mine. A few moments pass; there's nothing to say. He gives my hand a squeeze, and I hear him head for the door.

It's goofy how your mind works at a time like this. All I can think of is I'm really getting to dislike Yogi. Ya know…that fucken déjà vu thing with the eyes all over again! But this time I get the feeling it's going to be a hell of a lot harder.

I guess I don't really want any time alone; there really ain't all that much I want to think about right now, and anyway, my fascade is crumbling. I'm gonna try to sleep; sorry if I'm being rude.

*

"Are you awake?"

It's nice to be able to recognize a voice. "I am, Mr. Sheridan."

"How do you feel?"

"Actually, I feel pretty good, but then I figure I'm getting a boost from the I.V.," I say with a smile.

"No, you must be feeling pretty good on your own. I don't see any suspended bags or tubes."

"That's good to know. The doctor said I can go home tonight unless something unexpected happens, so hopefully they're starting to get me ready to check out."

"I'm glad to hear it."

"Dr. Milleckston told me you brought in a specialist from Mt Sinai Hospital; I really appreciate it."

"After talking with Dr. Milleckston, I wanted to make sure, and a second opinion was fine with him.

"I guess he's that confident of his diagnosis."

"Unfortunately, you're right, he is."

"Then you know it all?"

"Yes, I do, and we can dispense with the 'Mr. Sheridan.' My name is Howard, and I know you won't be coming back to the ballpark, Devon."

That takes me by surprise, not the informality. I didn't know he knew my name. Check that; I think he called me by name at the Forge and probably in Aspen, too. Anyway, it's interesting, almost a little scary, how quiet things are when you can't see anything. "I'm really sorry about all this, Howard. I let you down."

"It's not like you planned any of this; it's more like the fates planned it for you." He pauses. "I believe in fate. Do you?"

"No sir, I don't. I believe people make decisions and, for better or worse, deal with the consequences of those decisions."

He laughs. "That's close to something you said in Aspen. You still don't take yourself off the hook, do you?"

"I never should have been on that bike. The irony of it is that it was going to be my last ride…just a little cruise around the old neighborhood at only thirty miles per hour. "Well," I say reflectively, "I was right; it *was* my last ride."

"And you say you don't believe in fate?"

"Nope."

"Maybe you're right."

"I don't think it really matters. The end result's the same."

"Yes, it is," he says quietly. I get the feeling he's thinking about Lillian. If he chooses not to say anything, I'm not about to ask.

"I really don't know what happened," I say, changing the subject. "Have you talked to anyone?"

"That means the police haven't been in to get your statement?"

"No, they haven't. Do I have anything to worry about?"

"You certainly don't in terms of what happened. I've talked with the sergeant who was on the scene, and for the time being, they'll be content to have your statements communicated to them through my attorney."

"You're attorney?"

"Yes. His name is Preston Tannenbaum; he's a senior partner at Kirchenson and Kirchenson. I asked him to personally handle things, and he said he'd be more than glad to."

"Thanks, Howard. What kind of things?"

"I think very serious things, Devon. A young man in his mid twenties was driving his father's Mercedes-Benz. He had been drinking and was way over the limit. Just as he crossed the top of Hollywood Bridge, he swerved to the left and hit a white pick-up truck."

"I remember that part. The last thing I saw was the truck, flipping and coming at me."

"That's right, and it landed on you. Fortunately, the pick-up was a flat bed, so the only part that hit you was the rear side panel. The emergency medical guys figured if it had been any other kind of truck, you would have been killed instantly. Luckily, it was your bike that got totaled, not you. And thank God you were wearing a helmet. The police told me the visor was sheared off and your helmet was almost split in half."

So I'm thinking to myself, that explains the injuries to my eyes and the mild concussion as well. "What happened to the driver of the truck and the guy in the Mercedes?"

"The young man suffered nothing more than some minor cuts and bruises. You know how people get limp when they're drinking. In that respect, the young guy in the Benz was lucky."

"And what about the truck, was anyone hurt?"

"That's a much different story. A mother and daughter were in the truck. The mother was in her low 60's."

"Was?"

"She died on the way to the hospital."

"Damn, and her daughter?"

"She came out okay, which is great, because she's pregnant. So, like I said," he continues, "this is very serious. The police have charged the young man with, among other things, vehicular homicide; he was drunk and he killed a person. Preston tells me this is a Class C felony offense, so there's bound to be a criminal trial, and civil suits for wrongful death and injury. That's why he's going to work with you personally. I know this doesn't help right now, but there's going to be a lot of money involved."

"You're right. My mind isn't about to go there."

"I can understand that. I'm sure you're preoccupied with what's ahead of you.

"I am, but like I said, I let you down. Is there anything I can do?"

"And like I said, you didn't let me down, so put that away, okay?"

"Okay," I respond like a dutiful child.

He grunts approvingly. "But seeing as you mentioned it, you can do something for me. If you recall, in Aspen when we talked about the team, I welcomed your input, and I welcome it now."

"Regarding?"

"Regarding the coaching staff; who would you recommend regarding an interim manager?"

I think for a moment or two. "Other than Leo and Rusty, I don't think any of them see themselves as a manager. Confidentially, Rusty will be leaving at the end of the season. He's going to join a big electrical firm in an executive position."

"If that's what he wants, that's fine with me. How do you feel about Leo?"

"I know Leo would love to do it, and can do it, a lot better than me."

"I'd have to take issue with that, Devon. We've got a winning record, and from what Pepper tells Charley, the players respect you. And they're making tremendous strides."

"I appreciate it, but we're only a month into the season. It's going to be a long summer. Leo has the skill and experience to go the distance."

"I think I might have heard just a little hesitation in there."

"You did. Leo loves the game, but he's no spring chicken."

"So what are you suggesting?"

"I think he'd make a terrific general manager."

"And where would that leave Pepper?"

"He seems to really enjoy being on top of things. I know Charley always has his fingers in lots of pies, so I figure maybe he'd be comfortable with Pepper being his Executive Vice-President for Baseball Operations."

Sheridan doesn't say anything; maybe he's contemplating my input. "I think you've got some solid recommendations," he finally says, "and I tend to agree with you regarding both Leo and Pepper. But who's going to manage the team next year?"

"I think I've got a candidate for that one, too."

"Okay, shoot."

"Jamie Bell is the bench coach for the Jacksonville Suns. He was on his way to the Mets when he was sent to Vietnam…and wounded. He's been coaching for about five years so he's got experience on both sides of the game. I think he'd be perfect."

"Is he available?"

"He will be at the end of the season. The Suns just brought in a new guy to manage, so Jamie knows he's going to have to move on, and, I don't think he's going to be content at just the coaching level."

"So far, your judgments have been sound. I'll have Charley look into it. Do you have any other suggestions?"

"About the team, no sir, I don't"

"Sounds like you might have something to say about, maybe, the station? I don't think your situation changes anything, Devon."

"I'm sorry to disagree, Howard, but I do."

"Both Doctor Milleckston and Doctor Etting were in agreement that you should have some vision for awhile, so I don't see any reason why you can't handle being the sports director."

"Like I said, I do. If you recall our conversation in Aspen, you wanted me to come on board because I'm somewhat of a sports celebrity. And, to make sure the public remembered that, you named me manager of the Mets. I don't want to be the one-day wonder anymore, but there's more to it than that."

"What is it?" he says with concern.

"I was already having trouble with being manager. When Sam said our first road trip was somewhat successful, I just laughed. Obviously, I wanted to do better, but my job wasn't on the line. Some manager once said, Leo Durocher I think, that if you don't win, you're going to be fired. If you do win, you've only put off the day you're going to be fired."

"I see your point, but what does that have to do with the station?"

"It's a variation on the same theme. What was making the job tough was that, no matter what I did, I knew it would be over at the end of the season. If I come on board as your sports director, it will be the same thing. I know it will be over; it's just a matter of time. I don't think I can do that…and be good at it. I don't want to launch a deadend career. I'm sorry, Howard."

"I figured you might be thinking that way, and I think I've come to know you well enough not to try to talk you out of it. I'm almost embarrassed to admit that it crossed my mind yesterday, but of course, it's not as immediate as getting a manager to run the ball club."

"Do you have anyone in mind?"

"I might try to lure Tony Segreto away from WTVJ, or maybe I can get Edwin Pope. I'm hoping he might be interested in moving from the *Miami Herald* into television. Do you know of anyone you think could fill the bill?"

"For director, no, but for a sportscaster, as well as someone out of the studio, I've got a lulu for ya…if you're up to breaking new ground."

"That sounds interesting. Who do you have in mind?"

"It just so happens I know someone who was first team, Southeast Conference, in two sports, who also has a degree in broadcast journalism."

"That sounds great. But what's so special about him?"

"What's special is he's not a him; he's a her."

"You're kidding!"

"I'm dead serious. I know the sports world might not be ready for a woman, but lots more co-eds are participating at the NCAA level, and at the local level, the numbers of girls playing in soccer, tennis, volleyball, and basketball youth leagues are growing by leaps and bounds."

"You've got a good point. Do you think she'll present herself well on television?"

"With a degree in broadcasting, I figure she's got to be good at public speaking, and at just under six feet with a great figure and drop-dead looks, I don't see how she could miss."

"I suspect you're right."

"There is one other thing that makes her unusual?"

"In addition to being a woman?"

"Yeah, she's a Lakota Sioux."

Sheridan ponders this new piece of information, and then smiles "Is her name Jayleigh Burney Smith by any chance?"

"How did you know that?" I ask, astonished.

"Because Lillian agrees with you; she says she *is* drop-dead gorgous."

"When did Mrs. Sheridan meet her?"

"She didn't. She saw photographs of Ms. Smith in a piece in National Geographic. If I recall, she was working on a reservation somewhere."

"It was the Pine Ridge, in South Dakota."

"And how do you know her?"

"We went to high school together, right here in Hollywood."

"Another bonus, she's local. I'm beginning to think this might work. Do you think she might be interested?"

"I guarantee it. Right now, she's teaching second grade and loves her kids, but she's becoming concerned about some of the trends in elementary education. I think the school year ends in early June, so she'd be available then."

"That sounds good. Can you get me her phone number?"

"Sure."

"Thanks."

I hear a chair move. I'm going to have to get used to this. I didn't even know he was sitting down. Or, maybe he's not. Maybe someone else has been in the room all this time. I never even thought about that possibility.

"I'm sorry about the conversation, Devon," he says hesitantly. "I feel selfish, talking about the team and the station. I hope you know that I'm extremely concerned about what's happened to you."

"I know that. If you weren't, you wouldn't have called in a specialist or your attorney. And honestly, getting my mind on other things helps."

"Thank you for understanding…but I've taken up too much of your time. I've got to get going."

"Howard, I can't tell you how much I appreciate all you've done for me."

"I'd say it was my pleasure, but under the circumstances, that wouldn't be appropriate. But what I will say is that I think of you as family, and nothing's going to change that."

"Thank you. That means a lot."

"Are you going to be okay?"

"You bet."

"Of course you are," he says. I can hear the smile in his voice. "Samantha is waiting to see you. I wanted her to come in first, but she insisted on waiting. That way, she said, you'd be able to tell her everything we talked about."

"Did she seem okay to you?"

"She's fine, Devon, just fine. Oh, and Charley told me to offer you his best wishes. He's in St. Louis but will be back tonight. He said he'll visit you tomorrow."

"No he won't. I'm not going to be here", I say, trying not to laugh. Laughing and broken ribs are not compatible.

"I'll let him know. Take good care," he says. I hear him move toward the door and, leave the room. Suddenly, I'm all but panic-stricken. I'm not sure what's scaring me the most. Is Sam going to be mad as hell at me, or is she going to have second thoughts, what with this fucken diagnosis? I just don't know what to expect, sportsfans. I hear footsteps. I guess we're about to find out how she's gonna take this.

No more footsteps; I sense someone standing right next to me. I know it's Sam; I can smell her Estee Lauder Youth Dew. Without saying a word, she kisses me softly on the lips and lingers long enough for me to feel her warm tears on my cheek. She pulls away, but only enough to gently take hold of my shoulders. "Don't you ever do that to me again," she says, her voice cracking.

"I won't," I assure her.

"Cross your heart?"

"I can't. I've got some broken ribs, but I promise. I told you it was going to be my last ride. Hell, the bike was probably totaled; I can't even sell the damn thing."

"That's *not* what I'm talking about," she says, regaining her composure. "Don't you ever *frighten* me again."

"It's the last thing on earth I'd want to do. I'm so sorry, Sam. I never dreamed something like this could happen. After all the years of riding, I've never even come close to having a scratch."

"I think you mentioned that once. And even if you had perfect vision, there's no way you could have avoided what happened. Evel Knieval's a great bike daredevil, but from what I've been told about your accident, even he couldn't have gotten out of this one. I guess it was just fate," she says.

"You can talk to Howard Sheridan about fate. As for me, I ain't buying it."

She lightens up. "Neither am I; for me, it's just a saying."

"I'm glad to hear it. I think he might have left a chair next to the bed. Why don't you sit down, or did you just come to see how I am and do a quick hi and bye?"

"Very funny," she says as I hear the chair scrap the floor. "Has the doctor been in?"

"If you're referring to John, yeah, he was in first thing this morning. He doesn't like the formal stuff so we're on a first name basis. Have you talked to him?"

"Yes, he didn't want to at first; you know…immediate family and all that."

"So?"

"So, our secret isn't totally a secret any longer. I told him I'm your wife. I also asked him if he would keep it to himself, because it was a private ceremony and no one knows except my father."

"Is that true? Does Billy know?"

"Yes, I told him yesterday morning."

"How did he take it?"

"He didn't say a word. He just hugged me tight, and there were tears in his eyes. I know he's given you a tough time, but he does have a warm and wonderful side."

"After our chat at Ziggy's, I might have to agree with you."

"Have to?"

"You know what I mean, Sam."

"He told me about your conversation at Ziggy's about an hour before I got the phone call from the hospital yesterday morning. I told him about us right after that."

"How did they know to call you?"

"Mr. Sheridan told me one of the policemen knew who you were and a sergeant knew that you're the manager of the Mets. They called the business office and connected with Mr. Berston. Apparently, he told the Mets it was important to call me. I guess he thinks I'm more than your girlfriend."

"I don't know. I think it's pretty good to have a girlfriend and a wife all wrapped up in the same person."

"Well, don't get used to it. The girlfriend thing is over, as of today."

"And what's the status of the wife thing?"

"That starts today…for real."

"You said you talked to the doctor," I say more seriously. "Do you know everything, I mean, all of it?"

"Yes, Dev, I know all of it."

"And you're willing to deal with it, with me?"

"Until '*The Twelfth of Never.*'"

"Johnny Mathis, it was our song and he was right; that's a long, long time."

"It still is our song."

"I hope you can be happy, Sam, really, really happy."

"Of course I can. You're alive, aren't you?"

"It's gotta be more than that."

"It's much more than that. I came way to close to losing you for the second time."

"The second time, I don't understand?"

"I haven't told you this, but I actually saw you go down. I had a date and was at the SAE house at Florida. Some of the brothers went to Miami High and Gables and played against you. The game was being televised, and they wanted to watch it."

"And you saw it all?"

"From the very first pitch, you wouldn't believe how crazy the place went when you hit a dinger the first time you came up. The guys were chanting, 'D Jack jacked it.' They were thrilled for you. I heard one guy tell his date he couldn't believe he'd actually played against you. I mean, the whole place went nuts. And then you got two more hits and made a great throw to the plate in the eighth. And then…"

"And you remember all this?"

"Every moment of it."

More silence. I'm going to have to get used to this. More often than not, when people stop talking, non-verbal behavior kicks in. Ya know; a smile, a shrug, hands up in the air, whatever. I figure when these pads come off, I'm going to have some vision for awhile, impaired, but some. But like John said, the final diagnosis isn't a matter of if; it's a matter of when and it ain't gonna be that far down the road.

Sam interrupts my thoughts. "You've got quite a few bandages on your left forearm," she says, changing the subject. "Was that from the wreck?"

"I think it was from all the intravenous stuff. I guess it's a good sign the tubes are out. That should mean I'll be getting out of here early tonight. Do you know if they kept my clothes? There's probably a closet in here. Can you take a look?"

"I could, but even if they're in there, they're probably a mess. And it doesn't matter. When I was told late this morning that you'd probably be discharged, I went to your apartment and got you some jeans and a pullover."

"You went to my apartment? How did you know where it was, and how did you get in?"

"Rusty was here this morning hoping to see you. All the guys and the coaches signed a get-well ball. When he was told you couldn't have visitors until tomorrow, he gave me the ball. It's in my handbag. He said he'd be glad to go over to your place and get you some things if you needed them, but I asked him if it would be okay if I did it. He was fine with that, so he gave me your address and the keys."

I smile. "That was nice of the guys and John, too."

"What was nice of John?"

"I told him I needed some quiet time, so I guess he told Rusty and maybe some others I couldn't have visitors until tomorrow."

"And, of course, you won't be here tomorrow."

"That's right. I'll be safe and secluded at home."

"Speaking of which, I found your place to be, well, spartan at best. It reminded me more of a motel room than an apartment. Other than a picture of your dad, one of you and your mom, and one of me on a diving board, there was no way of telling you live there."

"I leased it when I started working at the Presidential. The job was sixteen hours a day, seven days a week. So, you're right. I didn't live there; I just slept there. I once kidded myself that I never even saw a sunrise or a sunset. It was dark when I went to work, and it was dark when I got back so there didn't seem to be a reason to make it a home."

"You said you still have about six months on your lease, right?"

"I think it's something like that. Why?"

"Do you think we could spruce her up alittle? You said it would be a great place for the kids to spend some time, on the beach and all, and it would be nice if it felt more like a home away from home for them."

"You're starting to sound like a wife," I say, with a little laugh. The morphine is definitely wearing off, and the broken ribs are starting to talk to me.

"Is that a bad thing?"

"Sam, it's undoubtedly the best thing that's ever happened to me."

I don't wait for a response. "So, are you hungry? They're going to treat me to my one hospital dinner and I'll be more than pleased, actually I'll be grateful, if you'll split it with me."

"Fine, as long as I don't have to eat jello. When I was in the hospital after I hit the board, I had to eat jello everyday. I haven't eaten it since."

"Fair enough, I'll eat the jello."

"Actually, I have a suggestion," she says enthusiastically. "I think you're going to be discharged pretty soon, so why don't we just pick at your supper and then get a bite to eat after you get out, if you think you're up to it?"

"I haven't been on my feet yet, but I think I can handle it. I don't really want to go home for awhile. That's what I did last time, for days, and it didn't feel very good. I don't mean to be melodramatic, Sam, but I'd just like to go somewhere…and feel alive. Just sitting quietly on the beach with some take-out would be fine with me."

"This is beginning to sound as if somebody wrote a script."

"What's that supposed to mean?"

"It means I was hoping you'd feel this way."

"You mean something like 'damn the torpedoes and full speed ahead?'"

"Exactly, but I think we could do a little more than sit on the beach. Actually, I thought we might go over to Sketch and catch Moon doing a set. I called, and he's playing tonight, and they have wine and a lite menu. I also asked him why he wanted to get in touch with you."

"What did he say?"

"He didn't say very much. He did say he wants to share something with you personally, and he sounded really excited about it."

"So you figured that 'something' might cheer me up? I'm not sure I'm physically ready to go out on the town or mentally ready to go out in public."

"Your doctor told me that, other than some discomfort with your ribs, you're healthy as a horse. They're going to take the pads off your eyes before you leave, and he told me the vision in your right eye is obviously going to be impaired, but it'll be functional from the git-go."

"You've certainly done your homework, haven't you Sam."

"Was I wrong?" she asks anxiously.

"This is all new territory, for me. I'm not bitchen' or moanen' or anything like that, but since my dad died, I've been on my own. I'm sure it's the way I wanted it, but there's been no one to lean on. That's what I had with my dad, and other than one brief moment in time, with you, those were the most terrific years of my life. I just didn't know it at the time."

"And what do you think now?"

"To answer your question, I know you're right. What's the expression, life is for the living? If that's the case, why wait until tomorrow? Let's go for the brass ring, Sam!" I say doing my best to sound positive and confident.

"Always, Dev."

Her tone is reassuring, but just between you and me guys, deep down I hope I'm not kidding myself. I hope this isn't the stiff upper lip thing, or maybe just a lot of false bravado, for her benefit, and maybe mine. Only time will tell, I guess.

"Dinner's served,"a female voice says pleasantly. I hear a cart being wheeled towards the bed.

"Do I get jello?"

"Of course you do. It's orange tonight."

"Great. That's my favorite. Can we get an extra one for my…uh…girlfriend?"

"I think so," the voice says. "I'll see what I can do."

"Thanks a lot."

"Yeah, Devon," Sam says. "Thanks, but no thanks. Yuck!"

XVI

SKETCH

Nobody goes there anymore
Because it's too crowded.
Yogi Berra, Manager
New York Yankees, New York Mets

Actually, Sketch doesn't seem to be all that crowded, but I'm sure that's because it's a weeknight. I dropped in once, on a Saturday, along with other music enthusiasts, and the place was wall-to-wall. It's that kind of joint. Oops, there I go again with 'joint.' It's really kind of low-key classy. I think I've already given you a picture of the place, but just in case, the bar has two beautiful mirrors that reflect the dark wood stools, tables, and chairs across from it. There are two rooms: the larger one is in front of the bar area, while the smaller one is towards the back, separated by a long, wooden planter with a brick base and real plants. The back room features more indirect lighting and houses the small bandstand in the far right corner. Well, let's be thankful for little things: my memory still works.

Right off, I've got to tell you that the vision in my right eye isn't as good as I'd hoped for. It's more than a little worse than before the wreck, but like John said, when he checked me out, it's at least functional. He wants to wait for two weeks before examining me again because that will be enough time for him to get a feel for the rate at which my vision will deteriorate. He also told me that if I experienced any sudden changes or discomfort, I was to call him immediately. All of this bothered me some, but I didn't say anything to Sam. I mean, two weeks seems like an awfully short time for him to see some deterioration. Candidly, it took me down a few notches on the "be positive" scale. When I think about it, being a pessimist is easier that being an optimist because with a negative prediction, if it goes south, you have the satisfaction of being right. If it goes north, you get the pleasantness of the unexpected; deep, huh?

Checking out of the hospital was quick and easy. Howard Sheridan had arranged for statements, bills, and the myriad of hospital paperwork that all too often greets a patient on the way out the door to be sent to Preston Tannenbaum. Having that out of the way was one hell of a relief. I remember when I came home from New York, I was stressing all the time over what was going to get paid or not, and by whom, particularly if I was the designated 'whom.' This always bothers me; how do people get healthy if they stay sick over trying to figure out how to pay their medical bills? I hope you never have to deal with it, but if you do, I hope you have people around to help carry the water bucket.

As usual, the drive to the beach was quiet. Sam did ask me if I wanted to stop by my apartment, to get anything, but I told her I was fine. So, here we are, sitting in the back room at still yet another corner table. When we arrived, the manager, a guy named Ben, told us the T-man had reserved the spot for us, figuring I would want as much privacy as possible. Good move.

I'm surprised I'm feeling pretty good. They gave me three pain pills for the road , a Demerol prescription for the busted ribs, and eye drops that I'm supposed to use until I go back to see John in two weeks. So far I've only had to take one pill but you know what that means, sportsfans: no VO tonight.

"Welcome to Sketch. My name is Josh. I'll be your waiter this evening. What can I get for you?" he asks.

"Do you have any red wine by the glass?" Sam inquires.

"Yes, ma'am, we have a cabernet sauvignon and a burgundy."

"I'll have a glass of the cabernet."

"And you sir?"

"I'd like a Pepsi.'

"Yes sir. Would you like to see a menu?"

"Yes, thank you," Sam replies.

"I'll get your drinks and be right back with some menus,"

"Just one will be fine," Sam says.

Josh nods and heads for the bar. Sam is smiling at me. "What's the big smile all about?"

"I was pleased you didn't order a VO. I've been on Demerol before and you only make the mistake of mixing it with booze once. It ain't fun."

"Have you taken any since we left the hospital?"

"I took one about an hour ago."

"And you're feeling okay?" shes asks sounding worried.

"Yeah, are you sure Moon is playing tonight?"

"He must be," she says, looking over my shoulder, "because he just waved to us, and he's heading our way."

I turn and see him approaching with a big smile and opened arms. I get to my feet and offer my hand. "No hugs, T Moon. I've got a couple of busted ribs."

We shake, and he smiles at Sam. "This guy looks too good to have been in a wreck." Then he looks at me. "Are you sure you were in the hospital today?"

"Could be, why don't you ask Sam if she liked the orange jello?"

"Don't bother, Charlie. The nurse did Devon a favor and got us two, and I was feeling sorry for him, so I insisted he eat mine."

"But you did save one bite for yourself." I add. "Ya gotta admit the orange was good, right Sam?"

"I wouldn't know. I hid it under the meatloaf and mashed potatoes you didn't eat."

"Okay, you two. I'm convinced. You definitely were in the hospital today. What did the doctors have to say?"

"You can guess…the standard stuff, rest and relaxation."

"That's great. Now we can spend some time together."

"Why would I want to spend some time with you, Moon?" I ask sarcastically. "Given a choice, I'd rather spend my time with Samantha."

"I'd rather spend some time with her, too," T says, "but I've been trying to get ahold of you the last couple of days. I think we've got something going."

"What do you mean, we?"

"I mean just that. Obviously, you haven't said anything to him, have you Sam?"

"No, I thought it would be better coming from you."

"Terrific," I interject. "It's some kind of conspiracy. What would be better coming from you, and how come you didn't say anything about whatever you two are talking about, Sam?"

"I was afraid I wouldn't get it right," Sam answers apologetically.

"Get what right?" I respond, with more than a hint of exasperation.

"I'm pretty sure a company wants to record our music," T says with a huge grin.

That stops me dead in my tracks. "You're kidding."

"No, I'm not. I met with a record producer named Riverton the day before yesterday. That's why I was trying to get ahold of you, so you could sit in on the meeting."

"Have you ever heard of this guy?"

"No, but Joe Smith sent him down here. Smith is the mover and shaker behind Elecktra records. Some of their recording artists are people like Joni Mitchell, Etta James, Judy Collins and…Harry Chapin!"

"That's a pretty impressive list."

"It is, and this guy Riverton told me they think the time is perfect for our story songs. That's because there aren't that many artists out there doing this kind of music. Other than Chapin, only guys like Dan Fogelberg, Billy Joel, and Jim Croce are doing folk-rock…and of course Croce's been gone now for about three years."

"Let's not forget Gordon Lightfoot, Charlie. My maternal grandmother was Canadian," Sam says with pride.

"You're right. Most Canadians consider him to be their greatest songwriter," Moon adds. "So what do you think, D Jack?"

"I think Howard Sheridan would add John Denver to the list. He was at Mrs. Sheridan's birthday party in Aspen this past December, and we even met the guy."

"Wonderful, but that's not what I was asking."

"Fine, then what do I think about what?"

"Riverton wants to put us in a sound studio as soon as possible. He's already located one in Miami. He wants us to do a demo, maybe half a dozen songs, so Smith and the brass at Elecktra can listen to it.

"Do they have studio musicians?"

"Yeah, I mean, this guy really wants us to get going?"

"And he sounds positive to you?"

"He thinks it's a done deal. He apologized, but he taped us a few times at the Bengal Lounge. That's why Joe Smith sent him down here. Smith's heard the tapes, and he likes 'em. So, what do you think?"

Ben, the manager, taps T on the shoulder and smiles. We've been so engrossed in our conversation we didn't realize he was standing right behind us. "I think it's time for you to earn your bar bill, Charlie," he says with a chuckle.

Moon doesn't acknowledge him but gets to his feet. "I know the timing really stinks, D Jack, but think about it, okay? I won't do it without you."

"You mean they really want us to do it, right?"

"I think they want our music; you can really take it to the bank."

"Hopefully, that's exactly where we'll take it."

"Is that a yes?"

"Is there such a thing as checkmate, almost?" I answer with a grin.

"I'll see you later, Mr. Jameison."

"Thanks, Mr. Moon."

"Ahhhh, Jameison and Moon…or Moon and Jameison; the new troubadours," Sam announces proudly.

T turns and heads for the bandstand, but Ben stays put. "There's something else Charlie didn't mention, D Jack. I realize we've never met, but he's been saying ever since he started here he was hoping you'd play some gigs with him."

"I know. We talked about it in January. I'm sure I would have enjoyed it, but the baseball thing was all I could handle."

"That sounds past tense to me?"

"It is."

"Then would you be willing to play here?"

"My mind's a little fuzzy right now. "

"That's understandable," he says sympathetically.

"But I'll certainly think about it, Ben."

"Good. In the meantime, do your best to enjoy your enforced vacation," he says.

"I don't think that'll take all that much effort," I say, glancing over at Sam.

I think he picks up on my unsaid words. "That sounds like a good plan, D Jack. There's a contract waiting for you on my desk. I'm ready when you are."

"Thanks, Ben."

He smiles and heads for the larger room. I'm thinking my circuits are flat-out overloaded. If Sam thought our conversation in the hospital sounded like a script, the past two days have turned into some kind of fucken movie!

Our waiter arrives. "Here are your drinks, and a menu. I'm sorry I took so long."

"That's okay, Josh," Sam says with her best smile. "We'll take a look at the menu, and let you know if we want anything to eat."

"That'll be fine, ma'am. I'll check back with you in a few minutes.

"Sounds good," she says. Then she turns to me. "Does anything sound good to you, Dev?"

"I don't know. What's on the menu?"

"I'm not talking about the menu, silly."

"I didn't think you were, but I don't know. This has all come at me pretty fast. I'm not sure this whole wreck thing has set in yet." I rub my hand across my forehead and shrug.

"Life isn't supposed to happen like this," I continue. "Three months ago I was hustling the rich and famous at the Presidental, and forty-eight hours ago I was managing a minor league ballclub. In six months, I was going to be a sports director for a television station. Now, all of a sudden, in maybe a year or two, I'm going to be totally…

"I know," Sam says as she takes my hand.

I give her a lame smile. "Am I on the clock? Have I started my alloted twenty-four hours of feeling sorry for myself?"

She returns my smile, but her's is genuine. "If you recall, I once gave myself a private pity party for a week."

"I don't want it."

Sam takes a sip of her drink. "What do you want, Dev?"

Ya know guys, I think what continually amazes me about Sam is her uncanny ability to get me focused on things I ought to be thinking about. She always likes to say you shouldn't waste your time processing stuff you have no control over. Okay, so when it comes to organized baseball and television, both of them have slid abrubtly and unexpectedly into a previous life. Well, not the television thing because it never happened.

Anyway, sometime, in the not-so-distant future, my vision will join them. And like Sam would say, I can't do a damn thing about it. And I know what else she'd say, because I've heard it; she'd say stressing over stuff like this takes a hell of a lot more energy than addressing things you can actually do something about.

"Devon," she says softly. "I asked you a question. I know you like to take your time and think before you talk, but fair is fair…time's up, okay?"

"Sorry. I was just thinking about some sage advice I often heard from someone."

"It must have been your father, right?"

"No, it was you. Lucky for me, it still is?"

"I'm confused; I haven't said anything yet?"

"That's the best part about it. You don't have to!"

"Am I that predictable?"

"On your view of life, you're damn right you are." Having offered that profound announcement, I take a hit on my drink, and shudder.

"Are you okay?"

"Yeah, I was expecting a welcomed slug of VO and got a mouthful of Pepsi. As you would say…yuck! Did you find something on the menu you'd like?"

"I'm not very hungry, Dev."

"Neither am I. And to tell you the truth, I'm not much in the mood to sit in on Moon's set. Do you think he'd be ticked if we left?"

"I don't think so. You've had a tough couple of days; I'm sure he'll understand. Do you want to go home?"

"Not right now. I think I'd like to sit on the beach. The sound of the waves will make it easier for me to take in that sage advice I'm about to get from the lovely lady sitting next to me."

"But you said I'm so predictable that I don't have to say a word," she says playfully.

"I lied!"

XVII

HEADING FOR HOME

It's what you learn
after you know it all
that counts.
Earl Weaver, Manager
Baltimore Orioles

There's something about this beach. I've been sitting here under these same palm trees for most of my life. About the only thing that's changed is the boardwalk; they paved it about ten years ago. Maybe that's why I find this haven so comforting. I guess you could call it my place of refuge. Nothing bad has ever happened to me here.

"I didn't really lie, ya know," I say to Sam, who's sitting next to me, hugging her knees. It's just a little nippy tonight.

"No shit, Dick Tracey. Is it time for the sage to start saging?"

"Go for it, sage me."

"I'd rather hear what Howard Sheridan had to say in the hospital."

"I know, because he told me that's why you wanted him to visit me before you did."

"Did it go okay?"

"I think it did. He was supportive when I told him I thought I'd let him down."

"What else did he say?"

"More or less, he said he thought it was just one of those things, something I had no control over. I think he was sincere. He knew for sure I wouldn't be managing the team anymore, but when I told him to find a new sports director he tried to convince me we could work around it."

"How did you handle that?"

"I told him I didn't want to start a new career both of us knew was a dead end."

"I hope he understood that."

"He did. But then he assured me he could find something at the station I could handle, so I nipped that one in the bud, too."

"And he wasn't angry or upset?"

"Nope. In fact, he apologized for bringing all this up, bad timing and all, and then he asked me for suggestions."

"About what?"

"He was most concerned about the television station, probably because he's more directly involved with that than he is with the Mets."

"Do you know anyone who could do the job?"

"No, I don't. He said he might take a crack at somebody at WTVJ or maybe another guy who writes sports for the Miami Herald."

"Then I guess you weren't much help to him."

"Well, I did have one suggestion."

"What was that?"

"I told him I knew someone who would be perfect for assignments out of the studio."

"You mean like doing interviews and stuff like that?"

"Yeah, the person I recommended was an all-conference athlete in college and has a BS in broadcast journalism."

"That sounds perfect," Sam says supportively. "Sheridan must have been thrilled."

"Actually, he sounded a little hesitant."

"Why so?"

"I recommended Jayleigh."

"Jayleigh, how did you know about her?"

"We talked at the picnic at Jefferson Park."

"I remember. I saw you sitting with her. But you didn't know anything about working for the television station back then."

"Right, I didn't. I bumped into her again at the Gold Coast after the opening game against the Orioles."

"Really, I thought you didn't like that place."

"I don't. But when Jilly the Ice says he wants to meet you there, you go, right?"

"Oh, boy, what did he want you to do? Fix games?"

I laugh. "That's exactly what I thought, but he just wanted me to sign a song a friend calligraphed for him."

"Was it one of yours and T's?"

"It was."

"Jilly's a scary-looking man, isn't he?"

"Yeah, I don't think I'd like to bump into him in a dark alley. But lucky for me, Jayleigh came in, so I waved to her and was able to use her as an excuse to get away from him."

"I suppose that's your story and you're sticking to it," she says with that cut little, wise-ass smirk of hers.

"You bet I am."

"And I'll bet she made a move on you," Sam says, but at least the smirk has turned into a foxy smile.

"Why do you say that?"

"Girls know things about girls, particularly when they really want something, and when they do, they go after it. I'll bet she kissed you, too, didn't she?"

"You'd win 'em both, but I didn't reciprocate."

"Are you telling me you rejected her advances?" she asks, big-eyed.

Ya know, guys, I think she's doing some kind of tease job on me, or maybe she's just playfully mocking me.

"I am…and I did."

The look on Sam's face tells me she's pleased; game over. "How did she handle it?"

"She took it in stride. That's why I figured she wasn't doing much more than making a casual pass at me."

"Are you saying she would have been more aggressive if she was serious?"

"You're the expert."

"Did she know you were going to talk to Sheridan?"

"How could she? At the time, I didn't know I was going to be talking with Sheridan today."

"That was silly, wasn't it? I wasn't thinking. Speaking of Sheridan, do you think he'd risk hiring an American Native female?"

"He seemed intrigued. I think there's a good chance he will."

"And what did you tell him about a new manager?" Sams asks, changing the subject. "I'm sure Leo could do it," she adds.

"So am I. He's a great baseball man, but he ain't getting any younger. I suggested he promote Pepper to VP to take some of the executive load off Charley Berston's plate, and bump Leo up to general manager."

"What did he think about that?"

"I think he liked it."

"Is Rusty going to manage the team?"

"No. He told me confidentially he's going to work for his father-in-law. And I don't think any of the other coaches are interested in running the club."

"So, who's left?"

"In house…no one. That's why I suggested Jamie Bell. I told Sheridan all about him, and Sheridan was very enthusiastic. He want's to get in touch with him as soon as possible."

"That's wonderful, Dev. Are you going to call him first?"

"Actually, I was thinking of going up to Jacksonville and talking it over with him. I think it would be a lot easier and more effective that way."

"That's a good idea. When do you think you'll fly up there to see him?"

"I was thinking of driving."

"You can't drive, silly."

"I know, but you can."

"That's an interesting way of inviting me to come with you," Sam says, sounding pleased, "but I really don't think I can leave the kids with Daddy, and I do have a job you know."

"So quit; now's the perfect time."

"But I just started. What would I tell them?"

"Tell them your boyfriend was seriously injured in a motorcycle wreck and taking care of him is going to be a full-time job."

"Is it?"

"I sure as hell hope so."

She smiles. "That actually sounds like a good idea but what about the kids?"

"Let's bring them with us? We'll make a mini-vacation out of it. We can stay in a hotel in Daytona, on the way up, and let them play around on the beach. On the way back, we could head over to Orlando and take them to Disneyworld."

"I think it's a wonderful idea, Dev. But wouldn't it be awkward?"

"Are you referring to hotel accommodations?"

"Yes."

"I don't see any problems. We can get a room with two queen sized beds. You can sleep with the girls, and I'll sleep with Sean."

She nods, and grins. "Remember earlier today you said I was starting to sound like a wife?"

"Yeah, I do."

"Well, you're starting to sound like a husband; I love it," she says affectionately. Then, she puts her hands on my shoulders. "And, Devon Jamesion," she says softly, "I love you…now, always, and forever."

"And I love you, Samantha, more than anything I've ever had, or dreamed about." I slowly take her hands from my shoulders and look at her.

"I know you're worried, and you care about me and I know at the Forge you said you still love me, but I don't want you to feel you have to say, well, you know, something way more, something you think I need to hear."

"It has nothing to do with the accident, Dev. I'm in love with you, and I'm more in love with you than I ever thought possible. I felt it at Greynolds Park, and then on the beach. I saw how attentive, even loving, you were with the children. But I was really sure a few nights ago, like you say, at the Forge. When we were talking about philosophy and religion and music, I was bowled over with how easy it was for us to talk and share things about each other. And I knew right then and there it was something I want to do for the rest of my life."

"Me too, Sam, and I've never felt that way about anyone."

"Not even your father?"

"Not fair, like you would say, that's a different kind of love. But for as much as I loved my dad, no, not even him. There were things I felt I couldn't share with him, probably because I didn't want to upset him."

"Like the time you told him you were scared?"

"Exactly, and I'll always regret it, because it was the last time we talked."

I pause, trying not to get too upset. I think everything's finally starting to catch up with me.

"There's something else, isn't there?"

"Yeah, there is. I told you he died when I was playing winter ball in Mexico. They found him in his bed with some paper and a pencil by his side. The only thing on the paper was my name written at the top so I'll never know what he wanted to say to me."

"I'm sure he wanted to reassure you that you could do it, and that you would become the big league ballplayer the two of you had dreamed about for so many years."

"Do you really think so?"

"I know it, deep in my heart. Your dad was on of the most caring, wonderful men I've ever met, and I loved him, almost as much as I love you."

"Sam, you asked me right before we got married if I knew what I was getting into, and today, I asked you the same question."

"I remember, and my answer this afternoon was the same as yours."

"I thought maybe you've had some time for all this to sink in. I'm not sure how many times I've kidded about Yogi's fork in the road, but this time there is no fork in the road. We both know there's only one way this thing can go."

"I'm aware of that," she replies firmly, "and it doesn't matter. I realize that sounds hard right now, but you've dealt with challenges before…and so have I. And even though I had Daddy and the kids, I had to wrestle with things on my own, things I couldn't share. And now, I know you had to do the same thing. But this time, it will be so much easier, because we'll do it together, if you'll let us. Do you think you can do that?"

I know I like to pick my words carefully before I say something, but not this time. "On New Years Eve, you told me that people have to have trust and faith in each other if they're going to travel through life together. So yeah, I can do that."

"Are you afraid, Dev?"

"Am I afraid of what?"

"Are you afraid of going blind?"

I don't think she's testing me, but if she is, it's an easy question, a no-brainer.

"Yeah, the thought of seeing black and never seeing anything else is frightening. I remember one of my philosophy professors talking about the human concept of never. If you dwell on it, he said, it can be one of the most daunting words in the English language."

"Not if you think about it as the 'Twelfth of Never.'"

Before I can reply, Sam puts her arms around me and kisses me, tenderly at first, then passionately. She presses her body against me, and I can feel her warmth; it's like she's trying to comfort or protect me. Her lips leave mine, but she continues to hold me.

"Dev, I remember what you said at Sheridan's party about focusing on good things that happen in your life. You said in so many words that eventhough your baseball career ended in your first major league game, your biggest thrill came in the same game when you hit a dinger into the left field stands at Shea."

"I remember."

"Was it really?"

"When it came to hitting homers, yes, it was…but I was always so intense when I played that I think the adrenaline rush was what I lived for."

"I don't understand," Sams says sounding confused.

"When I played, I didn't either, but at Arizona State I learned that when you're in a situation that's both fearful and exciting, your brain dumps adrenaline into your system and you can go beyond your limits…like maybe run faster."

"And what kind of situation did that for you?"

"The ones I remember most were when I'd be running for third and the coach would be yelling and waving frantically so I knew that when I was rounding third it was going to be a close play at home plate. And for just an instant I'd get that mixture of fear and excitement because I didn't know how it was going to end."

Sam turns her head upwards and looks at me. She's mostly shadows now, but I think I can see myself shining in her light-green eyes. Her arms are still around me, and she lays her head on my shoulder. I softly run my fingers through her hair. The gentle, tropical breeze barely rustles the palms rooted in the crushed seashell beach on the ocean side of the asphalt boardwalk. Through the serenity of the moment, she whispers, "I know how it's going to end. You're home, sweetheart."

**

EPILOGUE

"What's up there?"

We're stretched out next to each other on two large beach towels under, you guessed it, a couple of palm trees. There aren't a whole lot of people on the beach because evenings in early June are still a little nippy for the locals. Sam says most of the folks ambling along the boardwalk, are probably in their fifties or sixties, so I figure they're Canadians. Lots of snowbirds from cities like Quebec and Montreal have been coming here for years, but many are now buying homes and making the area their permanent residence. I can't say that I blame them. I know they're not from Aspen, but for as beautiful as it was out there this past December, it was awfully cold, and I wouldn't want to deal with the deep freeze there or in Canada or anywhere, for six months at a time. But then, Howard says the falls and summers are spectacular in the Rockies, so maybe it's worth it.

"Do you mean what's up in the sky or in the trees or what?" Sam asks in her typical cute, wise-ass fashion. She's been doing this a lot the last few months. It didn't take all that long for the two of us to get on the same page, the page being that of dealing with our challenge with humor. I know you might react to this pronouncement with some skepticism, but Sam and I have had only one brief conversation about the hand we've been dealt since getting out of the hospital. Simply stated, I'm alive, and we have a future; the woman in the white pick-up has neither, and her daughter doesn't have her mom. End of story.

"I mean the sky, Sam. What's up in the sky?"

"Are you asking me if I can see airplanes on a dark night?"

I'm on my back with my hands clasped under my head. Sam snuggles up against me and drapes her right arm across my chest. "I ain't deaf, ya know; I could hear a damn jet."

"Okay, then. I can't see the rings of Uranus."

"You mean Saturn, don't you?"

"Not as of last month. They discovered rings around Uranus."

"Terrific. I'm thrilled, but I want to know if there's a moon, ya know, celestial stuff ya can see with the naked eye."

"There's a moon."

"Crescent or full?"

"It's full, Dev, just above the horizon, and shining a path across the ocean right at us."

"That's sweet…and how about the stars?"

"Make a wish."

"I don't need to. I know Orion's belt is right up there, and those three stars are for lighting our way, not for wishing."

"You're right, on both counts. Orion *is* up there, and in about the same spot it was years ago, when we got serious and talked about what a great life we were going to have."

"I guess it took longer than we figured," I say reflectively. "But even if Orion wasn't up there," I quickly add, "I think you'd say it anyway, wouldn't you?"

"You know better."

"Yeah, Sam, I do."

It's quiet, but I can hear the soft rustling of the palm fronds above us. We've talked about it. As my vision has faded, more rapidly than John had predicted, Sam has increasingly become the eyes for both of us. I have to believe in her and trust that she'll tell me what *is*, and not something else, just because it might be the way I want it to be.

She tightens her arms around me. "Tomorrow is going to be one hell of day," she says enthusiastically.

"As if today wasn't?"

"You mean the call about you and Moon appearing on the Carson show next month?"

"That call came yesterday."

"Well, excuse me, o humble one." That remark is followed by a less than gentle squeeze. "Then it's the royalties check?" she inquires.

"No, it's stubbing my toe. Of course it's the check! I know it wasn't much, but it'll pay the bills along with the paycheck from Sketch. Maybe when all is said and done with the legal settlement, we could buy her."

"I think that's a good idea. That way, you won't have to argue with the owners if you don't feel like playing some night."

"True. So, what's so special about tomorrow?" I ask, matching her wise-ass response about what's in the sky.

"Very funny," she says, but this time she forgoes the gentle squeeze for a bona fide shot in the ribs. Thank God they've healed.

"Okay then, are the children excited?"

"Are you kidding? You've seen how giggly the girls have been around you since we told them we were getting married, and Sean is absolutely thrilled about us being his real mom and dad. And how about the way he looked at you when we told him? It was like…wow…D Jack's my dad! And, of course, one of your dreams has already come true."

"Yeah, I had a catch with my son. That was really special, but what was even more special was when he looked at you, knowing you're his mom. I'll never be able to put that into words…but it was as if the whole world had just embraced him. And you know, Sam? I feel the same way. Are we really getting married tomorrow?"

"Well, for us it's a renewing of vows, but as for as the public is concerned, yes, we are getting married."

"If the public is what you call exchanging rings in your living room in front of half a dozen people."

"Maybe our wedding will be a private one but it'll be in the papers, Dev. Story-song music lovers who bring their friends to hear you and Moon at *Sketch,* and of course Johnny Carson, are not going to let you go quietly into the night."

"Yeah, I guess not."

"And Daddy said this morning he wants to give me away," she adds gleefully.

"That's terrific, Sam. That means a lot to me," I say sincerely.

"It means a lot to me too."

It's peaceful. When I think of all that's happened, and where I'm at now, it's hard to believe that the one thing I truly thought I would never have is here with me, and in my arms. God, I love this woman.

Okay then, guys. I'm just going to have to disappoint you this one last time; I'm gonna gum up the moment with some philosophy, like you thought I really wouldn't do this, right? Anyway, Soren Kierkegaard, the other melancholy Dane, once said, *"most men pursue pleasure with such breathless haste that they hurry past it."*

"Are you up there with Orion, Dev?"

"Not really, I was just saying a little something…along with a goodbye to some guys."

That goes right over her head, so she must have her mind on something else. She gives me a big hug and a sweet, yummy kiss. "Eight years ago, I wanted desperately to say something to you."

"But you couldn't?"

"No, but I can now."

She sounds serious and determined, but something deep inside me says there's no need to be apprehensive, so I respond tenderly. "Just a few months ago, under these same stars and that same moon, you told me you loved me."

"Yes, I did…the fairy tale kind."

I laugh, and return her hug and precious kiss. "So Samantha Jameison, what can you say to me now that you couldn't say eight years ago?"

"Devon…I'm pregnant."

***

Acknowledgments

I would like to express my gratitude…to Dr. Richard Uecker who provided the veterinary diagnosis and surgical procedures described in Book I, Chapter XVIII; to Frank Shumer with whom I clashed on the handball court and learned the ins and outs of flying a Cessna; to Paul Jonart for fine-tuning the manuscript; and to Kathy Lake whose invaluable and *"super-enthusiastic"* editing transformed the somewhat sprawling nature of Books I and II into a more reader-friendly story. Finally, to my wife Lorrie, for her personal oral history of carny life and language and her countless hours of reading, suggesting, and encouraging, all of which enriched and brought to life the characters and events portrayed in this work.

Author's Note

As with many works of fiction, characters are frequently based upon real people and, although the details of his private life are purely ficticious, Samantha's father, Billy, was in real life, William "Billy" Outten, and he *was* The Diving Sensation.

For more than forty years, he was an independent who performed in such places as the Atlantic City Steel Pier, Coney Island, Kennywood, and yes, Palisades Park. He played fairs and carnivals and was among the most prominent athlete-performers of his time, a time (like that of the Park on the Palisades overlooking the Hudson River) that has faded into the past.

Was Billy's high dive really that spectacular? In the last Movietone News clip of daredevils shown in the movie, *The Right Stuff,* the entire feat is captured on film and I think you will agree that…Billy was the *only* guy who ever played his game…and that death defying game was fire-to-fire high diving!